Books are to be returned on or before
the last date below.

7 – DAY
LOAN

LIVERPOOL
JOHN MOORES UNIVERSITY
AVRIL ROBARTS LRC
TITHEBARN STREET
LIVERPOOL L2 2ER
TEL. 0151 231 4022

D0301560

THE ARCHAEOLOGY OF
HUMAN ANCESTRY

THEORETICAL ARCHAEOLOGY GROUP (TAG)

In this series:

THE ARCHAEOLOGY OF HUMAN ANCESTRY

Power, Sex and Tradition

Edited by James Steele and Stephen Shennan

London and New York

First published 1996
by Routledge
11 New Fetter Lane, London EC4P 4EE

Simultaneously published in the USA and Canada
by Routledge
29 West 35th Street, New York, NY 10001

© 1996 James Steele, Stephen Shennan and contributors

Typeset in Bembo by Florencetype Ltd, Stoodleigh, Devon

Printed and bound in Great Britain by
Redwood Books Ltd, Trowbridge, Wiltshire

All rights reserved. No part of this book may be reprinted or
reproduced or utilized in any form or by any electronic,
mechanical, or other means, now known or hereafter
invented, including photocopying and recording, or in any
information storage or retrieval system, without permission in
writing from the publishers.

British Library Cataloguing in Publication Data
A catalogue record for this book is available from the British Library

Library of Congress Cataloguing in Publication Data
A catalogue record for this book has been requested

ISBN 0–415–11862–X

CONTENTS

ILLUSTRATIONS

TABLES

CONTRIBUTORS

Michael Chance, Social Systems Institute, 12 Innage Road, Birmingham B31 2DX, UK.

Ben Cullen, Department of Prehistoric and Historical Archaeology, University of Sydney, Sydney, NSW 2006, Australia.

Robin Dunbar, Department of Psychology, University of Liverpool, PO Box 147, Liverpool L69 3BX, UK.

Robert Foley, Department of Biological Anthropology, University of Cambridge, Downing Street, Cambridge CB2 3DZ, UK.

Clive Gamble, Department of Archaeology, University of Southampton, Highfield, Southampton SO17 1BJ, UK.

John Gowlett, Department of Archaeology, The Hartley Building, University of Liverpool, PO Box 147, Liverpool L69 3BX, UK.

Paul Graves-Brown, Department of Psychology, University of Southampton, Highfield, Southampton SO17 1BJ, UK.

Kristen Hawkes, Department of Anthropology, The University of Utah, 102 Stewart Building, Salt Lake City, Utah 84112, USA.

Chris Knight, Anthropology Subject-Area, Faculty of Social Sciences, Brooker Building, University of East London, Longbridge Road, Dagenham, Essex RM8 2AS, UK.

Mark Lake, Department of Archaeology, University of Reading, Whiteknights, PO Box 218, Reading RG6 2AA, UK.

Phyllis Lee, Department of Biological Anthropology, University of Cambridge, Downing Street, Cambridge CB2 3DZ, UK.

Alexandra Maryanski, Department of Sociology, University of California, Riverside, Riverside, California 92521-0419, USA.

Henry M. McHenry, Department of Anthropology, University of California, Davis, Davis, California 95616-8522, USA.

Steven Mithen, Department of Archaeology, University of Reading, Whiteknights, PO Box 218, Reading RG6 2AA, UK.

Camilla Power, Department of Anthropology, University College London, Gower Street, London WC1E 6BT, UK.

Stephen Shennan, Department of Archaeology, University of Southampton, Highfield, Southampton SO17 1BJ, UK.

James Steele, Department of Archaeology, University of Southampton, Highfield, Southampton SO17 1BJ, UK.

Ian Watts, Department of Anthropology, University College London, Gower Street, London WC1E 6BT, UK.

GENERAL EDITOR'S PREFACE

Why does the world need archaeological theory? The purpose of the Theoretical Archaeology Group series is to answer the question by showing that archaeology contributes little to our understanding if it does not explore the theories that give meaning to the past. The last decade has seen some major developments in world archaeology and the One World Archaeology series provides a thematic showcase for the current scale of enquiry and variety of archaeological interests. The development of a theoretical archaeology series complements these thematic concerns and, by focusing attention on theory in all its many guises, points the way to future long-term developments in the subject.

In 1992 the annual Theoretical Archaeology Group (TAG) conference was held in Southampton. Europe and the world of archaeological theory was our theoretical theme at this EuroTAG conference. We stressed two elements in the structure of the three-day conference. In the first place, 1992 had for long been heralded as the time when the single market would come into existence combined with moves towards greater European unity. While these orderly developments could be planned for and sessions organized around the role of archaeology and the past in the construction of European identity, no one could have predicted the horror of what would occur in former Yugoslavia. Throughout 1992 and beyond, the ideologies of integration and fragmentation, federalism and nationalism vied with each other to use the resources of the past in vastly different ways.

The second element recognized that 1992 was a notable anniversary for theoretical archaeology. Thirty years before Lewis Binford had published his first seminal paper, 'Archaeology as Anthropology', in *American Antiquity*. This short paper was a theoretical beacon in an otherwise heavily factual archaeological world. From such beginnings came the influential processual movement which, in its early years, was referred to as the New Archaeology. Thirty years has clearly knocked the shine off such bright new futures. In the meantime archaeological theory had healthily fragmented while expanding into many areas of investigation previously regarded as off-limits to archaeologists and their mute data. Processualism had been countered by post-processualism to either the enrichment or irritation of by now partisan theoretical practitioners. EuroTAG marked the anniversary with a debate involving the views of Lewis Binford, Chris Tilley, John Barrett and Colin

Renfrew, supplemented by opinions from the floor. Their brief was to outline the theoretical challenges now set before the subject. The audience heard various programmes of where we might go as well as fears about an uncertain theoretical future. Both optimism and pessimism for another thirty years of theoretical excitement were to be found in almost equal measure. However, the clear impression, exemplified by the number of people (almost 800) who attended EuroTAG, was that the strength of any future theoretical archaeology now lies in its diversity.

How different in numbers attending and diversity of viewpoints from the early days of TAG, an organization whose aims have always been simple: to raise the profile of discussion about the theories of the past. The need for such a group was recognized at the first open meeting held in Sheffield in 1979 where the programme notes declared that 'British archaeologists have never possessed a forum for the discussion of theoretical issues. Conferences which address wider themes come and go but all too frequently the discussion of ideas is blanketed by the presentation of fact.' TAG set out to correct this balance and achieved it through an accent on discussion, a willingness to hear new ideas, often from people just beginning their theoretical careers.

EuroTAG presented some of the influences which must now contribute to the growth of theory in archaeology as the discipline assumes a central position in the dialogues of the humanities. As expected there was strong participation from European colleagues in sessions which focused on Iberia and Scandinavia as well as discussions of the regional traditions of theoretical and archaeological research in the continent, an archaeological perspective on theory in world archaeology, the identity of Europe and multicultural societies in European prehistory. Set beside these were sessions devoted to visual information, food, evolutionary theory, architecture and structured deposition. Two archaeological periods expressed their new-found theoretical feet. Historical archaeology argued for an escape from its subordination to history while classical archaeology embraced theory and applied it to its rich data. Finally, the current issues of value and management in archaeology were subjected to a critical examination from a theoretical perspective.

The potential of evolutionary theory as applied to human ancestry has only occasionally been the subject of a TAG session. This volume addresses that omission and concentrates on one of the least theoretical periods in archaeology – the Palaeolithic. Research into human origins and the Palaeolithic has increasingly become international in scope and multidisciplinary in approach. However, it has been directed to the recovery of data within ever more precise chronological and palaeoenvironmental frameworks rather than the development of new questions about our earliest ancestors. A truly interdisciplinary volume, such as this one, combines the methods and insights of a range of disciplines to examine areas which until recently were regarded as off-limits to researchers because of the nature of the data. This new research includes insights into social structure, social learning, cultural transmission, sex-based strategies and cognition. The result is a fresh agenda for human origins research and one where archaeology assumes an equal place with the palaeobiological sciences. Those who seek an answer to why we need archaeological theory, rather than more facts, need look no further.

Clive Gamble
April 1995

Acknowledgements

The editors would like to thank the EuroTAG committee, in particular Clive Gamble, for supporting this project during its initial stages. They also thank the team at Routledge, in particular Diana Grivas and Patricia Stankiewicz, for assistance with the preparation of the papers for publication.

The EuroTAG organizing committee consisted of Clive Gamble, Sara Champion, Simon Keay and Tim Champion. They were helped by many staff and students from the Department of Archaeology at the University of Southampton and particularly by Cressida Fforde and Olivia Forge who did the lion's share of the organization in the final days. Thanks are also due to Peter Philips who videotaped the debate and to Mike Corbishley, Peter Stone and Eric Maddern who organized videos and storytelling, while the art of Carolyn Trant and Sylvia Hays provided the art exhibition. Financial support was received from the Prehistoric Society, the TAG travel fund, Oxbow Books, Routledge and the University of Southampton.

J.S. expresses his appreciation to Adrienne, Oliver and Theo Steele for their forbearance when he was absorbed in the tasks of editing.

Figure 4.4 is reprinted from *Motor Learning and Performance* (p. 27) by Richard A. Schmidt, Champaign, IL: Human Kinetics Publishers. Copyright 1991 by Richard A. Schmidt. Reprinted by permission.

The cover incorporates part of a painting by Maurice Wilson, from *Human Evolution* by Peter Andrews and Chris Stringer, London: British Museum (Natural History). Copyright 1989 by British Museum (Natural History). Reprinted by permission.

INTRODUCTION

JAMES STEELE AND STEPHEN SHENNAN

The initial impetus for this book on the evolution of hominid culture and social systems has come from archaeologists. Milford Wolpoff (1994: 179) has suggested that 'archaeologists have become more concerned with the evolution of human behaviour than have biological anthropologists'. While the strong representation of biological anthropologists among the contributors belies this contention, it is also true that some social scientists currently seeking to ground their understanding of human social agency in a Darwinian framework are impatient with the laborious process of data-gathering and the niceties of data interpretation which characterize Palaeolithic archaeology. The 'evolutionary psychology' programme of Cosmides, Tooby and their collaborators (Barkow *et al.* 1992), which grounds human cognitive biases in the adaptive context of the 'Environment of Evolutionary Adaptedness', has developed free of any commitment to testing the validity of models of the EEA against archaeological evidence. Even Dunbar, whose ethological models of human conversational language use have given research on language origins such a new lease of life, has demonstrated this impatience, remarking of his group size model:

> That it may prove difficult to test such predictions from the archaeological record . . . is bad luck for the archaeologists, but is neither here nor there for my argument. At best, it affects one element in the story (and one that, from an evolutionary point of view, is the least interesting: the timing of a phenotypic change is only interesting in determining who might and who might not have inherited a particular character from a common ancestor).
>
> (Dunbar 1993: 725)

While we understand (and to some extent share) such impatience, we would dispute any dismissal of the archaeological contribution to understanding human social systems and their evolution. Evolutionary interpretations of human cognitive abilities and social predispositions are increasingly common in social science, and it is essential that space should be given in these programmes to testing such interpretations against the record of hominid behavioural evolution. Knowledge-gathering is, however, a collective enterprise, and archaeologists do not work in a theoretical vacuum. Just as evolutionary psychology is guided by a 'background' understanding of Pleistocene hominid social systems garnered from anthropology and archaeology, so archaeology is guided by a 'background' understanding of the cognitive and social behavioural correlates of fossil hominid anatomies which constrains the range of possible interpretations which archaeologists must consider in explaining a particular set of archaeological traces. As archaeologists, our responsibility to our colleagues in other disciplines is not just to listen to their own progress, but also to keep them up to date on ours. This book serves that dual purpose. Archaeological contributions serve to summarize the insight into hominid social systems which is offered, uniquely, by the archaeological record. Gamble, Gowlett and Mithen make this point particularly forcefully. Other contributions, from both biological anthropologists and archaeologists, review comparative evidence of living non-human primates and contemporary human foragers as a basis for specifying the 'degrees of freedom' in reconstructing hominid social systems which remain to be resolved by archaeological analysis. Not all imaginable social systems or cognitive adaptations were possible for any given hominid – these contributors identify aspects of anatomy and phylogeny which define the range of what is plausible in social reconstructions.

RECONSTRUCTING HOMINID SOCIAL SYSTEMS: METHODOLOGICAL ISSUES

The use of archaeological data for reconstructing hominid social systems: methodological considerations

Fossils and archaeological remains are the central elements in any reconstruction of the evolution of human social behaviour. Comparing the anatomy and behavioural repertoires of humans and of non-human primate species can give us a clear idea of the characteristics which were subject to strongest selection pressures, at least in that lineage of the hominid radiation which is ancestral to modern humans; but it is the remains themselves in their palaeoecological contexts which enable us to chart the course of that evolution, and to interpret it in terms of testable causal models (cf. Oliver *et al.* 1994).

Not all aspects of hominid behaviour have proved equally tractable to archaeological analysis, however. Blumenschine *et al.* (1994) have pointed out that reconstructions of hominid behaviour currently follow one of two approaches. First, there is the approach of taphonomic or middle-range research, exemplified by the work of Glynn Isaac and his research group, 'where archaeological remains and hominid bones are interpreted through models derived from taphonomic research (experimental or naturalistic), and biomechanical and functional analyses' (Blumenschine *et al.* 1994: 200). Middle-range research, in this context, denotes the documentation of linkages between a modern behavioural process and the traces it would leave in the archaeological, geological or palaeontological records. This approach has been fruitfully applied to elucidating the record of hominid behaviour in the fields of stone tool technology, diet and locomotor strategy.

Blumenschine *et al.* (1994: 200) point out, however, that other aspects of hominid social behaviour 'such as group size and composition, day range length, and mating systems are still largely beyond the resolution of middle range research'. These aspects remain largely the preserve of researchers using the second approach – general theory, applying 'general ecological principles relating aspects of the environment to behavioural responses in a wide range of species in different habitats' (Blumenschine *et al.* 1994: 201). According to Blumenschine *et al.*, while this approach has the considerable merit of extending current models in evolutionary ecology to the less tractable aspects of the behaviour of extinct species, it is compromised by the limited verifiability of predictions about hominid social behaviour derived from these general principles: 'many are tied too loosely to the available fossil evidence for activities and palaeoenvironment due to insufficient attention to middle range research' (Blumenschine *et al.*: 201).

The chapters in this book focus on those aspects of hominid behaviour which have yet to be resolved by middle-range research – group size, mating systems, the structure of social bonds and the origins of cultural traditions and social institutions. Consequently, there is a marked emphasis on general theory, and less emphasis on the verification of predictions by detailed analysis of some aspect of the artefactual record. Inevitably, some will criticize our choice of title for the volume, given this balance of emphasis on the general theoretical approach. Indeed, Palaeolithic archaeology has more than its share of methodological pessimists, who argue (with Bahn 1990: 75) that:

> I hate to break the news, but social organization is unexcavatable, when the best one can hope for is a hypothesis based on inference and analogy. . . . In fact it is quite possible that all the interpretations of Palaeolithic life yet put forward are hopelessly wrong, and in any case we shall never know which of them are correct.

We intend, in opposition to such methodological pessimism, that this book as a whole should enable identification of key areas for consolidation of middle-range research on these less tractable aspects of the social behaviour of hominids, including early modern humans. Group size, identified as a key component of some recent models of hominization (e.g. Dunbar 1993), needs to be re-evaluated archaeologically in the light of critiques of the 'site' as a discrete area of activity remains from a single episode, since this critique renders inference from site area to group size potentially invalid (cf. Isaac 1972, Hassan 1981). Possible fossil traces of group size identified in this book include lithic transport distances (Steele, 'On predicting hominid group sizes', chapter 8) and evidence of persistence in cultural traditions (Mithen, Shennan). Possible traces of mating systems, particularly the appearance of a sexual division of labour, are discussed by Graves, Knight, and by Power and Watts. Archaeological traces of mobility and information exchange between groups, particularly in relation to dispersal of mates, are discussed by Gamble (see also Steele 1994).

Gowlett, in an extremely useful review of the recent intellectual history of research on the archaeology of hominid social behaviour, reminds us of the difficulties of moving from general theory to middle-range research. However, the use of data from modern forager ethnography or from studies of living non-human primates also has its pitfalls, and we should be aware of these before yielding to general theory the central role of the fossil record in such reconstructions. In fact, the limitations of the comparative data-sets oblige us to press on with the task of building verifiable middle-range theory from these more general models.

The use of ethnographic data for reconstructing hominid social systems: methodological considerations

Modern forager ethnography has been a central element in general theories of ancestral human social systems since at least the 'Man the Hunter' conference (Lee and DeVore 1968). The social systems and economies of modern foragers are not 'living fossils' – they are adaptive and to some degree flexible systems, perhaps for the most part interlocked with the economies of their sedentary neighbours (cf. Shott 1992). Nevertheless, uniformitarian principles may well apply insofar as modern forager societies retain their cultural integrity and their systemic relationships to key evolutionary and ecological variables. For this reason, modern forager societies remain the closest extant models of the foraging systems of early modern humans: ethnoarchaeological work with modern foragers has supplied middle-range theory of the expected traces of their behaviour, especially subsistence behaviour, in the archaeological record. A number of contributors to this volume draw on the ethnographic record. Hawkes, Graves-Brown, Knight, and Power and Watts all discuss the evolution of modern human parenting strategies with reference to data on gender and foraging activity in modern forager societies. Gamble, Shennan and Dunbar cite data from forager ethnographies on group size and kinship systems to support their interpretations of Upper Palaeolithic adaptations.

Ethnography is not, however, a sufficient source for reconstructing the social systems even of early modern humans, let alone those of ancestral hominid taxa. Wobst (1978) pointed out nearly twenty years ago that ethnographic models have tended to underplay the spatial extent of social interactions in forager societies (see also Gamble, this volume). Foley argued both that 'the evolutionary ecology of earlier hominids and modern *Homo sapiens* was markedly divergent' (1988: 215), and also that 'the foraging and reproductive strategies of Pleistocene anatomically modern humans differed markedly from those of most modern hunter-gatherers' (1988: 219). In fact, as Shott (1992) points out, given the current revisionist mood in forager ethnography it is *archaeology* which must answer the question of the extent of continuity between modern forager adaptations and their ancestral forms (prior to the advent of sustained economic interactions with sedentary neighbours). Paradoxically, therefore, while forager ethnography remains central to our understanding of early human adaptations the validity of this source as a model for early humans must be verified by archaeological analysis of their prehistory. In Shott's view, this task remains problematic as long as 'archaeologists have still to give serious thought to how sociopolitical organization is registered in sparse remains like stone tools' (1992: 963).

The use of non-human primate data for reconstructing hominid social systems: methodological considerations

Non-human primate models have also played a central role in general theory, particularly about earlier hominid social systems, while contrasts between the social and economic systems of living non-human primates and modern foragers have defined models of the evolution of 'derived' features of human social behaviour (e.g. Isaac 1978). Thirty years ago Coles and Higgs (1969: 68) argued that 'as man is a primate, the assumption has usually been made that primate behaviour studies are most likely to yield valuable results. However, man, with his extensive range of adaptability, has probably behaved in the manner of animals other than primates, where his food supply has been akin to those of non-primates.' The implication – that Palaeolithic social systems might be better understood by analogy to a social carnivore model – is, however, flawed. Carnivore models of range area may be appropriate for explaining lithic transport distances in the Middle Palaeolithic (Steele, chapter 8, this volume), but *primate* models are needed to understand the character of social interactions in face-to-face networks. Cheney *et al.* (1987: 3–4) define three characteristics that make primates different from other animals. First, 'primates have unusually varied and diverse ways of expressing themselves socially', and they move easily between those behavioural 'currencies', trading a mount for tolerance at a food source, or a grooming bout for future support in an alliance. These may therefore provide a basis for complex reciprocal interactions. Second, 'the social organization of many primate species is unusually complex'. The complex networks of social interactions of individuals of different ages, sex, dominance rank and kin-relatedness, forming temporary alliances, subgroups, and long-term associations within and across categories, make the range of strategies used by individuals over the lifespan much more diverse. Finally, 'primates form various kinds of long-term social relationships'. Their long lifespans and intelligence enable interactions to be shaped by anticipations of outcomes which may not be realized immediately, as in the use of grooming interactions to service relationships which may only generate fitness-increasing outcomes in some future situation such as coalitional competition within or between groups.

A related reason for using primate models is the closeness of other primates to humans in their brain structure and cognitive abilities. While anthropologists continue to dispute the precise extent of the continuity between humans and other primates in these respects (cf. Passingham 1982, Deacon 1988), the basic proximities are accepted and shape discussions of, for example, the evolution of cultural learning in the hominid line (Tomasello *et al.* 1993). Many anthropologists would argue that since primate intelligence seems to be most selected for in the social domain, brain and social system characteristics have co-evolved: from this point of view, primate intelligence is a product of selection for living in complex social groups with diverse social communicative behaviours and long-term patterns of association (Byrne and Whiten 1988), to the extent that the cognitive capacity for cultural learning in humans is a product – if not a by-product – of selection for social monitoring of the intentions of other group members, and the manipulation of those intentions by social signalling.

Many contributors to this volume therefore draw on primate analogies to reconstruct hominid social systems, using one of two strategies. One is to identify similarities and differences in the behaviour of humans and great apes, and to attribute the similarities to conserved patterns retained by humans and great apes (and, by implication, earlier hominids) from their common ancestor. The differences are attributed to divergence in the evolution of the two groups: the problem becomes one of identifying the fossil taxon and the point in time where the divergence occurred. This cladistic method, adopted by Foley and Lee and by Maryanski, is based on the assumption that the 'degrees of freedom' available to hominid species in their social system evolution have been subject to phylogenetic constraints. The other strategy – used by contributors including McHenry, Steele and Dunbar – is to identify patterns of convergence between behavioural and anatomical traits in phylogenetically independent comparisons of primate taxa, and to derive predictions from these about the behaviour of extinct hominids on the basis of their fossil morphology. This second strategy attributes more 'degrees of freedom' to hominid social systems from the point of view of phylogenetic constraints, but ultimately attributes a more constraining role to ecological conditions influencing parameters such as group size or sexually dimorphic behaviours. The two strategies have the potential for conflicting with each other. For instance, Maryanski (this volume) argues from the phylogenetic constraint perspective that apes tend to live in small, weakly integrated groups, and that hominid group sizes only increased by virtue of evolving 'special mechanisms' for social integration such as kinship. However, Dunbar (1992, 1993) argues that in comparing primate grouping strategies the genus is a high enough taxonomic level to derive phylogenetically independent comparisons, and predicts group sizes for hominids including humans from their brain sizes: language is seen not as an ape 'special behaviour', but as an adaptation to order-wide allometric increases in time budgets for social relationship maintenance with very large groups (see also Dunbar, this volume; Aiello and Dunbar 1993). Steele (chapter 8) attempts to account for the apparent group size anomalies in the apes by modifying Dunbar's approach, but retains his commitment to the genus as the level for taxonomically independent comparisons. The most explicit discussions of this methodological problem are given by Foley and Lee; McHenry also raises the role of phylogenetic constraints in the evolution of varying primate sexual size dimorphisms in his discussion of the ecological significance of these morphological traits. The general methodological issues raised by such comparisons have been reviewed by Pagel and Harvey (1991).

If the problem of phylogenetically independent comparisons will not go away, nor will the problem of intraspecific variation in social systems. Both the approaches discussed in the previous paragraph assume that we can characterize primate species or higher taxa by their 'typical' social system – mean group size, competition level, sex-biased dispersal pattern. But a good deal of variation exists within and between populations of a given species in these traits, and affects comparisons between species – Melnick and Pearl (1987: 125), for example, found that 'even though the average bonnet macaque (*Macaca radiata*) group in south India is almost twice the size of the average Barbary macaque (*Macaca sylvanus*) group in Morocco, intraspecific variation in group size obscures this apparent difference' to the extent that it was not apparent in a simple one-way analysis of variance of the distribution of group size observations for the two species. As another instance, pygmy marmosets (*Cebuella pygmaea*) have been observed in groups of sizes between 1 and 15 individuals (n = 76, average = 6.4 individuals, Ferrari and Lopes-Ferrari 1989); gorillas (*Gorilla gorilla*) have been observed in groups of sizes ranging from 2 to 37 (n = 93, East and West African populations, median = 7–8 individuals, Harcourt *et al.* 1981). What is more important, the similarity in average group sizes, or the contrast in variance and in maximum group sizes? A strong central tendency in the distribution of observed group sizes may indicate an innate constraint (such as neocortex ratio, Dunbar 1992); a wide range of observed sizes may indicate an innate social flexibility responding to different habitat characteristics such as resource richness and patchiness. One very real question to be asked when we evaluate reconstructions of hominid social systems based on either of the two comparative methods just outlined is, therefore, 'How valid is the underlying characterization of the typical or modal values for social systems traits for the living taxa from which these reconstructions are derived?' Rowell proposes that social systems are *our* constructs, reifications of patterns of social interaction which are contingent on every individual reacting 'to perceived stimuli from the habitat and conspecifics according to the constraints and opportunities each stimulus provides at the moment' (Rowell 1993: 136). If there is a strong central tendency to the distribution of observed group sizes or mating patterns for a given species, therefore, it is only because some fundamental aspect of the species' adaptive repertoire (e.g. cognitive bias, locomotor limitations or dietary profile) is constraining individuals in different locations to make very similar decisions about reproduction, immigration and emigration in groups, or about mating tactics. While this critique does not negate the project of identifying typical social patterns for species, it does require us to focus our attention on the determinants of intraspecific *variability*.

There is, of course, a third problem with the comparative method, and like those of phylogenetically independent contrasts or intraspecific variation, it will not go away. This may be summarized succinctly by Barnett's apt recollection of 'a rebuke by an elderly philosopher: in his day, he said, he and his friends asked the inexhaustible question, what is man?; "but now all you young people can do is say, He *was* an ape"' (Barnett 1994: 171). Qualitatively unique behaviours that have emerged in hominid evolution, and which have no parallels among living non-human animals, demand an investigative methodology which draws primarily on observations of the behaviour and its ecological and anatomical correlates in contemporary human societies. Language, consciousness and social co-operation have often been cited as prototypical cases of this kind of behaviour. Here, we would simply point out the advances that have been made by searching for comparisons among living non-human primates, and warn against the premature drawing of Rubicon-like distinctions between the human and the non-human (see especially Gowlett and Dunbar, both in this volume). However, differences in cognitive abilities and social system properties which may have given rise to the evolution of a human 'knowledge economy' are extensively covered by contributors (see especially Shennan, Gamble, Knight, Power and Watts), and are discussed in more depth in the final section of this Introduction.

Thus the use of non-human primate data in reconstructing hominid social systems is subject to three methodological problems: (1) that of identifying the degrees of freedom from phylogenetic constraint available to hominids in differentiating from a great ape–human common ancestor; (2) that of quantifying the strength of central tendencies in the distribution of observed variants of a species' social system, when species traits are used in reconstructive inference; and (3) that of identifying the extent to which hominid behaviours depended on mechanisms which were qualitatively different from those of other, living primates.

ISSUES IN THE RECONSTRUCTION OF HOMINID SOCIAL SYSTEMS: SEXUAL DIVISION OF LABOUR, GROUP SIZE AND TIE STRUCTURE

To summarize, the ancestry of human society and the evolution of cultural traditions remain predominantly the domain of 'general theorists' working from comparative studies of fossil morphologies, of modern foragers and of living non-human primates. In order to test the general theories we need an intermediate set of hypotheses about how social systems leave their mark on the fossil and archaeological record. First of all, however, we need to be agreed that these issues are in principle *tractable*, and that general theory can reduce the number of 'degrees of freedom' in social models. In this section, three aspects of hominid social systems and their evolution are discussed: the sexual division of labour, group size and the structure of social bonds. The discussion concentrates on contributions to the renewal of debate on these issues which have come from within the discipline of palaeoanthropology and its related disciplines. While external sources of renewal in these debates have also come from philosophical critiques of the social construction of scientific knowledge, we are persuaded both that the most convincing elements of such critiques have been rapidly incorporated into the research programmes of workers in these focal disciplines, and that it is these workers who are best placed to advance the development of new models grounded firmly in the observed anatomy and ecological contexts of the hominids and the observed anatomy and behaviours of living primates, including humans.

The sexual division of labour

Increased male parental investment in child-rearing has often been seen as the most important social innovation in hominid evolution, and the one which removed the principal adaptive constraint on encephalization (the energetic cost to the mother of rearing such altricial and dependent offspring). Male provisioning effort has been particularly linked to the evolution of hunting, seen as the characteristic male foraging activity in forager bands, and to a sexual division of labour. One proposed correlate of this shift to more intensive male provisioning is the evolution of the monogamous pair bond: female continuous sexual receptivity and loss of oestrus signs have been held to reflect selection for sexual bonding mechanisms which reinforced that exclusive sexual and reproductive bond. Lovejoy (1981) argued that bipedalism in *Australopithecus afarensis* was an adaptation for provisioning – carrying food to the mate and offspring – and that human sexual behaviour reflected selection in early hominids of traits favouring monogamy and the 'nuclear family'. Isaac (1978) proposed a 'home base' model of archaeological site formation in the Lower Palaeolithic, associated with earliest *Homo*, which focused on food-sharing in small bands, and suggested that 'a mating system that involved at least one male in "family" food procurement on behalf of each child-rearing female in the group would have a clear selective advantage over, for example, the chimpanzees' pattern of opportunistic relations between the sexes' (1978: 106). He linked hunting and bipedality (which permitted carrying) into this general model.

The underlying assumptions of such arguments for male provisioning as the prime mover in hominid social evolution are highly debatable. Among the great apes, the closest parallel to human sexual traits such as continuous receptivity appears to come from the bonobos (*Pan paniscus*), among whom sex serves a wide range of social purposes including the building of affiliative bonds among unrelated females (Parish 1994). Common chimpanzees hunt (with bonobos they are the great ape species which are closest to humans in the proportion of female reproductive effort involved in the postnatal growth phase of their offspring), but co-operative hunting is restricted to specific combinations of circumstances (Boesch 1994), while at Gombe male chimpanzees appear to initiate hunting for red colobus monkeys primarily in response to the presence of oestrus females in the foraging party (who may receive the meat preferentially from them) – in other words, to acquire meat as a social and reproductive tool, perhaps as part of a process of female sexual selection (Stanford *et al.* 1994). Of non-human primate species living in multi-male groups, common chimpanzees are one of those among whom male care of young is reported least frequently (Busse 1985). Bipedality, which was earlier linked to provisioning, now seems more likely to have evolved in two phases – an initial emphasis on positional bipedalism in feeding (with analogies to chimpanzees), shifting with *Homo erectus* to an increased emphasis on thermoregulatory and locomotor efficiency associated with more extensive daytime ranging in a patchier habitat (cf. Hunt 1994, Wood 1993). Although these observations are not incompatible with a focus on the evolutionary significance of male provisioning effort, intensive male provisioning is inherently unstable as a strategy in multi-male groups, since it is a form of investment which is vulnerable to 'theft' by other males fertilizing the provisioned mate (Hawkes *et al.* n.d.): male reproductive interests are better served by concentrating on mating effort than by concentrating on care, except where either paternity can be assured to the male with relatively little effort in mate-guarding, or females exercise mate choice to favour caring males. Even in modern human foraging groups, Hawkes (1990) has suggested that male hunting may represent more a strategy for acquiring larger packets of resource for sharing outside the nuclear family than a family provisioning strategy, and suggested that the motive for this may be 'showing off' (thereby gaining preferential treatment from neighbours within a group).

> Among modern humans, men may acquire food for reasons quite different from family provisioning. Such patterns invite consideration of the role such reasons may have played among other hominids. . . . From the perspective of the showoff hypothesis, men's hunting may have more in common with the food calls of male chimpanzees (Wrangham 1977), than has otherwise been evident.
>
> (1990: 49)

In summary, the models of Lovejoy and Isaac favoured male provisioning effort as the key behavioural innovation which marked the emergence of a human pattern of society, but located the change respectively with early Australopithecine bipedalism and with the appearance of an archaeological record of early *Homo*. More recent theoretical and observational studies of chimpanzees and modern foragers suggest, however, that human family economics cannot be understood in isolation from the group-level dynamics of mate competition and alliance-building. In other recent models, male provisioning effort (where it is still understood as a form of parental investment) is seen as a very late addition to the social repertoire of hominid groups. Soffer (1994), noting that the origin of *Homo* has been displaced at centre of the stage in palaeoanthropology by debate on the origins of *Homo sapiens sapiens*, suggests that what characterized the Middle to Upper Palaeolithic transition in Eurasia was a social transformation – the appearance of the horizontally integrated, interdependent family and the sexual division of labour. She adduces a number of lines of evidence to support this hypothesis. Neanderthal archaeological remains are characterized by small, amorphous and undifferentiated sites with local raw material sources, an absence of symbolic items and a lack of food transport. Their skeletal remains indicate that both sexes were robustly built, that individuals experienced high levels of physical stress and that there was a high level of juvenile mortality. These characteristics indicate a social system of small, regionalized groups without a sexual division of labour or social differentiation. By contrast, the archaeological remains of early anatomically modern *Homo sapiens* are characterized by greater seasonal mobility across regional boundaries, variation in site types and sizes, food transport, the use of exotic resources and symbolic inventories. Their skeletal remains indicate that females became more gracile earlier than males, that males remained robust, and that individuals experienced lower levels of physical stress, lower juvenile mortality and increased longevity. Soffer interprets these contrasts as indicating that early anatomically modern humans in the northern latitudes of Eurasia lived in seasonally mobile groups of different sizes, with a sexual division of labour and social differentiation, and that this was the time of emergence of institutions of kinship. Soffer sees this social system not as the inevitable correlate of human biology or life-history, but as a sociocultural adaptation which emerged in northern latitudes and which became maintained as entrenched habitual practice at around the Middle to Upper Palaeolithic transition 'and generated the kind of an archaeological record we recognize as structurally similar to ethnographically known cases' (1994: 114–115).

McHenry (this volume) suggests that the degree of sexual dimorphism in *A. afarensis* and *A. africanus* is inconsistent with monogamy, and more likely reflects a multi–male, multi–female social system. The reduced sexual dimorphism of *Homo erectus* is attributed tentatively to selection for increased female body size, perhaps due to obstetric or metabolic constraints on production of large-brained offspring, or to biomechanical restraints on maximum body size in males. Gowlett (this volume) points out that the critique of Isaac's 'home base' model does not invalidate interpretation of dense artefact scatters as living floors – indeed, it would conflict with the observed lifeways of both non–human primates and modern foragers to deny hominids habitual use of favoured places as processing, feeding and/or sleeping sites. Foley and Lee (this volume) suggest that female reproductive energetics may have mandated pair-bonds and increased biparental investment with late *Homo erectus* (from about half a million years BP). Graves-Brown (this volume) suggests that male and female foraging roles evolved initially as more or less autonomous strategies, and suggests tentatively that the complementarity of a 'sexual division of labour' may only have emerged in ecological contexts like those of glacial Europe where such foraging autonomy became compromised by increased seasonality or increased efficiency in the technology of male foraging effort. Hawkes (this volume) extends this perspective, demonstrating that hunter-gatherer foraging effort differs by age, sex and ecology in ways that maximize the very different reproductive interests of males and females. Males may trade off parenting benefits for mating benefits, when the two are in conflict; females, whose foraging effort is concentrated on acquiring food resources to provision themselves and their offspring, may vary their foraging activity according to the ability of the offspring to participate in specific foraging activities.

Merlan (1992: 184–185) argued that in Australian aboriginal social systems,

> male–female separateness . . . provides the organizational basis for definition of spheres of action as male and female, not of each as a self-contained domain, but rather always one in relation to the other – always, as Strathern (1988: 334) has recently argued from Melanesian material, one kind of agent with the other 'in mind'.

Knight, and Power and Watts (both this volume), suggest both that the sexual division of labour appeared only with *Homo sapiens sapiens*, and that increased male provisioning effort was the result not of the pair-bond or of increased efficiency in hunting technology, but of female coercion through ritual regulation of sexual access. Their arguments for the effect of this social transformation on symbolic behaviour derive ultimately from a fusion of evolutionary ecology with Marxist theories of consciousness and collective action. But the idea that synchrony of reproductive timing in female co-residents of a group serves to increase male parenting effort is well-founded in observations of non-human primates:

1 Females may blur their estruses, thus inducing a situation of *scramble competition* between males. This may diminish the 'certainty of paternity' and reduce the likelihood of male infanticidal strategies.
2 Females can also make a polygynous male strategy become pointless by sharply synchronizing their estruses. Either method may have evolved to increase the option of female choice and seduce males to investment in services. Thus females may tip the balance towards special relationships or *monogamous bonds*.

(van Hooff and van Schaik 1994: 313–314)

The suggestion that apparent synchrony of female reproductive schedules in groups may have contributed to the evolution of male parenting stategies is, however, consistent with models other than those proposed by Knight and by Power and Watts (this volume). For instance, it is apparent that in human populations subject to seasonal resource scarcity, female conceptions peak at the beginning of the period of relative abundance, probably due to the effect of poor nutritional status on fertility during the period of scarcity (Ellison 1994). A recent survey of non-human primates living in temperate zones found that those species tend to have seasonal peaks in births (in spring), and increased levels of male parental care (even though the females mate with more than one male). 'It is all very well to impregnate and move on when there are abundant resources for mother and baby. But if neither get through the winter it's not a very sound strategy' (K. Cichy, quoted in Burne 1995). For *hominids* in zones with pronounced seasonal resource stress, increased male investment in parenting *and* birth seasonality may have evolved without any conscious synchronizing of reproductive effort by the females.

In summary, the evolution of a sexual division of labour and of increased male provisioning effort – formerly seen as the primary motor of hominid social systems – is increasingly being seen both as problematic (as a description of the dynamics of gendered foraging effort in contemporary hunter-gatherers) and as a late appearing trait of hominid foraging systems; it perhaps even appeared only as a cultural innovation in the Eurasian Upper Palaeolithic, unrelated to the selection pressures which had earlier produced the anatomically modern human morphology.

Group size

The evolution of hominid mating systems is, therefore, increasingly seen within the context of the evolution of large multi-male, multi-female groups, probably with a socionomic sex ratio approaching parity (cf.

McHenry, this volume). The evolution of hominid social cognitive abilities and of human patterns of social communication are also increasingly being seen in relation to the demands of living in increasingly large groups, and not those of living in small groups with a distinctive food-sharing foraging economy. This shift of emphasis in palaeoanthropology from a focus on male provisioning effort to one on cognitive adaptations to increasing group size has led to a renewed interest in 'magic numbers' or critical values for group size in different societies and task conditions.

Dunbar (this volume) summarizes evidence indicating that human groupings are limited by cognitive constraints, and argues that language evolved to service social relationships in large groups under time constraints. He presents new evidence from the study of human genealogical depth to support his contention that humans are naturally limited to face-to-face group sizes of a maximum of about 125–150 individuals. Steele (chapter 8) reanalyses some data used by Aiello and Dunbar (1993) to predict group sizes for extinct hominids, and having resolved some problems with the original analysis produces some new predictions which he proposes can be tested using raw material transport distances as indicators of minimum home range diameters (and thus group mass) in the Palaeolithic. Mithen (this volume) proposes that group size and cohesion affect the probability of persistence of cultural traditions, and links assemblage variation in the Lower Palaeolithic of southern England to ecological conditions which would have favoured either large, cohesive groups or smaller, less cohesive groups. Gamble (this volume) suggests that discussions of cognition and group size have ignored the spatial distribution of individuals in social groups, and proposes that the Upper Palaeolithic was characterized by an extension of the *spatial scale* of interactions. Shennan (this volume) discusses the implications of forager band structure, particularly the emergence of social inequality, for the persistence of cultural traditions. All these authors focus primarily on issues relating to group size, and the implications of varying group size for the evolution of cognitive capacity, coalition size, co-operative behaviour and cultural traditions.

Both non-human primates and humans form social aggregations in a hierarchy of increasing inclusiveness, each level serving different functions. Hull (1988: 22, 366) suggests that there is an analogy between the hierarchical structure of hamadryas baboon groups – small groups of a dozen or so for mating and care of young, feeding groups of 40–50, and sleeping groups of 125–750 primarily for predator avoidance – and that of scientific communities (where individuals form research groups of 'conceptual kin', which in turn make up 'conceptual demes' of dozens to several hundreds of scientists, depending on the discipline – a fourth level of inclusiveness being the 'invisible college'). As Caporael (1995) points out, such functionally differentiated hierarchies of core aggregations are pervasive in human societies, not least in the four-tier structure of foragers (dyad, task group, local band, regional band). An independent identification of such a pattern has also been made by social network analysts: Milardo (1992) identifies four levels of social network among individuals in contemporary urban industrialized states, of increasing size but whose members are progressively more 'distant', including the network of significant others (averaging about five members); the exchange network of people who are looked to for material or symbolic support (averaging about 19–20 members); the interactive networks of those with whom interactions typically occur (of widely varying sizes); and the global network of 'all people known to an individual' (again, a level with vastly different sizes of membership for different individuals). What is significant here is not just the existence of a hierarchy of levels of social network in many different social systems, but also the contrasting functions which the different levels of social network serve. One question we should bear in mind in examining the literature on hominid and human forager group sizes is, therefore, whether the group level in question corresponds to a cognitive grouping of 'all those of whom one has some social knowledge', or a cognitive grouping of 'all those with whom one can realistically hope to maintain intensive co-operative relations on a day-to-day basis'. The contrasting size-dependent cognitive demands for the social tasks implied by these two types of grouping will differ drastically, and this will affect the kinds of social interaction which can develop in groups of whatsoever size and cohesiveness.

Although large feeding or sleeping aggregations are common among terrestrial primates, game-theoretic simulations of the evolution of co-operation have shown that reciprocity is very hard to maintain in large groups due to the difficulty of tracking the intentions of so many different potential interaction partners (cf. Boyd and Richerson 1988, Glance and Huberman 1994). Williams (1981) pointed out that human working memory is evidently constrained by a storage limitation on the number of 'units' of information which can be held simultaneously in memory (5–7 units), and that this extended to the domain of social cognition. Williams suggested further that the household constitutes 'a chunk for economic, social, and political calculations in the everyday life of hunting peoples as in most societies' (1981: 249), and that the observed minimum band size of foraging groups, 25, corresponds to an aggregation of 5–7 such households. That humans may be constrained by cognitive limits in their social arrange-ments was further supported, for Williams, by evidence from a large study of urban student samples which found that the number of families which were classified as 'friend families' of the student's family was also always, on average, five 'friend families', and that this finding was almost invariant with respect to location and ethnic composition of the samples.

The most significant cognitive factor here is the constancy of the *size* of these groups or networks. Over time, their *composition* may be relatively fluid. In Williams' observation of the Birhor hunter-gatherers, foraging bands at the fission stage of the annual cycle change their composition according to transient minor disputes and frictions (1981: 250). In industrialized society, small informal voluntary groups based on 'organic solidarity' and sentimental ties are not necessarily characterized by universal strong ties among group members. Everyone in such a 'primary' group does not associate preferentially only with his or her fellows: individuals may interact 'as much or more with outsiders than they do with some of their fellow group members' (Freeman 1992a: 164). By implication, such a 'weak tie' structure means that voluntary group composition over time is likely to be much more fluid than in a group characterized by universal 'strong ties'. The *size* constant in human groups implies that cognitive constraints on group structure primarily reflect constraints on human capacity for *simultaneous integration* of social information from a large number of individuals, rather than constraints on the predictability of the outcome of interactions which are due to the degree of long-term 'familiarity' among group members (although we would assume that minimal foraging bands tend to be recruited from a stable community-level interaction network).

Johnson (1982: 393) reviewed evidence that,

1 The development of within-group leadership (hierarchical organization) appears to be most common in groups of six individuals.
2 Horizontally organized (non-hierarchical) groups of greater than six members appear to be under some kind of stress as evidenced by decreasing consensus in decision making and decreasing member satisfaction with group performance.
3 In groups of less than six members, not only does decision quality increase with group size, but horizontally organized groups may exhibit superior performance in comparison to hierarchically organized ones.

He also linked this group size effect to innate cognitive constraints on social information processing in co-operative groups, and gave extensive evidence that these constraints extend into group size and structure in societies with economies and population sizes greatly exceeding those of contemporary foragers. That large group size tends to have a negative effect on participation, cohesion and productivity, and to lead to increased conflict, is also the conclusion of a more recent review of group size effects in modern industrialized societies (Wheelan and McKeage 1993). In Johnson's view, while the stresses imposed on large groups in decision-making tasks can often lead to the evolution of simultaneous or 'sequential' hierarchies, reflected in the archaeological finding that 'it is now commonplace to suggest that many groups of egalitarian hunters and gatherers were not so egalitarian after all', a more common response to such large group size effects in pre-state societies is group fissioning (see also Boehm 1993). This is only prevented from occurring where the advantages of remaining voluntarily in large groups outweigh the costs, or where the group is socially or environmentally circumscribed – 'the fission products have no place to go' (Johnson 1982: 408).

Thus the scale of the relatively egalitarian, 'organic' human groups which are optimal for co-operative tasks appears to be much smaller than the group size predicted for humans by Dunbar (this volume) or by Steele (chapter 8, this volume). Dunbar is generalizing from observed brain/ group size correlations in other primates, and his prediction of mean human group size of about 150 individuals appears to be inconsistent with the much smaller size observed for human minimal foraging bands. But compared with other primates, human forager aggregation at the *community* level may be much more subject to seasonal fluctuations in resource concentrations, and this may bias our perceptions of the scale of the interaction networks in a human foraging community. Conversely, the focus on mean group size in Dunbar's work on the non-human primates should not distract us from the importance of subgroups and 'household'-type structures within such non-human primate groups (e.g. Quiatt 1985, 1986). Apparent contrasts between observed and predicted patterns in humans may simply reflect the greater proportion of the annual foraging cycle taken up by the fission phase in humans, and the relatively great importance placed on co-operation in foraging in human groups compared with those of other primate species. If there *is* a correlation between group size and brain structure across primates, including humans, then it is likely to reflect an adaptive component of social cognition which is common to all the primate genera: and this is more likely to relate to factors such as recognizing the long-term structure of affiliative ties within a community-level group (cf. Freeman 1992b), than to reflect the workload in computation of possible strategies and pay-offs in smaller groups whose members are playing a synchronous, repeated Prisoner's Dilemma-type co-operative game.

It is the latter which is the focus of explanatory models which focus on the '5–7 unit' human grouping, and on cognitive factors involved in the persistence of this smaller group size in human local foraging bands. It is quite possible, although as yet untested, that hominid foraging communities have been larger and more cohesive than the twenty-five individuals of the forager local band for much of the Palaeolithic and that the 'magic number twenty-five' only became typical of foraging groups in the Upper Palaeolithic, perhaps associated with a different economic strategy and a greater emphasis on more intensive sharing and norms of reciprocity within that smaller group.

Tie structure

The finding that larger groups tend to be more unstable applies to other anthropoid primates as well: Beauchamp and Cabana (1990) suggest that species living in large average group sizes, especially the terrestrial frugivores, tend to have a fission–fusion grouping pattern due to the groups' intrinsic instability. There are suggestions that for non-human primates, the possibility of fission may also be dependent on an absence of circumscription: where the costs of fission and dispersal of its 'products' are high, due to predation risk or the lack of empty adjacent territory, then animals may tolerate higher levels of dominance hierarchy. This idea – that community size may have different consequences for behavioural style according to the costs or frequency of temporary fission – is explored in various ways relating to human groups by Chance, Steele (chapter 4) and Shennan in this volume. Chance (this volume) contrasts two modes of social behaviour, the 'hedonic' and the 'agonic', and proposes that the 'hedonic' mode is the typical mode of human social life and that which characterized hominid social systems. The dichotomous classification of human social forms which he proposes has some similarities to Benedict's (1934) famous distinction between the Apollonian and the Dionysiac types; but in Chance's work, it is informed by ethological studies of the contrast between the social orders of great apes and Old World monkeys. Strum and Mitchell (1987) distinguished two rather similar pathways to social complexity in primates. One (typified by baboons) is that in which large groups with constant association among members, high density, high costs of aggression and impossibility of escape lead to selection for social manipulation and systems of reciprocity. The other (typified by chimpanzees) is that in which a fission–fusion social system leads to assessment problems in social encounters, leading to selection for an elaborate reassurance and appeasement repertoire, social intelligence and social manipulation within subgroups. The prediction that niche-specific variation in external constraints on group fissioning will affect the characteristic dominance pattern and 'emotional style' of species is also supported by van Schaik's (1989: 200) link of strong within-group feeding competition to a pattern of highly cohesive grouping associated with high vunerability to predation, and his suggestion that within-group feeding competition will be limited where predation risk is lessened (and where subgrouping to adapt to local patch richness thus becomes viable).

The evolution of hominid and human social groups involved, therefore, more than simply changes in the numerical limits on aggregation: the characteristic *structure of social bonds* can also be investigated. A number of contributions to this volume focus more specifically on the evolving structure of hominid social bonds, particularly in relation to sex. Foley and Lee (this volume) suggest that the conservatism of social system evolution makes male-kin bonded groups the best prototype for Australopithecine social organization, and that the close, long-term male–female bonds with prolonged biparental care and investment seen in modern humans may not have evolved at the most significant rate until about half a million years ago, with late *Homo erectus*. McHenry (this volume) suggests that the patterns of sexual size dimorphism seen in hominids are consistent with kin-related multi-male groups for *A. afarensis*, and that the reduced dimorphism seen in *Homo erectus* may either reflect biomechanical and reproductive factors favouring selective female body-size increase, or perhaps reduced male–male competition. Maryanski (this volume) argues that conserved features of great ape social systems – in this case, a pattern of high autonomy and generally relatively low sociality which is promoted by female migration from the natal group – shaped hominid social evolution, and that the shift to a more open habitat where denser groups were adaptive triggered the formation of the stabilizing institutions of kinship and economy (sexually segregated foraging roles). She proposes that the weak tie structure of African ape social systems is favourable to the maintenance of community-level relationships among larger numbers of individuals in dispersed local foraging groups. Steele (chapter 4) catalogues a range of features of modern human anatomy and behaviour which indicate a relaxed within-group dominance regime, and suggests that some at least of these traits can be traced back to *Homo erectus*. Chance (this volume) suggests that the affiliative and agonistic structure of social groups affects the level of creativity and the quality of individual learning of its members. As Foley and Lee point out (this volume), culture 'is concerned with the transmission of ideas and information through non-biological means, and as such it is transmitted largely through social channels'. As confidence increases in our ability to reconstruct the affiliative structure and interaction patterns of hominid groups on the basis of phylogenetic affinity and ecological niche, so we can begin to work on the effect of the organization of social interaction patterns on cultural transmission in hominid groups.

THE EVOLUTION OF HUMAN CULTURAL TRADITIONS

Reconstructing major aspects of hominid social systems is, therefore, a realistic scientific goal when the fossil and archaeological records are supplemented with evidence from living primates, and from modern hunter-gatherers. This leads on to the other main target of research in this field (at least from the perspective of the human sciences), which is to enable us to understand the emergence of a uniquely human pattern of adaptation – one which relies so heavily on the social transmission of information through cultural learning. The core of this transmission process is the activity of learning from conspecifics by imitation and instruction: through these processes, beliefs and practices may be transmitted from one (cultural) generation to the next and individuals do not have to learn everything they need to know by trial and error. This section considers some recent issues concerning the evolution of cognition and culture which provide the background to a number of the chapters in this book and which are central to any discussion of the nature of hominid cultural traditions.

Primate cognitive abilities and social learning

Social learning – defined as 'learning that is influenced by observation of, or interaction with, another animal (typically a conspecific) or its products' (Heyes 1994: 208) – is widespread among animals, and complements both genetically determined behaviour and learned behaviours which are acquired 'asocially' by individual trial-and-error learning. Empirical studies of such social transmission processes in birds and mammals suggest that the predominant mode of transfer is horizontal, between members of the same generation, and that the process is advantageous in environments which are rapidly changing and spatially heterogeneous (Laland 1993: 157). The prototypical example is social transmission of foraging information of transient value, which enables individuals 'rapidly to "home in" on appropriate behaviours' (Laland 1993: 157). Because of the speed at which behaviours are learned and transmitted socially, such a mode of information transfer can enable animals to respond to environmental novelty much more rapidly than is normally possible through genetic adaptation (Laland 1992). Social learning wins out over individual trial-and-error learning where individual learning is costly, but where there is a low probability that social transmission will propagate traits which reduce fitness (Laland 1993).

Much of human behaviour is under the control of socially learned concepts and mental representations, which are the product of cumulative modifications and re-transmissions of originally novel individually learned innovations. Indeed, many social scientists would argue that an individual's actions are entirely a construction of his or her social environment, with its sedimented layers of tradition written into the very fabric of every aspect of language and gesture. Thus *social learning theory* would seem to provide common ground for understanding aspects of both animal and human behaviour. There are, however, a number of different mechanisms of social learning, at least one of which appears to depend on high-order cognitive processes which remain to be demonstrated outside the hominoid (great ape–human) clade (cf. Galef 1988, Whiten and Ham 1992, Heyes 1994).

Work in this area has been shaped by the historical focus of social learning theory on the extent of the distribution among animals of imitative processes leading to 'matching behaviour', where the observing animal's behaviour comes to resemble that of the 'demonstrator' (social learning can also lead to other types of effect, Heyes 1994). An indication of the complexities involved in the interpretation of such 'matching behaviour' in animals is given by a recent review of the subject by Whiten and Ham (1992). They distinguish twelve different 'mimetic processes', where this means, 'all processes whereby some aspect of the behaviour of one animal, B, comes to be like that of another, A' (Whiten and Ham 1992: 246). If one excludes their four non-social processes, such as convergence and common descent, where matching arises without any social interaction of A and B, this still leaves another eight where some sort of social influence is involved. Among these, a distinction is made between 'social influence' and 'social learning'. Examples given of the former include 'contagion', defined as 'the unconditional release of an instinctive behaviour in one animal by the performance of the same behaviour in another animal' (Thorpe 1963, quoted in Whiten and Ham 1992: 252); 'exposure', where 'by simply being with (or following) A, B may be exposed to a similar learning environment and thus acquire similar behaviour' (Whiten and Ham 1992: 252); and 'social support', where 'B may be more likely to learn behaviour like A's in the mere presence of A and its learning environment, because A affects B's motivational state' (Whiten and Ham 1992: 253).

With the exception of contagion, which only involves the conditioned release of *instinctive* behaviours, these processes of social influence can lead to what is, in effect, cultural transmission, in which particular behaviour patterns spread through space and time without any corresponding genetic spread.

The same is, of course, true of the four mechanisms which the authors place under the heading of 'social learning'. From the point of view of the evolutionary study of 'imitation', perhaps the most misleading of these is 'stimulus (or local) enhancement'. It is this which is now believed to be behind the pattern of milk-bottle opening by tits (Fisher and Hinde 1949). Here subsequent work has shown that this does not necessarily involve imitation, in the sense of learning to do an act from seeing it done, but is explicable simply on the assumption that the birds learn to open milk bottles by a process of trial and error after their attention has been drawn to them by the activity of other birds (Sherry and Galef 1984). That is to say, they do not imitate, in the sense of learning from conspecifics *how* to open milk bottles. On the other hand, actually distinguishing the two mechanisms in practice may be extremely difficult.

Their second type of social learning Whiten and Ham refer to as 'observational conditioning': 'a form of classical conditioning in which an unconditioned response (e.g. fearful behaviour as a response to fearful behaviour in others) becomes associatively conditioned to a new stimulus (e.g. the presence of a snake)' (Whiten and Ham 1992: 250). Heyes (1994) has demonstrated that both these mechanisms of social learning can be understood within the terms of general animal learning theory.

Social influence and social learning processes of these kinds can certainly lead to the spread of behaviours through a population or sub-population of animals. Galef (1990) suggests that rather than calling such local distributions 'cultural traditions', we should initially refer to them as 'locale-specific' behaviours and avoid prejudging the issue of mechanism of spread. A cultural 'tradition', by contrast, seems to imply a process of transmission across generations, with cumulative modification due to individual learning; and this seems to imply some higher-order cognitive operations. Whiten and Ham's other two social learning mechanisms meet that condition. True imitation involves a process by which B 'learns some aspect(s) of the intrinsic form of an act from A' (Whiten and Ham 1992: 250), whether this involves acquiring a novel form of behaviour or using an existing form in response to another's use of it, 'where the form of the imitator's act is derived from the information gained in observing the other's act' (Whiten and Ham: 251). Imitation of this kind requires complex cross-modal analysis of inputs in which an animal must 'equate topographically visual input from its environment with response-generated kinaesthetic and/or proprioceptive stimulation' (Heyes 1993: 1006). For instance, Boesch (1993: 514, original italics) reports that '*copying the precise movement of the model* is very strong in the cultural behaviours of Taï chimpanzees'. There is some indication that such cognitive achievements are limited to the hominoid clade. The final category of social learning process is 'goal emulation', which involves reproducing not so much the behaviour of the model as the results achieved. Thus, Tomasello *et al.* (1987) discovered that chimpanzees who had seen others rake in out-of-reach food with a stick were quicker to do so themselves than others who had not seen this, but invented their own ways of using the stick to do it. As Whiten and Ham point out, this could be seen as a particularly intelligent form of learning from the activities of others precisely in that it involves recognizing a goal but not imitative copying. However, Nagell *et al.* (1993: 175) suggest that compared with true imitation, 'the limitation of emulation learning is that little if anything is learned about precisely how the model actually behaved'.

As an illustration of the issues involved in attributing mechanisms to an observed process of social learning we can take the supposedly 'classic case' of imitation and transmission in monkeys: the appearance and spread of potato-washing in a group of Japanese macaques at Koshima (Nishida 1987). Galef (1990) has recently proposed a number of alternative accounts of the spread of this behaviour through the troop, which do not involve 'true imitation' processes. For example, it is possible that the behaviour was independently discovered by many individuals, and it is likely that at least one of the persons provisioning the troop with sweet potatoes unconsciously reinforced the behaviour by feeding only those monkeys who washed them. This reinterpretation, in terms of simpler mechanisms, is supported by evidence from laboratory studies of macaques and of New World cebids (which are of a similar grade of brain size and organization) which suggest that these monkey species are not capable of the high-order cognitive operations involved in 'true imitation' (Visalberghi and Fragaszy 1990, Povinelli 1993).

Much of the field evidence for true imitation in chimpanzees can be explained in a similar way by stimulus enhancement: with regard to the well-known technique of using sticks to 'fish' for termites, even captive chimpanzees reared without access to models to imitate may show tendencies to poke sticks in holes (Whiten and Ham 1992). However, there are some chimpanzee behaviours in the wild which may be transmitted by imitation, such as the 'grooming handclasp' (McGrew 1992), and there have been reports of intentional instruction in which a mother showed her infant how to carry out nut-cracking with a hammer and anvil (Boesch 1991). Taken overall, the evidence suggests that chimpanzees and orangutans *can* imitate in the true sense but that monkeys probably cannot, or only in very limited ways (e.g. Visalberghi and Fragaszy 1990, Boesch 1993, Nagell *et al.* 1993, Russon and Galdikas 1993), and that this difference between the great apes and the monkeys lies in a broader pattern of cognitive distinctions. Chimpanzees have an ability 'to mentally represent another's mentality' (Whiten and Ham 1992: 271), evidenced in the fact that they engage in true pretend-play and 'mind-reading'; that is to say, both experiment and observation indicate that chimpanzees attribute intentional states to others. Imitation of complex actions of the kind of which chimpanzees are capable may require similar abilities.

Mechanisms of social transmission in human groups

If we now turn to humans, it is easy to accept that much social learning is the result of the simpler mechanisms. But it is generally agreed that it is learning based on imitation which is crucial to human social and cultural ontogeny, just as it is for the long-term processes of cultural evolution. Pelissier (1991), for example, shows how the human acquisition of culture (knowledge of norms, roles and skills) is shaped by the interactions of caregivers and children or novices, and is usually achieved (at least in cultures lacking formal schools) by a controlled 'legitimate peripheral participation' in activity, rather than by formal abstract instruction. Like Whiten and Ham, Tomasello *et al.* (1993) argue that perspective-taking is critical to real learning by imitation: 'in cultural learning, learners do not just direct their attention to the location of another individual's activity; rather, they actually attempt to see a situation the way the other sees it – from inside the other's perspective as it were' (Tomasello *et al.* 1993: 496). They propose that there are three stages in the ontogeny of human cultural learning. The first is true imitative learning involving object-directed actions and the use of communicative symbols, which occurs at around 9 months. The second, instructed learning, in the sense of 'the internalisation of adult instructions' (Tomasello *et al.* 1993: 499) is reached at around 4 years of age, while the social-cognitive foundations of their final stage, collaborative learning, do not emerge until the age of 6 to 7. Imitation also appears to play an important role on language acquisition (Braine 1994).

Three major differences between the cultural traditions of humans and other primates are suggested. The first is that 'all human groups have some cultural traditions that are learned by virtually all group members; any child who did not learn them would simply not be considered a normal member of the group' (Tomasello *et al.* 1993: 507). The second distinction is that human cultural traditions accumulate modifications over the generations – if a modification takes place, it is the modification that is passed on. The third difference is the mechanism of social learning in human groups, true imitation, which (they argue) permits the evolution of traditions. Like Whiten and Ham, they argue that most of the 'traditions' observed in non-enculturated primates are explicable in terms of mechanisms such as stimulus enhancement and other non–imitative (in the strict sense) social processes, which mean that there is very little real cultural accumulation of learned information – although as we have seen, this conclusion is disputed when applied to the great apes. The link between active social information transfer through teaching and the ability to attribute mental states to others also has been made explicit by Cheney and Seyfarth (1990), who suggested that primates who cannot separate their own beliefs and purposes from those of others cannot therefore attribute ignorance to others, and 'teach'. This led King (1991: 112) to advance a 'tentative explanation' for the evolved role of active social transmission in human groups: 'the increased ability to recognize and manipulate mental states of others, which conferred selective advantages on individuals interacting in complex social networks'.

The linkage of the capacity for true imitation to other 'high–order' cognitive processes in great apes is also supported by evidence in humans. Parker (1993) proposes that imitation and circular reactions (self-induced repetition of particular schemes) play an important role in the cognitive construction of causal understanding of actions and of the environment for actions, and sees these abilities as a derived trait of the great ape–human common ancestor. Smith and Bryson (1994) argue that the human autistic syndrome (seen in the symptomatic inability to imitate or to adopt another's perspective) relates to a basic information-processing deficit, namely an impaired ability to selectively attend to important aspects of the perceptual world and to shift the focus of attention in complex tasks, both within and across sensory modalities. Finally, Dawson *et al.* (1985) report psychophysiological evidence that facial and manual motor imitation are (like verbal tasks) predominantly under the control of the left cerebral hemisphere. This may relate to the possible functional specialization of that side of the brain for movement production tasks referenced to an internal body schema. Thus if the more simple processes of social learning can all be subsumed within general animal learning theory (Heyes 1994), true imitation appears to depend on high-order cognitive operations similar to those involved in perspective-taking, hierarchical object manipulation, and probably also in human language-processing.

There are signs, then, that the capacity for social information transfer *by imitation* may be limited to the hominoids. By implication, the relevant anatomical trait which differentiates them from the other anthropoid primates is likely to be the greater absolute brain size of the great apes and of humans. But is the existence of this cognitive capacity either a necessary or a sufficient condition for the evolution of cultural traditions? Can we attribute the possibility of human cultural evolution to the mechanism of true imitation alone? On the one hand, social transmission also requires initial input of high quality individually learned behaviours. On the other hand, the accumulation of modifications in a true 'cultural tradition' requires either that the information being transmitted has an adaptive value which is insensitive to local environmental variation, or that its transmission is insulated from extensive modification by individual learning (under the influence of local environmental variables). Imitation may be a more 'insulated' mechanism of social learning in that the learner need not interact with the environment at the time of acquisition, but nonetheless imitated behaviour declines and disappears subsequently in the face of aversive consequences (Heyes 1993). As Heyes (1993: 1005) puts it,

> if information acquired through imitation is as likely as information acquired through individual or [other processes of] social learning to be lost or revised as a result of the imitator's own interactions with its asocial environment, then imitation is no more likely than [other processes of] social learning to support culture.

The condition of high-quality individual learning, or at least 'creativity', certainly appears to be met by the great apes. Chance (this volume) links creativity in primates to neocortex size, and this link is supported by a plot of the scores for manipulative creativity in various primate species (from Parker 1974) against their absolute brain sizes, when the latter is used as a rough indicator of neocortex size (Figure 0.1). Similar comparative findings have been reported in a separate study of object manipulation patterns (Torigoe 1985) and in a study of curiosity in captive animals (Glickman and Sroges 1966). But the condition that imitative learning should be insulated from individual testing is not so easily demonstrated in non-human species: indeed, the evidence for creativity would suggest that hominoids will be very likely to test any imitatively learned behaviour, not necessarily purposively, before transmitting it. Heyes (1993: 1006) lists three processes which can lead to such 'insulation': they are the transmission of information about temporally and spatially remote objects and events or metaphysical entities, the adherence to social norms or moral beliefs promoting faithful transmission, and the storage of information exosomatically. All these processes buffer information against individual testing, the first because of the difficulty of testing it, the second because of normative attitudes to the status of

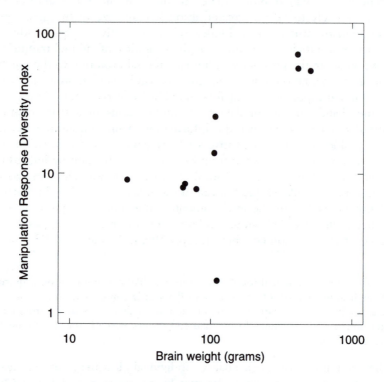

Figure 0.1 Adult brain size and manipulative creativity – the latter in a captive sample – of non-human primate genera (data from Parker 1974 and Harvey *et al.* 1987)

the information and the third because the stored information remains in the environment even after it may have been rejected by individuals. They would all support the move to a 'knowledge economy'. There has, however, been little success in identifying such processes at work in the 'traditions' of animals other than humans.

Thus while specific social learning capacities such as the ability to imitate may be constrained by the size and organization of the brain, the incorporation of such a capacity as the mechanism of retention of a cumulative cultural tradition requires other factors which ultimately pertain to *social systems*, such as the extension of scale of ranging areas and interaction networks, the appearance of social norms relating to information and its transfer, or the use of material cultural symbols as information stores. All these factors will insulate the information acquired by the imitator from testing against his or her own immediate experience. The alternative hypothesis would be that high-order social learners are psychologically predisposed to imitate models unevaluatively: but for humans and their hominid forebears, this is contradicted by evidence for a high order of curiosity and capacity to generate behavioural novelty in the hominoid clade.

In conclusion it seems, then, that cultural transmission by imitation is specific to the hominoids, and that within this clade it may be rare in the non-human great apes. The cognitive capacities entailed probably relate to encephalization and the evolutionary enlargement of the hominoid and hominid neocortex: insofar as they are specific to the social domain, they reflect a selection pressure for ability to succeed in manipulating relationships in complex social networks. Active teaching, in turn, appears to depend on the pre-existence of the same cognitive mechanisms involved in imitation – namely, the ability to model the physical postures and mental states of conspecifics. Insofar as both these processes will contribute to fidelity in cultural transmission, they are likely to lead to the evolution of cultural traditions. But as we have seen, there is in fact some cause to doubt that such imitative social learning capabilities are a *sufficient* condition for the evolution of cultural traditions. In fact, cultural traditions will only emerge if a further set of conditions are met, pertaining to the insulation of imitated behaviours from extinction due to short-term effects of individual trial-and-error learning.

Modelling the ecological preconditions and evolutionary dynamics of cultural transmission

While the study of the biological evolution of hominids has had a Darwinian evolutionary basis from the start, it is only relatively recently that an approach has been developed which looks rigorously at culture from the same perspective. The starting point for such work is the process of cultural transmission. If certain behaviours are transmitted from one generation to the next by processes of cultural learning, then cultural transmission represents a kind of inheritance mechanism, just as genetic transmission does. Furthermore, the frequencies of particular cultural variants will change through time – some will be more successful than others – just as in the case of genes. The question then becomes one of characterizing the specific mechanisms of cultural inheritance and their implications, and of investigating the mechanisms which result in changing frequencies.

A number of theorists have developed mathematical models of cultural transmission in recent years: the best-known contributions have come from Lumsden and Wilson (1981), Cavalli-Sforza and Feldman (1981) and Boyd and Richerson (1985). The approach has been most extensively developed by Boyd and Richerson (see especially Boyd and Richerson

1985, 1992), who identify several processes by which culture can come to have an adaptive role. These are summarized in Table 0.1.

Boyd and Richerson see the force of cultural bias as 'a culling process analogous to natural selection' (1992: 67). Imitative social learning is not blind, but selective, and the selectivity is guided by preferences which ought (in the main) to pick out the variant behaviours which are most likely to lead to maximizing inclusive fitness.

In parallel with this work defining the mechanisms of cultural evolution, theorists in this field have attempted to determine the ecological conditions which favour a dependence on imitative social learning (Rogers 1989, Boyd and Richerson 1992, Lake, this volume). Individual learning by trial and error is potentially costly, since there is a high probability of error; but it also enables the individual to sample local environmental variables to a degree which is unavailable to one dependent on the 'received wisdom' of models or demonstrators whose experience derives from environments which are spatially or temporally more remote.

Rogers (1989) assumed that cultural learning may be favoured because it cuts the cost of learning by trial and error. However, he shows that if everyone learns from others, the learning process is likely to become increasingly insensitive to environmental variables, so that people will do better if they go back to trial-and-error learning. The result will be an equilibrium mix of cultural and trial-and-error learners, since the adaptiveness of one or other strategy will be frequency-dependent; the specific equilibrium reached will depend on the amount of variation in the environment. Such an equilibrium is known as an 'evolutionarily stable strategy' (ESS), meaning that in the given circumstances it cannot be changed by natural selection; any deviation away from it will be countered by selective forces which bring the balance back to equilibrium.

Boyd and Richerson (1992: 71–74) developed an alternative model, in which there is also an equilibrium (ESS) involving a mixture of individual and cultural learning, with the balance moving towards cultural learning in environments which are more homogeneous in time and/or space. In this model, where individuals can (in contrast to Rogers' simple model) depend on a mix of social and individual learning, the average fitness of the individuals in the 'mixed strategy' population is actually greater than that of a population of purely individual learners. Cultural learning is favoured over genetic adaptation plus individual learning except where environmental stability is nearly constant or nearly random. The same conclusions apply to spatial environmental variation: here, the danger of cultural learning is that an individual in a particular situation where one specific strategy is best will imitate someone from another situation where a different strategy is more successful. Exploration of the implications of this (Boyd and Richerson 1993: 138–141) shows that the equilibrium amount of imitation depends on the relative quality of the information

Table 0.1 The principal mechanisms of adaptive cultural learning, according to Boyd and Richerson (1985, 1992)

Category	Mechanism	Psychological aspects	Consequences
Guided variation	Culturally learned beliefs about appropriate behaviour, modified through individual trial-and-error learning	Imitated behaviours are evaluated against local environment variables, and selectively modified or retained in the light of individual trial-and-error learning	Changing patterns of behaviour in successive generations
Biased transmission (a) Direct bias	Culturally available possibilities – for example, the behaviours of alternative possible 'models' in specific situations – are evaluated selectively in the light of preferences	Preferences may be governed by genetically determined predispositions, or may require more conscious 'calculation', but do not involve individual trial-and-error learning	Changing frequencies of pre-existing behaviours in successive generations
(b) Indirect bias	An individual is selected as a 'model' for imitation on the basis of cues concerning his or her reproductive success, such as greater personal prestige or wealth, and many features of his or her behaviour are imitated – not all of which may be fitness-enhancing	Models are selected on the basis of cues as to their reproductive success, leading to unselective imitation both of the behaviours contributing to that success and of other, contingently associated traits	Changing frequencies of pre-existing behaviours in successive generations, not all of which will correlate with reproductive success
(c) Positive frequency-dependent bias	The conformist tendency is exercised to adopt or imitate the version of a behaviour which is most common in the vicinity	'Conformism' is an adaptive response to situations where it is difficult to decide which of the available options is most conducive to enhancing fitness	Changing frequencies of pre-existing behaviours in successive generations, not all of which will correlate with reproductive success; may lead to group selection effects

obtained by trial and error as compared to that obtained by observing and selecting models:

> when the amount of mixing between environments is not too large and information is of low quality, individuals achieve the highest expected utility by relying mainly on tradition. We think that this combination of circumstances is not uncommon. The world is complicated and poorly understood and the effects of many decisions are experienced over the course of a lifetime.
>
> (Boyd and Richerson 1993: 140)

Even in these circumstances, however, some attention to trial-and-error learning from the environment is required so that tradition is kept 'honest', but the amount of such learning may be small.

Lake (this volume) comes to a similar conclusion in his simulation of the value of cultural learning of foraging techniques in temporally heterogeneous environments. He points out that Boyd and Richerson omitted to analyse the effects of varying levels of accuracy and precision of individually learned foraging decisions on the viability of social transmission of foraging information. He found that in individual learning there was an optimal weighting for the balance between attention to present circumstances and attention to past experience; this value placed on attention to past experience (which produced the best foraging yields for individual learners in heterogeneous environments) was also that which most strongly favoured the evolution of cultural learning in a 'mixed population' of cultural and individual learners. The implication of his model, of which the interim results are reported here, is that the fitness of a social learning strategy is dependent on the quality of individual learning in a population of 'mixed strategies', and that cultural evolution may therefore depend on the evolution of high-order individual learning ability. The same point, of course, is also likely to apply in reverse: as Laland (1993: 156) points out, 'any reduction in the accuracy of social learning, perhaps as a consequence of noisy transmission systems, is likely to favour increased reliance on individual learning'.

It must be said that the same arguments apply to the evolution of other social learning processes of a simpler kind than 'true imitation' and active teaching. The ecological conditions favouring social learning are, therefore, far from unusual, and it is not surprising that many animals in different taxa demonstrate some form of social learning (Mundinger 1980, Caro and Hauser 1992, Laland 1992, Heyes 1994). Laland (1993) suggests that such processes are generally characterized by horizontal transmission via some combination of biased transmission and individual learning: he suggests that horizontal social transmission – for instance, of foraging information – may be favoured in an unpredictable environment where individual learning would be costly, and where social learning will be adaptive provided that it does not propagate fitness-reducing traits. Transmission of foraging practices and food preferences is a focal social learning process which is widespread in mammals, and when we reflect on the complexity of the range of edible species eaten by the chimpanzees, for instance, we can readily appreciate the advantage of social learning as a means of acquiring preferences and knowledge of which plants are toxic and to be avoided (cf. Kortlandt 1984). Social learning of predator avoidance behaviour is also widespread, and here too we can readily appreciate that individual trial-and-error learning of the behavioural and dietary profile of other species is likely to be an inappropriate and costly strategy. If, as Heyes (1993) suggests, imitation is not intrinsically more likely to lead to faithful retention than other mechanisms of social learning, then evolved cognitive mechanisms may not in themselves be a sufficient cause of the evolution of the heavy dependence on cultural learning which characterizes humans. What seems to be specific to humans is both the nature of the transmission mechanisms – true imitation and active teaching – *and* the co-occurrence of factors 'insulating' imitated behaviours from extensive modification by individual trial-and-error learning. These include the spatial extension of social networks and of cultural representations of landscape beyond the range of everyday individual experience (Gamble, this volume); the regulation of knowledge transfer by norms and sanctions (Shennan, Knight, Power and Watts, all this volume); and the use of material culture as an external information store (Gamble, Cullen, this volume).

A key question for researchers reconstructing hominid evolution is, therefore, whether cultural traditions emerged with the evolution of genetically determined dispositions to 'imitate selectively' the most repro-ductively fit models in a social group, or whether a general evolution of high-order social-cognitive mechanisms leading, *inter alia*, to an increased curiosity, social attentiveness and behavioural generativity only became harnessed to faithful cultural transmission with the emergence of social systems in which the requisite 'insulating factors' were in place. Here, we may follow Alexandri (1995) in aspiring to test the two alternatives using the archaeological record. If bigger brains inevitably meant more depen-dence on cultural learning in hominids, then we would expect there to be a simple correlation between brain size and the stable evolution of cultural traditions (as seen most clearly in artefact series). If, by contrast, the stable evolution of cultural traditions required a further set of social preconditions, then we would expect a more complex pattern of partial covariation: there will be a partial decoupling of brain evolution and cultural evolution observable in comparisons of the fossil and artefactual records.

The archaeological record as a product of cultural learning processes: reconstructing the social and ecological conditions of cultural evolution

A number of the contributors to this book address these issues. Mithen's chapter on the cultural behaviour of late *Homo erectus* groups in southern

England contrasts simple 'core-and-flake'-based lithic assemblages with those containing handaxes, suggesting that the difference relates to a specific contrast in the types of environment in which they are found. Although the covariation of assemblage composition with habitat type might indicate that the contrasts represent functional adaptations of the hominids' tool kits, Mithen argues that the remarkable uniformity of handaxes over space and time indicates that the form was conditioned by tradition rather than by the functional needs of specific foraging and processing tasks. The relevance of the habitat contrast is indirect, through its expected effect on the grouping strategies of the hominids occupying open and more closed environments. Mithen argues that hominids in open habitats would have tended to live in larger and more cohesive groups, since larger groups are seen in non-human primates occupying open terrestrial habitats where there is an increased risk of predation. Handaxe assembages are more prevalent in what are believed to have been more open habitats; Mithen argues that this is because stable and cohesive groups with large numbers of demonstrators are a precondition of the evolution of persistent cultural traditions through social learning.

The proposal that grouping strategies have an effect on the evolution of cultural traditions is an intriguing one. Certainly, in other animals, we see this kind of effect. In colonial species of bird, 'there exists a potential for sharing individually acquired information, with the result that in species such as gulls, individual birds may give a higher priority to group allegiance than to standard habitat choice, and may relocate from their normal site' (Laland 1992: 90). In pigeons, social learning by naive subjects appears to be facilitated by higher ratios of tutors to observers (or by-standers) (Lefebvre and Giraldeau 1994). In primates, there is some empirical evidence that status and social group composition affects the spread of a new behaviour (Strayer 1976). Chance (this volume) points out that the structure of attention in primate groups affects the quality of individual learning about the environment, and it is clear that in a population of imitators, a mechanism that coerced the attention of subordinates towards dominant individuals would both degrade the quality of their 'asocial' learning and emphasize the behaviour of the dominants as models. If the details of handaxe morphology truly have no functional relevance, then their faithful transmission would appear to be a product of a process of indirect biased transmission (in Boyd and Richerson's terms). Steele (chapter 4, this volume) suggests that the fine motor control characteristic of stone tool production may have evolved as a by-product of temperament characteristics favourable to success in low-intensity status competition in hominid groups, so that indirect biased transmission – imitation of models who also coincidentally demonstrated high-order motor control in knapping skills – is indeed quite plausible as a partial explanation of this cultural pattern.

We have already seen that an increase in hominid average group sizes through the Quaternary is strongly indicated by the anatomical trend of increasingly large brains, with Dunbar (this volume) suggesting that language ability evolved to enable individuals to service an increasing number of social relationships under time constraints. His focus on everyday conversational language use as the best indicator of the original functions of the behaviour is persuasive, as is his finding that much of that everyday talk relates to social relationships and transactions. Indeed, in a study of one hunter-gatherer group, Eibl-Eibesfeldt (1989: 525–526, cited in Pinker and Bloom 1990) reported that a very high proportion of conversations were about food and procedures for equitable sharing of foraging yield:

> In both cultures [!Kung and Eipo], a great deal of talk centered on food, comprising 59 per cent of all !Kung conversations. . . . Some discussions concerned where food is found, which products are found in individual gathering areas, and in which gardens one should work. A larger part of the food conversations are concerned with the social aspects of nutrition. Topics include who gives what to whom, and criticisms of those who do not share their food. Three quarters of all words of the Mek-speaking In are based upon giving and taking.

'Gossip' as a form of social communication has an interest not just as an example of this kind of language use, but also because it is a potent mechanism of diffusion of information which has been studied empirically by a number of workers. Looking at the pattern of spread of gossip items may give insight into the channelling of such information spread through the tie structure of a social network. Gossip about out-group members can serve both to create in-group solidarity by manipulating symbolic representations of group identity, and to enhance self-esteem (e.g. Elias 1985, Eder and Enke 1991). Empirical study of the dissemination of personal or social 'news' in a modern US network has found that people linked by close ties, especially relatives, transmit news much faster than friends or acquaintances who are 'not close', and that women transmitted news faster than men (Shelley *et al.* 1990). Work in a closely related area, the study of rumour transmission, has found that dread rumours forecasting unpleasant outcomes are most virulent, and this may be due to the need for individuals to establish 'interpretive control' and social support when anxiety-inducing situations beyond their primary control seem likely to arise (Walker and Blaine 1991). Looking at these types of language use may seem less ennobling than the study of abstract reasoning or of the generativity of syntax, but it gives us an insight into the function of much everyday 'conversational work' – building cliques and social support networks, maintaining reciprocity, and minimizing the unpredictable and the threatening among possible social outcomes of existing situations. Increased group sizes, with the complicated tangle of interactions which they can entail, is clearly likely to favour such a mechanism of 'social grooming'.

In fact, as Shennan (this volume) points out, another consequence of increased group sizes is that co-operation through reciprocity becomes much harder to maintain without some kind of hierarchical structure (a point also made by Boyd and Richerson 1988). Gamble (this volume) implies that the pattern of spatial distribution of local hunter–gatherer bands can lead to the emergence of such a structure based on roles and symbolic tokens, while Shennan also argues (in effect) that a stable array of smaller social units within large hunter–gatherer groups is a way of simplifying the interaction patterns of group members. In both cases, consequences for the evolution of stable cultural traditions are indicated. Gamble, formulating a framework for analysing the processes whereby subjective representations of a landscape are construed from individual learning and from social transmission, argues that the landscapes of modern human hunter-gatherers, and of our hunter-gatherer forebears of the last glacial era, differed from the perceived worlds of hominids of earlier times in the scale of the social landscape, which now came to extend well beyond the scale of home ranges: it became impossible to acquire the 'social map' by individual learning by trial and error or 'guided variation'. He argues that the complexity of the social network which this increase in scale entailed was compensated for by a simplification of social roles: symbolic markers of status and role appear in the archaeological record at the same time that transport distances for lithic and other exotic material increase an order of magnitude beyond the range of the local band (see also Pickering 1994, Tacon 1994). It is provocative to note that these new factors, which Gamble discusses in the context of a discussion of group size and spatial structure, are also two of the three factors suggested by Heyes (1993) as possible 'insulators' of imitatively learned behaviours: transfer of information concerning the spatially or temporally remote, and use of material culture as a resilient medium of information storage. In this case, too, it is difficult to point to any anatomical markers of a greater innate ability for cultural learning in anatomically modern humans, as opposed to Neanderthals; rather, the evidence reviewed by Gamble points to a *social transformation* as the condition of the proliferation of cultural innovations into novel traditions which characterizes the archaeological record of the Upper Palaeolithic.

Shennan is also concerned with the effect of group structure on cultural transmission processes. He argues that hunter-gatherer societies with delayed-return foraging economies have intrinsic tendencies to foster the development of social inequalities based on ownership of resources, and points out that while mobility and an ethic of food-sharing prevent the expression of this inequality through material possessions, it finds its expression in the control of access to knowledge. He notes also that co-operation in large groups depends on the formation of stable subgroups, and proposes that these two intrinsic tendencies in co-operative, delayed-return foraging societies will promote a positive feedback loop reinforcing the spread and persistence of cultural behaviours which maintain a structure of authority. Like Gamble, he locates the origin of this confluence of economic and social preconditions at or shortly before the onset of the Upper Palaeolithic. Thus in Shennan's chapter, it is the spread of norms promoting faithful transmission – the third of Heyes' possible mechanisms for 'insulating' imitated behaviour from testing – that enables the spread and persistence of cultural behaviours relating to hierarchy formation.

These accounts all favour changes in the size, cohesion and spatial arrangement of social groups as the prime mover in the emergence of Upper Palaeolithic cultural traditions – as it were, of the human 'knowledge economy'. As we have seen, however, Knight, and Power and Watts, favour the move toward increased male parental investment as a prime mover in the evolution of human social systems, and their interpretations of the emergence of Upper Palaeolithic symbolic traditions reflect this theoretical perspective. Knight argues that collective representations – particularly the body of shared concepts and performances which reproduce a symbolic framework for group members' understanding of their own foraging and reproductive effort – emerge within groups in the process of realization of collective social agency. In his account, the collective agency is that of women, and the crucial economic transformation was the shift, within larger multi-male, multi-female groups, to a household economy based on the sexual division of labour. Power and Watts suggest that the increased incidence of red ochre in archaeological sites from southern Africa associated with early anatomically modern humans represents evidence supporting this account of 'symbolic origins'. These authors argue their case well, and their focus on the politics of reproduction within forager groups is a forceful reminder that a theoretical preoccupation with networking and the 'knowledge economy' should not cause us to distance ourselves too far from the underlying motive for most processes of cultural evolution, at least as this is understood in the models cited in the preceding section: namely, the maximization of reproductive fitness.

But not all cultural behaviours serve that end. The volume ends with a contribution which is at once lighter and more subversive. It has affinities with work which focuses on the spread of cultural behaviours such as fashions and fads (e.g. Bikhchandani *et al.* 1992). The host–pathogen relationship is one of the analogies which has been used for a subset of the possible processes whereby culturally learned behaviours spread. Cullen is concerned with following through the implications of seeing cultural phenomena as viruses affecting hosts, rather than as attributes of their bearers. The concrete explanatory value of this analogy remains to be explored but the idea is a liberating one in its initial apparent counter-intuitiveness. Once we become infected with it, it leads to a range of speculations, of interest perhaps to archaeologists in particular, because traditions of material culture have long been seen within the discipline as having a kind of independent existence from their makers. From Cullen's perspective the jibe often quoted about traditional archaeology, that pots seem to reproduce themselves, becomes no less than the truth.

REFERENCES

Aiello, L. and Dunbar, R. (1993) 'Neocortex size, group size, and the evolution of language.' *Current Anthropology* 34: 184–193.

Alexandri, A. (1995) 'The origins of meaning.' In I. Hodder, M. Shanks, A. Alexandri, V. Buchli, J. Carman, J. Last and G. Lucas (eds) *Interpreting Archaeology*, pp. 57–67. London: Routledge.

Ashton, N., McNabb, J., Irving, B., Lewis, S. and Parfitt, S. (1994) 'Contemporaneity of Clactonian and Acheulian flint industries at Barnham, Suffolk.' *Antiquity* 68: 585–589.

Bahn, P. (1990) 'Motes and beams – a further response to White on the Upper Paleolithic.' *Current Anthropology* 31: 71–76.

Barkow, J., Cosmides, L. and Tooby, J. (eds) (1992) *The Adapted Mind*. New York: Oxford University Press.

Barnett, S.A. (1994) 'Humanity as *Homo docens* – the teaching species.' *Interdisciplinary Science Reviews* 19: 166–174.

Beauchamp, G. and Cabana, G. (1990) 'Group size variability in primates.' *Primates* 31: 171–182.

Benedict, R. (1934) *Patterns of Culture*. London: Routledge.

Bikhchandani, S., Hirshleifer, D. and Welch, I. (1992) 'A theory of fads, fashion, custom, and cultural change as informational cascades.' *Journal of Political Economy* 100: 992–1026.

Blumenschine, R.J., Cavallo, J.A. and Capaldo, S.D. (1994) 'Competition for carcasses and early hominid behavioural ecology: a case study and conceptual framework.' *Journal of Human Evolution* 27: 197–213.

Boehm, C. (1993) 'Egalitarian behaviour and reverse dominance hierarchy.' *Current Anthropology* 34: 227–254.

Boesch, C. (1991) 'Teaching in wild chimpanzees.' *Animal Behaviour* 41: 530–532.

Boesch, C. (1993) 'Towards a new image of culture in wild chimpanzees?' *Behavioural and Brain Sciences* 16: 514–515.

Boesch, C. (1994) 'Cooperative hunting in wild chimpanzees.' *Animal Behaviour* 48: 653–667.

Boyd, R. and Richerson, P. (1985) *Culture and the Evolutionary Process*. Chicago: University of Chicago Press.

Boyd, R. and Richerson, P. (1988) 'The evolution of reciprocity in sizable groups.' *Journal of Theoretical Biology* 132: 337–356.

Boyd, R. and Richerson, P. (1992) 'Cultural inheritance and evolutionary ecology.' In E.A. Smith and B. Winterhalder (eds) *Evolutionary Ecology and Human Behavior*, pp. 61–92. New York: Aldine de Gruyter.

Boyd, R. and Richerson, P. (1993) 'Rationality, imitation and traditions.' In R.H. Day and Ping Chen (eds) *Nonlinear Dynamics and Evolutionary Economics*, pp. 131–149. New York: Oxford University Press.

Braine, M.D.S. (1994) 'Is nativism sufficient?' *Journal of Child Language* 21: 9–31.

Burne, J. (1995) 'Love in a cold climate dents monkeys' macho image.' *New Scientist* 5 Feb.: 15.

Busse, C.D. (1985) 'Paternity recognition in multi-male primate groups.' *American Zoologist* 25: 873–881.

Byrne, R. and Whiten, A. (eds) (1988) *Machiavellian Intelligence*. Oxford: Clarendon Press.

Caporael, L.R. (1995) 'Sociality: coordinating bodies, minds and groups.' *Psycoloquy*. 95.6.01.

Caro, T.M. and Hauser, M.D. (1992) 'Is there teaching in nonhuman animals?' *Quarterly Review of Biology* 67: 151–174.

Cavalli-Sforza, L.L. and Feldman, M.W. (1981) *Cultural Transmission and Evolution*. Princeton: Princeton University Press.

Cheney, D.L. and Seyfarth, R.M. (1990) *How Monkeys See the World*. Chicago: University of Chicago Press.

Cheney, D.L., Seyfarth, R.M., Smuts, B.B. and Wrangham, R.W. (1987) 'The study of primate societies.' In B.B. Smuts, D.L. Cheney, R.W. Wrangham and.T.T. Struhsaker (eds) *Primate Societies*, pp. 1–8. Chicago: University of Chicago Press.

Coles, J. and Higgs, E. (1969) *The Archaeology of Early Man*. London: Faber.

Dawson, G., Warrenburg, S. and Fuller, P. (1985) 'Left hemisphere specialization for facial and manual imitation.' *Psychophysiology* 22: 237–243.

Deacon, T. (1988) 'Human brain evolution: II. Embryology and brain allometry.' In H.J. Jerison and I. Jerison (eds) *Intelligence and Evolutionary Biology*, pp. 383–416. Berlin: Springer.

Dunbar, R. (1992) 'Neocortex size as a constraint on group size in primates.' *Journal of Human Evolution* 20: 469–493.

Dunbar, R. (1993) 'Co-evolution of neocortex size, group size, and language in humans.' *Behavioural and Brain Sciences* 16: 681–735.

Eder, D. and Enke, J.L. (1991) 'The structure of gossip: opportunities and constraints on collective expression among adolescents.' *American Sociological Review* 56: 494–508.

Eibl-Eibesfeldt, I. (1989) *Human Ethology*. New York: Aldine de Gruyter.

Elias, N. (1985) 'Remarques sur le commérage.' *Actes de la Recherche en Sciences Sociales* 60: 23–29.

Ellison, P.T. (1994) 'Advances in human reproductive ecology.' *Annual Review of Anthropology* 23: 255–275.

Ferrari, S. and Lopes-Ferrari, M. (1989) 'A re-evaluation of the social organization of the Callitrichidae, with reference to the ecological differences between genera.' *Folia Primatologica* 52: 132–147.

Fisher, J. and Hinde, R.A. (1949) 'The opening of milk bottles by birds.' *British Birds* 42: 347–357.

Foley, R. (1988) 'Hominids, humans and hunter-gatherers: an evolutionary perspective.' In T. Ingold, D. Riches and J. Woodburn (eds) *Hunters and Gatherers 1: History, Evolution and Social Change*, pp. 207–221. New York: Berg.

Freeman, L.C. (1992a) 'The sociological concept of "group": an empirical test of two models.' *American Journal of Sociology* 98: 152–166.

Freeman, L.C. (1992b) 'Filling in the blanks: a theory of cognitive categories and the structure of social affiliation.' *Social Psychology Quarterly* 55: 118–127.

Galef, B.G. Jr (1988) 'Imitation in animals: history, definitions, and interpretation of data from the psychological laboratory.' In T. Zentall and B. Galef (eds) *Social Learnng: Psychological and Biological Perspectives*, pp. 3–28. Hillsdale, NJ: Lawrence Erlbaum.

Galef, B.G. Jr (1990) 'Tradition in animals: field observations and laboratory analyses.' In M. Bekoff and D. Jamieson (eds) *Interpretations and Explanations in the Study of Behavior: Comparative Perspectives*, pp. 74–95. Boulder, CO: Westview Press.

Glance, N.S. and Huberman, B. (1994) 'Dynamics of social dilemmas.' *Scientific American* 270: 76–81.

Glickman, S.E. and Sroges, R.W. (1966) 'Curiosity in zoo animals.' *Behaviour* 26: 151–188.

Harcourt, A.H., Fossey, D. and Sabater-Pi, J. (1981) 'Demography of *Gorilla gorilla*.' *Journal of Zoology (London)* 195: 215–233.

Harvey, P.H., Martin, R.D. and Clutton-Brock, T.H. (1987) 'Life histories in comparative perspective.' In B.B. Smuts, D.L. Cheney, R.M. Seyfarth, R.W. Wrangham and T.T. Struhsaker (eds) *Primate Societies*, pp. 181–196. Chicago: University of Chicago Press.

Hassan, F. (1981) *Demographic Archaeology*. New York: Academic Press.

Hawkes, K. (1990) 'Showing off. Tests of an hypothesis about men's foraging goals.' *Ethology and Sociobiology* 12: 29–54.

Hawkes, K., Rogers, A.R. and Charnov, E.L. (n.d.) 'The male's dilemma: increased offspring production is more paternity to steal.' Ms, University of Utah.

Heyes, C.M. (1993) 'Imitation, culture and cognition.' *Animal Behaviour* 46: 999–1010.

Heyes, C.M. (1994) 'Social learning in animals: categories and mechanisms.' *Biological Reviews* 69: 207–231.

Hull, D.L. (1988) *Science as a Process*. Chicago: University of Chicago Press.

Hunt, K.D. (1994) 'The evolution of human bipedality – ecology and functional morphology.' *Journal of Human Evolution* 26: 183–202.

Isaac, G.L. (1972) 'Chronology and the tempo of cultural change during the Pleistocene.' In W.W. Bishop and J. Miller (eds) *Calibration of Hominid Evolution*, pp. 381–430. Edinburgh: Scottish Academic Press.

Isaac, G.L. (1978) 'The food-sharing behavior of protohuman hominids.' *Scientific American* 238: 90–108.

Johnson, G.A. (1982) 'Organizational structure and scalar stress.' In C. Renfrew, M. Rowlands and B. Segraves (eds) *Theory and Explanation in Archaeology*, pp. 389–421. London: Academic Press.

King, B.J. (1991) 'Social information transfer in monkeys, apes, and hominids.' *Yearbook of Physical Anthropology* 34: 97–115.

Kortlandt, A. (1984) 'Habitat richness, foraging range and diet in chimpanzees and some other primates.' In D.J. Chivers, B.A. Wood and A. Bilsborough (eds) *Food Acquisition and Processing in Primates*, pp. 119–159. New York: Plenum Press.

Laland, K.N. (1992) 'A theoretical investigation of the role of social transmission in evolution.' *Ethology and Sociobiology* 13: 87–113.

Laland, K.N. (1993) 'The mathematical modelling of human culture and its implications for psychology and the human sciences.' *British Journal of Psychology* 84: 145–169.

Lee, R. and DeVore, I. (eds) (1968) *Man the Hunter.* Chicago: Aldine.

Lefebvre, L. and Giraldeau, L.-A. (1994) 'Cultural transmission in pigeons is affected by the number of tutors and bystanders present.' *Animal Behaviour* 47: 331–337.

Lovejoy, C.O. (1981) 'The origin of man.' *Science* 211: 341–350.

Lumsden, C.J. and Wilson, E.O. (1981) *Genes, Mind, and Culture.* Cambridge, MA: Harvard University Press.

McGrew, W.C. (1992) *Chimpanzee Material Culture: Implications for Human Evolution.* Cambridge: Cambridge University Press.

Melnick, D.J. and Pearl, M.C. (1987) 'Cercopithecines in multimale groups: genetic diversity and population structure.' In B.B. Smuts, D.L. Cheney, R.M. Seyfarth, R.W. Wrangham and T.T. Struhsaker (eds) *Primate Societies*, pp. 121–134. Chicago: University of Chicago Press.

Merlan, F. (1992) 'Male–female separation and forms of society in Aboriginal Australia.' *Cultural Anthropology* 7: 169–193.

Milardo, R.M. (1992) 'Comparative methods for delineating social networks.' *Journal of Social and Personal Relationships* 9: 447–461.

Mundinger, P.C. (1980) 'Animal cultures and a general theory of cultural evolution.' *Ethology and Sociobiology* 1: 183–223.

Nagell, K., Olguin, R.S. and Tomasello, M. (1993) 'Processes of social learning in the tool use of chimpanzees (*Pan troglodytes*) and human children (*Homo sapiens*).' *Journal of Comparative Psychology* 107: 174–186.

Nishida, T. (1987) 'Local traditions and cultural transmission.' In B.B. Smuts, D.L. Cheney, R.M. Seyfarth, R.W. Wrangham and T.T. Struhsaker (eds) *Primate Societies*, pp. 462–474. Chicago: University of Chicago Press.

Oliver, J., Sikes, N.E. and Stewart, K.M. (eds) (1994) 'Early hominid behavioural ecology.' *Journal of Human Evolution* 27: 1–328.

Pagel, M. and Harvey, P. (1991) *The Comparative Method in Evolutionary Biology.* Oxford: Oxford University Press.

Parish, A.R. (1994) 'Sex and food control in the "uncommon chimpanzee": how bonobo females overcome a phylogenetic legacy of male dominance.' *Ethology and Sociobiology* 15: 157–179.

Parker, C.E. (1974) 'Behavioral diversity in ten species of nonhuman primates.' *Journal of Comparative and Physiological Psychology* 87: 930–937.

Parker, S.T. (1993) 'Imitation and circular reactions as evolved mechanisms for cognitive construction.' *Human Development* 36: 309–323.

Passingham, R.E. (1982) *The Human Primate.* Oxford: Freeman.

Pelissier, C. (1991) 'The anthropology of teaching and learning.' *Annual Review of Anthropology* 20: 75–95.

Pickering, M. (1994) 'The physical landscape as a social landscape: a Garawa example.' *Archaeology in Oceania* 29: 149–161.

Pinker, S. and Bloom, P. (1990) 'Natural language and natural selection.' *Behavioural and Brain Sciences* 13: 707–784.

Povinelli, D.J. (1993) 'Reconstructing the evolution of mind.' *American Psychologist* 48: 493–509.

Quiatt, D. (1985) 'The "household" in nonhuman primate evolution: a basic linking concept.' *Antropologia Contemporanea* 8: 187–193.

Quiatt, D. (1986) 'Juvenile/adolescent role functions in a rhesus monkey troop: an application of household analysis to non-human primate social organization.'

In J. Else and P.C. Lee (eds) *Primate Ontogeny, Cognition and Social Behaviour*, pp. 281–289. Cambridge: Cambridge University Press.

Rogers, A.R. (1989) 'Does biology constrain culture?' *American Anthropologist* 90: 819–831.

Rowell, T.E. (1993) 'Reification of social systems.' *Evolutionary Anthropology* 2: 135–137.

Russon, A.E. and Galdikas, B.M.F. (1993) 'Imitation in free-ranging rehabilitant orangutans (*Pongo pygmaeus*).' *Journal of Comparative Psychology* 107: 147–161.

Shelley, G.A., Bernard, H.R. and Killworth, P.D. (1990) 'Information flow in social networks.' *Journal of Quantitative Anthropology* 2: 201–225.

Sherry, D.F. and Galef, B.G. (1984) 'Cultural transmission without imitation: milk bottle opening by birds.' *Animal Behaviour* 32: 937–938.

Shott, M.J. (1992) 'On recent trends in the anthropology of foragers: Kalahari revisionism and its archaeological implications.' *Man* 27: 843–871.

Smith, I.M. and Bryson, S.E. (1994) 'Imitation and action in autism: a critical review.' *Psychological Bulletin* 116: 259–273.

Soffer, O. (1994) 'Ancestral lifeways in Eurasia – the Middle and Upper Paleolithic records.' In M.H. Nitecki and D.V. Nitecki (eds) *Origins of Anatomically Modern Humans*, pp. 101–119. New York: Plenum Press.

Stanford, C., Wallis, J., Mpongo, E. and Goodall, J. (1994) 'Hunting decisions in wild chimpanzees.' *Behaviour* 131: 1–18

Steele, J. (1994) 'Communication networks and dispersal patterns in human evolution: a simple simulation model.' *World Archaeology* 26: 126–143.

Steele, J., Quinlan, A. and Wenban-Smith, F. (1995) 'Stone tools and the linguistic capacities of earlier hominids.' *Cambridge Archaeological Journal* October.

Strathern, M. (1988) *The Gender of the Gift*. Berkeley: University of California Press.

Strayer, F.F. (1976) 'Learning and imitation as a function of social status in macaque monkeys.' *Animal Behaviour* 24: 835–848.

Strum, S. and Mitchell, W. (1987) 'Baboon models and muddles.' In W.G. Kinzey (ed.) *The Evolution of Human Behavior: Primate Models*, pp. 87–104. New York: SUNY Press.

Tacon, P.S.C. (1994) 'Socialising landscapes: the long-term implications of signs, symbols and marks on the land.' *Archaeology in Oceania* 29: 117–129.

Thorpe, W.H. (1963) *Learning and Instinct in Animals*. London: Methuen.

Tomasello, M., Davis-Dasilva, M., Camak, L. and Bard, K. (1987) 'Observational learning of tool-use by young chimpanzees.' *Human Evolution* 2: 175–183.

Tomasello, M., Kruger, A.C. and Ratner, H.H. (1993) 'Cultural learning.' *Behavioural and Brain Sciences* 16: 495–552.

Torigoe, T. (1985) 'Comparison of object-manipulation among 74 species of non-human primates.' *Primates* 26: 182–194.

van Hooff, J. and van Schaik, C.P. (1994) 'Male bonds: affiliative relationships among nonhuman primate males.' *Behaviour* 130: 309–337.

van Schaik, C.P. (1989) 'The ecology of social relationships among female primates.' In V. Standen and R. Foley (eds) *Comparative Socioecology*, pp. 195–218. Oxford: Blackwell Scientific.

Visalberghi, E. and Fragaszy, D. (1990) 'Do moneys ape?' In S. Parker and K. Gibson (eds) *'Language' and Intelligence in Monkeys and Apes*, pp. 247–273. Cambridge: Cambridge University Press.

Walker, C.J. and Blaine, B. (1991) 'The virulence of dread rumors: a field experiment.' *Language and Communication* 11: 291–297.

Wheelan, S.A. and McKeage, R.L. (1993) 'Developmental patterns in small and large groups.' *Small Group Research* 24: 60–83.

Whiten, A. and Ham, R. (1992) 'On the nature and evolution of imitation in the animal kingdom: reappraisal of a century of research.' *Advances in the Study of Behavior* 21: 239–283.

Williams, B.J. (1981) 'Hunters: the structure of bands and the structure of the brain.' *Anthropology UCLA* 7: 239–253.

Wobst, H.M. (1978) 'The archaeo-ethnology of hunter-gatherers or the tyranny of the ethnographic record in archaeology.' *American Antiquity* 43: 303–309.

Wolpoff, M. (1994) 'Visualizing the sweep of human evolution.' *American Scientist* 82: 178–179.

Wood, B.A. (1993) 'Four legs good, two legs better.' *Nature* 363: 587–588.

Wrangham, R. (1977) 'Feeding behaviour of chimpanzees in Gombe National Park, Tanzania.' In T.H. Clutton-Brock (ed.) *Primate Ecology*, pp. 508–538. New York: Academic Press.

PART I

COMPARATIVE APPROACHES TO HOMINID SOCIOECOLOGY

EDITORS' NOTE

The four chapters in this section illustrate the use of general principles to reconstruct hominid social systems based on analyses of primate behavioural ecology and phylogeny, and their impact on anatomy and social behaviour. For the most part, the evidential control on predictions of hominid social systems comes from fossil anatomy, although there is some reference to the psychology of manipulative behaviour as reflected in ancient artefacts, and to the ethnography of modern foragers.

Foley and Lee propose that natural selection acts on existing variation in the social domain as much as in the domains of locomotion or diet. Just as hominid bipedality was the characteristic adaptation of a climbing, partially brachiating ape morphology to the novel demands of a more open habitat (while the savannah baboons simply transferred their ancestral arboreal quadrupedalism into terrestrial quadrupedalism), so the evolution of hominid social systems is likely to have been constrained by the inferred ancestral state of a male kin-bonded social system with female dispersal. The novel social structures of the later hominids (from *Homo erectus* on), in foraging niches with a characteristic dependence on high levels of meat, selected for social intelligence, which in turn led to the addition of novel social behaviours – pair-bonding and increased biparental childcare – by the end of the Lower Palaeolithic, with the more highly encephalized later *Homo erectus* morphology.

Maryanski also identifies female dispersal as a major phylogenetic constraint on the evolution of social systems from the last common ancestor of the African great apes and the hominids, the legacy of its occupation of a specialized terminal-branch feeding adaptation which selected against large social aggregations. She proposes that the characteristic weak tie structure of African ape social systems prevented the evolution of cohesive hominid groups structured by female kin-based alliances on the model of Old World monkey social systems, and argues that the selection pressures on savannah hominids for increased sociality would have led to the appearance of social institutions (marriage, the sexual division of labour) as a means of stabilizing social interactions in a habitat favouring more cohesive and persistent social groupings.

McHenry proposes that the degree of sexual body size dimorphism found in early hominids indicates a regime of high-frequency, low-intensity male–male competition analogous to the pattern found among chimpanzees and other species (but contrasting with the highly agonistic pattern characteristic of many Old World monkeys). He suggests that patrilineal, multi-male groups were the most likely state for early Australopithecines, and points out that the relative increase in female body size with *Homo erectus* may reflect dietary changes and other factors as much as (if not rather than) reduced male–male competition.

Steele argues that hominid anatomical and behavioural traits (including the propensity for fine motor control evidenced by the artefactual record) indicate a characteristic 'dominance style' in hominid groups characterized by low-intensity competitive interactions, and a greater emphasis on cognitive and temperamental adaptations to complex social groups. He proposes that this pattern characterizes primate groups where low costs to dispersal, or low relatedness among members, prevent the evolution of kin-based 'despotic' dominance hierarchies.

All four chapters converge on a model of hominid social systems as deriving from an ape prototype social system characterized by the absence of strong ties among philopatric female kin. Common to these papers also is the proposal that an Old World monkey model of cohesive groups is inappropriate for savannah hominids, and that the social systems of the latter were likely to have been characterized by the low intensity of competitive dominance interactions within groups.

CHAPTER ONE

FINITE SOCIAL SPACE AND THE EVOLUTION OF HUMAN SOCIAL BEHAVIOUR

ROBERT FOLEY AND PHYLLIS LEE

SOCIAL EVOLUTION: A PROBLEM OF DEFINITION

Within the traditions of archaeology and anthropology, a common set of oppositions is that between the biological and the social. The putative contrast between what is biological and what is social has led to explanations for patterns of variation in human behaviour and in prehistory which are seen as competitive or mutually exclusive. The growth of 'social' archaeology, for example, might easily be seen as an alternative to the more ecological approaches that dominated in previous decades. If we are to investigate biologically based approaches to the evolution of social behaviour, it is clear that against this background it is necessary to find a way through a number of conflicting concepts and definitions of the term 'social'.

The most extreme interpretation of the term 'social' is that it is the antithesis of what is biological. Things are either social or they are genetic and biological. This view, indeed, conflates the term 'biological' to mean the same as genetic, a common fallacy within the social sciences (Ingold 1990). This is a strongly anthropological and non-evolutionary perspective, which implies that sociality is a unique part of the human world. It ignores the fact that the capacity for social behaviour is predicated upon physical and biochemical and indeed genetic characteristics, the widespread occurrence of social behaviour among other species, and the apparent trend towards marked sociality that can be found among the primates.

A second view is that the term 'social' refers specifically to the presence of elaborate cognitive skills. Among humans the variation in social behaviour is exemplified by cultural diversity, which in turn implies a strong association between the social and the cognitive and symbolic systems that humans have developed. While the previous view took the term 'social' away from that which is biological, within this second framework the concept of 'social' is removed from actual behaviour and focused on the cognitive capacities that generate behaviour. This view can be extended to include the idea that sociality is dependent upon the capacity for symbolic systems of thought and a sense of self-consciousness. While cognition is clearly an important element of any social behaviour, it is not the totality even if, as some have argued, the evolution of greater intelligence is related to social complexity (e.g. Humphrey 1976). The social world is actually played out in the realm of behaviour.

This perspective on the social is strongly linked to the general notion of culture in anthropology; indeed, the terms 'culture' and 'social' are often used in an almost interchangeable manner. Culture, it could be argued, is concerned with the transmission of ideas and information through non-biological means, and as such it is transmitted largely through social channels. This view conflates the cultural capacities of humans with the tendency towards social life: to be social requires non-biological means of passing on information, and culture in turn requires individuals to live in social groups. There is thus a positive feedback between the two (Foley 1991, McGrew 1992).

From the zoological end we have other notions of what is meant by the term 'social'. For some biologists it simply means group living – that is, a social species is any one where individuals do not lead solitary lives, and all groups can be considered as social groups. Clearly this greatly extends the meaning of the term, and takes the problem of social evolution away from anything very special to include an enormous variety of biological problems, from clonal colonies of bacteria to shoals of fish. While there may be advantages in this view, the generality is too great to have much explanatory power; while many species may aggregate into groups of conspecifics, it is not necessarily the case that their inter-actions are in any meaningful sense of the word social. It is probably the case that the majority of social species live in groups, but it is not the case that all groups are indeed social.

It is obvious that any attempt to model or explain social evolution is highly dependent upon the way in which the term 'social' is used. In adopting those that are more specifically anthropological and which exclude biology, the power of any evolutionary approach is greatly reduced. Expanding the definition to all associations loses the focus on that which makes humans, and other primates, unique.

The solution we have adopted here is that formulated by Hinde (1976, 1983). Sociality is seen not as a top-down system imposed by the charac-teristics of the group as a whole, but rather as an emergent property derived from the interactions between individuals. Social groups thus refer to groups where associations are maintained over time and space, where the individuals are consistently interactive, where individual recognition of others can be found, and where associations are patterned by familiarity and genetic relatedness. The interactions themselves typically can be classified into a number of simple categories. When these categories of interaction are patterned over time, repeated between individuals, and both the context and the content of the interaction are replicated, then social relationships emerge from simple rules of interaction. These relationships can also be patterned, maintain a stable context and content, and produce a form of social structure which is unique to that cluster of individuals. Such an approach does not ignore the perceptual, communicative or cognitive elements inherent in transactions; rather, in non-linguistic species it provides a basis for definition and comparison (Lee 1992). It also stresses the distinction between the mechanisms by which sociality is maintained (for example, cognition, behavioural cues, etc.) and the actual behaviour of being social. Indeed, Hinde's approach (see Hinde 1983) emphasizes the dialectic between the individual, the relationship and the emergent system. Again, the nature of the relationships, which themselves influence interactions, and so on, provides for a non-linear approach to understanding the complexity of sociality, at least for species with 'maintained sociality' (Lee, in press).

This means that the task of investigating the evolution of human sociality consists of determining the nature and extent of the repeated interactions that could have occurred in ancestral groups of hominids, the ecological, social and demographic conditions under which these may have changed, and the consequences of the interactions and subsequent sets of relationships for the emergence of human characteristics and behaviour. To this end we have developed a model of finite social space (Foley and Lee 1989, Lee, in press) that allows us to attempt to track the pathways of hominid social evolution and to explore its Darwinian basis.

FINITE SOCIAL SPACE: A MODEL OF SOCIAL OPTIONS

The central element of this model is that the range of options for social interactions, relationships and structure are finite and can be specified. This is in direct opposition to the widely held anthropological view that the range of social variation is infinite and therefore that reconstructing past states of sociality is an impossibility. In contrast, we have argued that because there are clear finite limits to what is possible socially, and because the conditions under which these variants may occur are relatively narrowly constrained, it is possible by a process of elimination to focus on the social options available for humans and their ancestors.

The assumptions of the model are predicated upon a biological constraint typical of mammalian and, indeed, many other species (Trivers

LIVERPOOL JOHN MOORES UNIVERSITY
LEARNING SERVICES

1972, Emlen and Oring 1977). This constraint can be simply stated as the differential costs of reproduction to males and females; male gamete production is relatively inexpensive in terms of time and energy, and a male's reproductive potential is limited by his access to potential mates. Females, on the other hand, produce more energetically costly gametes, bear the energy and time costs of internal gestation and subsequent lactation. Female reproduction is thus largely limited by time and energy, through her condition and nutritional intake. In using this basic premise, we are placing the biology of reproduction – the physiological, environmental and time costs – at the core of potential sociality, and have drawn on Wrangham's (1980) original premise for primate sociality. His framework argues that females need to ensure access to sufficient energy for reproduction, and the way in which energy (in the form of food resources) is distributed in the environment will ultimately determine the distribution of females in the environment, while male distributions will follow those of the females and take into account the number of other males also attempting to maximize access to reproductive females.

In terms of the model, other reasons for aggregating such as to avoid predation may influence group size. However, the fundamental *structure* of the group and its *maintenance* over time will depend on the options available to females to distribute themselves through a habitat in order to maximize foraging and nutritional intakes, thus ensuring reproduction and infant survival. Any female therefore can be limited to three simple options in their distribution with respect to other females. First females can be *alone*, without associating with other females. Second, females can associate with other females; here there are again only two options. Either they can be together with their other female kin, or they can be with females who are unrelated. This produces three 'social states' for females (Figure 1.1).

Males have the same options with respect to distributions of the same sex. Males can either be alone, relative to other males, with male kin or with male non-kin. Three options are thus available for male distributions. These three social states can be superimposed across the sexes, so that a total of nine permanently social states emerge, which combine the male and female options. Of course, there is no need for males and females to be continuously in association, and indeed among many mammals, as well as for some of the non-human primates, males and females live separately outside the mating periods. If the male–female associations can be categorized as stable or transitory, then the number of social options increases to eighteen (Figure 1.1). Among the primates, however, with one exception, all these species are among the strepsirhines (lemurs, galagos and lorises) where female receptivity is seasonal, of short duration within an oestrus period and where male–female co-residence provides few reproductive, foraging or anti-predator benefits to either sex. Among the higher primates, males and females are continuously co-resident, since

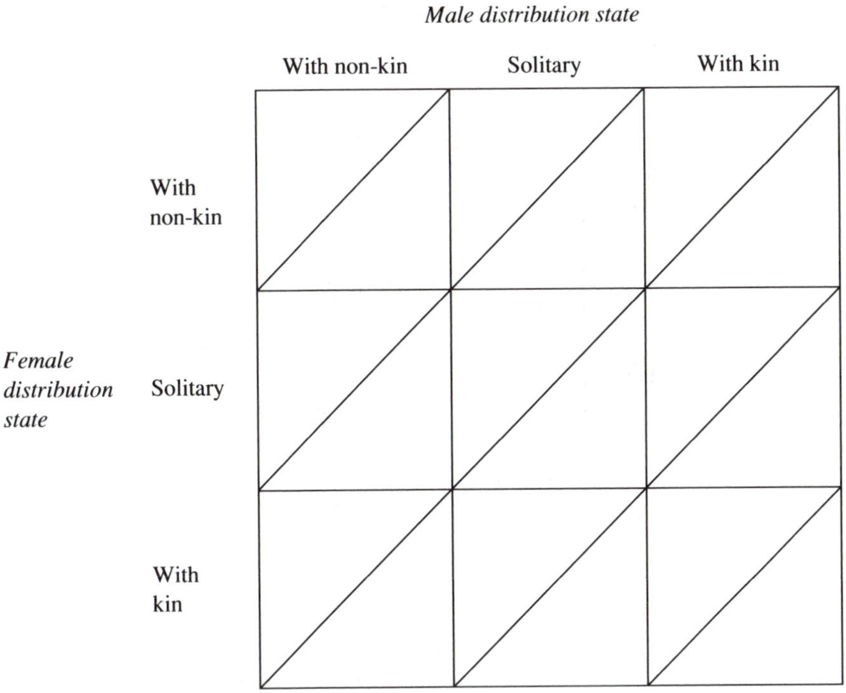

Male distribution state

Figure 1.1 Model of finite social space. The vertical axis shows how females associate with other females (solitary, with kin or with non-kin), and the horizontal axis shows how males similarly associate with other males. Interactions between the these two intra-sexual associational strategies provide the basis for social structure. A further dimension is added by allowing male–female reproductive associations to be either stable or transitory. The combinations yield a basic number of eighteen social structures derived from individual associations and distributional strategies. (Modified from Foley and Lee 1989)

these females have menstrual cycles of regular duration, are receptive for longer parts of the cycle, and show less marked seasonality to their cycling periods in any year. Under such conditions, male–female distributions have stabilized into the small range of options mentioned above.

These distribution states are, of course, purely hypothetical social states. They say little about the size of the group or the nature of the interactions which maintain the group. As a reduction of complexity to its bare minimum, they nonetheless highlight some interesting features. First, some social states are either rare or non-existent, while some are extremely common (Figure 1.2) across a range of mammalian species. For the most part, mammalian same-sex distributions appear to confirm the principles on which the model is based. Second, through comparisons between

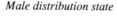

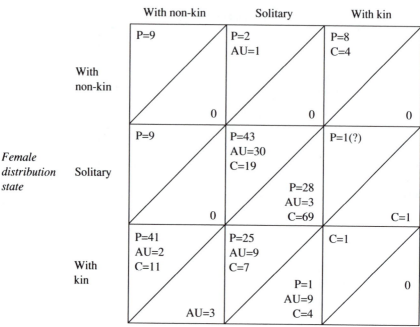

Figure 1.2 Frequency of social systems according to the finite social space model for a sample of three mammalian groups: Primates (P); African ungulates (AU) and Carnivores (C). The most frequent pattern is female kin-bonded groups (113/46.5%), followed by monogamy (92/37.9%). Male kin-bonding is the rarest structure (14/5.8%). (Modified from Lee, in press)

species with known ecological conditions, it becomes possible to specify the ecological conditions whereby some of these states will arise and stabilize. Finally, the model allows for complexity to be superimposed, in that the distributions define limits within which social complexity can flourish, and allows us to define the starting point for constructions of complexity.

FINITE SOCIAL SPACE AND SOCIAL EVOLUTION

This brief description of the finite social space model allows us to draw a number of inferences about the nature of social evolution, as well as to indicate a number of possible pathways for exploring the history of human sociality.

The main point of the model is that social variability in terms of male and female distributions is severely limited; within this model there are a maximum of eighteen possibilities. These have been extended by adding a number of more finely divided categories, such as recognizing the existence of inter-generational associations within kin groups (Foley and Lee 1989), or that inter-sex associations may vary more subtly than between just transient and stable. Even with these taken into account, though, the number of options remains limited.

Second, not all social systems are equally close to each other in evolutionary terms. For example, chimpanzees have a social system based on male residence and female dispersal – i.e. they are male kin-bonded – and inter-sexual relationships are both stable over the medium term while transient on a day-to-day basis. Gorillas, where there is a single male harem system, differ in two ways from chimpanzees – they are not male kin-bonded (males are solitary with respect to other males) and male–female relationships are stable. Orangutans, on the other hand, differ from gorillas and chimps by only one state change – relative to chimps in terms of male kin-bonding and relative to gorillas in terms of the stability of male–female relationships. Examining the 'distance' between social states allows us first to make estimates about the probability of various social states being ancestral to others and second about the probability of moving along particular evolutionary trajectories to certain end states.

The notion of evolutionary pathways is important, as one element of any evolutionary analysis is determining what has evolved from what. While this is relatively straightforward in principle at least in many evolutionary systems (for example, anatomy), its basis in social evolution is less well established. Put simply, it is generally accepted among evolutionary biologists that any evolutionary change is the outcome of the interaction between novel selective pressures and the existing structure or behaviour. Evolutionary change is therefore not just a product of a new environment, but of how the existing structures interact with the new environment. The same novel selective pressures can produce entirely different evolutionary responses because the initial conditions differ. For example, both apes and monkeys were faced with the selective challenge of declining forests and expanding grasslands in Africa in the later Miocene, but their responses were divergent: certain apes (hominids) became bipedal as this was the most cost-effective response in the context of a climbing, partially brachiating primate, while monkeys (baboons) simply transformed their arboreal quadrupedalism into terrestrial quadrupedalism. The same principles will hold for social evolution, and therefore in order to know how hominids evolved socially in response to new ecological and social conditions it is necessary to determine the ancestral states involved. Phylogeny and phylogenetic context are therefore of considerable importance and power within the finite social space model.

Third, while social states are partially constrained by phylogeny, they are also strongly influenced by immediate costs and benefits, and therefore can be analysed in terms of the principles of behavioural ecology. The 'bottom up' approach to sociality adopted here means that the occurrence of particular social structures will be the outcome of the costs and benefits of the following: (1) females forming groups with specific female compositions; (2) males forming more or less stable relationships with females; and (3) males and females tolerating the presence of other males. The costs and benefits of each of these will be a function of the resources available and utilized. Again, these costs and benefits will be dependent upon both the existing life-history parameters of the individuals and the external resources.

The significance of these last points lies in the logical conclusion that there is bound to be an ecological and energetic element for social evolution (as well as for setting the initial conditions for sociality), and that this will operate in ways that are dependent upon phylogenetic context. With this in mind we will now examine the phylogeny of human sociality and then its ecological context.

PHYLOGENETIC CONTEXT OF HUMAN SOCIALITY

The interpretation of the phylogenetic context of *Homo sapiens* has undergone considerable change recently. Two factors are mainly responsible: first, the increasingly unambiguous evidence from genetics and molecular biology that humans and the African apes are more closely related to each other than either is to the Asian orangutan; and second, the evidence that human evolution consists of a series of adaptive radiations and multiple taxa rather than a single unilinear trend. While there is considerable controversy beyond these points, both about terminology and details, nonetheless these two lines of evidence provide us with the basis for considering the phylogenetic context of the hominids and the way in which social behaviour fits into it (see also Ghiglieri 1987, Wrangham 1987, Foley 1989).

The living Old World anthropoids or Catarrhini are divided into two super-families, the Hominoidea and the Cercopithecoidea. The former comprise the apes and humans, the latter the monkeys (including macaques, baboons, mangabeys, guenons and the leaf-eating colobines and langurs). This evolutionary divide is seen in a number of physical, ecological and behavioural differences. There is also a marked difference in social strategy. Cercopithecoids are primarily characterized by male dispersal between groups and female residence. Where kin-based alliances occur, they are based on matrilines. In terms of the model, males are either solitary with respect to other males or co-resident with non-kin males. The exceptions to this pattern are found among the Colobinae, of which the red colobus

(*C. badius*) is the best studied example (Struhsaker and Leland 1987). The red colobus is unusual in forming groups with male kin and general female dispersal. Among some langurs, both sexes can disperse from the natal group to form new social units lacking any kinship. However, this is also the state that is reflected in monogamy, and is relatively simple to produce under the terms of the model.

In contrast to the typical female-kin residence pattern found among most cercopithecoid primates, among the Hominoidea stable female-kin residence is unknown. Both males and females can disperse, removing any potential degree of kin association, as in the monogamous gibbon (*Hylobates* spp.) and the solitary orangutan (*Pongo pygmaeus*). Among gorillas, again, females disperse prior to reproduction as do the majority of males, although some males remain resident with their fathers and these can ultimately inherit the harem (Harcourt and Stewart 1987). Among the common chimpanzee (*Pan troglodytes*) females generally disperse, while males remain co-resident with their male kin and form strong kin-based co-operative alliances (Goodall 1986). The situation among the pygmy chimpanzee or bonobo (*P. paniscus*) is interesting, in that females probably disperse and males remain co-resident, but the alliance structure seems to be concentrated on the male–female relationships rather than focused within the male kin units (Kano 1992).

This social distinction is striking. Using the model to define probable state changes from a solitary state to one of either male or female kin distributions produces a pattern where viable female kin units are far more likely to arise though a small number of state shifts than are male kin units (Foley and Lee 1989, Lee, in press). While the cercopithecoids display the mammalian conservative condition of female residence, the apes show the more derived form (Figure 1.3). Hanging the various social states on the most probable cladogram for the catarrhines allows us to identify the most probable social characteristics at the various branching points that have occurred in the evolution of the Hominoidea. Although homoplasies and reversals, as well as far greater diversity among the hominoids in the past is likely to complicate the picture, the following appears to be the most parsimonious interpretation of the social changes that have occurred during the evolution of the hominoids.

1 At the branching of the cercopithecoids and hominoids female residence seems to have lapsed. This is most likely to have occurred in the context of monogamy, in which both sexes disperse. This pattern is retained among the gibbons.

2 Increasing body size among the apes appears to have led to greater male tenure in harems, resulting in females dispersing to join successful males, thus re-emphasizing the break from female residence. This pattern is found in different ways among the gorillas (orthodox harem) and the orangutan (solitary or 'exploded' harem).

3 Under some circumstances males began to remain in their natal groups. The proposed mechanism for this is that with the break–up of the lush Miocene forested environments females began to range more widely for food, thus forcing males to shift from female defence to territorial defence. Under these circumstances male kin–based alliances would be a major advantage. This pattern is found in the common chimpanzee.

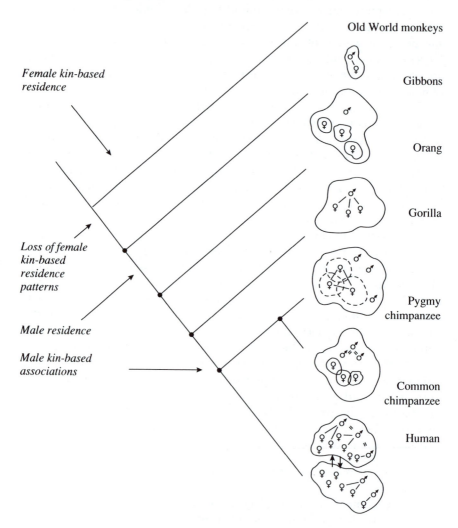

Figure 1.3 A cladistic phylogeny of catarrhine social systems. Female kin-based residence is considered to be the ancestral catarrhine system, which is lost in the hominoid clade. Male residence and male kin-bonding becomes established in the African ape/hominid clade

It can be argued that the shift from female to male kin-based systems is the result of increasing body size leading to greater longevity, which in turn led to longer male tenure in monogamous or polygynous situations (Clutton-Brock 1989). Under these conditions the probability of males being able to disperse and find mates would be greatly reduced, resulting in greater benefits arising from remaining with their kin. Once established, the advantages of switching back to a female kin-based system are likely to be greatly reduced, and the number of state shifts required increased. Thus one can relatively simply express the routes that would need to be taken, and the ecological and social consequences of these state shifts (see also Foley 1989, Foley and Lee 1989, Lee, in press).

The key inference to be drawn is that the distribution of social states among the living catarrhines provides us with a strong indication concerning the ancestral social organization of the first hominids. The best evidence suggests that chimpanzees are the sister clade of the hominids (see Figure 1.3). This means first that hominids, as hominoids, come from a lineage in which female residence is absent or rare. Furthermore, there is within the 'trends' of hominoid evolution from lesser apes to African apes a tendency to observe increased male residence and kin-based organization. The conclusion that should perhaps be drawn is that the phylogenetic context for the origins of the patterns of social behaviour to be found among modern humans is one where any descent and alliance groupings are more likely to be male-based than female-based.

Clearly a number of caveats should be borne in mind when considering this model. One of these is that living species are not necessarily a good basis for inferring the events of the past. However, it should be noted that it is not individual species that are being used to determine the ancestral state (in the form of an analogue model), but the overall pattern of variability. The second qualification is that while this may well have been the ancestral state of the first hominids, we know that there is subsequently a very high level of evolutionary diversity to be found among the hominids of the early Pleistocene, and consequently a considerable range of derived social patterns should be expected.

ECOLOGICAL CONTEXT OF HUMAN SOCIALITY

The phylogenetic context for human social evolution described above might be taken to imply two things; first, that there is an inner drive to social evolution, and that once set on a particular path evolution will continue along it. The second is that phylogenetic heritage or historical factors are the primary determinants of human social evolution. However, as stated above (see p. 54), it is not solely the ancestral state that determines evolutionary change, but the interaction of a particular state with novel selective conditions. To understand the direction human social evolution has taken it is necessary to examine the ecological context in which it has occurred.

It is widely accepted among evolutionary biologists that there is a primary relationship between the evolution of more complex sociality and the evolution of larger brain size. This relationship is thought to hold across the primates as a whole, among other groups of mammals, and would be a strong theory that could account for the rapid and marked encephalization found in hominids and the high level of sociality that occurs in modern humans. Quantification and elaboration of this model has been provided by Dunbar (1992, Aiello and Dunbar 1993, and see this volume, chapter 15). He has shown that neocortex ratio (the ratio of the neocortex, the part of the brain responsible for higher cognitive functions, to the size of the brain as a whole) correlates strongly with group size among anthropoid primates. According to this model there is a reciprocal relationship in which social group size is constrained by the level of intelligence of the species, and in which the demands of sociality drives up the size of the neocortex. The evolution of higher intelligence is therefore, as Humphrey (1976) originally argued, a function of sociality.

Again, this model might be seen to imply a directionality and inherent drive to social evolution, with social complexity and intelligence driving each other upwards. In order to see the proper context in which this may have occurred in human evolution it is necessary to ask a different question – why has this spiralling process not occurred in other species? Answering this question provides us with a more complete understanding of the context in which human social evolution has occurred.

Sociality, as we have seen (see p. 48) is quite rare in the animal kingdom. While there are many benefits that accrue from social and group living (increased anti-predator vigilance, enhanced searching abilities, increased scope for kin-selection, territorial defence, etc.), there are costs as well (Standen and Foley 1989). Increased conspicuousness to predators, increased risk of infection and increased competition for food are all likely to occur with group living (Lee, in press). For some species these costs are too high to establish maintained sociality, and it is only when the benefits exceed the costs that stable sociality will evolve. The conditions under which this will occur are relatively rare, and relate to ecology.

Social groups can occur and be large when resources are clumped in large patches or where they are very uniformly and evenly spread across a landscape, allowing for a number of individuals to jointly exploit the resources. The important element is that the resources are extensive enough to be shared between a number of conspecifics without a significant reduction in individual intake. Furthermore, when high-quality food occurs in large patches, groups of related females may form both to exploit and to defend the resource (Wrangham 1980). Under such conditions, groups of related females thus suffer a smaller individual cost from the partitioning of resources amongst kin (reduced over the actual costs by the degree of relatedness), while gaining the considerable advantage of being able to control the resource against females who are not co-resident or related. Clearly, co-feeding need not lead to sociality, but in the presence of others who are in competition for that same resource, individuals who maintain sociality will gain an advantage.

Alternatively, if there is little or no significant advantage to attempting to control large patches of resources, females are less likely to aggregate. If the resources are widely enough spread, then the males can group females, who will tolerate co-feeding as there are few costs, and distinct advantages from staying with one or more males. Once male co-residence develops on top of some level of female co-residence, then there is the potential for the development of male kin distribution.

Thus, the distribution and quality of resources influences both the size and nature of the social groups that can form. Once social groups do form, then sociality will itself become a factor in determining further patterns of social evolution, but nonetheless the evolution of sociality is predicated upon both the initial and the sustaining ecological conditions.

There are many occasions when resources do not allow for continuous shared exploitation, but do facilitate concentrations of individuals either in localities or through time. In such animals, the resource base sets the initial limitations to the consistency and size of aggregations, while other considerations such as control of mates or rearing strategies may come into play. These species tend to have same-sex and opposite-sex distributions more related to reproductive strategies than to foraging or competitive strategies, as in the male kin-bonded groups. The point remains that the ecological conditions either enable or constrain the options for individual distributions with respect to conspecifics. For humans to develop such extreme social complexity implies that ecological strategies pursued by hominids were associated with environments that simultaneously constrained the formation of female-kin groups, while nonetheless enabling the formation of many other types of social systems.

There is thus a reciprocal relationship between sociality and ecological conditions in the same way that there is a relationship between sociality and brain size or intelligence. A further dimension can be added when we consider the remaining relationship, that between intelligence and ecology.

A number of authors (Clutton-Brock and Harvey 1980, Milton 1988, Gibson 1986) have argued that an interaction occurs between ecological variables and brain size as a measure of intelligence. It has been shown that both absolute and relative brain size increases with such variables as home range size and food quality (Figure 1.4). Two explanations for this pattern have been proposed. One, that exploitation of complex food types (evasive prey, seasonal resources, patchily distributed resources or rare food types) demand a greater level of skill than easily obtainable foods. Forest

Taxonomic group

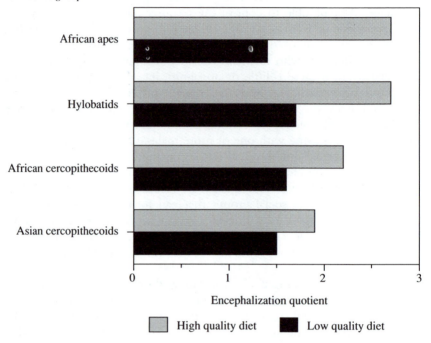

Encephalization quotient

☐ High quality diet ■ Low quality diet

Figure 1.4 Relationship between Encephalization Quotient (EQ) and dietary quality for a sample of catarrhine primates. For each of the major clades the highest and lowest quality feeders were selected and their EQs compared. In each case the species with the better quality diet has the higher EQ. (Modified from Foley and Lee 1991)

dwelling frugivorous primates would therefore be expected to have larger brains than folivores as their food type is less abundant. Alternatively, it has been argued that large brains are both metabolically expensive and isometrically related to metabolic rate. Animals with larger brains must therefore have a high quality and stable resource base.

In considering social evolution, therefore, we have a complex triangle of relationships. Sociality is clearly a major factor in driving the evolution of larger brains in primate and human evolution. However, the need to live in social groups is dependent upon the costs and benefits involved, and these are dependent upon the distribution of resources and the foraging strategies employed. Larger brains in turn require high levels of energy input, which means that their evolution can only occur under specific conditions of a high quality foraging strategy. Intelligence and sociality in turn both strongly influence the way in which resources can be exploited (Figure 1.5).

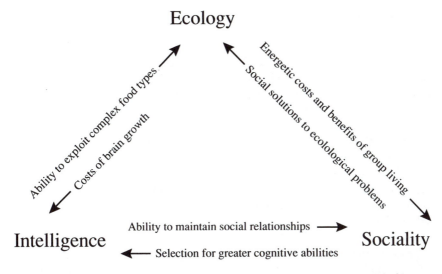

Figure 1.5 shown with labels: Ecology at top; Intelligence at bottom left; Sociality at bottom right. Arrows labelled "Ability to exploit complex food types", "Costs of brain growth", "Energetic costs and benefits of group living", "Social solutions to ecological problems", "Ability to maintain social relationships", "Selection for greater cognitive abilities".

Figure 1.5 The nature of the interactions between ecological factors, sociality and intelligence

LIFE-HISTORY THEORY AND A TENTATIVE TIMESCALE FOR HUMAN SOCIAL EVOLUTION

Two useful conclusions can be drawn from this discussion of the phylo-genetic and ecological context in which human sociality evolved. First, that human sociality is not the *de novo* origin of social behaviour, but is the addition of novel features onto existing strategies. This implies that any study of human social evolution should address the sequence and timing of the major changes that have occurred. Second, that sociality is not divorced from other biological elements, so that any consideration of social evolution should also address shifts in life-history strategy. This chapter will conclude with a brief discussion of these two problems.

Hominids diverged from the other African apes in the later Miocene (9–6 Myr), during a period of increasing climatic instability and aridity, and with an environmental shift away from forests towards more mosaic woodland and grassland. The ancestral conditions for the African hominoids can be surmised. In fully forested conditions there would have been a tendency towards closed, single male groups as is found today among gorillas. Resources would have been abundant and distributed in large and uniform patches. Females would have been able to survive within small home ranges, and in turn single males would be able to defend groups of females. In areas that were drier and as forests became less continuous and were replaced by woodland and savannah, the resources would become more dispersed and less uniformly distributed. Females would have to forage more widely, and males would thus no longer be able to employ a strategy of female defence. As is found among the common chimpanzee, larger communities would occur, with a breakdown of the classic harem system. With this females would no longer be attached to individual males, and related males would have to coexist to establish and maintain a territory. Thus it is in the late Miocene that male residence, female dispersal, male kin-bonding and larger communities became established as the basic social organization of the clade leading to both chimpanzees and humans.

During the Pliocene conditions in Eastern Africa became even drier and more seasonal. The effect of these new ecological conditions on the emerging hominid lineage can be seen in the establishment of bipedalism and other morphological changes, but there is increasing acceptance that for the most part the australopithecines are best thought of as bipedal apes rather than as anything very close to modern humans (Andrews and Martin 1991). There has, for example, at this stage been no significant increase in brain size. The same may well be true of their social organization which was most likely similar to that of the common chimpanzee. The main predicted effect would be a decrease in community size and an increase in community area – an effect that can be seen in chimpanzees across an environmental gradient (Foley 1993). However, caution should be exercised in this interpretation as among (mostly cercopithecoid) terrestrial and savannah primates there is a tendency towards larger group size, as a response either to the patchy resource distribution or to a higher incidence of predators.

The key change that needs to be incorporated into this model of social evolution is the change in the relationships between males and females. It can be argued that until this point – the 'australopithecine grade' – the only changes that have occurred lie within the potential range of variation for African apes, essentially variants on the theme of male kin-bonded groups. Patrilineal affinal kinship relationships may almost be said to be African ape plesiomorphies stretching back to the Miocene rather than unique human traits. In contrast, close and long-term bonding between males and females, with prolonged parental care and investment by both sexes, is unique to the human lineage. It is the timing of this that requires close examination.

Under what conditions should the bonding of males and females become more prolonged? Such bonding – and it should be noted that this is not necessarily implying exclusive monogamous bonds, but can apply equally to polygyny – is normally seen as evidence for increased parental, especially paternal, investment or effort. Male reproductive success is better served by close attention to the survivorship of putative offspring than in pursuing a more philandering strategy. This implies, as Lovejoy (1981) has pointed out, that infant survivorship is at stake and critical to male reproductive success. This led him to consider monogamy and the evolution of higher reproductive rates as critical. Two other factors seem more plausible. The first is that there may be a greater incidence of infanticide, and it may be the case that males are investing more to reduce the risk of infanticide by strange males. With the proposed model of a male kin-bonded social system this may seem unlikely, although the possibility of inter-group encounters cannot be excluded.

Alternatively, paternal investment might be increased if the infant survivorship became increasingly dependent upon the quality of resources, and male protection or provisioning could offset the risks. The key question becomes under what conditions might this occur and how does any such change relate to the timing of human evolutionary changes.

Apart from the shift to bipedalism the other major change in hominid evolution is increased brain size. Rather than being a hominid trait this is in fact unique to the genus *Homo* and occurs predominantly in the last million years (i.e. the last 20 per cent of the hominid fossil record) (Foley 1992). Above it was argued that increased brain size imposes major metabolic costs on both mother and infant, and requires a stable and high quality resource base. In ecological terms this means that encephalization is dependent upon high quality resource availability, and without this it is unlikely that the extremely costly infants could be sustained. It is in this context that changes in male–female relationships should have occurred, with both males and females investing more in individual offspring.

In terms of the timing of these events a number of points can be made. First, the first significant increase in brain size in the hominid lineage occurs around 2.0 Myr, at about the time there is evidence for greater levels of meat-eating. With the establishment of *Homo erectus* there seems to be little doubt that some hominids were effective foragers for meat. Meat, it should be noted, constitutes a highly nutritious resource, especially in the seasonally variable African savannah environment. Second, models estimating the energetic costs of various levels of encephalization have shown that unless there are major changes in the rates of growth involved, the mother of an offspring with a far smaller brain than a modern human infant would face significantly greater costs (Foley and Lee 1991). In other words, changes in life-history parameters such as growth rates are integrally related to the brain size of the hominids. This implies that there is a close relationship between changing foraging strategies, life-history strategies and social behaviour in hominid evolution.

Attempting to pinpoint exactly when the critical changes occurred is problematic. Initial increases in male–female bonding may have occurred with the beginnings of brain size expansion, but the most significant effects are unlikely to occur until later. Modelling suggests that a cranial capacity of about 1,000 cc is the critical threshold where human growth rates are required (Foley and Lee 1991). This occurs in 'late *Homo erectus*', or around half a million years ago. Aiello and Dunbar (1993) have also argued that this is both the brain size when primate systems of social relationship maintenance would break down, and when there is also evidence for an acceleration in the rate of encephalization. Furthermore, there is dental evidence that the rate of growth in early *Homo erectus* (>1.0 Myr) is still much faster than that of modern humans, but that by later *H. erectus* the life-history changes were already in place (Smith 1989, 1992, Foley and Lee 1991). All this points to the possibility that while some changes in sociality were gradual throughout the Pleistocene, the late middle Pleistocene represents a significant point of inflection both biologically and behaviourally. This fact should be remembered in considerations of the context in which the so-called 'human revolution' of the Upper Palaeolithic occurred.

CONCLUSIONS

This brief consideration of the possible timing of the key events in human social evolution has led to the suggestion that some human social features are best considered as deep plesiomorphies from our hominoid ancestry, but that others may have occurred much later in conjunction with shifts in both ecology and life-history strategies. Affinal kinship structures are likely to lie further back in the hominid ancestry (and indeed be ultimately hominoid) than male–female mating strategies. In summary, we have argued that social evolution in humans has been predicated upon both ecological conditions and life-history parameters, rather than being a process divorced from other evolutionary changes. The fact that sociality is a major force in evolution does not mean that the potential for social behaviour and the actual social strategies pursued are not subject to biological constraints. As we have seen, the elaboration of social behaviour that is so characteristic of our own species is deeply dependent upon the phylogenetic and ecological context in which we evolved. Human social behaviour, far from being a tapestry of infinite variety, lies within the finite social space that constrains all mammals, and has not been built from new but is a continuation of the highly successful primate strategy of solving ecological problems by social means.

REFERENCES

Aiello, L.C. and Dunbar, R.I.M. (1993) 'Neocortex size, group size and the evolution of language.' *Current Anthropology* 34: 184–193.

Andrews, P. and Martin, L. (1991) 'Hominoid dietary evolution.' *Philosophical Transactions of the Royal Society (London) Series B* 334: 199–209.

Clutton-Brock, T.H. (1989) 'Female transfer, male tenure and inbreeding avoidance in social mammals.' *Nature* 337: 70–72.

Clutton-Brock, T.H. and Harvey, P.H. (1980) 'Primates, brains and ecology.' *Journal of Zoology* 190: 309–323.

Dunbar, R.I.M. (1992) 'Neocortex size as a constraint on group size in primates.' *Journal of Human Evolution* 22: 469–493.

Emlen, S.T. and Oring, L.W. (1977) 'Ecology, sexual selection and the evolution of mating systems.' *Science* 197: 215–223.

Foley, R.A. (1989) 'The evolution of hominid social behaviour.' In V. Standen and R.A. Foley (eds) *Comparative Socioecology*, pp. 473–494. Oxford: Blackwell Scientific Publications.

Foley, R.A. (1991) 'How useful is the culture concept in early human studies?' In R.A. Foley (ed.) *The Origins of Human Behaviour*, pp. 25–28. London: Unwin Hyman.

Foley, R.A. (1992) 'Evolutionary ecology of fossil hominids.' In E.A. Smith and B. Winterhalder (eds) *Evolutionary Ecology and Human Behavior*, pp. 131–164. Chicago: Aldine de Gruyter.

Foley, R.A. (1993) 'The influence of seasonality on hominid evolution.' In S.J. Ulijaszek and S. Strickland (eds) *Seasonality and Human Ecology*, pp. 17–37. Cambridge: Cambridge University Press.

Foley, R.A. and Lee, P.C. (1989) 'Finite social space, evolutionary pathways and reconstructing hominid behavior.' *Science* 243: 901–906.

Foley, R.A. and Lee, P.C. (1991) 'Ecology and energetics of encephalization in hominid evolution.' *Philosophical Transactions of the Royal Society (London) Series B* 334: 223–232.

Ghiglieri, M.P. (1987) 'Sociobiology of the great apes and the hominid ancestor.' *Journal of Human Evolution* 16: 319–357.

Gibson, K.R. (1986) 'Cognition, brain size and the extraction of embedded food resources.' In J. Else and P.C. Lee (eds) *Primate Ontogeny, Cognition and Social Behaviour*, pp. 93–105. Cambridge: Cambridge University Press.

Goodall, J. (1986) *The Chimpanzees of Gombe*. Cambridge, MA: Belknap Press.

Harcourt, A. and Stewart, K. (1987) 'The influence of help in contests on dominance rank in primates: hints from gorillas.' *Animal Behaviour* 35: 182–190.

Hinde, R.A. (1976) 'Interactions, relationships and social structure.' *Man* 11: 1–17.

Hinde, R.A. (1983) *Primate Social Relationships: An Integrated Approach*. Oxford: Blackwell.

Humphrey, N.K. (1976) 'The social function of intellect.' In P.P.G. Bateson and R.A. Hinde (eds) *Growing Points in Ethology*, pp. 303–317. Cambridge: Cambridge University Press.

Ingold, T. (1990) 'An anthropologist looks at biology.' *Man* 25: 208–229.

Kano, T. (1992) *The Last Ape: Pygmy Chimpanzee Behaviour and Ecology*. Palo Alto: Stanford University Press.

Lee, P.C. (1992) 'Biology and behaviour in human evolution.' *Cambridge Archaeological Journal* 1: 207–226.

Lee, P.C. (in press) 'Social structure and evolution.' In P. Slater and T. Halliday (eds) *Behaviour and Evolution*. Cambridge: Cambridge University Press.

Lovejoy, C.O. (1981) 'The origin of man.' *Science* 211: 341–50.

McGrew, W.C. (1992) *Chimpanzee Material Culture*. Cambridge: Cambridge University Press.

Milton, K. (1988) 'Foraging behaviour and the evolution of primate intelligence.' In R. Byrne and A. Whiten (eds) *Machiavellian Intelligence*, pp. 285–305. Oxford: Clarendon.

Smith, B.H. (1989) 'Dental development as a measure of life history in primates.' *Evolution* 43: 683–688.

Smith, B.H. (1992) 'Life history and the evolution of human maturation.' *Evolutionary Anthropology* 1: 134–142.

Standen, V. and Foley, R.A. (eds) (1989) *Comparative Socioecology: The Behavioural Ecology of Humans and Other Mammals.* Special Publication of the British Ecological Society No. 8. Oxford: Blackwell Scientific.

Struhsaker, T. and Leland, L. (1987) 'Colobines: infanticide by adult males.' In B. Smuts, D.L. Cheney, R.M. Seyfarth, R.W. Wrangham and T. Struhsaker (eds) *Primate Societies*, pp. 83–97. Chicago: Chicago University Press.

Trivers, R.L. (1972) 'Parental investment and sexual selection.' In B. Campbell (ed.) *Sexual Selection and the Descent of Man*, pp. 139–179. Chicago: Aldine.

Wrangham, R.W. (1980) 'An ecological model of female-bonded primate groups.' *Behaviour* 75: 262–300.

Wrangham, R.W. (1987) 'The significance of African apes for reconstructing human evolution.' In W.G. Kinzey (ed.) *The Evolution of Human Behavior: Primate Models*, pp. 28–47. Albany: SUNY Press.

CHAPTER TWO

AFRICAN APE SOCIAL NETWORKS

A blueprint for reconstructing early hominid social structure

ALEXANDRA MARYANSKI

INTRODUCTION

When a lineage of proto-hominids left the forest for the savannah, the process of hominidization was initiated. Armed with bags of fossil bones, such influential scholars as Jolly (1970) with his 'seed-eating hypothesis', Lewis (1972) with his 'brachiation hypothesis' and Washburn (1971) with his 'knuckle-walking hypothesis' have all utilized skeletal materials to chronicle the emergence of the Hominidae, or the family of bipedal primates that includes direct and near ancestors and modern humans. More recently, the excavation of several hominid-rich fossil sites has now equipped researchers with enough tangible remains to fashion a physical portrait of early hominids. This reproduction conveys the impression that the first hominids evolved in Africa, closely resembled apes in facial features and cranial capacity, evidenced body size sexual dimorphism, and had successfully adapted to an open country niche as habitual bipeds long before manufacturing stone tools (see Falk 1983, Rak 1983, Stern and Susman 1983, Stringer 1984, White and Suwa 1987, Fleagle 1988, Grine 1988, Potts 1993). While any reconstruction of early hominid evolution must ultimately rest on the fossil and archaeological records, these assemblages are inadequate by themselves when it comes to reassembling the social ways of early hominids. This realization has forced scholars to consider secondary sources such as the rich social data now available on non-human primate societies. In particular, researchers have highlighted the Hominoidea, or the superfamily that includes apes and humans, and especially chimpanzees (*Pan*) and gorillas (*Gorilla*) because their phyletic closeness to humans would seem to allow us to glimpse ourselves in a truly 'distant mirror'. Of course, *Pan* and *Gorilla* are the evolutionary end points of their own equally long lineages. However, although the African forest belt shrunk in response to cooler climatic conditions, the interior is believed to have remained relatively stable since the Miocene and niche theory would predict more relaxed selection, especially for primary forest chimpanzees (Simonds 1974).

Unfortunately, using African ape societies to reconstruct early hominid societies is hampered by the nagging problem of why such closely related genera reveal such disparate organizational features – an enigma that continues to fuel debates on whether phylogeny is relevant at all for understanding hominoid social organization. Undoubtedly, the observed differences reflect diverse environmental pressures from the time these genera last shared a common ancestor. For although chimpanzees and gorillas both inhabit equatorial rainforest, each exploits a distinctive kind of forest (Jones and Sabater-Pi 1971, Dixson 1981, Tuttle 1986). Chimpanzees typically live in mature canopy woodland or forest–savannah mosaic regions, and although as many as a hundred chimpanzees can share a home range, individuals rarely congregate as one spatially bounded unit. Instead, adult chimpanzees travel alone or episodically gather into momentary 'subgroups' or 'parties' which make up the fluid internal segments of a more inclusive organizational structure (Nishida 1979, Goodall 1983, Chapman and Wrangham 1993). In contrast, gorillas typically live in secondary or montane forests, and reveal two distinct spatial patterns: (1) relatively stable heterosexual groups which are typically organized around one mature silverback male and a number of adult females with dependent offspring; and (2) residential lone adult males who move about at large within a regional home range which is shared with three or more heterosexual groupings, all of which occasionally affiliate and even mingle temporarily (Fossey 1972, Weber and Vedder 1983, Watts 1990). *Pan* and *Gorilla* breeding patterns also differ, with a casual promiscuous pattern for chimpanzees and a rather stable but still fluid 'polygynous' pattern for gorillas (since up to four potential sexual partners may be available to a female in a residential group) (see Watts 1992, Sicotte 1993).

The first objective of this chapter is to develop the hypothesis that despite major contrasts in African ape organization, both pongids converge in their underlying network structure. In short, the results of a social network analysis indicate that while *Pan* and *Gorilla* are clearly set apart by many lifestyle differences, both genera are predisposed towards high autonomy and, with few exceptions, relatively low degrees of sociality. These traits are underscored by a social network structure of weak over strong ties which is maintained, in part, by female-biased dispersal at puberty and the resulting absence of kinship-based group continuity over time. The second objective of this chapter is to use African ape network data to highlight some possible structural and institutional aspects of early hominid organization.

Essentially, I shall argue that early proto-hominids were, like their hominoid relatives, predisposed towards weak ties and low density networks. However, a shift from forest to a more open-country habitat triggered an initial phase of hominid tie-building strategies to enhance survival and reproductive success. In turn, selection for greater network density facilitated the emergence of the first hominid social institutions – a kinship institution to codify stable, high density network cliques and an economic institution to codify bonds between males and females through segregated economic roles.

A COMPARATIVE ANALYSIS OF CHIMPANZEE AND GORILLA SOCIAL STRUCTURE

The social network approach

A social structure can be conceptualized by considering either (1) the attributes and behaviours *of* individuals, or (2) the patterns of relationships *among* individuals (Hinde 1976, 1983). Primate research is usually guided by the traditional attribute approach. That is, observations made on individuals or classes of individuals are usually described and classified in terms of such attributes as age, sex, rank, body size, personality, etc., or the social behaviours of alpha and beta males, cycling females, subordinate males and lactating females are recorded. While the attributes described vary, the point of concentration is on the properties and qualities of individuals and their corresponding social behaviours.

In comparison, a social network approach is guided by a relational perspective which demarcates social behaviours and social relations as different foci, with the former seen as a sequence of actions by individuals towards each other, while the latter is seen as a regular and persistent association produced by some of these social behaviours. In network theory, the established tie or relation is the basic unit of analysis. Moreover, this approach defines social structure in a very narrow way to refer *solely* to *the forms of relations* among members of a given unit of study. Admittedly, much organizational data is ignored by this approach, but it is essentially designed to supplement the traditional attribute perspective by illuminating what are often hidden social configurations among a population of individuals. Thus, in network analysis only those behaviours implicated in the creation and maintenance of patterned and stable forms of linkages among individuals are crucial (e.g. dominant–subordinate relations). Such a focus often reveals underlying structural properties which cannot be easily detected by studying either the attributes of individual members or their social behaviours (Knoke and Kuklinski 1982, Freeman *et al.* 1989, Maryanski and Turner 1991).

For this research, network analysis was used to examine only one crucial property of African ape social structure: the strength of social bonds and the effects of dispersal on these bonds. The findings will suggest that the close biological affinities of chimpanzees and gorillas are paralleled by a far greater congruity in their respective social structures than has been previously hypothesized.

Materials and methods

Although individuals can either ignore or interact with one another, little is known about the evolution of primate sociality. We do know, however, that extant primates seek out particular classes of individuals rather than conspecifics in general. These predilections vary among species, making possible characteristic profiles of attachment – from strong antagonism to strong attraction – for sex and age classes (for discussions, see Sade 1972, Hinde 1976, 1983, Cheney *et al.* 1986, and especially Carpenter 1934, 1942, who was first to consider primate organization from a relational perspective). For this study, relational data on *Pan troglodytes*[1] and *Gorilla gorilla* were compiled through a complete literature review of African ape field data, although this chapter contains only a synopsis and a small sample of citations (see Maryanski 1986 for a full and comprehensive data analysis). To represent these data a qualitative network technique was employed, because investigators used such a variety of observational techniques that quantitative techniques could not be appropriately applied. In addition, these data were made roughly equivalent by comparing very closely related genera, by using the 'relation' as a common yardstick, by weighing carefully the inferences drawn by each investigator, and by using rates of interaction as a measure of tie strength with tie strength itself assessed as a somewhat continuous variable.

To analyse *Pan* and *Gorilla* ties required two consolidation procedures: first, social bonds are assumed to be symmetrical and, overall, to be positive. Second, social ties are described using a simple scale of tie strength: (1) absent ties, (2) weak ties, (3) moderate ties and (4) strong ties. To amplify, individuals without ties have opportunity for social exchange but seldom if ever interact. Those with weak ties interact in a positive way from time to time as the occasion demands; those with moderate ties affiliate closely for a time but without great intensity or endurance (at least for adults); and those with strong ties evidence extensive physical contact (e.g. grooming), mutual social support, high rates of interaction and have very stable relationships over time. This basic ordinal scale for assessing tie strength worked best because it fully accommodated the data of investigators without having to make undue inferences. For it is standard procedure for researchers to assess ties between dyads on the basis of time spent together, spatial proximity, frequency of physical contact (although sexual contact is usually excluded), food-sharing, supportive alliances, intensity and endurance.[2]

The strength of ties ranges, then, from negligible attraction to binding intimacy. It should be mentioned that scaling the intensity of African ape linkages was an uncomplicated procedure because, with few exceptions, investigators agreed upon the degree of attraction among and between age and sex classes. Some classes were lumped (because researchers usually considered them together); however, these classes have equivalent bonding patterns. One limitation must be noted: the relational data on gorillas are extensive only for Eastern gorillas, with some gorilla and chimpanzee ties classified as a 'null' tie. A null tie means the relation is a nonentity (e.g. father–son relations when mating is promiscuous) or is so rare it has not been observed with enough regularity for coding purposes. For example, a few cases of gorilla father–son ties have been suspected when a mature silverback and a young blackback exhibit an especially close attachment to each other in the same residential group. In the rows of Table 2.1, the *predominant patterns* of common chimpanzee and gorilla social ties are arrayed with respect to: (1) kin-based and voluntary ties; and (2) age and sex classes.

Analysis of tie patterns among chimpanzees and gorillas

What generalizations can be drawn from the relational data in Table 2.1? First, if we shift our normal vantage point and take an aerial view of a chimpanzee regional population – that is, if we imagine a collection of conspecifics moving about in a single inhabited block of forest – the emerging picture is of a widely dispersed ape colony composed of unattached individuals, mothers with dependent young, and momentary groups which vary in size, composition and stability. This hang-loose 'community' structure is reflected in the nature of ties from which chimpanzee social structure is built. Only a mother and her dependents are in continual spatial proximity, but this unit dissolves when dependents mature and disperse (Baldwin *et al.*). While mother–daughter ties are strong in early adolescence, this bond is interrupted when a female transfers either temporarily or permanently into a neighbouring community. Seemingly this relation is forever weakened, with rare exceptions, for should a daughter return to her natal community, she still remains mostly aloof, with only her dependents for company (Wrangham and Smuts 1980, Plooij 1984: 17, Goodall 1986: 168, Nishida and Hiraiwa-Hasegawa 1987, Hayaki 1988, Chapman and Wrangham 1993). Mother–son ties are strong, for although an adult son moves independently of his mother after puberty, both share the same ranging area and are frequently seen together feeding, grooming and assisting each other in conflict situations (Nishida 1979, Pusey 1983, Tuttle 1986). Brother–sister bonds are strong, but following Pusey (1980) they are likely to lessen as the sister matures. Among adult males, the strongest ties are between siblings, who constitute the most companionable and enduring

Table 2.1 African ape tie patterns compared among age-sex classes

	Pan troglodytes		Gorilla gorilla	
	Kin-blood ties	Voluntary ties	Kin-blood ties	Voluntary ties
(1) Adult male–adult male	Null tie between father and son Strong sibling ties 1, 2, 3, 4, 5, 11, 38, 39, 47	Weak to moderate ties with other males 4, 6, 7, 8, 9, 10, 11, 12, 13, 33, 36, 39, 56, 57, 60, 64	Null ties between father and son Null sibling ties	Weak ties with other males 14, 15, 16, 17, 18, 19, 20, 30, 40, 58, 63
(2) Adult male–adult and adolescent female	Strong mother–son ties Strong brother–sister ties, weakening after maturity Null tie between father and daughter 1, 2, 4, 6, 7, 8, 22, 37	Weak ties between male-adult/adolescent females 4, 5, 6, 7, 21, 33, 47, 57, 59	Mother–son and sibling ties null after puberty Null ties between father and daughter	Moderate to strong ties among leader male and females with offspring Weak ties among all males and females without offspring 16, 17, 23, 24, 25, 40, 41, 53, 54, 65
(3) Adult male–adolescent male	Strong sibling ties 1, 4	Weak ties between adults and adolescent males 1, 4, 6, 7, 39, 42, 43, 47	Null sibling ties	Weak ties silverbacks and blackbacks 17, 24, 26, 27, 40
(4) Adult male–juvenile and infant	Strong ties among siblings 29, 32, 42	Absent to weak ties adult males and juveniles/infants 1, 6, 47	Null ties among siblings	Moderate to strong ties between leader male and juveniles/infants Weak ties all other silverbacks 16, 17, 23, 24, 25, 26, 30, 31, 40

	Pan troglodytes		Gorilla gorilla	
	Kin-blood ties	Voluntary ties	Kin-blood ties	Voluntary ties
(5) Adult/adolescent female–adult/adolescent female	Strong mother–daughter ties, usually weakening after puberty. Strong sibling ties, weakening at maturity. 1, 4, 6, 7, 22, 36, 37, 42, 48	Absent to weak ties among females 4, 6, 7, 8, 9, 33, 44, 47	Strong mother–daughter ties, usually weakening after puberty Null sibling ties 25, 40, 54	Absent to weak ties among females 16, 17, 24, 25, 30, 40, 41, 54, 62
(6) Adult/adolescent female–adolescent male	Strong mother–son ties Strong sibling ties, weakening over time 1, 7, 22, 29	Weak ties between adult/adolescent females and adolescent males 34	Null mother–son and sibling ties	Weak ties for adult/adolescent females and blackbacks 30, 40
(7) Adult/adolescent female–juveniles and infants	Strong mother–offspring and sibling ties 1, 7, 22, 29, 31, 32, 34, 35, 39, 42, 45, 46, 49, 50, 51, 52, 60	Absent to weak ties for adult/adolescent females and juveniles and infants 12, 34, 38	Strong mother–offspring ties Null sibling ties 16, 30, 31	Weak ties for adult/adolescent females and juveniles and infants 16, 31, 41
(8) Adolescent male–adolescent male	Null sibling ties	Weak to moderate ties for adolescent males 4, 10, 39, 45	Null sibling ties	Weak ties for blackbacks 17, 24, 40
(9) Adolescent male–juveniles and infants	Strong sibling ties 4, 11, 29, 61	Absent to weak ties adolescent male–juveniles and infants 39	Null sibling ties	Weak ties for blackbacks and juveniles and infants 24, 30, 31
(10) Juveniles/infants–juveniles/infants	Strong sibling ties 4, 11, 29, 51	Weak ties among juveniles/infants 39	Strong sibling ties 30, 31, 40	Weak to moderate ties among juveniles 30, 31, 40, 55

LIVERPOOL
JOHN MOORES UNIVERSITY
AVRIL ROBARTS LRC

male–male interactions. Although strong 'friendship' ties are reported between adult males (Goodall 1967, and see Mitani and Nishida 1993), most male ties are typically weak to moderate with interactions as infrequent as once in a period of weeks or months (see Goodall 1986, Tuttle 1986, Nishida and Hiraiwa-Hasegawa 1987). Adult male–adult female ties are also weak since stable relations between unrelated adult males and females are never reported (Nishida and Hiraiwa-Hasegawa 1987). Adult female–adult female ties are absent to weak with most researchers agreeing that voluntary female relations are either inconsequential or constitute what Goodall (1986: 176) calls a 'neutral relationship', that is, one that cannot be described as friendly or unfriendly (Halperin 1979, Nishida 1979, Nishida and Hiraiwa-Hasegawa 1987). Father–offspring ties are void in a promiscuous mating system.

Table 2.1   Sources

1 Goodall-Lawick, J. (1975)
2 Riss, D. and Busse, C. (1977)
3 Riss, D. and Goodall, J. (1977)
4 Goodall, J. (1986)
5 Bygott, J.D. (1974)
6 Nishida, T. (1979)
7 Nishida, T. and Hiraiwa-Hasegawa, M. (1987)
8 Bygott, J. (1979)
9 Halperin, S. (1979)
10 Sugiyama, Y. (1968)
11 Teleki, G. (1973)
12 Nishida, T. (1983)
13 Simpson, M. (1973)
14 Cousins, D. (1978)
15 Casimir, M.J. (1975)
16 Schaller, G. (1972)
17 Schaller, G. (1962)
18 Dixson, A. (1981)
19 Fossey, D. (1970)
20 Fossey, D. (1976)
21 McGinnis, P. (1973)
22 Pusey, A. (1983)
23 Harcourt, A.H. (1979a)
24 Yamagiwa, J. (1983)
25 Stewart, K. and Harcourt, A.H. (1987)
26 Harcourt, A.H. and Fossey, D. (1981)
27 Harcourt, A.H. (1979d)
29 Goodall-Lawick, J. (1968a)
30 Stewart, K. (1981)
31 Fossey, D. (1979)
32 Teleki, E., Hunt, E. and Pfifferling, J. (1976)
33 Bauer, H. (1976)
34 Silk, J. (1979)
35 McGrew, W.C. (1975)
36 Nishida, T. and Kawanaka, K. (1972)
37 Pusey, A.E. (1980)
38 Goodall-Lawick, J. (1968b)
39 Goodall, J. (1965)
40 Harcourt, A.H. (1979c)
41 Harcourt, A.H. (1977)
42 Hayaki, H. (1988)
43 Pusey, A. (1977)
44 Wrangham, R.W. and Smuts, B.B. (1980)
45 Reynolds, V. and Reynolds, F. (1965)
46 Plooij, F. (1984)
47 Nishida, T. (1970)
48 Nishida, T. (1968)
49 Silk, J. (1978)
50 Izawa, K. (1970)
51 Goodall-Lawick, J. (1973)
52 Tutin, C.E.G., McGrew, W.C. and Baldwin, P. (1983)
53 Harcourt, A.H. (1978)
54 Harcourt, A.H. (1979b)
55 Fossey, D. (1967–1968)
56 Wrangham, R. (1979a)
57 Wrangham, R. (1979b)
58 Veit, P. (1982)
59 Wrangham, R. (1975)
60 Ghiglieri, M. (1985)
61 Goodall, J. (1983)
62 Watts, D. (1990)
63 Sicotte, P. (1993)
64 Mitani, J. and Nishida, T. (1993)
65 Watts, D. (1992)

Second, if we imagine a regional population of gorillas moving about in a solid block of forest, our image converts to that of four or more groups and some lone males foraging on the same home range. While gorilla groups fluctuate in size and composition, with some containing up to four adult males at times, the stable core is a silverback leader and a number of mothers and their dependents (Harcourt 1978). However, if we now drop our reliance upon parcelling gorillas into discrete groups, and instead consider only the linkages of individuals over time, the following network configuration emerges: a mother and dependents are strongly tied but after puberty son and daughter disperse. After daughter leaves, she will 'seldom interact' with her mother or any close relatives. Instead, she will transfer to another group or a lone silverback, often moving out of her natal regional population to a neighbouring population (Harcourt et al. 1980, Pusey and Packer 1987: 253, Stewart and Harcourt 1987). After son departs he usually becomes a solitary traveller or a transient group visitor but, unlike his sister, he usually remains within the boundaries of his natal home range (Watts 1990). In regard to other ties, silverbacks usually have weak bonds with each other (Schaller 1972, Cousins 1978, Dixson 1981: 114, Fossey 1983). Adult male and female ties are generally weak, although mothers with dependents are moderately to strongly tied to the leader silverback. Yet this tie is reported to weaken as offspring mature, with a mother's degree of attachment to a leader male (indexed primarily by spatial proximity) reported to be inversely proportional to the age and condition of her offspring, with the birth of an infant having an immediate effect on the time a female spends near a leader male (Stewart and Harcourt 1987, Harcourt 1979a, Yamagiwa 1983). Ostensibly, only when a mother is successful in raising offspring does she engage in a long-term relationship with a silverback male. Otherwise, she is inclined to transfer on her own to a lone silverback, blackback, or another group (Harcourt 1977, Stewart 1981). To be sure the stability of a gorilla group rests upon a nucleus of mothers and a silverback male. But because gorilla females 'rarely' interact with each other (Schaller 1962, Harcourt 1977, 1979b, Yamagiwa 1983), most adult ties in a gorilla group are weak. Indeed, in the core network of mothers and the leader male, the configuration is star-shaped because the only supportive adult ties are those that directly link females with the silverback (see top of Figure 2.1 for an illustration of this low-density star-shaped structure).

While gorilla tie patterns are surprising (given the traditional notion of a tight-knit gorilla group), they help to account for the easy and often sudden departure of a female from her residential group (Harcourt et al. 1976). Moreover, the high proportion of weak bonds among gorillas is reflected in the 'small number of overt social interactions' within a residential group − a fact which Schaller (1972: 103) considered to be 'a most striking aspect of gorilla intragroup behavior'.

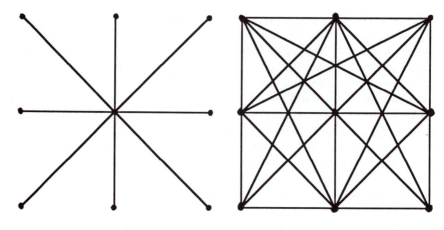

Low Density Network   High Density Network

Figure 2.1 Visualizing network density. Density is the number of ties as a proportion of all possible social ties among actors. Also of relevance is the strength of the ties connecting actors; and in this study, strength was measured in terms of the extent to which ties involved conspecifics in particular age and sex classes who could be found in spatial proximity, who socially groomed each other, who shared food, who formed alliances, and who provided social support. Thus, for the purposes of this study, density is viewed as a joint function of the number of ties (as a proportion of all possible ties) and the strength of these ties.

Thus, despite major contrasts in social organization, the majority of network ties for both chimpanzees and gorillas are constructed primarily from weak rather than strong linkages. If we assume that strong ties represent 'dense' patterns of interactions and weak ties 'sparse' patterns of interactions, both pongids can be characterized as having low-density networks, composed of a few strong ties and many weak ties. In contrast, the social structures of Old World cercopithecines have, on average, many more strong ties and two intriguing regularities are apparent. First, most monkeys (and also prosimians) reveal male-biased dispersal and female-bonded networks, a format that with few exceptions exists regardless of the primate species and the mating arrangement (Greenwood 1980). And, second, monkey groups normally reveal a number of supportive matrifocal cliques, a configuration that embeds individuals in networks that define relational boundaries, restricts individual mobility and ensures inter-generational continuity over time. For example, among the well-studied common baboons (*Papio*) and macaques (*Macaca*), natal males transfer into non-natal troops, slowly working their way into an all-male hierarchy of dominant–subordinate relations. In turn, adult females remain in natal cliques with up to four generations of mothers, daughters and sisters. These kinship networks are the anchors for the stability and cohesion of a baboon or macaque troop (for discussions see Altmann 1980, Greenwood 1980, Fedigan 1982, Smuts 1985, Cheney *et al.* 1986, Pusey and Packer 1987, Ray and Sapolsky 1992, Bernstein *et al.* 1993). Such a high-density clique is illustrated in Figure 2.1.

In contrast, African ape females emigrate at puberty with female gorillas, perhaps in line with female chimpanzees, often moving through multiple transfers outside their natal range into a neighbouring population (Stewart and Harcourt 1987). The result is to block, in most cases, the formation of matrifocal cliques. While gorilla males also disperse, they usually become solitary within their natal home range. In the case of chimpanzee networks, strong ties continue between mother and son and between male siblings. While sons and mothers could, in theory, generate extended blood-ties, they rarely mate with each other (Pusey 1980), and 'patrifocal' cliques cannot exist without male parental care and stable heterosexual bonds. Thus, even in a community organization where only females are dispersing, until males can be linked by 'patrifocal' kinship relations, voluntary ties must assume more importance than kinship ties. As a result, for both gorillas and chimpanzees, there are few nested and enduring strong-tie cliques.

What might account for this convergence in low-density tie patterns for both gorillas and chimpanzees? At this point it is important to state that a predominance of weak ties is apparent not only for the African apes but is common to all non-human hominoids. Indeed, despite what are otherwise striking differences in organizational arrangements, all extant ape genera – gorilla, chimpanzee, gibbon (*Hylobates*) and orangutan (*Pongo*) – evidence low-density networks, with the gibbon isolated into nuclear families and the near solitary ways of adult orangutans generating the sparsest network patterns of any living monkey or ape (see Rodman and Mitani 1987, Mitani 1990, and Maryanski and Turner 1992 for a network analysis of gibbon and orangutan network ties). Additionally, on the basis of an earlier cladistic/network analysis of hominoid relations, a configuration of the organizational tendencies of the Last Common Ancestor (LCA) was drawn (Maryanski 1992, Maryanski and Turner 1992). In light of these data and the successful application of the 'regularity' and 'relatedness' hypotheses, a striking conclusion became apparent: in line with contemporary hominoids, the Last Common Hominoid Ancestor (LCA) population evidenced a social structure of very weak ties, with low sociality, transient mating and a lack of group continuity over time (see Maryanski 1992, Maryanski and Turner 1992). The ultimate cause for hominoid low-density networks is seemingly correlated with the rapid extinction of ape genera in the Miocene, the adaptive radiation of monkey species and their movement into the original hominoid niche during the middle Miocene, and the subsequent adaptation of hominoids to a peripheral zone where selection promoted anatomical modifications for forelimb dominant locomotion and other novel skeletal features (see Andrews 1981, Temerin and Cant 1983 for discussions). The thesis argued in this earlier network research was that a terminal-branch feeding niche or any marginal niche with sparsely distributed and limited resources would also select against dense organizational structures with stable cliques (see Maryanski 1992). But to generate such a low-density social structure prompted a departure from the normal anthropoid pattern of 'high sociality' and instead involved (1) a tendency for relative low sociality among most adults and (2) a systematic bias for female dispersal in the hominoid line (a pattern which is rare among mammals in general, and primates in particular) (Pusey and Packer 1987). In turn, this disruption of the mother–daughter bond through female-biased dispersal blocked genealogical ties through female lines and disrupted group recursiveness. While a network/cladogram reconstruction of the LCA population suggested a very sparse social network (rather similar to contemporary orangutans), descendant hominoid species who later moved into new habitats undoubtedly underwent selection pressures for increased density in social support networks. Yet, for unknown reasons, female dispersal at puberty was retained which forced succeeding ape species to build social structure through unconventional bonding patterns. All present-day apes evidence novel organizational arrangements (relative to monkeys and to each other) in their adaptation to different habitats, in part because they forged ties within the constraints of female dispersal. Indeed, a network analysis of all extant hominoid organization plainly revealed an across-the-board strengthening of ties in ways that manifestly worked around female dispersal, making it a formidable ancestral character (Maryanski 1992, Maryanski and Turner 1992) (see footnote 1 for why G-G rubbing in female bonobos does not constitute a real exception to this pattern).

Thus, if we assume that the trend in *hominoid* organization after the LCA has been the building of supportive ties in response to ecological circumstances, what type of social structure was possible for early proto-hominids in light of this legacy?

EARLY HOMINID SOCIAL STRUCTURE

The savannah is a vastly different habitat than the rainforests where African hominoids originally evolved. With drier climatic conditions creating open woodlands and savannahs beginning in the Miocene, some hominoid (and cercopithecoid) populations moved out to more open terrain (Malone 1987). While the adaptation of proto-hominids to an open-country niche was most certainly constrained by earlier anatomical and neurological features that had once enhanced hominoid survival and reproductive success in a rainforest (see Maryanski 1992, 1993), the questions to be considered here are purely sociological: what kinds of social network ties did early proto-hominids bring to the African savannah? And, which ones served as the organizational building blocks for what would later evolve into the distinctly human hunting and gathering society? To help answer these questions, the social networks and dispersal patterns of African apes are relevant, but only the chimpanzee will be used here as the prototype for early proto-hominid society, in part because recent molecular data point to human and chimp as each other's closest *living* relative[3] (Goodman *et al.* 1990, Gould *et al.* 1993).

Thus in considering a chimpanzee social network as a blueprint for the proto-hominid condition, we begin with a relatively 'hang-loose' community structure where individuals freely mingle with conspecifics or move about alone within a defined block of forest. But on the open savannah, such predilections would be modified, in part because of predator pressures and the concomitant loss of arboreal safety zones. Instead, pressures would likely promote a more codified organization with increased sociality for predator defence and social support (see Anderson 1986, Dunbar 1988, Steele 1989).[4] However, it is unlikely that such pressures worked to make hominoid networks more like their monkey counterparts (e.g. *Papio* and *Macaca*) whose ancestral legacy would appear to have incorporated male-biased dispersal and strongly tied matrifocal cliques (see Maryanski and Turner 1992 for a cladistic/network analysis of bonding patterns among selected Old World monkeys). Indeed for the problem at hand a cercopithecine strategy would seem counter-productive since it would first require a neutralization of male–male bonds, a read-option of male-biased dispersal and a curtailing of female-biased dispersal. Instead, if we assume that early proto-hominids carried with them the social propensities of their chimpanzee relatives, the future hominid line required an adaptive strategy which could weigh anchor against the current of an ancestral background of few strong ties between adults, female transfer, an unstable mating system and father-absent child-rearing. Even if we assume that proto-hominids evidenced more tie-formation tendencies than common chimpanzees, their biological nature was still, in all likelihood, biased towards the pan-hominoid legacy of relatively low sociality, weak ties and female-biased dispersal.

One solution to this organizational problem is the creation of social institutions. From a purely structural perspective, a social institution can be viewed as composed of networks of status positions in which individuals are incumbent (and to which normative and value elements are attached). These networks of positions are organized into diverse types of social units (e.g. groups, lineages, clans), with each institution focused on a specific set of adaptive problems faced by a society. However, given the hominoid legacy, coupled with intense selection pressures for increased support networks, what institutional structures could be initially fashioned from a fluid, weak-tie network base with pressures for increased social support?

The pioneer institution: kinship

If we use chimpanzee society as an approximation of the network structure of our hominid ancestors, the core support ties already in place consisted of: (a) strong ties between mother and young, but with female-biased dispersal out of the natal community at puberty; (b) continued strong ties between mother and adult son (since males remain within the same ranging area); (c) strong ties between male siblings; (d) selected 'friendship ties' between male dyads (see Maryanski 1993 for a detailed discussion). Yet, how can a kinship-based support network with inter-generational continuity be constructed in light of a mother–son 'incest' taboo and, to a lesser extent, brother–sister sexual avoidance, a non-existent father-role, and the regular migration of daughters (in every extant ape species) from their mothers and sisters after puberty (thereby excluding stable matrilines)?

One strategy is to foster a more enduring breeding pattern in conjunction with what was likely a polygynous 'family' arrangement. A stable coupling of one male with two or more females is a reasonable assumption to entertain because it is consistent with the evidence of sexual dimorphism among early hominids (Johanson 1980, Wood 1985, McHenry 1991), the well-documented rarity of monogamy among Old World primates, and the fact that polygyny has been recorded as the preferred choice in 70 per cent of the world's human societies (Murdock 1967, and see Maryanski 1993 for a discussion). Thus, contrary to most sociological arguments on the 'incest taboo' as the cornerstone of the kinship institution (Davis 1949), the reproductive data on primates would suggest that this 'taboo' is already rooted in our primate heritage, since sexual avoidance between primary relatives is well-documented among Old World higher primates in general (Pusey and Packer 1987) (although among humans it was to be considerably elaborated upon culturally when lineages and clans were created in horticultural societies). Instead, the major institutional step was not a normative 'incest rule' preventing sexual relations between primary kin but rather a 'marriage rule' (or an initial attachment strategy) to reinforce a stable breeding pattern and, in turn, activate father–offspring ties to make patrilocal residence a reality. Yet, alternations in reproductive arrangements from a transitory mating arrangement to 'family units' with dependent offspring would have to overcome the genetic propensity for weak male–female ties as well as reduce, to some extent, the promiscuity of males and females. For this to have occurred, selection pressures for anchoring relationships must have been intense. But such a kinship system with a residential bias of patrilocal residence, female-biased dispersal (or female exogamy), and conjugal family units without unilineal descent is what typifies bands of hunter-gatherers (Murdock 1967, Ember 1978, Martin and Stewart 1982, Bailey and Aunger 1990, Maryanski 1993). Thus, stabilization of male-female mating, and not the incest taboo, was the cornerstone of the first hominid institution.

The economic institution

In conjunction with a kinship system, an institution for economic production was also likely developing. This institution would further strengthen gender-role relations and reinforce the family as the basic unit of production through the creation of mutual dependencies. Here a key adaptive strategy was the organization of a sexual division of labour: males hunt, females gather. Economic task allocation by sex is characteristic of all hunting and gathering societies (Murdock 1949). Moreover, gender-based role segregation in subsistence activities is compatible with the support ties already in place among adult males. And, in a social system where females are already predisposed to disperse, the retention of natal males on their home-ground for mutual aid and defence is the least disruptive arrangement. Additionally, the future success of 'big game hunting' as is documented in the Upper Paleolithic record (Olsen 1989) was probably facilitated by the good fellowship among hominid natal males (as is the case among present-day male chimpanzees who hunt co-operatively).

Finally, in line with segregated conjugal roles for economic co-operation, other economic rules, however informal at first, would come to govern hominid social relations in a general fashion. One such rule is a broad 'principle of reciprocity', which is universal to band-level societies and is a social correlate to the economic sexual division of labour. The addition of an expanded economic pattern that involves a balance of giving and receiving would provide a necessary counter-balance to the hominoid legacy of high individualism and self-reliance by linking individuals through co-operative food-getting, and, in turn, intensify a 'sense of community' among all resident members. It is probably not coincidental that the 'nuclear family' and the 'community' are the only social networks that are 'genuinely universal' and 'occur in every known human society' (Murdock 1949: 79).

SUMMARY AND CONCLUSIONS

Any hypothesis on hominid evolution must work hand-in-hand with the empirical findings of archaeology and palaeoanthropology. Yet, how can reconstruction of hominid lifeways be put on a sound empirical footing when concrete social arrangements can only partly be gleaned from empirical findings? One answer is to examine the social structures of Old World anthropoids, especially the African apes. For hominid history was constructed by a primate, with the hominization process itself driven by biological and sociological processes which led to the emergence of *Homo sapiens*. In this chapter, network analysis was used to compare African ape social structure, which highlighted an underlying convergence in chimpanzee and gorilla linkages and dispersal dynamics. A predominance of weak ties over strong ties was then associated with a conservative ancestral trait of female dispersal, a pan-hominoid character. Finally, chimpanzee network ties were used as a blueprint to consider early hominid social structure and it was hypothesized that to overcome the basic hominoid legacy of weak ties and a lack of group continuity, the first social institutions of kinship and the economy emerged, which over time evolved into the innovative hunting and gathering society.

In contrast to the above thesis, Dunbar (1993) recently proposed that hominid populations achieved organizational stability through selection for language which evolved to replace social grooming as the basis of integration when group size increased in *Homo* populations. Dunbar's thesis is rooted in the assumption that all primates are highly social, and grooming is the primary mechanism to service social relationships. These generalizations can be supported for Old World monkeys but they cannot be easily sustained for hominoids, as adult grooming is rare among gorillas and orangutans, and in chimpanzees only males frequently groom (see Goosen 1991 for a discussion). Hence, if our closest relatives rarely groom, it is unlikely that speech evolved in *Homo* to supplement grooming as a cohesive strategy. Instead, it might be more fruitful to consider this issue using Granovetter's (1973) 'weak/strong tie' theory of integration and suppose that selection operated to shift hominid relations from a weak to a stronger tie mode where, once social structure was altered, language later operated to further promote tie-building. For example, Dunbar is correct that integration in Old World monkeys is accomplished mostly by strong ties rather than weak ties (as indexed by female grooming cliques). This generates a high degree of integration at the micro-group level but a low degree of integration at the macro-regional level (i.e. monkeys tend to have cohesion within groups with little integration between groups). But for apes, weak ties predominate over strong ties. This means less cohesion at the micro-group level, but, as often happens, a higher degree of integration at the macro–population level. In chimpanzees, weak ties permit the linking of dispersed members within a fluid regional population with the result that chimpanzees possess a 'sense of community' but not a strong 'sense of subgroup affiliation'. Thus there *is* a strength in weak ties because when individuals are not locked into cliques a greater number of individuals come into contact. This gives structural cohesion to a regional level of organization which would be difficult to achieve on the basis of strong ties alone. In addition, gorillas might also be organized (or were) at the regional population level (see Emlen and Schaller 1960, Imanishi 1965, Reynolds 1966: 444, Goodall and Groves 1977, Maryanski 1987). The sharing of a home range by dispersed groups, the 'visiting' and overlapping of groups, and the easy movement in and out of groups by males and females all hint that, in relatively undisturbed habitats, gorilla groups are merely segments of a larger established community network with weak ties connecting members of different groups and lone males within the same community. Thus, integration is possible with either weak or strong ties, with hominoids clearly predisposed to form low-density networks. Indeed, Dunbar's (1992: 490) speculation that orangutans might 'live in a more complex social world' is a plausible assumption in light of their low-density social networks. Moreover orangutan integration on the basis of weak ties might help to resolve the enigma Dunbar (1992) found between a large neocortical volume and a small group size in the red ape.

In conclusion, it is gratifying that the network findings outlined here are compatible with the recent work of other investigators who used different conceptual tacks to arrive at similar findings on early hominid social structure. For example, McHenry (1991, this volume) maintains that *A. afarensis* evidenced only a moderate degree of sexual dimorphism, which he links to a polygynous mating pattern and a patrilocal kinship structure. The early hominid profiles of Foley and Lee (1989) and Wrangham (1987) are also consistent with the proposed network model. Wrangham suggests that female dispersal and a lack of female–female bonding in hominoids are conservative phyletic characters derived from the LCA population, while Foley and Lee's behavioural model also views male–female bonds and male–male consanguinity as pivots for early hominid social structure.

In turn, the above research is congruent with the classic 'residential hypothesis' that Pleistocene hunters and gatherers were organized into patrilocal bands with female-biased dispersal, a position favoured by such scholars as Service (1962), Radcliffe-Brown (1930), Williams (1974), Ember (1978) and Martin and Stewart (1982). It should also come as no surprise that the overwhelming majority of studied human societies have favoured patrilocal residence and female exogamy (Ember 1978, Murdock 1967). Finally, whether evolution is cultural or biological it is important to consider that any particular form must have grown out of an ancestral form and on this score it is not difficult to appreciate that a residence pattern of patrilocality might eventually give rise to a system of descent, with patrilineality the usual outcome with this residential rule (Murdock 1967). Thus, step by step with the steady accumulation of 'social knowledge,' we are drawing closer to a more graphic representation of early hominid organization which is supported by a growing number of scholars.

NOTES

1 I should note that the network ties analysed here are those of the widespread, common chimpanzee (*P. troglodytes*). The species *P. paniscus*, or bonobos, an isolated population that inhabits the Zaire River basin, is not included here because their tie patterns vary somewhat from the common chimpanzee, requiring a separate classification for a few ties, even though bonobos evidence

a community organization and female-biased dispersal. Most importantly, G-G rubbing presents a problem as a measure of tie strength. While it seemingly functions to promote female–female sociality, it is not really an affect activity (as social grooming is, for example), but rather a ritualized contact activity to 'reduce tension' among unrelated females (see White 1989: 162). Yet, the rather bizarre and unique G-G rubbing is understandable as a means to promote greater tolerance among unrelated females when selection favoured greater network density in the bonobo habitat, a hypothesis to be discussed later in the chapter.

2   These measures are independent of each other, but they are probably inter-correlated.

3   The most recent molecular data points to chimpanzees and humans sharing a common ancestor, with the gorilla line branching first, although on the basis of both molecular and morphological characters, all three share a close phyletic relationship (see Ciochon 1987, Goodman *et al.* 1990, Sibley *et al.* 1990).

4   Anderson found in her review of primate predation that the higher the rate of predation, the less likely were individuals to move about alone, and the more likely they were to cluster together.

REFERENCES

Altmann, J. (1980) *Baboon Mothers and Infants.* Cambridge, MA: Harvard University Press.

Anderson, C. (1986) 'Predation and primate evolution.' *Primates* 27: 15–39.

Andrews, P. (1981) 'Species diversity and diet in monkeys and apes during the Miocene.' In C.B. Stringer (ed.) *Aspects of Human Evolution.* London: Taylor and Francis.

Bailey, R. and Aunger, R. (1990) 'Humans as primates: the social relationships of Efe pygmy men in comparative perspective.' *International Journal of Primatology* 11: 127–145.

Baldwin, P. J., McGrew, W.C. and Tutin, C.E.G. (1982) 'Wide-ranging chimpanzees at Mt. Assirik, Senegal.' *International Journal of Primatology* 3: 367–385.

Bauer, H. (1976) 'Ethological aspects of Gombe chimpanzee aggregations with implications for hominisation'. Dissertation, Stanford University.

Bernstein, I., Judge, P. and Ruehlmann, T. (1993) 'Kinship, association, and social relationships in rhesus monkeys (*Macaca mulatta*).' *American Journal of Primatology* 31: 41–53.

Bygott, J. (1974) 'Agonistic behaviour and dominance in wild chimpanzees'. Dissertation, University of Cambridge.

Bygott, J. (1979) 'Agonistic behavior, dominance, and social structure in wild chimpanzees of the Gombe National Park.' In D. Hamburg and E. McCown (eds) *The Great Apes*, pp. 405–428. California: Benjamin/Cummings.

Carpenter, C.R. (1934) 'A field study of the behavior and social relations of howling monkeys.' *Comparative Psychology Monographs* 10: 168.

Carpenter, C.R. (1942) 'Societies of monkeys and apes.' *Biological Symposia* 8: 177–204.

Casimir, M. (1975) 'Feeding ecology and nutrition of an eastern gorilla group in the Mt. Kahuzi Region (République du Zaire).' *Folia Primatologica* 24: 81–136.

Chapman, C. and Wrangham, R. (1993) 'Range use of the forest chimpanzees of Kibale: implications for the understanding of chimpanzee social organization.' *American Journal of Primatology* 31: 263–273.

Cheney, D., Seyfarth, R. and Smuts, B. (1986) 'Social relationships and social cognition in nonhuman primates.' *Science* 234: 1361–1366.

Ciochon, R. L. (1987) 'Cladistics and the ancestry of modern apes and humans.' In R. Ciochon and J. Fleagle (eds) *Primate Evolution and Human Origins*. New York: Aldine de Gruyter.

Cousins, D. (1978) 'Aggressive behavior in gorillas.' *Ratel* 5: 10–13.

Davis, K. (1949) *Human Society*. New York: Macmillan.

Dixson, A. (1981) *The Natural History of the Gorilla*. New York: Columbia University Press.

Dunbar, R.I.M. (1988) *Primate Social Systems*. London: Croom Helm.

Dunbar, R.I.M. (1992) 'Neocortex size as a constraint on group size in primates.' *Journal of Human Evolution* 20: 469–493.

Dunbar, R.I.M. (1993) 'Coevolution of neocortical size, group size and language in humans.' *Behavioral and Brain Sciences* 16: 681–735.

Ember, C. (1978) 'Myths about hunter-gatherers.' *Ethnology* 17: 439–448.

Emlen, J. and Schaller, G. (1960) 'Distribution and status of the mountain gorilla.' *Zoologica* 45: 41–52.

Falk, D. (1983) 'Cerebral cortices of East African early hominids.' *Science* 222: 1072–1074.

Fedigan, L. (1982) *Primate Paradigms: Sex Roles and Social Bonds*. Canada: Eden Press.

Fleagle, J. (1988) *Primate Adaptation and Evolution*. New York: Academic Press.

Foley, R. and Lee, P.C. (1989) 'Finite social space, evolutionary pathways, and reconstructing hominid behavior.' *Science* 243: 901–906.

Fossey, D. (1967–1968) 'Mountain-gorilla research.' *National Geographic Society Research Reports* 131–140. Washington: National Geographic Society.

Fossey, D. (1970) 'Making friends with mountain gorillas.' *National Geographic Magazine* 137: 48–67.

Fossey, D. (1972) *Living with Mountain Gorillas*. Washington: National Geographic Society.

Fossey, D. (1976) 'The behaviour of the mountain gorilla'. Dissertation, University of Cambridge.

Fossey, D. (1979) 'Development of the mountain gorilla (*Gorilla gorilla beringei*): the first thirty-six months.' In D. Hamburg and E. McCown (eds) *The Great Apes*, pp. 139–184. Menlo Park: Benjamin/Cummings.

Fossey, D. (1983) *Gorillas in the Mist*. Boston: Houghton Mifflin Company.

Freeman, L., White, D. and Romney, A.K. (1989) *Research Methods in Social Network Analysis*. Fairfax, VA: George Mason University Press.

Ghiglieri, M. (1985) 'The social ecology of chimpanzees.' *Scientific American* 252 (6): 84–90.

Goodall, A. and Groves, C. (1977) 'The conservation of eastern gorillas.' In Prince Rainier III of Monaco and G. Bourne (eds) *Primate Conservation*, pp. 559–637. New York: Academic Press.

Goodall, J. (1965) 'Chimpanzees of the Gombe Stream Reserve.' In I. DeVore (ed.) *Primate Behavior*, pp. 425–473. New York: Holt, Rinehart and Winston.

Goodall, J. (1967) *My Friends: The Wild Chimpanzees*. Washington: National Geographic Society.

Goodall, J. (1983) 'Population dynamics during a 15-year period in one community of free-living chimpanzees in the Gombe National Park.' *Zeitschrift für Tierpsychologie*. 61: 1–60.

Goodall, J. (1986) *The Chimpanzees of Gombe*. Cambridge, MA: Belknap Press.

Goodall-Lawick, J. (1968a) 'The behaviour of free-living chimpanzees in the Gombe Stream Reserve.' *Animal Behaviour Monographs* 1: 161–311.

Goodall-Lawick, J. (1968b) 'Behavior of free-ranging chimpanzees, Tanzania 1968.' *National Geographic Society Research Reports* 147–155. Washington: National Geographic Society.

Goodall-Lawick, J. (1973) 'Cultural elements in a chimpanzee community.' In W. Montagna (ed.) *The Symposia of the Fourth International Congress of Primatology* 1: 145–174.

Goodall-Lawick, J. (1975) 'The behavior of the chimpanzee.' In G. Kurth and I. Eibl-Eibesfeldt (eds) *Hominisation and Behavior*, pp. 74–134. Stuttgart: Gustav Fischer Verlag.

Goodman, M., Tagle, D.A., Fitch, D.H.A., Bailey, W., Czelusnak, J., Koop, B., Benson, P. and Slightom, J.L. (1990) 'Primate evolution at the DNA level and a classification of hominids.' *Journal of Molecular Evolution* 30: 260–266.

Goosen, C. (1991) 'Social grooming in primates.' In M.E. Stephens and J.D. Paterson (eds) *The Order Primates*. Iowa: Kendall/Hunt Publishing.

Gould, K., Young, L., Smithwick, E. and Phythyon, S. (1993) 'Semen characteristics of the adult male chimpanzee (*Pan troglodytes*).' *American Journal of Primatology* 29: 221–232.

Granovetter, M. (1973) 'The strength of weak ties.' *American Journal of Sociology* 78: 1360–1380.

Greenwood, P. (1980) 'Mating systems, philopatry, and dispersal in birds and mammals.' *Animal Behaviour* 30: 1140–1162.

Grine, F. (1988) *Evolutionary History of the 'Robust' Australopithecines*. New York: Aldine de Gruyter.

Halperin, S. D. (1979) 'Temporary association patterns in free-ranging chimpanzees: an assessment of individual grouping preferences.' In D. Hamburg and E. McCown (eds) *The Great Apes*, pp. 491–499. Menlo Park: Benjamin/Cummings.

Harcourt, A. (1977) 'Social relationships of wild mountain gorillas.' Dissertation, University of Cambridge.

Harcourt, A. (1978) 'Strategies of emigration and transfer by primates, with particular reference to gorillas.' *Zeitschrift für Tierpsychologie* 48: 401–420.

Harcourt, A. (1979a) 'Social relationships between adult male and female mountain gorillas in the wild.' *Animal Behaviour* 27: 325–342.

Harcourt, A. (1979b) 'Social relationships among adult female mountain gorillas.' *Animal Behaviour* 27: 251–264.

Harcourt, A. (1979c) 'The social relations and group structure of wild mountain gorillas.' In D. Hamburg and E. McCown (eds) *The Great Apes*, pp. 187–194. Menlo Park: Benjamin/Cummings.

Harcourt, A. (1979d) 'Contrasts between male relationships in wild gorilla groups.' *Behavioral Ecology and Sociobiology* 5: 39–49.

Harcourt, A. and Fossey, D. (1981) 'The Virunga gorillas: decline of an "island" population.' *African Journal of Ecology* 19: 83–97.

Harcourt, A., Stewart, K. and Fossey, D. (1976) 'Male emigration and female transfer in wild mountain gorilla.' *Nature* 263: 226–227.

Harcourt, A., Fossey, D., Stewart, K. and Watts, D. (1980) 'Reproduction in wild gorillas and some comparisons with chimpanzees.' *Journal of Reproduction and Fertility* (Suppl.) 28: 59–70.

Hayaki, H. (1988) 'Association partners of young chimpanzees in the Mahale Mountains National Park, Tanzania.' *Primates* 29: 147–161.

Hinde, R. (1976) 'Interactions, relationships and social structure.' *Man* (n.s.) 11: 1–17.

Hinde, R. (ed.) (1983) *Primate Social Relationships*. Oxford: Blackwell.

Imanishi, K. (1965) 'The origins of the human family: a primatological approach.' In S.A. Altmann (ed.) *Japanese Monkeys. A Collection of Translations*, pp. 113–136. Atlanta, GA: S.A. Altmann.

Izawa, K. (1970) 'Unit groups of chimpanzees and their nomadism in the savanna woodland.' *Primates* 11: 1–44.

Jolly, C. (1970) 'The seed-eaters: a new model of hominid differentiation based on a baboon analogy.' *Man* 5: 5–26.

Johanson, D.C. (1980) 'Early African hominid phylogenesis: a re-evaluation.' In L.K. Konigsson (ed.) *Current Argument on Early Man*, pp. 31–69. Oxford: Pergamon Press.

Jones, C. and Sabater-Pi, J. (1971) *Comparative Ecology of Gorilla gorilla (Savage and Wyman) and Pan troglodytes (Blumenbach) in Rio Muni, West Africa*. New York: S. Karger.

Knoke, D. and Kuklinski, J. (1982) *Network Analysis*. Beverly Hills: Sage.

Lewis, O.J. (1972) 'Osteological features characterizing the wrists of monkeys and apes, with reconsideration of this region in *Dryopithecus (Proconsul) africanus*.' *American Journal of Physical Anthropology* 36: 45–58.

McGinnis, P. (1973) 'Patterns of sexual behaviour in a community of free-living chimpanzees.' Dissertation, Cambridge University.

McGrew, W. C. (1975) 'Patterns of plant food sharing by wild chimpanzees.' Proceedings of the 5th Congress of the International Primatological Society (Nagoya, Japan), pp. 304–309. Basel: Karger.

McHenry, H. (1991) 'Sexual dimorphism in *Australopithecus afarensis*.' *Journal of Human Evolution* 20: 21–32.

Malone, D. (1987) 'Mechanisms of hominid dispersal in Miocene East Africa.' *Journal of Human Evolution* 16: 469–481

Martin, J. and Stewart, D. (1982) 'A demographic basis for patrilineal hordes.' *American Anthropologist* 84: 79–96.

Maryanski, A. R. (1986) 'African ape social structure: a comparative analysis'. PhD dissertation, University of California, Irvine.

Maryanski, A.R. (1987) 'African ape social structure: is there strength in weak ties?' *Social Networks* 9: 191–215.

Maryanski, A.R. (1992) 'The last ancestor: an ecological network model on the origins of human sociality.' *Advances in Human Ecology* 1: 1–32.

Maryanski, A.R. (1993) 'The elementary forms of the first protohuman society: an ecological/social network approach.' *Advances in Human Ecology* 2: 215–241.

Maryanski, A. and Turner, J. (1991) 'Network analysis.' In J. Turner (ed.) *The Structure of Sociological Theory*, 5th edn, pp. 540–572. Belmont, CA: Wadsworth.

Maryanski, A. and Turner, J. (1992) *The Social Cage: Human Nature and the Evolution of Society*. Stanford: Stanford University Press.

Mitani, J. (1990) 'Experimental field studies of Asian ape social systems.' *International Journal of Primatology* 11: 103–126.

Mitani, J. and Nishida, T. (1993) 'Contexts and social correlates of long-distance calling by male chimpanzees.' *Animal Behaviour* 45: 735–746.

Murdock, G. (1949) *Social Structure*. New York: Macmillan.

Murdock, G. (1967) *Ethnographic Atlas*. Pittsburgh, PA: University of Pittsburgh Press.

Nishida, T. (1968) 'The social group of wild chimpanzees in the Mahale Mountains.' *Primates* 9: 167–224.

Nishida, T. (1970) 'Social behavior and relationships among wild chimpanzees of the Mahale Mountains.' *Primates* 11: 47–87.

Nishida, T. (1979) 'The social structure of chimpanzees of the Mahale Mountains.' In D. Hamburg and E. McCown (eds) *The Great Apes*, pp. 73–121. Menlo Park: Benjamin/Cummings.

Nishida, T. (1983) 'Alpha status and agonistic alliance in wild chimpanzees (*Pan troglodytes schweinfurthi*).' *Primates* 24: 318–336.

Nishida, T. and Hiraiwa-Hasegawa, M. (1987) 'Chimpanzees and bonobos: cooperative relationships among males.' In B. Smuts, D. Cheney, R. Seyfarth, R. Wrangham and T. Struhsaker (eds) *Primate Societies*, pp. 165–180. Chicago: University of Chicago Press.

Nishida, T. and Kawanaka, K. (1972) 'Inter-unit group relationships among wild chimpanzees of the Mahale Mountains.' *Kyoto University African Studies* 7: 131–169.

Olsen, S. (1989) 'Solutré: a theoretical approach to the reconstruction of Upper Paleolithic hunting strategies.' *Journal of Human Evolution* 18: 295–327.

Plooij, F. (1984) *The Behavioral Development of Free-living Chimpanzee Babies and Infants*. New Jersey: Ablex Publishing.

Potts, R. (1993) 'Archaeological interpretations of early hominid behavior and ecology.' In D.T. Rasmussen (ed.) *The Origin and Evolution of Humans and Humanness*, pp. 49–73. Boston: Jones and Bartlett.

Pusey, A. (1977) 'The physical and social development of wild adolescent chimpanzees.' Dissertation, Stanford University.

Pusey, A. (1980) 'Inbreeding avoidance in chimpanzees.' *Animal Behaviour* 28: 543–552.

Pusey, A. (1983) 'Mother-offspring relationships in chimpanzees after weaning.' *Animal Behaviour* 31: 363–77.

Pusey, A. and Packer, C. (1987) 'Dispersal and philopatry.' In B. Smuts, D. Cheney, R. Seyfarth, R. Wrangham and T. Struhsaker (eds) *Primate Societies*, pp. 250–266. Chicago: University of Chicago Press.

Radcliffe-Brown, A.R. (1930) 'The social organization of the Australian tribes.' *Oceania* 1: 1–63, 206–246.

Rak, Y. (1983) *The Australopithecine Face*. New York: Academic Press.

Ray, J. and Sapolsky, R. (1992) 'Styles of male social behavior and their endocrine correlates among high-ranking wild baboons.' *American Journal of Primatology* 28: 231–250.

Reynolds, V. (1966) 'Open groups in hominid evolution.' *Man* 1: 441–452.

Reynolds, V. and Reynolds, F. (1965) 'Chimpanzees of the Budongo Forest.' In I. DeVore (ed.) *Primate Behavior*, pp. 368–424. New York: Holt, Rinehart and Winston.

Riss, D. and Busse, C. (1977) 'Fifty-day observation of a free-ranging adult male chimpanzee.' *Folia Primatologica* 28: 283–297.

Riss, D. and Goodall, J. (1977) 'The recent rise to the alpha-rank in a population of free-living chimpanzees.' *Folia Primatologica* 27: 134–151.

Rodman, P. and Mitani, J. (1987) 'Orangutans: sexual dimorphism in a solitary species.' In B. Smuts, D. Cheney, R. Seyfarth, R. Wrangham and T. Struhsaker (eds) *Primate Societies*, pp. 146–154. Chicago: University of Chicago Press.

Sade, D. (1972) 'Sociometrics of *Macaca mulatta*: linkages and cliques in grooming matrices.' *Folia Primatologica* 18: 196–223.

Schaller, G. (1962) 'The ecology and behavior of the mountain gorilla.' Dissertation, University of Wisconsin.

Schaller, G. (1972) 'The behavior of the mountain gorilla.' In P. Dolhinow (ed.) *Primate Patterns*, pp. 85–123. New York: Holt, Rinehart and Winston.

Service, E. (1962) *Primitive Social Organization*. New York: Random House.

Sibley, C., Comstock, J. and Ahlquist, J. (1990) 'DNA hybridization evidence of hominoid phylogeny: a reanalysis of the data.' *Journal of Molecular Evolution* 30: 202–236.

Sicotte, P. (1993) 'Inter-group encounters and female transfer in mountain gorillas: influence of group composition on male behavior.' *American Journal of Primatology* 30: 21–36.

Silk, J. (1978) 'Patterns of food sharing among mother and infant chimpanzees at Gombe National Park, Tanzania.' *Folia Primatologica* 29: 139–141.

Silk, J. (1979) 'Feeding, foraging, and food sharing behavior of immature chimpanzees.' *Folia Primatologica* 31: 123–142.

Simonds, P. (1974) *The Social Primates*. New York: Harper and Row.

Simpson, M. (1973) 'The social grooming of male chimpanzees.' In R. Michael and J. Crook (eds) *Comparative Ecology and Behaviour of Primates*, pp. 411–505. London: Academic Press.

Smuts, B. (1985) *Sex and Friendship in Baboons*. New York: Aldine.

Steele, J. (1989) 'Hominid evolution and primate social cognition.' *Journal of Human Evolution* 18: 421–432.

Stern, J.T., Jr. and Susman, R.L. (1983) 'The locomotor anatomy of *Australopithecus afarensis*.' *American Journal of Physical Anthropology* 60: 279–317.

Stewart, K. (1981) 'Social development of wild mountain gorillas'. Dissertation, University of Cambridge.

Stewart, K. and Harcourt, A. (1987) 'Gorillas: variation in female relationships.' In B. Smuts, D. Cheney, R. Seyfarth, R. Wrangham and T. Struhsaker (eds) *Primate Societies*, pp. 155–164. Chicago: University of Chicago Press.

Stringer, C.B. (1984) 'Human evolution and biological adaptation in the Pleistocene.' In R. Foley (ed.) *Hominid Evolution and Community Ecology*. London: Academic Press.

Sugiyama, Y. (1968) 'Social organization of chimpanzees in the Budongo Forest, Uganda.' *Primates* 9: 225–258.

Teleki, G. (1973) *The Predatory Behavior of Wild Chimpanzees*. Lewisburg: Bucknell University Press.

Teleki, G., Hunt, E.E., Jr. and Pfifferling, J.H. (1976) 'Demographic observations (1963–1973) on the chimpanzees of Gombe National Park, Tanzania.' *Journal of Human Evolution* 5: 559–598.

Temerin, A. and Cant, J. (1983) 'The evolutionary divergence of Old World monkeys and apes.' *American Naturalist* 122: 335–51.

Tutin, C.E.G., McGrew, W.C. and Baldwin, P.J. (1983) 'Social organization of savannah-dwelling chimpanzees, *Pan troglodytes verus*, at Mt. Asserik, Senegal.' *Primates* 24: 154–173.

Tuttle, R. (1986) *Apes of the World*. New Jersey: Noyes Publications.

Veit, P. (1982) 'Gorilla society.' *Natural History* 91 (3): 48–58.

Washburn, S. (1971) 'The study of human evolution.' In P. Dolhinow and V. Sarich (eds) *Background for Man*, pp. 82–117. Boston: Little, Brown and Co.

Watts, D. (1990) 'Ecology of gorillas and its relation to female transfer in mountain gorillas.' *International Journal of Primatology* 11: 21–45.

Watts, D. (1992) 'Social relationships of immigrant and resident female mountain gorillas. 1. Male–female relationships.' *American Journal of Primatology* 28: 159–181.

Weber, A.W. and Vedder, A. (1983) 'Population dynamics of the gorillas: 1959–1978.' *Biological Conservation* 26: 341–366.

White, F.J. (1989) 'Ecological correlates of pygmy chimpanzee social structure.' In V. Standen and R.A. Foley (eds) *Comparative Socioecology*. Oxford: Blackwell.

White, T. and Suwa, G. (1987) 'Hominid footprints at Laetoli: facts and interpretations.' *American Journal of Physical Anthropology* 72: 485–514.

Williams, B.J. (1974) 'A model of band society.' *American Antiquity* 39 (2), Memoir 29.

Wood, B. (1985) 'Sexual dimorphism in the hominid fossil record.' In J. Ghesquiere, R.D. Martin and F. Newcombe (eds) *Human Sexual Dimorphism*, pp. 105–123. London: Taylor and Francis.

Wrangham, R. (1975) 'The behavioral ecology of chimpanzees in Gombe National Park, Tanzania.' PhD dissertation, Cambridge, England.

Wrangham, R. (1979a) 'On the evolution of ape social systems.' *Social Science Information* 18: 334–368.

Wrangham, R. (1979b) 'Sex differences in chimpanzee dispersion.' In D. Hamburg and E. McCown (eds) *The Great Apes*, pp. 481–489. Menlo Park: Benjamin/Cummings.

Wrangham, R. (1987) 'The significance of African apes for reconstructing human social evolution.' In W.G. Kinzey (ed.) *The Evolution of Human Behavior: Primate Models*. Albany: State University of New York Press.

Wrangham, R. and Smuts, B.B. (1980) 'Sex differences in the behavioral ecology of chimpanzees in the Gombe National Park, Tanzania.' *Journal of Reproduction and Fertility* (Suppl.) 28: 13–31.

Yamagiwa, J. (1983) 'Diachronic changes in two eastern lowland gorilla groups (*Gorilla gorilla graueri*) in the Mt. Kahuzi Region, Zaire.' *Primates* 25: 174–183.

CHAPTER THREE

SEXUAL DIMORPHISM IN FOSSIL HOMINIDS AND ITS SOCIOECOLOGICAL IMPLICATIONS

HENRY M. MCHENRY

'The law of battle for the possession of the females appears to prevail throughout the whole great class of mammals', wrote Darwin (1892: 552). 'Most naturalists will admit that the greater size, strength, courage, and pugnacity of the male, his special weapons of offence, as well as his special means of defence, have been acquired or modified through that form of selection which I have called sexual.' These are prophetic words in the sense that after more than a century of study, most naturalists *do* accept sexual selection as the cause of sexual dimorphism.

The purpose of this paper is to review the sexually dimorphic characters in the fossil record and how they might be interpreted in the context of our current understanding of primate socioecology.

AUSTRALOPITHECUS AFARENSIS

Size variation among individuals referred to as *A. afarensis* is striking (Aiello 1990, Aiello and Dean 1990, Frayer and Wolpoff 1985, Hartwig-Scherer 1993, Johanson *et al.* 1978, Johanson *et al.* 1982, Johanson and White 1979, Jungers 1988, Leutenegger 1982a, b, Leutenegger and Shell 1987, Lovejoy *et al.* 1989, McHenry 1982, 1983, 1986, 1988, 1991a, b, 1992a, b). Signifi-cant shape variation between the large and small individuals may be present as well (e.g. Senut 1978, 1980, 1986, Senut and Tardieu 1985, Stern and Susman 1983, Susman *et al.* 1984, Tardieu 1981, 1983, 1986, Zihlman 1985). Many have suggested that more than one species of hominid is represented in the Hadar and Laetoli collections from strata dated between

3.7 and 2.9 Myr (e.g. Coppens 1981, 1983, Falk 1986, Hartwig–Scherer 1993, Olson 1981, 1985, Schmid 1983, Senut and Tardieu 1985, Tuttle 1981, Zihlman 1985), but there is strong evidence that only one species is represented (e.g. Johanson and White 1979, Johanson *et al.* 1978, Kimbel 1984, 1986, Kimbel and White 1988b, Kimbel *et al.* 1982, McHenry 1983, 1991a, 1992a, White 1985, White *et al.* 1981).

If this sample is a single species, as a majority of scholars who work directly with the material maintain, then one estimate of the degree of body weight dimorphism based on hindlimb joint size is 1.5 (assuming a human-like relationship between hindlimb joint size and body weight as explained in McHenry 1991a, 1992a). Table 3.1 presents estimates of body weight for this and other species of early hominids. This degree of dimorphism is above modern *H. sapiens* (1.2) and species of *Pan* (1.4), but below *Gorilla* (2.1) and *Pongo* (2.0). Jungers (1988) and Lovejoy *et al.* (1989) find a similar degree of body size variation using different methods.

A palaeontological sample like that attributed to *A. afarensis* provides invaluable insights into the nature of hominids of the past, but is inevitably limited. All inferences must be built on the tenuous ground of current available evidence. The sample is small and spread over at least 0.5 Myr and 800 km (i.e. Laetoli to Hadar). This means that the size variation observed within *A. afarensis* should not be expected to have a range like that of a modern species. But there are two palaeontological discoveries that are as close as one can expect to ever get to sampling the variability within a population of 3.7 to 2.9 Myr hominids: The G trails of Laetoli footprints and the sample in the A.L. 333 site of Hadar preserve records of body size variability within single populations. The G trails were left by three individuals. The smallest footprints (G-1) correspond to an individual standing about 1.22 m tall and the largest (G-3) had a foot size matching a 1.41 m tall individual (Tuttle 1991). The body weights of individuals of these statures are 27.8 kg and 40.1 kg respectively (calculated from the power curve given in Jungers and Stern 1983). The ratio of large to small is 1.44 which is similar to the male/female ratio in *Pan* (1.4), above that in modern *H. sapiens* (1.2) and below that in *Gorilla* and *Pongo* (2.0–2.1). Unfortunately, one cannot know the age of maturity of the individuals; they may have been children or two children and a parent. Fortunately the 333 site of Hadar does contain the evidence needed to ascertain maturity. At least thirteen individuals appeared to have died at one time (Johanson *et al.* 1982, White and Johanson 1989). This number is based on the number of preserved jaws. The postcrania reveal the presence of at least three large adult individuals (represented by three left distal fibulae [A.L. 333-9B, -85, -333w-37]) with fused epiphyses which are presumably males. Two adult small-bodied individuals (presumably females) are present as shown by two left tibia (A.L. 333-6 and 96). There are also one or more large sub-adults (A.L. 333w-33, -333w-14/15 and -333-95). The range of size variation is well above that seen in any

Table 3.1 Body weight dimorphism in species of Hominoidea[1] and fossil hominids[2]

Species	Male	Female	Ratio
A. afarensis	44.6	29.3	1.5
A. africanus	40.8	30.2	1.4
A. boisei	48.6	34.0	1.4
A. robostus	40.2	31.9	1.3
H. habilis sensu lato[3]	51.6	31.5	1.6
H. habilis sensu stricto[3]	37.0	31.5	1.2
H. rudolfensis[3]	59.6	50.8	1.2
early African H. erectus (= H. ergaster)[3]	62.7	52.3	1.2
Neanderthal[4]	60.1	51.8	1.2
Early a.m. H. sapiens[4]	70.0	56.8	1.2
H. sapiens	64.9	53.2	1.2
P. troglodytes	54.2	39.7	1.4
P. paniscus	47.8	33.1	1.4
G. gorilla	157.9	75.4	2.1
P. pygmaeus	78.8	38.8	2.0
H. syndactylus	11.3	11.3	1.0
H. lar	5.5	5.2	1.1

Notes
1 From McHenry (1991a).
2 From McHenry (1992a) except where indicated.
3 From McHenry (1994).
4 Derived from stature estimates in Feldesman et al. (1990) by regression formulae for male and female given in Table 11 of Ruff and Walker (1993). These body weights are probably underestimates of the true values, because these hominids were much more robust than the modern humans from whom the stature/weight formulae are derived. Adding 10 kg or even 20 kg does not appreciably affect the male/female ratio, however, since both sexes were robust.

modern human population. The largest hindlimb specimen, A.L. 333-3, corresponds to a modern human of about 50 kg and the smallest hindlimb specimen (A.L. 333-96) is as small as a 33.5 kg Pygmy.

The moderate level of body size variation is reflected in the jaws and teeth. This is significant because the sample sizes of jaws and teeth are much better. There are eleven mandibular and ten maxillary canines whose breadths can be measured reliably, and the variability (as measured by the coefficient of variation) is well below that of *Gorilla*, *Pongo* and *Pan troglodytes*, although lower canines in *Pan paniscus* are similar to *A. afarensis* in variability (Kimbel and White 1988a). The postcanine teeth do not exhibit unusually high degrees of variation (e.g. the CVs of their breadths are mostly below *Gorilla* and above *H. sapiens*; Kimbel and White 1988a). The robusticity of their mandibles is also not unusual (Kimbel and White 1988a).

There is much greater variation in forelimb size, however. The difference between large and small ulnae, radii and capitates is as great or greater than that between male and female means of the most dimorphic apes (McHenry 1986). If forelimb size is used to predict body weight, the result is a high level of variation that may imply very strong dimorphism or the existence of two species. Hartwig-Scherer (1993), for example, concludes that specimens referred to as *A. afarensis* may derive from more than one species because by her estimates, the degree of body weight sexual dimorphism based on both fore- and hindlimb size falls outside the range seen in modern species of hominoid. She predicts a female weight of approximately 30 kg which is similar to what most other authors have predicted, but a male weight of over 60 kg. The latter is based on the midshaft circumferences of one radius (A.L. 333w-33, predicting a weight of 68 kg) and one humerus (A.L. 333-107 predicting weights between 89 and 99 kg). McHenry (1986) reports unexpectedly large forelimbs as well, especially the mediolateral diameter of the proximal ulna. The ratio between this measure in the largest specimen of *A. afarensis* (A.L. 333w-36) and the smallest (A.L. 33x-5) is greater than the ratio of male to female sizes in the most dimorphic great apes (*Pongo* and *Gorilla*). McHenry (1991a) notes that the smallest radial head (A.L. 288-1p) corresponds to a human weighing 28 kg and the largest (A.L. 333x-14/15) matches a 62 kg *H. sapiens*. The same pattern is apparent at Maka with an exceptionally large humerus (MAK-VP-1/3) and a small ulna (MAK-VP-1/111; White *et al.* 1993) associated with *A. afarensis* at 3.4 Myr.

Why are forelimbs apparently more dimorphic than jaws, teeth or hindlimbs? There are at least four possible explanations. One explanation might be sampling bias (i.e. in the small sample of postcrania, smaller individuals are represented by hindlimbs and larger ones by forelimbs). While this is possible, the 333 site contains fore- and hindlimb specimens of both large and small morphs. If this is truly a simultaneous burial of a single group, then the big morph did have proportionately larger forelimbs than the small morph. A second explanation is that there are two species represented. Senut and Tardieu (1985) note, for example, that although the large distal humerus, A.L. 333w-29, is badly weathered, it appears to have a lateral epicondyle that projects more weakly and is in a lower position than is apparent in the smaller specimens (A.L. 137-48A, A.L. 288-1M&S, and A.L. 322-1) and the anterior lateral trochlear crest is only moderately developed in the large morph. My own observations of the original specimens do not confirm or deny these distinctions, because the key large specimen (A.L. 333w-29) is too badly abraded. Another problem with considering the two size morphs as two species is the fact they both occur at the 333 site.

A third possibility is that male *A. afarensis* had proportionately larger forelimbs than females because of selection for utilization of different ecological niches. From this point of view, males climbed more than females. This is just the opposite of the view so elegantly presented by Stern and Susman (1982). Related to this is the unlikely view that males differed from females because they needed large forelimbs to gather and carry more food to their less mobile female mates and offspring.

Finally, an explanation for larger forelimbs in males can be assessed from the point of view of sexual selection. Here one can invoke Darwin's words about canine reduction and remember that early hominids had free forelimbs.

> The free use of the arms and hands, partly the cause and partly the result of man's erect position, appears to have led in an indirect manner to other modifications of structure. The early male forefathers of man were, as previously stated, probably furnished with great canine teeth; but as they gradually acquired the habit of using stones, clubs, or other weapons, for fighting with their enemies or rivals, they would use their jaws and teeth less and less. In this case, the jaws, together with the teeth, would become reduced in size, as we may feel almost sure from innumerable analogous cases.
>
> (Darwin 1892: 53)

AUSTRALOPITHECUS AFRICANUS

Body size variability is also high in *A. africanus* (e.g. Aiello and Dean 1990, Feldesman and Lundy 1988, Geissmann 1986, Jungers 1988, McHenry 1974, 1975, 1976, 1988, 1991a, b, 1992a, b, Robinson 1972, Steudel 1980, Wolpoff 1973, 1975). Hindlimb joint-size predicts a male weight of 40.8 kg and female weight of 30.2 kg (McHenry 1992a). As in *A. afarensis*, there appears to be very strong dimorphism in forelimb size with some specimens (e.g. Stw 326, 390 and 418) corresponding in size to a 28 kg human Pygmy and others (e.g. Sts 7, Stw 113, 382 and 432) as large or larger than the equivalent elements in a 55 kg *H. sapiens*.

Dental and mandibular size dimorphism in *A. africanus* is similar to that seen in *A. afarensis*, although maxillary M2 breadths divide the thirty available specimens into two essentially non-overlapping groups (Kimbel and White 1988a). Facial and basicranial structure is exceptionally variable and may imply that two species are represented (Clarke 1988, Kimbel and Rak 1993, Kimbel and White 1988a). Variability in endocranial volume is quite low, however (Holloway 1970).

AUSTRALOPITHECUS BOISEI

The sample of postcrania of the hyper-robust hominid of East Africa is small because taxonomic attribution of isolated elements is difficult. Fortunately there is one partial associated skeleton found with a taxonomically diagnostic bit of jaw (KNM-ER 1500). There are a few specimens from a site (Arca 6A, Ileret) which has produced only *A. boisei* craniodental material. From these specimens the male is estimated to weigh 48.6 kg and the female 34 kg, assuming human proportions (McHenry 1992a). These are very tenuous estimates because of the lack of material and the uncertainty about proportions and attributions. The ratio of male to female is 1.4 which is similar to that found in modern species of chimpanzee. Forelimbs may have been strongly dimorphic, but species attribution of isolated specimens precludes any certainty. The associated partial skeleton has small hindlimb joints corresponding to a 34 kg human, but its radial head is matched by a 50 kg human. There are several very large isolated forelimb fossils that may belong to the male *A. boisei*. For example, the KNM-ER 739 humerus has a distal end as large as what would be expected in a 72 kg male (McHenry 1992a) and its shaft circumference predicts a body weight of 79 kg (Hartwig-Scherer 1993).

Dental and mandibular variability in *A. boisei* is no greater than in earlier species of *Australopithecus* (Kimbel and White 1988a). The 'robust' features of the female face (KNM-ER 732) are less strongly developed than in the adult male (KNM-ER 406; Rak 1983).

AUSTRALOPITHECUS ROBUSTUS

Body size dimorphism in the South African 'robust' australopithecine species appears to have been only moderate. The estimate for males is 40.2 kg and females 31.9 kg, which yields a ratio of 1.26 which is similar to modern humans (McHenry 1992a). There is no evidence that male forelimbs were proportionately larger than those of females (McHenry 1991c). Variability in mandibular robusticity is below that seen in *A. afarensis*, *A. africanus* and species of African ape (Kimbel and White 1988a). Dental variability is also relatively moderate.

EARLIEST HOMO (H. HABILIS AND RUDOLFENSIS)

Two very different size morphs have been attributed to the earliest specie(s) of *Homo*. The small morph is represented by material from Olduvai Gorge such as the O.H. 8 partial foot (part of the paratype of *Homo habilis*), the tibia and fibula (O.H. 35) and the O.H. 62 partial skeleton. These specimens yield a body weight estimate of 31.5 kg (McHenry 1992a). The large morph is represented by specimens from Koobi Fora including the KNM-ER 1481 partial hindlimb, the KNM-ER 1472 femur, and the KNM-ER 3228 os coxa. A body weight of 51.6 kg is predicted from these fossils (McHenry 1992a). If these two morphs represent the male and female of *H. habilis sensu lato*, then their ratio is 1.6 (above modern chimps).

There is a growing concern, however, that two species are represented by these two morphs. Wood (1992) presents the most extensive work on this problem and concludes that the Olduvai early *Homo* is *H. habilis* and the large morph at Koobi Fora is *H. rudolfensis*. By this classification, some of the smaller specimens from Koobi Fora, such as the partial skeleton KNM-ER 3735 are *H. habilis*. Using Wood's (1992) classification, McHenry (1994) estimates the male *H. habilis sensu stricto* to be 37.0 kg and the female, 31.5 kg which yields a ratio of 1.2 (similar to modern humans). The estimate for the male *H. rudolfensis* is 62.7 kg and the female, 52.3 kg, making a ratio of 1.2 (McHenry 1994).

Unfortunately, it is difficult to assess dimorphism in the earliest *Homo* because the taxonomy is still unresolved. Tobias (1991) presents a thorough review of *H. habilis* at Olduvai Gorge and concludes that the Koobi Fora early *Homo* can be accommodated into that species. Wood (1991) finds evidence for two species as do many others (e.g. Groves 1989, Kimbel and Rak 1993, Leakey and Leakey 1978, Lieberman *et al.* 1988, Rightmire 1993, Stringer 1986, Wood 1992, 1993). A major difficulty is that these and other authors often disagree on which specimens belong together in a single species and which do not. For example, the well preserved KNM-ER 1813 is *H. habilis* to Wood (1992), *H. ergaster* to Groves (1989) and *Homo* but not *H. habilis* to Stringer (1986) and Rightmire (1993).

EARLY AFRICAN *HOMO ERECTUS*

The well preserved cranium, KNM-ER 3733, is usually attributed to *H. erectus* (e.g. Howell 1978, Leakey and Walker 1976, Rightmire 1990, Walker and Leakey 1978, Walker 1981,) and its early date, 1.8 Myr. (Fiebel *et al.* 1989), places it as the earliest of that species. The earliest postcranial fossils attributed to *H. erectus* are at 1.7 Myr (Fiebel *et al.* 1989). As with pre-*erectus Homo* there is debate on specimen attribution and species name (e.g. Groves 1989, Kimbel and Rak 1993, Rightmire 1990, Wood 1991). *Homo ergaster* is often used for early specimens previously attributed to *H. erectus* (e.g. Groves 1989, Wood 1992).

Despite these disagreements about craniodental taxonomy, analysis of the postcranial remains is less problematical for early African *H. erectus* than it is for earlier *Homo*. This is due to the fact that there are several partial skeletons including the nearly complete specimen, KNM-WT 15000. Ruff and Walker (1993) give estimated body weights for many of these specimens. Assuming that the large specimens are male, a weight of 62.7 kg is appropriate for early *H. erectus* (McHenry 1994). The smaller specimens average 52.3 kg and may be close to the female average (McHenry 1994). The ratio is 1.2. The apparent dimorphism in relative forelimb size seen in earlier species is not present in *H. erectus*. The forelimbs of the male specimen, KNM-WT 15000, are relatively quite small. Unfortunately the sample is too small to make meaningful dental or mandibular comparisons in early African *H. erectus*, but in later members of that species (especially those from North Africa and Java) there appears to be quite strong sexual dimorphism in mandibular size (Frayer and Wolpoff 1985, Tyler 1991, Wolpoff 1980).

NEANDERTHALS AND EARLY ANATOMICALLY MODERN *HOMO SAPIENS*

Table 3.1 also presents estimates of body size in male and female Neanderthals and early anatomically modern *Homo sapiens*. These estimates are based on femoral length and its relationship to stature (Feldesman *et al.* 1990) and body weight (Ruff and Walker 1993). Like all estimates of body weight in fossil samples there is much room for error, but it is clear that the high level of body size dimorphism characteristic of early *Australopithecus* has disappeared. The degree of body weight dimorphism is about the same as modern *H. sapiens* (i.e. with a male/female ratio of 1.2), but interesting subtleties are present in the pattern of sexual dimorphism (Frayer 1980).

SEXUAL SELECTION AND MATING SYSTEM

What does the degree of dimorphism apparent in *A. afarensis*, *A. africanus*, and other species of early hominid imply about behaviour and ecology? It may be interpreted as indicating a polygynous mating system, but such a simple extrapolation needs considerable caution.

In general, mammalian species with polygynous mating systems have a higher level of sexual dimorphism in body weight, canine size and other features than do species with monogamous mating systems (Alexander and Hoogland 1979, Clutton-Brock 1989, Clutton-Brock and Vincent 1991, Clutton-Brock *et al.* 1977, Frayer and Wolpoff 1985, Gaulin and Sailer 1984, Harvey and Bennett 1985, Harvey *et al.* 1978, Lande 1980, Leutenegger 1977, 1978, 1982a, b, Leutenegger and Kelly 1977, Plavcan and van Schaik 1992, Rodman and Mitani 1987, Willner and Martin 1985).

But can one predict mating system in extinct species? According to Rowell and Chism (1986: 111) 'we do not think it is possible to infer the social systems or mating patterns of extinct species from the degree of sexual dimorphism shown by their fossils'. The problem is that there is a great deal of variability in the relationship between social system and degree of sexual dimorphism.

A general trend is clear: monogamous species have very low levels of body weight sexual dimorphism and polygynous species have higher dimorphism. Clutton-Brock *et al.* (1977) show this by comparing the socionomic index (number of adult females per male) with body weight ratio. The association holds up relatively well. Within the Order Primates, monogamous species are always monomorphic and polygynous species are usually dimorphic with males often weighing twice as much as females. Trivers (1972) explains how selection may drive the evolution of dimorphism in polygynous species. By this view male/male competition to monopolize the reproductive potential of females tends to favour greater size, strength, display and other sexually dimorphic characteristics among males. When the male impregnates a female, he monopolizes her reproductive potential for a long time and excludes other males. The potential exists for one male to impregnate several females, if he can exclude other males. Selection operates differently for the female, however, because of the vastly greater energetic cost of reproduction for the females (i.e. the energetics of gestation and lactation). Smaller females are not at the same disadvantage as small males in the competition for mates. In monogamous species, the difference disappears because the male cannot monopolize the reproductive potential of more than one female. Among primates, monomorphism is always associated with monogamous mating systems. The level of sexual dimorphism is not, however, closely associated with the degree of polygyny. Some polygynous species have high levels of dimorphism and some do not. The differences may have to do with the quality of male/male competition.

Plavcan and van Schaik (1992) fine tune the analysis by classifying four types of male/male competition and its relationship with canine dimorphism. Type 1 by their analysis (low-frequency and low-intensity competition) includes monogamous primates such as *Hylobates*, *Callicebus* and *Saguinus*. Type 2 is high-frequency, low-intensity inter-male competition and includes *Pan*, *Ateles*, *Lagothrix* and *Pithecia*, although there is little known about the social behaviour of the latter two. Type 3 is low-frequency, high-intensity and type 4 is high-frequency, high-intensity. Calculating the male/female ratio of body weight in these categories (correcting for taxonomic artefact following Pagel and Harvey 1988) leads to the following: competition type 1 has a male/female body weight ratio of 1.01; type 2 has 1.18; type 3 has 1.55; and type 4 has 1.51.

These results show (1) that there is a striking relationship between the intensity of male/male competition and the degree of sexual dimorphism in canine and body size and (2) that there is a clear difference in body weight dimorphism between species of low and high frequency of inter-male competition, among the species with low intensity competition. The degree of body size sexual dimorphism in early hominids fits well within competition type 2 (high-frequency, low-intensity like *Pan* and *Ateles*).

But even with fine-tuning, the relationship between sexual dimorphism and social behaviour is not simple. Among primates, several groups provide challenges. Species of the suborder Anthropoidea hold fairly well to the rule of monogamy/monomorphism and polygyny/sexual dimorphism. Exceptions appear (e.g. *Cercopithecus neglectus* is sexually dimorphic in body size but early reports gave its mating system as monogamous), but further information substantiates the generalization

(*C. neglectus* is polygynous, Leutenegger and Lubach 1987, Wahome *et al.* 1993). Prosimians are another matter altogether.

Mating systems among Prosimii range from strict monogamy to polygyny with multi-male/multi-female groups. Size varies from 60 g to 10 kg in living Malagasy lemurs and up to 150 kg in the subfossil, *Megaladapis* (Fleagle 1988, Godfrey *et al.* 1993). But there is no sexual dimorphism in body size (Godfrey *et al.* 1993, Richard 1992). Several explanations for this are possible (reviewed in Godfrey *et al.* 1993 and Richard 1992). Godfrey *et al.* (1993: 331) suggest that 'hypometabolism and intersexual resource competition during a critical period in the repro-ductive cycle of females may have constrained the evolution of sexual size dimorphism in Malagasy lemurs'.

OTHER CORRELATES TO DIMORPHISM

Although sexual selection appears to be an important cause of sexual dimorphism in anthropoid primates, other factors may be involved. Oxnard (1983) stresses the need to understand the multifactorial causes of dimorphism. Body size itself explains much of the variance in sexual dimorphism according to Leutenegger (1982a, b) and Leutenegger and Cheverud (1982, 1985), although body size has only a minor effect according to other studies (Gaulin and Sailer 1984, Plavcan and van Schaik 1992). Predation pressure may be important (Harvey *et al.* 1978, Rowell and Chism 1986). Phylogenetic inertia has been emphasized particularly by Cheverud *et al.* (1985, 1986), but Ely and Kurland (1989) challenge this view. Dietary constraints may be important (Demment 1983, Milton 1985). The dispersion of food sources, mobility of males and philopatry may be related to reduced dimorphism in chimpanzees (Rodman 1984). Economic and non-economic role differences which result in the division of labour by sex may be important in explaining sexual dimorphism in many primates, especially hominids (Frayer and Wolpoff 1985).

BEHAVIOURAL AND ECOLOGICAL CORRELATES OF DIMORPHISM IN EARLY HOMINIDS

Although the relationship between body size sexual dimorphism and mating system is not exact in anthropoid primates, the degree of dimorphism apparent in *A. afarensis* and *A. africanus* makes it unlikely that these species were monogamous (*contra* Lovejoy 1981, 1988). It is likely, although less certain, that male/male competition was less intense than that seen in the highly dimorphic primates such as *Gorilla* and *Pongo*. While it is possible that these species lived in groups comprising a single breeding male and several adult females with dependent offspring (i.e. like *Gorilla*), patrilineal, multi-male groups seem more likely (Foley and Lee 1989). If it is true that the 333 site of Hadar samples a single population at one point in time, then the group composition was multi-male/ multi-female. If they did live in kin-related, multi-male groups, it is odd that their descendants have relative low testes weights unlike one of our close biological relatives, chimpanzees (Harcourt *et al.* 1981). Perhaps the testes size of modern humans is not what it used to be.

Although taxonomic uncertainty obscures a clear picture of sexual dimorphism in *H. habilis sensu lato*, by 1.7 Myr the degree of body size and forelimb size dimorphism in *Homo erectus* is substantially reduced from that seen in its ancestors. Small-bodied hominids all but disappear from the East African fossil record at 1.7 Myr and the body size within early *H. erectus* is similar to that seen in modern *H. sapiens*. This change was due to an increase in both female and male body size by as much as 22 kg from that seen in *Australopithecus*. The effect of this equal increase in the two sexes results in a reduced ratio.

What behavioural and/or ecological factors might be correlated with the dramatic change in body weight sexual dimorphism that occurred with the appearance of *H. erectus*? Certainly it is not related to species body size change, because it reverses the trend (i.e. *H. erectus* is larger than *A. afarensis* and *A. africanus* but has a lower level of sexual dimorphism). Nor can phylogenetic inertia be invoked because of the ancestor–descendant relationship between *A. afarensis–A. africanus–*early *Homo* (Skelton and McHenry 1992). Reduced intensity of male/male competition might be involved and may explain the reduced forelimb size dimorphism, but the reduced body size dimorphism seen in *H. erectus* is due to both male and female body size increase and not to a reduction in male body size.

Perhaps the relaxation of dietary constraints is related to the change in body weight dimorphism apparent in *H. erectus*. It appears that *H. erectus* was less restricted in habitat usage than was *Australopithecus* (Shipman and Harris 1988) and may have incorporated more animal products (meat and/or marrow) into the diet (Potts 1988). The larger body size and especially longer hindlimbs of *H. erectus* would allow greater travel distances between more widely distributed food sites. Another possible explanation for increased body weight is related to increased frequency and intensity of interdemic conflict. In this case selection favoured larger-bodied individuals and their close kin who were successful in aggressive encounters with conspecifics. Related to this could be the appearance of the Acheulian handaxe and its use as a projectile.

More difficult to explain is the proportionately greater increase in size of the *H. erectus* female. The male *H. erectus* is about 50 per cent larger than his *Australopithecus* ancestors, but the female is more than 70 per cent larger. Perhaps the greater increase in female body size was due to selection for physiological mechanisms to produce larger brains. The expected neonatal brain size predicted from the female body weight of *A. africanus* is 166 g and for early *H. erectus*, 270 g (McHenry 1994). This would probably have been related to a change in diet. Another explanation for the reduced male/female body weight ratio in *H. erectus* might be related to biomechanical restraints on maximum body size. Males who exceeded 60–70 kg were selected against because of physical failures such as back injuries that continue to plague this bipedal animal. In this regard it is interesting to note that KNM-WT 15000 had relatively small lumbar vertebrae (in cross-sectional area) unlike the augmented size of modern humans of equivalent body weight (Latimer and Ward 1993).

CONCLUSIONS

Body weight sexual dimorphism in *A. afarensis* is above that seen in modern humans and chimps, but well below that characteristic of gorillas and orangs. As in other animals, sexual selection probably accounts for this dimorphism and is most likely related to a polygynous mating system. The level of body weight dimorphism in *A. afarensis* corresponds to what might be expected from moderate intensity male/male competition. Kin-related multi-male groups are most likely based on the composition of the A.L. 333 site at Hadar and on theoretical considerations.

Canine dimorphism in *A. afarensis* is well below that seen in the great apes (except for the lower canines in *Pan paniscus*), but forelimb size dimorphism is apparent. This may be related to the fact that forelimbs were freed from any role in terrestrial locomotion and thereby took over the role of threat and aggression previously played by the canines.

Body weight dimorphism declines through time from *A. afarensis* to *A. africanus* to *A. robustus* with a dramatic reduction in *H. erectus*. Taxonomic attributions of specimens formerly assigned to *H. habilis* obscure the analysis of dimorphism in pre-*erectus Homo*, unfortunately.

The dramatic reduction in body weight sexual dimorphism at 1.7 Myr with the appearance of *H. erectus* is due to increase in both male and female body size. The cause of this change is probably related to the release of dietary constraints on body size, selection for larger brains and biomechanical constraints on maximum male body size. It may also be due to reduced male/male competition.

Sexual dimorphism is very high in some traits such as mandibular size in later *H. erectus*, but there are too few postcranial remains of later *H. erectus* and early *H. sapiens* to assess body weight dimorphism. Weight dimorphism in Neanderthals and early anatomically modern *H. sapiens* is as low as that seen in modern humans.

ACKNOWLEDGEMENTS

The author thanks R.E. Leakey and M.G. Leakey and the staff of the National Museums of Kenya, M.D. Leakey, F.C. Howell, D.C. Johanson and the staff of the Cleveland Museum of Natural History and the

Institute of Human Origins, Tadessa Terfa, Mammo Tessema, Berhane Asfaw and the staff of the National Museum of Ethiopia, C.K. Brain and the staff of the Transvaal Museum, P.V. Tobias and the staff of the Department of Anatomy and Human Biology, University of Witwatersrand, for permission to study the original fossil material in their charge and for numerous kindnesses. The author also thanks D.R. Howlett, C. Powell-Cotton and staff of the Powell-Cotton Museum; M. Rutzmoser and staff of the Museum of Comparative Zoology, Harvard University; R. Thorington and the staff of the Division of Mammalogy, Smithsonian Institution; D.J. Ortner and the staff of the Department of Anthropology, Smithsonian Institution; D.F.E.T. van den Audenaerde and M. Lovette and the staff of the Musée d'Afrique Centrale, Tervuren; R.D. Martin and the staff of the Anthropologische Institut, Zurich; W.W. Howells and the staff of the Peabody Museum, Harvard University; C. Edelstamm and the staff of the Natur Historiska Rismuseet, Stockholm; R.L. Susman and W.L. Jungers for many kindnesses and for permission to study the comparative material in their charge; L.J. McHenry, L. Digby, A.H. Harcourt, and P.S. Rodman for insightful comments on early drafts. J. Martini for her help in preparing this paper; and Stephen Shennan and James Steele for inviting me to participate in this symposium. Partial funding was provided by the Committee of Research, University of California, Davis.

REFERENCES

Aiello, L.C. (1990) 'Patterns of stature and weight in human evolution.' *American Journal of Physical Anthropology* 81: 186–187.

Aiello, L. and Dean, C. (1990) *An Introduction to Human Evolutionary Anatomy.* London: Academic Press (Harcourt Brace Jovanovich).

Alexander, R.D. and Hoogland, J.L. (1979) 'Sexual dimorphisms and breeding systems in pinnipeds, ungulates, primates, and humans.' In N.A. Chagnon and W. Irons (eds) *Evolutionary Biology and Human Social Behavior*, pp. 402–435. North Scituate: Duxbury Press.

Cheverud, J.M., Low, M.M. and Leutenegger, W. (1985) 'The quantitative assessment of phylogenetic constraints in comparative analysis – sexual dimorphism in body weight among primates.' *Evolution* 39: 1335–1351.

Cheverud, J.M., Low, M.M. and Leutenegger, W. (1986) 'A phylogenetic auto-correlation analysis of sexual dimorphism in primates.' *American Anthropologist* 88: 916–922.

Clarke, R.J. (1988) 'A new *Australopithecus* cranium from Sterkfontein and its bearing on the ancestry of *Paranthropus*.' In F.E. Grine (ed.) *Evolutionary History of the 'Robust' Australopithecines*, pp. 285–292. New York: Aldine de Gruyter.

Clutton-Brock, T.H. (1989) 'Mammalian mating systems.' *Proceedings of the Royal Society of London B* 236: 339–372.

Clutton-Brock, T.H. and Vincent, A.C.J. (1991) 'Sexual selection and the potential reproductive rates of males and females.' *Nature* 351: 58–60.

Clutton-Brock, T.H., Harvey, P.H. and Rudder, B. (1977) 'Sexual dimorphism, socionomic sex ratio and body weight in primates.' *Nature* 269: 797–800.

Coppens, Y. (1981) 'Le cerveau des hommes fossiles.' *Comptes Rendues de l'Academie des Sciences, Paris: Supplément à la vie académique* 3–24.

Coppens, Y. (1983) 'Systematics, phylogeny, environment and culture of the Australopithecines, hypothesis and synthesis.' *Bulletin et Mémoires de la Société d'Anthropologie de Paris* 13: 273–284.

Darwin, C. (1892) *The Descent of Man, and Selection in Relation to Sex*, new edition. New York: D. Appleton and Company.

Demment, M.W. (1983) 'Feeding ecology and the evolution of body size of baboons.' *African Journal of Ecology* 21: 219–233.

Ely, J. and Kurland, J.A. (1989) 'Spatial autocorrelation, phylogenetic constraints, and the causes of sexual dimorphism in primates.' *International Journal of Primatology* 10: 151–171.

Falk, D. (1986) 'Evolution of cranial blood drainage in hominids: enlarged occipital/marginal sinuses and emissary foramina.' *American Journal of Physical Anthropology* 70: 311–324.

Feldesman, M.R. and Lundy, J.K. (1988) 'Stature estimates for some African Pliocene–Pleistocene fossil hominids.' *Journal of Human Evolution* 17: 583–596.

Feldesman, M.R., Kleckner, J.G. and Lundy, J.K. (1990) 'Femur/stature ratio and estimates of stature in Mid- and Late-Pleistocene fossil hominids.' *American Journal of Physical Anthropology* 83: 359–372.

Fiebel, C.S., Brown, F.H. and McDougall, I. (1989) 'Stratigraphic context of fossil hominids from the Omo Group Deposits: Northern Turkana Basin.' *American Journal of Physical Anthropology* 78: 595–622.

Fleagle, J.G. (1988) *Primate Adaptation and Evolution*. New York: Academic Press.

Foley, R.A. and Lee, P.C. (1989) 'Finite social space, evolutionary pathways, and reconstructing hominid behavior.' *Science* 243: 901–906.

Frayer, D.W. (1980) 'Sexual dimorphism and cultural evolution in the Late Pleistocene and Holocene of Europe.' *Journal of Human Evolution* 9: 399–415.

Frayer, D.W. and Wolpoff, M.H. (1985) 'Sexual dimorphism.' *Annual Review of Anthropology* 14: 429–474.

Gaulin, S.J.C. and Sailer, L.D. (1984) 'Sexual dimorphism in weight among the primates: the relative impact of allometry and sexual selection.' *International Journal of Primatology* 5: 515–535.

Geissmann, T. (1986) 'Estimation of Australopithecine stature from long bones: A.L.288-1 as a test case.' *Folia Primatologica* 47: 119–127.

Godfrey, L.R., Lyon, S.K. and Sutherland, M.R. (1993) 'Sexual dimorphism in large-bodied primates: the case of the subfossil lemurs.' *American Journal of Physical Anthropology* 90: 315–334.

Groves, C.P. (1989) *A Theory of Human and Primate Evolution*. Oxford: Clarendon Press.

Harcourt, A.H., Harvey, P.H., Larson, S.G. and Short, R.V. (1981) 'Testis weight, body weight, and breeding system in primates.' *Nature* 293: 55–57.

Hartwig-Scherer, S. (1993) 'Body weight prediction in early fossil hominids: towards a Taxon-"Independent" approach.' *American Journal of Physical Anthropology* 92: 17–36.

Harvey, P.H. and Bennett, P.M. (1985) 'Sexual dimorphism and reproduction strategies.' In J. Ghesquiere, R.D. Martin and F. Newcombe (eds) *Human Sexual Dimorphism*, pp. 43–59. London: Taylor and Francis.

Harvey, P.H., Clutton-Brock, T.H. and Kavanagh, M. (1978) 'Sexual dimorphism in primate teeth.' *Journal of Zoology, London* 186: 475–485.

Holloway, R.L. (1970) 'New endocranial values for the Australopithecines.' *Nature* 227: 199–200.

Howell, F.C. (1978) 'Hominidae.' In V.J. Maglio and H.B.S. Cooke (eds) *The Evolution of African Mammals*, pp. 154–248. Cambridge, MA: Harvard University Press.

Johanson, D.C. and White, T.D. (1979) 'A systematic assessment of early African hominids.' *Science* 203: 321–330.

Johanson, D.C., White, T.D. and Coppens, Y. (1978) 'A new species of the genus *Australopithecus* (Primates: Hominidae) from the Pliocene of Eastern Africa.' *Kirtlandia* 28: 1–14.

Johanson, D.C., Taieb, M. and Coppens, Y. (1982) 'Pliocene hominids from the Hadar Formation, Ethiopia (1973–1977): stratigraphic, chronologic, and paleoenvironmental contexts, with notes on hominid morphology and systematics.' *American Journal of Physical Anthropology* 57: 373–402.

Jungers, W.L. (1988) 'New estimations of body size in australopithecines.' In F.E. Grine (ed.) *Evolutionary History of the 'Robust' Australopithecines*, pp. 115–126. New York: Aldine de Gruyter.

Jungers, W.L. and Stern, J.T. (1983) 'Body proportions, skeletal allometry and locomotion in the Hadar hominids: a reply to Wolpoff.' *Journal of Human Evolution* 12: 673–684.

Kimbel, W.H. (1984) 'Variation in the pattern of cranial venous sinuses and hominid phylogeny.' *American Journal of Physical Anthropology* 63: 243–264.

Kimbel, W.H. (1986) 'Calvarial morphology of *Australopithecus afarensis*: a comparative phylogenetic study.' Dissertation, Kent State University.

Kimbel, W.H. and Rak, Y. (1993) 'The importance of species taxa in paleoanthropology and an argument for the phylogenetic concept of the species category.' In W.H. Kimbel and L.B. Martin (eds) *Species, Species Concepts, and Primate Evolution*, pp. 461–483. New York: Plenum Press.

Kimbel, W.H. and White, T.D. (1988a) 'Variation, sexual dimorphism and the taxonomy of *Australopithecus*.' In F.E. Grine (ed.) *Evolutionary History of the 'Robust' Australopithecines*, pp. 175–192. New York: Aldine de Gruyter.

Kimbel, W.H. and White, T.D. (1988b) 'A revised reconstruction of the adult skull of *Australopithecus afarensis*.' *Journal of Human Evolution* 17: 545–550.

Kimbel, W.H., Johanson, D.C. and Coppens, Y. (1982) 'Pliocene hominid cranial remains from the Hadar Formation, Ethiopia.' *American Journal of Physical Anthropology* 57: 453–500.

Lande, R. (1980) 'Sexual dimorphism, sexual selection and adaptation in polygenic characters.' *Evolution* 34: 292–305.

Latimer, B. and Ward, C.V. (1993) 'The thoracic and lumbar vertebrae.' In A. Walker and R. Leakey (eds) *The Nariokotome Homo erectus Skeleton*, pp. 266–293. Cambridge, MA: Harvard University Press.

Leakey, R.E.F. and Leakey, M.G. (1978) *The Fossil Hominids and an Introduction to their Context 1967–1974. Koobi Fora Research Project, 1.* Oxford: Clarendon Press.

Leakey, R.E.F. and Walker, A.C. (1976) 'Australopithecus, Homo erectus and the single species hypothesis.' Nature 261: 572–574.

Leutenegger, W. (1977) 'Sociobiological correlates of sexual dimorphism in body weight in South African Australopiths.' South African Journal of Science 73: 143–144.

Leutenegger, W. (1978) 'Scaling of sexual dimorphism in body size and breeding system in primates.' Nature 272: 610–611.

Leutenegger, W. (1982a) 'Scaling of sexual dimorphism in body weight and canine size in primates.' Folia Primatologica 37: 163–176.

Leutenegger, W. (1982b) 'Sexual dimorphism in nonhuman primates.' In R.L. Hall (ed.) Sexual Dimorphism in Homo sapiens, pp. 11–36. New York: Praeger.

Leutenegger, W. and Cheverud, J. (1982) 'Correlates of sexual dimorphism in primates: ecological and size variables.' International Journal of Primatology 3: 387–402.

Leutenegger, W. and Cheverud, J.M (1985) 'Sexual dimorphism in primates: the effects of size.' In W.L. Jungers (ed.) Size and Scaling in Primate Biology, pp. 33–50. New York: Plenum Press.

Leutenegger, W. and Kelly, J.T. (1977) 'Relationship of sexual dimorphism in canine size and body size to social, behavioral, and ecological correlates in anthropoid primates.' Primates 18: 117–136.

Leutenegger, W. and Lubach, G. (1987) 'Sexual dimorphism, mating system, and effect of phylogeny in De Brazza's monkey (Cercopithecus neglectus).' American Journal of Primatology 13: 171–179.

Leutenegger, W. and Shell, B. (1987) 'Variability and sexual dimorphism in canine size of Australopithecus and extant hominoids.' Journal of Human Evolution 16: 359–368.

Lieberman, D.E., Pilbeam, D.R. and Wood, B.A. (1988) 'A probabilistic approach to the problem of sexual dimorphism in Homo habilis: a comparison of KNM-ER 1470 and KNM-ER 1813.' Journal of Human Evolution 17: 503–512.

Lovejoy, C.O. (1981) 'The origin of man.' Science 211: 341–350.

Lovejoy, C.O. (1988) 'Evolution of human walking.' Scientific American November: 118–126.

Lovejoy, C.O., Kern, K.F., Simpson, S.W. and Meindl, R.S. (1989) 'A new method for estimation of skeletal dimorphism in fossil samples with an application to Australopithecus afarensis.' In G. Giacobini (ed.) Hominidae: Proceedings of the 2nd International Congress of Human Paleontology Turin, September 28–October 3 1987, pp. 103–108. Milan: Jaka.

McHenry, H.M. (1974) 'How large were the Australopithecines?' American Journal of Physical Anthropology 40: 329–340.

McHenry, H.M. (1975) 'Fossil hominid body weight and brain size.' Nature 254: 686–688.

McHenry, H.M. (1976) 'Early hominid body weight and encephalization.' American Journal of Physical Anthropology 45: 77–84.

McHenry, H.M. (1982) 'The pattern of human evolution: studies on bipedalism, mastication and encephalization.' Annual Review of Anthropology 11: 151–173.

McHenry, H.M. (1983) 'The capitate of Australopithecus afarensis and Australopithecus africanus.' American Journal of Physical Anthropology 62: 187–198.

McHenry, H.M. (1986) 'Size variation in the postcranium of Australopithecus afarensis and extant species of Hominoidea.' Journal of Human Evolution 15: 149–156.

McHenry, H.M. (1988) 'New estimates of body weights in early hominids and their significance to encephalization and megadontia in "robust" australopithecines.' In F.E. Grine (ed.) *Evolutionary History of the 'Robust' Australopithecines*, pp. 133–148. New York: Aldine de Gruyter.

McHenry, H.M. (1991a) 'Sexual dimorphism in *Australopithecus afarensis*.' *Journal of Human Evolution* 20: 21–32.

McHenry, H.M. (1991b) 'Femoral lengths and stature in Plio-Pleistocene hominids.' *American Journal of Physical Anthropology* 85: 149–158.

McHenry, H.M. (1991c) 'Petite bodies of the "robust" australopithecines.' *American Journal of Physical Anthropology* 86: 445–454.

McHenry, H.M. (1992a) 'Body size and proportions in early hominids.' *American Journal of Physical Anthropology* 87: 407–431.

McHenry, H.M. (1992b) 'How big were early hominids?' *Evolutionary Anthropology* 1: 15–19.

McHenry, H.M. (1994) 'Behavioral ecological implications of early hominid body size.' *Journal of Human Evolution* 27: 77–87.

Milton, K. (1985) 'Multi-male mating and absence of canine tooth dimorphism in woolly spider monkeys (*Brachyteles arachnoides*).' *American Journal of Physical Anthropology* 68: 519–524.

Olson, T.R. (1981) 'Basicranial morphology of the extant hominoids and Pliocene hominoids: the new material from the Hadar Formation, Ethiopia, and its significance in early human evolution and taxonomy.' In C.B. Stringer (ed.) *Aspects of Human Evolution*, pp. 99–128. London: Taylor and Francis.

Olson, T.R. (1985) 'Cranial morphology and systematics of the Hadar formation hominids and *"Australopithecus" africanus*.' In E. Delson (ed.) *Ancestors: The Hard Evidence*, pp. 102–119. New York: Alan R. Liss, Inc.

Oxnard, C.E. (1983) 'Anatomical, biomolecular and morphometric views of the primates.' In V. Navaratnam and R.J. Harrison (eds) *Progress in Anatomy, 3*, pp. 113–142. Cambridge: Cambridge University Press.

Pagel, M.D. and Harvey, P.H. (1988) 'The taxon-level problem in the evolution of mammalian brain size: facts and artifacts.' *American Naturalist* 132: 344–359.

Plavcan, J.M. and van Schaik, C.P. (1992) 'Intrasexual competition and canine dimorphism in anthropoid primates.' *American Journal of Physical Anthropology* 87: 461–477.

Potts, R. (1988) *Early Hominid Activities at Olduvai*. New York: Aldine de Gruyter.

Rak, Y. (1983) *The Australopithecine Face*. New York: Academic Press.

Richard, A.F. (1992) 'Aggressive competition between males, female-controlled polygyny and sexual monomorphism in a Malagasy primate, *Propithecus verreauxi*.' *Journal of Human Evolution* 22: 395–406.

Rightmire, G.P. (1990) *The Evolution of Homo Erectus*. Cambridge: Cambridge University Press.

Rightmire, G.P. (1993) 'Variation among early *Homo* crania from Olduvai Gorge and the Koobi Fora region.' *American Journal of Physical Anthropology* 90: 1–33.

Robinson, J.T. (1972) *Early Hominid Posture and Locomotion*. Chicago, IL: University of Chicago Press.

Rodman, P.S. (1984) 'Foraging and social systems of orangutans and chimpanzees.' In P.S. Rodman and J.G.H. Cant (eds) *Adaptations for Foraging in Nonhuman Primates*, pp. 136–159. New York: Columbia University Press.

Rodman, P.S. and Mitani, J.C. (1987) 'Orangutans: sexual dimorphism in a solitary species.' In B.B. Smuts, D.L. Cheney, R.M. Seyfarth, R.W. Wrangham and T.T. Struhsaker (eds) *Primate Societies*, pp. 146–154. Chicago: University of Chicago Press.

Rowell, T.E. and Chism, J. (1986) 'Sexual dimorphism and mating systems: jumping to conclusions.' In M. Pickford and B. Chiarelli (eds) *Sexual Dimorphism in Living and Fossil Primates*, pp. 107–111. Il Sedicesimo: Giugno.

Ruff, C.B. and Walker, A. (1993) 'Body size and body shape.' In A. Walker and R. Leakey (eds) *The Nariokotome Homo erectus Skeleton*, pp. 234–265. Cambridge, MA: Harvard University Press.

Schmid, P. (1983) 'Eine Rekonstruktion des skelettes von A.L. 288-1 (Hadar) und deren Konsequenzen.' *Folia Primatologica* 40: 283–306.

Senut, B. (1978) 'Revision de quelques pièces humerales Plio-Pleistocene Sud-Africaines.' *Bulletins et Mémoires de la Société d'Anthropologie de Paris* 5: 223–229.

Senut, B. (1980) 'New data on the humerus and its joints in Plio-Pleistocene hominoids.' *Collection Anthropologie* 4: 87–93.

Senut, B. (1986) 'Long bones of the primate upper limb: monomorphic or dimorphic?' *Human Evolution* 1: 7–22.

Senut, B. and Tardieu, C. (1985) 'Functional aspects of Plio-Pleistocene hominoid limb bones: implications for taxonomy and phylogeny.' In E. Delson (ed.) *Ancestors: The Hard Evidence*, pp. 193–201. New York: Alan R. Liss, Inc.

Shipman, P. and Harris, J. (1988) 'Habitat preference and paleoecology of *Australopithecus boisei* in eastern Africa.' In F.E. Grine (ed.) *Evolutionary History of the 'Robust' Australopithecines*, pp. 343–382. New York: Aldine de Gruyter.

Skelton, R.R. and McHenry, H.M. (1992) 'Evolutionary relationships among early hominids.' *Journal of Human Evolution* 23: 309–349.

Stern, J.T. and Susman, R.L. (1983) 'The locomotor anatomy of *Australopithecus afarensis*.' *American Journal of Physical Anthropology* 60: 279–318.

Steudel, K. (1980) 'New estimates of early hominid body size.' *American Journal of Physical Anthropology* 52: 63–70.

Stringer, C.B. (1986) 'The credibility of *Homo habilis*.' In B. Wood, L. Martin and P. Andrews (eds) *Major Topics in Primate and Human Evolution*, pp. 266–294. Cambridge: Cambridge University Press.

Susman, R.L., Stern, J.T. and Jungers, W.L. (1984) 'Arboreality and bipedality in the Hadar hominids.' *Folia Primatologica* 43: 113–156.

Tardieu, C. (1981) 'Morphofunctional analysis of the articular surfaces of the knee-joint in primates.' In A.B. Chiarelli and R.S. Corruccini (eds) *Primate Evolutionary Biology*, pp. 68–80. Berlin: Springer-Verlag.

Tardieu, C. (1983) *L'articulation du genou. Analyse morpho-fonctionelle chez les primates et les hominides fossiles.* Paris: Cahiers de Paléoanthropologie. Editions du CNRS.

Tardieu, C. (1986) 'The knee joint in three hominoid primates: application to Plio-Pleistocene hominids and evolutionary implications.' In D.M. Taub and F.A. King (eds) *Current Perspectives in Primate Biology*, pp. 182–192. New York: Van Nostrand Reinhold.

Tobias, P.V. (1991) *Olduvai Gorge Volume 4: The Skulls, Endocasts and Teeth of Homo habilis.* Cambridge: Cambridge University Press.

Trivers, R.L. (1972) 'Parental investment and sexual selection.' In B. Campbell (ed.) *Sexual Selection and the Descent of Man*, pp. 136–179. Chicago: Aldine.

Tuttle, R.H. (1981) 'Evolution of hominid bipedalism and prehensile capabilities.' *Philosophical Transactions of the Royal Society of London B* 292: 89–94.

Tuttle, R.H. (1991) 'Laetoli toes and *Australopithecus afarensis.*' *Human Evolution* 6: 193–200.

Tyler, D.E. (1991) 'A taxonomy of Javan hominid mandibles.' *Human Evolution* 6: 401–420.

Wahome, J.M., Rowell, T.E. and Tsingalia, H.M. (1993) 'The natural history of de Brazza's monkey in Kenya.' *International Journal of Primatology* 14: 445–466.

Walker, A. (1981) 'The Koobi Fora hominids and their bearing on the origins of the genus *Homo.*' In B.A. Sigmon and J.S. Cybulski (eds) *Homo erectus,* pp. 193–215. Toronto: University of Toronto Press.

Walker, A. and Leakey, R.E.F. (1978) 'The hominids of East Turkana.' *Scientific American* 239: 54–66.

White, T.D. (1985) 'The hominids of Hadar and Laetoli: an element-by-element comparison of the dental samples.' In E. Delson (ed.) *Ancestors: The Hard Evidence,* pp. 138–152. New York: Alan R. Liss, Inc.

White, T.D. and Johanson, D.C. (1989) 'The hominid composition of Afar locality 333: some preliminary observations.' In G. Giacobini (ed.) *Hominidae: Proceedings of the 2nd International Congress of Human Paleontology Turin, September 28–October 3 1987,* pp. 97–102. Milan: Jaka.

White, T.D., Johanson, D.C. and Kimbel, W.H. (1981) '*Australopithecus africanus:* its phylogenetic position reconsidered.' *South African Journal of Science* 77: 445–470.

White, T.D., Suwa, G., Hart, W.K., Walter, R.C., WoldeGabriel, G., de Heinzelin, J., Clark, J.D., Asfaw, B. and Vrba, E. (1993) 'New discoveries of *Australopithecus* at Maka in Ethiopia.' *Nature* 366: 261–265.

Willner, L.A. and Martin, R.D. (1985) 'Some basic principles of mammalian sexual dimorphism.' In L.J. Ghesquiere, R.D. Martin and F. Newcombe (ed.) *Human Sexual Dimorphism.* London: Taylor and Francis.

Wolpoff, M.H. (1973) 'Posterior tooth size, body size, and diet in South African gracile australopithecines.' *American Journal of Physical Anthropology* 39: 375–394.

Wolpoff, M.H. (1975) 'Sexual dimorphism in the Australopithecines.' In R.H. Tuttle (ed.) *Paleoanthropology, Morphology and Paleoecology,* pp. 245–284. The Hague: Mouton.

Wolpoff, M.H. (1980) 'Cranial remains of Middle Pleistocene European hominids.' *Journal of Human Evolution* 9: 339–358.

Wood, B.A. (1991) *Koobi Fora Research Project IV: Hominid Cranial Remains From Koobi Fora.* Oxford: Clarendon.

Wood, B.A. (1992) 'Origin and evolution of the genus *Homo.*' *Nature* 355: 783–790.

Wood, B. (1993) 'Early *Homo:* How many species?' In W.H. Kimbel and L.B. Martin (eds) *Species, Species Concepts, and Primate Evolution,* pp. 485–522. New York: Plenum Press.

Zihlman, A. (1985) '*Australopithecus afarensis:* two sexes or two species?' In P.V. Tobias (ed.) *Hominid Evolution: Past, Present and Future,* pp. 213–220. New York: Alan R. Liss, Inc.

CHAPTER FOUR

ON THE EVOLUTION OF TEMPERAMENT AND DOMINANCE STYLE IN HOMINID GROUPS

JAMES STEELE

DOMINANCE STYLE AND TEMPERAMENT IN NON-HUMAN PRIMATES

Dominance relationships are an important feature of primate and human societies. The pattern of social relationships in multi-male, multi-female primate groups is characterized by co-operative and competitive dynamics. 'Dominance', in this context, is a term denoting an attribute of dyadic relationships within a social group. When, in repeated agonistic inter-actions, one individual is consistently the winner and the other consistently yields rather than escalate the contest, then the winning individual is the dominant and the other is the subordinate (Drews 1993). Although this definition relates to dyadic interactions, it does not preclude recognition of the effects of support from other individuals on the outcome of the contest, as in coalitional behaviour. Furthermore, not all dyadic interactions demon-strate a dominance relationship: some will be unresolved or balanced in nature. Finally, whereas dominance status is a relational attribute of individ-uals with respect to specific dyadic relationships, observer attribution of dominance rank is the product of a calculation of the dominance hierarchy within a group on the basis of observed dyadic contest outcomes. It is possible for dominance statuses to exist in a group without there being a single ordinally ranked dominance hierarchy.

'Dominance style' refers to the characteristic pattern of escalatory and conciliatory behaviour which group members demonstrate in agonistic contests (see also Chance, this volume). Comparisons of closely related species of primate have shown that they can nonetheless differ markedly in their reconciliation behaviour (de Waal 1989). Stumptail macaques (*Macaca arctoides*) interact within groups with a pattern of high-frequency, low-intensity aggression, and have a richer repertoire of appeasement and reassurance gestures, while rhesus macaques (*Macaca mulatta*) form rigid dominance hierarchies enforced by low-frequency, high-intensity aggression. Similarly, whereas common chimpanzee females (*Pan troglodytes*) have a generally antagonistic pattern of interactions with other females, bonobo females (*Pan paniscus*) associate with one another more frequently and have a richer repertoire of tension-reducing behaviours (which include non-conceptive sex both with males and with other females).

It seems that these contrasts are products of a feedback loop linking ecology, group composition and behaviour in a cycle which can lead over evolutionary time to the genetic fixing of population and species-level traits relating to temperament and dominance style. Microevolutionary studies of this process can be made comparing temperament between individuals and populations of the same species. At the level of individuals, Sapolsky (1990) has found that dominant males in an olive baboon troop can be differentiated into high-stress and low-stress groups according to their personality style, with correlates in both social information-processing style and in endocrine gland activity levels. He argues that the hormonal profiles of both the subordinate males and (by implication) the high-stress group among the dominants expose them to fitness-reducing consequences in terms of lowered immune status and heightened risk of heart disease. In competitive social environments, there is thus a direct fitness advantage to a personality style which enables individuals to predict and control the outcomes of social interactions and to find outlets for tension.

These dynamics can also be observed in a population-level study of two populations of squirrel monkeys (*Saimiri sciureus*) from different regions in South America, with different patterns of resource patchiness and consequently differences in levels of feeding competition and need for social vigilance against aggression for each population: they were also found to show different levels of physiological reactivity in laboratory settings. The explanation appears to be that the animals from the population with a higher level of social feeding competition have developed a greater stress response with higher baseline levels of plasma cortisol (Clarke and Boinski n.d.). This study demonstrates potential socio-ecological conditions for allopatric divergence in evolved temperament characteristics, of the sort which can come to distinguish species over a longer span of evolutionary time.

At the level of species comparisons, Thierry (1990) suggests that despotic macaque social systems evolve when social bonds are mostly based on kinship, while egalitarian macaque social systems are less kin-based and animals keep affiliative ties with all members of the group – 'the individual retains a certain degree of freedom in relation to the power of kin networks' (1990: 511). Moore (1992) has argued that the low levels of escalated aggression which characterize the dominance style of stumptail macaques (and also bonnet and Barbary macaques) may reflect richer habitats in which decreased feeding competition permits males to coexist in troops without intense sexual competition for access to females, resulting in the high male: female ratios characteristic of these species (where observed, typically nearly 1:1). Rhesus macaques by contrast may inhabit niches with lower quality diet, low male: female ratios (since females will favour marginalization or emigration by subordinate males and thus fewer mouths to feed), and high levels of escalated aggression. The contrast between common chimpanzees and bonobos may also relate to underlying contrasts in their feeding ecology over evolutionary time (current thinking puts the bonobo–common chimpanzee split at about 2.5 Myr BP, Morin *et al.* 1994), with the forest-dwelling bonobos inhabiting an environment with richer background levels of food availability and periodically aggregating into larger feeding groups at fruiting trees – and managing the competitive tensions which this generates with a suite of species-specific affiliative and reconciliatory behaviours (cf. Blount 1990). The evolved anatomical and physiological basis of the contrasts in behavioural style between the two chimpanzee species is less well understood, but may involve some component or correlate of the more paedomorphic traits which characterize the bonobos.

Despite the resilience of these contrasts in dominance style as species-specific traits even in laboratory-reared animals, they do not merely reflect hard-wired genetic programs of behaviour. For instance, de Waal and Johanowicz (1993) have reported that co-housing juvenile rhesus monkeys with stumptails for a 5-month period resulted in the rhesus monkeys manifesting much higher levels of reconciliations after fights, suggesting that 'the reconciliation behavior of juvenile non-human primates is susceptible to manipulation of the social environment', even if the rhesus monkeys retained many other elements of their distinctive behavioural style (1993: 907; see also Clarke and Boinski n.d.).

A coherent synthesis of the comparative socioecology of dominance style in primates is needed, and recent work is moving in that direction (e.g. Vehrencamp 1983, van Schaik 1989, Thierry 1990, Kappeler and van Schaik 1992, Moore 1992, Clarke and Boinski n.d., Plavcan *et al.* in press). It seems that where a stable set of selection pressures favours group living and coalition formation in a species, and yet where there are relatively low costs to individuals subgrouping or dispersing out of groups when dominant animals are imposing excessive negative fitness differentials on subordinates, then a pattern of social behaviour characterized by a 'relaxed' dominance style with low levels of escalated aggression might be expected to emerge. In the remainder of this chapter, I want simply to highlight some pointers to the role of temperament and dominance style in hominid evolution and raise the question of what socioecological variables could have driven a feedback loop leading to their evolution as heritable species-level traits.

POINTERS TO THE EVOLUTION OF
DOMINANCE STYLE IN HOMINIDS

Sexual dimorphism

Ratio indices of sexually dimorphic traits such as body size and canine size have often been used in the past as indices of the degree of intensity of male–male competition for access to reproductive females. In fact, as Plavcan *et al.* (in press) have demonstrated, it is quite misleading to take female values for such traits as baselines since in the case of canine tooth size there is almost as much variance between females as between males in comparisons across primate species.

Studies of these traits in closely related species suggest that they co-vary with the intensity of agonistic interactions between individuals of one or both sexes. For instance, common chimpanzees and bonobos differ in that bonobos are less sexually dimorphic in body weight and canine size (Plavcan and van Schaik 1992): furthermore, whereas male common chimpanzees have relatively larger canines than either *Gorilla* or *Pongo*, bonobo males have the smallest canines of any hominoid (Plavcan *et al.*, in press). This suggests a relaxation in the course of bonobo evolution of selection pressures favouring male canine enlargement. These pressures for larger canines derive from socioecological variables underlying manifest high levels of intensity of within or between group contest competition where outcomes are based on individual fighting ability (Plavcan *et al.*, in press).

Similar anatomical indications of dominance style exist among the macaque species. Stumptails have a much higher 'conciliatory tendency' than rhesus macaques (Kappeler and van Schaik 1992), and they are also much less sexually dimorphic in body size (male/female body weight ratios are 1.15 for stumptails, 2.07 for rhesus, data in Harvey *et al.* 1987). Comparison of Tonkean macaques with rhesus macaques, another such comparison between sister species of contrasting dominance styles (Thierry 1986, Petit *et al.* 1992), shows that the conciliatory species (Tonkean macaques) are also much less sexually dimorphic in canine dimensions (Plavcan and van Schaik 1992: Table 1).

These case studies suggest that sexually dimorphic fossil traits can be used to infer dominance style, and the character of agonistic interactions, in hominid groups. Plavcan and van Schaik (1994) have argued that the reduced male canine size and reduced canine dimorphism seen in Australopithecines is indicative of a low-intensity pattern of male–male agonistic interactions, in which coalitionary behaviour was likely to have been more important than individual fighting ability for the outcome of dominance contests. However, they note that the apparent high levels of sexual body size dimorphism are hard to reconcile with this pattern and may reflect the selective consequences of male predator defence in open environments (if indeed there are not two modestly dimorphic species in the currently recognized *Australopithecus afarensis* taxon). McHenry (this volume) argues that the low level of canine dimorphism seen in *A. afarensis* indicates relaxed selection pressure for this component of fighting ability, but suggests that the relatively high level of body size dimorphism implies some other component of male dominance-seeking behaviour must have evolved in compensation – he proposes such a role for the forelimbs. He notes also that the low level of body size dimorphism in *Homo erectus* is consistent with a pattern of reduced male–male competition.

A parsimonious explanation of this set of dimorphic traits in hominids is that the pattern in *Australopithecus afarensis* indicates a male-bonded social system on the chimpanzee pattern, and that a distinctive pattern of low-intensity dominance interactions had evolved at least by the time of the appearance of early *Homo erectus* in Africa (if not earlier).

Endocrine gland weight scaling

Dominance rank has both costs and benefits for a high-ranking individual. The benefits include enhanced access to feeding resources and to fertile females, and the costs can include sequelae to the stress which dominants experience in establishing and maintaining their rank – such as depressed immune function (Masataka *et al.* 1990) and impaired cognitive performance (Bunnell *et al.* 1980, Bunnell and Perkins 1980). It is intriguing to note suggestions that elevated levels of serum testosterone, which are associated with high dominance rank (and increased metabolism of glucose in muscles) in male primates, in humans may correlate inversely with cerebral metabolic rate and that compared with males human females consistently show 10–20 per cent more regional cerebral blood flow in studies of cognitive physiology across task conditions (Vernikos-Danellis 1972, Wendt and Risberg 1994).

Although serum and saliva sampling of hormone levels is routinely carried out in studies of dominance style and dominance behaviour in primates, there is less work on endocrine gland weight scaling across primates as an indicator of cross-species variance in normal thresholds of physiological reactivity. However, it is evident from single-species studies that heightened adrenocortical activity and hypertrophy of the adrenal glands is a correlate of subordinate status in adult male macaques (*Macaca fascicularis*, Shively and Kaplan 1984), and that heightened testosterone levels and enlarged testes correlate with dominance and increased access to reproductive females in mandrills, the largest of the monkey species (*Mandrillus sphinx*, Wickings and Dixson 1992).

This aspect of comparative anatomy is highly relevant for studies of hominid evolution. At various times it has been suggested that humans are characterized by markedly different normal levels of circulating adrenal and gonadal hormones to those of non-human primates, and even by disproportionately large endocrine glands, and this has clear relevance for understanding hominid dominance style. Thus Spuhler (1979) argued that humans have greatly enlarged adrenals as an adaptation for sustained high rates of metabolism of energy reserves during endurance running, and that female continuous sexual receptivity is a secondary consequence of this (since most testosterone is secreted by the adrenals in human females, and testosterone was postulated to be the principal female 'libido hormone'). Smith (1984: 626) asserted that human males have proportionately large testes relative to the great apes (though less so than chimpanzees). However, no explicit inferences are drawn about the cognitive and behavioural consequences of these contrasts in gonadal scaling when the gonads are viewed as endocrine glands.

In fact, with respect to Spuhler's arguments about the causes of the supposedly continuous human female sexual receptivity, more recent work has failed to replicate the association of female primate 'libido' with adrenal testosterone levels, and has implicated effects of varying levels of ovarian hormones – estradiol and progesterone (Michael and Zumpe 1993: 223). There is little data on variance in proportional size of primate female ovaries, but data compiled in Table 4.1 suggest that the mean size of human ovaries may not be significantly larger (relative to body size) than that of the great apes. However, to confirm that observation these raw ratios would need more careful adjusting for allometric factors and for sample size and bias.

Data on adrenal gland weights and body weights for eighteen primate species were collected by Crile and Quiring (1940), and are summarized in the Appendix to this chapter. As Figure 4.1 shows, human mean adrenal weight scales to body weight are consistent with the general trend for the primates. Least squares regression (chosen because of the greater expected probability of measurement error in the adrenal weights) of log adrenal weight against log body weight for this dataset gives a slope coefficient of 0.77, which suggests a relationship between adrenal scaling

Table 4.1 Ovary weights of female primates as a percentage of body weight, according to various sources

Inay et al. (1940)		Short (1979, 1981)		Pearl et al. (1936: 117)	
Macaca	0.008				
Cercocebus	0.0054				
		Pongo	0.006		
		Gorilla	0.012		
Pan	0.0087	Pan	0.010		
		Homo	0.014	Homo	0.0102

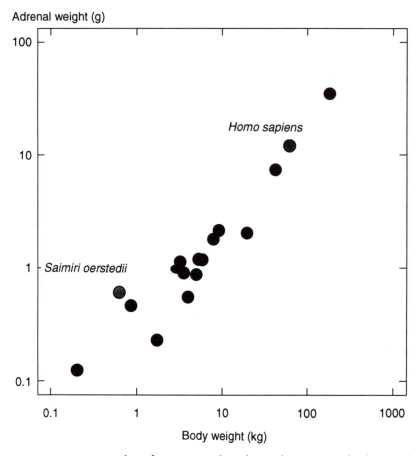

Adrenal weight (g)

Body weight (kg)

Figure 4.1 Scatterplot of primate adrenal weights against body weight, with both axis scales logged (data from Crile and Quiring 1940, reproduced in Appendix)

and metabolic rate scaling, and consistent with this it is the squirrel monkey (*Saimiri*) which shows the greatest positive residual variation in relative adrenal size (cf. Steele, this volume; the *Saimiri* data in Crile and Quiring 1940 came from Panama, which is within the region of the less stressed ('Gothic') group with lower baseline cortisol levels, see p. 111 and Clarke and Boinski n.d.). It is interesting in this context to note that the temperament of the squirrel monkey is distinctive, the squirrel monkeys having been described in a paired comparison with titi monkeys (*Callicebus moloch*) as more active, opportunistic, impulsive and bolder, as well as having a higher baseline heart rate and cortisol level (Clarke and Boinski n.d.: 14). Because of the small samples used for many of these species data, no further statistical analysis will be attempted here.

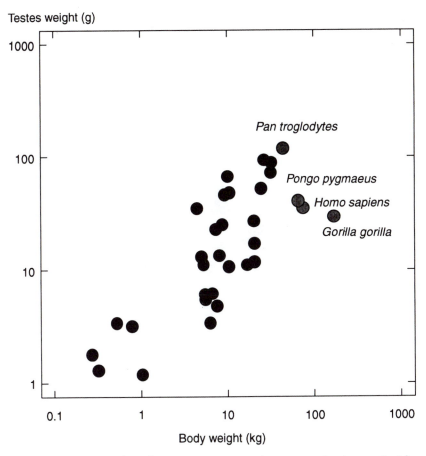

Figure 4.2 Scatterplot of primate testes weights against body weight (data from Harvey and Harcourt 1984: 592; both axis scales logged)

Gonadal weight scaling studies have focused on male traits, and in contrast with Smith's emphasis (1984) a recent study suggests that human testes weight is consistent with that of other apes with one-male mating systems when effects of variation in the morphology of the female reproductive tract are taken into account (Dahl *et al.* 1993). The chimpanzees differ in having relatively larger testes, and the gorillas appear to have anomalously small testes relative to body size. Studies differentiating the great ape species by temperament date from at least the Yerkes' day (Yerkes and Yerkes 1929), and it is plausible to expect that differences in reproductive hormone gland sizes affect baseline serum hormone levels in a way which may account for some of these differences. The Yerkes found gorillas to be diffident and shy, orangutans withdrawn and brooding, and chimpanzees outgoing, expressive and impulsive

Brain weight (g)

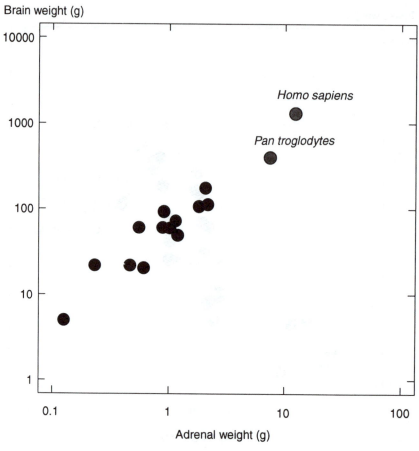

Figure 4.3a Scatterplot of primate brain weights against adrenal weights (data from Crile and Quiring 1940, see Appendix; both axis scales logged)

(Clarke and Boinski n.d.): cognitive style is likely primarily a reflection of the proportion of metabolic energy allocated to the brain, as opposed to other 'expensive' tissues such as the gut, in these species, but it is suggestive that the great ape species are also differentiable by endocrine weight scaling.

As Figure 4.2 shows, human males are not particularly anomalous among primates in their testes size relative to body weight, and cluster with orangutans for this trait. However, the contrast with chimpanzees is noteworthy since they are our closest living relatives: the divergence in relative testes size in these two lines may therefore have had consequences for male temperament and dominance style due to the expected consequent variation in baseline serum testosterone levels, with the male

Brain weight (g)

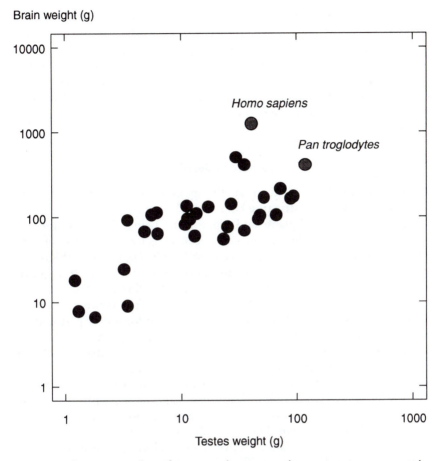

Figure 4.3b Scatterplot of primate brain weights against testes weights (data from Harvey and Harcourt 1984: 592, and Harvey *et al.* 1987; both axis scales logged)

hominid pattern expected on the basis of the foregoing review to correlate with higher baseline levels of cerebral activation and lower levels of aggression.

Humans are most anomalous among the primates in their gonad weight/brain weight scaling, since the relatively enlarged human brain is so anomalous with respect to body size – an effect which is less noticeable for adrenal weight/brain weight scaling (Figures 4.3a, b). This effect is particularly noticeable in the scaling of male testes to brain weight, which suggests (contrary to folk wisdom!) that cognition in the human male cannot be wholly under the control of gonadal hormones. The implication here is that human reproductive behaviour, temperament and dominance style, insofar as these are mediated by the behavioural effects of circulating hormone levels, are more under control of the central nervous system and of cognitive processes than is the case for any other living primate (cf. Worthman 1990). While no soft tissue data on gland weights of fossil hominids are available, relative brain size increased in early *Homo* and then again with later *Homo erectus* and *Homo sapiens*, suggesting that this pattern of increased cognitive control of hormonal factors involved in male aggression dates from the earliest evolution of genus *Homo*.

Cerebral laterality

Humans demonstrate a trend at the population level for correlated asymmetries in brain structure and in behavioural organization, with the left cerebral hemisphere and right hand being dominant for fine motor tasks. This handedness bias has been detected in patterns of early artefact production probably associated with early *Homo* (Toth 1985), and is associated with the evolution of morphological asymmetry (the greater development of the left lobes of the brain, Falk 1987).

Tucker and Williamson (1984) have argued that the neurochemistry of the brain promotes a left hemisphere specialization for motor preparedness with a cognitive pattern of limited span of visuospatial attentiveness, but more intensive involvement of memory and anticipation. This is contrasted with the right cerebral hemisphere's specialization for arousal and orienting to novelty in the immediate visuospatial environment. The evolution of technological skill in the Palaeolithic, with increasingly fine motor skills demonstrated in the production of lithic artefacts, therefore reflects the evolution of this pattern of cerebral dominance since there is an inverse correlation between optimal arousal level for motor performance and the degree of fine motor skill and cognitive complexity which the task involves (Schmidt 1991: 26–30, see Figure 4.4).

Cerebral dominance of the left hemisphere involving selective inhibition of the right hemisphere arousal system could also underlie certain evolved temperament characteristics in genus *Homo*. Reactivity to novel or stressful stimuli is an important aspect of temperament, and studies of reactivity in non-human primates suggest that low reactivity is a trait which may facilitate attainment of a high dominance rank (Clarke and Boinski n.d.). A number of studies of different anthropoid species have found an inverse correlation between dominance rank and fearfulness or impulsivity, with higher-ranking animals scoring higher for social confidence and 'controlledness' (Clarke and Boinski n.d.). This pattern may also be detectable using physiological measures, with more dominant animals usually showing characteristic patterns of hormonal reactivity to stress. The evolution of cerebral dominance in *Homo* is therefore capable of explanation as the product of selection for temperament characteristics relating to reactivity to stress. Seen in this perspective, the capacity

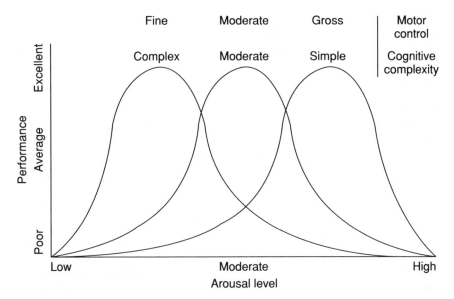

Figure 4.4 Model of relationship between optimal arousal levels and the degrees of motor control and cognitive complexity entailed in a task (from Schmidt 1991: Figure 2.6)

for the fine motor performance seen in Palaeolithic technologies is a by-product of temperamental characteristics relating to ability in 'low-key' social dominance contests, and not itself a primary object of positive natural selection.

Speech

Understanding the evolution of the human language capacity has too often been reduced to an exercise in reverse engineering of the brain's hardware and software. Important though this is, it draws attention away from the real problems which language evolution poses for theories of the evolution of co-operation. Language behaviour involves the co-operative exchange of large quantities of information which may have significant consequences for the fitness of some or all of the participants, and a proto-linguistic hominid community would therefore have been vulnerable to invasion by cheaters (who decoded the information being broadcast by others, but withheld such co-operative signals themselves).

Because of this, there is particular value in studies which examine the way in which human conversational exchanges serve not only for information exchange, but also for parallel processes of affiliative bonding and testing of relationship quality. The strength of an affiliative bond and the power structure of a relationship would be expected to be crucial considerations which an individual should evaluate before and during such an exchange, as a guide to decisions about the quality of information which he or she should broadcast to the other conversational participants. Dunbar's work (1993, this volume) on human conversational cliques and on topic choice in conversational groups has been a crucial contribution to such studies, as has his emphasis on the persuasive analogy between human everyday language use and non-human primate social grooming: similar theoretical problems arise in understanding social grooming as an apparently altruistic behaviour of the groomer, and have led to fresh insights into the role of grooming in primate social systems (cf. Spruijt et al. 1992).

A number of aspects of human conversational exchanges (cyclicity, repetition, turn-taking routines, mutual adaptation of parameters such as voice pitch and amplitude) have properties which tend to reinforce the affiliative quality of a relationship (cf. Steele 1995). Rather than viewing language purely as a means of transmitting unique strings of information between signaller and receiver, the new emphasis is on 'tonic' properties of language as a communication system (Schleidt 1977). If language is seen as having its origins in a species-specific grooming behaviour (on an analogy with female bonobo G–G rubbing, for example), then we should expect conversational interactions to be capable of analysis using the same tools used in analysing primate social grooming. Dunbar (1993, this volume) has already undertaken work on a number of relevant parameters of which the most notable relate to clique size and structure. A parallel tradition of work on primate social grooming has focused on its endocrine sequelae (e.g. Keverne 1992, Spruijt et al. 1992). Grooming has properties which 'de-arouse' the recipient animal, and these properties may underlie its development as a key component of primate social relationships. By analogy, we would expect the same to apply to linguistic interactions, and it is important that this topic should be explored in experimental situations in the future.

There is scope for much further work on conversational exchanges in these ethological paradigms, before we can gain a clear picture of the closeness of the analogy between human language and primate social grooming. Existing evidence on the physiological correlates of talking is limited, and we still need to understand the evolved role of social touch and of behaviour directed at the outer body surface in hominid social relationships (cf. respectively Tardy 1993 and Thayer 1986). However, it is evident that language could not have evolved in the context of social relationships which were other than tolerant, relaxed, and with a low level of escalated hostile vocal signalling. The pattern of hominid language capacities and their evolution remains unclear, and much evidence favours a late evolution of modern levels of language ability with *Homo sapiens*:

but if patterns of cerebral lateralization found in hominid endocasts are taken as indicators of selection for proto-language behaviours, then this process was underway at least by the appearance of early *Homo* in Africa (cf. Falk 1987, Gibson and Ingold 1993).

Stone tools, culture and the evolution of dominance style in hominid groups

The conventional emphasis in palaeoanthropology on hominid cognitive ability and brain size increase implies that we should expect a linear increase in exploratory and innovative behaviour throughout the Lower and Middle Palaeolithic. In fact the evidence is inconsistent with such expectations, with the high level of repetition and conservatism in artefact forms leading some scholars to speculate that cultural traditions in *Homo erectus* groups were 'the product of complex forms of imitative behavior in a pattern no longer to be found among the Hominidae' (Jelinek 1977: 15, cited by Klein 1989). Others have argued that the stone tools demonstrate either that before *Homo sapiens*, hominid cognitive evolution was domain-specific and there was no communication between the parts of the brain processing different types of problem (Mithen 1994 and this volume), or that the domain-specificity of human cognitive evolution led to an increased language ability without a corresponding increase in the complexity of tool-making or tool-use (Wynn 1993).

The emphasis in this chapter has been on temperamental and cognitive adaptations to living in relatively egalitarian social groups. In this context, a high level of imitative fidelity in stone tool traditions should not be seen as necessarily reflecting a deficit in hominid capabilities. First, as Tomasello *et al.* (1993) have pointed out, imitative learning in unenculturated non-human primates is rare and difficult to demonstrate, such that the ability for true imitation may itself be one of the hallmarks of hominid evolution. Indeed, cultural learning is also dependent on the co-operative 'scaffolding' of the environment of the learner by the experienced members of a group (Tomasello *et al.* 1993). Thus Lower Palaeolithic artefact traditions must be treated as the central witnesses to the evolution of sociocultural learning processes, and not as a puzzling anomaly (see Lake, this volume). Second, imitation is itself an affiliative behaviour which enhances the predictability of an interaction for the participants (cf. Roberts 1980). If the emphasis in studies of hominid behaviour shifts from the individual to the social structure of the group, then the high level of imitative fidelity seen in Lower Palaeolithic artefact assemblages may come to be seen not as indicative of an unexplained cognitive deficit, but as another component of the distinctive affiliative behavioural style which has characterized the evolution of genus *Homo*.

Summary

I have argued that dominance style can be inferred from a number of anatomical and behavioural markers including sexual dimorphisms, endocrine gland weight scaling, aspects of manipulative and communicative behaviour, and the presence or absence of imitation. The underlying theme has been that of the importance of temperament or 'style' of behaviour management as a differentiating trait in species-level comparisons of primates in social groups.

The study of emotions and emotion management has become increasingly common in the social sciences: Wouters (1992: 230) attributes this heightened interest to the parallel development of a 'social process of intensified status competition within increasingly dense networks of interdependency' in Western societies. Dabbs (1992) has recently reported that males with high levels of serum testosterone tend to have lower status occupations in the US, perhaps because among humans dominance depends more on mastering cultural rules and skills than on aggression, which can interfere with this process (assuming that variance in baseline testosterone levels is genetically heritable, and not an adaptive developmental response to different patterns of work). In this context, it is interesting to note that male foragers have consistently lower salivary testosterone levels than are found in settled or Western populations, perhaps due to nutritional factors (Bribiescas 1994) and that lowered salivary testosterone is also associated in foragers (at the inter-individual level) with paedomorphic anatomical traits (Winkler and Christiansen 1991), since the modern foraging economy of hunter-gatherers is the closest extant approximation to that of Pleistocene hominids. The implication is that significant parallels exist between the emerging emotion management style of modern Western societies and that of the 'environment of ancestral adaptation'.

SOCIOECOLOGY OF DOMINANCE STYLE IN HOMINID EVOLUTION

A number of correlates of contrasts in temperament between primate species have been proposed in the literature, focused either on group composition and dispersal patterns or on foraging technique and responsiveness to predation risk (Clarke and Boinski n.d.). With respect to dominance style and social structure Vehrencamp (1983) proposed that biased resource allocation favouring dominant individuals could only evolve in populations to the extent that there remained net gains to grouping for subordinates, and that the degree of 'despotism' exercised by dominants would be a function of the degree of relatedness among group members, the costs to subordinates of dispersal out of the group, and the costs of solitary living.

Explanations of the benefits of group living for primates include protection from predators, increase in foraging efficiency and defence of rich clumped food patches from other competing groups: of these, predator defence has proved the most consistent with observed variation in primate grouping strategies (e.g. van Schaik 1983, and see Rodman 1988). A number of authors (see especially Dunbar, Mithen, Steele, all in this volume) have proposed that hominid evolution was characterized by a trend for living in larger and larger social groups. However, others have also argued that these groups were characterized by a social structure elaborated from a male-bonded fission–fusion social system as the ancestral state (see especially Foley and Lee, Maryanski, this volume). Janson and van Schaik (1988) point out that limited existing evidence suggests that one form of 'despotism', aggressive behaviour by dominants leading to depressed food intake by subordinates, does not appear to increase with group size. In fact, among Old World monkeys large groups appear to be more unstable and prone to fission and fusion than small groups, a feature which enables individuals to adapt to widely dispersed and unpredictable food distributions (Beauchamp and Cabana 1990): but the instability may also reflect the inability of dominant individuals to control large hierarchies. Finally, large groups will also contain larger proportions of individuals who are not closely related, a condition unfavourable for the evolution of despotism in Vehrencamp's model (1983). Hominids in groups with a fission–fusion structure and increasingly large community sizes would therefore be expected to have undergone selection not for individual fighting ability, but for cognitive and temperamental traits favourable for the formation of coalitions and co-operative alliances. This also seems to imply a dietary adaptation which permitted such aggregation without excessive feeding competition. Such a pattern is certainly consistent with recent arguments from ethnography that male–male relationships in the ancestral human social structure were characterized by a 'reverse dominance hierarchy' (Boehm 1993), and by specific palaeodietary evidence suggesting that the physical basis for male dominance rank (as indexed by muscularity and age in skeletal males) was unrelated to feeding benefits in a human Mesolithic hunter-gatherer community (Jacobs 1994). If it is accepted that temperament and dominance style are important aspects of human 'evolved psychology', then the job of tracking their evolution in the details of the hominid fossil and cultural records will become more and more worthwhile.

ACKNOWLEDGEMENTS

I am very grateful to the following colleagues for discussions and/or for providing pre-prints of their work: Susan Clarke, Ellen Ingmanson, Kenneth Jacobs and Michael Plavcan. They are not, however, responsible for any mistakes in the synthesis presented here, which remain uniquely mine.

APPENDIX

Summary of Crile and Quiring's data (1940)

Species	Sample size	Body weight (kg)	Adrenal weight (g)	Brain weight (g)
Alouatta palliata	38	5.8	1.190	49.4
Aotus zonalis	17	9.1	2.159	112.2
Ateles dariensis	17	9.1	2.159	112.2
Ateles geoffroyi	83	7.9	1.805	107.0
Cebus capucinus	23	3.2	1.139	72.3
Cercopithecus aethiops	4	4.0	0.554	60.9
Cercopithecus mitis	4	2.9	1.020	60.0
Cercopithecus sp.	2	4.9	0.878	60.7
Galago senegalensis	1	0.2	0.125	5.0
Gorilla gorilla	1	181.0	35.0	n/a
Homo sapiens	36	61.9	12.17	1320.3
Lagothrix humboldti	1	5.3	1.20	86.2
Lemur catta	1	1.7	0.232	21.8
Leontocebus geoffroyi	16	0.8	0.465	22.0
Macacus rhesus	11	3.5	0.907	92.6
Pan troglodytes	3	42.2	7.440	398.5
Papio cynocephalus	1	19.5	2.050	175.0
Saimiri oerstedii	66	0.6	0.608	20.4

Note
Data are weighted means for both sexes, adults only; species names are as given by Crile and Quiring.

REFERENCES

Beauchamp, G. and Cabana, G. (1990) 'Group size variability in primates.' *Primates* 31: 171–182.

Blount, B.G. (1990) 'Issues in bonobo (*Pan paniscus*) sexual behavior.' *American Anthropologist* 92: 702–714.

Boehm, C. (1993) 'Egalitarian behaviour and reverse dominance hierarchy.' *Current Anthropology* 34: 227–254.

Bribiescas, R.G. (1994) 'Salivary testosterone levels in a population of Aché agriculturalists in eastern Paraguay [Abstract].' *American Journal of Physical Anthropology* S18: 59.

Bunnell, B.N. and Perkins, M.N. (1980) 'Performance correlates of social behavior and organization: social rank and complex problem solving in crab-eating macaques (*M. fascicularis*).' *Primates* 21: 515–523.

Bunnell, B.N., Gore, W.T. and Perkins, M.N. (1980) 'Performance correlates of social behavior and organization: social rank and reversal learning in crab-eating macaques (*M. fascicularis*).' *Primates* 21: 376–388.

Clarke, A.S. and Boinski, S. (n.d.) 'Temperament and responsivity in non-human primates.' *American Journal of Primatology*, submitted.

Crile, G. and Quiring, D.P. (1940) 'A record of the body weight and certain organ and gland weights of 3690 animals.' *Ohio Journal of Science* 40: 219–259.

Dabbs, J.M. (1992) 'Testosterone and occupational achievement.' *Social Forces* 70: 813–824.

Dahl, J.F., Gould, K.G. and Nadler, R.D. (1993) 'Testicle size of orang-utans in relation to body size.' *American Journal of Physical Anthropology* 90: 229–236.

Drews, C. (1993) 'The concept and definition of dominance in animal behaviour.' *Behaviour* 125: 283–313.

Dunbar, R.I.M. (1993) 'Coevolution of neocortex size, group size and language in humans.' *Behavioural and Brain Sciences* 16: 681–735.

Falk, D. (1987) 'Hominid paleoneurology.' *Annual Review of Anthropology* 16: 13–30.

Gibson, K.R. and Ingold, T. (eds) (1993) *Tools, Language and Cognition in Human Evolution.* Cambridge: Cambridge University Press.

Harvey, P.H. and Harcourt, A. (1984) 'Sperm competition, testes size, and breeding system in primates.' In R.L. Smith (ed.) *Sperm Competition and the Evolution of Animal Mating Systems*, pp. 589–600. Orlando: Academic Press.

Harvey, P.H., Martin, R.D. and Clutton-Brock, T.H. (1987) 'Life histories in comparative perspective.' In B.B. Smuts, D. Cheney, R. Seyfarth, R. Wrangham and T. Struhsaker (eds) *Primate Societies*, pp. 181–196. Chicago: University of Chicago Press.

Inay, M., Ruch, T.C., Finan, S. and Fulton, J.F. (1940) 'The endocrine weights of primates.' *Endocrinology* 27: 58–67.

Jacobs, K. (1994) 'Meat, muscularity, and Mesolithic social status: evaluating their association at Olenii ostrov (Karelia) [Abstract].' *American Journal of Physical Anthropology* S18: 115.

Janson, C.H. and van Schaik, C.P. (1988) 'Recognizing the many faces of primate food competition: methods.' *Behaviour* 105: 165–186.

Jelinek, A. (1977) 'The Lower Palaeolithic: current evidence and interpretations.' *Annual Review of Anthropology* 6: 11–32.

Kappeler, P. and van Schaik, C.P. (1992) 'Methodological and evolutionary aspects of reconciliation among primates.' *Ethology* 92: 51–69.

Keverne, E.B. (1992) 'Primate social relationships: their determinants and consequences.' *Advances in the Study of Behavior* 21: 1–37.

Klein, R.G. (1989) *The Human Career.* Chicago: University of Chicago Press.

Masataka, N., Ishida, T., Suzuki, J., Matsumura, S., Udono, S. and Sasaoka, S. (1990) 'Dominance and immunity in chimpanzees (*Pan troglodytes*).' *Ethology* 85: 147–155.

Michael, R.P. and Zumpe, D. (1993) 'A review of hormonal factors influencing the sexual and aggressive behavior of macaques.' *American Journal of Primatology* 30: 213–241.

Mithen, S.J. (1994) 'From domain-specific to generalized intelligence: a cognitive interpretation of the Middle/Upper Palaeolithic transition.' In C. Renfrew and E. Zubrow (eds) *The Ancient Mind: Elements of a Cognitive Archaeology*, pp. 29–39. Cambridge: Cambridge University Press.

Moore, J. (1992) 'Dispersal, nepotism, and primate social behavior.' *International Journal of Primatology* 13: 361–378.

Morin, P.A., Moore, J.J., Chakraborty, R., Jin, L., Goodall, J. and Woodruff, D.S. (1994) 'Kin selection, social structure, gene flow, and the evolution of chimpanzees.' *Science* 265: 1193–1201.

Pearl, R., Goch, M., Miner, J.R. and Freeman, W. (1936) 'Studies on constitution, IV. Endocrine organ weights and somatological habitus types.' *Human Biology* 8: 92–125.

Petit, O., Desportes, C. and Thierry, B. (1992) 'Differential probability of "co-production" in two species of macaque (*Macaca tonkeana, M. mulatta*).' *Ethology* 90: 107–120.

Plavcan, J.M. and van Schaik, C.P. (1992) 'Intrasexual competition and canine dimorphism in anthropoid primates.' *American Journal of Physical Anthropology* 87: 461–477.

Plavcan, J.M. and van Schaik, C.P. (1994) 'Implications of canine and body size dimorphism in Australopithecines [Abstract].' *American Journal of Physical Anthropology* S18: 160–161.

Plavcan, J.M., van Schaik, C.P. and Kappeler, P.M. (in press) 'Competition, coalitions and canine size in primates.' *Journal of Human Evolution.*

Roberts, M.C. (1980) 'On being imitated: effects of levels of imitation and imitator competence.' *Social Psychology Quarterly* 43: 233–240.

Rodman, P.S. (1988) 'Resources and group sizes of primates.' In C.N. Slobodchikoff (ed.) *The Ecology of Social Behavior*, pp. 83–108. London: Academic Press.

Sapolsky, R.M. (1990) 'Stress in the wild.' *Scientific American* 262: 106–113.

Schleidt, W. (1977) 'Tonic properties of animal communication systems.' In B.M. Wenzel and H.P. Ziegler (eds) *Tonic Functions of Sensory Systems. Annals of the New York Academy of Sciences* 290: 43–49.

Schmidt, R.A. (1991) *Motor Learning and Performance.* Champaign, IL: Human Kinetics Books.

Shively, C. and Kaplan, J. (1984) 'Effects of social factors on adrenal weight and related physiology of *Macaca fascicularis*.' *Physiology and Behavior* 33: 777–782.

Short, R.V. (1979) 'Sexual selection and its component parts, somatic and genital selection, as illustrated by man and the great apes.' *Advances in the Study of Behaviour* 9: 131–158.

Short, R.V. (1981) 'Sexual selection in man and the great apes.' In C.E. Graham (ed.) *Reproductive Biology of the Great Apes*, pp. 319–341. New York: Academic Press.

Smith, R.L. (1984) 'Human sperm competition.' In R. L. Smith (ed.) *Sperm Competition and the Evolution of Animal Mating Systems*, pp. 601–659. Orlando: Academic Press.

Spuhler, J.N. (1979) 'Continuities and discontinuities in anthropoid-hominid behavioral evolution: bipedal locomotion and sexual receptivity.' In N.A. Chagnon and W. Irons (eds) *Evolutionary Biology and Human Social Behavior: An Anthropological Perspective*, pp. 454–461. North Scituate, MA: Duxbury Press.

Spruijt, B.M., van Hooff, J.A.R.A.M. and Gispen, W.H. (1992) 'Ethology and neurobiology of grooming behavior.' *Physiological Reviews* 72: 825–852.

Steele, J. (1995) 'Talking to each other: why hominids bothered.' In I. Hodder, M. Shanks, A. Alexandri, V. Buchli, J. Carman, J. Last and G. Lucas (eds) *Interpreting Archaeology*, pp. 81–86. London: Routledge.

Tardy, C.H. (1993) 'Biological perspectives on language and social interaction.' *American Behavioral Scientist* 36: 339–358.

Thayer, S. (1986) 'History and strategies of research on social touch.' *Journal of Nonverbal Behavior* 10: 12–28.

Thierry, B. (1986) 'A comparative study of aggression and response to aggression in three species of macaque.' In J.G. Else and P.C. Lee (eds) *Primate Ontogeny, Cognition, and Social Behaviour*, pp. 307–313. Cambridge: Cambridge University Press.

Thierry, B. (1990) 'Feedback loop between kinship and dominance: the macaque model.' *Journal of Theoretical Biology* 145: 511–521.

Tomasello, M., Kruger, A.C. and Ratner, H.H. (1993) 'Cultural learning.' *Behavioral and Brain Sciences* 16: 495–552.

Toth, N. (1985) 'Archaeological evidence for preferential right-handedness in the Lower and Middle Pleistocene, and its possible implications.' *Journal of Human Evolution* 14: 607–614.

Tucker, D.M. and Williamson, P.A. (1984) 'Asymmetric neural control systems in human self-regulation.' *Psychological Review* 91: 185–215.

van Schaik, C.P. (1983) 'Why are diurnal primates living in groups?' *Behaviour* 87: 120–144.

van Schaik, C.P. (1989) 'The ecology of social relationships amongst female primates.' In V. Standen and R.A. Foley (eds) *Comparative Socioecology*, pp. 195–218. Oxford: Blackwell.

Vehrencamp, S.L. (1983) 'A model for the evolution of despotic versus egalitarian societies.' *Animal Behaviour* 31: 667–682.

Vernikos-Danellis, J. (1972) 'Effects of hormones on the central nervous system.' In S. Levine (ed.) *Hormones and Behavior*, pp. 11–60. New York: Academic Press.

de Waal, F.B.M. (1989) *Peacemaking among Primates*. Cambridge, MA: Harvard University Press.

de Waal, F.B.M. and Johanowicz, D.L. (1993) 'Modification of reconciliation behavior through social experience: an experiment with two macaque species.' *Child Development* 64: 897–908.

Wendt, P.E. and Risberg, J. (1994) 'Cortical activation during visual spatial processing: relation between hemispheric asymmetry of bloodflow and performance.' *Brain and Cognition* 24: 87–103.

Wickings, E.J. and Dixson, A.F. (1992) 'Testicular function, secondary sexual development, and social status in male mandrills (*Mandrillus sphinx*).' *Physiology and Behavior* 52: 909–916.

Winkler, E.-M. and Christiansen, K. (1991) 'Anthropometric-hormonal correlation patterns in San and Kavango males from Namibia.' *Annals of Human Biology* 18: 341–355.

Worthman, C.M. (1990) 'Socioendocrinology: key to a fundamental synergy.' In T.E. Ziegler and F.B. Bercovitch (eds) *Socioendocrinology of Primate Reproduction*, pp. 187–212. New York: Wiley-Liss.

Wouters, C. (1992) 'On status competition and emotion management – the study of emotions as a new field.' *Theory, Culture & Society* 9: 229–252.

Wynn, T. (1993) 'Layers of thinking in tool behavior.' In K.R. Gibson and T. Ingold (eds) *Tools, Language and Cognition in Human Evolution*, pp. 389–406. Cambridge: Cambridge University Press.

Yerkes, R.M. and Yerkes, A.W. (1929) *The Great Apes: A Study of Anthropoid Life*. New Haven: Yale University Press.

PART II

ORIGINS OF THE ARCHAEOLOGICAL RECORD

EDITORS' NOTE

The chapters in this section relate to the appearance of a cultural record of hominid activities. As Gowlett points out, it is at this point (c. 2 million years ago in Africa) that general comparative models of hominid socio-ecology come up against the highly specific evidence of direct behavioural traces – artefacts and scatters in their environmental contexts. This contrast in types of evidence and inferential procedures continues to create challenges for integrating social models with the archaeological record.

Gowlett makes robust arguments for the central importance of archaeological data in reconstructing hominid social systems. He notes an emerging consensus that these data can inform us both about range use, and about cognitive and functional aspects of the organization of activities within sites. He argues that a positive feedback loop of gene-behaviour co-evolution in response to climatic change or change in competitive regimes may prevent taxa going extinct, and proposes that the rule-governed cultural systems of hominids from Olduvai onwards represented a robust transmission system which was coupled to behavioural flexibility. His quantification of the parameters of socially learned behaviour offers a window on the complexity of such rule-based systems in the African Lower Palaeolithic.

Lake also asks what conditions favoured the evolution of cultural learning as an adaptive hominid strategy. He follows up the suggestion that the precondition for such a strategy is that environmental hetero-geneity should have been neither too great for cultural learning to track it any more efficiently than individual learning alone, nor too little for cultural learning to have any advantage over genetic adaptation in highly canalized behaviour patterns. His simulation model is designed to overcome existing limitations in the formal definitions of environ-mental heterogeneity and of the quality of individual learning. He reports initial experimental findings that cultural learning would have been favoured where individual learning (cf. Gowlett's behavioural flexibility) was of a fairly high quality, and where environments were temporally homogeneous. This approach may also enable archaeologists to assess the extent to which the poor temporal resolution of Lower Palaeolithic archaeological landscapes limits inferences about range use: if the data are themselves the product of a robust cultural learning system, then their presence may imply an adaptation which was stable across time, and which would therefore have left a persistent type of signature on the landscape across an unconnected series of depositional events.

Mithen addresses the question of the proximate mechanisms promoting robust cultural transmission of behavioural traditions. Following recent work which suggests both that hominid cognitive evolution was linked to the increasing average size of social groups, and that cognitive adaptations are often domain-specific, he argues that robust cultural transmission of artefact production traditions may initially have been decoupled from functional considerations, with early artefact traditions in effect indirectly tracking the size and cohesiveness of social groups.

Steele also analyses the evidence for group sizes of hominids, although his paper is principally a statistical study of non-human primate behavioural and anatomical data. His predictions of hominid group sizes are linked to estimates of the ranging areas of primate and carnivore groups of different total bio-mass, and his suggestion that raw material transport data can be used to test these predictions offers a new method for integrating comparative social models with the archaeological record.

Gamble's chapter also discusses artefact provenance data as indicators of range use and of the scale of social networks, and his distinction between the Local Hominid Network and the Social Landscape, with the symbolic structures which underwrite the latter, links these group size debates to longer-standing discussions of the evidence for a great extension of the spatial scale of social networks at the beginning of the Upper Palaeolithic. What all five chapters have in common is the attempt to link the cultural record of Palaeolithic archaeology to the social parameters of the general modellers, by developing theories of the cognitive and social preconditions for those robust hominid cultural transmission systems to which the archaeological record testifies so eloquently.

CHAPTER FIVE

THE FRAMEWORKS OF EARLY HOMINID SOCIAL SYSTEMS

How many useful parameters of archaeological evidence can we isolate?

JOHN GOWLETT

> Attention has shifted from technology to resource exploitation, demography, settlement location, interaction and mating networks.
>
> (Gamble 1979: 35)

As originally conceived, this chapter aimed to examine the problems of relating technical and social information in the archaeology of earlier hominids, and specifically to examine the number of individual cultural traits that could be identified in early material. It has been widened to take a broader look at social models in human evolution, but I try to follow the same theme: how many lines of evidence do we have about early hominids that can be related as knowledge? Scrutiny of these may cast light on relationships between social structure and the more directly cultural (archaeological) evidence.

Gamble's quotation above indicates some of the profound changes in approaches to the Palaeolithic: these have had even greater consequences for its early stages, because of the great alterations in framework and new finds of fundamental importance (e.g. the 4.5 million-year-old hominids reported by White *et al.* 1994).

Plainly a social phase has come to dominate archaeology, after earlier cultural, economic and processual focuses. But for early times there are difficulties in applying it because the record is so technological. It is not surprising that technology has made something of a fight-back since Gamble's comment, but it is more socially dressed (Sinclair and Schlanger 1990). Static, classificatory, typology is out. A dynamic approach to technology as social practice is in contrast much favoured, perhaps suspiciously so: Reynolds (1991) has decried it as a new tyranny. Ideally the several aspects should be brought together, as in the 'palaeoethnology' of studies at Pincevent (Leroi-Gourhan and Brezillon 1972), but for the earliest Palaeolithic that is less possible.

The strands of evidence – if we are honest – militate against an integrated approach. The fossils lend themselves to studies of locomotion and diet, and next towards being arranged in taxonomies – and, with more difficulty, phylogenies. Ecological studies aim to set this information into a context of life – of animals, plants and interspecies relations. They suffer from a surfeit of free play, because animal behaviour in an environment is actually very flexible. Conventional environmental science hits a similar problem – it is often too general or too specific to explain an archaeological context. Archaeology itself comes in too late to tell us about early hominization, and though typological approaches no longer dominate the scene, squeezing life from the hard stones is still a gruelling occupation.

Essentially two approaches are possible: first, is to use the framework of archaeology, standing in its own right, to look at the early past. This is like using a telescope, illuminating the subject with some analogy, but blanking out the surroundings. The second is to use comparative method, long a mainstay of biology (e.g. Alexander 1979). In this we set up a framework for evolution that includes other relevant species and their ecology; which studies locomotion, dietary adaptation and DNA. This approach is interdisciplinary, but disciplines such as hominid palaeontology often fit within it more comfortably than they relate to archaeology. From the potential conflict of approaches one could draw an extreme view:

- Social modellers have the right theme, but too much free play in their variables – building an archaeology-free archaeology; they should go out and dig some sites.
- Archaeology is largely irrelevant, because it is merely technology; Spatial information is gone – with Binford's criticisms – in the hydraulic jumble.

But it would be absurd to argue that human evolution could be sorted out by one approach without the other. The archaeologist sees this dramatically expressed when new finds of hominid fossils reach areas that archaeology cannot touch. But conversely, and paradoxically, the great majority of socially based studies are brought to bear on just that early period of the Pleistocene when artefacts had just appeared. If the archaeology informs us so little, how surprising that so much work focuses on 1.8 rather than 3.8 million years ago.

The interdisciplinary approach now involves the majority of researchers, simply because it embraces several disciplines. Our challenge is to integrate the different approaches, since archaeological evidence is valuable, but difficult to handle in isolation. On the other hand, a comparative approach can reach wrong conclusions. Anthropologists have a long history of

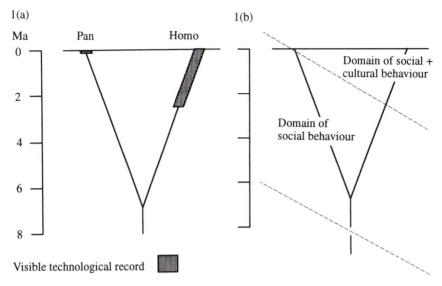

Figure 5.1   Simple model of the general and archaeological/technological record of divergence between hominids and a common ancestor with the chimpanzee

mistrusting comparative work, since it fails to handle much of the cultural variation seen in modern *Homo*, and it would fail to resolve any unique component of earlier human behaviour, including perhaps cultural changes seen in early *Homo*.

This chapter reviews models relevant to both the early (pre-archaeology) and later periods. I hope this brings out the difficulty of change of gradient between the comparative or general model, and the highly specific evidence which archaeology presents when it arrives (Figure 5.1).

The concept of models was introduced to archaeology by David Clarke (1968) and the new archaeology. It then seemed difficult to see how the subject had done without the term for more than a hundred years. But now, the word 'model' has almost gone out of fashion. This emphasizes the notion of tradition in our own ideas, but also our subject's propensity to change interests, often linked with the arrival of new ideas from other sciences. One effect common to other science is that we often quit problems before they are resolved, by-passing debates to come to newer topics (Arber 1985).

THE FRAMEWORK OF IDEAS

Models and simplification

Any model is a simplification – especially an archaeological model – but at the moment we seem to live in a time which favours *esprits simplistes*

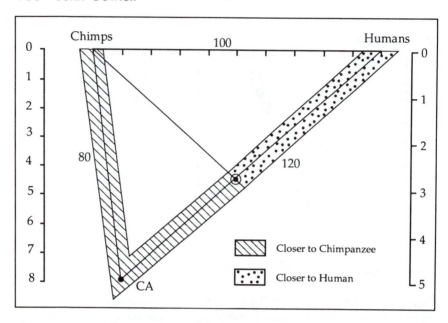

Figure 5.2 A divergence model showing how chimpanzees might be closer analogues than modern humans for modelling early hominid behaviour before around 3.5 million years ago – a model 'to kick against'. Distances, arbitrarily assigned, are Chimp–Human: 100; Chimp–Common Ancestor: 80; Human–CA: 120. Two possible timescales are provided in millions of years (after Gowlett 1993a).

(cf. Lovejoy 1936). At the least we need set procedures for optimizing the simplification. It is far from certain that archaeology has these, in spite of attempts to put modelling on a rational basis (e.g. Clarke 1968). Science has long had its procedures. Huxley (1955) gave a penetrating critique of anthropology for failing to establish similar agreed principles. In hard science, there is normally a community of shared interpretation, but in archaeology there is a spectrum of views at every level. Archaeology tends now to the simplification that there was traditional archaeology, then new archaeology, then post-processual archaeology. Most work before 1960 can be dismissed. This view is plainly flawed, and in any case less relevant to studies of human evolution, where the exposure to other disciplines has been different.

One of our difficulties is to balance lines of evidence in any objectively simplified way. As an illustration I include a diagram which I published recently to test a point in McGrew (1993). McGrew has argued that chimpanzees represent a better model for early hominid evolution than humans. The model makes simple assumptions about chimpanzee/hominid divergence, using distance measures (Figure 5.2; Gowlett 1993a:

299). This is simply a model to kick against, and as such needs no defence. It is designed to assign units of divergence in cultural behaviour, and therefore it omits:

- other species,
- physical aspects of evolution,
- social aspects,
- differential rates of change,
- geography and time management.

That is, the model is limited in dimensions and in its number of nodes, and is adjusted to a long timescale without short-term considerations. But how do we bring all those things in? Most current models are primarily economic/social to the extent that they omit species considerations; or on the other hand they are preoccupied with cultural evidence.

Figure 5.3 is intended to give some idea of the range of models which we can bring together. They vary in dimensions, scales and content. The general systems model of David Clarke (1968) seems indispensable, though the size and 'reality' of the system is a question which I come to again below. I have considered previously the contrast in the literature between 'kick' models that alter a state, and feedback models which trace an alteration of some state through a period (Gowlett 1984). Kick models seem too simple, though they could start off a feedback cycle in a 1–2 sequence. Feedback models have been favoured by numerous authors concerned with human evolution (e.g. Isaac 1972a; Alexander 1979, 1989; Tobias 1981, 1991; Wilson 1983).

When Darwin noted that the free use of the arms and hands was 'partly the cause and partly the result of man's erect position' he was recognizing both the nature of feedback loops and the difficulties of disentangling variables (Darwin 1874: 80).

Perhaps the more complete explanation is to postulate that species tend to be fairly stable systems, in which changes in one parameter tend to be controlled or countered by stabilizing forces (reviewed by Dean 1992); but when a parameter such as climate or competition changes too much, there will be a system change, which may be reinforced in a feedback loop. There is a curious contrast between the flexibility of behaviour which many species exhibit, and the high numbers of extinctions which are likely to have been due to sudden changes of environment: it may be that only a minority of species have a pathway of positive feedback change open to them.

The feedback models have normally taken a long timescale view of human evolution. Alongside them, archaeology was seeking detailed documentation, including a search for better-defined entities. These needed to do their modelling with elements larger than the individual – industries, cultural groups, traditions and species. The definitions are a difficulty, especially with archaeology, although issues of continuity/discontinuity are

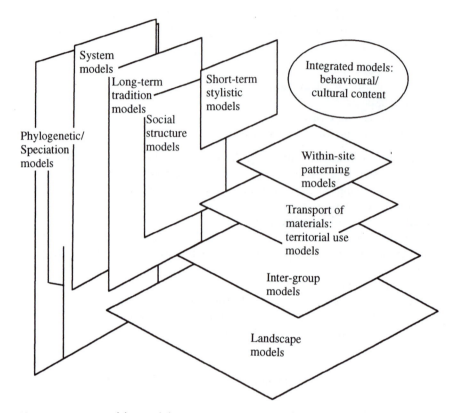

Figure 5.3 Possible models on varying scales of time and space which can be brought together in human evolution

also well-known to evolutionary biology (e.g. Smith 1975). It is not surprising that the subject has tended to turn away from these 'fuzzy building blocks' as Gamble (1986) described them. Even so, 'characterization' is important, for otherwise we do not actually know what our subject matter is (Ingold 1992). In parallel developments, there has been a reaction against the idea of 'progression' (discussed in Bowler 1986), and with the advent of behavioural ecology much modelling has become concerned with understanding the short term, the slice across evolutionary time. The intention is that these past systems should be studied for their own sake, rather than because they lead to us modern humans.

I turn now to examine the major models of human evolution, with particular consideration of their social implications. This involves starting with older literature, because it is helpful to see the contexts in which models were first introduced. Comparative modelling can be said to start with Darwin. At present it may seem as if an intense phase of archaeological work has been superseded by one of comparative approach, but the latter has been active throughout. The point of going back to older work is that when new finds are made they inform general models, but introduce new biases. When these are eventually corrected, the subject surprisingly often readopts older standpoints.

Models in the 1950s

Sometimes a book is produced at a moment when it provides an invaluable snapshot. Desmond Clark's *Prehistory of Southern Africa* is illuminating because it was published in 1959, immediately pre-dating the major hominid discoveries at Olduvai, and the interpretations of *Ramapithecus* as an early hominid. Even then Clark had twenty years of experience in Africa, knew the contexts of the Australopithecine finds, and through his work at Kalambo Falls had done much to develop the idea of 'living floors'. After discussing early 'generalized' apes such as *Proconsul* of the early Miocene Clark (1959: 59) gives us this outline:

> During the late Miocene and early Pliocene several different, and more specialized, forms of ape had developed, adapted to an arboreal life. Still others took to life on the ground in the open country and this allowed their forelimbs to develop once they no longer had to use them for locomotion. As a result the pelvic girdle and hind limbs became adapted to movement on the back legs only so that these creatures gradually began to walk in an upright posture. The fossil evidence for these creatures is provided by the remarkable discoveries made in the northern Cape and the Transvaal from 1924 onwards . . . These discoveries have proved conclusively that it was as a result of the upright carriage that man was able to expand his brain and develop a mind capable of conceptual thought.

The only documented links between Oldowan stone tools and the Australopithecines at this time were some tools found at Sterkfontein in 1957, and Clark relied more on general bone evidence for interpretation:

> Whether or not the Australopithecines were carnivores to the extent that Dart and others have suggested hinges on the interpretation of the way in which accumulations of bones found their way into the old caves. Some favour the belief that they represent the remains of the meals of the Australopithecines while others believe that they are the debris left in the lair of some extinct carnivore and that Australopithecus himself was thus one of the victims. . . . The former theory does not necessarily imply that the slenderly built Australopithecus was capable of killing the largest as well as the smallest beasts. It is much more probable that when it came to a meat diet he was to a great extent a scavenger who collected the remains left over from some carnivore's kill, or the body of a beast that had died, and carried selected parts back to his den to eat at his leisure.

Clark and other authors took a different view of hunting and scavenging when it came to the Acheulian. Here it seemed plain that the more capable early *Homo* were 'big game hunters', on the basis of Olduvai sites such as BK. Clark also emphasized the value of 'living floors' where careful excavation methods allowed artefacts to be recovered undisturbed in primary context.

Such work is evidence against a unilineal development of archaeological thought. Binford (1972) notes how Clark's appreciation of contemporary variation in the Acheulian anticipates the New Archaeology. His work also presents a more modern view than was possible once the major Olduvai finds and *Ramapithecus* had firmly set a long timescale. Clark saw in 'early communal banding the basis of the development of hunting techniques'. Indeed, most social theory of this time was based on the hunting hypothesis, owed originally to Carveth Read (1920). It was developed by Dart in relation to Australopithecus, underpinned by the bone finds at Makapansgat and the claimed 'Osteodontokeratic' culture (Dart 1957). Clark's caution was not shared at a more popular level, where authors such as Ardrey (1961) popularized the notion of the 'killer ape' (and then the 'territorial imperative' as a further explanation of human aggression, see Ardrey 1967, 1976; other views on aggression are given in Montagu 1973 and Holloway 1974).

For Washburn and Howell (1960) the central question was whether the Australopithecines were the hunters or the hunted. They felt the issue was answered by the association of artefacts and bones at Olduvai, and placed hunting as the motor of human evolution: 'Those areas of the cortex associated with persistent motivation, memory, anticipation, and imagination are greatly expanded in the human brain. These abilities are essential to complicated social life.' (Washburn and Howell 1960: 51).

Although the direct archaeological evidence strengthened the pre-occupation with hunting, modelling on a more general level led to broader social issues, as seen in Irving Hallowell's paper of 1960. This demonstrates an extraordinary continuity with recent work in its general frame, which tackles the need for more refined analysis and broaches the 'dimension of social structure'. Hallowell complained that anthropology's concentration on culture had led to its re-erection as a barrier between humans and other primates, a gulf which the evolutionary frame had seemed to bridge – and which we still struggle with.

The Olduvai event

There is widespread agreement that the discoveries of Olduvai Bed I in 1959/60 offer a kind of basepoint for assessing the early Pleistocene archaeological record (Leakey 1967, Leakey 1971, Binford 1981). They brought together early hominid remains, stone artefacts and radiometric dates of about 1.8 Myr. This was the first important use of K–Ar dating

(Evernden and Curtis 1965, Leakey 1967). The re-dating also had the result of sundering Africa from Europe and Asia in the Pleistocene record. Only recently have the other continents managed to lay claim to an archaeological record of anything like this length.

Mary Leakey's exemplary work was characterized by sound excavation, innovation in classification and cautious suggestions of analogy. Her typology has been seen as traditional and conservative relative to newer analyses, but it was far more appropriate to the African material than that of François Bordes, and is largely descriptively neutral.

The new finds also introduced a bias (cf. Clark 1959). They seemed to emphasize meat-eating, and placed more emphasis on hunting. Equally, the discovery of early *Homo* (the new species *Homo habilis*) had the effect of putting the Australopithecines on one side as the poor relations. The Olduvai Bed I finds are no longer strictly 'the early hominids' – new finds are more than twice as old – but time and again the phrase 'early hominids' implicitly refers to this period, rather than the preceding 3 million years.

Mary Leakey's own classification offers a starting point for basic analysis. For her, the Oldowan sites can be divided into four groups (Leakey 1971):

- living floors (limited vertical distribution),
- butchery or kill sites (one or more animals),
- sites with diffused material,
- river or stream channel sites.

Others have used, criticized or developed her scheme, noting that the categories are not exclusive (e.g. Isaac 1972a, 1984, Binford 1981).

Leakey's interpretations are on a modest scale, occasionally making use of analogy, as when she made comparisons with bushmen, and drew these conclusions about social life:

> it seems likely that the groups of early hominids were never very large, but comprised a sufficient number of active males to form hunting bands and to protect the females and young in case of attack. Hunting and fishing were unquestionably practised . . . but it is probable that scavenging from predator kills was also a method of obtaining meat.
>
> (1971: 259)

Leakey's site categories reflect that both the depth of sediments containing artefacts, and the density of finds, vary extensively at Olduvai so that there is 'unfortunately, no means either of assessing the length of time during which any camp site was occupied or of estimating the number of resident hominids'. This remains a serious problem: we have absolute dates, but no internal timescale. Re-dating at Olduvai has given some extra precision, but in tens of thousands of years at best (Walter *et al.* 1991).

MODELS OF HOMINIZATION

The hominid/hominoid framework

Human evolution is often seen in relation to the Olduvai Benchmark of 2 million years ago, not only by archaeologists. The ideas of camp sites and hunting at this unexpectedly early date led many to look for a longer timescale for hominization as a whole. For the early stages, this was conveniently provided by the supposed early hominid *Ramapithecus*, on a 15-million-year timescale (Simons 1967).

Now that *Ramapithecus* is relegated to being merely a Miocene ape (once more), new Pliocene finds help us to see, as in the 1950s view, that the Australopithecines are in many respects very ape-like. If we seek to establish an overall frame for hominid evolution, it will need to operate on the basis of the good fit now obtained between DNA and fossil evidence, with an implied timescale of some 6–8 million years (Goodman *et al.* 1989; for reviews see Jeffreys 1989; Chamberlain 1991). It will need to provide documentation for, or account for a number of key parameters. These would include:

- divergence from a common ancestor,
- geographical/ecological aspects of speciation,
- reduction of canines,
- evolution of bipedalism,
- changes in control systems (e.g. endocrine system),
- possible reorganization of brain in Australopithecines, and documented enlargement of brain in *Homo*;

and on a behavioural level development of:

- technological abilities,
- social institutions,
- other cultural traits,
- language (which must be underpinned by new capabilities of the brain).

Lists of characteristics have often been provided (e.g. Washburn and DeVore 1961, Holloway 1972, Isaac 1983). These are useful summaries, but have the limitation that they do not necessarily discriminate between independent and linked variables. Nor are they always exclusive, nor do they embrace different levels of explanation.

I now turn to examine more specific problems. All primates are social, and it is ever more plain that the comparative framework of African apes is vital. Issues of social structure, locomotion and other behaviour can all be studied in their context, with the obvious proviso that hominids in the first stages of culture may have features shared by no living species. (Simply to base models on a single animal such as the chimpanzee, is as

Hill [1994] notes, a dead end.) Even so, as Figure 5.2 suggests, a chimpanzee model may be at least as relevant as modern humans for the period from about 3.5 million years backwards, a view argued cogently by McGrew (1993) on behavioural grounds.

The relationship with archaeology in these models is tenuous: but when archaeology does appear, it provides documentation of and many insights into changes which must have happened by at least 2.5 Myr.

Social structure as a context

Social interactions are well known to characterize primates and other 'advanced' mammals. Monkey groups, for example, tend to exist in stable and rather close groups, 'where they co-operate not only in breeding and rearing young but in finding food and defending the group against predators' (MacKinnon 1978). Strong bonds between adults are delineated by social hierarchy, but reinforced by activities such as grooming, play, feeding and sexual activity.

Social factors are therefore likely to have played an important part in human evolution. Social structure was considered by Hallowell (1960), and in relation to chimpanzees by Reynolds (1966). Hinde (1979) has noted that in primate studies much work has centred on group size and sex ratio. These seem to him inadequate to account for selection and the resulting evolutionary patterns. He sees a hierarchical arrangement of the interactions between individuals (the primary basis of study); the relationships indicated by these; and social structure, which he sees as an abstract phenomenon. For an anthropologist this has echoes of Kroeber who regarded culture in similar terms of abstractions. In respect of culture, White (1959) criticized this view, asserting that we do not know what we mean by an abstraction. The problem is a more general one, mentioned above: how 'real' is any social structure or institution? The question has often been argued, sometimes as a philosophical issue. Systems models are of some help, although they too suffer from 'fuzziness' problems. In their essence, groups and institutions exist because they are mapped in the minds of the individuals who make them up.

For the African apes and humans some kind of comparative framework can be established. For example, Wrangham has indicated that relative to ecology chimps have larger core areas than gorillas/orangutans (Pusey 1979, Wrangham 1979). This may be linked, according to Wrangham, with the more patchy nature of resources. Compared with gorillas, chimpanzees show a more definite social grouping of males, fewer interactions between females, and considerable female transfer between groups. Wrangham wondered what justification there was for seeing the community as a bisexual social unit, and concluded that in effect the males formed alliance-groups, but that females had a more dispersed distribution, and were liable to move from group to group.

Table 5.1 Patterns of social structure in the African apes and human hunter-gatherer societies[1]

Gorillas	Chimpanzees	Humans
Stable groups (2–20)	Loose band structure (30–80)	Flexibly organized bands (30–80)
Silverback as leader	Association of males in hunting/defence	Co-operation of males
Less dominant males present		
Females as stable members of group	Females less bonded to group	Closely bonded female groups
Few interactions between females	Few interactions between females	Long-term permanent male/female relationships within band and as mobile unit
	Strong relationships between siblings	Strong father–offspring relationships
Other males in solitary existence		Extra institutional layer of structure: the 'people' (approx. 500–2000)
Generally stable relations between groups	Often antagonistic relations between groups	Stable or antagonistic relations between groups

Note

1 Compiled after multiple sources, e.g. in Lee and DeVore (1968), Dixson (1981), Wrangham (1979). Chimpanzees may be more similar to humans in that the major group may include subgroups which sometimes detach, such as consort pairs or smaller foraging parties.

Some main characteristics of African ape and human social patterning are listed in Table 5.1. It seems plain that there are linked questions of territory, mating patterns, patterns of resources, and the physical adaptations that go with them: social implications impinge on key issues such as bipedalism and sexual dimorphism, including canine reduction. Human groups appear to be most like chimpanzees in terms of male society, but they differ through having correspondingly tight links between females, plus the additional non-territorial male–female pair bond (Reynolds 1966).

Whereas out-movement is characteristic of males in monkey societies, that of females is common in ape societies. Wrangham (1979) defines the range of a community as the area occupied by all its males. In the Gombe area he referred to the overlapping areas of two bands. N and S were partially separate, occupying 13 and 10 sq. km respectively. These areas are fairly small in relation to daily movement, so that 'over a four-day period prime males sometimes approached all four boundaries'. But female travel distances were considerably shorter. The result was of males and females nesting separately at night, but often maintaining vocal contact. This practice would be safe in the forest, where there are few predators, but would seem a risky strategy for hominids in more open bush.

It seems likely that changes in social structure, perhaps in response to altered environment, provide a background to hominization. Sexual dimorphism and size are linked (e.g. McHenry 1994), and so is size with the ability to range over a larger territory. As so often it is not plain which is cause and which effect, but Wrangham observes that the cost of locomotion is a major determinant of the capacity for group territoriality. The incentive for a larger range in chimpanzees is therefore primarily social, but adjusted to cost in effort. This suggests a delicate balance between social needs and economy. Human foragers operate at low density, without rigorous social 'packing' of territories. In hominids who required raw materials, the primary motivation of larger range may be (technologically) economic, perhaps stemming from social arrangements adapted to fairly dry conditions, but altered feeding patterns must play a part.

A principal challenge to archaeologists has been to see that chimpanzees embrace many characteristics which were previously attributed to 'hominization'. Some of the continuities between chimpanzee and human behaviour can be listed after Goodall (1976) and McGrew (1993); these are all behaviours of chimpanzees which also occur in humans (Table 5.2).

It is also necessary to reconcile this behaviour with the brain enlargement visible in *Homo*. Apes can clearly do a great deal with 500 cc of brain, to the extent that they can be said to be 'in the same world' as us (Mason 1979). Brain enlargement cannot easily be ascribed to the needs of social intelligence; there are also difficulties in ascribing it to technology. Language may have a role (cf. Aiello and Dunbar 1993; see p. 167).

Table 5.2 Some elements of behaviour shared by chimpanzees and humans

Tool-use
Tool-making
Re-use of stone tools at work sites
Processing of bones with tools
Hunting and eating of meat
Extracting and eating of insects
Scavenging of carcasses from other predators
Food sharing
Prolonged period of maturation
Social learning
Close family relationships
Non-verbal communication
Symbol use (in captivity)

Sources: Goodall (1976), McGrew (1993), Savage-Rumbaugh (1986), Boesch (1993)

Early stages of hominization: bipedalism and other changes

Bipedalism was certainly one of the earlier developments of hominization. The reduction of the canines and changes in tooth enamel have often been considered alongside this. Finds are not complete enough to document a precise sequence. The fossils from Hadar show bipedalism already established, but the upper body was still decidedly ape-like (Johanson *et al.* 1987, Hunt 1994).

The recent finds of *Australopithecus ramidus* from Aramis cast no more light on bipedalism, because lower body parts have not yet been found, but they show canines distinctly larger than in *A. afarensis*. In relative size the canines approach those of female gorillas, although they are more hominid-like in morphology. If an ancestor–descendant relationship between *ramidus* and *afarensis* can be assumed, the particular interest of the finds lies in the fairly rapid change over a million years.

Changes in locomotion have been considered since Darwin (1871), who took a 'long view', asserting that all the apes were in a transitional state. Huxley (1963) made the point that all the apes very definitely have feet, rather than a second pair of hands. This development probably goes with adoption of a relatively upright trunk posture, and reflects weight transmission as much as locomotion. Thus as a starting possibility we have the suggestion that locomotion is a compromise adaptation involving all four limbs, and as Huxley urges we must take into account the complete adaptation (Huxley 1963). Hunt (1994) reminds us that most primates may spend at least half their time in feeding. To be able to do this conveniently may be more important than longer-distance movement, or flight, except where predators are important. The main factors affecting the compromise may be:

- The feeding environment, including nature of collected food, the vertical range of foods from ground to canopy, and patchiness of the vegetation involved;
- Length of total travel distances;
- Predator avoidance/predation;
- Carrying needs.

Recent years have seen two major hypotheses, those of Hunt and Wheeler. Hunt's work is based on observation of bipedalism in chimpanzees, and study of skeletal adaptations (e.g. 1994). He supports earlier hypotheses based on feeding adaptations (the Jolly/Rose/Wrangham hypothesis). Hunt demonstrates that most chimpanzee bipedalism is seen in feeding contexts, often linked with arm-hanging, or support. It is especially helpful where the feeding involves collecting many small objects, such as fruits. An environment with a preponderance of small trees within ground reach would therefore probably act as a stimulus. Hunt notes that early bipedal adaptations were less efficient for locomotion than those of humans.

Wheeler, in contrast, supports a thermoregulatory basis for bipedalism, pointing out the heat-saving and thus water-saving benefits of walking upright, particularly during the hotter hours of the day (e.g. Wheeler 1984, 1994). Hunt (1994) criticizes this view on several grounds, finding elements which it cannot account for, such as the long period for which hominids retained long arms alongside bipedalism.

It is not plain, however, that both explanations are not feasible. Evolution is not teleological: humans would not become bipedal so as later to range widely, carry artefacts and hunt prey. The adaptation would have to work validly at every intermediate stage. It seems a favoured habit of evolution to adjust an existing adaptation gradually for one set of reasons, then to use it for new purposes.

The second phase – the Wheeler model – might well be linked with larger territories, and the evidence of carrying which can be seen in the early archaeological record. According to Hunt, tool-carrying does not imply bipedalism. He argues that carrying is not a relevant component, because chimpanzees can carry objects well. But McGrew (1993) notes that chimp tripedalism is awkward, and used only over short distances. Chimps carry objects when they need them, but they do not do so habitually. The transport of a termite fishing stick from nest to nest is quite literally a lightweight example.

Bipedal creatures have a greater chance of having an object to hand. Predator avoidance may not have been a first stimulus, but since chimpanzees readily pick up sticks when threatened (Kortlandt 1980), there may have been more incentive for early hominids to do so steadily in a more predator-ridden environment. Lovejoy (1981) saw the ability to carry food as an important element in a provisioning model for bipedalism.

The upheavals of Miocene climate have often been invoked as an explanation for the development of bipedalism (e.g. Ardrey 1967). (The background is explained by Van Couvering and Van Couvering 1976.) Hunt (1994) cites Pickford (1991), to the effect that the raising of the Ruwenzori block disturbed air currents and created new climatic patterns, extending the savannah. This idea is appealing, but was critically examined by Bishop (1976), who examined evidence from all Miocene and Pliocene localities of East Africa. He concluded that there was an essential continuity of fauna, flora and climatic evidence.

As with the flow of archaeological ideas, the problem lies partly in invoking a unilineal sequence. General temperature dropped during the Miocene, and forest cover may have decreased, but it is likely that there was always regional diversity, and certainly always a range of climatic and altitudinal zones. Geographic separation is one of the best-established modes of speciation, and so may be invoked for testing against the evidence (Foley 1987). Is it possible to see the hominids as a regional adaptation? One difficulty is to explain their distribution in relation to the African apes and European dryopithecines. We know that there were gorilla-like apes in Greece about 10 million years ago (Dean and Delson 1992); we also know that there was a phase of hyperaridity in which the Mediterranean dried up about 6 million years ago. The following is therefore offered as a possible rough outline for the origins of bipedalism (Figures 5.4 and 5.5):

1 There was a largely continuous distribution of forest-cover and apes across Africa–Middle East–Europe in the middle Miocene.
2 From about 8–6 million years this range was broken by intense aridity around the Mediterranean and North Africa, leading to greater regional differentiation of apes.
3 Terrestrialization of habits of African apes, as upper gallery opportunities in forest are limited/eliminated, and other niches are taken by monkeys.
4 The hominids differentiated in the more arid zone, which may have included North-east Africa and the Middle East, and perhaps the Sahara area. A feeding adaptation based on small trees and clumped resources created the bipedalism of the lower body.
5 This constituted a preadaptation for other niches, exploited in different ways by different species, such as early *Homo* and the robust australopithecines. Thermoregulatory changes. Incipient carrying.
6 The continued Rift formation, including the lifting of the Ruwenzori block (often invoked in explaining hominid origins) broke the forest cover across central Africa, establishing a savannah corridor to the south. Hominids expanded through this into the drier parts of southern Africa, appearing there before 3 million years ago.

Figure 5.4 Scenarios of bipedalism: (a) feeding positions in which bipedalism is favoured; (b) a quadrupedal animal encounters a dilemma in managing resources, a defensive artefact and offspring; (c) a specialization of bipedalism

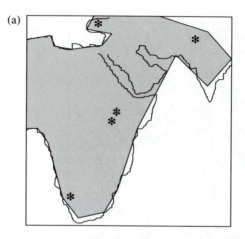

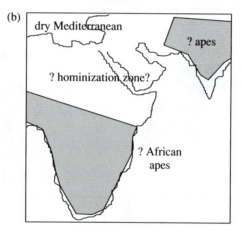

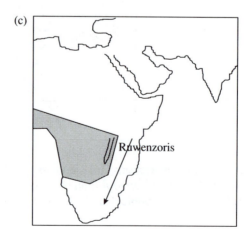

This model (or better, scenario) which contains elements of many others, would fit the timescale of hominid evolution, and also its speciations. It is important not to be naive about past environmental diversity. As Williams (1979, 1984) has emphasized, forest cover in Africa has not been continuous in the past even in regions now forested: glacial cycles have had profound effects.

MODELS OF EARLY HOMINID BEHAVIOUR IN THE EARLY PLEISTOCENE

Archaeology comes into the picture with the earliest documented stone artefacts, dated to about 2.5 million years (Roche 1980, Harris 1983, Toth 1985). Further early sites have been reported by Asfaw *et al.* (1992) and Kibunjia (1994). The artefacts might be regarded as initially no more than a minor cultural trait, but they rapidly become common and lead to a concentrated focus of study, in which archaeology is the lynch pin. The Olduvai evidence appeared to extend campsites or 'living floors' to early times. On these foundations the food-sharing model of Glynn Isaac became the most important generalizing model of the 1970s to 1980s. The background of his work can be traced through his 1968 paper, which traces inspiration from Washburn (e.g. 1960, 1963, 1967).

The essential aspect of Washburn's idea was that stone tools clinched the link between australopithecines and hunting in some form. The australopithecines themselves, in South Africa and at Olduvai, were found ingrassland environments (it was thought; the Olduvai environments mayhave been wetter and more wooded). Baboons had adapted to a terrestrial savannah life; hominids had gone through a similar process. Thus, analogies could be made, but also similarities and differences could be set out in list form. The similarities would provide comparative models (the role of the baboons) but the differences would point to unique human characteristics. 'The tool-using, ground-living hunting way of life created the large human brain rather than a large-brained man discovering certain new ways of life' (Washburn and Howell 1960: 49). These ideas, concentrating on the importance of hunting, were set out in a number of papers (Washburn 1963, Washburn and DeVore 1961, Washburn and Lancaster 1968).

Figure 5.5 Maps suggesting possible geographic origins and progression of bipedalism: (a) suggested relatively continuous distribution of apes in Miocene forests c. 10–15 Myr; (b) distribution of forests and apes broken by hyperaridity of Mediterranean zone, c. 6 Myr; (c) postulated southwards movement of hominids in Pliocene as mountain-building and climate/ vegetation changes open savannah corridor perhaps c. 4 Myr

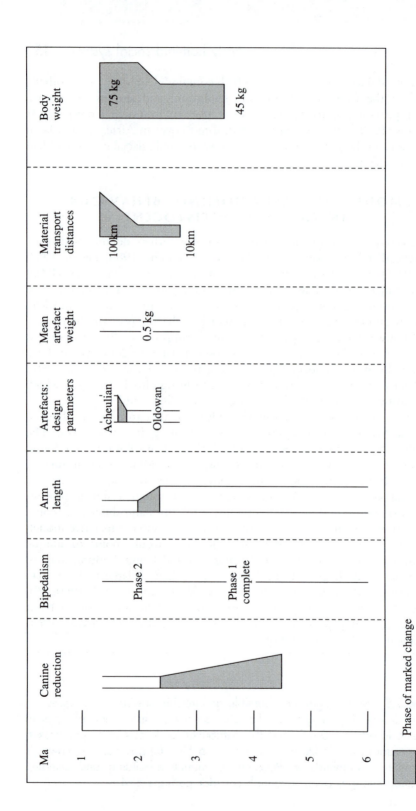

Figure 5.6 Some characters of hominization highlighting documented phases of major change

Background to the food-sharing model

The food-sharing model was anticipated by Le Gros Clark (1967), who saw it as a major step in hominization, and perhaps a precondition for the evolution of cultural abilities. Isaac felt that there were many topics which could not be investigated archaeologically but he believed that Washburn (1965) and Washburn and DeVore (1961) had selected questions that might be answered from the archaeological record: the existence of home bases; the size of cohabiting groups; territorial ranges and population densities, these all being matters in which human and primate behaviour were seen consistently to be separated. Isaac believed that archaeological methods 'must stand on their own merits' (like Binford 1968), but he also felt that the 'most useful and economic hypotheses will be suggested by situations that are better documented than prehistoric ones' (Isaac 1968). This can be seen as a call for analogy, but also for an examination of archaeological evidence by new means.

Isaac's views on these topics certainly began to take shape when he was working at Olorgesailie in the 1960s, but their gestation can also be linked with his work at Koobi Fora, where he began work in 1969. The period was marked by two important theoretical papers (1972a and b), followed by the full food-sharing thesis (Isaac 1976: the draft had been prepared in 1974). In part Isaac's formulation may have been a response to the published views of scholars in other disciplines. As he said, it had 'become fashionable for all kinds of research workers to present models'. These included a number of expositions based on a single discipline or primate model: Lancaster (1967) – primate studies; Fox (1967) – social anthropology; Reynolds (1966) – chimpanzees; Jolly (1970) – the seed eating model (baboons).

Several other compilations were more convincing to Isaac because they shared 'the practice of treating anatomy, diet, tool involvement and behaviour as interrelated parts of an integrated system of adaptation'. These models, advanced by Washburn (e.g. 1965), Campbell (1966) and Pilbeam (1972), were 'not very specific' on archaeology, which Isaac wished to tie in. The essential components of the resulting food-sharing model were:

- home bases,
- food-sharing,
- the concept of a 'protohuman' phase followed by a human phase,
- earliest technology,
- division of labour,
- cultural elaboration based on a feedback loop of these other elements.

The rationale was the need for models that took into account complete systems, not just one component. The source of this integrated approach was apparently multiple: Isaac was bringing together comparative approaches derived from primate studies, cultural approaches, and the concepts of systems models, as also discussed by David Clarke (1968).

Although this work was centred on archaeology, in principle Isaac found 'it easiest to approach the model building proposition by way of a comparison of human behaviour with the behaviour of man's closest living relatives, the African apes'. In effect he was drawing contrasts, listing them. He emphasized differences in range, the concept of the home base, and food-sharing, which apes did not have. He saw the interactions as the basis for later technological evolution and refinement of the system. It may thus be seen as a multiple feedback system.

The model could have been criticized on several grounds, for example that other primates have home bases, or that they have food-sharing. The main ground actually used in criticism was the archaeological evidence for/against home bases. The chief but not only critic was Lewis Binford (e.g. the *Bones* book of 1981). His concern with challenging assumptions and 'just-so' stories was derived partly from the perspective of modern ethnography in the arctic, and partly from a more general preoccupation of the 'New Archaeology' – transforming archaeology from traditional culture-history to the 'processual'. His evident interest in African archaeology (Binford 1972) was expanded in his Olorgesailie book review (Binford 1977).

According to Binford, Isaac's arguments about food-sharing and home bases depended on the accuracy of the 'assumption that the integrity of the deposits is great'. Binford was sceptical, believing that 'All the facts gleaned from the deposits interpreted as living sites have served as the basis for making up "just-so stories" about our hominid past'. The main thrust of these criticisms was methodological, and Binford was rarely concerned to present an alternative model explicitly. He goes so far as to describe the hominids as 'the most marginal of scavengers', but saw this as a direct implication of the evidence of the bones: 'Our ancestors were simply taking advantage of matter abandoned and/or ignored by other animals.' In other respects, he appears to think of them as baboon-like, roaming across the landscape in troops, perhaps focused by the natural features of the landscape and its resources into 'routed foraging' (Potts 1994).

The critiques and responses developed over a period of years. Glynn Isaac stimulated a number of research studies, largely centred on site formation processes and taphonomy. His earlier ideas were victim as much of his own analyses and those of his students as of Binford. An example is provided by the classic study of the East Turkana site FxJj50 (Bunn *et al.* 1980). Here it was possible to document limited disturbance, for example through re-fitting of artefacts and bones. The authors argued that some specimens had been fractured on the spot, and that the fracture patterns on some of the bones suggested breakage with hammers. As on other sites cutmarks were found on some bones. It was admitted that scavenging carnivores had been present, as well as the tool-making hominids. Although there seemed an ideal case here for clinching the model of the home base, Isaac and his colleagues were concerned not to do so: they expressed uncertainty as to whether this was a home-base camp, or simply a 'locality used for meat-eating and tool-making'. They talk about multiple influences contributing to a complex input–output system.

Later thoughts on Olorgesailie and Olduvai have shown more than one oscillation of views. Shipman *et al.* (1981) argued for human involvement in the killing of the Olorgesailie *Theropithecus* baboons, but the patterns of bone breakage did not convince Binford and Todd (1982). More recently, the studies of Koch (1990) have strengthened the idea that butchery is not the explanation. The conjunction of many handaxes and the splintered bones of *Theropithecus* at Olorgesailie is still difficult to explain. The enigmatic situation is one for specialists in bone taphonomy to argue, but the majority of large Acheulian sites are found with no fauna, or a mixed bag. Thus the Olorgesailie circumstances are so far unique (rather like the Olduvai DK circle) and cannot safely be used as a plank of interpretation.

Olduvai has similarly been the centre of more work. The DK circle in Bed I was explained by Mary Leakey as a possible hut base. Its status as a structure, and the extent of hominid involvement in the Bed I bone assemblages have both been debated. Binford's view of a minimal hominid role was in effect extended to the DK stone circle. Bunn and Kroll have claimed a more intense hominid involvement in the site, on the basis of cutmarks (Bunn 1981, 1986, Bunn and Kroll 1986) and are supported by the work of Oliver (1994). Potts has emphasized the dangers of the lake shore, and developed a stone cache model, on the basis of computer simulations (Potts 1988). This would see hominids as bringing stones to concentrations in the dangerous areas over a period. In this view the DK circle can be explained as a large stone cache; or alternatively as disturbance caused by tree roots.

Models based on bones have paid little direct attention to the stone circle. The difficulty in omitting it is that the stone circle is objectively a real feature (Figure 5.7). No geological explanation has been offered for it, and the critiques have not offered a detailed archaeological analysis. The tree roots hypothesis does not explain either the scale of the feature or the density of the stone distribution, or the small piles of stones which Mary Leakey recorded around the margins. The circle is about 0.5 metres above a lava substratum. Basalt often weathers into large numbers of cobbles, which can migrate and be rearranged by natural agencies: but could such forces have created the distribution which Mary Leakey has excavated?

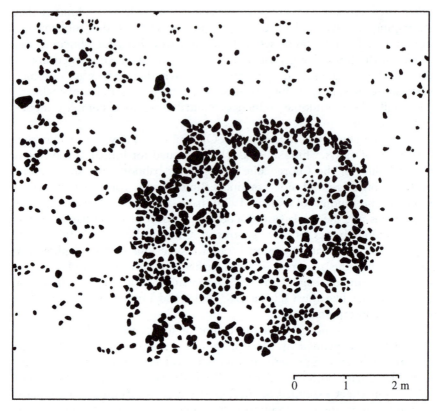

0   1   2 m

Figure 5.7 The Olduvai circle from site DK in Bed I (redrawn after Leakey 1971)

Central place foraging

In later papers Isaac abandoned the terminology of his classic formula: home bases were replaced by the idea of 'central place foraging' (1984). Recent work, such as that by Hunt on bipedalism or Schick on site formation, has suggested that larger trees would make an attractive environment, in which hominids would have adequate protection against carnivores. This is the 'favoured places' hypothesis of Schick – a natural descendant of Isaac's 'sand between the toes' idea that hominids would like the combination of sandy channels and access to the fringing gallery forest, but without the co-operative implications of 'food-sharing' (Schick 1987). Even this does not avoid controversy, since work by O'Connell *et al.* (1988) on Hadza butchery suggests that concentrations of bones in such channels may not represent occupation sites. Sept, considering debris and nests left by wild chimpanzees, takes another line: 'chimpanzees are known to return to localized groves of nesting trees and favourite feeding sites in a range of different habitat types' (1992). Old nests show that the areas are revisited. Thus individual episodes add up to a pattern, which contrasts with the 'traditional' home base idea. Wrangham (1992) asks 'But what is the contrast? The idea that hominid archaeological sites could have arisen through repeated returns to sleep in a limited area seems close to the concept of a home base or central place for foraging.' The wheel is near to coming full circle: Foley (1977, 1981) used the language of home bases then in vogue, but presciently plotted out artefact distributions which indicated favoured places. Many primates show 'long-term loyalty to particular sleeping sites' (Anderson 1984), and it seems unlikely that they select these without reference to local foraging opportunities.

Critiques of the home-base/food-sharing model in archaeology by-passed some of the new problems which they raised. Home bases became regarded as implausible, because they had not been proven. The implication is that only later humans would have the abilities to structure local environments in this way (Stringer and Gamble 1993), but this seems to fly in the face of evidence of chimpanzees and baboons, who are highly familiar with the positions of their sleeping sites (Anderson 1984: 189). Archaeology is tending to replace assumptions about sites with alternatives that make assumptions about abilities. There is a danger of making interpretations that would route the early hominids regularly through the sites, allow them to drop myriad objects from trees, inflict cutmarks on bone, but effectively banish them at night – without any evidence that some other roosting place was safer or more desirable.

The hydraulic jumble argument, suggesting that all sites are disturbed, because they are found in sediments laid by water, was not the most powerful element of Binford's critique. Tests such as those applied by Schick, Toth and others show that relatively undisturbed sites can be recognized (Schick 1991, Schick and Toth 1993). But ethnographic studies also show that large numbers of bones can be amassed in a short period by hunter-gatherers, and that bones can also accumulate without human agency. Thus the problem is more one of unravelling multiple events and palimpsests. Isaac realized this, as did Diane Gifford-Gonzalez at East Turkana (Isaac 1989). The potential bias of the data is evident, but the problem of establishing an internal timescale has until recently been an unspoken problem. It has now been raised in a different guise as 'time-averaging' (Stern 1994).

What then was the effect of the Binford critique? Above all it made people think about the sites in fresh terms. The debate itself was fought on rather misleading terms. Isaac claimed there were home bases that had a specific importance, as a foundation for evolution of hominid abilities. Binford argued that existence of the home bases had not been proven. If we structure the situation logically, it becomes clear that:

1 home bases are not unique to humans;
2 flaked artefact production is unique to hominids but not necessarily linked with home bases;
3 but even if no existing sites are unequivocally home bases on the basis of our sample, this does not mean that such sites do not exist;
4 home bases and food-sharing cannot be put in a one-to-one relation: either can occur without the other.

Binford's contribution was in part to shake the kaleidoscope. The pieces have come together again in another but not altogether dissimilar form.

RECENT DEVELOPMENTS IN HOMINID PALAEOECOLOGY

Debates about early sites have not always centred on these issues. It is too easy to see 'early hominid studies' as restricted to Africa, or to a world of English-speaking scholars. The recent work at Boxgrove, the analyses of bones from Aridos, the excavations of Roche and colleagues at Isenya, or the final publication of Ubeidiya, are examples which help to strike a balance (Roberts 1986, Roche et al. 1988, Villa 1990, Bar-Yosef and Goren-Inbar 1992).

Increasingly, new research has tackled general problems rather than single sites, and recently discussion of the general issues has converged into a tangible 'hominid behavioural ecology' (e.g. Foley 1984, 1987, papers in Oliver et al. 1994). Such work must involve studying every aspect of an ecosystem, and has led to a series of questions:

- What models do we have of land use?
- What habitats were preferred?
- What information do faunal remains yield?
- What is the role of scavenging, and how intense was competition over carcasses?
- Is there a fundamental plant niche of early hominids?
- What structure is retained in early archaeological occurrences, on macro- and micro-scale?
- What is the time relationship between sediment series and sites?

Research on these topics has been carried out increasingly in an actualistic frame – based on experiments, or on observation of relevant living systems. Access to early sites for excavation has become difficult. The word 'actualistic' should not hide that this is once more a comparative frame. It bears the risk that it may tell us what hominids might have done, not what they did. But it brings us closer to some real world, through being based on present actualities. To what extent are the alternatives models? They are listed by Potts (1994) as:

- central place foraging,
- stone cache,
- routed foraging,
- riparian woodland.

One may argue that these are not all clearly formulated models, nor again mutually exclusive. This view is compatible with Potts' observation that the ideas tend to become regarded as rival hypotheses, and miss the point of the need to study variability in the ancient record (which may encompass more than one of them). Potts supports a search for behavioural ecological variables, of which he lists five (resource transport; tethering; habitat heterogeneity; predation potential and social aggregation). It is interesting that one of these, social aggregation, is a secondary character: not dependent primarily on ecological evidence – but on archaeology. Transport of resources and 'tethering' do not seem logically separable. Table 5.3 makes a comparison of the variables listed by Isaac (1972a) with those isolated by Potts. Not only is there an overlap across the years, but the earlier set seems to make a tighter distinction between primary evidence and inference. On the other hand, behavioural ecology is largely concerned with mapping out a complete set of relations in the past, so it may be fair to express variables that are sought, as well as those easily available.

TIME FOR REAPPRAISAL? OTHER APPROACHES: THE ARTEFACTS

The bones debate, or the food-sharing debate, may have led research away from questions that would be easier to solve. It was based on set piece oppositions, but the possibilities are clearly not exclusive (cf. McBrearty 1989). Bone studies often bring stone age archaeology to life, informing us about economy. For Binford (1981), they are far more important than stones. Nevertheless, the idea that animal bones are central to studying early human behaviour is not yet borne out by conclusions for this period. Arguably the recent debates distracted attention from earlier systematic studies of artefact evidence, such as that of Clark (1969) at Kalambo Falls, Howell and colleagues at Isimila (Howell *et al.* 1962, Kleindienst 1962, Howell and Clark 1963), Leakey (1971) at Olduvai and Isaac (1977) at Olorgesailie. That work had a concern with precise documentation of variability which was remarkably forward-looking (cf. Binford 1972). Table 5.4 presents a list of the aspects that have been studied then and more recently, and suggests the number of dimensions that can be reached via technology.

Ecological language aside, behaviour may be seen fundamentally as 'what things do'. The archaeological material is organized in space and time, and thus is an index to behaviour, to what has been done – if not

Table 5.3   Criteria for modelling early Pleistocene hominid behavioural systems: a comparison of elements from Isaac (1972a) and Potts (1994)[1]

Isaac 1972a

Archaeologically observable phenomena	*Possible interpretations*
(+) Location and density of sites and relicts	(+) Aspects of demographic arrangement, land-use and ecology
(O) Site sizes and internal structure	(O) Estimates of community size and aspects of organization
N Seasonality and duration of occupation	Patterns of movement and aspects of economic strategy
N Food refuse and faeces	Aspects of diet and subsistence practices
( ) Introduced materials	Range of movement or contact
N Artefact forms	Aspects of role in economy/society
Level of complexity of material culture	Rule systems (in part)
Propagation patterns of material culture	Traditions (historical, geographic and sociological implications)

Potts 1994

Ecological variables
( ) Resource transport: the tendency of hominids to carry resources from one place to another
( ) Tethering: the proximity of debris to known stationary resources
(+) Habitat heterogeneity: the degree to which debris concentrations correspond with distinctive habitats or vegetation zones
N   Predation potential: the overlap between carnivores and hominids in their use of carcasses and space
(O) Strength of social aggregations: tendency for a primary social focus to which kin and other group members return
(O) Material evidence: shelters, hearths or other distinctive features or spatial patterns

---

Note
1   Symbols indicate variables which appear to be essentially the same or highly related in the two analyses. Some expanded statements of description have been omitted.

all of it, at least part of it. It therefore has a potential for cognitive studies, as is now widely recognized (cf. papers in Gibson and Ingold 1993). Numbers of authors have made studies of early artefact form, with implicit or explicit recognition of psychological aspects (e.g. Wynn 1979, 1985, 1989, 1991, Gowlett 1982, 1984, Robson Brown 1993, Belfer-Cohen and Goren-Inbar 1994). They have adopted various approaches, but in recent years there seems to have been a convergence of values and basic

Table 5.4 Examples of lines of archaeological research in Lower Palaeolithic studies over the last generation

Site spatial configuration Howell and Clark (1963) Leakey (1971) Roberts (1986)	Toth (1985) Bradley and Sampson (1986) Bar-Yosef and Goren-Inbar (1992)
Definition of entities Bishop and Clark (1967) Clarke (1968) Isaac (1977)	*Artefacts – morphology* Roe (1968) Isaac (1977) Wynn (1979) Wynn (1981, 1985) Wynn and Tierson (1990)
Regional/assemblage variation Kleindienst (1962) Isaac (1977) Bar-Yosef and Goren-Inbar (1992) Wynn and Tierson (1990)	*Artefacts – modalities in design* Gowlett (1988) *Artefacts – allometry* Crompton and Gowlett (1993) Gowlett and Crompton (1994)
Artefacts – typology Kleindienst (1962) Leakey (1971) Isaac (1977)	*Artefacts – transport* Hay (1976) Clark (1980) Wilson (1988) Bunn (1994)
Artefacts – technology/replication Roche (1980)	

conclusions (Gowlett, in press). The material offers potential of this nature:

1 Landscape: artefacts provide an indication of raw material sources, how well they were known, how exclusive they were; how far material was brought. They thus give an indication of ranging behaviour, travel duration and artefact curation.
2 Within site, artefacts provide information about design content, function and an index of concentrations of activities, with indications of duration of activities.

The information can be strung into routines or chains, which show us how organisms navigate through space and time. Weight of material transported has the potential to provide information about biomechanics and costs. Distance of transport tells us about time expended. Concentrations give us an idea of how much there was return to a set place. Site BK at Olduvai, or 10/5 at Chesowanja, are examples where vast quantities of artefacts have been brought to one 'favoured place' over a long period (Leakey 1971, Gowlett *et al.* 1981).

The artefacts allow us to map out navigation in time and space, and thus provide a schema of decision making (Gowlett 1984). In this large sites are as important as small, although the latter are now more favoured in study. Most analyses of early material concentrate on a few Oldowan sites, but there is little reason for analyses to be restricted to the earliest Pleistocene and to Africa: a much better comparative frame would be obtained by combining the Oldowan and Acheulian, and by beginning to compare Africa, Europe and Asia.

Most artefact research is now geared towards analysis of the dynamics of assemblage formation, rather than to the old static classifications of typology. This exercise may be highly successful, but early hominids, like chimpanzees, were probably not making or using technology all the time. Technology is only one aspect of ancient hominid life, and this poses the question: how much of a system remains? How much can we reconstruct other aspects of life from it?

An analysis by L.A. White remains useful. He conceived culture as divisible into these aspects – sociological, technological and philosophical (ideological) (White 1943, 1947/1984: 117, 1954/1987: 215). Technology mediates between humans and nature; the sociological aspect between humans and humans. The philosophical provides knowledge and structure, overlapping the others. For White technology was far the most important, because of the mastery of the environment that it allowed: he saw it as an independent variable, with the social as a function of it. Anthropologists are less likely to agree today. Figure 5.8 attempts to place the elements in a frame. The sociological is easier to see as an independent variable, as it occurs in other primate societies without culture (Hallowell 1960), and thus is the foundation. But cultural rules filter down into it, and restructure it. The philosophical must structure the technological,

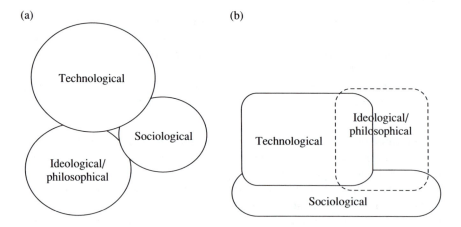

Figure 5.8 The technological, sociological and philosophical (ideological) domains of culture: (a) after L.A. White; (b) re-arranged according to the argument of this chapter

offering a framework of information including stylistic elements. The model need not be applied too rigorously, but if the fundamentals of the analysis have value, then the archaeology may be seen not merely as technology, but as one domain exhibiting 'connectivity' with the others.

An Acheulian example

Implicitly the artefacts can be used to recover information in the other domains. These are summarized in Tables 5.3 and 5.4. How important is the technology? To assess this we can aim to set up another set of variables through detailed study. The approach can be applied to the early industries of the Oldowan (down to about 1.5 Myr), but the succeeding Acheulian is more amenable because of the greater number of sites, and the more evident complexity of material. Kilombe is offered as an example (Table 5.5). On this large site complex in Kenya, probably in the age range 0.8–1.0 million years, there is a vast concentration of material, distributed on an extended surface, and consisting largely of bifaces and cobbles (Gowlett 1978, 1991, 1993b). Small flakes and scrapers are also present. Variability is restricted on the main surface, but evident elsewhere. Table 5.5 is intended to list the parameters of evidence.

Cultural rule systems in technology

The bifaces and their rule systems remain a puzzle, although recent work has explored new aspects of variation (Wynn and Tierson 1990, Crompton and Gowlett 1993, Gowlett and Crompton 1994). Many bifaces were evidently made for immediate or near-immediate use in butchery, as at Boxgrove (Roberts 1986). But others were transported for long distances (e.g. obsidian specimens at Olorgesailie, Kilombe and Gadeb; Isaac 1977, Clark 1980, Gowlett 1993b). When raw material is transported to site, pre-working is now well documented (Toth 1985, Schick 1991), it is more economical to carry blanks which will be good for tool-making. This may also give some hint of why some bifaces are made better than necessary. One can postulate a contrast between *ad hoc* specimens and those made for curation. The makers may have paid more attention to the latter, knowing that they would be used over a period, and a more idealized view of them may have crept in, precisely because they were more separated from immediate function. Use of good raw material provides insufficient explanation for well-made specimens: the maker has more control over good material, but is under no compulsion from the material to carry on working to impose a fine state of finish.

It seems likely that the basic rules in handaxe manufacture are functionally governed, though largely culturally transmitted. The rules may be reinforced by the individual maker's experience (Gowlett, in

Table 5.5 Kilombe as an example of parameters of evidence. There is no consensus over a basic unit of cultural information: the techno-units of Oswalt, memes of Dawkins, or even mind-bytes. Nevertheless, over 30 fairly distinct parameters of knowledge can be recognized. These must be far fewer than actually existed.

Assemblage variability	Number of parameters of knowledge
A,B,C and D variants of Kleindienst	? = 4 parameters known to makers
Manuports	
• cobbles	1
• hammerstones	1
Artefacts	
• heavy duty (linked with knowledge of pounding, etc.)	1
• scrapers (knowledge of retouching, position of retouch)	2
• flake properties: knowledge of sharp edges	1
Bifaces	
• knowledge of size (normal distribution)	1
• knowledge of planes of Length, Breadth and Thickness	3
• pointedness	1
• allometry – four adjustments	4
• categories, e.g. handaxes and cleavers, 'large' group and 'small' group[1]	4 (+)
• chains of procedure (routines)	1 (+)
Transport – knowledge of properties of/distance of	
• trachyphonolite (local)	
• trachyte (c. 3–5 km)	
• olivine basalt (c. 15 km)	
• obsidian	(?) = 8 parameters or more
Physical geographic environment	
• multiple parameters, not definable	??
Fauna	
• possible knowledge of habits, presence, etc.	?? of multiple species

Note
1 Isolated by cluster analysis.

press). The following is an example of a 'rule' which appears to be observed: in general the Acheulian knappers appear to have been pre-occupied with keeping the tip area thin, even and especially in those specimens where a substantial mass was required. Beyond direct functional requirements, however, there seems to have been an area of free play, which was subject to variation. This element was considered by Isaac (1972a), who thought that local craft traditions might drift in a random or stochastic manner. This observation seems to have been borne out by more recent studies, which sometimes indicate that biface sets very far apart in space and time may be very similar (e.g. the Kariandusi obsidian bifaces and the Cunette series from Sidi Abderrahman in Morocco, Gowlett 1993b).

Language origins

To consider the number of variables recorded in the artefacts at sites such as Kilombe leads naturally towards the study of language origins, because it raises the question of whether so much information could be transmitted without language. Language is of fundamental importance in the human condition, but very different opinions have been expressed about its origins and significance in shaping the mind (e.g. Deacon 1992, Duff et al. 1992, Davidson and Noble 1993, Lieberman et al. 1992), and it must be admitted that there is no direct evidence from the early periods of archaeology (Graves 1994). Comparative approaches, such as that of Aiello and Dunbar (1993), dealing with brain size and group size, as well as the symbolic/conceptual element, seem as powerful as those dealing with fossil evidence.

To what extent, if any, do the archaeological data offer a guide to the presence of language, and cultural identity in an exclusive stylistic sense? The number of parameters may just possibly offer some guide to interpreting the archaeological material. If we can find so many rule systems that they could not easily be conveyed by copying alone, this might be a hint, but not a stronger one than is provided by anatomical evidence in any case (cf. Tobias 1991). More convincing would be a demonstration that there are rules embedded in the material that would not be visually obvious to the maker, and so which could not be transmitted by simple copying. It is possible that some of the allometric adjustments observed by Crompton and Gowlett (1993) meet such criteria, but an alternative position would be that they are functionally enforced.

Thus language may well remain elusive in the archaeological evidence, but the evidence has other value: it demonstrates that a great deal of information was being transmitted culturally, regardless of the channel of communication.

The idea of progression

Ideally we could weld together archaeological and other models for human evolution. This would entail grasping the problems of relating levels of biological and cultural evolution (cf. Lee 1992). The distinctions between these were fairly well defined by evolutionary biologists of a previous generation, but are blurred both by the extensive middle ground of learned behaviour in many mammals, and the difficulties of distinguishing between single 'cultural traits' and a 'culture'. Both levels have been linked with 'progression', and both have tended to kick against that link.

In the archaeology the case for progression is that 2 or 3 million years ago, hominids were 'half-brained' as Hallowell (1960) put it, and now the surviving hominid has a greatly enlarged brain. Technology was rudimentary, and is now dauntingly complex. Social institutions have similarly grown. Against this, we must admit that some modern peoples have technology no more complex than that of the Oldowan; and that non-industrial ways of life may have equal value. Also that the Pleistocene record itself shows much variation, rather than any steady progression. It is tempting to discard the idea of progression altogether, but naive if we do so formally and then keep resurrecting it implicitly. Everybody 'knows' that the simplest populations of recent times have great complexities of social behaviour that were probably not shared by *Homo habilis*.

Here too we can seek to tabulate the possibilities:

1 greater complexity can be documented objectively, e.g. as numbers of steps in sequential operations, or as neurones in a brain;
2 overall there have been trends towards greater complexity, regardless of how this is valued;
3 this long-term development can be seen indubitably in both humans and their technology, if we restrict ourselves initially to comparing simply a startpoint and endpoint (3 million years ago and now);
4 present-day peoples with simple technologies or institutional structures need not offer a problem: if pressures leading towards complexity are relaxed in a particular environment, different solutions may be favoured;
5 the record must follow a trajectory from the startpoint to the endpoint, but there may be much variation counter to this overall trend, which can be roughly summarized as 'noise'.

If there were no such 'progression' then there would be no value in any of the feedback models that have been discussed; there would be no trajectories, except a random jumping around. In practice the archaeological record includes elements of progression (Figure 5.9), and other elements which show just such an apparently random variation (e.g. hand-axe shape). If we term this 'noise' it emphasizes its mysteriousness, but closer study may explain much of the variation more directly. Wynn and

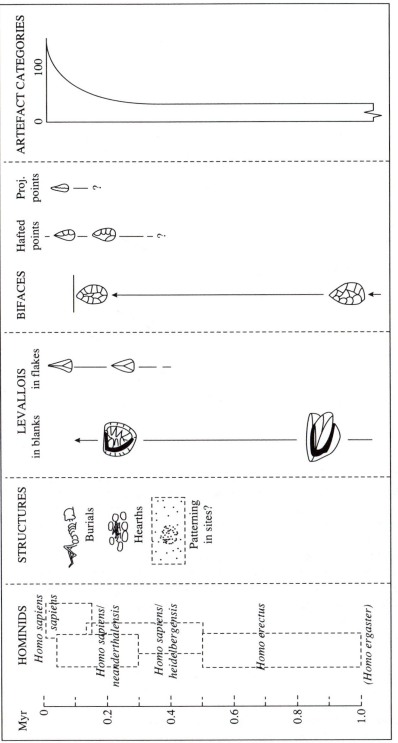

Figure 5.9 Culture and biology: some major developments in the archaeological record over the last million years. Levallois technique as such appears around 0.2–0.3 Myr, but the ideas are implicit in much earlier production of biface blanks. The timescale of change suggested here contrasts markedly with that envisaged by Stringer and Gamble (1993), who place most major changes between 80 and 40 Kyr BP (after Gowlett in press)

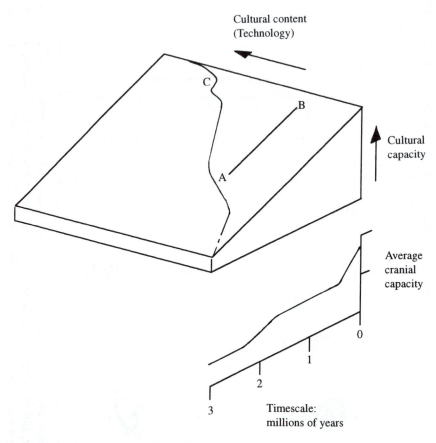

Figure 5.10 Culture and biology: an attempt to separate cultural capacity and cultural content as expressed by stone technology onto separate axes. As a simplification, increase in cultural capacity is represented as linear with time (we have no means of measuring it directly and a feature such as cranial capacity does not necessarily provide a good index). The axis of cultural content indicates approximately the maximum complexity of ideas current in stone-working, together with examples of the range found in any one period. The level of content found in the Developed Oldowan (A) is much the same as that found in some recent simple industries (B). (C) indicates an apparent plateau following the development of Levallois industries. (Modified after Gowlett 1990, in Sinclair and Schlanger 1990)

Tierson (1990) have demonstrated a regional element, and Crompton and Gowlett (1993) have isolated allometric variation; perhaps other components will be explained in due course.

Through the Pleistocene, artefact systems have points in common between sites, but also show points of difference. This underlines that we need many sites for a fuller understanding. They indicate so far a combination of robust cultural transmission coupled with flexibility. Factors underlying this combination have been explored by, for example, Isaac (1972a, b) and Steele (1994). Many authors have noted increased regional variation in the last 100,000 years, as well as greater refinement and faster rates of change (e.g. Otte 1990, Reynolds 1991, Clark 1993, Mellars 1993). New lines of evidence such as bone artefacts, burials and art appear. Recent thinking links a cultural explosion with the start of the Upper Palaeolithic about 40,000 years ago, rather than with the appearance of modern humans per se. But if we accept that dissociation, we also have to admit that the new traits do not all appear together in a package. Hence the suggestion by Reynolds (1991) that we should concentrate on 'scheduling' or sequencing rather than a 'before and after' approach. On that basis, the beginnings of the speeding-up go back to the start of Levallois technology for flakes, about 250,000 years ago (Figure 5.9). If the Tabun burial is as old as some suspect, these too may go back much beyond 100,000 years (Bar-Yosef 1993). For some authors the speeding-up is the central problem, but for many others the greater difficulty is the earlier lack of change. Either way, the last major event in human evolution is almost universally accepted to be concerned with this change of gear.

In analysing this, it is important to reassert that Upper Palaeolithic change was nowhere near as rapid as modern cultural (fashion) change. Modern change is visible within a lifetime. But for the individual there is likely to be no apparent difference between a society where change comes every thousand years, and one where it comes once in a hundred thousand years. Indeed only hindsight shows us whether the change, when it comes, is directional and cumulative, or a random movement within cultural free play.

Analytically, we can say that change can only come about through accident or through deliberate innovation. In the early periods of great stability in cultural traits it follows that either: there was no innovation; or innovation was selected against by cultural rules; or innovations were eliminated by clashes with environmental constraints (that is, they always tended to be selectively disadvantageous).

We cannot yet discriminate between these possibilities, although it is possible to simulate outcomes. But both innovation as the result of accident and deliberate innovation call for a mind which can appreciate alternatives. Conceivably the easiest way for culture to change is additively, and the greater the amount of information to be transferred, the higher the chance that it will be varied in transmission. The human spread around the globe may have raised the chance of cultural variation, partly because more humans had to adapt to extreme conditions, but also because the system became larger, increasing the chances for change to operate.

IDEAS ALONG AND ACROSS THE TIMESCALE:
AN APPRAISAL

The aim of this chapter was to consider how many lines of evidence are available in the investigation of early hominid behaviours and, second, to see whether progress can be made in formulating general models for human evolution, on the basis of the evidence accumulated in recent years.

Different levels of models have been considered for different periods. There is no obvious agreed relationship between these various levels – no easy transect from the physical to the behavioural to the cultural. Once culture is in the frame, it allows immense changes that are otherwise unpredictable, akin to the pilot effects of Popper and Eccles (1977). Culture can buck environment completely in some circumstances. Activities conducted solely for the purpose of exchange are a good example (Paton 1994); here the social requirements are far more important than the apparent utility of artefacts. Such activities are postulated for the Upper Palaeolithic (Gamble 1986, Barton *et al.* 1994), but few authors would suggest on present evidence that they go back more than 40,000 years.

Nor can any all-embracing model for human evolution be worked out, integrated along the timescale. The multiple species of early hominids rule out such possibilities, for what is true for one cannot always be so for another. There are potentially more lines of evidence than are currently studied. For example, the evolution of the thumb has particular importance (Susman 1988). Social parameters are numerous (Table 5.1). It is certain, however, that archaeology brings in more lines of evidence than can be studied for any earlier period.

The wealth of comparative work in several disciplines is equally indispensable for building a framework, but sometimes it does too little to trawl in the archaeological evidence that we have. With or without language as a context, technology (archaeological evidence) offers connectivity to other areas. Apart from comparative work we can aim to mesh actual data with models in a feedback process. At present we are probably not trying hard enough to use a lot of the data that has been accumulated with difficulty over the last thirty years. Specialist fields of study are needed, but not a human evolution divided into sub-fields which refer chiefly to their own data-sets and problems.

Comparative studies – primatology, ethnoarchaeology and palaeoecology – have scarcely yet been reapplied to considering long timescale problems, with rare exceptions such as Rogers *et al.* (1994). The long perspective was important in much past research, but recent work has tended to emphasize slices across time (akin perhaps to studies in 'Pleistocene Park'). The justification is that we must work towards understanding the short term before long-term developments can be comprehended. The long term, indeed, is made up of increments of short-term change, so it is crucial to analyse the elements militating towards stability and change respectively. This involves levels of genetic, behavioural and cultural change. Very small changes of parameters could have major effects. The readiest distinction must be between models that are merely written down, and those that are constructed so as to work: Steele (1994), Wobst (1974) and Potts (1988) have provided examples of these. Such mathematical models are valuable because their strengths and frailties are explicitly exposed to scrutiny.

CONCLUSION

In terms of the theme of this volume – power, sex and tradition – two developments in human evolution are perhaps more important than any others: first, the social change which has added at least one extra tier to human social structure: in apes we find individual/band; in humans, individual/band/maximum band – the nature of band society has no doubt also altered through changed roles of the sexes; second, the symbolic explosion mentioned above.

At first glance the evidence might encourage us to think that these developments were separated by more than a million years. Decreased sexual dimorphism and the long transporting distances of *Homo erectus* suggest a social transformation as much as 1.5 million years ago (Leakey 1994). But convincing evidence of externally projected symbolism is elusive more than a hundred thousand years ago. And yet the maximum band in recent societies is linked with language and social identity in a highly symbolic way.

I deliberately selected an example slap in the middle of the intervening time, asking: how many measurable parameters? I have argued that at Kilombe – taken as an example of a site about a million years ago – systematic transmission may involve some fifty characters. These may not all occur on all Acheulian sites, or in any one part of a site, but comparisons suggest the situation is typical. I would argue that the number of parameters documented points to the external projection of rules, in a manner that may point the way to later symbolism. A handaxe made by one human would certainly be recognizable as such to another, and hence it would fulfil the criteria of 'bestowed meaning' used by White (1962) for defining a symbol. Although the definition of symbol needs further exploration, there may be far more continuity between social structuring (whether by apes or humans) and formal symbolism than is generally recognized.

Next we might assess the number of parameters in other periods. McGrew has attempted this comparatively between humans and chimpanzees, using Oswalt's techno-units (citing Oswalt 1976). But in that scheme, a handaxe would count as one techno-unit, although it clearly stems from the conjunction of several ideas. This is one example of our scope for developing improved analyses.

In spite of difficulties discussed above, space and time remain vitally important in our record. Archaeological potential can be exploited more fully if we deal with them more explicitly. At the moment, little more than assumption tells us that the periods 1.5, 1.0 and 0.5 and 0.25 Myr are substantially different in their archaeology. Just as the CLIMAP project aimed to provide us with a world-wide view of the environment 18,000 years ago, and archaeology provided a cultural content (Soffer and Gamble 1990), so we might aim specifically to assemble a series of global snapshots, starting at 1.8 million year ago, and incorporating some of these other timelines.

In the last few years interest has focused on two problems relating to temporal sequence: human origins and the origins of modern humans. In principle, the transition to our own species, *sapiens*, should be the most important one, at about 0.5 Myr. But on this point hominid palaeontologists now seem hopelessly divided. Some see *Homo sapiens* beginning at 0.5 Myr, others only with the so-called Proto-Cro-Magnons 100,000 years ago; others see no important distinction between *erectus* and *sapiens*. Archaeology must therefore act independently. As resolution improves, it can hope to repair the decided lack of long-term and inter-continent comparisons, and consider the results against other evidence. If there is a unifying frame for all the models and their components, it surely must be in determining how natural selection has operated to produce such rapid change in the hominids, with such an emphasis on the accumulation and transmission of information.

REFERENCES

Aiello, L.C. and Dunbar, R.I.M. (1993) 'Neocortex size, group size, and the evolution of language.' *Current Anthropology* 34: 184–193.

Alexander, R.D. (1979) *Darwinism and Human Affairs*. London: Pitman.

Alexander, R.D. (1989) 'Evolution of the human psyche.' In P. Mellars and C. Stringer (eds) *The Human Revolution: Behavioural and Biological Perspectives on the Origins of Modern Humans*, pp. 455–513. Edinburgh: Edinburgh University Press.

Anderson, J.R. (1984) 'Ethology and ecology of sleep in monkeys and apes.' *Advances in the Study of Behavior* 14: 166–229.

Arber, A. (1985) *Mind and the Eye*. Cambridge: Cambridge University Press.

Ardrey, R. (1961) *African Genesis*. London: Collins.

Ardrey, R. (1967) *The Territorial Imperative*. London: Collins.

Ardrey, R. (1976) *The Hunting Hypothesis*. London: Collins.

Asfaw, B., Beyene, Y., Suwa, G., Walter, R.C., White, T.D., Woldegabriel, G. and Yemane, T. (1992) 'The earliest Acheulean at Konso-Gardula.' *Nature* 360: 732–735.

Barton, C.M., Clark, G.A. and Cohen, A.E. (1994) 'Art as information: explaining Upper Palaeolithic art in western Europe.' *World Archaeology* 26: 185–207.

Bar-Yosef, O. (1993) 'The role of western Asia in modern human origins.' In M.J. Aitken, C.B. Stringer and P.A. Mellars (eds) *The Origin of Modern Humans and the Impact of Chronometric Dating*, pp. 132–147. Princeton: Princeton University Press.

Bar-Yosef, O. and Goren-Inbar, N. (1992) 'The lithic assemblages of the site of Ubeidiya, Jordan Valley.' Jerusalem: Qedem 34.

Belfer-Cohen, A. and Goren-Inbar, N. (1994) 'Cognition and communication in the Levantine Lower Palaeolithic.' *World Archaeology* 26: 144–157.

Binford, L.R. (1968) 'Methodological considerations of the archaeological use of ethnographic data.' In R.B. Lee and I. DeVore (eds) *Man the Hunter*, pp. 268–273. Chicago: Aldine.

Binford, L.R. (1972) 'Contemporary model building: paradigms and the current state of Palaeolithic research.' In D.L. Clarke (ed.) *Models in Archaeology*, pp. 109–166. London: Methuen.

Binford, L.R. (1977) 'Olorgesailie deserves more than an ordinary book review.' *Journal of Anthropological Research* 33: 493–502.

Binford, L.R. (1981) *Bones: Ancient Men and Modern Myths*. New York: Academic Press.

Binford, L.R. and Todd, L.C. (1982) 'On arguments for the "butchering" of giant geladas.' *Current Anthropology* 23: 108–110.

Bishop, W.W. (1976) 'Pliocene problems relating to human evolution.' In G.L. Isaac and E. McCown (eds) *Human Origins: Louis Leakey and the East African Evidence*, pp. 139–154. Menlo Park, CA: Benjamin.

Bishop, W.W. and Clark, J.D. (eds) (1967) *Background to Evolution in Africa*. Chicago: University of Chicago Press.

Boesch, C. (1993) 'Aspects of transmission of tool-use in wild chimpanzees.' In K.R. Gibson and T. Ingold (eds) *Tools, Language and Cognition in Human Evolution*, pp. 171–183. Cambridge: Cambridge University Press.

Bowler, P.J. (1986) *Theories of Human Evolution: A Century of Debate, 1844–1944.* Baltimore: The Johns Hopkins University Press.

Bradley, B. and Sampson, C.G. (1986) 'Analysis by replication of two Acheulian artefact assemblages from Caddington, England.' In G.N. Bailey and P. Callow (eds) *Stone Age Prehistory*, pp. 29–45. Cambridge: Cambridge University Press.

Bunn, H.T. (1981) 'Archaeological evidence for meat-eating by Plio-Pleistocene hominids from Koobi Fora and Olduvai Gorge.' *Nature* 291: 574–576.

Bunn, H.T. (1986) 'Patterns of skeletal representation and hominid subsistence activities at Olduvai Gorge, Tanzania, and Koobi Fora, Kenya.' *Journal of Human Evolution* 15: 673–690.

Bunn, H.T. (1994) 'Early Pleistocene hominid foraging strategies along the ancestral Omo River at Koobi Fora, Kenya.' In J.S. Oliver, N.E. Sikes and K.M. Stewart (eds) Special Issue 'Early Hominid Behavioural Ecology.' *Journal of Human Evolution* 27: 247–266.

Bunn, H.T. and Kroll, E.M. (1986) 'Systematic butchery by Plio-Pleistocene hominids at Olduvai Gorge, Tanzania.' *Current Anthropology* 27: 431–452.

Bunn, H., Harris, J.W.K., Isaac, G.L., Kaufulu, Z., Kroll, E., Schick, K., Toth, N. and Behrensmeyer, A.K. (1980) 'FxJj50: an early Pleistocene site in northern Kenya.' *World Archaeology* 12: 109–136.

Campbell, B. (1966) *Human Evolution*. Chicago: Aldine.

Chamberlain, A. (1991) 'A chronological framework for human origins.' *World Archaeology* 23: 137–146.

Clark, J.D. (1959) *The Prehistory of Southern Africa.* Harmondsworth: Penguin.

Clark, J.D. (1969) *Kalambo Falls Prehistoric Site 1, Vol. I. The Geology, Palaeontology and Detailed Stratigraphy of the Excavations.* Cambridge: Cambridge University Press.

Clark, J.D. (1980) 'The Plio-Pleistocene environmental and cultural sequence at Gadeb, northern Bale, Ethiopia.' In R.E. Leakey and B.A. Ogot (eds) *Proceedings of the 7th Pan-African Congress of Prehistory and Quaternary Studies. Nairobi,* pp. 189–193. Nairobi: TILLMIAP.

Clark, J.D. (1993) 'African and Asian perspectives on the origins of modern humans.' In M.J. Aitken, C.B. Stringer and P.A. Mellars (eds) *The Origin of Modern Humans and the Impact of Chronometric Dating,* pp.148–178. Princeton: Princeton University Press.

Clark, W.E. Le Gros (1967) 'Human food habits as determining the basic patterns of economic and social life.' In J. Kuhnau (ed.) *Proceedings of the 7th International Congress of Nutrition Vol. 4,* pp. 18–24. Braunschweig: Viewig and Sohm.

Clarke, D.L. (1968) *Analytical Archaeology.* London: Methuen.

Crompton, R.H. and Gowlett, J.A.J. (1993) 'Allometry and multidimensional form in Acheulean bifaces from Kilombe, Kenya.' *Journal of Human Evolution* 25: 175–199.

Dart, R.A. (1957) 'The osteodontokeratic culture of *Australopithecus prometheus.*' *Memoirs of the Transvaal Museums* 10: 1–105.

Darwin, C. (1871) *The Descent of Man and Selection in Relation to Sex.* London: John Murray. (2nd edn 1874.)

Davidson, I. and Noble, W. (1993) 'Tools and language in human evolution.' In K.R. Gibson and T. Ingold (eds) *Tools, Language and Cognition in Human Evolution,* pp. 363–388. Cambridge: Cambridge University Press.

Deacon, T. (1992) 'Biological aspects of language.' In S. Jones, R. Martin and D. Pilbeam (eds) *The Cambridge Encyclopedia of Human Evolution,* pp. 128–133. Cambridge: Cambridge University Press.

Dean, D. (1992) 'The interpenetration of dialectic and hierarchy theory: a hominoid paleobehavioral example.' In E. Tobach and G. Greenberg (eds) *Levels of Social Behavior: Evolutionary and Genetic Aspects,* pp. 33–49. Wichita: Wichita State University.

Dean, D. and Delson, E. (1992) 'Second gorilla or third chimp?' *Nature* 359: 676–677.

Dixson, A.F. (1981) *The Natural History of the Gorilla.* London: Weidenfeld and Nicolson.

Duff, A.I., Clark, G.A. and Chadderton, T.J. (1992) 'Symbolism in the early Palaeolithic: a conceptual odyssey.' *Cambridge Archaeological Journal* 2: 211–229.

Evernden, J.F. and Curtis, G.H. (1965) 'Potassium-argon dating of late Cenozoic rocks in East Africa and Italy.' *Current Anthropology* 6: 343–385.

Foley, R. (1977) 'Space and energy: a method for analysing habitat values and utilization in relation to archaeological sites.' In D.L. Clarke (ed.) *Spatial Archaeology,* pp. 163–187. London: Academic Press.

Foley, R. (1981) 'A model of regional archaeological structure.' *Proceedings of the Prehistoric Society* 47: 1–17.

Foley, R. (ed.) (1984) *Hominid Evolution and Community Ecology*. London: Academic Press.

Foley, R. (1987) *Another Unique Species*. London: Longman.

Fox, R. (1967) 'In the beginning: aspects of hominid behavioural evolution.' *Man* (n.s.) 2: 415–433.

Gamble, C.S. (1979) 'Hunting strategies in the central European palaeolithic.' *Proceedings of the Prehistoric Society* 45: 35–52.

Gamble, C.S. (1986) *The Palaeolithic Settlement of Europe*. Cambridge: Cambridge University Press.

Gibson, K.R. and Ingold, T. (eds) (1993) *Tools, Language and Cognition in Human Evolution*. Cambridge: Cambridge University Press.

Goodall, J. (1976) 'Continuities between chimpanzee and human behaviour.' In G.L. Isaac and E. McCown (eds) *Human Origins: Louis Leakey and the East African Evidence*, pp. 80–95. Menlo Park, CA: Benjamin.

Goodman, M., Koop, B.F., Czelusniak, J., Fitch, D.H.A., Tagle, D.A. and Slighton, J.L. (1989) 'Molecular phylogeny of the family of apes and humans.' *Genome* 31: 316–335.

Gowlett, J.A.J. (1978) 'Kilombe – an Acheulian site complex in Kenya.' In W.W. Bishop (ed.) *Geological Background to Fossil Man*, pp. 337–360. Edinburgh: Scottish Academic Press.

Gowlett, J.A.J. (1982) 'Procedure and form in a Lower Palaeolithic industry: stoneworking at Kilombe, Kenya.' *Studia Praehistorica Belgica* 2: 101–109.

Gowlett, J.A.J. (1984) 'Mental abilities of early man: a look at some hard evidence.' In R. Foley (ed.) *Hominid Evolution and Community Ecology*, pp. 167–192. London: Academic Press.

Gowlett, J.A.J. (1988) 'A case of Developed Oldowan in the Acheulean?' *World Archaeology* 20: 13–26.

Gowlett, J.A.J. (1990) 'Technology, skill and the psychosocial sector in the long term of human evolution.' *Archaeological Review from Cambridge* 9: 82–103.

Gowlett, J.A.J. (1991) 'Kilombe – review of an Acheulean site complex.' In J.D. Clark (ed.) *Approaches to Understanding Early Hominid Life-Ways in the African Savannah*, pp. 129–136. UISSP, 11 Kongress, Mainz, 1987, Monographien Band 19. Bonn: Dr Rudolf Habelt GMBH.

Gowlett, J.A.J. (1993a) 'Chimpanzees deserve more than crumbs of the palaeo-anthropological cake.' *Cambridge Archaeological Journal* 3: 297–300.

Gowlett, J.A.J. (1993b) 'Le site Acheuléen de Kilombe: stratigraphie, géochronologie, habitat et industrie lithique.' *L'Anthropologie* 97: 69–84.

Gowlett, J.A.J. (in press) 'Mental abilities of early *Homo*: elements of constraint and choice in rule systems.' In P.A. Mellars and K.R. Gibson (eds) *Modelling the Early Human Mind*. Cambridge: McDonald Institute.

Gowlett, J.A.J. and Crompton, R.H. (1994) 'Kariandusi: Acheulean morphology and the question of allometry.' *African Archaeological Review* 12: 1–40.

Gowlett, J.A.J., Harris, J.W.K., Wood, B.A. and Walton, D. (1981) 'Early archaeological sites, hominid remains and traces of fire from Chesowanja, Kenya.' *Nature* 294: 125–129.

Graves, P. (1994) 'Flakes and ladders: what the archaeological record cannot tell us about the origins of language.' *World Archaeology* 26: 158–171.

Hallowell, A.I. (1960) 'Self, society and culture in phylogenetic perspective.' In S. Tax (ed.) *Evolution after Darwin, Vol. II*, pp. 309–372. Chicago: University of Chicago Press.

Harris, J.W.K. (1983) 'Cultural beginnings: Plio-Pleistocene archaeological occurrences from the Afar, Ethiopia.' *African Archaeological Review* 1: 3–31.

Hay, R.L. (1976) *Geology of the Olduvai Gorge: a study of sedimentation in a semi-arid basin.* Berkeley: University of California Press.

Hill, A. (1994) 'Early hominid behavioral ecology: a personal postscript.' In J.S. Oliver, N.E. Sikes and K.M. Stewart (eds) Special Issue 'Early Hominid Behavioural Ecology.' *Journal of Human Evolution* 27: 321–328.

Hinde, R.A. (1979) 'The nature of social structure.' In D.A. Hamburg and E.R. McCown (eds) *The Great Apes*, pp. 295–315. Menlo Park, CA: Benjamin.

Holloway, R.L. (1972) 'Australopithecine endocasts, brain evolution in the Hominoidea, and a model of human evolution.' In R. Tuttle (ed.) *The Functional and Evolutionary Biology of Primates*, pp. 185–203. Chicago: Aldine.

Holloway, R.L. (ed.) (1974) *Primate Aggression, Territoriality, and Xenophobia: A Comparative Perspective.* New York: Academic Press.

Howell, F.C. and Clark, J.D. (1963) 'Acheulian hunter-gatherers of sub-Saharan Africa.' In F.C. Howell and F. Bourlière (eds) *African Ecology and Human Evolution*, pp. 458–533. Chicago: Aldine.

Howell, F.C., Cole, G.H. and Kleindienst, M.R. (1962) 'Isimila, an Acheulean occupation site in the Iringa Highlands, Southern Highlands Province, Tanganyika.' In G. Mortelmans and J. Nenquin (eds) *Actes du IVe Congrès Pan-Africain de Préhistoire*, pp. 43–80. Tervuren, Belgium.

Hunt, K.D. (1994) 'The evolution of human bipedality: ecology and functional morphology.' *Journal of Human Evolution* 26: 183–202.

Huxley, J. (1955) 'Evolution, cultural and biological.' Guest editorial, *Yearbook of Anthropology.* New York: Wenner Gren.

Huxley, J. (1963) *Evolution: The Modern Synthesis*, 2nd edn. London: Allen and Unwin.

Ingold, T. (1992) 'Foraging for data, camping with theories: hunter-gatherers and nomadic pastoralists in archaeology and anthropology.' *Antiquity* 66: 790–803.

Isaac, B. (ed.) (1989) *The Archaeology of Human Origins: Papers by Glynn Isaac.* Cambridge: Cambridge University Press.

Isaac, G.L. (1968) 'Traces of Pleistocene hunters: an East African example.' In R.B. Lee and I. DeVore (eds) *Man the Hunter*, pp. 253–261. Chicago: Aldine.

Isaac, G.L. (1972a) 'Early phases of human behaviour: models in Lower Palaeolithic archaeology.' In D.L. Clarke (ed.) *Models in Archaeology*, pp. 167–199. London: Methuen.

Isaac, G.L. (1972b) 'Chronology and the tempo of cultural change during the Pleistocene.' In W.W. Bishop and J.A. Miller (eds) *The Calibration of Hominoid Evolution*, pp. 381–430. Edinburgh: Scottish Academic Press.

Isaac, G.L. (1976) 'The activities of early African hominids: a review of archaeological evidence from the time span two and a half to one million years ago.' In G.L. Isaac and E. McCown (eds) *Human Origins: Louis Leakey and the East African Evidence*, pp. 483–514. Menlo Park, CA: Benjamin.

Isaac, G.L. (1977) *Olorgesailie: Archaeological Studies of a Middle Pleistocene Lake Basin.* Chicago: University of Chicago Press.

Isaac, G.L. (1983) 'Aspects of human evolution.' In D.S. Bendall (ed.) *Evolution from Molecules to Men*, pp. 509–543. Cambridge: Cambridge University Press.

Isaac, G.L. (1984) 'The archaeology of human origins: studies of the lower Pleistocene in East Africa, 1971–1981.' *Advances in World Archaeology* 3: 1–87.

Jeffreys, A.J. (1989) 'Molecular biology and human evolution.' In J.R. Durant (ed.) *Human Origins*, pp. 217–252. Oxford: Clarendon Press.

Johanson, D.C., Masao, F.T., Eck, G.C., White, T.D., Walter, R.C., Kimbel, W.H., Asfaw, B., Manega, P., Ndessokia, P. and Suwa, G. (1987) 'New partial skeleton of *Homo habilis* from Olduvai Gorge, Tanzania.' *Nature* 327: 205–209.

Jolly, C. (1970) 'The seed-eaters: a new model of hominid differentiation based on a baboon analogy.' *Man* (n.s.) 5: 5–26.

Kibunjia, M. (1994) 'Pliocene archaeological occurrences in the Lake Turkana basin.' In J.S. Oliver, N.E. Sikes and K.M. Stewart (eds) 'Early Hominid Behavioural Ecology.' *Journal of Human Evolution* 27: 159–171.

Kleindienst, M.R. (1962) 'Components of the East African Acheulian assemblage: an analytic approach.' In G. Mortelmans and J. Nenquin (eds) *Actes du IVe Congrès Pan-Africain de Préhistoire*, pp. 81–105. Tervuren, Belgium.

Koch, C.P. (1990) 'Bone breakage, differential preservation and *Theropithecus* butchery at Olorgesailie, Kenya.' In S. Solomon, I. Davidson and D. Watson (eds) *Problem Solving in Taphonomy*, Vol. 2, pp. 158–166. University of Queensland, Anthropology Museum, Tempus.

Kortlandt, A. (1980) 'How might early hominids have defended themselves against predators and food competitors?' *Journal of Human Evolution* 12: 231–278.

Lancaster, J.B. (1967) 'The evolution of tool-using behavior.' *American Anthropologist* 70: 56–66.

Leakey, L.S.B. (1967) *Olduvai Gorge 1951–1961, Vol 1*. Cambridge: Cambridge University Press.

Leakey, M.D. (1971) *Olduvai Gorge. Vol. III: Excavations in Beds I and II, 1960–1963*. Cambridge: Cambridge University Press.

Leakey, R.E. (1994) *The Origin of Humankind*. New York: Basic Books.

Lee, P.C. (1992) 'Biology and behaviour in human evolution.' *Cambridge Archaeological Journal* 1: 207–226.

Lee, R.B. and DeVore, I. (eds) (1968) *Man the Hunter*. Chicago: Aldine.

Leroi-Gourhan, A. and Brezillon, M. (1972) 'Fouilles de Pincevent: essai d'analyse ethnographique d'un habitation magdalenien.' 7th Supplement to *Gallia Préhistoire*. Paris: CNRS.

Lieberman, P., Laitman, J.T., Reidenberg, J.S. and Gannon, P.J. (1992) 'The anatomy, physiology, acoustics and perception of speech: essential elements in analysis of the evolution of human speech.' *Journal of Human Evolution* 23: 447–467.

Lovejoy, A.O. (1936) *The Great Chain of Being*. Cambridge, MA: Harvard University Press.

Lovejoy, C.O. (1981) 'The origin of man.' *Science* 211: 341–350.

McBrearty, S. (1989) 'Cutlery and carnivory [Lead Review].' *Journal of Human Evolution* 18: 277–282.

McGrew, W.C. (1993) *Chimpanzee Material Culture: Implications for Human Evolution*. Cambridge: Cambridge University Press.

McHenry, H.M. (1994) 'Behavioral ecological implications of early hominid body size.' In J.S. Oliver, N.E. Sikes and K.M. Stewart (eds) Special Issue 'Early Hominid Behavioural Ecology.' *Journal of Human Evolution* 27: 77–87.

MacKinnon, J. (1978) *The Ape Within Us*. London: Collins.

LIVERPOOL
JOHN MOORES UNIVERSITY
AVRIL ROBARTS LRC
TEL. 0151 231 4022

Mason, W.A. (1979) 'Environmental models and mental modes: representational processes in the great apes.' In D.A. Hamburg and E.R. McCown (eds) *The Great Apes*, pp. 277–293. Menlo Park, CA: Benjamin.

Mellars, P. (1993) 'Archaeology and the population-dispersal hypothesis of modern human origins in Europe.' In M.J. Aitken, C.B. Stringer and P.A. Mellars (eds) *The Origin of Modern Humans and the Impact of Chronometric Dating*, pp. 196–216. Princeton: Princeton University Press.

Montagu, A. (ed.) (1973) *Man and Aggression*. 2nd edn. Oxford: Oxford University Press.

O'Connell, J.F., Hawkes, K. and Blurton-Jones, N.B. (1988) 'Hadza hunting, butchering and bone transport and their archaeological implications.' *Journal of Anthropological Research* 44: 113–161.

Oliver, J.S. (1994) 'Estimates of hominid and carnivore involvement in the FLK Zinjanthropus fossil assemblage: some socioecological implications.' In J.S. Oliver, N.E. Sikes and K.M. Stewart (eds) Special Issue 'Early Hominid Behavioural Ecology.' *Journal of Human Evolution* 27: 267–294.

Oliver, J.S., Sikes, N.E. and Stewart, K.M. (eds) (1994) Special Issue 'Early Hominid Behavioural Ecology.' *Journal of Human Evolution* 27 (1–3).

Oswalt, W.H. (1976) *An Anthropological Analysis of Food-getting Technology*. New York: Wiley.

Otte, M. (1990) 'From the Middle to the Upper Palaeolithic: the nature of the transition.' In P. Mellars (ed.) *The Emergence of Modern Humans: An Archaeological Perspective*, pp. 438–456. Edinburgh: Edinburgh University Press.

Paton, R. (1994) 'Speaking through stones: a study from northern Australia.' *World Archaeology* 26: 172–184.

Pickford, M. (1991) 'Growth of the Ruwenzoris and their impact on palaeo-anthropology.' In A. Ehara, T. Kimura, O. Takenaka and M. Iwamoto (eds) *Primatology Today*, pp. 513–516. New York: Elsevier.

Pilbeam, D.R. (1972) *The Ascent of Man*. New York: Macmillan.

Popper, K.R. and Eccles, J.C. (1977) *The Self and its Brain*. Berlin: Springer International.

Potts, R. (1988) *Early Hominid Activities at Olduvai*. New York: Aldine de Gruyter.

Potts, R. (1994) 'Variables versus models of early Pleistocene hominid land use.' In J.S. Oliver, N.E. Sikes and K.M. Stewart (eds) Special Issue 'Early Hominid Behavioural Ecology.' *Journal of Human Evolution* 27: 7–24.

Pusey, A. (1979) 'Intercommunity transfer of chimpanzees in Gombe National Park.' In D.A. Hamburg and E.R. McCown (eds) *The Great Apes*, pp. 465–479. Menlo Park, CA: Benjamin.

Read, C. (1920) *The Origin of Man*. Cambridge: Cambridge University Press.

Reynolds, T.E.G. (1991) 'Revolution or resolution? The archaeology of modern human origins.' *World Archaeology* 23: 155–166.

Reynolds, V. (1966) 'Open groups and hominid evolution.' *Man* (n.s.) 1: 441–452.

Roberts, M. (1986) 'Excavation of the Lower Palaeolithic site at Amey's Eartham Pit, Boxgrove, West Sussex: a preliminary report.' *Proceedings of the Prehistoric Society* 52: 215–245.

Robson Brown, K. (1993) 'An alternative approach to cognition in the Lower Palaeolithic: the modular view.' *Cambridge Archaeological Journal* 3: 231–245.

Roche, H. (1980) *Premiers Outils Taillés d'Afrique*. Paris: Société d'Ethnographie.

Roche, H., Brugal, J.-P., Lefevre, D., Ploux, S. and Texier, P.-J. (1988) 'Isenya: état des recherches sur un nouveau site acheuléen d'Afrique orientale.' *African Archaeological Review* 6: 27–55.

Roe, D.A. (1968) 'British lower and middle Palaeolithic handaxe groups.' *Proceedings of the Prehistoric Society* 34: 1–82.

Rogers, M.J., Harris, J.W.K. and Feibel, C.S. (1994) 'Changing patterns of land use by Plio-Pleistocene hominids in the Lake Turkana basin.' In J.S. Oliver, N.E. Sikes and K.M. Stewart (eds) Special Issue 'Early Hominid Behavioural Ecology.' *Journal of Human Evolution* 27: 139–158.

Savage-Rumbaugh, E.S. (1986) *Ape Language: From Conditioned Response to Symbol.* New York: Columbia University Press.

Schick, K.D. (1987) 'Modelling the formation of stone artifact concentrations.' *Journal of Human Evolution* 16: 789–807.

Schick, K.D. (1991) 'On making behavioral inferences for early sites.' In J.D. Clark (ed.) *Approaches to Understanding Early Hominid Life-Ways in the African Savannah*, pp. 79–107. UISSP, 11 Kongress, Mainz 1987, Monographien Band 19. Bonn: Dr Rudolf Habelt GMBH.

Schick, K.D. and Toth, N. (1993) *Making Silent Stones Speak: Human Evolution and the Dawn of Technology.* New York: Simon and Schuster.

Sept, J. (1992) 'Was there no place like home? A new perspective on early hominid archaeological sites from the mapping of chimpanzee nests.' *Current Anthropology* 33: 187–207.

Shipman, P.L., Bosler, W. and Davis, K.L. (1981) 'Butchering of giant geladas at an Acheulian site.' *Current Anthropology* 22: 257–268.

Simons, E.L. (1967) 'The earliest apes.' In S.H. Katz (ed.) *Biological Anthropology: Readings from Scientific American*, pp. 28–35. San Francisco: W.H. Freeman.

Sinclair, A. and Schlanger, N. (eds) (1990) 'Technology in the humanities.' *Archaeological Review from Cambridge* 9(1): 3–157.

Smith, J. Maynard. (1975) *The Theory of Evolution*, 3rd edn. Cambridge: Cambridge University Press.

Soffer, O. and Gamble, C. (eds) (1990) *The World at 18000 BP* (2 vols). London: Unwin Hyman.

Steele, J. (1994) 'Communication networks and dispersal patterns in human evolution: a simple simulation model.' *World Archaeology* 26: 126–143.

Stern, N. (1994) 'The implications of time-averaging for reconstructing the land-use patterns of early tool-using hominids.' In J.S. Oliver, N.E. Sikes and K.M. Stewart (eds) 'Early Hominid Behavioural Ecology.' *Journal of Human Evolution* 27: 89–105.

Stringer, C. and Gamble, C.S. (1993) *In Search of the Neanderthals: Solving the Puzzle of Human Origins.* London: Thames and Hudson.

Susman, R.L. (1988) 'Hand of *Paranthropus robustus* from Member 1, Swartkrans: fossil evidence for tool behaviour.' *Science* 240: 781–784.

Tobias, P.V. (1981) 'The emergence of man in Africa and beyond.' *Philosophical Transactions of the Royal Society of London, Series B* 292: 43–56.

Tobias, P.V. (1991) 'The emergence of spoken language in hominid evolution.' In J.D. Clark (ed.) *Approaches to Understanding Early Hominid Life-Ways in the African Savannah*, pp. 67–78. UISSP, 11 Kongress, Mainz 1987, Monographien Band 19. Bonn: Dr Rudolf Habelt GMBH.

Toth, N. (1985) 'The Oldowan reassessed: a close look at early stone artefacts.' *Journal of Archaeological Science* 12: 101–121.

Van Couvering, J.A.H. and Van Couvering, J.A. (1976) 'Early Miocene mammal fossils from East Africa: aspects of geology, faunistics and paleoecology.' In G.L. Isaac and E. McCown (eds) *Louis Leakey and the East African Evidence*, pp. 155–207. Menlo Park, CA: Benjamin.

Villa, P. (1990) 'Torralba and Aridos: elephant exploitation in Middle Pleistocene Spain.' *Journal of Human Evolution* 19: 299–309.

Walter, R.C., Manega, P.C., Hay, R.L., Drake, R.E. and Curtis, G.H. (1991) 'Laser-fusion $40_{Ar}/39_{Ar}$ dating of Bed I, Olduvai Gorge, Tanzania.' *Nature* 354: 145–149.

Washburn, S.L. (1960) 'Tools and human evolution.' *Scientific American* 203: 63–75.

Washburn, S.L. (1963) 'Behaviour and human evolution.' In S.L. Washburn (ed.) *Classification and Human Evolution*, Viking Fund Publications in Anthropology, 37. Chicago: University of Chicago Press.

Washburn, S.L. (1965) 'An ape's-eye view of human evolution.' In I. DeVore (ed.) *The Origin of Man*. New York: Wenner Gren Foundation.

Washburn, S.L. (1967) 'Behaviour and the origin of man.' *Proceedings of the Royal Anthropological Institute for 1967*: 21–27.

Washburn, S.L. and DeVore, I. (1961) 'Social behaviour of baboons and early man.' In S.L. Washburn (ed.) *Social Life of Early Man*, pp. 91–105, Viking Fund Publications in Anthropology, 31. Chicago: University of Chicago Press.

Washburn, S.L. and Howell, F.C. (1960) 'Human evolution and culture.' In S. Tax (ed.) *Evolution after Darwin*, Vol. II, pp. 33–56. Chicago: University of Chicago Press.

Washburn, S.L. and Lancaster, C.S. (1968) 'The evolution of hunting.' In R.B. Lee and I. DeVore (eds) *Man the Hunter*, pp. 293–303. Chicago: Aldine.

Wheeler, P.E. (1984) 'The evolution of bipedality and loss of functional body hair in hominids.' *Journal of Human Evolution* 13: 91–98.

Wheeler, P.E. (1994) 'The thermoregulatory advantages of heat storage and shade-seeking behaviour to hominids foraging in equatorial savannah environ- ments.' *Journal of Human Evolution* 26: 339–350.

White, L.A. (1943) 'Energy and the evolution of culture.' *American Anthropologist* 45: 335–356.

White, L.A. (1947/1987) 'Evolutionism and anti-evolutionism in American ethnological theory.' *Calcutta Review* 104: 147–159, 105: 29–40, 161–174. Reprinted in B. Dillingham and R.L. Carneiro (eds) *Leslie A. White's Ethnological Essays*, pp. 97–122. Albuquerque: University of New Mexico Press.

White, L.A. (1954/1987) 'The energy theory of cultural development.' In K.M. Kapadia (ed.) *Ghurye Felicitation Volume*, pp. 1–10. Bombay: Popular Book Depot. Revised 1975 and reprinted in B. Dillingham and R.L. Carneiro (eds) *Leslie A. White's Ethnological Essays*, pp. 215–221. Albuquerque: University of New Mexico Press.

White, L.A. (1959) 'The concept of culture.' *American Anthropologist* 61: 227–251.

White, L.A. (1962) 'Symboling: a kind of behavior.' *Journal of Psychology* 53: 311–317.

White, T.D., Suwa, G. and Asfaw, B. (1994) '*Australopithecus ramidus*, a new species of early hominid from Aramis, Ethiopia.' *Nature* 371: 306–312.

Williams, M.A.J. (1979) 'Droughts and long-term climatic change: recent French research in arid North Africa.' *Geography Bulletin*, September: 82–96.

Williams, M.A.J. (1984) 'Late Quaternary prehistoric environments in the Sahara.' In J.D. Clark and S.A. Brandt (eds) *From Hunters to Farmers*, pp. 74–83. Berkeley: University of California Press.

Wilson, E.O. (1983) 'Sociobiology and the Darwinian approach to mind and culture.' In D.S. Bendall (ed.) *Evolution from Molecules to Men*, pp. 545–553. Cambridge: Cambridge University Press.

Wilson, L. (1988) 'Petrography of the lower Palaeolithic tool assemblage of the Caune de l'Arago (France).' *World Archaeology* 19: 376–387.

Wobst, H.M. (1974) 'Boundary conditions for Palaeolithic social systems: a simulation approach.' *American Antiquity* 39: 147–178.

Wrangham, R.W. (1979) 'Sex differences in chimpanzee dispersion.' In D.A. Hamburg and E.R. McCown (eds) *The Great Apes*, pp. 481–489. Menlo Park, CA: Benjamin.

Wrangham, R.W. (1992) 'Comment on Sept, J., Was there no place like home? A new perspective on early hominid archaeological sites from the mapping of chimpanzee nests.' *Current Anthropology* 33: 201–202.

Wynn, T. (1979) 'The intelligence of later Acheulian hominids.' *Man* (n.s.) 14: 371–391.

Wynn, T. (1981) 'The intelligence of Oldowan hominids.' *Journal of Human Evolution* 10: 529–541.

Wynn, T. (1985) 'Piaget, stone tools and the evolution of human intelligence.' *World Archaeology* 17: 32–43.

Wynn, T. (1989) *The Evolution of Spatial Competence*. Urbana: University of Illinois Press.

Wynn, T. (1991) 'Tools, grammar and the archaeology of cognition.' *Cambridge Archaeological Journal* 1: 191–206.

Wynn, T. and Tierson, F. (1990) 'Regional comparison of the shapes of later Acheulean handaxes.' *American Anthropologist* 92: 73–84.

CHAPTER SIX

ARCHAEOLOGICAL INFERENCE AND THE EXPLANATION OF HOMINID EVOLUTION

MARK LAKE

Archaeology has a vital role to play in the wider palaeoanthropological endeavour to understand hominid evolution since it provides the only direct evidence for the behaviour of our ancestors and their relatives. As Glynn Isaac (1972, 1976a, 1983) made clear, the ultimate goal of hominid archaeology is to stimulate and test explanations for hominid evolution. Over the past twenty years researchers have sought to accomplish this ultimate goal through the intermediate goal of behavioural reconstruction (e.g. Isaac 1978). While very real advances have been made in identifying specific hominid activities, it is still proving difficult to reconstruct the wider behavioural context of such activities. The source of this difficulty has been identified by recent work on the structure of the East African Lower Palaeolithic archaeological record which suggests that the goal of behavioural reconstruction is not commensurable with the nature of the available evidence. This chapter assesses the implications of the mismatch between goals and data for the attempt to explain hominid evolution. First, a review of the current inferential strategy leads to the conclusion that inference about the wider organization of hominid activities is unreliable owing to a debilitating lack of temporal resolution. The second section argues that progress will require a greater understanding of the mechanisms and rates of hominid behavioural change. Only then will it be possible to establish whether the conflation of behavioural episodes across tens of thousands of years is acceptable. The final section argues that computer simulation has a vital role to play in exploring the mechanisms underlying behavioural change, and thus in assessing the viability of behavioural reconstruction as a route to the explanation of hominid evolution.

INFERRING HOMINID BEHAVIOUR

The origin of the current goals and inferential framework of early hominid archaeology can be traced back to the early 1970s, when Glynn Isaac joined Richard Leakey's exploration of fossil hominid bearing strata in the east Turkana Basin in northern Kenya. There have undoubtedly been important developments over the past two decades, but these essentially represent refinements in method rather than a radical alteration of Isaac's project. Isaac aimed to reconstruct the 'basic features of Early Pleistocene life' (1969: 8). It is in this sense that current goals were referred to as 'reconstructionist', which is not to deny that Isaac was interested in wider evolutionary questions – indeed, Isaac's recognition of the need to test models of human evolution against the archaeological record will surely prove to be one of his most enduring contributions to palaeoanthropology. Rather, the term 'reconstructionist' is used to highlight the way in which Isaac and subsequent researchers have relied upon largely synchronic behavioural reconstructions to make the link between archaeological evidence and evolutionary models. The first section of this chapter explores the problems encountered in making such reconstructions.

A good example with which to identify the pitfalls of behavioural reconstruction is the archaeological research conducted to test Isaac's so-called home base hypothesis (e.g. Bunn *et al.* 1980, Binford 1981, Bunn and Kroll 1986, Shipman 1986, Potts 1988). Isaac (1976b, 1978) postulated that the early hominid behavioural complex included food-sharing and a division of labour. Animal foods, obtained by males, and plant foods, obtained by females, were redistributed at a central place (home base), which was also the site of stone tool manufacture. These strategies developed in evolutionary feedback with pair-bonding, increasing sociality, increasingly prolonged infant dependency and ultimately increased brain size. Isaac argued that the East African archaeological record provided evidence supporting this hypothesis. Specifically, faunal remains indicate that hominids transported meat-bearing bones away from kill sites, while their spatial association with clusters of stone tools indicates use of a central place.

The process of testing a behavioural model such as the home base hypothesis involves making a series of inferences from archaeological data. As both Potts (1988) and Gifford-Gonzalez (1991) make clear, these inferences are necessarily hierarchical. Following Potts' scheme, archaeologists must begin by demonstrating that sites really do exist and that they are at least partly the result of hominid activity; these are first-order or taphonomic inferences. Second-order inferences attempt to establish the specific activities of hominids: for example, did they hunt or scavenge to obtain the bones transported to sites, how much meat was available on those bones and so on. Third-order inferences make the leap from specific activities to the organization of those activities; they answer questions such as: who was hunting, were they sharing with other members of the group, was this part of a reciprocal relationship and what were the other features of that relationship? Later in this chapter it is argued that any behavioural reconstruction intended to inform debate about hominid evolution must include information about both specific activities and their wider organization. Thus useful behavioural reconstruction is only possible if sound inferences can be obtained at all three levels in Potts' hierarchy. Unfortunately, inadequacies in the archaeological data-set render third-order inference unreliable. In order to understand the nature and implications of this limit to knowledge it is necessary to investigate what we can learn from first and second-order inference.

First-order inference

Three major questions fall within the domain of first-order or taphonomic inference. First, are the clusters of bone and stone really anomalous accumulations whose existence requires explanation? Both the density of material and the faunal assemblage composition at the sites lead the majority of researchers to agree that this is indeed the case (e.g. Isaac 1984, Potts 1988, but see also Binford 1981). The second taphonomic question that must be answered concerns the duration over which the assemblages accumulated. The most convincing argument (Potts 1986, 1988), based on bone weathering data and the agents responsible for accumulation, is that bones were introduced to each site intermittently over a period of at least five to ten years. The third taphonomic question concerns the agent or agents of accumulation. There are three aspects: distinguishing between physical and behavioural agents, identifying which behavioural agents have at some stage been involved with the assemblages and, finally, assessing their relative contributions. The first and second tasks are relatively straightforward. Physical processes, such as water flow, appear to have played a relatively small role in assemblage formation, but both carnivores and hominids played a more substantial role (Isaac 1984, Potts 1988). The third task is altogether more difficult. Potts (1988) concedes that we will only be able to distinguish between 'primarily hominid' sites and 'primarily carnivore' sites. To place sites in the appropriate category Potts uses what he calls the contextual approach, a method that brings together the faunal and the artefactual evidence:

> At the five artefact sites, tools and stone raw materials are concentrated at the same delimited locus as the bones, and these accumulations are well beyond that expected on a landscape over time through the casual discard of artefacts. In other words, these sites were specific foci to which hominids brought artefacts. The final point is that it remains doubtful at best that hominids repeatedly transported stone tools and raw materials to places of bone concentration that, if they were not primarily hominid areas of bone transport,

served as major foci of bone accumulation of carnivores. Hominids, thus, are considered to have been primarily responsible for the accumulation of bones at the artefact sites.

(1988: 144)

Strictly speaking, given a five-to-ten year accumulation period, the contemporaneity of stone transport episodes and bone transport episodes cannot be demonstrated. Thus it is logically possible that hominids could have transported stone artefacts to particular locations in years when carnivores where not using them as, for example, dens. It could then be argued that the co-occurrence of stone artefacts and faunal remains is not evidence that hominids were largely responsible for bone transport at artefact sites. Even the presence of cutmarks on bones does not strictly permit refutation of this alternative scenario. Nevertheless, the interpretation that hominids and carnivores alternated over the short term in their use of the same location does seem unlikely.

Thus first-order inference allows archaeologists to state with reasonable certainty that there are anomalous clusters of faunal and artefactual material, that these accumulated over a period of five to ten years, that many of them are the result of both hominid and carnivore activity, and that hominids are largely, even if not wholly, responsible for those accumulations where stone artefacts are present. It is, however, possible to learn more.

Second-order inference

Whether hominids hunted or scavenged is a good example of the kind of question that falls within the domain of second-order inference. It is also a question which, despite considerable attention, remains unanswered. Archaeologists have available two sources of evidence about the means by which hominids acquired animal tissue: bone modification and body part representation. Neither provide an unambiguous distinction between hunting and primary scavenging (early access to a carcass resulting from natural death or carnivore predation). This difficulty led Potts to abandon the question of hunting or scavenging *per se* and to concentrate instead on the relative timing of carnivore and hominid access to animal tissue. He attempted to establish the timing of hominid access to carcasses by comparing the body part representation at primarily hominid sites with that at primarily carnivore sites (Potts 1988). This residual approach requires comparison between sites which are neither contemporary nor spatially coincident. Nevertheless, if it can be demonstrated that carnivore behaviour has remained relatively consistent across time and space then the lack of contemporaneity and spatial coincidence will not undermine the project to identify distinctly hominid carcass access patterns. Even if there are reasons to doubt the persistence of carnivore behaviour, inferences based on Potts' residual approach can be strengthened by appeal to the ecological principles for carnivore behaviour such as those that have been presented by Blumenschine (1986a, b). Thus it is possible to learn something about the ability of hominids to gain early access to carcasses. In general, it seems likely that second-order inferences which rely on comparison between hominid behaviour and other animal behaviour will be reasonably secure provided that the animal behaviour has either remained constant or can be modelled by a relatively simple set of ecological principles.

Third-order inference

While first-order inference provides reasonably secure knowledge and second-order inferences must be judged on an individual basis, all third-order inference currently appears to be unreliable. Unlike first-order inference, which is largely site based, third-order inference about the organization of hominid behaviour invariably requires landscape-wide knowledge of hominid activity (Isaac 1981, Potts 1988, 1989a, b, Stern 1991). Thus it must make use of data from both the high-density sites and the isolated occurrences (known as scatters) of archaeological material spread over much of the modern landscape. Several researchers, notably Blumenschine and Potts (Gibbons 1990), have initiated research with the aim of surveying a palaeolandscape in order to identify the particular topographic and ecological contexts of specific behaviours. This in turn should facilitate reconstruction of more inclusive behaviours such as food-sharing.

Such optimism is misplaced for two reasons. First, reliable inference is once again thwarted by the inadequate temporal resolution of the archaeological record. Nicola Stern's research at Koobi Fora (1991, 1993) has shown that an increased spatial sample of hominid activity is won at the expense of temporal control. There are some laterally extensive deposits such as the KBS and Morotot tuffs, but, presumably because they were laid down relatively quickly, they contain little archaeological material. These tuffs do provide broad chronological markers for the faunal remains and artefacts found in the sediments sandwiched between them. Broad, however, means of an order of magnitude of 100,000 years. Sedimentary units deposited between these chronological markers do not outcrop over very large areas. Consequently, a 'palaeolandscape' is typically made up of a series of discontinuous sediments such that stratigraphic correlation rapidly becomes impossible as one travels away from a given point. Thus sampling a greater range of topographic and ecological contexts renders the contemporaneity of their associated activities more doubtful. A reconstruction of hominid subsistence strategy based on the full range of inferred activities might well conflate some that were never practised by any one group of hominids. In this case the reconstruction would represent a hominid way of life which never actually existed.

The second potential problem with the landscape approach stems from uncertainty as to whether the archaeological record does in fact provide evidence for spatially discrete activities. It will be recalled that the first step in testing the home-base hypothesis was to establish whether the sites represent anomalous clusters of archaeological material. This chapter accepted that the methods employed led to reasonably certain knowledge that this is indeed the case. Nevertheless, it is important to understand just what was tested. The composition of the site faunal assemblages was compared with a theoretical model (derived from modern attritional death assemblages) of an untransported assemblage (Potts 1988). This comparison allowed the inference that the sites are the result of transport behaviour. In addition, the greater density of the site faunal assemblages when compared with the Plio-Pleistocene scatters allowed the further inference that transport behaviour occurred repeatedly at certain locations which we know as the sites. But, because the *composition* of the site faunal assemblages was not compared with that of the scatters, it cannot be inferred that, *in the past*, the transport behaviour which occurred repeatedly at certain locations occurred *only* at those locations. Similarly, site artefact assemblages were compared with the scatters in terms of density, but not composition, hence they too do not allow inference that some behaviours occurred only at certain locations in the landscape. According to Stern (1993) the scatters and sites share the same assemblage composition (but see Bunn and Kroll 1993). Consequently, the scatters and sites differ, not in the range of activities they represent, but in the frequency with which a whole suite of activities were carried out in different parts of the landscape.

DEVELOPING EXPLANATIONS FOR HOMINID EVOLUTION

Archaeologists have sought to stimulate and test explanations for hominid evolution through the intermediate goal of behavioural reconstruction. The apparent unreliability of third-order inference undermines these ultimate aims because explanations based on behavioural reconstruction require information about the wider organization of activities as well as the existence of specific activities. It is argued below that a greater understanding of the rate of hominid behavioural change is required in order to assess the reliability of third-order inference. In addition, consideration of the mechanisms for change reveals that the role of behavioural reconstruction in evolutionary explanation is not as straightforward as has generally been assumed because evolution operates at more than one level. Thus the central message is that archaeologists can no longer afford to view hominid land-use and subsistence strategies in isolation from issues of learning and cultural transmission.

Third-order inference and evolutionary explanation

Neo-Darwinian evolutionary theory currently provides the only scientific framework within which to understand hominid evolution (Foley 1987). The central tenet of neo-Darwinian theory is evolution by natural selection. Organisms better suited to their ecological niche enjoy greater reproductive success, thereby increasing the prevalence of their genotype. Providing the phenotypic properties conferring reproductive success are genetically encoded they will gradually spread through the population as a whole. Accordingly, understanding of a particular evolutionary trajectory results from showing that the novel phenotypic properties increased the fitness of the organisms that possessed them, in other words that the traits were adaptive. As Ernst Mayr (1982) argues, satisfactory explanations of biological phenomena do not invoke general laws – unlike in the physical sciences – but instead employ central concepts (such as adaptation) which are articulated with the factual aspects of a given case. Hence the apparent circularity of evolutionary explanation must be overcome by a rich networking of data and concepts. In palaeoanthropology this strategy can be mobilized by predicting hominid morphology, physiology or behaviour on the basis of the selective pressures which the hominids faced. Demonstration that the predicted properties did indeed evolve confirms that the selective pressures have been correctly identified. In reality prediction and testing are conducted in a process of feedback because a phenotype is both a response to and a cause of selective pressures. This feedback process can be considered to have arrived at an adequate explanation when it meets three criteria: (1) it specifies a set of novel phenotypic features which can reasonably be regarded to confer reproductive success on an organism confronted by a specified set of selective conditions, (2) those phenotypic features actually evolved and (3) the selective conditions also existed. When the phenotypic features in question are behavioural, archaeology has a vital role in testing whether the second and third criteria are met.

Thus Gifford-Gonzalez (1991: 243) states that archaeologists are engaged in 'reconstructing past states of systems [which] relate to historical narratives, both as cases demanding an evolutionary account and as challenges to existing narratives'. In other words, the goal of behavioural reconstruction is to identify the novel phenotypic properties which must be explained and to test the subsequent explanation by reconstructing the selective conditions which supposedly favoured them. At the moment this goal cannot be achieved because of the inferential problems encountered in attempting to make behavioural reconstructions. Archaeology does allow certain behaviours (phenotypic properties) to be identified, but these tend to be activities which must be placed in a wider context before they can form part of an evolutionary explanation. For example, it is reasonably certain that some hominids made stone tools and transported bones, nevertheless, these are not activities which directly increase the fitness of the individuals engaged in them. Evolutionary explanations require an assessment of adaptive value, but this is not an intrinsic property of the kinds of behaviour identified through first-order inference. Adaptive value is a property of the more inclusive behaviours which are reconstructed through second- and third-order inference. Some second-order inferences can be made without a debilitating degree of uncertainty (the example discussed above was the timing of access to animal tissue). Even so, this extra information is insufficient to test an evolutionary explanation. Imagine that the use of stone tools enabled hominids to detach meat-bearing bones and transport them away from the kill site for consumption in relative safety. Intuitively, this scenario confers an adaptive advantage on its protagonists because it increases the efficiency of their foraging behaviour which in turn can be expected to contribute to increased reproductive success (Dunbar 1988). Whether this intuition is correct, however, depends upon the wider behavioural context of the foraging strategy in question: is it part of a group effort to drive away the initial carnivore consumers, does it involve sharing the spoils, does it increase reproductive success through provisioning the young or through increased sexual access, and so on. A satisfactory evolutionary explanation is one which shows *that* a behaviour was adaptive by describing *how* it was adaptive. Unfortunately the requisite wider behavioural context can only be reconstructed through third-order inference which, as has been argued, is currently unreliable.

It will be recalled that the major problem undermining third-order inference is the need to conflate behavioural episodes across tens or possibly hundreds of thousands of years. This renders inference about wider behavioural organization unreliable owing to the risk of conflating activities from separate land-use or subsistence strategies into one strategy which never actually existed. The notion of risk serves to emphasize that the unreliability of third-order inference stems as much from archaeologists' ignorance of the quality of data required to support their interpretations as it does from the actual quality of the data which is available. For instance, it could be that hominid behaviour changed so slowly that conflating activities separated by tens of thousands of years would not result in an erroneous reconstruction of hominid behavioural adaptation. Equally, the converse might be true. Clearly then, given the nature of the archaeological record, the reliability of third-order inference depends upon the rate of hominid behavioural change. In order to understand how rapidly hominid behaviour might have changed it is necessary to reconsider the nature of the evolutionary process.

Mechanisms for behavioural change

Biologists and philosophers of science writing from an evolutionary epistemological perspective (e.g. Campbell 1974, Hull 1982, Odling-Smee 1983) have argued that evolution by natural selection is just one implementation of a more general process of knowledge gain which occurs at several levels. At each level a common algorithm is implemented through a unique mechanism. The common algorithm is a continuous alternation of processes which generate variety and processes which winnow that variety by selection and retention. Odling-Smee (1983) describes four levels of knowledge gain each characterized by a specific mechanism: at level 1 populations gain knowledge through the genetic mechanism of evolution by natural selection; at levels 2 and 3 organisms gain knowledge through variable epigenesis and individual learning respectively; and finally, at level 4, it is once again populations which gain knowledge, but this time through the mechanism of cultural evolution. All four mechanisms result in their corresponding unit of knowledge-gain acquiring a better way of existing in a given environment. Nevertheless, one important way in which they differ is in the rate and scope of the resulting change. For instance, the major morphological and physiological changes required for hominid bipedalism evolved relatively slowly through natural selection. Individual hominids probably benefited from a more rapid, but equally irreversible, fine-tuning of those changes through variable epigenesis. By contrast, individual learning would have provided hominids with the ability to alter their behaviours reflexively over a relatively short timescale. Finally, any persistence of reflexively learned behaviour across time and space may have been the result of cultural learning.

This evolutionary epistemological perspective suggests that the maximum rate at which hominid land-use and subsistence strategies changed would have depended upon whether they were genetically determined, individually learned or culturally learned. Given that the viability of pursuing evolutionary explanation through behavioural reconstruction depends upon the reliability of third-order inference, and that this in turn depends upon the rate of change of hominid behaviour, it is imperative that archaeologists investigate the balance between individual and cultural learning present at different stages in hominid evolution. The next section suggests how this might be achieved through the use of computer simulation. But first, identification of the mechanisms underlying hominid behavioural change carries another implication for the role of behavioural reconstruction in evolutionary explanation.

The balance between individual and cultural learning at different stages in hominid evolution alters the requirements for an adequate evolutionary explanation. For instance, suppose that early hominids did not possess a genetic blueprint for a neurologically hardwired programme which instructed them in the art of using stone tools to gain early access to meat. Instead they evolved the neurological capacity for complex and flexible behaviour (Foley 1987), that is, an increased degree of individual and possibly cultural learning. This capacity for complex and flexible behaviour evolved through natural selection, but thereafter the existence of many specific behaviours would only be immediately explicable in terms of faster mechanisms of information gain. According to this scenario, hominid evolution became a two-tier process whose explanation involves reconciling the immediate causality of organism learning with the ultimate causality of natural selection. Thus it is no longer adequate to show that and how particular hominid behaviours were adaptive; in addition it must be demonstrated that and how the particular way in which these behaviours 'evolved' was adaptive. Explanations for each of the two tiers of hominid evolution must be tested over different timescales. In the case of the evolution of flexible behaviour the adaptation that results from genetic evolution is not a particular behaviour or suite of behaviours, but a means of controlling and altering behaviour. Thus demonstrating the adaptive value of individual learning requires showing that and how learned behaviour varies with changing selective conditions. By contrast, the adaptation that results from organism learning is a particular behaviour or suite of behaviours whose adaptive value is demonstrated in the context of the particular selective conditions which favoured them. Consequently, it can be seen that the use of behavioural reconstruction to test evolutionary explanations requires at least two series of reconstructions of hominid behaviour, each generated over a different time-frame.

THE SIMULATION OF INDIVIDUAL LEARNING AND CULTURAL LEARNING IN HOMINID EVOLUTION

Information about the mechanisms and rate of hominid behavioural change is required both to assess the reliability of third-order inference and to ensure that behavioural reconstructions are made at the appropriate timescales. The remainder of this chapter describes the use of computer simulation to explore the role of individual and cultural learning in hominid evolution. Both Mithen (1991) and Stern (1991) have noted the potential utility of simulation for hominid studies, but despite their observations the only published example remains Potts' (1988) investigation of the energetic costs of different bone transport strategies. Nevertheless, computer simulation provides the ideal method for exploring the cumulative effect of differently scaled processes because its experimental nature allows the investigator to alter the rates of those processes and the way in which they interact.

The term 'individual learning' refers to the process by which individual hominids learn about their natural and social environment through their own trial and error. In other words, based on their own knowledge, they make decisions about the appropriate course of action, for example where to forage, and then adjust that knowledge in the light of subsequent experience. Cultural transmission, on the other hand, refers to the outcome of cultural learning, a process in which hominids acquire information from and/or copy the decisions of others. The extent to which individual learning and cultural learning are distinct at a psychological level is currently the subject of considerable debate (e.g. Tomasello *et al.* 1993). Nevertheless, at a phenomenological level there can be little doubt that the two are distinct, both in terms of their effect and in terms of the associated costs to the learner.

The effect and significance of cultural learning has been succinctly described by Tomasello *et al.* (1993: 495):

> Many animal species live in complex social groups; only humans live in cultures. Cultures are most clearly distinguished from other forms of social organisation by the nature of their products – for example, material artefacts, social institutions, behavioural traditions, and languages. These cultural products share, among other things, the characteristic that they accumulate modifications over time.

By contrast, behaviours and material artefacts resulting from individual learning must be constantly reinvented if they are to persist across space and time, and there is no sense in which they can accumulate modifications. Thus one might expect a subsistence strategy based on individual learning to show greater variability across space and time and little or no cumulative change. Persistence of individually learned traits will only be found where there are strong external constraints such as genetic determination, the properties of available raw materials, or very specific problems posed by the environment.

Individual learning and cultural learning also differ in their costs to the learner. This is true even if, as Heyes and Plotkin argue (1989), the process of cultural learning is psychologically little different from that of other learning forms. As they point out, 'what one [cultural learner] learns is in part a function of what some other person or animal has learned' (1989: 149); consequently, while possibly subject to the same cognitive costs as the individual learner, the cultural learner will not incur the energetic costs, loss of time and risk associated with trial-and-error learning. Admittedly this is only true if the learned information or behaviour is both correct and relevant – a point to which I will return – but assuming that this condition is fulfilled it would, for example, be possible for a hominid to forage in rich resource patches without wasting time and energy sampling poor patches. This cost differential provides the basis for understanding the conditions under which a propensity for cultural learning might be expected to evolve by natural selection.

Boyd and Richerson (1985) have analysed the conditions favouring the evolution of cultural learning. As just noted, there is little to be gained from acquiring information which is inaccurate or out of date. Boyd and Richerson's analysis suggests that a propensity for cultural learning should evolve where the spatial and temporal heterogeneity of an environment is neither so great that culturally learned information is misleading, nor so little that the genetic mechanism provides a cheaper (since it does not incur the developmental and metabolic costs of a large brain) way of storing and altering information. Thus, in order to establish likely rates of behavioural change, archaeologists need to ascertain what balance of individual and cultural learning would have been favoured in the environments inhabited by the hominids in question. Boyd and Richerson's analysis provides a strong theoretical basis for this investigation; however, from an archaeological perspective it presents two practical problems. The first is that Boyd and Richerson characterize environmental heterogeneity in terms of an autocorrelation coefficient: unfortunately it is difficult to estimate this parameter from palaeoenvironmental reconstruction. The second problem concerns individual learning. It has already been noted that the viability of cultural learning depends upon the quality of the information which is learned, and that one factor affecting this is the degree of environmental heterogeneity. Another factor is the accuracy of the individual learning that originally generated the information later culturally transmitted. Boyd and Richerson characterize the error in individual learning as the variance of a normally distributed random variable: needless to say, the variance of error terms in hominid knowledge is simply unknown.

The challenge facing archaeologists is to build a computer simulation model which embodies the principles of Boyd and Richerson's formal model, but allows investigation of the effect of individual learning abilities on foraging in environments characterized by the type of information which is actually available from palaeoenvironmental reconstruction. Figure 6.1 is a flow-chart depicting just such a simulation. In the inner shell hominids forage in an environment made up of resource patches, each of which is characterized by a reward with an associated probability and a cost of search. This latter allows the model to incorporate factors such as temperature stress and the need for vigilance against predators. In the course of foraging hominids must decide which patches to exploit on the basis of their knowledge about those patches. Hominid decision criteria are modelled using principles derived from optimal foraging theory (see, for example Stephens and Krebs 1986) although it is not assumed that they make optimal decisions, instead they satisfice, that is, make 'good enough' decisions (Mithen 1990: 45). The simulation model assumes that hominids have reasonable knowledge of the value of resources that they might encounter; what they have to learn is the probability of encounter. The way in which a given hominid learns about

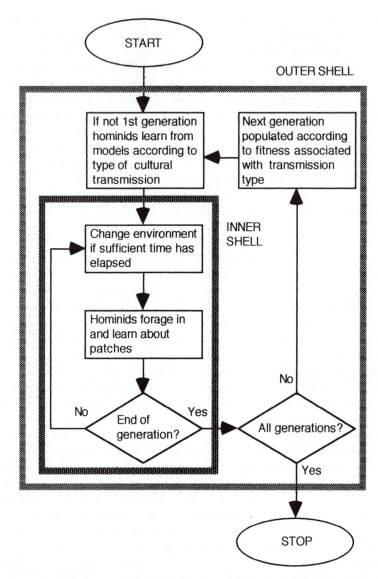

Figure 6.1 Flow-chart of a computer simulation model incorporating Boyd and Richerson's formal principles, but permitting investigation of the effect of individual learning abilities in realistic foraging environments

its environment depends upon whether its 'genotype' specifies a strong propensity for individual learning or a strong propensity for cultural learning. In the case of individual learning the hominid adjusts its expected probability of encounter for each resource according to how often it has encountered the resource on previous visits to the patch. In the case of cultural learning the hominid imitates the foraging behaviour of another hominid who appears to be fitter than average; this is an implementation of what Boyd and Richerson term 'indirect biased transmission' (1985: 135). The outer shell of the model allows the relative frequency of the two 'genotypes' for learning propensity to vary by natural selection, that is, according to their relative fitness in the population.

It must be stressed that experimentation with the simulation model is not yet complete, thus the following discussion is intended as an illustration of potential rather than a rigorous presentation of firm conclusions. Figure 6.2 shows the change over 200 generations in relative frequency of hominids possessing the 'genotype' for cultural learning (indirect biased transmission). The population was initialized with 50 per cent of 'genotypes' specifying cultural learning and 50 per cent specifying individual learning. It was then allowed to evolve in environments ranging from temporally homogeneous to temporally heterogeneous (characterized by high and low autocorrelation coefficients respectively). It can be seen that temporal homogeneity favours cultural learning while temporal heterogeneity favours individual learning. This makes sense because in a temporally homogeneous environment information and behaviours which are beneficial to one generation are likely to be beneficial to the next, thus learning from the previous generation is a viable shortcut enabling its practitioners to divert more time and energy to provisioning the young or finding a mate. By contrast, in a temporally heterogeneous environment hominids who adhere to the knowledge and behaviours of the previous generation are likely to have committed themselves to a life of costly error. These runs of the computer simulation were made using environments of known autocorrelation in order to establish the theoretical validity of the simulation model by checking that evolution occurs in the manner predicted by Boyd and Richerson's formal model. Once the simulation model has been validated in this way it can be put to use by inputting a series of more realistic palaeoenvironmental parameters in order to establish what balance of the two learning types would have been favoured in hominid populations.

The second reason cited above for building a simulation model of hominid individual and cultural learning was that it would facilitate investigation of the relationship between individual learning ability and the viability of cultural learning. Figure 6.3 suggests that the quality of individual learning does alter the viability of cultural learning. The quality of individual learning has been modelled in terms of the amount of information a hominid uses in learning what to expect from a given patch. While it can be argued that this does not constitute a model of different cognitive abilities in the sense of different computational abilities, it does have the virtue of modelling differing rates of tracking the environment, and it is this which is most likely to affect the viability of cultural transmission since, as the evolutionary epistemological perspective reveals, different learning mechanisms are geared to coping with different rates of

LIVERPOOL JOHN MOORES UNIVERSITY
LEARNING SERVICES

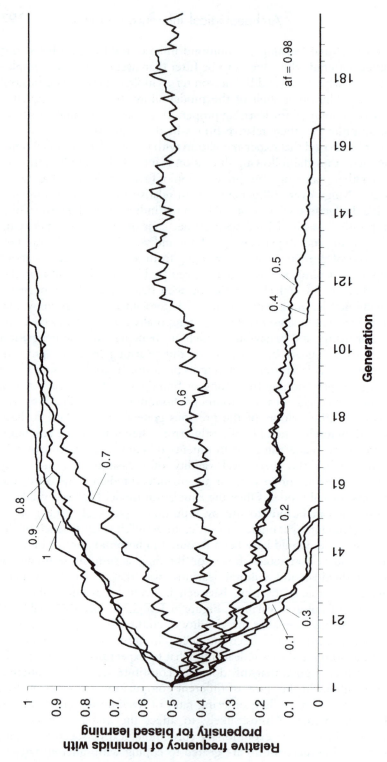

Figure 6.2 Change in relative frequency of hominids with biased transmission according to autocorrelation of environmental change

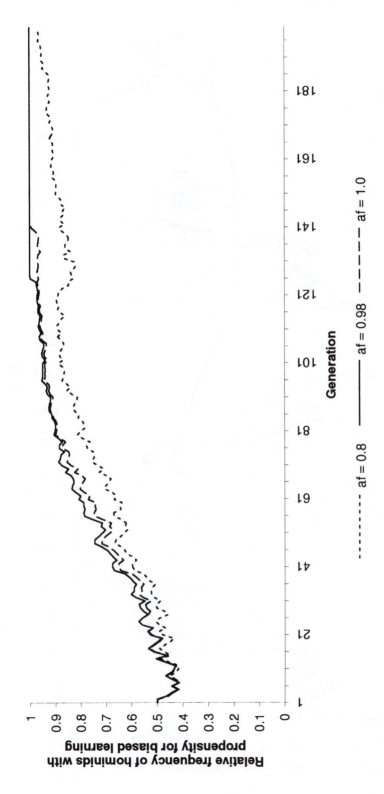

Figure 6.3 Selective pressure for cultural learning is affected by attention paid to past experience

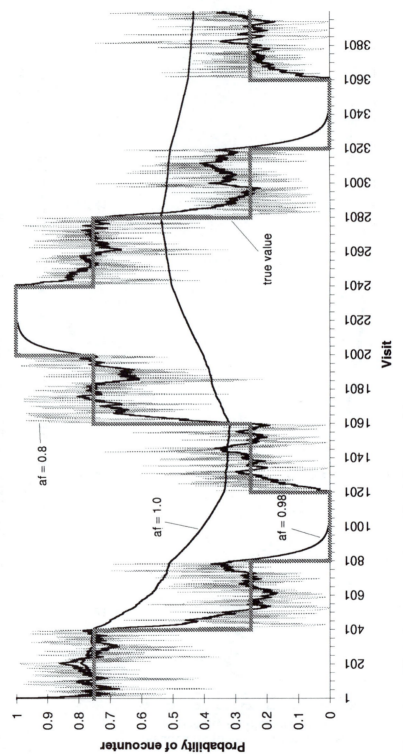

Figure 6.4 Effect of memory on hominid's ability to model environment

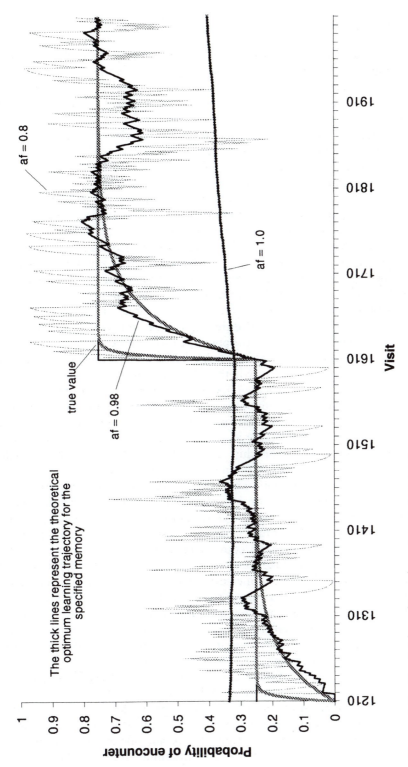

Figure 6.5 Hominid tracking changing environment

change. Figure 6.3 shows that the rate at which the 'genotype' for cultural learning spreads through a population depends upon the extent to which hominids make use of past experience when individually learning about their environment. Cultural learning is most strongly favoured in the population whose members pay about twice as much attention to their most recent experience compared to their experience of 30 days ago (af = 0.98). Cultural learning is less strongly favoured in populations where hominids pay either more (af = 1.0) or less (af = 0.8) attention to past experience.

Figure 6.4 provides some clues as to why cultural learning is less favoured in populations of hominids paying either very considerable or very little attention to past experience. The graph shows how closely a hominid is able to track a changing environment according to the amount of attention it pays to past experience. Clearly there is a trade-off between the speed of response to environmental change and the precision of the knowledge which a hominid gains. In the following discussion a distinction is made between accuracy and precision. The former refers to the extent to which hominid estimates cluster around the true value of the probability of encounter as opposed to some other (erroneous) value. The latter refers to the degree of dispersion around the mean value of the estimates, irrespective of whether that value is close to the true value. Figure 6.6 illustrates how accuracy and precision combine to influence the overall quality of the hominid's knowledge (better knowledge is represented by a lower standard deviation). The three sets of statistics relate to the entire duration of Figure 6.4, but are better understood if viewed alongside Figure 6.5. The thin lines in Figure 6.5 represent a single hominid's actual estimates of the new probability of encounter. The thick lines represent the optimum adjustment towards the changed probability of encounter based solely on the elapsed time since the environmental change. This optimum provides a close approximation to a moving average of the actual hominid estimates; thus the distance between the optimum and the true value provides a convenient measure of the accuracy of the hominid's knowledge. Likewise, the distance between the optimum and actual estimates provides a measure of the precision of the hominid's knowledge. These distances are given as standard deviations in Figure 6.6, which clearly shows that while paying much attention to past experience (af = 1.0) results in a precise estimate of the environment, that estimate may actually be highly inaccurate if the environment is changing. On the other hand, paying much less attention to past experience (af = 0.8) improves the accuracy of the estimate, but drastically reduces its precision. The best compromise turns out to be the degree of attention to past experience which most strongly favoured cultural learning (af = 0.98).

By using the computer simulation just described it should be possible to draw some conclusions regarding the balance between individual and cultural learning at different stages in hominid evolution. This will be

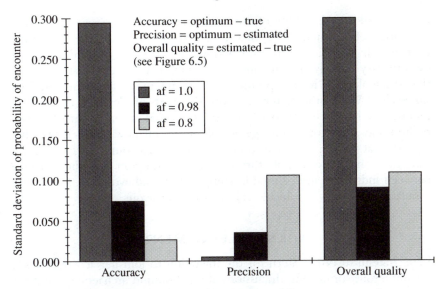

Figure 6.6 *Standard deviation as a measure of the accuracy and precision of hominid model of environment*

achieved by running the simulation with environmental parameters similar to those of the palaeoenvironments in which hominids were living. It should be noted that specification of such parameters does not require knowledge of exact probabilities of encounter of different resource types in the palaeoenvironment, but rather a more general understanding of magnitudes and rates of change of such probabilities. In addition, as is already evident from the results described above, the balance between individual and cultural learning favoured in the simulations will partly depend on the wider cognitive abilities attributed to the hominids. These abilities must be compatible with information gleaned from the study of hominid stone tool technology and ape cognition (see, for example, papers in Gibson and Ingold 1993). The balance between individual and cultural learning established in the simulations can then be used to assess the reliability of third-order inference, and thus the viability of using behavioural reconstruction to stimulate and test evolutionary explanations.

CONCLUSION

Archaeologists will not be able to fulfil their aim of contributing to our understanding of hominid evolution in the absence of a greater understanding of the mechanisms and rate of hominid behavioural change. This is not to suggest that all aspects of the current research paradigm are inappropriate. First- and second-order inferences remain important because they provide reasonably certain knowledge about some specific hominid activities such as tool-making and bone transport. Nevertheless, it is essential that the utility of third-order inference be reassessed through two lines of research. The first is an investigation of the timescales over which behavioural reconstructions are required in order to test evolutionary models. The second must establish whether the structure of the archaeological record permits reliable inference over the requisite timescales. While the latter involves the sort of detailed field study reported at length by Nicola Stern (1991, 1993), research into the rate of hominid behavioural change is still in its infancy. This chapter has argued that the appropriate timescales for behavioural reconstruction can only be determined through an exploration of the balance between individual and cultural learning in hominid evolution. Computer simulation will play a valuable role in this endeavour.

ACKNOWLEDGEMENTS

I am grateful to Nikki Stern for the invitation to join her at Koobi Fora, for numerous stimulating discussions about hominid archaeology, and for comments on an earlier draft of this chapter. I was able to gain first-hand experience of the nature of the East African Lower Pleistocene archaeological record with the help of financial support from the Science and Engineering Research Council, the Boise Fund (University of Oxford), King's College Cambridge and the Dorothy Garrod Travel Fund (University of Cambridge). I also thank Stephen Shennan and James Steele for inviting me to contribute to this book and for their advice. Finally, I am particularly grateful to Steven Mithen for his encouragement and for asking some simple but awkward questions.

REFERENCES

Binford, L. (1981) *Bones: Ancient Men and Modern Myths.* New York: Academic Press.

Blumenschine, R.J. (1986a) Early Hominid Scavenging Opportunities. *British Archaeological Reports International Series* 283. Oxford: B.A.R.

Blumenschine, R.J. (1986b) 'Carcass consumption sequences and the archaeological distinction of scavenging and hunting.' *Journal of Human Evolution* 15: 639–660.

Boyd, R. and Richerson, P.J. (1985) *Culture and the Evolutionary Process.* Chicago: Chicago University Press.

Bunn, H.T. and Kroll, E. (1986) 'Systematic butchery by Plio-Pleistocene hominids at Olduvai Gorge, Tanzania.' *Current Anthropology* 27: 431–452.

Bunn, H.T. and Kroll, E. (1993) '*CA* comment on N. Stern. The Structure of the Lower Pleistocene Archaeological Record: a case study from the Koobi Fora formation.' *Current Anthropology* 34: 216–217.

Bunn, H.T., Harris, J.W.K., Isaac, G.L., Kaufulu, Z., Kroll, E., Schick, K., Toth, N. and Behrensmeyer, A.K. (1980) 'FxJj50: an early Pleistocene site in northern Kenya.' *World Archaeology* 12: 109–136.

Campbell, D.T. (1974) 'Evolutionary epistemology.' In P.A. Schlipp (ed.) *The Philosophy of Karl Popper Book 1*. La Salle, IL: The Open Court Publishing Company.

Dunbar, R.I.M. (1988) *Primate Social Systems*. Beckenham, England: Croom Helm.

Foley, R.A. (1987) *Another Unique Species: Patterns in Human Evolutionary Ecology*. Harlow: Longman Scientific and Technical.

Gibbons, A. (1990) 'Palaeontology by bulldozer (research news).' *Science* 247: 1407–1409.

Gibson, K.R. and Ingold, T. (eds) (1993) *Tools, Language and Cognition in Human Evolution*. Cambridge: Cambridge University Press.

Gifford-Gonzalez, D. (1991) 'Bones are not enough: knowledge and interpretative strategies in zooarchaeology.' *Journal of Anthropological Archaeology* 10: 215–254.

Heyes, C.M. and Plotkin, H.C. (1989) 'Replicators and interactors in cultural evolution.' In M. Ruse (ed.) *What the Philosophy of Biology Is*, pp. 139–162. Dordrecht: Kluwer Academic Publishers.

Hull, D.L. (1982) 'The naked meme.' In H.C. Plotkin (ed.) *Development and Culture: Essays in Evolutionary Epistemology*, pp. 273–327. Chichester: Wiley.

Isaac, G. (1969) 'Studies of early culture in East Africa.' *World Archaeology* 1: 1–28.

Isaac, G. (1972) 'Early phases of human behaviour: models in lower Palaeolithic archaeology.' In D.L. Clarke (ed.) *Models in Archaeology*, pp. 167–199. London: Methuen.

Isaac, G. (1976a) 'Early hominids in action: a commentary on the contribution of archaeology to understanding the fossil record of east Africa.' *Yearbook of Physical Anthropology for 1975*, pp. 19–35. Washington DC: AAPA.

Isaac, G. (1976b) 'The activities of early African hominids.' In G. Isaac and E. McCown (eds) *Human Origins*, pp. 483–514. Menlo Park, CA: Benjamin.

Isaac, G. (1978) 'The food sharing behaviour of proto-human hominids.' *Scientific American* 238: 90–108.

Isaac, G. (1981) 'Stone age visiting cards: approaches to the study of early land-use patterns.' In I. Hodder, G. Isaac and N. Hammond (eds) *Pattern of the Past*, pp. 131–155. Cambridge: Cambridge University Press.

Isaac, G. (1983) 'Aspects of human evolution.' In D.S. Bendall (ed.) *Evolution from Molecules to Men*, pp. 509–543. Cambridge: Cambridge University Press.

Isaac, G. (1984) 'The archaeology of human origins: studies of the Lower Pleistocene in east Africa 1971–1981.' *Advances in Old World Archaeology* 3: 1–87.

Mayr, E. (1982) *The Growth of Biological Thought: Diversity, Evolution and Inheritance*. Cambridge, MA: Belknap Press.

Mithen, S.J. (1990) *Thoughtful Foragers: A Study of Prehistoric Decision-making*. Cambridge: Cambridge University Press.

Mithen, S.J. (1991) 'Home bases and stone caches: the archaeology of early hominid activities (review article).' *Cambridge Archaeological Journal* 1: 277–283.

Odling-Smee, F.J. (1983) 'Multiple levels in evolution: an approach to the nature–nurture issue via applied epistemology.' In G.C.L. Davey (ed.) *Animal Models of Human Behaviour*, pp. 135–158. Chichester: Wiley.

Potts, R. (1986) 'Temporal span of bone accumulations at Olduvai Gorge and implications for early hominid foraging behaviour.' *Palaeobiology* 12: 25–31.

Potts, R. (1988) *Early Hominid Activities at Olduvai*. New York: Aldine de Gruyter.

Potts, R. (1989a) 'Ecological context and explanations of hominid evolution.' *Ossa* 14: 99–112.

Potts, R. (1989b) 'Olorgesailie: new excavations and findings in Early and Middle Pleistocene contexts, southern Kenya rift valley.' *Journal of Human Evolution* 18: 477–484.

Shipman, P. (1986) 'Scavenging or hunting in early hominids: theoretical framework and tests.' *American Anthropologist* 88: 27–43.

Stephens, D.W. and Krebs, J.R. (1986) *Foraging Theory*. Princeton: Princeton University Press.

Stern, N. (1991) 'The scatters between the patches: a study of early hominid land-use patterns in the Turkana Basin, Kenya.' Unpublished PhD dissertation, Harvard University.

Stern, N. (1993) 'The structure of the Lower Pleistocene archaeological record: a case study from the Koobi Fora formation.' *Current Anthropology* 34: 201–225.

Tomasello, M., Kruger, A.C. and Ratner, H.H. (1993) 'Cultural learning.' *Behavioural and Brain Sciences* 16: 495–552.

CHAPTER SEVEN

SOCIAL LEARNING AND CULTURAL TRADITION

Interpreting Early Palaeolithic technology

STEVEN MITHEN

INTRODUCTION

The problem archaeologists face when interpreting the stone tools of modern humans is that tools are made under the joint influences of tradition and current needs. As these are not easily separated, the interpretation of stone tools requires extensive reference to both cultural tradition and patterns of economic, social and symbolic behaviour – a daunting task for the archaeologist. My argument in this chapter is that for the Early Palaeolithic the task is perhaps less complex, for tradition heavily outweighed a consideration of current needs in the minds of early tool-makers. This derives, I will argue, from the domain-specific mentality of early humans which prevented the complex integration of thought about technology, social interaction and environmental adaptation that is pervasive among modern humans (Mithen 1994a). In this regard, to further our understanding of early technology, archaeologists need to develop their understanding of 'tradition' – how it arises, how it is transmitted and how it is transformed. Key foci must be the processes of social learning, how these vary between individuals and groups and how this variability influences Early Palaeolithic technology. As a contribution to this task, I will suggest a model for the relationship between social learning, group size and hominid technology and attempt to evaluate it by two case studies from the Early Palaeolithic. Prior to this, I must briefly consider the interaction between tradition and the process of adaptation in modern humans and why this appears to have been absent among early humans.

TRADITION, ADAPTATION AND
MODERN TECHNOLOGY

A modern knapper partly acquires his/her skill by social learning and is therefore influenced by the 'traditional' way of making tools. But he/she is also producing tools for specific functional tasks which may be different to those faced by previous generations – perhaps the type of game is different and the 'traditional' form of a projectile point is no longer effective. As such the cultural tradition may evolve in a direction which results in tools becoming more appropriate for the current ecological context. At any one time the form of a stone tool, and the manner in which it is made, is likely to result from a complex interplay between the influences of tradition and the process of adaptation.

The difficulty this creates for the interpretation of stone tools is exacerbated because the technology of hunter-gatherers is deeply embedded in multiple domains of behaviour. For instance, Wiessner (1983) described how the arrows of the !Kung play significant roles in the economic domain, as they are used to supply meat; in the social domain, for the provider of meat is responsible for its distribution; and in the domain of myth and folklore, for arrows were used for hunting the eland – an animal of symbolic significance for the !Kung. Consequently when a tool is made, the traditional form of an artefact may be modified not only in light of the changing functional requirements, but also due to the changing social and symbolic contexts in which tools are used.

The embedding of technology in multiple behavioural domains creates substantial problems for interpretation, as can be seen from the Upper Palaeolithic. There are numerous well-preserved late glacial settlements which have been excavated in sufficient detail to allow the re-fitting of a substantial number of flakes, blades and cores, such as at Etiolles (Pigeot 1987) and Hengistbury Head (Barton 1992). These re-fitted cores allow us to monitor the actions of individual flint knappers and to reconstruct the specific choices they made when reducing a nodule of flint. Those choices would have been influenced not only by the acquired cultural tradition but by the intended use of the artefacts in economic, social and symbolic spheres. As we have limited information about late glacial behaviour in each of these, the interpretation of why specific technical decisions were made is difficult. It appears impossible to separate out the features of a stone tool that may be attributed to the following of tradition, the imposition of style and functional utility (Sackett 1982). The task of interpretation is further complicated when we take into account the influence of raw material availability and fracture dynamics on the technological options available to a tool-maker.

According to this argument, as we move from the Later to the Earlier Palaeolithic the interpretation of stone tools ought to become more difficult. As the Earlier Palaeolithic record has a poorer chronological resolution and inferences about social and economic behaviour are generally more difficult, it becomes even more unlikely that we can reconstruct the many factors influencing the decision-making of early tool-makers – if these were similar to those of modern humans. This would remain the case even when the particular decisions are seen with as much clarity as in the Upper Palaeolithic (e.g. from the re-fitted cores of Maastricht-Belvedere, Roebroeks 1988). The argument developed in this chapter is that such pessimistic views are unwarranted.

My argument will be that early technology is fundamentally different in character to that of modern humans and was not embedded in multiple behavioural domains. Indeed, I will suggest that rather than emerging from the joint influences of tradition and adaptation, early technology was heavily dominated by the first of these alone; concerns about creating a functionally efficient tool for a specific task or investing it with social information and symbolic meanings played a minimal role in the decisions of early tool-makers. Consequently, when interpreting the imposed form of early stone tools archaeologists need to make relatively extensive reference to tradition but relatively little reference to function and adaptation.

The ecological context certainly influenced technology. Factors such as raw material availability, transport costs, mobility patterns and the duration of occupation at sites influenced the nature and extent of core and tool reduction (e.g. Rolland and Dibble 1990, Kuhn 1991). But these factors simply defined the constraints under which early tool-makers worked. As I have discussed elsewhere (Mithen, in press) their technology provides a passive reflection of the ecological constraints as opposed to constituting an active means to restructure the ecological context, as is characteristic of modern technology.

The principal reason for this is likely to be cognitive: the early human mind appears to have had a much higher degree of domain-specific thought resulting in a technological behaviour being relatively isolated from other behavioural domains (Mithen 1994a, in press). Consequently when decisions about making tools were made, these were not influenced by thought about specific foraging tasks or the need to imbue an artefact with social and symbolic information. Without these influences, tradition, together with ecological constraints, must be seen as the principal influence over artefact form.

DOMAIN-SPECIFIC INTELLIGENCE AND EARLY TECHNOLOGY

It has long been argued that Early Palaeolithic technology is fundamentally different in character to that of modern humans. The limited technological variability across time and space during the Lower and Middle Pleistocene suggests that it is not being used to adapt to environments in the same way as modern technology and does not carry social and symbolic information. Binford (1989) characterized it as an 'aid to', rather than the 'means of' adaptation. Isaac (1972) argued that much of Middle Pleistocene technological variability may be no more than a 'random walk pattern', while Foley (1987) argued that early tools should be analysed as if they were biological, rather than cultural, traits of early hominids. Several archaeologists have suggested that early technology has more in common with that of modern apes, rather than modern humans (e.g. Wynn and McGrew 1988, Davidson and Noble 1993).

The problem with these interpretations is that they do not account for the high levels of technological skill and investment involved in many early industries. The manufacture of a fine, symmetrical Acheulian handaxe, or a Levallois core, is unlikely to have been any less complex than Upper Palaeolithic blade tools. Indeed the production of Oldowan tools required an understanding of fracture mechanics far in advance of that displayed by modern apes (Toth and Schick 1993, Toth *et al.* 1993). Moreover, it is also clear that *in some contexts* early humans were imposing specific forms onto their tools, likely to reflect mental templates of desired artefacts (Gowlett 1984).

The paradox faced by Palaeolithic archaeologists is that when the spatial and temporal variability of early technology is examined, it looks very different to that of modern humans, but when the technological skill and imposition of form (found in some but not all industries) is considered, the technology appears to be very similar to that of modern humans. A resolution of this paradox may be found in the nature of the early human mind.

There has been considerable discussion during the last decade as to the extent to which the minds of modern humans and non-human primates are modular, possessing a 'domain specific intelligence'. The notion of mental modularity was largely introduced by Fodor (1983) who argued that the processes of perception (in which he included language) were encapsulated from each other, 'hard wired', and dependent upon inde- pendent neural circuits. Gardner (1983) applied similar ideas to the notion of intelligence by suggesting that the human mind is constituted by multiple intelligences, such as that relating to language use, musical ability and spatial thought. A more extreme approach has been adopted by Cosmides and Tooby (1987, cf. Tooby and Cosmides 1989, Barkow *et al.* 1992) who argue that the mind is composed of very many discrete modules, each dedicated to an adaptive problem faced by humans in their evolutionary environment. Within studies of non-human primates the notion of a distinct 'social intelligence', deriving from the work of Humphrey (1976) and Jolly (1966), has been very powerful for under- standing primate cognition and behaviour. Contrasts have been drawn between the relative levels of social and non-social intelligence among vervet monkeys (Cheney and Seyfarth 1990).

Rozin (1976, Rozin and Schull 1988) argued that the course of human evolution has involved a trend from a 'domain-specific' to a generalized intelligence. Similarly, Gibson (1993) argued that 'hierarchization' – a process by which new and complex cognitive processes are constructed from the interaction of those which will become lower in a cognitive hierarchy – is a critical theme for the evolution of the human mind. I have recently argued that the patterning in the archaeological record appears to confirm these ideas – the minds of early humans appear to have a much greater degree of domain-specific thought than those of modern humans (Mithen 1994a, in press). Indeed, I have argued that the Middle/Upper Palaeolithic transition marks a major cognitive development towards a generalized intelligence in which cognitive processes which had evolved with regard to very specific activities, such as mediating social interaction, become accessible to thought about other activities. From this increased cognitive accessibility, new capacities developed, such as visual symbolism (Mithen 1994a). This transition from a domain-specific to a generalized mentality is likely to have been a gradual process, with complex relationships to other cognitive developments (such as language). There are likely to have been substantial changes during the course of the Early Palaeolithic and *Homo erectus* may have had a substantially different degree of domain-specific intelligence than, say, Neanderthals. But in this chapter my concern is with the gross contrast between the Early and the Upper Palaeolithic and between a domain-specific and a generalized intelligence.

The essence of this argument is that during the Early Palaeolithic hominids appear to have had a capacity for complex thought about behaviour in numerous domains, such as technology, social interaction and the natural world, but a limited capacity to integrate such thought. For instance, the detailed understanding of animal behaviour that such hominids required to survive in harsh northern landscapes was not integrated with understanding about lithic technology to produce tools specialized for exploiting specific types of game in specific locations. Such tools only appear after the start of the Upper Palaeolithic. This can be illustrated by weapon tips. During the Upper Palaeolithic and Mesolithic there was an impressive variety of points (e.g. Peterkin 1993, Pike-Tay and Bricker 1993), which can be interpreted as partly deriving from an active engagement with the natural world, such as to cope with time stress or to exploit the specific attributes of game species (Torrence 1983, Bleed 1986, Straus 1990). In contrast, the weapon tips created by Neanderthals in Europe during the Middle Palaeolithic were 'remarkably monotonous' reflecting little functional variation (Kuhn 1993) even though Neanderthals lived in a diverse range of environments. Nevertheless, to manufacture Mousterian and Levallois points appears to have involved an equivalent level of technical intelligence to that for making those points of the Upper Palaeolithic. Neanderthals were not generally 'less intelligent', but were unable to integrate their multiple intelligences in the manner of modern humans (Mithen, in press).

The presence of a domain-specific intelligence during the Lower Palaeolithic can be illustrated by comparing the Clactonian and the Acheulian industries of South East England, an example I will return to below. These industries involve a different range of artefact types and different degrees of knapping skill, although there is likely to be a technological continuum rather than sharp divide between them (Ashton 1992). In spite of previous interpretations that these industries were different components of a single 'tool kit' (e.g. Ohel 1979, Roebroeks 1988) it is now clear that they are chronologically independent and were manufactured in different environments with the Clactonian restricted to the Hoxnian interglacial (Wymer 1988), as illustrated in Figure 7.1. Yet there appears to be limited functional differentiation between these industries. Microwear analysis suggests that the core tools (Acheulian handaxes and Clactonian choppers) were used for a similar diverse range of tasks (Keeley 1980) and were not produced for specific tasks appropriate for the resources and structure of those very different environments. In contrast, the technology of modern humans made in glacial and interglacial environments shows dramatic differences (Gamble 1984).

The contrast between the technology of modern and early humans reflects different degrees of integrated thought. For early humans with a high degree of domain-specific thought, technology played a limited active role in adaptive strategies to either the natural or the social environment. While tools were made for functional purposes, these remained at a very generalized level – tools with sharp edges, or which had a substantial mass. Without the influence of thought about the social and natural worlds playing a significant role when tools were being produced, their character was a passive reflection of the ecological and social contexts in which they were produced. Imposed form largely derived from cultural tradition. Consequently, to interpret early technology we need to understand the processes by which tradition is generated and transformed – in other words, the processes of social learning.

SOCIAL LEARNING AND TOOL-MAKING

Humans learn by a variety of processes which can be placed into two classes: individual and social. The division is one of emphasis rather than kind – all human learning takes place in a social context or uses mechanisms that developed during the course of social interaction. Individual learning involves trial and error and the ill-defined processes of 'thought', 'insight' and 'understanding'. Other learning processes are more explicitly social, notably imitation and tuition. It is likely that people are predisposed to use social and individual learning for different tasks (Rogers 1988). With regard to the development of tradition these are

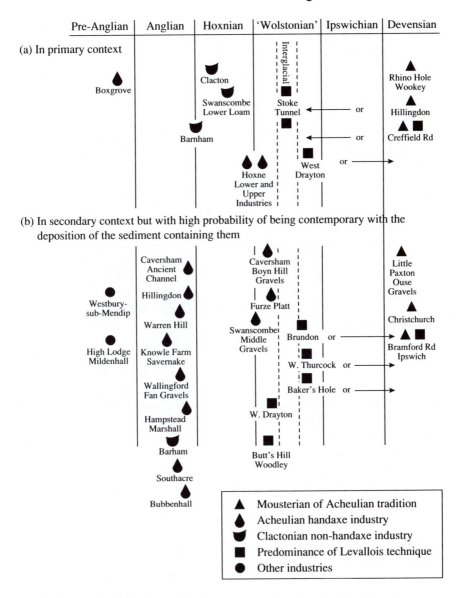

Figure 7.1 Proposed relationship between Lower Palaeolithic assemblages and Pleistocene environmental stages in S.E. England (after Wymer 1988)

pulling in different ways – social learning to propagate traditions, individual learning to dissipate them as people engage in the process of adaptation (Mithen 1989, 1990).

During the last decade there has been considerable interest in the processes of social learning among humans and non-human primates (e.g.

Boyd and Richerson 1985, Whiten 1989). This has led to the collapse of many assumptions and the recognition of the complexity of social learning. In the following I will highlight some of the major themes in these recent discussions, selecting those which are of particular significance for understanding the acquisition of technological knowledge by early humans.

The principle mechanism of social learning among modern humans is imitation (Meltzoff 1988). The urge to imitate is extremely powerful during early stages of child development (Meltzoff and Moore 1989) and imitation is the basis for the acquisition of cultural behaviour. A decade ago it had been assumed that imitation was also prevalent among non-human primates and led to the spread of cultural behaviours such as food-washing, placer-mining and stone-handling (e.g. Kawamura 1959, Huffman 1984, Nishida 1987). The extent to which this is the case has recently been questioned (Galef 1988, 1990) and many primatologists now regard imitation as either absent, or at least very rare, among both monkeys and apes (e.g. Fragaszy and Visalberghi 1990, Visalberghi and Fragaszy 1990, Tomasello 1990, Tomasello *et al.* 1987, 1993, Whiten 1989). Others disagree and point to apparently clear instances of imitative behaviour among wild chimpanzees (e.g. Boesch 1993) or point to the difficulties in recognizing either the presence or absence of imitation (e.g. Byrne 1993, Hauser 1993). This controversy partly reflects the difficulty of arriving at a workable definition for imitation. Tomasello *et al.* (1993) suggest three criteria: (a) the acquisition of behaviour that is novel for the imitator; (b) the reproduction of the actual behavioural strategies of the model; (c) behaviour that is directed towards the same goal as the model. But such definitions may be unworkable in practice and can be questioned in principle (e.g. Heyes 1993). One of the difficulties that a domain-specific cognitive perspective creates is that the ability to imitate as a means of social learning may be present in some domains, but absent in others.

The demise of imitation as an explanation for the spread of cultural behaviour among extant non-human primates has promoted an interest in alternative processes of social learning which are likely to play a major role in both human and non-human societies. The definition of these is plagued by terminological distinctions (Galef 1976) but Byrne (in press) has suggested that there are three principal processes which complement imitation. *Stimulus enhancement* refers to the increase in the probability that an individual will approach or contact something in the environment when a conspecific is observed with it. This is now thought to be a major process by which cultural behaviours are acquired, but it does not imply that the learner is attempting to acquire the specific goals or methods possessed by the model. *Response facilitation* refers to an increase in the probability that an individual will perform a certain act, once a conspecific is observed performing it. This is crucially different from stimulus enhancement, because the actual actions of the model are repeated, and from imitation because these actions must already be in the animal's behavioural repertoire. *Emulation* is a further process of social learning in which an individual copies the goal, but not the methods of a conspecific. This is known to be prevalent among humans and is likely to play a significant role in explaining the results of chimpanzee tool-use experiments (e.g. Tomasello *et al.* 1987).

The above forms of social learning are imitative in nature, even if they do not constitute true imitation. A common feature is that there is no active instruction from the model to the learner. Yet, among humans at least, instructed learning also plays a major role in the generation of cultural traditions. Tomasello *et al.* (1993) suggest that instructed learning is a second stage in the ontogeny of cultural learning and can only arise after the child has developed a theory of mind that enables him/her to understand that another person may have a different mental perspective than his/her own. This generally occurs at around the age of 4 years. Instructed learning takes many forms ranging from simply providing the child with the facilities to encourage his/her own learning to providing a set of instructions, usually by the spoken word.

Tomasello *et al.* (1993) suggest that chimpanzees in the wild do not engage in instructed learning; they also doubt the validity of claimed examples of instructed learning among captive chimpanzees. Boesch (1993) has provided possible evidence for instructed learning among wild chimpanzees by describing two instances in which a mother appears to instruct her juveniles in the most appropriate manner to use tools for opening nuts. Even if this is an instance of active instruction (Tomasello *et al.* 1993 deny this) it is perhaps most notable for being so rare – only two out of 977 observed instances of social interaction. Tomasello *et al.* (1993) suggest that the rarity, or possible absence of instructed learning among chimpanzees is because they cannot conceive of others as mental agents, having thoughts and beliefs that may contrast with their own. This runs counter, however, to a growing body of literature that describes how chimpanzees are capable of deception, which requires a developed theory of mind (e.g. Byrne and Whiten 1988, Whiten 1991).

SOCIAL LEARNING AMONG EARLY HOMINIDS

As described above there is a marked contrast between the social learning capacities of modern humans and non-human primates. This contrast may be qualitative, if imitation is truly absent among non-human primates, or more probably simply quantitative if imitation is present but very rarely expressed. The social learning of non-human primates appears to be dominated by processes of social enhancement and response facilitation. These are also pervasive among modern humans, together with emulation, but are outweighed in significance by imitation.

What were the social learning capacities of pre-modern hominids, *Homo erectus* and archaic *Homo sapiens*? As these share a common ancestor with the chimpanzee we must at least attribute them with capacities for social enhancement and response facilitation. It would also appear, however, that imitation played a significant role in the transmission of technical knowledge – *in some instances*. Perhaps the most remarkable feature of the Acheulian is the similarity in the form and manufacturing processes of handaxes across wide areas (e.g. Wynn and Tierson 1990). Within individual assemblages the similarity between artefacts is often so remarkable that a single knapper may be responsible for several artefacts (e.g. Tyldesley 1986). Yet it is more likely that this simply reflects the presence of strong social learning involving imitation in the transmission of technical knowledge. Indeed, the technical skill required to make some handaxes may suggest that instructed learning was necessary (Dennell 1994), which in turn has implications for the evolution of language.

It is clear, however, that in many assemblages there is a marked absence of typological and technological similarity between artefacts. The Clactonian provides a classic example in which, although some technical features are shared, it is difficult to identify 'types' and the reduction methods are highly variable (Wymer 1974, 1985, Newcomer 1979, Ohel 1979, Roe 1979, 1981). Moreover, the level of technical skill is relatively low, compared to that required to manufacture a handaxe. It would appear that imitation and instructed learning are not playing significant roles in the transmission of technical knowledge. The technical traditions of the Clactonian may be accounted for by weak social enhancement and/or response facilitation alone.

In this regard a major dimension of the variability in Early Palaeolithic assemblages may be accounted for by the variability in the expression of social learning capacities and consequently the role of tradition in artefact manufacture. No doubt other variables are also playing a role, such as variability in raw material quality and availability. But if archaeologists are to explain the variability in the archaeological record, they need to understand the conditions under which the various processes of social learning will be expressed. Under what conditions, for instance, will imitation play a significant role in the transmission of technical knowledge? One possibility, which I will now explore, is when hominids are living in relatively large groups.

GROUP SIZE, SOCIAL INTERACTION AND SOCIAL LEARNING

Non-human primates live in groups which vary markedly in their size, although each species appears to have a modal value for group size (Dunbar 1988, 1991). This variability in group size – whether between or within species – has been interpreted by ecologists as reflecting the adaptive strategies of individual animals. Living in large social groups may provide considerable benefits. It may substantially decrease the chance of predation and/or increase foraging efficiency if resources are patchily distributed in large clumps (Clutton-Brock and Harvey 1977, van Schaik 1983, see Dunbar 1988 for a review of causes of group size). On the other hand there are disadvantages to living in a large group in terms of competition for resources (Wrangham 1987). The frequency of aggressive encounters appears to be directly correlated with group size and the extent to which food is clumped (Dunbar 1988: 113–115). Living in large groups requires extensive social knowledge about other group members and requires the investment in time to service the key relationships which maintain group stability (Dunbar 1991, Aiello and Dunbar 1993).

As a consequence there are often intense relationships between individuals within large groups. The high level of stress may lead to intense bonding within kin groups and the formation of coalitions between kin and non-kin. Specific forms of social interaction, such as grooming, are likely to play an important role in maintaining relationships; Dunbar (1991) has noted that the time spent grooming appears to be positively correlated with group size. The risk of harassment by conspecifics, and/or the risk of predation, may promote paternal care of infants, possibly as a means to maintain relationships with a female (Whitten 1987). Predator risk may promote high levels of social cohesion in general (Kummer et al. 1985) and Dunbar (1988: 303) has noted particularly high levels of social interaction in populations which form unusually large groups.

These causes and consequences of large group size are likely to be as applicable to hominids as to any other large terrestrial primate. But one further consequence, especially significant for hominids with their reliance on stone tools and capacity for strong social learning, is that as group size increases we should expect the opportunities for social learning (of whatever form) to increase. The frequency of innovation is likely to decrease as juveniles will be encouraged to feed with and remain spatially close to adults, especially their kin, due to the high level of social harassment and the clumping of food. Consequently, the relative role of social to individual learning will increase. Similarly, the rate of cultural transmission will increase. Individuals will be able to observe the actions of other individuals, such as their manipulation of objects more frequently and in more detail when living in large groups, due to the importance of intense kin-bonding, coalitions and the high frequency of visual monitoring and social interaction in general. This increased opportunity for observation will increase the extent of stimulus enhancement, response facilitation, true imitation and emulation. It may also increase the probability that individuals will engage in instructed learning.

GROUP SIZE AND INDUSTRIAL VARIABILITY

The implications of the changing patterns of social learning between small and large groups for hominid technology are substantial (Mithen 1994b). When living in small groups knapping procedures are likely to be diverse due to the absence, or weak influence, of cultural traditions of artefact manufacture. Similarly, artefact form will be diverse and heavily influenced by raw material characteristics. Knapping skill will also be limited since the 'ratchet' effect deriving from cumulative technical experience will be constrained by the low degree of social learning. As with modern primates, each generation may be struggling to reach the level of technical skill achieved by the preceding generation.

In contrast, when hominids are living in larger groups, social learning will become more significant – the rate of innovation will decrease, while the transmission of a new cultural trait will increase. The consequences for technology are that common knapping procedures and artefact forms will be found throughout the group and a relatively high level of technical skill may develop due to cumulative experience. We should still expect artefacts displaying low levels of technical skill and shared features to be produced, as the artefacts deriving from the shared cultural traditions of the group are likely to be additions to, rather than replacements of, the technological repertoire.

The influences of increased social learning on hominid technology will only be realized if raw material characteristics are appropriate. If a material with poor flaking characteristics is being worked (such as a coarse-grained quartzite), so that it is very difficult to remove a flake of a specific size and shape, there will be a constraint upon the expression, and consequently transmission and development of technical skill and shared artefact forms. With such materials, the technology of hominids in large groups, experiencing strong social learning, may be indistinguishable from that of hominids in small groups with weak social learning.

EVALUATING THE MODEL: HOMINID GROUP SIZE DURING THE EARLY PALAEOLITHIC

The above model has set up some expectations concerning how hominid technology should vary with hominid group size under the joint conditions of a domain-specific intelligence and raw materials which allow the expression of technological skill and the imposition of form. Evaluating the model requires that we can make estimates for past hominid group size.

This is, perhaps, one of the most difficult tasks for the Palaeolithic archaeologist. In the vast majority of sites the extent of post-depositional disturbance has been so substantial that we have little idea about original site structure. And even when extensive areas of *in situ* remains are preserved, we lack any methodology to move from that data to past group size. Due to the difference in the cognitive characteristics I have outlined above, it is unlikely that those methods which may allow us to estimate the hunter-gatherer group size from site structure (e.g. O'Connell 1987) of modern humans will be applicable to the early Palaeolithic. The spatial behaviour and resulting site structure of early humans appears to be principally episodic in nature and in marked contrast to that of modern humans (Stringer and Gamble 1993).

A consequence of the absence of a methodology for inferring past group size directly from archaeological data is that we need to turn to indirect evidence. There are two sources: hominid brain size and palaeoenvironments. The first may allow us to make an estimate for the absolute modal group size of a hominid species, while the second allows us to estimate the relative group size for the same species when living in different environments.

GROUP SIZE AND NEOCORTEX RATIO: THE OLDOWAN AND ACHEULIAN

Dunbar (1992) has shown that among living primates there is a strong positive correlation between group size and the neocortex size. As there is also a correlation between brain size and neocortex size, and the brain size of hominids can be derived from fossil endocasts, estimates for the modal group size of early Palaeolithic hominids can be made. In this regard we can make an indirect estimate for the modal group size of past hominids.

According to the figures provided by Aiello and Dunbar (1993) the modal group size for *Homo habilis/rudolfensis* is c. 82, that for *Homo erectus* is c. 111 and that for Archaic *Homo sapiens* c. 137, the last being not significantly different to that of modern humans. Here we should focus on the contrast between *Homo habilis/rudolfensis* and *Homo erectus* and note that as group size is significantly larger for the later species, we should expect an increase in the extent of social learning, and consequently cultural tradition should be a more pervasive influence over technology and artefact form. I am not concerned with the accuracy of the specific figures for group size that Aiello and Dunbar propose. The derivation of their figures involves several assumptions about appropriate statistical methods and the importance of their work for this chapter is simply that group size of *Homo erectus* is predicted to be significantly larger than that for *Homo habilis/rudolfensis* – the extent of the difference is open to debate.

Although it is possible that Australopithecines were making early artefacts (Susman 1991), the Oldowan is conventionally attributed to *Homo habilis/rudolfensis*, while the developed Oldowan and the Acheulian were produced by *Homo erectus*. In spite of the disagreement about the complexity of both Oldowan and Acheulian technologies (e.g. Toth 1985, Wynn and McGrew 1988, Davidson and Noble 1993, Toth and Schick

1993, Toth *et al.* 1993), there can be little doubt that the latter displays a higher level of technical skill and cultural traditions in artefact form. 'Types' are likely to be absent in the Oldowan (Toth 1985, Potts 1988), while with the early Acheulian, bifaces are being produced with imposed form, probably resulting from mental templates (Gowlett 1984, Wynn 1989).

While the Oldowan/Acheulian contrast follows our expected pattern of technological change with group size, mediated by increased social learning, it may also be accounted for by other factors. We may be witnessing a general increase in the overall capacity for social learning between *Homo habilis* and *Homo erectus*, rather than simply an increase in its expression. *Homo habilis* may well have possessed a repertoire of social learning capacities more similar to modern apes, in which, as discussed above, imitation may be absent. A second problem, is that the Acheulian is a very diverse industry with marked variability in technological skill and the extent of shared artefact form. Moreover, *Homo erectus* and archaic *Homo sapiens*, in some areas and at some times, had a pebble/flake industry which was more similar to the Oldowan than the Acheulian (e.g. Vértesszöllös, Bilzingsleben, Isernia, Clacton – Wymer 1974, Vértes 1975, Svoboda 1987). This level of technological variability may be accounted for by variation in group size within species, and provides a more effective evaluation of the proposed model.

GROUP SIZE AND PALAEOENVIRONMENTS: THE ACHEULIAN AND CLACTONIAN

As noted above, primate group size is likely to be relatively large under conditions of high predator risk and resource clumping. Both of these tend to be associated with open, rather than closed (i.e. wooded) landscapes. Trees provide a means to hide and escape from predators, while in open landscapes primates remain at high risks of detection. In wooded landscapes both animal and plant resources are likely to be more dispersed and to come in smaller packages than in open landscapes. In these, hominids are likely to have been dependent upon meat, possibly scavenged from carcasses (Gamble 1987). Consequently, we should expect hominids to have lived in relatively larger groups in open rather than closed landscapes.

We know that the extent of tree cover has varied markedly during the Pleistocene. At a gross level, we know there to have been at least eight glacial/interglacial cycles during the Middle and Upper Pleistocene and these involved the environment switching from open to closed landscapes (Shackleton and Opdyke 1973, West 1977). Within any one glacial or interglacial phase there was also substantial environmental variability through time and space. As the environments changed during the course of the Pleistocene, hominids adapted their behaviour to fit the changing

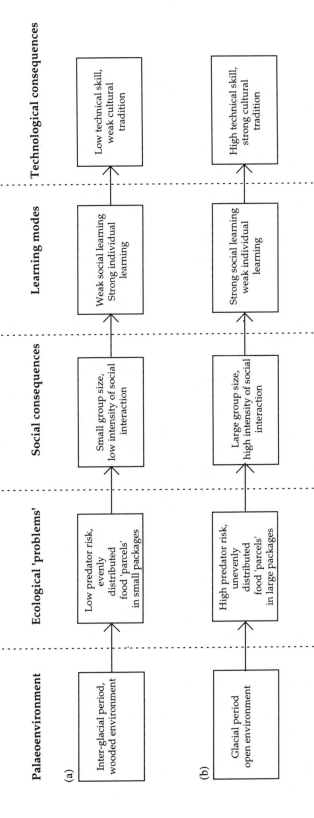

Figure 7.2a Proposed causal relationships between closed (i.e. wooded) environments and early hominid technology, as mediated by social interaction and social learning. This scenario is suggested as applicable to the Lower Palaeolithic Clactonian industry of S.E. England

Figure 7.2b Proposed causal relationships between open environments and early hominid technology, suggested as being applicable to Lower Palaeolithic Acheulian industry in S.E. England

conditions. Unlike modern humans, they appear to have been unable to cope with the extreme conditions of either very thickly wooded or barren tundra landscapes at the peak of an interglacial or glacial (Gamble 1986, 1992, Roebroeks *et al.* 1992).

One response of the hominid populations to changing environments is likely to have been an adjustment in group size for the reasons of predator defence and/or resource exploitation as described above. Consequently, according to the above model, we should expect to find some correlation between technological variability and palaeoenvironments, with hominid group size and social learning as the mediating factors (Figure 7.2). During periods in which landscapes were relatively treeless, we should expect hominids to have formed relatively large groups and for social learning to have played a substantial role in the acquisition of technical knowledge. As a result, and if raw materials are suitable, we should expect to find artefacts which display high levels of skill, morphological and technological similarity. In contrast, during periods in which the landscape was wooded, hominid group size is likely to have been low, social learning weak and technology to have remained relatively simple. We should expect artefacts to display considerable variability in form and manufacturing process.

This hypothesized relationship between stone tool technology and palaeoenvironments is straightforward, but not easy to test. It requires a detailed understanding of the sequence of technological and environmental change in one region in which raw materials are found which may express the changing levels of social learning. The character of the Middle Pleistocene archaeological record makes such opportunities very rare (Villa 1991). One region where this appears possible is South East England during the Middle Pleistocene (Mithen 1994b).

There has been a long history of research on the industrial and environmental sequence of South East England. Both of these have been subject to a major re-evaluation in recent years as the complexity of Pleistocene environmental change has been recognized and clear evidence for pre-Anglian occupation acquired (e.g. Roberts 1986, Ashton *et al.* 1992). The variability in the lithic assemblages has been summarized by identifying two major industrial types, the Clactonian and the Acheulian, whose technological features have been well described and subject to numerous interpretations.

Wymer's (1988) re-evaluation of the environmental and industrial sequence has suggested that the Clactonian can now be confidently placed in the Hoxnian interglacial. Palaeoenvironments during the Hoxnian were thickly wooded (Turner 1970, Kerney 1971, Stuart 1982) and we should expect hominids to have formed relatively small social groups and social learning to have been weakly present. Acheulian assemblages appear to have been only manufactured in the relatively open environments of the glacial phases, when group size is likely to have been large and social learning strong. These industrial/environmental associations fit with the expectations of the model proposed in this paper. The Clactonian involves limited technological skill, lacks artefacts with imposed and shared form, and exhibits a diverse range of knapping methods (Wymer 1974, 1979, Newcomer 1979, Ohel 1979, Roe 1981). In contrast, the Acheulian assemblages involve artefacts which required considerable technical skill to manufacture and which often display strong similarities in form and technology – in other words they exhibit a strong cultural tradition.

CONCLUSION

Neither of the two case studies briefly described in this chapter are perfectly suited to testing the model concerning hominid technology and group size proposed in this chapter. In both cases group size can only be estimated by indirect evidence, relying on relationships found among modern primates.

Although Palaeolithic archaeologists deal with a vast time span of human prehistory for which there is an extremely poor chronological resolution, they must devote more effort to developing models for micro-scale processes – the decisions and actions of individuals (Mithen 1994c). It was from these that cultural traditions developed and the process of adaptation was accomplished. Similarly, greater attention must be paid to children and the means by which they acquire technical knowledge, to balance the current dominant concern with the manner in which adults exploit such knowledge to make tools. Recent developmental studies of humans, apes and monkeys (e.g. Parker and Gibson 1990, Tomasello et al. 1993) suggest that there is considerable potential for the construction of archaeological models for the cognitive development of juvenile early humans.

For modern humans cultural tradition (acquired by social learning) and the process of adaptation (achieved by individual learning) are likely to have played equivalent roles in the decision-making of tool-makers. Their technology was embedded in multiple domains of behaviour and played active roles in the exploitation of the natural world, social interaction and symbolic communication. In contrast, for early humans there appears to have been a greater degree of independence between behavioural domains and while they possessed a high level of technical intelligence, tools were made for generalized purposes and passively reflected the ecological and social conditions of manufacture. As such, their form could become heavily influenced by tradition in contexts when the degree of social interaction – particularly between adults and juveniles – was intense, resulting in strong social learning.

REFERENCES

Aiello, L.C. and Dunbar, R.I.M. (1993) 'Neocortex size, group size and the evolution of language.' *Current Anthropology* 34: 184–193.

Ashton, N.M. (1992) 'The High Lodge flint industries.' In N.M. Ashton, J. Cook, S.G. Lewis and J. Rose (eds) *High Lodge: Excavations by G. de G. Sieveking 1962–68 and J. Cook 1988*, pp. 124–163. London: British Museum Press.

Ashton, N.M., Cook, J., Lewis, S.G. and Rose, J. (eds) (1992) *High Lodge: Excavations by G. de G. Sieveking 1962–68 and J. Cook 1988*. London: British Museum Press.

Barkow, J., Cosmides, L. and Tooby, J. (eds) (1992) *The Adapted Mind: Evolutionary Psychology and the Generation of Culture*. Oxford: Oxford University Press.

Barton, N. (1992) *Hengistbury Head, Volume 2. The Later Upper Palaeolithic and Mesolithic Sites*. Oxford: Oxford Committee for Aerial Photography.

Binford, L. (1989) 'Isolating the transitions to cultural adaptations.' In L. Binford, *Debating Archaeology*, pp. 423–436. New York: Academic Press.

Bleed, P. (1986) 'The optimal design of hunting weapons: maintainability or reliability?' *American Antiquity* 51: 737–747.

Boesch, C. (1993) 'Aspects of transmission of tool-use in wild chimpanzees.' In K. Gibson and T. Ingold (eds) *Tools, Language and Cognition in Human Evolution*, pp. 171–183. Cambridge: Cambridge University Press.

Boyd, R. and Richerson, P. (1985) *Culture and the Evolutionary Process*. Chicago: Chicago University Press.

Byrne, R.W. (1993) 'Hierarchical levels of imitation.' *Behavioural and Brain Sciences* 16: 516–517.

Byrne, R.W. (in press) 'The evolution of intelligence.' In P.J.B. Slater and T.R. Halliday (eds) *Behaviour and Evolution*. Cambridge: Cambridge University Press.

Byrne, R.W. and Whiten, A. (eds) (1988) *Machiavellian Intelligence: Social Expertise and the Evolution of Intelligence in Monkeys, Apes and Humans*. Oxford: Oxford University Press.

Cheney, D.L. and Seyfarth, R.M. (1990) *How Monkeys see the World*. Chicago: Chicago University Press.

Cosmides, L. and Tooby, J. (1987) 'From evolution to behaviour: evolutionary psychology as the missing link.' In J. Dupre (ed.) *The Latest on the Best: Essays on Evolution and Optimality*, pp. 277–306. Cambridge, MA: MIT Press.

Clutton-Brock,T.H. and Harvey, P.H. (1977) 'Primate ecology and social organisation.' *Journal of the Zoological Society of London* 183: 1–39.

Davidson, I. and Noble, W. (1993) 'Tools and language in human evolution.' In K. Gibson and T. Ingold (eds) *Tools, Language and Cognition in Human Evolution*, pp. 363–389. Cambridge: Cambridge University Press.

Dennell, R. (1994) 'Comment on Mithen, S.J. "Technology and society during the Middle Pleistocene".' *Cambridge Archaeological Journal* 4: 24–25.

Dunbar, R.I.M. (1988) *Primate Social Systems*. London: Croom Helm.

Dunbar, R.I.M. (1991) 'Functional significance of social grooming in primates.' *Folia Primatologica* 57: 121–131.

Dunbar, R.I.M. (1992) 'Neocortex size as a constraint on group size in primates.' *Journal of Human Evolution* 22: 469–493.

Fodor, J. (1983) *The Modularity of Mind.* Cambridge, MA: MIT Press.

Foley, R. (1987) 'Hominid species and stone tool assemblages: how are they related?' *Antiquity* 61: 380–392.

Fragaszy, D. and Visalberghi, E. (1990) 'Social processes affecting the appearance of innovative behaviours in Capuchin monkeys.' *Folia Primatologica* 54: 155–165.

Galef, B.G. (1976) 'Social transmission of acquired behaviour: a discussion of tradition and social learning in vertebrates.' In J.S. Rosenblatt, R.A. Hinde, E. Shaw and C.G. Beer (eds) *Advances in the Study of Behaviour*, Vol. 6, pp. 77–100. New York: Academic Press.

Galef, B.G. (1988) 'Imitation in animals: history, definition and interpretation of data from the psychological laboratory.' In T.R. Zentall and B.G. Galef (eds) *Social Learning: A Comparative Approach*, pp. 3–28. Hillsdale, NJ: Erlbaum.

Galef, B.G. (1990) 'Tradition in animals: field observations and laboratory analysis.' In M. Bekoff and D. Jamieson (eds) *Methods, Inferences, Interpretations and Explanations in the Study of Behaviour*, pp. 74–95. Boulder, CO: Westview Press.

Gamble, C. (1984) 'Regional variation in hunter-gatherer strategy in the Upper Pleistocene of Europe.' In R. Foley (ed.) *Human Evolution and Community Ecology*, pp. 237–260. London: Academic Press.

Gamble, C. (1986) *The Palaeolithic Settlement of Europe.* Cambridge: Cambridge University Press.

Gamble, C. (1987) 'Man the shoveler: alternative models for Middle Pleistocene colonization and occupation in northern latitudes.' In O. Soffer (ed.) *The Pleistocene Old World*, pp. 81–98. New York: Plenum Press.

Gamble, C. (1992) 'Comment on "Dense forests, cold steppes, and the Palaeolithic settlement of Northern Europe" by W. Roebroeks, N.J. Conrad and T. van Kolfschoten.' *Current Anthropology* 33: 569–571.

Gardner, H. (1983) *Frames of Mind: The Theory of Multiple Intelligences.* New York: Basic Books.

Gibson, K. (1993) 'Tool use, language and social behaviour in relationship to information processing capacities.' In K. Gibson and T. Ingold (eds) *Tools, Language and Cognition in Human Evolution*, pp. 251–270. Cambridge: Cambridge University Press.

Gowlett, J. (1984) 'The mental abilities of early man: a look at some hard evidence.' In R. Foley (ed.) *Human Evolution and Community Ecology*, pp. 167–192. London: Academic Press.

Hauser, M.D. (1993) 'Cultural learning: are there functional consequences?' *Behavioural and Brain Sciences* 16: 524.

Heyes, C. (1993) 'Imitation without perspective-taking.' *Behavioural and Brain Sciences* 16: 524–525.

Huffman, M. (1984) 'Stone play of *Macaca fuscata* in Arashiyana B troop: transmission of a non-adaptive behaviour.' *Journal of Human Evolution* 13: 725–735.

Humphrey, N. (1976) 'The social function of intellect.' In P.P.G. Bateson and R.A. Hinde (eds) *Growing Points in Ethology*, pp. 303–317. Cambridge: Cambridge University Press.

Isaac, G.L. (1972) 'Chronology and the tempo of cultural change during the Pleistocene.' In W.W. Bishop and J. Miller (eds) *Calibration of Hominid Evolution*, pp. 381–430. Edinburgh: Scottish Academic Press.

Jolly, A. (1966) 'Lemur social behaviour and primate intelligence.' *Science* 153: 501–506.

Kawamura, S. (1959) 'The process of sub-culture propagation among Japanese macaques.' *Primates* 24: 43–60.

Keeley, L. (1980) *Experimental Determination of Stone Tool Uses: A Microwear Analysis.* Chicago: Chicago University Press.

Kerney, M.P. (1971) 'Interglacial deposits in Barnfield pit, Swanscombe, and their molluscan fauna.' *Journal of the Geological Society of London* 127: 69–93.

Kuhn, S.L. (1991) ' "Unpacking" reduction: lithic raw material economy in the Mousterian of west central Italy.' *Journal of Anthropological Archaeology* 10: 76–106.

Kuhn, S.L. (1993) 'Mousterian technology as adaptive response: a case study.' In G.L. Peterkin, H.M. Bricker and P. Mellars (eds) *Hunting and Animal Exploitation in the Later Palaeolithic and Mesolithic of Eurasia.* Archaeological Papers of the American Anthropological Association 4: 2–31.

Kummer, H., Banaja, A., Abo-khatwa, A. and Ghandour, A. (1985) 'Differences in social behaviour between Ethiopian and Arabian Hamadryas baboons.' *Folia Primatologica* 45: 1–8.

Meltzoff, A.N. (1988) '*Homo imitans.*' In T.R. Zentall and B.G. Galef (eds) *Social Learning: A Comparative Approach*, pp. 319–342. Hillsdale, NJ: Erlbaum.

Meltzoff, A.N. and Moore, M.K. (1989) 'Imitation in newborn infants: exploring the range of gestures imitated and the underlying mechanisms.' *Developmental Psychology* 25: 954–962.

Mithen, S.J. (1989) 'Evolutionary theory and post-processual archaeology.' *Antiquity* 63: 483–494.

Mithen, S.J. (1990) *Thoughtful Foragers; A Study of Prehistoric Decision-making.* Cambridge: Cambridge University Press.

Mithen, S.J. (1994a) 'From domain-specific to generalised intelligence: a cognitive interpretation of the Middle/Upper Palaeolithic transition.' In C. Renfrew and E. Zubrow (eds) *The Ancient Mind*, pp. 29–39. Cambridge: Cambridge University Press.

Mithen, S.J. (1994b) 'Technology and society during the Middle Pleistocene.' *Cambridge Archaeological Journal* 4: 3–33.

Mithen, S.J. (1994c) 'Individuals, groups and the Palaeolithic record: a reply to Clark.' *Proceedings of the Prehistoric Society* 59: 393–398.

Mithen, S.J. (in press) 'Domain-specific intelligence and the Neanderthal mind.' In P. Mellars and K. Gibson (eds) *Modelling the Early Human Mind*, MacDonald Institute for Archaeological Research Monograph 1. Cambridge: Cambridge University Press.

Newcomer, M. (1979) 'Comment on "The Clactonian: an independent entity or an integral part of the Acheulian", by M.Y. Ohel.' *Current Anthropology* 20: 717.

Nishida, T. (1987) 'Local traditions and cultural transmission.' In B.B. Smuts, D.L. Cheney, R.M. Seyfarth, R.W. Wrangham and T.T. Struhsaker (eds) *Primate Societies*, pp. 462–474. Chicago: University of Chicago Press.

O'Connell, J. (1987) 'Alyawara site structure and its archaeological implications.' *American Antiquity* 52: 74–108.

Ohel, M.Y. (1979) 'The Clactonian: an independent entity or an integral part of the Acheulian.' *Current Anthropology* 20: 685–726.

Parker, S.T. and Gibson, K. (eds) (1990) *'Language' and Intelligence in Monkeys and Apes*. Cambridge: Cambridge University Press.

Peterkin, G.L. (1993) 'Lithic and organic hunting technology in the French Upper Palaeolithic.' In G.L. Peterkin, H.M. Bricker and P. Mellars (eds) *Hunting and Animal Exploitation in the Later Palaeolithic and Mesolithic of Eurasia*. Archaeological Papers of the American Anthropological Association 4: 49–68.

Pigeot, N. (1987) *Magdaléniens d'Étiolles: Economie de Debitage et Organisation Sociale* (Suppl. 25 Gallia Préhistoire). Paris: CNRS.

Pike-Tay, A. and Bricker, H. (1993) 'Hunting in the Gravettian; an examination of evidence from southwestern France.' In G.L. Peterkin, H.M. Bricker and P. Mellars (eds) *Hunting and Animal Exploitation in the Later Palaeolithic and Mesolithic of Eurasia*. Archaeological Papers of the American Anthropological Association 4: 127–144.

Potts, R. (1988) *Early Hominid Activities at Olduvai*. New York: Aldine de Gruyter.

Roberts, M. (1986) 'Excavations of the Lower Palaeolithic site at Amey's Eartham pit, Boxgrove, West Sussex.' *Proceedings of the Prehistoric Society* 52: 215–245.

Roe, D. (1979) 'Comment on "The Clactonian: an independent entity or an integral part of the Acheulian", by M.Y. Ohel.' *Current Anthropology*, 20: 718–719.

Roe, D. (1981) *The Lower and Middle Palaeolithic Periods in Britain*. London: Routledge and Kegan Paul.

Roebroeks, W. (1988) 'From flint scatters to early hominid behaviour: a study of Middle Palaeolithic riverside settlements at Mastrict-Belvedere.' *Analecta Praehistorica Leidensae* 21.

Roebroeks, W., Conrad, N.J. and van Kolfschoten, T. (1992) 'Dense forests, cold steppes, and the Palaeolithic settlement of Northern Europe.' *Current Anthropology* 33: 551–586.

Rogers, A.R. (1988) 'Does biology constrain culture?' *American Anthropologist* 90: 818–831.

Rolland, N. and Dibble, H.L. (1990) 'A new synthesis of Middle Palaeolithic variability.' *American Antiquity* 55: 480–499.

Rozin, P. (1976) 'The evolution of intelligence and access to the cognitive unconscious.' In J.N. Sprague and A.N. Epstein (eds) *Progress in Psychobiology and Physiological Psychology*. New York: Academic Press.

Rozin, P. and Schull, J. (1988) 'The adaptive–evolutionary point of view in experimental psychology.' In R.C. Atkinson, R.J. Herrnstein, G. Lindzey and R.D. Luce (eds) *Stevens' Handbook of Experimental Psychology, Vol. 1: Perception and Motivation*, pp. 503–546. New York: John Wiley and Sons.

Sackett, J. (1982) 'Approaches to style in lithic archaeology.' *Journal of Anthropological Archaeology* 1: 59–112.

Shackleton, N.J. and Opdyke, N.D. (1973) 'Oxygen isotope and palaeomagnetic stratigraphy of equatorial Pacific core, V28-238.' *Quaternary Research* 3: 39–55.

Straus, L.G. (1990) 'The original arms race: Iberian perspectives on the Solutrean phenomenon.' In J. Kozlowski (ed.) *Feuilles du Pierre: Les Industries à Pointes Foliacées du Paléolithique Supérieur Européen*, pp. 425–447, ERAUL 42. Liège: Université de Liège.

Stringer, C. and Gamble, C. (1993) *In Search of the Neanderthals*. London: Thames and Hudson.
Stuart, A.J. (1982) *Pleistocene Vertebrates in the British Isles*. New York: Longman.
Susman, R.L. (1991) 'Who made Oldowan tools? Fossil evidence for tool behaviour in Plio-Pleistocene hominids.' *Journal of Anthropological Research* 47: 129–151.
Svoboda, J. (1987) 'Lithic industries of the Arago, Vértesszöllös, and Bilzingsleben hominids: comparisons and evolutionary interpretation.' *Current Anthropology* 28: 219–227.
Tomasello, M. (1990) 'Cultural transmission in tool use and communicatory signalling of chimpanzees.' In S. Parker and K. Gibson (eds) *Language and Intelligence in Monkeys and Apes: Developmental Perspectives*, pp. 274–311. Cambridge: Cambridge University Press.
Tomasello, M., Davis-Dasilva, M., Camak, L. and Bard, K. (1987) 'Observational learning of tool use by young chimpanzees.' *Human Evolution* 2: 175–183.
Tomasello, M., Kruger, A.C. and Ratner, H.H. (1993) 'Cultural learning.' *Behavioural and Brain Sciences* 16: 495–552.
Tooby, J. and Cosmides, L. (1989) 'Evolutionary psychology and the generation of culture, part I.' *Ethology and Sociobiology* 10: 29–49.
Torrence, R. (1983) 'Time budgeting and hunter-gatherer technology.' In G. Bailey (ed.) *Hunter-Gatherer Economy in Prehistory: A European Perspective*, pp. 11–22. Cambridge: Cambridge University Press.
Toth, N. (1985) 'The Oldowan reassessed: a close look at early stone artefacts.' *Journal of Archaeological Science* 12: 101–120.
Toth, N. and Schick, K. (1993) 'Early stone industries and inferences regarding language and cognition.' In K. Gibson and T. Ingold (eds) *Tools, Language and Cognition in Human Evolution*, pp. 346–362. Cambridge: Cambridge University Press.
Toth, N., Schick, K., Savage-Rumbaugh, S., Sevcik, R.A. and Rumbaugh, D.M. (1993) 'Pan the tool-maker: Investigations into the stone tool-making and tool-using capabilities of a Bonobo (*Pan paniscus*).' *Journal of Archaeological Science* 20: 81–91.
Turner, C. (1970) 'The Middle Pleistocene deposits at Marks Tey, Essex.' *Philosophical Transactions of the Royal Society, B* 257: 373–440.
Tyldesley, J. (1986) *The Wolvercote Channel Handaxe Assemblage: A Comparative Study*. Oxford: British Archaeological Reports, British Series 152.
van Schaik, C.P. (1983) 'Why are diurnal primates living in groups?' *Behaviour* 87: 120–144.
Vértes, L. (1975) 'The Lower Palaeolithic site of Vértesszöllös, Hungary.' In R. Bruce-Mitford (ed.) *Recent Archaeological Excavations in Europe*, pp. 287–301. London: Routledge and Kegan Paul.
Villa, P. (1991) 'Middle Pleistocene prehistory in southwestern Europe: the state of our knowledge and ignorance.' *Journal of Anthropological Research* 47: 193–217.
Visalberghi, E. and Fragaszy, D. (1990) 'Do monkeys ape?' In S. Parker and K. Gibson (eds) *Language and Intelligence in Monkeys and Apes: Developmental Perspectives*, pp. 247–73. Cambridge: Cambridge University Press.
West, R.G. (1977) *Pleistocene Geology and Biology*. New York: Longman.
Whiten, A. (1989) 'Transmission mechanisms in primate cultural evolution.' *Trends in Ecology and Evolution* 4: 61–62.

Whiten, A. (ed.) (1991) *Natural Theories of Mind: Evolution, Simulation and Development of Everyday Mindreading.* Oxford: Basil Blackwell.

Whitten, P. (1987) 'Infants and adult males.' In B.B. Smuts, D.L. Cheney, R.M. Seyfarth, R.W. Wrangham and T.T. Struhsaker (eds) *Primate Societies*, pp. 343–357. Chicago: University of Chicago Press.

Wiessner, P. (1983) 'Style and social information in Kalahari San projectile points.' *American Anthropologist* 48: 253–276.

Wrangham, R. (1987) 'Evolution of social structure.' In B.B. Smuts, D.L. Cheney, R.M. Seyfarth, R.W. Wrangham and T.T. Struhsaker (eds) *Primate Societies*, pp. 283–296. Chicago: University of Chicago Press.

Wymer, J. (1974) 'Clactonian and Acheulian industries in Britain: their character and significance.' *Proceedings of the Geological Association* 85: 391–421.

Wymer, J. (1979) 'Comment on "The Clactonian: an independent entity or an integral part of the Acheulian," by M.Y. Ohel.' *Current Anthropology* 20: 719.

Wymer, J. (1985) *Palaeolithic Sites of East Anglia.* Norwich: GeoBooks.

Wymer, J. (1988) 'Palaeolithic archaeology and the British Quaternary sequence.' *Quaternary Science Reviews* 7: 79–98.

Wynn, T. (1989) *The Evolution of Spatial Competence.* Urbana: University of Illinois Press.

Wynn, T. and McGrew, W. (1988) 'An ape's eye view of the Oldowan.' *Man* (n.s.) 24: 383–398.

Wynn, T. and Tierson, F. (1990) 'Regional comparison of the shapes of later Acheulian handaxes.' *American Anthropologist* 92: 73–84.

CHAPTER EIGHT

ON PREDICTING
HOMINID GROUP SIZES

JAMES STEELE

INTRODUCTION

Reconstructing the social systems of extinct hominids is one of the fundamental goals of palaeoanthropology and of Palaeolithic archaeology. It is also an important field of research for the many social scientists who are currently seeking to ground their models of human 'evolved behavioural predispositions' in the selective context of Pleistocene foraging bands. However, the uses of the archaeological record for this purpose are being re-evaluated, as a new generation of field workers comes to recognize the limited temporal resolution available in the archaeological record for reconstructing snapshots of Lower Palaeolithic patterns of range use, and the constraints this places on validating models like Isaac's 'home base' (Stern 1993, Lake, this volume).

Because of this, other reconstructive methodologies are urgently being sought to complement the long-term perspective which archaeology provides on human behavioural evolution. One promising field involves the use of observations of living primates to make predictions about the socioecology of extinct hominids. This is exemplified by McHenry's use of studies of sexual dimorphism in living primates to make inferences about the levels of male–male competition in hominid groups on the basis of hominid sexual size dimorphisms (this volume).

One very innovative attempt to apply this methodology to extinct hominid social systems is Aiello and Dunbar's (1993) derivation of a predictive model for fitting expected average group sizes to hominid fossils on the basis of their brain size and organization. The model is based on a bivariate regression analysis of the relationship between two variables, group size and relative neocortex size, across extant primate genera (Dunbar 1992), and uses the equation which describes a best-fit line for this covariation as a prediction equation for hominids of known cranial capacities. The strength of the original observed correlation was taken by Dunbar (1992) to indicate a causal relationship between the complexity of primate group life and the cognitive resources required by group members. Group sizes predicted for these living non-human primate genera using Dunbar's equation have a good fit with observed values ($r^2 = 77.26$, mean group size observed vs. mean group size predicted with both variables logged, n = 35 genera, data from Dunbar 1992: Table 1). Consequently, even if the hypothesis of a direct causal link is mistaken, the predictive value of the equation may remain, since any latent variables affecting both cortex ratio and average group sizes might appear to have a fairly constant effect on each variable across the primate order.

Aiello and Dunbar extend the predictive scope of this equation by interpolating steps to derive an expected 'cortex ratio' from measurements of the endocranial capacity of primate or hominid skulls. The arguments justifying this extension of the model are given in their paper, but without testing it against primate species of known cranial capacities and known average group sizes. In this chapter, which is conceived of as an extended footnote to their work, I shall ask four simple questions in the course of validating and extending this method of predicting behavioural variables from anatomical form. How confidently can we predict cortex ratios from endocranial capacity data? How confidently can we use the Reduced Major Axis line for predicting group size from cortex ratios? What other methods exist for deriving causal models of the relationships between anatomical and behavioural variables in living taxa? And finally, how can the accuracy of such predictive exercises be checked using archaeological evidence?

HOW CONFIDENTLY CAN WE PREDICT CORTEX RATIOS FROM ENDOCRANIAL CAPACITY DATA?

Aiello and Dunbar (1993) predicted the mean group sizes of extinct hominids, living humans and living great apes using a Reduced Major Axis equation describing the fit between generic mean group size and neocortex ratio, across thirty-five primate genera (Dunbar 1992: Eq. 1). For the fossils, neocortex ratio was predicted from estimates of total brain volume, which were in turn derived from measurements of endocranial capacity. Although the original equation correlating group size with neocortex ratio was derived from comparing generic averages, Aiello and Dunbar use it to predict specific (and intraspecific) values of the missing variable (group size) on the basis of estimates of the cortex ratios of extinct hominids of known cranial capacity. This assumes that there is no decrease in goodness-of-fit for the relationship between cortex ratio and group size when we compare congeneric species for these attributes. One simple way of testing this assumption is to take a random sample of one species from each of the genera used in the original study (Dunbar 1992), and compare the group sizes for them predicted by Aiello and Dunbar's procedure with those observed in the field.

Table 8.1 Observed and predicted group sizes for the great apes, from Aiello and Dunbar (1993)

Genus	Brain volume (cc)[1]	Mean group size (predicted)[2]	Mean group size (observed)[3]
Pan	400,000	60.42	53.5
Pongo	397,000	60.11	2
Gorilla	469,000	67.2	7

Notes
1 From Ashton and Spence (1958).
2 Predicted from Aiello and Dunbar (1993: Eqs 1 ,3, 4).
3 From Dunbar (1992: Table 1) and Mackinnon (1974).

A first approximation at a test of their model is given by Aiello and Dunbar themselves (1993), in their use of great ape cranial capacity data from Ashton and Spence (1958) to predict average group sizes. As can be see from the fit of these predictions with observed values, this exercise is not too encouraging (see Table 8.1). Additional data on the cranial capacities of twenty-five haplorhine primate species are given in Martin (1989: 362), and these have been used to derive predicted average group sizes using Aiello and Dunbar's procedure (1993: Eqs 1, 3, 4). The predicted group sizes are given in Table 8.2, with observed average group sizes extracted from the literature[1]. Almost all of these cranial capacity data are for species which were sampled for the generic means used by Dunbar – indeed, in sixteen cases these species were the only species sampled for their respective generic means – so it might be thought that the fit of the model would be particularly good. However, the goodness-of-fit between observed and expected group size figures as given by the coefficient of determination is poor ($r^2 = 0.11$, both variables logged). This discovery that at least 89 per cent of variation between these species in average group size was missed by the predictive model is disappointing.

A more controlled test of Aiello and Dunbar's predictive model would be to start with generic mean cranial volume data for the genera sampled in Dunbar's original paper (1992), and to loop back and predict group sizes using Aiello and Dunbar's equations (1993: Eqs 1, 3, 4). This would simply assess how much 'noise' has been introduced into the cortex ratio/group size relationship (as originally observed) by introducing extra steps into the predictive exercise, using endocranial volume rather than observed neocortex ratios as the predictor. Unfortunately, good quality endocranial volume data is not available from mature adults of all of the species sampled for Dunbar's database (i.e. the primate species represented in Stephan et al.'s data-set, 1981). Data is, however, available on total brain volumes for these species, and was used by Dunbar to derive the original predictive equation. Table 8.3 summarizes the goodness-of-fit of predicted

Table 8.2 Cranial capacity data from Martin (1989: 362) used to derive group size predictions (see p. 232). Fit of observed to predicted group sizes: $r^2 = 0.11$

Species	Cranial capacity (cc)	Mean group size (predicted)[1]	Mean group size (observed)[2]
Tarsius spp.	3.0	2.3	1
Aotus trivirgatus	16.9	7.3	3.8
Callicebus moloch	18.3	7.7	3.3
Saimiri sciureus	23.6	9.1	32.5
Cebus apella	76.2	19.9	13
Ateles spp.	108.8	25.3	17
Lagothrix lagotricha	97.2	23.5	23.4
Alouatta seniculus	60.3	17.1	7.1
Callimico goeldii	11.1	5.5	7.3
Cebuella pygmaea	6.1	3.7	6
Callithrix jacchus	7.2	4.1	8.5
Saguinus spp.	9.9	5.1	9.3
Miopithecus talapoin	39.0	12.7	65.5
Cercopithecus ascanius	63.4	17.6	28.2
Cercocebus albigena	96.9	23.4	15.4
Macaca mulatta	83.0	21.1	39.6
Papio anubis	177.0	35	51.2
Theropithecus gelada	133.0	28.9	n/a
Colobus badius	61.6	17.3	35
Hylobates lar	99.9	23.9	3.4
Hylobates syndactylus	123.7	27.6	3.8
Pongo pygmaeus	418.0	62.2	2
Pan troglodytes	393.0	59.7	53.5
Gorilla gorilla	465.0	66.8	7
Homo sapiens	1409.0	140.2	n/a

Notes
1 From Aiello and Dunbar (1993: Eqs 1, 3, 4).
2 From Dunbar (1992) and Smuts et al. (1987).

group sizes for these primate genera derived from total brain volume data (Aiello and Dunbar's Eq. 3). The fit of this predictive model is given by the coefficient of determination, $r^2 = 0.34$, observed vs. predicted average group sizes (both variables logged, n = 25 haplorhine genera, data from Dunbar 1992: Table 1). In other words, more than half of the predictive power of Dunbar's original equation linking cortex ratio and mean group sizes has been lost by introducing total brain volume as the point of extrapolation for the calculation. It may be expected that using endocranial capacity as a predictor of total brain volume has only introduced a further source of error.

Table 8.3 Mean group sizes as predicted from total brain volume, and as observed (see p. 233). Fit of observed to predicted group sizes: $r^2 = 0.34$

Genus	Total brain vol. (mm^3)[1]	Mean group size (predicted)[2]	Mean group size (observed)[3]
Tarsius	3,393	2.5	1
Callithrix	7,241	4.1	8.5
Cebuella	4,302	2.9	6.0
Saguinus	9,537	5.0	5.2
Callimico	10,510	5.3	7.3
Aotus	16,195	7.1	3.8
Callicebus	17,944	7.6	3.3
Pithecia	32,867	11.5	3.6
Alouatta	49,009	15.1	8.2
Ateles	101,034	24.6	17.0
Lagothrix	95,503	23.7	23.4
Cebus	66,939	18.6	18.1
Saimiri	22,572	8.9	32.5
Macaca	87,896	22.2	39.6
Cercocebus	97,603	24.0	15.4
Papio	190,957	37.8	51.2
Cercopithecus	67,035	18.6	23.9
Miopithecus	37,776	12.6	65.5
Erythrocebus	103,167	24.9	28.1
Pygathrix	72,530	19.6	n/a
Nasalis	92,797	23.2	14.4
Procolobus	73,818	19.9	35.0
Hylobates	97,505	24.0	3.4
Gorilla	470,359	69.7	7.0
Pan	382,103	60.6	53.5

Notes
1 From Stephan et al. (1981).
2 From Aiello and Dunbar (1993: Eqs 1, 3).
3 From Dunbar (1992: Table 1).

This second result makes it evident that total brain volume is a relatively poor predictor of neocortex/rest of brain ratios. This is a finding which goes against a common received view that anthropoid primates have neocortex ratios which are tightly scaled to absolute brain size at the level of interspecific or intergeneric comparisons (e.g. Passingham 1982, Deacon 1988). However, if we regress the log of Dunbar's cortex ratio for haplorhine genera (excluding *Homo*) against the log of total brain volume, the goodness-of-fit is less than perfect ($r^2 = 0.82$, n = 25 haplorhine genera, data in Dunbar 1992). The same is even more true if

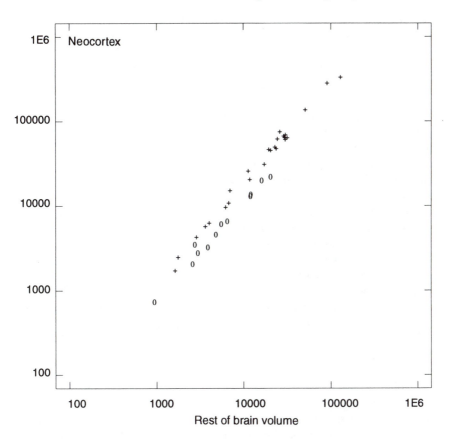

Figure 8.1 Neocortex plotted against rest of brain volume for 37 primate genera; + are haplorhines, 0 are strepsirhines (data, in mm³, are from Stephan *et al.* 1981)

we use the ratio of log(neocortex) to log(rest of brain volume), which is the other way to derive a cortex ratio ($r^2 = 0.63$, alternative cortex ratio vs. total brain volume, same data-set). This is a puzzling finding, and one which requires explanation.

One possible explanation lies in the association between the brain and basal metabolic rates. The grade difference between haplorhines and strepsirhines for neocortex/whole-brain ratios, graphed by Aiello and Dunbar (1993, cf. Figure 8.1), mirrors the separation of primates into these two groups seen for the relationship between total neonate body weight and maternal weight, and for the relationship between cranial capacity and body weight (Martin 1989: 447, 366, Armstrong 1990, cf. Figures 8.2 and 8.3). Martin (1989: 449) suggests that the grade difference in relative neonate body weight between haplorhines and strepsirhines may derive from differences in maternal basal metabolic rate, while

Armstrong (1990: 172) shows how the grade difference in relative cranial capacity disappears when body weights are adjusted for specific metabolic rates (the amounts of O_2 consumed per unit of tissue). These studies point to the possibility that variation in relative neocortex size (controlled for total brain volume) might also relate to underlying variation in metabolic rate.

We can specify a more detailed model of the specific metabolic constraints on relative neocortex size. Recent work on cerebral glucose metabolism shows that rates of glucose uptake per unit volume are considerably greater in grey matter than in white matter. This variation correlates closely with variation in the density of capillary blood vessels per unit volume. Borowsky and Collins (1989) found that in rats, grey matter has a density of capillary vessels of three to five times that found in white matter: they also found that there was a strong positive correlation between regional capillary density and glucose utilization ($r = 0.88$, $p < 0.001$ for data sampled across eighteen grey and five white matter sites). In the grey matter of the human cerebral cortex, it is estimated that the density of the capillary network is approximately 3.3 times that of the white matter of the hemispheres (Blinkov and Glezer 1968). Collins (1991) suggests (for the rat data) that this pattern derives from the higher firing rates of synapses which characterize the resting or control state in these more densely vascularized areas of the brain.

Armstrong (1985) has shown that brain size scales isometrically to available metabolic energy (body mass × specific basal metabolic rate), with a slope very close to 1.0 across mammal species. The same is true for neocortical sheet surface area in primates. This can be demonstrated if we take the slopes of the two Reduced Major Axis lines fitted to the generic mean neocortex/rest-of-brain data for strepsirhines and haplorhines (Figure 8.1), as given by the following regression equations (all data from Stephan et al. 1981).

For strepsirhines (n = 12 genera):

Log_{10} Neocortex (mm^3) =

$$-0.460 + 1.125 \,(Log_{10} \text{ Rest of Brain, mm}^3).r^2 = 0.985. \qquad [1]$$

For haplorhines (n = 25 genera, excl. *Homo*):

Log_{10} Neocortex (mm^3) =

$$-0.523 + 1.20 \,(Log_{10} \text{ Rest of Brain, mm}^3).r^2 = 0.992. \qquad [2]$$

In mammals with convoluted neocortices, total cortical surface area scales to total volume of gray matter to the power of 0.89, while total volume of gray matter scales to total neocortical volume to the power of 0.933 (Hofman 1989). Thus neocortical surface area scales to neocortex

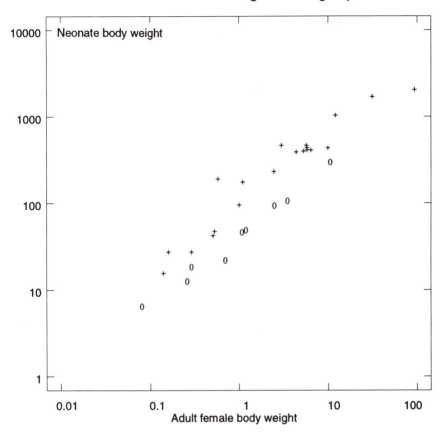

Figure 8.2 Neonate body weight (g) plotted against female adult body weight (kg) for 32 primate genera; + are haplorhines, 0 are strepsirhines (data from Harvey *et al.* 1987)

volume to the (compounded) power of 0.83. Since neocortex volume scales to the rest of the brain to the powers of 1.12 (strepsirhines) and 1.20 (haplorhines), we can derive the observation that for haplorhines, at any rate, neocortical surface area – an index of the proportion which is the metabolically expensive grey matter – scales isometrically with total brain volume (1.20 × 0.83 = 0.996). The scaling factor for strepsirhines is 0.93.

Because of the characteristic folded, 'gyrified' pattern of neocortical grey matter, which evidently represents an adaptation of this structure to the constraints of a quasi-spherical endocranial space under selection for optimization of sheet surface area, the ratio of superficial grey to white matter in this area can be expected to decrease with size less markedly than in other, non-convoluted brain structures (the only close parallel is with the cerebellum, which appears in fact closely to track the neocortex

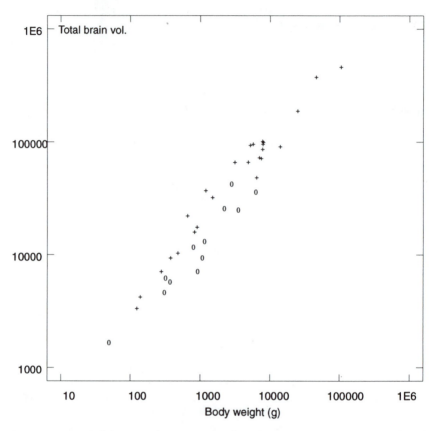

Figure 8.3 Total brain volume (mm³) plotted against body weight (g), for 37 primate genera; + are haplorhines, 0 are strepsirhines (data from Stephan *et al.* 1981)

in its volume scaling ratios). This means that an increase in the relative size of the neocortex (controlled for total brain volume) will incur an increase in the total metabolic needs of the brain. It follows that neocortex size and cerebellum size (relative to total brain volume) should co-vary with the overall capacity of the organism to deliver oxygen and glucose to the brain (which, following Armstrong 1990, we expect to be a function of body size and specific basal metabolic rate). This leads us to a testable 'metabolic constraints' hypothesis of the variance in the cortex ratio–total brain volume relationship, which has so drastically reduced the predictive power of Dunbar's original group size/cortex ratio equation. As has been shown to be the case for total brain volume in mammals (Armstrong 1985), the neocortex ratio is expected to scale isometrically to available metabolic energy, calculated as the product of body mass and specific basal metabolic rate (sBMR). Cases such as *Gorilla*, which have large bodies, but not especially great relative brain size or cortex ratio, would be expected to also have a relatively low specific BMR.

It is worth noting here that residual variation in neocortex size (controlled for brain size) shows some degree of correlation with relative brain size (controlled for body size). In both cases, residuals for non-human haplorhines were derived as the distance from a datum to a point perpendicular to it on the Reduced Major Axis line, as suggested by Martin and Barbour (1989).

The following are the Reduced Major Axis lines used for this exercise, and the equation used to derive values for the residuals:

$$\text{Log}_{10} \text{ Neocortex Ratio} = -0.61 + 0.20(\text{Log}_{10} \text{ Total Brain Volume, mm}^3) \quad [3]$$

($r^2 = 81.6$, n = 25 non-human haplorhine genera, data in Stephan *et al.* 1981)

$$\text{Log}_{10} \text{ Total Brain Volume (mm}^3) = 2.102 + 0.735(\text{Log}_{10} \text{ Body Weight, g}) \quad [4]$$

($r^2 = 96.3$, data as for Eq. 3)

$$\text{For } i = 1 \ldots n, \ L_i \text{ (residual)} = (y_i - a - bx_i) \sqrt{\frac{\Sigma(x_i - \bar{x})^2}{\Sigma(y_i - \bar{y})^2 + \Sigma(x_i - \bar{x})^2}} \quad [5]$$

(where a and b are respectively the intercept and the slope coefficient of the RMA equation).

Results are given in Table 8.4. Of the five genera with the greatest negative residual variation from the neocortex ratio/total brain volume line, four also made up the group with the greatest negative residual variation from the total brain volume/body mass line (*Alouatta, Gorilla, Nasalis* and *Tarsius*). Contrariwise, *Saimiri* and *Miopithecus* were among the three genera with the greatest positive residual variation from both these lines. If these two sets of genera were also distinguished by their contrastive relative BMRs, it would support the suggestion that cortex ratio variation is subject to metabolic energy constraints. Low sBMR species will have brains with relatively little of the grey-matter intensive, metabolically expensive neocortex, while high sBMR species will be able to 'afford' both encephalization, and a higher proportion of neocortex than their brain size would lead us to expect.

Saimiri is, in fact, the only primate for which good resting metabolism data is available which has a relatively high BMR for its size (compared with the general mammal trend) (Ross 1992). There is some reason to expect this to be the case for *Miopithecus* too, since in addition to the relatively large brain and high cortex ratio, this species has a fairly high ratio of neonate to maternal body weight (Napier and Napier 1985),

Table 8.4 Residuals analysis, using data from Stephan *et al.* (1981) and Dunbar (1992); values for *Homo* also interpolated (see p. 239)

Genus	Residuals (cortex ratio, controlled for total brain volume)	Genus	Residuals (total brain volume, controlled for body weight)
Saimiri	0.090	[Homo]	[0.356]
Erythrocebus	0.087	Miopithecus	0.170
Miopithecus	0.069	Saimiri	0.144
Cebuella	0.045	Cebus	0.126
Macaca	0.045	Lagothrix	0.118
Cercopithecus	0.040	Hylobates	0.101
Saguinus	0.029	Pithecia	0.064
Callithrix	0.027	Pan	0.042
Callimico	0.018	Erythrocebus	0.040
[Homo]	[0.015]	Ateles	0.026
Pan	0.012	Cerocebus	0.018
Cebus	0.009	Cercopithecus	0.012
Papio	0.004	Saguinus	0.015
Cercocebus	− 0.002	Macaca	− 0.016
Procolobus	− 0.008	Callicebus	− 0.016
Ateles	− 0.011	Aotus	− 0.031
Callicebus	− 0.016	Callithrix	− 0.033
Aotus	− 0.022	Cebuella	− 0.037
Lagothrix	− 0.029	Callimico	− 0.042
Pithecia	− 0.035	Papio	− 0.044
Pygathrix	− 0.040	Procolobus	− 0.049
Tarsius	− 0.053	Pygathrix	− 0.073
Nasalis	− 0.055	Tarsius	− 0.091
Alouatta	− 0.057	Gorilla	− 0.098
Hylobates	− 0.060	Nasalis	− 0.147
Gorilla	− 0.089	Alouatta	− 0.169

which Martin (1989) suggests may be a marker of high relative BMR. Contrariwise, *Gorilla*, which has relatively small brain size and low cortex ratio, and also has a relatively low ratio of neonatal to maternal body weight (Martin and Maclarnon 1988), is expected on ecological grounds to have a low relative BMR (Ross 1992: 19).

Interestingly, *Saimiri* and *Miopithecus* are also among the three haplorhine genera for which group size is most underestimated by Dunbar's equation, while *Gorilla* is the genus for which the equation most overestimates the parameter (cf. Table 8.5 – residual deviation of observed mean group size from that predicted by Dunbar 1992: Eq. 1). *Saimiri* and *Miopithecus* are small – *Saimiri* is the smallest New World cebid monkey, *Miopithecus* is the smallest Old World monkey – and they have both been

Table 8.5 Residuals from the predicted group sizes from Dunbar's Equation 1 (1992)

Genus	Residuals (group size, controlled for cortex ratio using Dunbar's Eq. 1)
Miopithecus	0.137
Procolobus	0.079
Saimiri	0.072
Callithrix	0.062
Cebuella	0.044
Papio	0.035
Lagothrix	0.029
Macaca	0.028
Callimico	0.021
Nasalis	− 0.004
Cercopithecus	− 0.008
Cebus	− 0.011
Alouatta	− 0.018
Saguinus	− 0.024
Pan	− 0.025
Ateles	− 0.034
Cercocebus	− 0.052
Aotus	− 0.057
Tarsius	− 0.062
Erythrocebus	− 0.069
Callicebus	− 0.088
Pithecia	− 0.109
Hylobates	− 0.181
Gorilla	− 0.194

observed in very large groups of up to 200 individuals. According to Napier and Napier (1985), they both have complex social systems subdivided into adult male bands, mother–infant bands and juvenile bands, and the closest parallels for each is with the other, rather than with a more closely genetically related species. *Gorilla*, *Hylobates*, *Pithecia* and *Tarsius* are among the seven genera which have greatest negative residual deviation of neocortex ratio from total brain volume, and also among the six genera which have the greatest proportional 'underperformance' on group size compared with that predicted from their neocortex ratio using Dunbar's equation. The implication is that investment in a higher or lower proportion of the metabolically costly neocortex may co-vary with group size, perhaps due to the effect of some confounding variable – probably dietary quality and abundance – affecting both sBMR and the cost/benefit balance of larger feeding aggregations.

These analyses have shown that the variance in the brain size/cortex ratio relationship, which causes a 50 per cent loss in predictive power for

Dunbar's group size equation when brain size is used, can be explained in part by a model of energetic constraints affecting corticalization. How much does this observation affect Aiello and Dunbar's group size predictions for extinct hominids? In Table 8.4 I have interpolated figures for the residual deviation of *Homo sapiens sapiens'* brain volume and cortex ratio from the lines fitted to non-human haplorhine brain and body size data (*Homo* was omitted from the original calculations due to claims that *Homo* is anomalous among haplorhines in the cortex ratio, Deacon 1988). It will be seen that modern human anatomy makes *Homo* an extreme outlier for brain/body size, but not an outlier in terms of neocortex ratio. Humans also have a basal metabolic rate which is fairly normal for body weight among haplorhines. This suggests that predictions of cortex ratio from absolute brain size in fossil hominid taxa will not be hopelessly wide of the mark, and will likely err on the side of underestimation. However, the cumulative error attaching to these calculations makes the specific group size predictions of Aiello and Dunbar for *Australopithecus* and *Homo* (including *Homo sapiens sapiens*) unreliable other than as broad indicators of a tendency in hominid social system evolution. It seems, then, that we can use endocranial capacity data to predict cortex ratios with only a limited degree of confidence.

HOW CONFIDENTLY CAN WE USE THE REDUCED MAJOR AXIS LINE FOR PREDICTING GROUP SIZE FROM CORTEX RATIOS?

Another question mark attaching to such group size predictions concerns the use of Reduced Major Axis line equations in predicting missing values of the Y-variable (see also Smith 1994). Prediction in regression analysis is usually done using the least-squares model, since in this model error variance is restricted to the dependent variable. Values of the dependent variable can therefore be predicted from the known value of the independent variable, to a confidence interval specified from analysis of the error variance in the original data for the dependent variable. With the reduced major axis, however, error is supposed to be distributed equally in both variables, with the consequence that the fitted line usually has a significantly steeper slope than that fitted by the least-squares method. However, no procedure exists for attaching a confidence interval to estimates of the Y-variable derived from observed values of the X-variable in the Reduced Major Axis model. Some heuristic estimates of the confidence interval for the slope and intercept parameters exist: Draper (1992) suggests that the two least-squares regression slopes (Y on X, and X on Y, appropriately transformed) might be taken as approximate indicators of the confidence interval for the slope, while Davis (1986: 204, Eqs 4.45 and 4.47) gives formulae for the standard errors of the intercept and slope for the reduced major axis line which can be used to determine an approximate confidence interval around these values. As an approximate guide to the confidence interval for the intercept and slope of Dunbar's original cortex ratio/group size equation (1992: Eq. 1) I have used both these methods. The results for the least-squares method (Draper 1992: 9) put outer limits for the intercept at 0.177–0.012, and for the slope as 2.96–3.86, while calculation of the standard error for the same parameters using Davis' method gives a range for the intercept of 0.29–0.215, and for the slope of 3.11–3.67. But these confidence intervals for the RMA line parameters cannot be used to derive confidence intervals for predictions. As Janson (1993) points out, if conventional least-squares regression had been used to predict an average group size for humans, the 95 per cent confidence interval would cover the range 23–446 individuals! So we can use the RMA line for prediction with only very limited confidence, pending further work on the methodology. It is evident that this aspect of allometric analysis needs further attention if we are to undertake predictive modelling based on RMA line-fitting.

WHAT OTHER METHODS EXIST FOR DERIVING CAUSAL MODELS OF THE RELATIONSHIPS BETWEEN ANATOMICAL AND BEHAVIOURAL VARIABLES IN LIVING TAXA?

We have seen that there are problems in predicting hominid average group sizes from cortex ratios, due partly to the difficulty in reliably estimating cortex ratios of individuals of extinct species for whom only endocranial capacity data is available, and partly to the limitations of the Reduced Major Axis model as a prediction equation. Although the problem of the lack of a confidence interval for RMA predictions remains, the variables used in the prediction equation can be varied to try to increase the fit of observed to estimated Y-values for living primates, using anatomical data which can be recovered from fossils.

In this section, I shall outline an alternative prediction equation for estimating hominid average group size. The model is that of multiple regression. Multiple regression analysis of the data set in Table 8.6 (cf. Figure 8.4) suggests that average group size can be predicted (albeit with limited reliability) from a combination of adult female body weight and adult total brain volume data (multiple $R^2 = 0.59$). This is not surprising, since our analyses have shown that cortex ratio (which is an even stronger predictor of group size) varies both with total brain volume and with relative brain size (relative both to body size and to maternal body weight). The multiple regression equation for this model, calculated by the least squares method, is as follows:

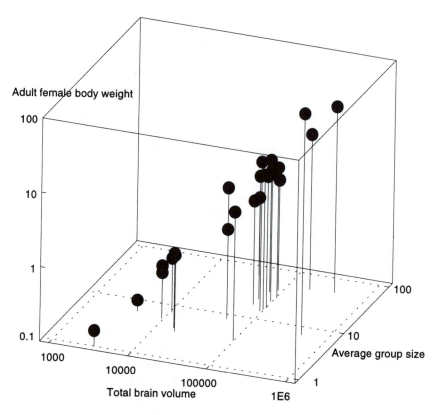

Figure 8.4 Scatterplot of data on female adult body weight (kg), total brain volume (mm³) and average group size for 25 haplorhine genera (data in Table 8.6)

$$\text{Log}_{10} \text{ Mean Group Size} = -8.525 + 2.20 \text{ Log}_{10} \text{ Total Brain Vol. (mm}^3)$$
$$- 1.45 \text{ Log}_{10} \text{ Adult Female Body Weight (kg)}. \qquad [6]$$

This gives a fit of $r^2 = 0.63$ between predictions and the observed haplorhine group sizes in Dunbar's data set, which is a marked improvement on the fit of Aiello and Dunbar's model derived from total brain volume alone (observed/predicted haplorhine group sizes, $r^2 = 0.34$, see p. 233). It will be seen that the fit for the apes is still not perfect, although *Gorilla* has become separated out by its predicted small group size. Parenthetically, we may also record that if the partial regression coefficients for the slopes of the predictor variables in Eq. 6 had been derived from RMA line-fitting for the underlying bivariate regressions, the correlation of the predicted and observed haplorhine group sizes would have been much worse ($r^2 = 0.35$), suggesting that in this case more of the error

Table 8.6 Data and predictions for average group sizes of 25 living haplorhine genera from my Equation 6 (see p. 244). Generic means are for species for which total brain volume data was available. Values for *Homo* interpolated. The r^2 for the correlation between observed and predicted group sizes is 0.63

Genus	Female adult mass (kg) [1]	Total brain vol. (mm³) [2]	Mean group size (predicted by Eq. 6)	Mean group size (observed) [3]
Tarsius	0.16	3,393	2.5	1.0
Callithrix	0.29	7,241	5.6	8.5
Cebuella	0.14	4,302	5.1	6.0
Saguinus	0.51	9,537	4.5	5.2
Callimico	0.53	10,510	5.3	7.3
Aotus	1.0	16,195	5.4	3.8
Callicebus	1.05	17,944	6.4	3.3
Pithecia	n/a	32,867	n/a	3.6
Alouatta	5.7	49,009	5.0	8.2
Ateles	5.8	101,034	23.9	17.0
Lagothrix	5.8	95,503	21.1	23.4
Cebus	2.47	66,939	33.3	18.1
Saimiri	0.58	22,572	24.9	32.5
Macaca	3.0	87,896	45.7	39.6
Cercocebus	6.4	97,603	19.2	15.4
Papio	12.0	190,957	33.7	51.2
Cercopithecus	4.4	67,035	14.4	23.9
Miopithecus	1.1	37,776	30.5	65.5
Erythrocebus	5.6	103,167	26.3	28.1
Pygathrix	n/a	72,530	n/a	n/a
Nasalis	9.9	92,797	9.1	14.4
Procolobus	5.8	73,818	12.0	35.0
Hylobates	5.3	97,505	25.2	3.4
Gorilla	93.0	470,359	12.6	7.0
Pan	31.1	382,103	39.0	53.5
[Homo]	[40.1]	[1,251,847]	[367.3]	[n/a]

Notes
1 From Harvey *et al.* (1987).
2 From Stephan *et al.* (1981).
3 From Dunbar (1992).

variance is contained in the behavioural than the anatomical observations (see also Smith 1994).

In Table 8.7 a sample of hominid taxa are listed with their estimated female body weights, total brain volumes, and with average group sizes as predicted from my Equation 6 and from Aiello and Dunbar's equations (1993). The cumulative error likely in the derivations of total brain volume

Table 8.7   Data and predictions for average group sizes of various fossil hominid taxa,[1] using predictive equations from Aiello and Dunbar (1993) and Steele (Equation 6)

Species	Female adult body weight (kg) [2]	Total brain volume (mm³) [3]	Average group size predicted by Aiello and Dunbar (1993)	Average group size predicted from Eq. 6
A. afarensis	29.3	411,976	63.7	50.2
A. africanus	30.2	429,491	65.5	52.7
A. boisei	34.0	486,914	71.4	58.4
H. habilis s.s.	31.5	567,100	79.1	91.3
H. rudolfensis	50.8	709,497	92.1	74.7
early African H. erectus	52.3	853,403	104.2	107.6
Neanderthal	51.8	1,369,351	143.7	308.7
early a.m. H. sapiens	56.8	1,462,391	150.4	312.1
H. sapiens	53.2	1,293,718	138.4	262.1

Notes
1   Fossils used for total brain volume estimates and Aiello and Dunbar's group size estimates are as follows. *A. afarensis*: AL333-45, AL162-28, AL333-105J. *A. africanus*: Sts5, Sts19/58, Sts60, Sts71, MLD1, MLD37/38. *A. boisei*: KNMER406, KNMER732, OH5. *H. habilis s.s.*: OH13, OH16, OH24, KNMER1805, KNMER1813. *H. rudolfensis*: KNMER1470. Early African *H. erectus*: KNMER3733, KNMER3883, OH9. Neanderthal: Amud 1, Le Moustier, La Chapelle, Neanderthal, Gibraltar 1, Shanidar 1, Guattari 1, La Quina 5, Spy 1, Spy 2, La Ferrassie 1, Krapina B, Tabun C1, Saccopastore 1, Saccopastore 2. Early a.m. *H. sapiens*: Cro-Magnon, Skhul 4, Skhul 5, Skhul 6, Qafzeh 6. Data from Aiello and Dunbar (1993).
2   From McHenry, this volume. Estimates.
3   From Aiello and Dunbar (1993). Estimates.

and body weight estimates for the fossil hominids suggests that they should be used only as illustrations of the differences the use of the new prediction equation makes. However, it will be apparent that use of Equation 6 has markedly affected the predictions for group sizes for Neanderthals and *Homo sapiens*. Indeed, this predictive model would support a 'late spurt' account of hominid social system evolution, whereas Aiello and Dunbar's predictions (1993) were used to support a gradualist account.

This does not necessarily invalidate Dunbar's use of the cortex ratio to predict a group size of 148 for modern *Homo sapiens* (Dunbar 1993, this volume). After all, my new equation responds to problems with predictions for haplorhine genera with large residual deviations from the neocortex/ total brain volume scaling trend, and this is not a problem either for *Pan* or for *Homo*. Group sizes predicted from hominid endocranial volumes are therefore less likely to be subject to such sources of error than would be predictions from skull volumes of (for instance) extinct saimirids, or of ancestral apes like *Sivapithecus* or *Proconsul*. It does, however, illustrate the uncertainty attaching to such predictions when outlier values are used as predictors, since the average group size predicted for humans by my Equation 6 (which uses total brain volume and adult female body weight as predictor variables) is about twice that predicted from neocortex ratio by Dunbar using his Equation 1 (1992). In fact, if (for consistency with the living primate genera) we use Harvey *et al.*'s (1987) datum for human adult female body weight, and Stephan *et al.*'s (1981) datum for human total brain volume, then we get an alternative, even greater prediction from Equation 6 of an average human group size of 367 (see Table 8.6). The difference between this figure and that of 262 given in Table 8.7 reflects the sensitivity of Equation 6 to variation in estimates of mean human adult female body mass. By way of complete contrast Martins (1993), who used least squares regression to predict human mean group size from neocortex ratio, derived a prediction for *Homo* of 42.9. The differences hang on the statistical line-fitting technique used and the method used to factor out phylogenetic constraints.

CONCLUSIONS REGARDING THE PREDICTION MODELS

In this chapter, I have taken the view that regression equations describing strong correlations between anatomical and behavioural variables in living primates have the potential to be used as prediction equations for missing values of the behavioural variable in extinct hominid taxa. The attempt to infer average group sizes from the relative size of the neocortex is an example of such predictive modelling. As has been shown, there are pitfalls in the inference of cortex ratio from endocranial capacity in haplorhines which hinder this project, although this represents a tractable problem: some of the variance in the neocortex/brain volume relationship may relate to variance in total metabolic energy budgets between primates of the same body size.

Additionally, there is considerable variance in the average group sizes of living primate genera which is not accounted for either by the neocortex ratio or by the joint effects of brain size and female body mass, and this further complicates the predictive exercise. Because of this, it seems that group sizes cannot yet be predicted for extinct hominids with any great degree of certainty, even within a fairly wide confidence interval. However, progress has already been made to improve the model's predictive accuracy, both here and elsewhere (cf. Dunbar 1993 with peer commentaries). In part such development must come from a closer look at the data from which average group size estimates for the living primates were derived. This case looks like a good 'laboratory' for evaluating the use of predictive equations derived from primate allometry, and we may hope for continuing improvement in our understanding of the causal structure of the brain–social system relationship in primates, and of its implications for reconstructing the lifeways of our hominid predecessors.

TOWARDS ARCHAEOLOGICAL TESTS OF HOMINID GROUP SIZE PREDICTIONS

In his response to peer commentaries on an earlier paper, Dunbar (1993: 725) challenged that archaeological evidence suggesting prehistoric forager groups were of the order of 25–50 people is uninformative, since it tells us nothing about the possible higher levels of integration which may have characterized these Palaeolithic societies. As we have seen, however, different techniques result in very different predictions of human and hominid group sizes: Martins (1993) predicts ancestral human groups of the scale of the foraging local band (25–50 persons); Dunbar (1993) predicts groups on the scale of an intermediate level of integration between the minimum and the maximal band (c. 125–150 persons); and my own equation predicts groups on the scale approximating to the human foragers' maximal band (c. 300 persons). Clearly there is a need for independent sources of evidence which would enable us to test the validity of these varying predictions. Dunbar's strategy is to take a theoretically derived number for human group sizes, and to search the *social scientific literature* for confirmation that this number represents an empirical limit on grouping patterns of a certain level of integration. This is a wholly valid procedure. My alternative strategy here is to take theoretically derived numbers, and to search the *archaeological record* for new means of confirmation that they do or do not represent limits on hominid and early modern human grouping patterns.

The archaeological evidence most often used to estimate group sizes is site area and number of hearths, used to predict the size of the bands using the site on the basis of equations describing the relationship between settlement area and group size in modern foraging societies. Thus Hassan (1981: 93) gives such estimates of the forager band sizes inhabiting sites from the basal Pleistocene (FlK1, Olduvai) to the early Holocene (Kebaran, Natufian) which converge on an average estimate of about 20 persons (range 1–48, excluding large sites from the Natufian). Dunbar's objection, quite rightly, is that there may be higher levels of spatial integration which existed in the Palaeolithic but which have left no archaeological trace (see also Gamble, this volume).

Site area is not, however, the only potential source of archaeological evidence. Raw material transport is an indicator of the minimum diameters of home ranges, and home range area scales to group mass (the total biomass of a social group of animals) with a fairly tightly correlated positive relationship in mammals (Grant *et al.* 1992), such that it is possible to predict the diameter of an idealized circular home range where the area (in square kilometres) has been derived from prediction equations from group mass. Adult body weight estimates have been given for the Hominidae by McHenry (1994, this volume). Group mass can be worked out for a given group size if (following Clutton-Brock and Harvey 1977) we assume group composition with a ratio of one male : one female : two juveniles, and a mean body weight for juveniles of half the mean adult body weight. We can therefore predict home range diameters for the various members of the hominid series for given group sizes, and test these predictions against the maximum distances of raw material transport found in the archaeological record associated with these fossil taxa (Table 8.8, see also Gamble and Steele, in prep.).

Foley (1987) has pointed out that the home range sizes indicated by lithic transport distances at Olduvai Gorge, and associated with the earliest

Table 8.8 Group mass and home range diameter for selected hominid species. Body weight data from McHenry, this volume. Prediction equations for home range areas of primates and for carnivores with undefended ranges from Grant *et al.* (1992: Figures 3, 5)

Species	Group size	Group mass (kg)	Home range diameter (km), primate model	Home range diameter (km), carnivore model
H. habilis s.s.	25	642	3.0	26.2
H. habilis s.s.	125	3,211	5.9	53.2
H. habilis s.s.	300	7,706	8.5	78.0
H. rudolfensis	25	1,035	3.6	32.4
H. rudolfensis	125	5,175	7.2	65.5
H. rudolfensis	300	12,420	10.4	96.2
early African H. erectus	25	1,078	3.7	32.9
early African H. erectus	125	5,391	7.3	66.7
early African H. erectus	300	12,937	10.6	97.9
Neanderthal	25	1,049	3.6	32.6
Neanderthal	125	5,245	7.2	65.9
Neanderthal	300	12,589	10.5	96.8
early a.m. H. sapiens	25	1,189	3.8	34.4
early a.m. H. sapiens	125	5,944	7.6	69.6
early a.m. H. sapiens	300	14,265	11.0	102.2

stone tool making hominids at the beginning of the Lower Palaeolithic, are greater than those expected for a mammal of that body mass. One possible explanation is that the group sizes being sustained by this range area were also anomalously high. However, we must note a complicating factor. The maximum lithic transport distances reported for the European Middle Palaeolithic (c. 100 kilometres, Gamble, this volume) are in the order of magnitude characteristic for carnivore home ranges, and greatly in excess of those of a primate (cf. Table 8.8). The complication of dietary niche and trophic level as a determinant of range area, in addition to body mass and group size, must therefore be take into consideration when using these lithic transport data as information about group mass and ranging strategies (see Gamble and Steele, in prep., for a more extensive treatment of this data set and its associated problems).

In summary, Aiello and Dunbar (1993) have proposed an intriguing and original way of teasing socioecological information out of the palaeoanthropological record. This chapter, seen as a footnote to that work, proposes both an alternative prediction equation to get at the same behavioural variable, and a category of archaeological evidence which may complement the empirical literature on contemporary human groupings which has been used to date by Dunbar as an independent test of these predictions.

ACKNOWLEDGEMENTS

I am most grateful to Philip Prescott for help with the formulae for the RMA equation, and for deriving the formula for RMA residuals (Eq. 5).

NOTE

1 In a number of cases the group size averages extracted from the main source used by Dunbar (1992), which was Smuts et al. (1987), differed slightly from those which I estimated from the same data. In such cases, I have used the estimated mean group sizes given by Dunbar.

REFERENCES

Aiello, L.C. and Dunbar, R.I.M. (1993) 'Neocortex size, group size, and the evolution of language.' Current Anthropology 34: 184–193.

Armstrong, E. (1985) 'Allometric considerations of the adult mammalian brain with special emphasis on primates.' In W.L. Jungers (ed.) Size and Scaling in Primate Biology, pp. 115–146. New York: Plenum.

Armstrong, E. (1990) 'Brains, bodies and metabolism.' Brain, Behavior and Evolution 36: 166–176.

Ashton, E.H. and Spence, T.F. (1958) 'Age changes in the cranial capacity and foramen magnum of hominoids.' Proceedings of the Zoological Society of London 130: 169–181.

Blinkov, S.M. and Glezer, I.I. (1968) *The Human Brain in Figures and Tables: A Quantitative Handbook*. New York: Basic Books.

Borowsky, I.W. and Collins, R.C. (1989) 'Metabolic anatomy of brain: a comparison of regional capillary density, glucose metabolism, and enzyme activities.' *Journal of Comparative Neurology* 288: 401–431.

Clutton-Brock, T.H. and Harvey, P.H. (1977) 'Primate ecology and social organization.' *Journal of Zoology (London)* 183: 1–39.

Collins, R.C. (1991) 'Basic aspects of functional brain metabolism.' *Ciba Foundation Symposia* 163: 6–22.

Davis, J.C. (1986) *Statistics and Data Analysis in Geology*, 2nd edn. New York: John Wiley and Sons.

Deacon, T.W. (1988) 'Human brain evolution II: embryology and brain allometry.' In H. Jerison and I. Jerison (eds) *Intelligence and Evolutionary Biology*, pp. 383–416. Berlin: Springer.

Draper, N.R. (1992) *Straight Line Regression when Both Variables are Subject to Error*. Technical Report No. 890, Dept of Statistics, University of Wisconsin, Madison, WI.

Dunbar, R.I.M. (1992) 'Neocortex size as a constraint on group size in primates.' *Journal of Human Evolution* 20: 469–493.

Dunbar, R.I.M. (1993) 'Co-evolution of neocortex size, group size, and language in humans.' *Behavioral and Brain Sciences* 16: 681–735.

Foley, R.A. (1987) *Another Unique Species*. Harlow: Longman.

Gamble, C.S. and Steele, J. (in prep.) 'Group mass and home range area of hominids: an archaeological evaluation of the group size debate.'

Grant, J.W.A., Chapman, C.A. and Richardson, K.S. (1992) 'Defended versus undefended home range size of carnivores, ungulates and primates.' *Behavioral Ecology and Sociobiology* 31: 149–161.

Harvey, P.H., Martin, R.D. and Clutton-Brock, T. (1987) 'Life histories in comparative perspective.' In B.B. Smuts, D.L. Cheney, R.M. Seyfarth, R.W. Wrangham and T.T. Struhsaker (eds) *Primate Societies*, pp. 181–196. Chicago: University of Chicago Press.

Hassan, F.A. (1981) *Demographic Archaeology*. New York: Academic Press.

Hofman, M.A. (1989) 'On the evolution and geometry of the brain in mammals.' *Progress in Neurobiology* 32: 137–158.

Janson, C.H. (1993) 'Primate group size, brains and communication: a New World perspective.' *Behavioural and Brain Sciences* 16: 711–712.

McHenry, H.M. (1994) 'Tempo and mode in human evolution.' *Proceedings of the National Academy of Sciences (USA)* 91: 6780–6786.

Mackinnon, J.R. (1974) 'The behaviour and ecology of wild orang-utans (*Pongo pygmaeus*).' *Animal Behaviour* 22: 3–74.

Martin, R.D. (1989) *Primate Origins and Evolution*. London: Chapman and Hall.

Martin, R.D. and Barbour, A.D. (1989) 'Aspects of line-fitting in bivariate allometric analyses.' *Folia Primatologica* 53: 65–81.

Martin, R.D. and Maclarnon, A. (1988) 'Comparative quantitative studies of growth and reproduction.' *Symposia of the Zoological Society of London* 60: 39–80.

Martins, E.P. (1993) 'Comparative studies, phylogenies and predictions of co-evolutionary relationships.' *Behavioural and Brain Sciences* 16: 714–716.

Napier, J.R. and Napier, P.H. (1985) *The Natural History of the Primates*. London: British Museum (Natural History)/Cambridge University Press.

Passingham, R.E. (1982) *The Human Primate*. San Francisco: Freeman.

Ross, C. (1992) 'Basal metabolic rate, body weight and diet in primates: an evaluation of the evidence.' *Folia Primatologica* 58: 7–23.

Smith, R.J. (1994) 'Regression models for prediction equations.' *Journal of Human Evolution* 26: 239–244.

Smuts, B.B., Cheney, D.L., Seyfarth, R.M., Wrangham, R.W. and Struhsaker, T.T. (eds) (1987) *Primate Societies*. Chicago: University of Chicago Press.

Stephan, H., Frahm, H. and Baron, G. (1981) 'New and revised data on volumes of brain structures in insectivores and primates.' *Folia Primatologica* 35: 1–29.

Stern, N. (1993) 'The structure of the Lower Pleistocene archaeological record.' *Current Anthropology* 34: 201–225.

CHAPTER NINE

MAKING TRACKS

*Hominid networks and the evolution of the
social landscape*

CLIVE GAMBLE

INTRODUCTION

Many of the dimensions of early hominid behaviour remain obscure. In particular, the link between estimates of group size and foraging areas, essential to several arguments about language origins and the elaboration of social intelligence have hardly been explored. The spatial dimension is either ignored (e.g. Dunbar 1993) in the analysis of social and demographic evolution, or is treated qualitatively, using terms such as 'local' and 'distant', to examine changes in decision-making (e.g. Rolland and Dibble 1990, Andrefsky 1994). Neither are the temporal dimensions of these actions adequately considered. The result is a piecemeal approach to human evolution with little integration of the various multidisciplinary insights. Consequently, each discipline emphasizes its own favoured prime-mover as the appropriate explanation for the timing and direction of change.

What is required is a unifying concept to focus the multidisciplinary enterprise. In this contribution I will explore regional social units which have been identified by specialists in several fields as critical in understanding variation in behaviour at the local level. Archaeologists have been particularly reluctant to take more than a 'worm's-eye view of sociocultural evolution' (Wobst 1976: 49). They have concentrated on the analysis of settlements in their local setting and attributed local variation to local factors. But the same approach can also be seen in primate studies (Rowell 1991), where the space–time limits of the system to which any local group belongs are currently unknown, and in much anthropological research (Hill 1978).

But while it is easy to assert the importance of regional systems on local outcomes it is more difficult to characterize the dimensions of those units. Here archaeology has a distinct advantage over primate and anthropological studies since we have the regional record of such inter-actions preserved in the distribution of material culture (Gamble 1986). Moreover these patterns have time-depth so that we can study changes in the temporality of action as well as the use of space by past hominids.

I will examine such regionally based, population-wide studies with two models, the Local Hominid Network and the Social Landscape. These concepts are both spatially and temporally based since these are the domains for adaptation and selection, both biological and cultural. They are regional in scale since they concern the mobility of individuals and their constructions of society. The archaeological record is used to supply the dimensions of these systems as well as to identify the points of flexure in later hominid evolution. As Steele (in press) has recently argued, we need to develop interdisciplinary techniques to study variations in the hominid record which are relevant to quantitative parameters such as mean group size and home range area. Without an appropriate analytic unit to investigate space–time, such parameters will remain ill-defined. This means our ability to investigate many of the research questions in this volume, for example the evolution of learning strategies, degree of planning depth, memory and patterns of cultural transmission, will be seriously compromised.

THE LOCAL HOMINID NETWORK (LHN)

A Local Hominid Network (Gamble 1993a) identifies a common structure in the space–time behaviour of foragers, past and present. It encompasses both subsistence and social behaviour. The network contains other hominids, non-hominid competitors and resources. It is centred on the individual and the decisions she/he must make. In this sense it is the immediate spatial forum for the negotiation and reproduction of social life. These everyday routines also have a temporal sequence that structures the contexts of interaction. This continuous process involves interactions between individuals where negotiation is achieved through display, gesticulation, grooming, language, performance, sign and symbol. Hominids, like other primates, do not enter a stable social structure but rather, as Strum and Latour maintain (1987: 788), negotiate what that structure will be.

From earliest prehistory the form of hominid societies is expected to be variable and therefore difficult for archaeologists to either specify or reconstruct. For this reason attention is focused here on the networks which supported this social variety. These component networks are likewise variable in the use of space and resources. However, the latter can be investigated for qualitative and quantitative changes in the flows and use of materials, particularly lithics. These items define the networks which contributed to the negotiation of society at particular times and places.

A local hominid network (LHN) is not, however, a Palaeolithic society by another name. It is instead a means to introduce social concepts into an archaeological period that has traditionally not considered such issues. Indeed, the study of society has a different agenda in the Palaeolithic than in other archaeological periods (Gamble 1993b). It is assumed that the Palaeolithic, prior to modern humans, deals with societies so far outside ethnographic experience they are not even on the bottom rung of some evolutionary stepladder (Yoffee 1993: Figure 6.1). The purpose of the LHN is to bridge this step-wise thinking and bring discussion of Palaeolithic societies into the archaeological fold. Once admitted they can be sheltered from the tyranny of evolutionist schemes (Wobst 1978). Only then can the discussion of social evolution (Ingold 1986a) for this period commence.

While such LHNs link individuals and form the struts in all hominid societies, in another sense the local network is also the environment of the hominid. It is its niche, constructed to assist its survival. It contains the resources necessary for social and biological reproduction. During hominid evolution, as stated previously,

> a useful distinction can be drawn between the *local hominid network*, where life routines, assisted by tools, are played out sequentially, and the construction of *social landscapes* where local networks are linked together by negotiation. While all hominids share the organizational framework of a local network only modern humans have elaborated and reticulated them into diverse social landscapes.
>
> (Gamble 1993a: 42)

The idea of social landscapes will be examined below. At the outset it is important to distinguish between the two concepts in terms of their applicability to the span of human evolution. An LHN is germane to all human evolution. Within its structure lies a rich variety of negotiated social behaviour that can only be described as *complex* (Strum and Latour 1987: 790). Complex in this sense means to embrace many objects and where the capacity for simultaneous transactions sets a limit to what can be achieved in terms of social arrangements (Rowell 1991: 260). For Strum and Latour, baboons have complex sociality because 'when they construct and repair their social order, they do so only with limited resources, their bodies, their social skills and whatever social strategies they can construct' (1987: 790).

By contrast, I will argue that social landscapes are restricted to the social revolution associated with modern humans some 50,000 years ago. In Strum and Latour's terms it is at this time that we first see *complicated* social life. 'Something is "complicated" when it is made of a succession of simple operations' (1987: 791). Social life is in fact made more simple by negotiating one variable at a time but where, crucially, the negotiations are less complex in themselves. Such complicated social life draws on the use of symbol, place and object to achieve this simplification. Complex social life by contrast relies on just the hominid body and associated social skills which are limited to negotiating one factor at a time. With this distinction in mind, some major changes are expected in the spatial organization of these differently constructed social lives.

Scale

The dimensions of the LHN are readily ascertained from the archaeological record. Recent studies of the distributions of raw materials from a number of ecologically diverse areas, and associated with a wide variety of hominids and cultural assemblages (Bíró 1981, Gowlett 1984, Hiscock 1986, Geneste 1988a, b, Roebroeks *et al.* 1988, Turq 1988, 1992, 1993, Féblot-Augustins 1990, 1993, Floss 1990, 1991, Franco 1990, 1991, 1994, McNiven 1990, Bar-Yosef 1991, Potts 1991, Kuhn 1992, Lebel 1992, Pasda 1992, Perlès 1992, Petitt 1992, Rensink 1993), has produced consistent results. These concern both the distances over which materials were regularly transported and the effect this has on the quantity and morphology of stone implements in archaeological sites.

The distances from Geneste's important study (1988a, b) are summarized in Table 9.1, where the proportions of different raw materials are also indicated.

Table 9.1 Proportions of raw materials present and utilized on Middle Palaeolithic sites in S.W. France (Geneste 1988a, b). The same relationships hold for Upper Palaeolithic material and in many different regions (see text for references)

Km radius from site	% of stone on site	% utilized, made into tools
'Local' = within 5 km	55–98	1–5
'Region' = 5–20 km	2–20	1–20
'Exotic' = 30–80 km	< 5	74–100

These studies have led to the following general principle concerning the use of raw material by foragers: *distant raw materials are represented by the later stages of the reduction sequence* (Gamble 1993a: 36). In particular the work of Geneste (1988a, b) has supplied a figure of between 30–80 km to quantify the term 'distant'. These distances fix the operating limits of the LHN. For most purposes the raw material data indicate an LHN with a radius of 40 km and an upper limit of 100 km (Gamble 1993a: 42). Within this radius we can refer to all activities as local in terms of their social and organizational implications. The raw material principle is the result of mobile hominids optimizing an aspect of their provisioning strategies. It expresses a simple relation between mobility and the distance separating resources. For much of human evolution, when hominids were assisted by tools rather than using them to pursue cultural strategies, this raw material principle is sufficient to understand most of the variation in lithic assemblages.

DISCUSSION

The LHN, as described above, raises several points concerning archaeological concepts of space–time and territory which need further discussion. The issues addressed here are territorial analysis, off-site analysis of continuous behaviour and the resource transport hypothesis. Underlying these issues is the recurrent theme of complexity and inferences concerning organizational ability.

Territorial analysis: boundaries, perception and environments

It might, for example, be suggested that the LHN concept is merely an elaboration of site catchment analysis (Vita-Finzi and Higgs 1970, Bailey and Davidson 1983) which has been widely used in prehistoric archaeology. This is not so for the following reasons. The LHN is regionally rather than site based. Its specification is designed to encompass behaviour rather than provide, as site catchment analysis does, explanations of site-by-site circumstances. In that regard the concept is concerned with linkages between places rather than with the shape of surface-area territories. The LHN is also concerned with boundaries since their construction and maintenance are part of the social skills employed by the individual hominids as they negotiate the social structure (e.g. Hodder 1982). These boundaries are assumed to result from complex interactions (as defined above, p. 255) among the hominids in the LHN. The purpose of the LHN (and subsequently the social landscape) is to investigate the spatial component that arises from such negotiations. The expectation is that social life in an LHN, associated with a complex system of negotiation, will be local and predominantly exclusive in terms of boundary maintenance. These principles are also supported by traditions which relied on shallow temporal depth to support such regional units.

Moreover, the rationale behind the LHN is to unite social and subsistence concerns rather than to give primacy to the latter, as is the case with site catchment analysis. While both models may aim to understand the patterning produced by hominid spatial decisions, they differ in that the LHN expects the hominids it contains to potentially exhibit a variety of social behaviours. Site catchment analysis on the other hand expects all hominids to be essentially the same, ecologically driven creatures who only varied in terms of subsistence and not social relations.

Therefore, the concept of an LHN, by stressing individuals and their linkages, is not attempting a territorial analysis where boundaries are established on a simple cost surface stemming from a fixed exploitation point. Most importantly, the LHN takes a rather different view of how hominids use space. The LHN can be conceived as the *environment* of the hominid and is constructed as a result of mobility, what Gibson (1979) referred to as *ambulatory perception*. It is by moving around with a head that swivels on a neck and eyes that look forward that we perceive the world. This is how we pick up information and orient ourselves to the environment in a mutual relationship (Graves n.d.). Ambulatory perception is above all the mode of engagement of people with the world (Ingold 1992: 44).

Any understanding of such a mutual relationship between hominid/ environment needs to acknowledge that it is 'mainly rigid but partly nonrigid, mainly motionless but partly movable, a world that is both changeless in many respects, and changeable in others but is neither dead at one extreme nor chaotic at the other' (Gibson 1979: 14). This is the environment which we, and all hominids before us, have perceived, interpreted, used and changed. This is only possible through *direct perception*; what is visible to the eye rather than under the microscope. As a result we can 'apprehend the same things that our human ancestors did before they learned about atoms and galaxies' (Gibson 1979: 10). This unifying approach provides a further bridge to re-instate the discussion of Palaeolithic society into more general agendas on social evolution and change.

But while Gibson deals very succinctly with the ecology of perception he has less to say about the substance of social change. While the environment provides many affordances (1979: 127) it is their changing uses that are of interest for an historical discipline. An affordance is a use-value (Ingold 1992: 48) where 'the environment is given, to the extent that it is real, but it only affords us anything to the extent that it is *congruent* with our actions; it is an affordance by acting rather than for acting' (Graves n.d.: 9).

Direct perception may unite *Australopithecus* with ourselves but it is the evidence for the construction of different environments within and between hominid species which is of prime interest. To this end the LHN provides a framework for assembling the evidence for change and a context for its interpretation.

Off-site approaches: paths, tracks and places

The LHN also modifies existing approaches to the regional study of Palaeolithic behaviour. For example, the importance of mobility in the construction of an LHN suggests, in archaeological terms, an off-site approach to the use of a region. But while such off-site approaches correctly identify behaviour as spatially continuous (Foley 1981) they have too frequently assigned the physical environment a dominant role in shaping hominid decisions and their regional archaeological signatures. This relationship can be questioned if we consider how any sentient creature perceives its environment and the mutual relationship which is so expressed (Gibson 1979). I would emphasize again the importance of ambulatory perception, which is the consequence of mobility and a feature common to all hominids and animals, for exploring and creating the meanings of the environment. These meanings can either be social or physical since they are not perceived as different. They are part of an animal's complex life routines (Richards 1989) and have been discussed by Gosden (1994: 188) in terms of *habitual action*.

> Habit derives from the human body's involvement with the world and habitual action carries forward the bulk of our lives. The complexity of human life arises not from the sophistication of our cognition, but rather because we can operate so well in the world and towards others, without thought.

Among foragers these mutual environments are not surface-area territories, as traditionally conceived, but rather *paths* and *tracks* between places. Hence the suitability of network analysis with its vocabulary of nodes and links (Barnes 1972, Milroy 1987). In an important discussion of hunter-gatherer territoriality from a Gibsonian perspective, Ingold (1986b: 152) makes the point that a person's life in such a society is a passage along a well-established track. Tenure in such societies 'is not of surface-area, but of sites and paths within a landscape' (1986b: 153). For example,

> if the movements of these major [Dreamtime] personages . . . could be shown on a map of Australia, the result would be a complicated criss-crossing of mythical tracks, dotted with a multitude of sites . . . And these tracks, especially when they cover routes from one waterhole to another, coincide closely with the traditional pathways that people themselves used when moving across the country.
>
> (Berndt and Berndt 1983: 54–55)

Foraging is likewise concerned with intersection points where the paths of gatherers and hunters either cross those of their prey or encounter a plant resource. The sites and paths, rather than the surface-area territories which surround them, are the important elements in the foragers' socially constructed landscapes. The flow of goods through such negotiated paths (e.g. McBryde 1993) is a feature of the LHN and will be discussed further under social landscapes.

Resource transport hypothesis

But how appropriate is it to study the dimensions of LHNs through the distribution of stone materials? It might be argued that the use of stone only deals with a technological aspect of behaviour and is therefore insensitive to wider environment/hominid concerns. For example, in a recent review of the major inferences which can be made about hominid behaviour and ecology, Potts (1993: 332) only lists when stones were first carried. He does not specify either the distances or the effect this has on stone reduction sequences. This underplaying of the archaeological evidence seems strange, since elsewhere he has developed a *resource transport hypothesis* whereby 'behaviours involving more complicated movement of resources were enabled, but not dictated, by the making of tools' (Potts 1991: 169). And yet his preferred model for early hominid activity in East Africa (1991: Figure 6) has no scale for the activities which involved moving resources.

Paradoxically, Potts' reluctance to specify the spatial dimensions of early hominid behaviour which involved the use of stone resources, highlights their importance. Since such stones are incorporated in the basic life routines of hominids from 2.5 Myr ago they provide the only independent means to observe how hominids moved around and, in so doing, created their local environment by engaging with its affordances.

What I am suggesting is that in order to appreciate the analytical value of the LHN, as studied through raw material transfers (Gamble 1986: 331), we need to turn the analysis of such transfers inside out. It has become customary to identify the sources in a site and draw arrows to them. However, the same lithic catchment area can be reversed and the sources and site presented as nodes in a network. The distances of the transfers from source to site are important measures, but should not prevent the potential for regional analysis by concentrating exclusively on a catchment approach.

THE SOCIAL LANDSCAPE (SL)

If the emphasis in an LHN is upon the individual then in a Social Landscape (SL) the focus changes to the group and what we mean by that term in an archaeological context. The main point about the SL is that it splices LHNs together. The group therefore consists of a number of LHNs and is constructed by negotiation. In the SL these negotiations are fixed, not just by interaction but by the *possibility* of interaction, although this may never take place. These are societies of distant relatives and comparative strangers. The hominid environment is therefore truly extended beyond either a foraging or subsistence scale. It transcends habitual action and the pattern of life routines contained in the LHN. Most importantly the SL saw a shift from social life being complex to becoming complicated in the sense discussed by Strum and Latour (see p. 255). In essence this replaced, 'a complexity of shifting, often fuzzy and continuous behaviours, relationships and meanings with a complicated array of simple, symbolic, clear-cut items' (1987: 791). The distinction is well made by Rowell (1991: 260), 'By use of symbols and material resources [complicated societies] can separate social problems into a series of simpler tasks, and this allows each individual to handle a greater elaboration of social arrangements.'

Moreover, alongside social elaboration we also find both synchronic and diachronic variety as the mechanism of negotiation leads to exaptive social outcomes. Among the social problems Rowell refers to are those which arise from infrequent encounters and the ability of individuals to recognize a network of acquaintance (Rowell 1991: 266).

But how can a population-wide system be maintained without the sort of complex and frequent interactions which are needed to negotiate its structure? This is certainly a limiting factor for the LHN, where social life was characterized as local and exclusive. The solution is that in addition to exclusive systems, the SL entertains the possibility of including others in an extended network (Gamble 1993a). As a result social life in an SL, that incorporates several LHNs, and which is associated with a complicated system of negotiation, will be regional, as well as local, and either *inclusive* or *exclusive* in terms of boundary maintenance. An important element in achieving these outcomes is the use of objects in the 'performing' of social structure and the exercise of individual power at a distance (Gosden 1994). This leads to the crucial point made by Strum and Latour (1987: 796) that with the creation of symbolic and material bonds the actors now *appear* to be entering a pre-existing social structure rather than creating it.

Scale

There are no upper limits to the spatial dimensions of the SL. The American flag still stands on the Moon and Voyager II heads out of the galaxy. It is not so much where hominids have been but where they can potentially go. This potential has not, however, been a characteristic of all hominids during prehistory and the limiting factor reverts to their different negotiation of social life (Gamble 1993c).

Among recent foragers this potential for spatial extension can readily be assessed by the movement of resources. A review by Féblot-Augustins and Perlès (1991) of stone and other transported materials indicates distances well beyond the 30–80 km of the LHN. Transfer of materials over 600–2,000 km among hunters and gatherers can be readily documented.

A classic example of such extended networks among recent foragers is provided by the Australian axe trade (McBryde 1978). In her study McBryde found that stone from the greenstone quarries of Victoria was being moved as much as 800 km and on average 228 km from the Mt William source. While such stone might be regarded as utilitarian and necessary for the manufacture of stone hatchets it is clear from McBryde's work that we have now moved beyond the LHN and into a domain of social value where the objects are items for negotiation and affiliation to extended networks.

Writing about the exchange systems of Lake Eyre where goods can move 2,000 km, McBryde notes (1993) that

> The [distribution] system is embedded not in the economic or subsistence regimes of the societies concerned, but in their social and ceremonial life in which material goods and exchange play substantial roles. The meanings of the goods and the significance of their source location are explained and maintained over time by the stories that also map the symbolic and geographical world of these long distance transactions.

At this level the mode of transfer (exchange, visiting, partnership, kin-based, etc.) is of less importance than demonstrating the existence of the extended social landscape where the tracks which define it are now longer, and more varied, than the ambulatory perception of any individual. What can be said is that local dispersal, those tracks associated with the habits and routines of the LHN, is no longer the only mechanism to explain the generation of spatial patterning in material culture.

A review of the archaeological information on the distances goods were transported indicates that the SL was a late development in human prehistory. The date for this development can be fixed at 50,000 years ago with the first appearance of items which came from these greater distances. This was matched by the exaptive explosion of stone tools and raw materials such as antler, bone and ivory into items of display and their use as symbolic markers in the environment (Stringer and Gamble 1993). Before this date there are instances of raw materials being moved distances greater than 100 km (Floss 1990, Kuhn 1992, Féblot–Augustins 1993). However, these are exclusively stone resources and the number of cases are rare. Items such as shell, ochre, fossils and ivory, referred to by Féblot–Augustins and Perlès (1991) as *Biens Fortement Valorisés* (BFV), the 'prestige goods' of a 'non-prestige good' economy, are not transported prior to 50,000 years ago. Whether they are transferred as raw materials or pieces of sculpture, jewellery or ornaments is not important compared to the clear demonstration they provide of extended social networks. The fossil shells found 650 km from their source in Ukrainian Palaeolithic sites (Soffer 1985: 253) is an example, 14,000 years ago, of a small step for a hominid but a giant leap forward for social organization.

DISCUSSION

The SL, as described above, raises several points concerning archaeological concepts of groups which need further investigation. The issues briefly addressed here are demographic norms, patterns of dispersal and issues of time. Underlying these themes is the notion of complicated social behaviour and cognitive thresholds.

Demographic 'magic numbers': groups and spatial knowledge

The demographic limits to foraging are often presented in terms of the 'magic numbers' which surround the interactions and information capacity of mobile foragers. The best known is Birdsell's 500 person dialect tribe (1953, 1958, 1968, Tindale 1974, Kosse 1990, Meehan and White 1990, Constandse-Westermann and Newell 1991).

An example of the 'magic numbers' applied to the spatial knowledge of foragers is provided by Hunn (1994) who has explored the capacity of oral traditions to process information about places. From a geographically diverse sample Hunn shows that individual place-name repertoires normally consist of 500 localities. Kosse (1990: 277) notes similar numerical sizes in ethnobiological taxonomies and relates such a figure to the limits incurred by regional networks which rely on face-to-face interaction. She sets the maximal face-to-face group at 500 ± 100 (Kosse 1990: 291). This limit, she argues, is set by cognitive problems in coping with the information generated by, and necessary to run, such a network. Accordingly, social evolution involves larger population units and more complex means of information-processing involving hierarchies and ritual.

Such developmental models of complexity are commonplace in the archaeological literature. In contrast to this cognitive view, Gibson's mutualistic approach to hominids and their surrounding environments offers an instructive alternative, and one that echoes Birdsell's (1968: 232) explanation for the existence for 500-person dialect tribes as dependent upon 'competence in speech [and] mobility on foot'.

Gibson argues that due to animal mobility the perception of places and movable objects are quite different. 'Places merge into adjacent places, whereas objects have boundaries. Orientation to hidden places with their attached objects can be learned once and for all, whereas orientation to movable objects has to be relearned continually' (1979: 199).

Perception rather than cognitive maps (Tolman 1948) helps explain why rats are so good at learning mazes or chimpanzees at solving the travelling salesman problem (Menzel 1984: 518). The latter experiment involved hiding food in a field and only showing its location to some of the chimps. The lucky ones were carried around the field as the burying took place. When released the informed ones not only found nearly all the food but did this by taking different but very efficient routes, in terms of distance and time, to those when they had been carried. Similar spatial problem-solving was found among Tai forest chimps who remember the location of hammer stones and minimize the transportation distances to nut trees (Boesch and Boesch 1984).

We can conclude from such studies that the knowledge of places and the use of space is part of complex behaviour, but no more complex than other animals exhibit. We do not need to discuss the issue in terms of cognitive thresholds, memory, planning depth or increased organizational abilities involving language.

However, the complications to such behaviour come when the movement of individuals has to be tracked, rather than finding them attached to places, like the broom in the broom closet. To that extent the LHN is comparable to a 'place' with hominids attached, albeit ones making habitual tracks through a local network. By contrast, the SL encompasses defined places through which hominids navigate as they negotiate their regional social structures. From this perspective the re-learning of moveable objects (people) to which Gibson refers, also involves the negotiation of social structure.

But some units do not change. Studies of mating networks (Williams 1974, Wobst 1974) have shown the minimum numbers needed to survive stochastic fluctuations and ensure long-term reproductive success. For these reasons the 500-person unit underwrites both the LHN and SL. In the former it was associated with complex hominid societies and mobility was a limiting factor. With the latter it formed the basis for negotiating extended networks among complicated social structures.

Within the group of 500 an individual probably has detailed social knowledge of only a third of its members but an ability to form additional alliances with the remainder (e.g. Colson 1978). These alliances are based on a wide variety of transactions – for example trade, ritual partnership and fictive kinship. They form negotiated relationships of various degrees of commitment and duration (e.g. Peterson 1993). However, an individual is able to construct from these alliances an SL using the different degrees of knowledge within this 500-person unit. The difference between such basic demography in the LHN and SL is expressed socially in the exclusive and exclusive + inclusive boundaries, as already discussed.

Such SLs do literally consist of making tracks between individuals as well as between places. These people in turn become named 'places' in the sense that they form a social network – their associations and movements providing the meanings of their, and others', environment. Moreover, the association of people with physical places is the basis for generating social contexts for action. These are variously constituted by the numbers and kinds of people in the network who visit and interact. It is through the knowledge of these paths and places, either for sacred or secular purposes, that the SL is constructed and the movement along paths between places conceptualized. Once again, these places are effectively people in the landscape.

Dispersal and larger-scale social units

The role of dispersal has received comparatively little attention in studies of hominid evolution (but see Gamble 1993c, Lahr and Foley in press). Its importance for understanding network structure has recently been modelled by Steele (1994) in a simulation study of the effects of different dispersal patterns on the distribution of cultural traits. He contrasts three networks which express different degrees of connectivity between nodes – Poisson, Low-Density and Tribal. The nodes can be treated as local groups linked in an hexagonal lattice through mate exchange. The simulation examines the diffusion of cultural traits through the three networks (each experimental lattice containing ninety nodes) via this mechanism of dispersal.

The results suggest that studies of hominid evolution have ignored the importance of larger-scale social units. Palaeolithic archaeologists have instead developed models of local home bases rather than regional systems with which to interpret their data (Isaac 1978). However, Steele contends there are good reasons to link the evolution of role segregation (and possibly the sexual division of labour) with the causal influence of patterns of dispersal and philopatry at the population–wide scale.

The differences proposed here between the LHN and the SL would make a similar point about population and spatial scale. In both systems the larger social units would be critical for understanding hominid evolution. The distinction would be the means by which they were constructed. One suggestion is that with Social Landscapes, temporal depth is extended so that the past is used more to shape the future (cf. Gosden 1994). Another would be that the SL has additional mechanisms which involve strangers who have either to be included or excluded from the social structure. Dispersal within the SL can take on a purposive rather than habitual form. As Helms (1988) has argued, the knowledge and information obtained of distant places and customs confer prestige on the traveller. Such purposive construction of the SL in a spatially extended form (when compared to the LHN), now contains the seeds of making the environment differentially knowable or observable to all. The possibility of asymmetries of knowledge and power is thereby produced (Mackie, pers. comm.).

One consequence of mobility and dispersal within regional networks is the problem of reintegrating temporary strangers (Strum and Mitchell 1986). Since social and spatial distance are not the same thing the category of stranger is not easily defined by the distribution of materials. The existence of boundaries, and determining whether they are inclusive or exclusive, might pose problems. However, earlier I adopted the view that society is created rather than entered. Consequently the problem of absence and the reintegration of individuals, however long they are away, becomes another question for negotiation. The LHN with its complex approach to such negotiation sets limits on the benefits for extended dispersal and travel by individuals. Not only might the socially far-distance traveller never be adopted into another regional group (LHN) but also they might run the risk of failing to reintegrate with their own LNH. The complicated negotiation attendant on a SL would facilitate both problems. Extended absence, which now could involve long-distance travel, would be possible (Gamble 1993c). As Gosden has remarked, 'Looked at archaeologically, we should expect to see the effects of colonization not only in areas of new settlement but also back in the "homelands"' (1994: 24). This property would not be expected under a pattern of range extension where only the LHN was involved.

The importance of larger-scale social units has been discussed by Hill (1978) in terms of area-level adaptations that deal, in Tindale's phrase, with 'tracks, travel, trespass and trade' (1974: 75). These regional adaptations, revealed through a study of linguistic exogamy,

> are highly significant clues to the existence of systematically maintained long-distance contact networks in which we must see phenomena like refugee movements *and trespass as systematic rather than as accidents or failures of the local level of adaptation.*
>
> (Hill 1978: 9, emphasis added)

This social environment may seem truly mutual to the hominids which created, perceived and used it. But any distinction from the physical environment is ultimately unhelpful since, as Gibson pointed out (1979: 8), the essence of an environment is that it surrounds an individual. Such surrounding is done both physically and socially. The existence of hominids presupposes environments of both types just as these combined environments imply the existence of a hominid. The extended character of such environments is explained as follows,

> Although it is true that no two individuals can be at the same place at the same time, any individual can stand in all places, and all individuals can stand in the same place at different times. Insofar as the habitat has a persisting substantial layout, therefore, all its inhabitants have an equal opportunity to explore it. In this sense the environment surrounds all observers in the same way that it surrounds a single observer.
>
> (Gibson 1979: 43)

The SL therefore addresses the difficult issue of how a group environment can exist. Mobility allows individuals to both participate in and perceive the environment available to all others. What is significant are the different interpretations of those tracks and places which are available to visitors and acquaintances in an inclusive system. A group environment is not uniform but varies as a result of 'performing' the social structure by different actors with very different knowledge bases. This would seem to necessitate a move from complex to complicated societies, where the role of objects takes on another dimension (Strum and Latour 1987).

Time, materials and memory

Materials serve the two systems of LHN and SL in different ways. Both offer affordances, or use values (Ingold 1992), but only the SL provides a structure for their interpretation as symbols. If the structure of the LHN can be understood as stemming from habit and complex negotiations, then the SL is based upon habit-*plus* and complicated negotiations. I shall argue here that the habit-*plus* refers to concepts of time and the symbolic use of objects.

Gosden (1994) has provided a thorough review of the importance of time in archaeological interpretation. This is not the measured time of radiocarbon-based chronologies upon which so many archaeological resources are spent but rather the temporality of action. His central principle is that life operates through recursiveness, where we make use of the past to create present and future action (1994: 188). This creation also involves raw materials and artefacts:

> Human and material involvements are inextricably linked: we only have such a depth of social relations because we can bring material things into the creation of social relations in fundamental ways; we only have such a depth of material involvements because we can combine socially to change the world. It is the two-way penetration of material and social involvements which differentiates us from other species.
>
> (Gosden 1994: 188)

This interpenetration is illustrated through Ricoeur's concept of *public time* which makes portions of an individual's private time accessible. Public time can be understood as a means of coping with the problems of habit (Gosden 1994: 189). Indeed it gains legitimacy from the unthought actions of habit but is open to manipulation once in the public arena. Public time can therefore create social space (LHNs and SLs) and organize materials within it as the problems of habit dictate. It is in this temporal dimension that strangers can be defined and the boundaries which attend the social structures of inclusion and exclusion can be maintained. Such obvious social complication requires simplification which is provided by objects and the power they derive from the tensions of habitual action and their use in the performance of public time. The process is exaptive. For example, stone tools have existed for 2.5 Myr. Since then they have been part of hominid habit and instrumental in supporting and creating the varied LHNs. However, as we have seen in terms of the spatial dimensions of these networks, hominid involvement with materials (either unmodified or modified) never rose above that expected from habitual action. The changes in social structure 50,000 years ago transformed the use of these same materials through their role in the performance of public time. The stylistic explosion which followed marks the transition to complicated social life.

Archaeologists have conceived of this transition in terms of memory and the selective management of time as a currency for efficient, optimal or security-based behaviour (Gamble, in press). Much discussion has recently been directed to Binford's organizational approach that the transition can be understood in terms of planning depth, defined as: 'The potentially variable length of time between anticipatory actions and the actions they facilitate, [and the] amount of investment in anticipatory actions' (1989: 19).

Increased planning depth is seen as a characteristic of modern populations along with *tactical depth*, the variable capacity to find, based on memory, more than one way to skin a cat, and *curation* which refers to the degree to which technology is maintained (1989: 19–20). This last concept is dependent upon the presence of planning depth. When combined, these three organizational elements provide a signature of modern behaviour, expressed in raw material selection, tool manufacture and discard locations.

A fundamentally different view of behaviour comes from Gibson who argues that it is controlled by perception and not by memory, conceived either as stored knowledge (Binford 1989) or long-term memory (Kosse 1990). Accordingly anticipation, or foresight, is not memory-based but the perception of an affordance (Gibson 1979: 232). This view depends on information being 'out there' in the present, and available via direct perception.

However, I agree with Menzel who has taken this extreme view to task (1984: 528). He points out that animals require some mechanism of information-processing and that direct perception and memory are both available. The cost to the animal will determine which mechanism is selected. The point is relevant to the dichotomy I have been drawing between LHNs and SLs with their complex and complicated, habit and habit-*plus* structures. Direct perception may well be sufficient for the *landscape of habit* (Gosden 1994: 182) of the LHN. Memory, as a guide to behaviour, comes with the manipulation of objects in enhanced public time where the SL is created. In that sense memory depends upon the simplification that comes from complicated rather than complex behaviour. This provides a rather different gloss on planning depth and curation. The latter most probably arises from habit and, given the earlier discussion that all distances within the LHN should be regarded as local, probably has limited explanatory force for past systems of technological organization. On the other hand planning depth only has meaning through memory since part of that anticipation will be to track individuals (the moveable objects) through the structure of the SL.

CONCLUSION: SOCIAL EVOLUTION IN THE PALAEOLITHIC

Steele (in press) has recently proposed that we reconstruct the *normal social environment* for hominids. Establishing the spatial dimensions for hominid behaviour is part of that process. Such normal social environments involve a regional approach and variation is expected both synchronically and diachronically. In this chapter I have explored the basis for understanding the regularities in behaviour which might permit reconstruction of a normal social environment as well as investigating variation in social structure through the mechanism of individual negotiation.

The two networks discussed here set the spatial framework for further discussions of such normal social environments. The Local Hominid Network establishes an upper limit of 80–100 km for the minimum regional scale of interaction during all of hominid evolution. Obviously individuals travelled much larger distances during seasonal rounds and over their lifetimes. But the total distance covered by a hominid only becomes significant if those local networks are spliced together in the extended form of network I have termed a Social Landscape. One expectation of such splicing is that strangers are now an aspect to either be included or excluded. The archaeological evidence for Social Landscapes dates to after 50,000 years ago when distances for raw material transfers regularly exceed 500 km. It is associated with other evidence for ocean voyaging and the colonization of habitats such as Siberia where sociality, measured as the frequency of interaction, would be stretched to the limit due to the distribution of resources (Gamble 1993c). Such separation requires a social system which affords both mobility and reintegration on return. The Social Landscape is capable, through splicing, of almost unlimited spatial extent.

The Social Landscape therefore provides two types of normal social environment – exclusive and inclusive. The former places the emphasis on closure and the maintenance of boundaries. Total demographic closure is neither desirable nor possible and an upper limit of 85 per cent of all marriages occurring within the group seems exceptional (Birdsell 1976). In such systems spatially 'exotic' items, the BFVs (Féblot-Augustins and Perlès 1991), are used to pay membership dues (Gamble 1993a). The use of BFVs for boundary maintenance makes the exclusive social networks which they help define very different to those discussed earlier in terms of the LHN. One reason for this is that the range of normal social environments has changed from the position where social structure was created solely through the LHN. With the SL, inclusive systems can also be negotiated where openness and individual mobility are common. Here the BFVs serve a further function of paying insurance premiums so that tolerated trespass in times of shortage can occur. Hill sums this up well when she points out that in Australia the focus on lexicon as opposed to phonological differentiation, 'cannot be predicted by the dialect tribe model, but appears to result from interpenetration into the properties of local systems by area systems of adaptation' (1978: 18).

The variety of Australian social systems shows, at a continental scale, the two poles of social structure, inclusive/exclusive (Peterson 1986, Gamble 1993a: Table 4.2). These negotiated outcomes can in part be understood, as Peterson (1986) argues, by different ecological circumstances setting the conditions of existence. But these normal social environments are not inevitable. The prehistory of Australia makes this abundantly clear (Cosgrove *et al.* 1990, Smith *et al.* 1993) as different responses to environment and climate are traced at a regional scale.

We can find parallels for this interpenetration of systems with different social and spatial scales in Milroy's (1987) study of social networks in urban communities. Language is also used as a means of measuring interaction and maintaining boundaries. A high-density personal network forms closed, exclusive units predicated on economic and social ties and enforced through heavy dialect. The density of the networks is expressed through four key relationships: kin, neighbourhood, occupation and voluntary association. The closed groups have dense, multiplex links, which express the content of the interaction and the number of strands which define it. The ties which bind individuals as kin are normally more elaborate (multiplex) than those which bind individuals in an occupational network (uniplex). While you may visit the greengrocer more often than you do your sister the content of the interaction with the former will generally be uniplex and with the latter multiplex in character.

By contrast a low-density personal network forms an open system which facilitates geographically and socially mobile sections of communities. The interactions are sparse and uniplex in content. The symbolic/ritual code associated with such systems is elaborated (Douglas 1973: 77–8), where meaning can be detached from local contexts, rather than restricted, where pre-arranged coded forms exist, as is the case with the closed systems. Here the parallel with Helms' (1988) travels to acquire knowledge for prestige purposes is noteworthy.

Changing patterns of raw material transfers provide the means to trace archaeologically the Local Hominid Network and Social Landscape. The development of two normal social environments 50,000 years ago is well brought out in Kuhn's (1991, 1992) studies of the contrasted provisioning strategies of Neanderthal and anatomically modern populations in Italy. He draws the distinction between strategies which aimed to provision places with raw materials and those where individuals were provisioned. As he points out, Neanderthals regularly moved artefacts more than 10–15 km thereby demonstrating that they regularly anticipated needs from one day to the next (1992: 193). These distances, as we have seen, are a feature of the Local Hominid Network, which makes it possible to agree with Kuhn that his Neanderthals, and other archaic hominids, 'regularly carried tools as a hedge against unforeseen, generalized needs' (1992: 206). These are individuals provisioning themselves. It is evidence for complex behaviour based on habit. Such perception (rather than cognition as many prefer) is something we share with all hominids just as we are subject to the selective forces which produce the repeated dimensions of the Local Hominid Network.

However, the data for Neanderthals provisioning places are currently elusive and their lack contrasts strongly with such behaviour after 50,000 years ago. On this point it might be argued that Potts' (1991) savannah resource transport model, where distances are unspecified but short, is a much earlier example of place provisioning. But in essence Potts' observation is similar to those of Tai forest chimps (Boesch and Boesch 1984) and their solution of marrying up nuts and hammerstones in a habitat where visibility is only 20 m. These chimps and the earliest tool-assisted East African hominids are engaged in provisioning themselves. They are both creatures of habit, although most emphatically the former does not serve as an analogue for understanding the society of the latter.

The contrast with place provisioning after 50,000 years ago is dramatic. For example, Webb (1993) describes the lithification, starting during the Pleistocene, of a stone-free, sandy habitat around Lake Cawndilla in semi-arid western New South Wales. Large cobbles were brought from a minimum distance of 40 km and acted as 'portable quarries' as well as anvils and grindstones (Webb 1993: Plate 1). Lithification, setting up stone caches, would, according to the models presented here, be associated with Social Landscapes. It is not expected that such behaviour will be found prior to evidence for BFVs, which are present at Cawndilla, and other indications that the Local Hominid Networks have now been spliced into a Social Landscape.

The challenge for future studies of hominid social evolution can now be seen clearly to be that of investigating variability in the two normal social environments among prehistoric foragers, variability which hinges on the negotiated principles of exclusion and inclusion. With Gosden's perspective on the different uses of the past to structure action we can see that the Local Hominid Network is essentially a landscape of habit as much as one of thought. As applied to the resource transport hypothesis (see p. 259), it assumes complex chains of actions which created social structure from negotiations between individuals. The role of objects in such landscapes of habit was to assist and structure such relations but not to manipulate them in what public time existed.

By contrast the Social Landscape involves a more developed sense of public time, something Gosden also attributes to the post-50,000 BP social revolution (1994: 183). Deliberate manipulation of people and social structures now takes place supported by objects such as ornaments and art, attached both to places and people.

> The new social and material relations did not develop because people could think further into the future or construct broader spaces in their mind than ever before, but mainly because people could create broader forms of time and space *without thinking about it*. Habit carried them further in time and space.
>
> (1994: 184)

Social evolution in the Palaeolithic, as discussed in this chapter, is therefore about the continual and differential construction of the hominid environment. This involves issues of perception, rather than cognition, and properties of extending such environments to include other hominids in complicated societies. Perception rather than memory has been put forward in this chapter as central to our future understanding of these environments. In particular paths, places and landscapes are the doors of Palaeolithic perception. We need to recognize that hominids operated within a niche constructed by others and by preceding generations (Odling-Smee 1993). These affordances in the environment set up distinctive trajectories, particularly when reinforced, as they were in Social Landscapes, by objects which spanned the generations, representing not only power at a distance but ultimately control by the ancestors. The process of change was exaptive where negotiation drew on existing resources, such as stone tools and the landscapes of habit where raw materials were moved around. Time was elaborated and extended and in the process tracks were made towards a global Social Landscape.

ACKNOWLEDGEMENTS

This chapter benefited from the insights and comments of Quentin Mackie, James Steele, Steve Shennan, Richard Cosgrove, Yvonne Marshall, Paul Graves-Brown and Chris Gosden. Any woolliness that remains is entirely mine.

REFERENCES

Andrefsky, W. (1994) 'Raw-material availability and the organization of technology.' *American Antiquity* 59: 21–34.

Bailey, G.N. and Davidson, I. (1983) 'Site exploitation territory and topography: two case studies from Palaeolithic Spain.' *Journal of Archaeological Science* 10: 87–115.

Bar-Yosef, O. (1991) 'Raw material exploitation in the Levantine Epi-Paleolithic.' In A. Montet-White and S. Holen (eds) *Raw Material Economies among Prehistoric Hunter-gatherers,* pp. 235–250. University of Kansas Publications in Anthropology 19.

Barnes, J.A. (1972) *Social Networks.* Addison-Wesley Module in Anthropology 26. Reading, MA: Addison-Wesley.

Berndt, C.H. and Berndt, R.M. (1983) *The Aboriginal Australians: The First Pioneers.* Carlton: Pitman Books.

Binford, L.R. (1989) 'Isolating the transition to cultural adaptations: an organizational approach.' In E. Trinkaus (ed.) *The Emergence of Modern Humans,* pp. 18–41. Cambridge: Cambridge University Press.

Birdsell, J.B. (1953) 'Some environmental and cultural factors influencing the structuring of' Australian Aboriginal populations.' *American Naturalist* 87: 171–207.

Birdsell, J.B. (1958) 'On population structure in generalized hunting and gathering populations.' *Evolution* 12: 189–205.

Birdsell, J.B. (1968) 'Some predictions for the Pleistocene based on equilibrium systems among recent hunter-gatherers.' In R. Lee and I. DeVore (eds) *Man the Hunter*, pp. 229–240. Chicago: Aldine.

Birdsell, J.B. (1976) 'Realities and transformations: the tribes of the Western Desert of Australia.' In N. Peterson (ed.) *Tribes and Boundaries in Australia*, pp. 95–120. Canberra: AIAS.

Bíró, T.K. (1981) 'A Kárpát-Medencei obszidiánok Vizsgálata.' *Különlenyomat az Archeologiai Ertesito* 108: 194–205.

Boesch, C. and Boesch, H. (1984) 'Mental maps in wild chimpanzees: an analysis of hammer transports for nut cracking.' *Primates* 25: 160–170.

Colson, E. (1978) 'A redundancy of actors.' In F. Barth (ed.) *Scale and Social Organization*, pp. 150–162. Oslo: Universitetsforlaget.

Constandse-Westermann, T.S. and Newell, R.R. (1991) 'Social and biological aspects of the western European Mesolithic population structure: a comparison with the demography of North American Indians.' In C. Bonsall (ed.) *The Mesolithic in Europe*, pp. 106–115. Edinburgh: Edinburgh University Press.

Cosgrove, R., Allen, J. and Marshall, B. (1990) 'Palaeo-ecology and Pleistocene human occupation in south central Tasmania.' *Antiquity* 64: 59–78.

Douglas, M. (1973) *Natural Symbols*. Harmondsworth: Pelican Books.

Dunbar, R.I.M. (1993) 'Coevolution of neocortex size, group size and language in humans.' *Behavioural and Brain Sciences* 16: 681–735.

Féblot-Augustins, J. (1990) 'Exploitation des matières premières dans l'Acheuléen d'Afrique: perspectives comportementales.' *Paléo* 2: 27–42.

Féblot-Augustins, J. (1993) 'Mobility strategies in the late middle Palaeolithic of central Europe and Western Europe: elements of stability and variability.' *Journal of Anthropological Archaeology* 112: 211–265.

Féblot-Augustins, J. and Perlès, C. (1991) 'Perspectives ethno-archéologiques sur les échanges à longue distance.' Unpublished ms. Colloques 'Éthnoarchéologie' Antibes.

Floss, H. (1990) 'Rohmaterialversorgung im Paleolithikum des Mittelrhein-gebietes.' Dissertation, Köln.

Floss, H. (1991) 'Sur l'approvisionnement des matières premières au Magdalénien et Paléolithique final en Rhenanie (Bassin de Neuwied).' In A. Montet-White (ed.) *Les bassins du Rhin et du Danube au Paléolithique supérieur*. Colloque UISPP, Mainz 1986. *Eraul* 43: 104–113.

Foley, R.A. (1981) *Off-site Archaeology and Human Adaptation in Eastern Africa.* Oxford: British Archaeological Reports International Series 97.

Franco, N. (1990) 'El aprovisionamiento de los recursos liticos por parte de los grupos del area interserrana Bonaerense.' In H. Nami (ed.) *Estudios liticos en Argentina: vias de analisis y desarrollo actual*, pp. 39–51. S.F. del V. de Catamarca.

Franco, N. (1991) 'Algunas tendencias distribucionales en el material litico recuperado en el area interserrana Bonaerense.' *Boletín de Centro* 1 (3): 72–9.

Franco, N. (1994) 'Maximizacion en el aprovechamiento de los recursos liticos: un caso analizado en el area interserrana Bonaerense.' In L.A. Borrero and J.L. Lanata (eds) *Arqueología de cazadores-recolectores: limites, casos y aperturas*, pp. 75–88. Buenos Aires: Arqueología Contemporánea 5.

Gamble, C.S. (1986) *The Palaeolithic Settlement of Europe*. Cambridge: Cambridge University Press.

Gamble, C.S. (1993a) 'Exchange, foraging and local hominid networks.' In C. Scarre and F. Healy (eds) *Trade and Exchange in Prehistoric Europe*, pp. 35–44. Oxford: Oxbow Monograph 33.

Gamble, C.S. (1993b) 'Ancestors and agendas.' In N. Yoffee and A. Sherratt (eds) *Archaeological Theory: Who Sets the Agenda?*, pp. 39–52. Cambridge: Cambridge University Press.

Gamble, C.S. (1993c) *Timewalkers: The Prehistory of Global Colonization*. Far Thrupp: Alan Sutton.

Gamble, C.S. (in press) 'Lithics and social evolution.' In J. Schofield (ed.) *Lithics in Context*. Oxford: Oxbow Books.

Geneste, J.-M. (1988a) 'Systèmes d'approvisionnement en matières premières au paléolithique moyen et au paléolithique supérieur en Aquitaine.' *L'Homme de Néandertal* 8: 61–70.

Geneste, J.-M. (1988b) 'Les industries de la Grotte Vaufrey: technologie du débitage, économie et circulation de la matière première lithique.' In J.-P. Rigaud (ed.) Special Issue 'La Grotte Vaufrey à Cenac et Saint-Julien (Dordogne), Paléoenvironments, chronologie et activités humaines.' *Mémoires de la Société Préhistorique Française* 19: 441–518.

Gibson, J.J. (1979) *The Ecological Approach to Visual Perception*. Hillsdale, NJ: Erlbaum.

Gosden, C. (1994) *Social Being and Time*. Oxford: Blackwell.

Gowlett, J.A.J. (1984) 'Mental abilities of early man: a look at some hard evidence.' In R. Foley (ed.) *Hominid Evolution and Community Ecology*, pp. 167–192. London: Academic Press.

Graves, P. (n.d.) 'The doors of perception: a mutualist account of entrances and exits.'

Helms, M.W. (1988) *Ulysses' Sail: An Ethnographic Odyssey of Power, Knowledge, and Geographical Distance*. Princeton: Princeton University Press.

Hill, J.H. (1978) 'Language contact systems and human adaptations.' *Journal of Anthropological Research* 34: 1–26.

Hiscock, P. (1986) 'Raw material rationing as an explanation of assemblage differences: a case study of Lawn Hill, Northwest Queensland.' In G. Ward (ed.) *Archaeology at Anzaas 1984*, pp. 178–190. Canberra: Canberra Archaeological Society/Department of Archaeology and Prehistory, Australian National University.

Hodder, I. (1982) *Symbols in Action*. Cambridge: Cambridge University Press.

Hunn, E. (1994) 'Place-names, population density and the magic number 500.' *Current Anthropology* 35: 81–85.

Ingold, T. (1986a) *Evolution and Social Life*. Cambridge: Cambridge University Press.

Ingold, T. (1986b) *The Appropriation of Nature: Essays on Human Ecology and Social Relations*. Manchester: Manchester University Press.

Ingold, T. (1992) 'Culture and the perception of the environment.' In E. Croll and D. Parkin (eds) *Bush Base: Forest Farm. Culture, Environment and Development*, pp. 39–56. London: Routledge.

Isaac, G. (1978) 'The food-sharing behaviour of proto-human hominids.' *Scientific American* 238: 90–108.

Kosse, K. (1990) 'Group size and societal complexity: thresholds in the long-term memory.' *Journal of Anthropological Archaeology* 9: 275–303.

Kuhn, S.L. (1991) ' "Unpacking" reduction: lithic raw material economy in the Mousterian of West-Central Italy.' *Journal of Anthropological Archaeology* 10: 76–106.

Kuhn, S.L. (1992) 'On planning and curated technologies in the Middle Palaeolithic.' *Journal of Anthropological Research* 48: 185–214.

Lahr, M.M. and Foley, R. (in press) 'Multiple dispersals and modern human origins.' *Evolutionary Anthropology*.

Lebel, S. (1992) 'Mobilité des hominides et systèmes d'exploitation des ressources lithiques au paléolithique ancien: La Caune de l'Arago (France).' *Canadian Journal of Archaeology* 16: 48–69.

McBryde, I. (1978) 'Wil-im-ee Moor-ring: or, where do axes come from?' *Mankind* 11: 354–382.

McBryde, I. (1993) ' "The landscape is a series of stories". Grindstones, quarries and exchange in aboriginal Australia: a case study from the Cooper/Lake Eyre Basin, Australia.' In A. Ramos-Millán (ed.) *Siliceous Rocks and Culture: Proceedings of the VIth International Flint Symposium*. Granada: Madrid University.

McNiven, I.J. (1990) 'Prehistoric aboriginal settlement and subsistence in the Cooloola region, coastal southeast Queensland.' PhD thesis, University of Queensland.

Meehan, B. and White, N. (eds) (1990) *Hunter-gatherer Demography: Past and Present*. Oceania Monographs, University of Sydney.

Menzel, E. (1984) 'Spatial cognition and memory in captive chimpanzees.' In P. Marler and H.S. Terrace (eds) *The Biology of Learning*, pp. 509–531. Berlin: Springer Life Sciences Research Report 29.

Milroy, L. (1987) *Language and Social Networks*, 2nd edn. Oxford: Blackwell.

Odling-Smee, F.J. (1993) 'Niche construction, evolution and culture.' In T. Ingold (ed.) *Companion Encyclopedia of Anthropology: Humanity, Culture and Social Life*, pp. 162–196. London: Routledge.

Pasda, C. (1992) 'Das Magdalenein in der Freiburger Bucht.' Thesis, Tübingen University.

Perlès, C. (1992) 'In search of lithic strategies: a cognitive approach to prehistoric chipped stone assemblages.' In J.-C. Gardin and C. Peebles (eds) *Representations in Archaeology*, pp. 223–247. Bloomington and Indianapolis: Indiana University Press.

Peterson, N. (1986) *Australian Territorial Organisation*. Oceania Monograph 30.

Peterson, N. (1993) 'Demand sharing: reciprocity and the pressure for generosity among foragers.' *American Anthropologist* 95: 860–874.

Petitt, P.B. (1992) 'Reduction models and lithic variability in the middle Palaeolithic of southwest France.' *Lithics* 13: 17–32.

Potts, R. (1991) 'Why the Oldowan? Plio-Pleistocene toolmaking and the transport of resources.' *Journal of Anthropological Research* 47: 153–176.

Potts, R. (1993) 'The hominid way of life.' In S. Jones, R. Martin and D. Pilbeam (eds) *The Cambridge Encyclopedia of Human Evolution*, pp. 325–334. Cambridge: Cambridge University Press.

Rensink, E. (1993) 'Moving into the north: Magdalenian occupation and exploitation of the loess landscapes of northwestern Europe.' Proefschrift, Leiden University.

Richards, G. (1989) 'Human behavioural evolution: a physiomorphic model.' *Current Anthropology* 30: 244–255.

Roebroeks, W., Kolen, J. and Rensink, E. (1988) 'Planning depth, anticipation and the organization of Middle Palaeolithic technology: the "archaic natives" meet Eve's descendants.' *Helinium* 28: 17–34.

Rolland, N. and Dibble, H. (1990) 'A new synthesis of Middle Palaeolithic variability.' *American Antiquity* 55: 480–499.

Rowell, T.E. (1991) 'What can we say about social structure?' In P. Bateson (ed.) *The Development and Integration of Behaviour*, pp. 255–269. Cambridge: Cambridge University Press.

Smith, M.A., Spriggs, M. and Frankhauser, B. (1993) *Sahul in Review: Pleistocene Archaeology in Australia, New Guinea and Island Melanesia*. Canberra: Department of Prehistory RSPacS.

Soffer, O. (1985) *The Upper Palaeolithic of the Central Russian Plain*. New York: Academic Press.

Steele, J. (1994) 'Communication networks and dispersal patterns in human evolution: a simple simulation model.' *World Archaeology* 26: 126–143.

Steele, J. (in press) 'Weak modularity and the evolution of human social behaviour.' In H. Maschner (ed.) *Darwinian Archaeologies*. New York: Plenum.

Stringer, C. and Gamble, C. (1993) *In Search of the Neanderthals: Solving the Puzzle of Human Origins*. London: Thames and Hudson.

Strum, S.S. and Latour, B. (1987) 'Redefining the social link: from baboons to humans.' *Social Science Information* 26: 783–802.

Strum, S.S. and Mitchell, W. (1986) 'Baboon models and muddles.' In W.G. Kinzey (ed.) *The Evolution of Human Behaviour: Primate Models*, pp. 87–104. Albany: State University of New York Press.

Tindale, N.B. (1974) *Aboriginal Tribes of Australia*. Los Angeles: University of California Press.

Tolman, E.C. (1948) 'Cognitive maps in rats and men.' *Psychological Review* 55: 189–208.

Turq, A. (1988) 'L'approvisionnement en matières premières lithiques du Magdalénien du Quercy et du Haut-Agenais: étude préliminaire.' *Colloque de Chancelade, 10–15 Octobre 1988*: 301–308.

Turq, A. (1992) 'Le Paléolithique inférieur et moyen entre les vallées de la Dordogne et du Lot.' Thèse, L'Université de Bordeaux I. 2 volumes.

Turq, A. (1993) 'L'approvisionnement en matières premières lithiques au Moustérien et au début du Paléolithique supérieur dans le nord-est du bassin Aquitain (France).' In V. Cabrera Valdes (ed.) *El origen del hombre moderno en el suroeste de Europa*, pp. 315–325. Madrid: Universidad de Educacion a Distancia.

Vita-Finzi, C. and Higgs, E.S. (1970) 'Prehistoric economy in the Mount Carmel area of Palestine, site catchment analysis.' *Proceedings of the Prehistoric Society* 36: 1–37.

Webb, C. (1993) 'The lithification of a sandy environment.' *Archaeology in Oceania* 28: 105–111.

Williams, B.J. (1974) *A Model of Band Society*. Memoir of the Society for American Archaeology 29. Washington, DC: Society for American Archaeology.

Wobst, H.M. (1974) 'Boundary conditions for Paleolithic social systems: a simulation approach.' *American Antiquity* 39: 147–178.

Wobst, H.M. (1976) 'Locational relationships in Paleolithic society.' *Journal of Human Evolution* 5: 49–58.

Wobst, H.M. (1978) 'The archaeo-ethnology of hunter gatherers or the tyranny of the ethnographic record in archaeology.' *American Antiquity* 43: 303–309.

Yoffee, N. (1993) 'Too many chiefs? (or, safe texts for the 90s).' In N. Yoffee and A. Sherratt (eds) *Archaeological Theory: Who Sets the Agenda?*, pp. 60–78. Cambridge: Cambridge University Press.

PART III

THE SEXUAL DIVISION OF LABOUR IN MODERN HUMAN FORAGING SOCIETIES

EDITORS' NOTE

The four chapters in this section all focus on the nature and evolutionary history of the sexual division of labour in human foraging societies. However, in contrast to past approaches which have seen the economic interdependence of the family unit as the key to understanding the social basis of all Pleistocene hominid evolution, the concentration here is on continuities between human foragers and other primates in types of provisioning behaviour when this is seen as a reproductive strategy (Hawkes), and on discontinuities in the emergence of early anatomically modern human societies in Southern Africa and elsewhere (Power and Watts, Knight, Graves-Brown).

Hawkes demonstrates, by careful comparative analysis of foraging data from different modern foraging societies, that the sexual division of labour derives from the contrastive fitness-maximizing strategies of men and women. Hunting appears to enable men to maximize mating opportunities, while women's foraging is oriented to contributing to the welfare of their children. These observations challenge received views of the family as the prototypical common-interest group: Hawkes notes that the archaeological implications remain to be explored.

Power and Watts develop a theoretical model of the costs of male philandering to females when the energetic investment in rearing offspring constitutes a major burden. They note that the seasonal birth peaks seen in many forager societies may have the effect of synchronizing the female reproductive cycle and thus decreasing the benefits to males of philandering, but argue that additionally, through behavioural synchrony, menstruation – the principal visual cue to female fertility status – became converted into a collective symbolic resource for females whose coalitionary strategies enforced male provisioning effort. They locate this social transition at the time of the first appearance of modern humans in Southern Africa, and point to possible supporting evidence in increased symbolic use of red ochre at that time.

Knight and Graves-Brown both develop accounts of the Upper Palaeolithic transition based on theoretical models of male and female foraging roles. But whereas Knight sees male provisioning as a crucial, coerced strategy to enable females to decrease the energetic burden of reproduction, and sees the 'symbolic revolution' as a consequence of the intensely solidaristic female coalitions which were the basis of this coercion, Graves-Brown argues that male and female foraging roles evolved separately as the outcome of their contrasting reproductive interests, coming together into a relationship of complementarity in the Upper Palaeolithic. Graves-Brown, however, is fairly sceptical about the possibility of detecting confirmatory evidence of the evolution of gender roles in the Pleistocene archaeological record.

CHAPTER TEN

FORAGING DIFFERENCES BETWEEN MEN AND WOMEN

Behavioural ecology of the sexual division of labour

KRISTEN HAWKES

Non-human primates forage mostly to feed themselves. Since this is not true of human foragers, a sexual division of labour and regular food-sharing have been nominated as the evolutionary keys to a distinctively human way of life (e.g. Washburn and Lancaster 1968). The evident economic co-operation among men and women is used to justify the view that families or larger social groups are units of common interest with members deployed to meet group needs. Here I provide theoretical and empirical justification for the contrary view that the interests of individuals, and the way these vary with sex, age and ecology, can better explain human foraging patterns and the social strategies of which they are part.

To set the problem, I begin with a summary of the influential scenario that makes a sexual division of labour the key transition in human evolution. This is followed by a brief sketch of the general orientation of behavioural ecology and some of its primary conceptual and modelling tools, especially those that apply to understanding behavioural differences between the sexes. After this I review some sex-biased foraging and social strategies among other primates as a means of illustrating these tools in use and providing a background for their application to human patterns. I then consider some examples of recent work on foraging practices among hunter-gatherers that focus on fitness-related trade-offs and the way they differ with sex, age and ecology. This work shows that differences between the sexes are as important among people as they are among other primates. Females trade off alternatives that give different benefits to their children; males trade off parenting benefits for benefits in mating competition. This view of the sexual division of labour locates it more clearly within the general primate variation. It also underlines similarities in the conflicts of interest arising among men and women who forage for a living and the sexual conflicts among people who make a living in other ways.

HUMAN EVOLUTION

The substantial contribution men make to feeding children distinguishes human social arrangements from those of other primates. Washburn saw this as a consequence of the switch made by ancestral males to hunting, creating 'a wholly new set of interpersonal bonds. When males hunt and females gather, the results are shared and given to the young, and the habitual sharing between a male, a female, and their offspring becomes the basis for the human family' (Washburn and Lancaster 1968: 301). Lancaster and Lancaster put it this way: 'The division of labor between human males and females and the regular sharing of food represents the true watershed for differentiating ape from human life ways' (1983: 36). They noted that male care of young is more frequent in primates than other mammals, but the one thing they do not do is regularly bring food to their mates and offspring – 'the evolution of the role husband/father is unique to the human species and represents major ecological and social specializations' (1983: 42).

> . . . the fundamental platform of behavior for the genus *Homo* was the division of labour between male hunting and female gathering, which focused on a unique human pattern of parental investment – the feeding of juveniles. The importance of contributions by both the male and female parent toward juvenile survival reduced the significance of sexual selection in human reproductive strategies and emphasized parental investment and parental partnerships for the rearing of children.
>
> (1983: 51)

This scenario compellingly ties an array of salient features into a coherent package, linking ecological changes to shifts in resource exploitation and consequent social strategies, all through appeal to adaptive advantages. Possible conflicts of interest among family members seem overshadowed by longer-term common interests. But the problem with the argument is that explanatory appeals to natural selection require careful attention to distinctions between individual and group benefits. Despite extensive discussion of the importance of this distinction (e.g. Williams 1966a), and influential demonstrations of pervasive conflicts of interest between mates and among closest kin (Trivers 1972, 1974), anthropologists continue to think of small kin-based communities, especially the families composing them, as units of common interest. Reasons to revise this widely accepted view of the economic and social basis of the sexual division of labour continue to accumulate.

BEHAVIOURAL ECOLOGY

Two sets of ideas are fundamental to behavioural ecology. First is the assumption that, as the products of evolution, living things have been designed by natural selection (Williams 1966a). This warrants the expectation that individuals will tend to do things likely to enhance their own fitness. (For extended discussion of applications to human behaviour see, e.g., Alexander 1979, Betzig, *et al.* 1988, Borgerhoff Mulder 1991, Chagnon and Irons 1979, Cronk 1991, Daly and Wilson 1983, Smith and Winterhalder 1992, Symons 1979). This has an important entailment: the fitness interests of individuals are rarely perfectly coincident, hence conflicts of interest among family or group members can result in outcomes that do not maximize group benefits or average benefits among members.

The second distinctive feature of behavioural ecology is its explicitly economic perspective (Maynard Smith 1978a, Parker and Maynard Smith 1990). Because time and energy are limited, individuals always face allocation problems. More to one thing means less to something else. Every action exacts the opportunity cost of missed benefits from alternatives foregone. Using the working assumption that individuals have been designed to choose options likely to give them higher net fitness, investigators seek to explain a pattern by discovering how it serves the fitness of those displaying it better than available alternatives. This involves posing hypotheses about (1) the particular (fitness-related) effects it has, the 'goal', (2) the constraints on achieving that goal and (3) the currency in which the options are evaluated. Simple optimality models are used when the pay-offs for a strategy do not depend on how many others adopt it. When the pay-offs vary as others use the same strategy, frequency-dependent optimality models that take mutual adjustments into account are appropriate. Evolutionary game theory (Maynard Smith 1982) has proven especially useful.

The tools of optimality modelling require investigators to be quite explicit about their construal of any pattern of interest. This is both a peculiar strength of the approach and the source of what some see as its irritating inflexibility. Investigators make biologically informed guesses about the fitness-related problem the subject is trying to solve. This requires hypotheses about the effects or goals of the behaviour, and about the costs and benefits of alternative means to achieve that goal. Formal models serve to show what individuals would necessarily do to achieve a particular goal under specified constraints. If subjects don't behave as modelled they are not meeting that goal, and/or they face other constraints. Models that have proven most useful have focused on very simple trade-offs, use readily measured currencies to assess alternatives and incorporate few constraints. For example, the prey model of foraging theory (Stephens and Krebs 1986) shows which resources a forager will pursue to maximize its mean rate of energy capture if it can only spend time either searching for or handling resources (so this is the only trade-off), and if resources with known average handling rates are encountered sequentially at a known rate (these are the only constraints). Lack's (1947) model of optimal clutch size is another example, where the trade-off is between clutch size and survivorship per offspring (because daylight constrains parents in the total amount of food they can deliver to the nest) and the hypothesized goal is maximum number of surviving offspring per clutch. The utility of the models is not just a matter of whether or how often subjects seek these goals under these constraints. The simplicity of the models, and the relative ease with which key variables can be measured, makes patterns in falsification themselves informative (e.g., Lessells 1991, Stephens and Krebs 1976). For example, bird and insect clutches are often smaller than the size that would maximize the number of survivors per clutch, leading to hypotheses about different goals and trade-offs (Charnov and Krebs 1974, Williams 1966b).

SEX DIFFERENCES

Understanding the fundamentally different ways in which males and females gain reproductive success supplies a foundation for expecting differences in a wide array of phenotypic strategies. In all sexually reproducing populations, including humans, each individual has both a mother and a father. Although each contributes half the genetic material, males and females can differ enormously in the other investments they must make to produce offspring. Trivers (1972) recognized that the extent of this difference determines the power of sexual selection, the aspect of selection that spreads characters according to their effects on competition for mates (Darwin 1871). The measure best capturing the key sex difference is the relative rate of offspring production (Clutton-Brock 1991). The slower reproducing sex necessarily limits the rate of offspring production. In humans for example, only the number of women determines the possible rate of baby production. A population including exactly 100 women can produce a maximum of about 100 babies a year, whether it includes 10 men or 10,000. One man could potentially monopolize all the paternity. Since all babies have a mother and a father, imbalanced sex ratios make average reproductive success higher for the rare sex. If, for example, females are rare, so that mothers get more grandchildren on average through daughters than through sons, then selection favors biasing toward daughters. As a consequence, equilibrium sex ratios are usually even, making the mean reproductive success of males and females equal (Charnov 1982, Fisher 1930). Then when any male gains higher reproductive success than the average female, other males must have reproductive success lower than the female mean. Because male fitness can be so much more strongly affected by differential success at getting mates, it is selection on males that often favours allocating reproductive expenditure to mating effort. So Darwin noted widespread patterns of male–male combat, in which males compete to displace each other from mating opportunities, and female choice, in which males have been selected to display characteristics that females prefer in mates.

Maynard Smith's model of the evolution of parental care illustrates mating and parenting trade-offs that could be important in shaping reproductive strategies among animals generally (Maynard Smith 1977). He showed that each of the four possible patterns: female and male care (common among birds), female only care (common among mammals), male only care (not uncommon among fish) and no care (also frequent among fish) could be evolutionarily stable depending only on the values of three variables: offspring survivorship as a function of the number of 'parents' caring; number of offspring a female can produce depending on whether or not she devotes effort to care; and probability that a male will successfully mate again if he does not stay to care.

A particularly interesting feature of the model is that certainty of paternity plays no role (Maynard Smith 1978b, cf. 1982); i.e. male care can be an evolutionarily stable strategy (ESS) even if paternity certainty is very low, and no care or female only care can be an ESS even if certainty of paternity is very high. Recently new techniques to assess paternity have uncovered astonishingly high rates of 'extra pair paternity' in birds (Birkhead and Møller 1992), even though 'monogamy' with 'biparental' care is common. Relationships between care and probable paternity have been observed in some species (e.g. Davies 1992), but cross-species comparisons show paternal probability to be a poor predictor of male care (Møller and Birkhead 1993).

Maynard Smith's model highlights key differences between the sexes in the trade-offs they may face in committing a unit of reproductive effort. For males, parental care may cost the missed opportunity of additional matings, while females trade off increases in quality for quantity of offspring. The model's great virtue is in deriving so much from so little, and flagging what may be key differences between the sexes. But some of the empirical patterns we wish to explain add complications. Direct offspring care may not be the only way females expend parental effort and males may sometimes gain mating advantages by providing care.

OTHER PRIMATES

The distinction between parental and mating effort seems quite straightforward: expenditure aimed to increase the number and/or fitness of offspring vs. that aimed to increase success at gaining mates. Much work over the past fifteen years focused on primate reproductive strategies has revised prior expectations about the character of these two kinds of expenditure. Primate females, like other mammals, reproduce at a slower rate than males can, so males are expected to compete for matings and females to be choosy. Yet some primate females are extremely libidinous, actively seeking copulations with many males. While extra copulations might increase the number of offspring produced by a male they cannot have that effect for females. Hrdy (1979) suggested that multiple copulations by females are actually parenting effort. Males are often a source of danger or aid to infants and juveniles and differentially so depending on their possibility of paternity. Thus a female may increase the survivorship of her offspring by spreading the possibility of paternity widely (Hrdy and Whitten 1987).

The key link in this argument between male behaviour toward infants and juveniles and their probability of paternity has been challenged. While the relative frequency with which primate males care for infants has been generally assumed to be a function of the possibility of paternity and labelled paternal investment, males often contribute to the welfare of infants unlikely to be their own. Smuts (1985) noted that baboon males who made such contributions had greater chances of being chosen to mate by the infant's mother. Reviewing the patterns of male care across primate species Smuts and Gubernick (1992) found that probability of paternity was not clearly linked to the probability of care and concluded that their evidence 'calls into question the hypotheses that male–infant caregiving in non-human primates is primarily a form of paternal investment and suggests, instead, that male–infant care is sometimes a form of mating effort' (1992: 20). Male care of infants and juveniles may be mating effort even among monogamous primates (Price 1991, Whitten 1987).

The kind of care males provide rarely involves food delivery. But males of some species hunt. This is more frequent among chimpanzees than previously supposed and may earn mating pay-offs. Goodall (1968) early reported hunting at Gombe, and Teleki noted that males preferentially shared meat with oestrous females (1973). Boesch and Boesch (1989) reported more frequent hunting among chimpanzees at Tai. Females hunt much less often than males although they can be as successful at it as males are. Re-analysis of the frequency of hunting at Gombe (Wrangham and Bergmann-Riss 1990) showed overall rates to be about as high as those at Tai. Additional data and analysis provided by Stanford et al. (1994) shows marked short-term and seasonal variation in hunting frequency at Gombe and some similar patterning in this variation between Gombe and Tai as well as between Gombe and Mahale (Takahata et al. 1984). In addition to individual differences in hunting frequency, Stanford et al. show that there is a marked association between the number of males in a group, the number of oestrous females in the group and the frequency of hunts. They suggest that it is not variation in prey profitability or encounter rates but 'social' factors that account for hunting 'binges'. Social benefits could be either direct preferential treatment by females or preferential alliances with hunters by other males, the latter in turn advantageous in mating competition. A related supposition comes from Nishida *et al.*'s report of the long-term pattern of meat-sharing by one male at Mahale, suggesting that 'it may be a political strategy, used to establish and reinforce alliances' (1992: 160).

In addition to the fact that male chimpanzees hunt and share their prey, other sex differences in foraging patterns (e.g. Boesch and Boesch 1984, 1989, Galdikas and Teleki 1981, Goodall 1986, McGrew 1992, Strum 1981) and food-sharing (Feistner and McGrew 1989, Silk 1978, Strum 1981) occur among chimpanzees and other primates. Altman (1980) showed how much nursing infants interfere with the foraging of baboon mothers and how dramatically mortality risks shift from mother to offspring at weaning. Fifteen years ago Wrangham (1979) pointed out that the key determinants of reproductive success for male and female primates are so different that explanations for varying 'social systems' should begin with those determinants. For females the main problem is access to food and so the characteristics of food resources should largely determine how they are distributed. The distribution of females determines the main problem for males: how much paternity they can gain (or lose) in competition with other males.

The work on other primates shows that for females parental trade-offs shape behaviour generally, including foraging activities. Males, by contrast, may hunt, share meat and care for infants not to invest in offspring but rather to gain mating advantages. This work highlights the potential for mistaking the benefits individuals gain from their behaviour. Recent work on hunter-gatherers corroborates the importance of the problem and shows how sex-specific trade-offs affect foraging strategies.

HUNTER-GATHERERS

From the perspective of behavioural ecology people are expected to adjust their activity patterns as the pay-offs for alternative allocations of time and effort vary. If so, ethnographic patterns should differ accordingly. Differences in the character, distribution, and abundance of local plants and animals affect the rates of nutrient acquisition for different foraging strategies. Differences in the ways men and women can enhance their own fitness affect the trade-offs they face in choosing foraging tasks.

The accumulating quantitative picture of foraging activities among people who depend on wild foods shows that there can be substantial overlap in the resources taken by men and women (e.g. Dwyer and Minnegal 1991, Goodman *et al.* 1985) and that under some circumstances spouses spend large fractions of their foraging time working together (Bailey and Aunger 1989, Hart and Hart 1986, Hewlett 1992, Stearmen 1987). Sometimes men and women both hunt and gather. Satisfactory explanations will need to account for the variation in the extent of the overlap between the foraging practices of women and men.

To illustrate how the exploration of sex-specific trade-offs can help explain ethnographic variation, I summarize two sets of ethnographic comparisons that employ this perspective. Women's foraging patterns and the way these are affected by child welfare goals and trade-offs between components of parenting are reviewed first. I then consider men's trade-offs.

Women's foraging

Trade-offs between foraging and child care: the example of the Hiwi and the Ache

Acquisition (and/or processing) of some resources but not others may be effectively carried out in combination with child care. Resource choice often requires women to trade-off higher nutrient acquisition rates for child care benefits (Brown 1970, Hurtado *et al.* 1985, Murdock and Provost 1973). The extent of these trade-offs could be represented as one variable, the potential nutrient acquisition rates as another. Imagine the first variable as a continuum. At one extreme the two activities are mutually exclusive, at the other they are so perfectly compatible that a unit of time spent on one can also be spent on the other, with no loss of efficiency in either. Between these extremes tasks differ across the range of mutual interference.

The benefits expected for child care will also vary. Hurtado *et al.* (1992) report some of the ways trade-offs between foraging and child care benefits vary among Ache and Hiwi women. Differences in the environments of the two populations affect foraging opportunities, and also the prevalence of health threats to children that can be reduced by close supervision. The Ache inhabit the subtropical forests of eastern Paraguay in which resources are relatively abundant and evenly distributed throughout the year (Hill *et al.* 1984). Insect pests are also ubiquitous and cleared spaces minimal at daytime rest spots in the forest and in temporary foraging camps usually occupied for only a single night. These features 'make the forest a very unsafe area for unsupervised infants and children the year round' (Hurtado *et al.* 1992: 191). The Hiwi live in the savannahs of western Venezuela where resource distribution varies markedly in both space and time (Hurtado and Hill 1990). Main camps are occupied continuously for many years while temporary seasonal camps are used during the 'almost entirely pest-free' dry season, 'making camps an extremely safe area for infants and children' (Hurtado *et al.* 1992: 190). Hiwi women have less to gain from child care than Ache women do. On the other hand the acquisition rates they can earn are much lower than those available to Ache women.

Individual vs. team foraging rates: the example
of the Hadza and the !Kung

In addition to the trade-offs with child care that may adjust the resources women choose to exploit and the time they devote to food acquisition, there is a third way in which child welfare may guide women's strategies. Women may promote larger collective daily totals of food for their family's consumption by enlisting their children in nutrient acquisition and/or processing. Under some circumstances this could entail high costs in child welfare, but sometimes that trade-off might be slight and women might best serve their own fitness by adjusting their foraging to maximize the 'team rate' they jointly earn with the participation of their children. The importance of this 'team rate' is illustrated in the food acquisition patterns of Hadza foragers in northern Tanzania and in the quite different patterns of !Kung speakers foraging in the Dobe area of northwestern Botswana in the 1960s.

The Hadza inhabit the East African savannah, the Dobe !Kung the northern edge of the Kalahari. Annual rainfall patterns are similar and both regions are home to the plant and animal species of the arid African tropics. In broad terms their environments are alike. However the rocky hill country of the Hadza with many visible landmarks and long vistas differs from the much flatter sandy terrain of the Dobe area. The Hadza have many more surface water sources, large ungulates are more abundant, more baobabs dot the hills, and patches of berries and nutrient-dense tubers are more extensive. There are no mongongo groves.

When foraging was the main subsistence activity !Kung children acquired little food themselves until their teenage years (Draper 1976, Draper and Cashdan 1988, Lee 1968). In contrast, Hadza children are energetic foragers providing substantial amounts of their nutritional requirements by their own efforts while very young (Blurton Jones *et al.* 1989, Hawkes *et al.*, in prep.).

Models based on measurement of the rates of nutrient acquisition that women and children can earn for alternative foraging strategies in these two settings show that the differences in the distribution and character of local resources account for the behavioural differences. Experimental foraging excursions around Dobe (Blurton Jones *et al.* 1994, forthcoming) and measurements of Hadza children's return rates near base camps (Blurton Jones *et al.* 1989, Hawkes *et al., in prep.*) showed that near-camp foraging is profitable for Hadza but not !Kung children, explaining why Hadza but not !Kung youngsters forage unaccompanied by adults.

Hadza children also join adults in long forays to distant resource patches, travelling as far as !Kung women do when they visit the mongongo groves. The rates of caloric acquisition that children and adults earn both near camp and in the berry patch explain why Hadza women take their children older than 5 or 6 years on these long trips (of nearly ten hours, duration including about an hour and a half of travel each way). Children can earn a rate much closer to the adult rate when picking berries. Since a child consumes food it acquires itself as well as that provided by its mother, the amount of food a woman makes available to her children depends not just on her own rate but on her 'team rate', the rate she and her children earn collectively. The choice that maximizes the team rate of a woman and a child on long foraging excursions is to travel to the berries.

The 'team rates' to be earned by a woman and her children foraging around Dobe also explain why !Kung youngsters didn't go to the mongongo groves. The main dry season resource here is the mongongo nut. While experimental foraging trips showed that the nut groves provided foraging return rates substantially higher than any closer patches, mongongo nuts, unlike either berries or tubers, require substantial processing (Hawkes and O'Connell 1981, 1985). Lee reports that 'children over eight *and all adults of both sexes* do most of their own cracking. Children 4 to 7 eat smaller quantities of nuts and these are cracked for them by their parents or older siblings' (Lee 1979: 277–278, original emphasis). Blurton Jones *et al.* (forthcoming) show that if a child were to travel with mother to the nut grove and carry (and then crack) enough nuts to cover its own nutritional requirements, the mother–child team rate would be *lower* than it is when the child devotes that amount of food related work time just to cracking nuts. By refusing to take children to the groves, leaving them at home to crack nuts for themselves and younger siblings, !Kung mothers maximize the rate at which their 'team' compiles edible nutrients.

Trade-offs between childbearing and feeding and caring for grandchildren: the issue of menopause

Women's foraging practices vary with ecological differences in the costs and benefits of various contributions they can make to the welfare of children. This has implications for understanding menopause and age-specific differences in women's foraging practices. A woman's childbearing years end sharply at about the middle of maximum life span (Pavelka and Fedigan 1991). From the perspective of life-history theory this is a striking puzzle. Williams (1957) addressed it when he elaborated a theory to explain how natural selection could account for senescence and its wide variation across the living world. Among the predictions of life-history theory Williams noted that there should be no 'post-reproductive' life and suggested that when there was a long period of juvenile dependency, mothers who stopped bearing offspring as their pregnancies got riskier with age might gain the benefit of increased survival for their last born. However menopause is absent among other primates (Pavelka and Fedigan 1991) even though late pregnancies can cost the survival of older and still dependent offspring (e.g. chimpanzees; Goodall 1986, 1989). Long juvenile dependence is common among primates, menopause is not.

Post-menopausal Hadza women spend more time digging tubers, the most energetically expensive resource women take, than do women of childbearing age. To explain this as a consequence of fitness trade-offs we suggested an amendment to Williams' 'grandmother hypothesis' that focuses on a way in which women but not other female primates can earn substantial fitness benefits from helping their daughters (Hawkes *et al.* 1989).[1] When juveniles depend on their mothers for food, this changes the fitness trade-offs not only for the mothers of small children but for the mothers of those mothers. The more a female forages to feed her children the more help in either child care or food acquisition can affect the limits these place on her reproductive success. The more valuable this help, the more fitness a woman can gain by helping her adult daughter. By this argument the important fitness benefits for post-menopausal women come from the increases they promote in reproductive success of adult daughters.

Such a verbal argument about the direction in which important parameters might vary is one thing, constructing models with reasonable values that actually give the expected outcome is another. One evolutionary model shows that reduced childbirth mortality cannot account for menopause, although increases in children's reproductive success might (Rogers 1993). Another, using values for variables derived from the Ache, shows it possible but unlikely that the benefits of grandmothering in that case are higher than the benefits of continuing to bear children (Hill and Hurtado 1991). Alternative models and estimators remain to be tried.[2]

These examples show that many aspects of women's foraging practices, the resources they choose, the time they spend foraging, and the ways these vary by age and among ethnographic cases, can be explained by considering how women can best contribute to the welfare of their children. Trade-offs between different components of parenting differ by age and among ethnographic settings; the character and amount of women's labour differs accordingly.

Men's foraging

Resources that men preferentially acquire often come in large packages, with high day-to-day variance in foraging success (Hawkes 1990, Hawkes *et al.* 1991, Kaplan and Hill 1985a). When men target these resources they bring home little or nothing on many, sometimes most, days, and when they are successful their capture is widely shared. Thus many of the daily nutrients consumed by women and children in foraging communities are acquired by men who are not their husbands or fathers, while husbands and fathers are contributing little, and that undependably, to their own families. Since men could adopt the same foraging practices that women do, which would often mean bringing home a larger, steadier contribution to family consumption (Hawkes 1990, 1991, 1993), an obvious hypothesis is that instead of maximizing child welfare, they are, at least sometimes, serving a different goal. As noted above for males generally, men may have something to gain (or lose) depending on the effort they devote to mating competition.

Mating benefits that men might earn for their foraging practices remain largely unmeasured. It is easier to show that they are not choosing foraging targets that would give higher family earnings (Hawkes 1991, 1993, Hill et al. 1987), than to show mating pay-offs. Empirical support for the hypothesis that men earn mating benefits for their foraging is strongest for the Ache where better hunters are more often reported as sexual partners by women (Kaplan and Hill 1985b). Modelling can clarify the possibilities. Since the benefits a man can earn from trying to gain additional mates depend on what other men do, the pay-offs for alternative strategies are frequency dependent. Game theory models can accommodate both the zero-sum competition with other men for paternity and also the non-zero-sum pay-offs for increasing the number of offspring women can raise. One such model (Hawkes 1990) shows the relative success of the alternative male strategies of family provisioner (who brings in a steady amount of food varying little from day to day so that it reliably supports a family but never much extra) and show-off (who brings in wildly varying amounts, no reliable minimum to support a family, but occasional bonanzas much greater than a family can consume making a feast for the neighbours as well). When values estimated from Ache data are assigned to the variables in that model, 'showing off' is a robustly stable strategy.

Hadza men are primarily big game specialists. Hunting and scavenging large carcasses (O'Connell et al. 1988), they capture an extremely high average rate of 4.9 kg of prey per day (Hawkes et al. 1991). But hunters also commonly fail to kill or scavenge anything for weeks, sustaining an average 0.97 probability of failure each day (Hawkes et al. 1991). When they are successful, the carcass is shared throughout the camp and with neighbouring camps as well, only a small fraction going to the hunter's own family. If a man sought to feed his offspring, other available strategies, including hunting and trapping small animals (Hawkes et al. 1991) or gathering fruits and tubers as women do (Hawkes 1993) would be better choices.

!Kung men around Dobe in the 1960s hunted large animals, also with high failure rates (Lee 1979, Yellen 1977: Appendix B). In Lee's month-long quantitative record only one hunter succeeded in taking any large animal. These men also hunted and trapped small animals and gathered vegetable food (Hawkes 1987, Lee 1979, Yellen 1977: Appendix B). To the extent the smaller and more reliable packages of the latter were less widely shared, they contributed more directly to family provisioning. !Kung men may have had relatively more to gain from parental investment (and less from mating effort), and so, in terms of the 'provisioner/show-off' model, pursued a mixed strategy, allocating some effort to each (Hawkes 1990: 163–165). The wide variation in foraging activity among the men in Lee's group of subjects (Hawkes 1993, Lee 1979) might be due to individual differences in the benefits a man expects from each kind of effort.

In the case of the Hiwi, men spend little time in foraging and 'share most of the meat and other foods they acquire with their spouse and offspring only' (Hurtado and Hill 1992: 40). This may be a case in which a man has very limited mating opportunities beyond his current spouse. It is important to note that it need not imply little mating effort. Women can be unavailable as potential mates because they are absent, because they refuse or because they are effectively guarded or defended by other men. A general pattern of monogamy could be the result of intense mating competition, with men unable to attract more than one mate or defend more than one.

Comparison of these four ethnographic cases suggests that where men have more mating opportunities they allocate more time to foraging practices that garner widely shared foods. They do this instead of maximizing the amount of food they supply to their own families. Hurtado and Hill (1992) have described the marked contrast in mating opportunities available to Ache and Hiwi men. Among the Ache amicable inter-band relations facilitate frequent visiting and so increase the pool of possible mates. The Ache have high female fertility, a growing population with relatively large young age cohorts, and a nearly even adult sex ratio through middle age, all of which increase the number of reproductive opportunities an Ache man can have. In addition, sexual joking and intimate interactions are common among Ache men and women who are not spouses. By contrast, among the Hiwi visiting is little tolerated, female fertility is lower and the sex ratio is strongly male biased through middle age (Hurtado and Hill 1992: 39). Interaction among Hiwi men and women not married to each other is very restricted. 'While serial monogamy and extramarital promiscuity is very common among the Ache, stable lifetime monogamous unions with almost no extramarital copulation is the normative mating pattern among the Hiwi' (Hurtado and Hill 1992: 40). Associated with these differences are marked differences in foraging effort. Ache men spend long hours foraging (Hill *et al.* 1985), nearly seven hours a day every day, for resources that are widely shared (Hawkes 1991, Kaplan and Hill 1985a). Hiwi men, by contrast, do not forage every day – about two days a week in the dry season (Hurtado and Hill 1987), and an average of less than three hours a day in any season (Hurtado and Hill 1990). The food they acquire goes mostly to their wives and children (Hurtado and Hill 1992).

Contrasts between the Hadza and the !Kung are not as extreme but they are notable. Hadza work effort is yet to be reported although a provisional tabulation (Hawkes *et al.* 1987) shows men to spend about thirty-four hours a week foraging compared to the twenty-two hours reported by Lee (1979: 278) for the !Kung. In the 1960s the !Kung hunted large animals only a few days a week in some seasons (Hawkes 1987, Lee 1979, Yellen 1977) and spent substantial fractions of their foraging time gathering vegetable food and hunting and trapping small animals. Hadza men hunt almost every day for big game. They usually forgo small animals and rarely bring home vegetable food. These differences could follow a higher pay-off for mating effort among Hadza men. Three other differences suggest that Hadza men do have more mating opportunities. First, Hadza women have higher fertility (Blurton Jones *et al.* 1992). Second, 10 per cent of !Kung women in Howell's record were married to Bantu (Howell 1979) whereas only 4 per cent of Hadza women are married to villagers (Blurton Jones *et al.* in prep.) implying that the !Kung face stiffer mating competition from outsiders. Third, while only 8 per cent of !Kung women between 20 and 45 were unmarried, the proportion of unmarried Hadza women in that age range is 24.5 per cent (Blurton Jones *et al.,* in prep.).

THE BROAD PATTERN OF VARIATION

In the ethnographic cases here, as among most hunter-gatherers, monogamy is the usual pattern. The explanation commonly given for its prevalence among foragers is that a husband and wife form 'a generalized economic group constituted to produce the local conception of livelihood' (Sahlins 1972: 79). That view of the sexual division of labour is challenged here. Cultural anthropologists have also recognized that marriage assigns mating rights in a particular woman to a particular man (Goodenough 1970). If marriage is often about mating competition among males (Wilson and Daly 1992), the common monogamy of the Ache, Hadza, Hiwi and !Kung should not obscure differences among these cases in the extent to which males can successfully monopolize access to mates. The role sperm competition has played in shaping aspects of human physiology and behaviour is only just emerging (Baker and Bellis 1993, Smith 1984), but it shows that 'extra pair' copulations and defence against them have long been important options.

Men sometimes do expend substantial effort in parenting, and differential risks of physical harm to children from step- and genetic fathers (Daly and Wilson 1988) provide clear evidence of the important role that confidence of paternity may play in men's behaviour toward children. Concern about probable paternity seems to be widespread (Daly and Wilson 1982), perhaps especially where economic property rights are important. Scholars have noted that men take less responsibility for their wives' children when confidence of paternity is low (Alexander 1974, Hartung 1985, Kurland 1979). The array of sometimes extreme practices to ensure paternity certainty (Wilson and Daly 1992), especially elaborated when differential wealth and power can be transferred (Dickemann 1979a), seems aimed to prevent paternal effort from going astray. But sometimes the clear effect is to prevent other men from gaining mating access, whether or not any paternal effort follows (e.g. Dickemann 1979b: 175–176). Large differences can exist in both the parenting and mating options open to men of different classes (Lancaster and Kaplan 1992). The two kinds of effort need not always interfere. For example, men may be much more likely to care for a child they have fathered when they expect future matings with its mother. The extent of the interference and the extent to which the probable pay-offs differ may vary especially widely with the large wealth differences in stratified societies.

Some aspects of male behaviour that have generally been assumed to be paternal investment among both people and other primates may be mating effort instead. The assumption that men forage largely to provide for their families obscures similarities in two directions, those between some foraging practices and activities of other primates that earn social benefits, as well as similarities between foraging for widely shared resources and other 'status-seeking' activities associated with different subsistence patterns. Men may sometimes have more to gain from mating than parenting and they may trade off parenting benefits when the two interfere with each other.

The trade-offs for women are quite different. Modelling and measuring the many ways females can affect the welfare of their offspring continues to generate promising hypotheses to explain diverse aspects of female behaviour, from multiple copulations (Hrdy 1988) to styles of parenting (Blurton Jones 1993). An appreciation of the role that children's abilities can play in women's foraging practices may have large implications for understanding the constraints on other primates. As with humans, juveniles are not as competent in food acquisition as adults (Janson and van Schaik 1993). To the extent that youngsters' competence varies with resource type, primate mothers might sometimes increase their own fitness by foregoing resources that maximize their own rate of nutrient acquisition to exploit resources that offspring can acquire more efficiently. This highlights one of the consequences that human nutrient acquisition efficiency has for feasible foraging opportunities. When women can acquire food at a rate high enough to feed their weaned children, they can afford to make greater use of resources that juveniles cannot competently exploit.

The general analytical framework here directs attention to the trade-offs women face when different components of parenting interfere with each other and the trade-offs men face when parenting and mating interfere with each other. From this perspective the sexual division of labour is the outcome of males and females each pursuing their own fitness interests. The small sample of cases was chosen to illustrate the use of those conceptual tools. For each case the patterns observed provoke questions about the available alternatives and their probable pay-offs to individual actors. The analytical framework can, in principle, guide investigation to ever finer precision in description and explanation, a potential especially useful to ethnographers seeking to account for particular cases. When the larger goal is to construct hypotheses about the past, however, more precision increases the difficulty and inflates the likelihood of failure. The more variables that must be estimated, the more chances to be wrong. The work discussed here converges on some important differences between the sexes and their patterned interaction with features of ecology. From this perspective the sexual division of labour, its character and variation, is the outcome of men and women facing different fitness trade-offs. To the extent that observed patterns can be explained in these terms, received views of families, or larger social groups, as units of common interest will be revised. Robust archaeological implications remain to be elaborated but the challenge to common assumptions about hunting and nuclear families is clear. Large effects on the activity patterns of women and children appear to follow from differences in the acquisition and processing requirements of broad categories of plant resources. Continuing work will show whether we can develop models with a few key variables that can give us testable hypotheses about the past.

ACKNOWLEDGEMENTS

For helpful criticism and advice on earlier drafts of this paper I thank R. Bliege Bird, N. Blurton Jones, M. Borgerhoff Mulder, E. Cashdan, D. Grayson, H. Harpending, D. Metcalfe, J. O'Connell and L. Rogers.

NOTES

1 This is in marked contrast to the reduced foraging among older !Kung women in the 1960s reported by Lee (1985), a difference that may turn on the high processing requirements of mongongo nuts. Older women foraging in the Dobe area may increase the food production rates of their adult daughter's team more by staying in camp to crack nuts. Among the Hiwi, senior women are, like the Hadza, more active tuber diggers (Hurtado and Hill 1987). The Ache population has few senior women due to the heavy death toll on elders in the 1970s.

2 Arguments that the fitness pay-offs through increased reproductive success of daughters account for menopause (whether the mismatch between the end of childbearing and general senescence is seen as 'stopping early' or living longer) imply a particular pattern of sex-biased dispersal. Adult daughters would have to stay with their mothers, a pattern opposite to the male philopatry/female dispersal surmised to be characteristic of hunter-gatherers on ethnographic grounds (Ember 1978), general among hominids on phylogenetic grounds (Foley and Lee 1989, Ghiglieri 1987, Wrangham 1987), and increasingly taken

as an established fact (e.g. Manson and Wrangham 1991, Rodseth *et al.* 1991). By the argument here, menopause is a piece of evolutionary evidence inconsistent with a phylogenetic history of male philopatry. There is also some relevant evidence from molecular studies. Melnick and Hoelzer (1993) provide a provocative summary of work on mitochondrial DNA in which they note that the pattern of variation in 'small aboriginal human populations' is similar to that seen in the highly female philopatric macaques, and differs notably from the genetic structure consistent with female dispersal found in human groups with a long history of property-holding.

REFERENCES

Alexander, R.D. (1974) 'The evolution of social behaviour.' *Annual Review of Ecology and Systematics* 5: 325–383.

Alexander, R.D. (1979) *Darwinism and Human Affairs*. Seattle: University of Washington Press.

Altman, J. (1980) *Baboon Mothers and Infants*. Cambridge, MA: Harvard University Press.

Bailey, R. and Aunger, R. (1989) 'Net hunters vs. archers: variation in women's subsistence strategies in the Ituri Forest.' *Human Ecology* 17: 273–297.

Baker, R. and Bellis, R. (1993) 'Human sperm competition: ejaculate adjustment by males and the function of masturbation.' *Animal Behavior* 37: 861–885.

Betzig, L., Borgerhoff Mulder, M. and Turke, P. (1988) *Human Reproductive Behavior: A Darwinian Perspective*. New York: Cambridge University Press.

Birkhead, T. and Møller, A. (1992) *Sperm Competition in Birds: Evolutionary Causes and Consequences*. London: Academic Press.

Blurton Jones, N. (1993) 'The lives of hunter-gatherer children: effects of parental behavior and parental reproductive strategy.' In M. Perreira and L. Fairbanks (eds) *Juvenile Primates: Life History, Development, and Behavior*, pp. 309–326. Oxford: Oxford University Press.

Blurton Jones, N., Hawkes, K. and Draper, P. (1994) 'Difference between Hadza and !Kung children's work: original affluence or practical reason?' In E.S. Burch (ed.) *Key Issues in Hunter-gatherer Research*, pp. 189–215. Oxford: Berg.

Blurton Jones, N., Hawkes, K. and Draper, P. (forthcoming) 'Foraging returns of !Kung adults and children: why didn't !Kung children forage?' *Journal of Anthropological Research*.

Blurton Jones, N., Hawkes, K. and O'Connell, J.F. (1989) 'Modelling and measuring costs of children in two foraging societies.' In V. Standen and R. Foley (eds) *Comparative Socioecology: The Behavioural Ecology of Humans and Other Mammals*, pp. 367–390. Oxford: Basil Blackwell.

Blurton Jones, N., Hawkes, K. and O'Connell, J.F. (in preparation) 'The global process and local ecology: how should we explain differences between the Hadza and the !Kung?' In S. Kent (ed.) *Cultural Diversity among Twentieth Century Foragers: An African Perspective*.

Blurton Jones, N., Smith, L., O'Connell, J., Hawkes, K. and Kamuzora, C. (1992) 'Demography of the Hadza, an increasing and high density population of savannah foragers.' *American Journal of Physical Anthropology* 89: 159–181.

Boesch, C. and Boesch, H. (1984) 'Possible causes of sex differences in the use of natural hammers by wild chimpanzees.' *Journal of Human Evolution* 13: 415–440.

Boesch, C. and Boesch, H. (1989) 'Hunting behavior of wild chimpanzees in the Tai National Park.' *American Journal of Physical Anthropology* 78: 547–573.

Borgerhoff Mulder, M. (1991) 'Human behavioural ecology.' In J. Krebs and N. Davies (eds) *Behavioural Ecology: An Evolutionary Approach,* 3rd edn, pp. 69–98. Oxford: Blackwell Scientific Publications.

Brown, J. (1970) 'A note on sexual division of labor.' *American Anthropologist* 72: 1073–1078.

Chagnon, N. and Irons, W. (eds) (1979) *Evolutionary Biology and Human Social Behavior: An Anthropological Perspective.* North Scituate, MA: Duxbury Press.

Charnov, E. (1982) *The Theory of Sex Allocation.* Princeton: Princeton University Press.

Charnov, E. and Krebs, J. (1974) 'On clutch size and fitness.' *Ibis* 116: 217–219.

Clutton-Brock, T. (1991) *The Evolution of Parental Care.* Princeton: Princeton University Press.

Cronk, L. (1991) 'Human behavioral ecology.' *Annual Review of Anthropology* 20: 25–53.

Daly, M. and Wilson, M. (1982) 'Whom are new-borns said to resemble?' *Ethology and Sociobiology* 3: 69–78.

Daly, M. and Wilson, M. (1983) *Sex, Evolution and Behavior.* Boston: Willard Grant Press.

Daly, M. and Wilson, M. (1988) *Homicide.* New York: Aldine de Gruyter.

Darwin, C. (1871) *The Descent of Man and Selection in Relation to Sex.* London: John Murray.

Davies, N. (1992) *Dunnock Behaviour and Social Evolution.* Oxford: Oxford University Press.

Dickemann, M. (1979a) 'Female infanticide, reproductive strategies and social stratification: a preliminary model.' In N. Chagnon and W. Irons (eds) *Evolutionary Biology and Human Social Behavior: An Anthropological Perspective,* pp. 321–367. North Scituate, MA: Duxbury Press.

Dickemann, M. (1979b) 'The ecology of mating systems in hypergynous dowry systems.' *Social Science Information* 18: 163–195.

Draper, P. (1976) 'Social and economic constraints on child life among the !Kung.' In R. Lee and I. DeVore (eds) *Kalahari Hunter Gatherers,* pp. 199–217. Cambridge, MA: Harvard University Press.

Draper, P. and Cashdan, E. (1988) 'Technological change and child behavior among the !Kung.' *Ethology* 27: 339–365.

Dwyer, P. and Minnegal, M. (1991) 'Hunting in a lowland tropical rainforest: towards a model of non-agricultural subsistence.' *Human Ecology* 19: 187–211.

Ember, C. (1978) 'Myths about hunter-gatherers.' *Ethnology* 17: 439–448.

Feistner, A. and McGrew, W. (1989) 'Food sharing in primates: a critical review.' In P. Seth and S. Seth (eds) *Perspectives in Primate Biology.* New Delhi: Today and Tomorrow's Press.

Fisher, R. (1930) *The Genetical Theory of Natural Selection.* Oxford: Clarendon Press.

Foley, R. and Lee, P. (1989) 'Finite social space, evolutionary pathways, and reconstructing hominid behavior.' *Science* 243: 901–906.

Galdikas, B. and Teleki, G. (1981) 'Variations in subsistence activities of male and female pongids: new perspectives on the origins of human labor division.' *Current Anthropology* 22: 241–256.

Ghiglieri, M. (1987) 'Sociobiology of the great apes and the hominid ancestor.' *Journal of Human Evolution* 16: 319–358.

Goodall, J. (1968) 'Behavior of free-living chimpanzees of the Gombe stream area.' *Animal Behavior Monographs* 1: 163–311.

Goodall, J. (1986) *The Chimpanzees of Gombe: Patterns of Behavior.* Cambridge, MA: Harvard University Press.

Goodall, J. (1989) 'Gombe: highlights and current research.' In P. Heltne and L. Marquardt (eds) *Understanding Chimpanzees*, pp. 2–21. Cambridge, MA: Harvard University Press.

Goodenough, W. (1970) *Description and Comparison in Cultural Anthropology.* Chicago: Aldine.

Goodman, M., Estioko-Griffin, A., Bion-Griffin, P. and Grove, J. (1985) 'Compatibility of hunting and mothering among the Agta hunter-gatherers of the Philippines.' *Sex Roles* 12: 1199–1209.

Hart, T. and Hart, J. (1986) 'The ecological basis of hunter-gatherer subsistence in African rain forests: the Mbuti of Zaire.' *Human Ecology* 14: 29–55.

Hartung, J. (1985) 'Matrilineal inheritance: new theory and analysis.' *Behavioral and Brain Sciences* 8: 661–688.

Hawkes, K. (1987) 'How much food do foragers need?' In M. Harris and E. Ross (eds) *Food and Evolution: Toward a Theory of Human Food Habits.* Philadelphia: Temple University Press.

Hawkes, K. (1990) 'Why do men hunt? Some benefits for risky strategies.' In E. Cashdan (ed.) *Risk and Uncertainty*, pp. 145–166. Boulder: Westview Press.

Hawkes, K. (1991) 'Showing off: tests of another hypothesis about men's foraging goals.' *Ethology and Sociobiology* 11: 29–54.

Hawkes, K. (1993) 'Why hunter-gatherers work: an ancient version of the problem of public goods.' *Current Anthropology* 34: 341–361.

Hawkes, K. and O'Connell, J. (1981) 'Affluent hunters? Some comments in light of the Alyawara case.' *American Anthropologist* 83: 622–626.

Hawkes, K. and O'Connell, J. (1985) 'Optimal foraging models and the case of the !Kung.' *American Anthropologist* 87: 401–405.

Hawkes, K., O'Connell, J.F. and Blurton Jones, N. (1987) 'Hadza foraging time.' Paper delivered at the 86th Annual Meeting of the AAA, Chicago.

Hawkes, K., O'Connell, J.F. and Blurton Jones, N. (1989) 'Hardworking Hadza grandmothers.' In V. Standen and R.A. Foley (eds) *Comparative Socioecology: The Behavioural Ecology of Humans and Other Mammals*, pp. 341–366. Oxford: Basil Blackwell.

Hawkes, K., O'Connell, J.F. and Blurton Jones, N. (1991) 'Hunting income patterns among the Hadza: big game, common goods, foraging goals, and the evolution of the human diet.' *Philosophical Transactions of the Royal Society London, Series B* 334: 243–251.

Hawkes, K., O'Connell, J.F. and Blurton Jones, N. (in preparation) 'Hadza children's foraging.'

Hewlett, B. (1992) 'Husband–wife reciprocity and the father–infant relationship among Aka Pygmies.' In B. Hewlett (ed.) *Father–Child Relations: Cultural and Biosocial Contexts*, pp. 153–176. New York: Aldine de Gruyter.

Hill, K., Hawkes, K., Hurtado, A.M. and Kaplan, H. (1984) 'Seasonal variance in the diet of Ache hunter-gatherers in Eastern Paraguay.' *Human Ecology* 12: 145–180.

Hill, K. and Hurtado, A.M. (1991) 'The evolution of premature reproductive senescence and menopause in human females: an evaluation of the "Grandmother Hypothesis".' *Human Nature* 2: 313–350.

Hill, K., Kaplan, H., Hawkes, K. and Hurtado, A.M. (1985) 'Men's time allocation to subsistence work among the Ache of Eastern Paraguay.' *Human Ecology* 13: 29–47.

Hill, K., Kaplan, H., Hawkes, K. and Hurtado, A.M. (1987) 'Foraging decisions among Ache hunter-gatherers: new data and implications for optimal foraging models.' *Ethology and Sociobiology* 8: 1–36.

Howell, N. (1979) *Demography of the Dobe !Kung*. New York: Academic Press.

Hrdy, S. (1979) 'Infanticide among mammals: a review, classification, and examination of the implications for the reproductive strategies of females.' *Ethology and Sociobiology* 1: 13–40.

Hrdy, S. (1988) 'The primate origins of human sexuality.' In R. Bellig and G. Stevens (eds) *The Evolution of Sex*. Nobel Conference XXIII: 101–136. San Francisco: Harper and Row.

Hrdy, S. and Whitten, P. (1987) 'Patterning of sexual activity.' In B. Smuts, D. Cheney, R. Seyfarth, R. Wrangham and T. Struhsaker (eds) *Primate Societies*, pp. 370–384. Chicago: University of Chicago Press.

Hurtado, A. and Hill, K. (1987) 'Early dry season subsistence ecology of Cuiva (Hiwi) foragers of Venezuela.' *Human Ecology* 15: 163–187.

Hurtado, A. and Hill, K. (1990) 'Seasonality in a foraging society: variation in diet, work effort, fertility, and the sexual division of labor among the Hiwi of Venezuela.' *Journal of Anthropological Research* 46: 293–346.

Hurtado, A. and Hill, K. (1992) 'Paternal effect on offspring survivorship among Ache and Hiwi hunter-gatherers: implications for modelling pair-bond stability.' In B. Hewlett (ed.) *Father-Child Relations*, pp. 31–76. New York: Aldine de Gruyter.

Hurtado, A., Hill, K., Kaplan, H. and Hurtado, I. (1992) 'Trade-offs between female food acquisition and childcare among Hiwi and Ache foragers.' *Human Nature* 3: 185–216.

Hurtado, A., Hawkes, K., Hill, K. and Kaplan, H. (1985) 'Female subsistence strategies among the Ache of Eastern Paraguay.' *Human Ecology* 13: 1–28.

Janson, C. and van Schaik, C. (1993) 'Ecological risk aversion in juvenile primates: slow and steady wins the race.' In M. Perreira and L. Fairbanks (eds) *Juvenile Primates: Life History, Development, and Behavior*, pp. 57–76. Oxford: Oxford University Press.

Kaplan, H. and Hill, K. (1985a) 'Food-sharing among Ache foragers: tests of explanatory hypotheses.' *Current Anthropology* 26: 223–245.

Kaplan, H. and Hill, K. (1985b) 'Hunting ability and reproductive success among male Ache foragers.' *Current Anthropology* 26: 131–133.

Kurland, J. (1979) 'Paternity, mother's brother, and human sociality.' In N. Chagnon and W. Irons (eds) *Evolutionary Biology and Human Social Behavior: An Anthropological Perspective*, pp. 145–180. North Scituate, MA: Duxbury Press.

Lack, D. (1947) 'The significance of clutch size.' *Ibis* 89: 302–352.

Lancaster, J. and Kaplan, H. (1992) 'Human mating and family formation strategies: the effects of variability among males in quality and the allocation of mating effort and parental investment.' In T. Nishida, W. McGrew, P. Marler, M. Pickford and F. de Waal (eds) *Topics in Primatology, Vol. 1*, pp. 21–33. Tokyo: University of Tokyo Press.

Lancaster, J. and Lancaster, C. (1983) 'Parental investment: the hominid adaptation.' In D. Ortner (ed.) *How Humans Adapt: A Biocultural Odyssey.* Washington, DC: Smithsonian Institution Press.

Lee, R. (1968) 'What hunters do for a living, or, how to make out on scarce resources.' In R. Lee and I. DeVore (eds) *Man the Hunter*, pp. 30–48. Chicago: Aldine.

Lee, R. (1979) *The !Kung San: Men, Women, and Work in a Foraging Society.* Cambridge: Cambridge University Press.

Lee, R. (1985) 'Work, sexuality and aging among Kung women.' In J. Brown and V. Kerns (eds) *In Her Prime: A View of Middle-Aged Women*, pp. 23–36. South Hadley, MA: Bergen and Garvey Publishers.

Lessells, C. (1991) 'The evolution of life histories.' In J. Krebs and N. Davies (eds) *Behavioural Ecology: An Evolutionary Approach*, pp. 32–68. Oxford: Blackwell Scientific Publications.

McGrew, W. (1992) *Chimpanzee Material Culture: Implications for Human Evolution.* Cambridge: Cambridge University Press.

Manson, J. and Wrangham, R. (1992) 'Intergroup aggression in chimpanzees and humans.' *Current Anthropology* 32: 369–390.

Maynard Smith, J. (1977) 'Parental investment: a prospective analysis.' *Animal Behaviour* 25: 1–9.

Maynard Smith, J. (1978a) 'Optimization theory in evolution.' *Annual Review of Ecology and Systematics* 9: 31–56.

Maynard Smith, J. (1978b) *The Evolution of Sex.* Cambridge: Cambridge University Press.

Maynard Smith, J. (1982) *Evolution and the Theory of Games.* Cambridge: Cambridge University Press.

Melnick, D. and Hoelzer, G. (1993) 'What is mtDNA good for in the study of primate evolution?' *Evolutionary Anthropology* 2: 2–10.

Møller, A. and Birkhead, T. (1993) 'Certainty of paternity covaries with paternal care in birds.' *Behavioral Ecology and Sociobiology* 33: 261–268.

Murdock, G. and Provost, C. (1973) 'Factors in the division of labor by sex.' *Ethnology* 12: 203–225.

Nishida, T., Hasegawa, T., Hayaki, H., Takahata, Y. and Uehara, S. (1992) 'Meat-sharing as a coalition strategy by an alpha male chimpanzee.' In T. Nishida, W. McGrew, P. Marler, M. Pickford and F. de Waal (eds) *Topics in Primatology, Vol. 1*, pp. 159–174. Tokyo: University of Tokyo Press.

O'Connell, J.F., Hawkes, K. and Blurton Jones, N. (1988) 'Hadza scavenging: implications for Plio-Pleistocene hominid subsistence.' *Current Anthropology* 29: 356–363.

Parker, G. and Maynard Smith, J. (1990) 'Optimality theory in evolutionary biology.' *Nature* 348: 27–33.

Pavelka, M. and Fedigan, L. (1991) 'Menopause: a comparative life-history perspective.' *Yearbook of Physical Anthropology* 34: 13–38.

Price, E. (1991) 'Infant carrying as a courtship strategy of breeding cotton-top tamarins.' *Animal Behaviour* 40: 784–786.

Rodseth, L., Wrangham, R., Harrigan, A. and Smuts, B. (1991) 'The human community as a primate society.' *Current Anthropology* 32: 221–254.

Rogers, A. (1993) 'Why menopause?' *Evolutionary Ecology* 7: 406–420.

Sahlins, M. (1972) *Stone Age Economics.* Chicago: Aldine.

Silk, J. (1978) 'Patterns of food sharing among mother and infant chimpanzees in Gombe National Park.' *Folia Primatologica* 31: 12–42.

Smith, E. and Winterhalder, B. (eds) (1992) *Evolutionary Ecology and Human Behavior.* New York: Aldine de Gruyter.

Smith, R. L. (1984) 'Human sperm competition.' In R. L. Smith (ed.) *Sperm Competition and the Evolution of Animal Mating Systems*, pp. 601–659. Orlando: Academic Press.

Smuts, B. (1985) *Sex and Friendship in Baboons.* New York: Aldine.

Smuts, B. and Gubernick, D. (1992) 'Male–infant relationships in non-human primates: paternal investment or mating effort?' In B. Hewlett (ed.) *Father–Child Relations: Cultural and Biosocial Contexts*, pp. 1–29. New York: Aldine de Gruyter.

Stanford, C., Wallis, J., Mpongo, E. and Goodall, J. (1994) 'Hunting decisions in wild chimpanzees.' *Behaviour* 131: 1–18.

Stearmen, A. (1987) 'Making a living in the tropical forest: Yuqui foragers in the Bolivian Amazon.' *Human Ecology* 19: 245–259.

Stephens, D. and Krebs, J. (1986) *Foraging Theory.* Princeton: Princeton University Press.

Strum, S. (1981) 'Processes and products of change: baboon predatory behavior at Gilgil, Kenya.' In R. Harding and G. Teleki (eds) *Omnivorous Primates: Gathering and Hunting in Human Evolution.* New York: Columbia University Press.

Symons, D. (1979) *The Evolution of Human Sexuality.* New York: Oxford University Press.

Takahata, Y., Hasegawa, T. and Nishida, T. (1984) 'Chimpanzee predation in the Mahale Mountains from August 1979 to May 1982.' *International Journal of Primatology* 5: 213–233.

Teleki, G. (1973) *The Predatory Behavior of Wild Chimpanzees.* Lewisburg, PA: Bucknell University Press.

Trivers, R. (1972) 'Parental investment and sexual selection.' In B. Campbell (ed.) *Sexual Selection and the Descent of Man 1871–1971*, pp. 136–179. Chicago: Aldine.

Trivers, R. (1974) 'Parent-offspring conflict.' *American Zoologist* 14: 249–262.

Washburn, S. and Lancaster, C. (1968) 'The evolution of hunting.' In R. Lee and I. DeVore (eds) *Man the Hunter*, pp. 293–303. Chicago: Aldine.

Whitten, P. (1987) 'Infants and adult males.' In B. Smuts, D. Cheney, R. Seyfarth, R. Wrangham and T. Struhsaker (eds) *Primate Societies*, pp. 343–357. Chicago: University of Chicago Press.

Williams, G. (1957) 'Pleiotropy, natural selection, and the evolution of senescence.' *Evolution* 11: 398–411.

Williams, G. (1966a) *Adaptation and Natural Selection: A Critique of Some Current Evolutionary Thought.* Princeton: Princeton University Press.

Williams, G. (1966b) 'Natural selection, the costs of reproduction and a refinement of Lack's Principle.' *American Naturalist* 100: 687–690.

Wilson, M. and Daly, M. (1992) 'The man who confused his wife with a chattel.' In J. Barkow, L. Cosmides and J. Tooby (eds) *The Adapted Mind: Evolutionary Psychology and the Generation of Culture*, pp. 289–322. New York: Oxford University Press.

Wrangham, R. (1979) 'On the evolution of ape social systems.' *Social Science Information* 18: 334–368.

Wrangham, R. (1987) 'The significance of African apes for reconstructing human social evolution.' In W. Kinzey (ed.) *The Evolution of Human Behavior: Primate Models*, pp. 51–71. Albany: State University of New York Press.

Wrangham, R. and Bergmann-Riss, E. (1990) 'Rates of predation on mammals by Gombe chimpanzees, 1972-1975.' *Primates* 31: 157–170.

Yellen, J. (1977) *Archaeological Approaches to the Present: Models for Reconstructing the Past*. New York: Academic Press.

CHAPTER ELEVEN

FEMALE STRATEGIES AND COLLECTIVE BEHAVIOUR

The archaeology of earliest Homo sapiens sapiens

CAMILLA POWER AND IAN WATTS

When and why did symbolic behaviour become 'an integral part of adaptation' (Chase and Dibble 1987: 285)? Can we model within a neo-Darwinian framework preadaptations to ritual and other symbolic activity? Few theories of the origin of symbolic cognition have ventured predictions which are testable against symbolic evidence. This chapter is in two parts. The first aims to model selection pressures promoting quasi-ritual collective behaviour in late archaic *Homo sapiens*. The second examines some of the model's predictions in the light of Southern African archaeological and ethnographic data.

COSTS OF ENCEPHALIZATION

If the central strand in the story of human evolution is encephalization, the materialist subtext must be how females fuelled the production of increasingly large-brained and hence burdensome offspring. We know the basic answer: in the course of *Homo*'s 2 million years of evolution, mothers extracted what by primate standards are unprecedented levels of male energetic investment. Models which address the fine-grained evolutionary mechanisms by which females drove this process may yield fruitful lines of enquiry, helping to explain not only some basic features of human reproductive physiology, but also underlying motives to symbolism. Dawkins and Krebs (1984) demonstrate the function of deceptive signalling in exploiting the muscle power of other animals. On this basis, we propose a hypothesis. *Symbolism emerged as a set of deceptive sexual signals aimed by kin-coalitions of females at their mates for the purpose of exploiting male muscle-power.*

The extra costs arising from encephalization include the metabolic demands on the mother for sustaining brain growth in the infant (Foley and Lee 1991), and the increased energetic requirements of foraging for a higher quality diet. Humans compensate for their expensive brains by having correspondingly small, and energetically cheap, guts (Aiello and Wheeler, in press). This is only compatible with high quality diet, which in turn requires larger foraging areas (Clutton-Brock and Harvey 1977), with increased overall energy expenditure (Leonard and Robertson 1992).

Because hominid mothers bore these escalating costs, we must suppose that it was females who developed strategies to meet them. As the pressures to encephalization placed maternal energy budgets under strain, natural selection would have acted on two key areas of reproductive physiology: first, on life-history variables (cf. Foley and Lee 1991) – factors critical in partitioning the energy costs of reproduction – and second, on features of the reproductive cycle. As females drove a process of sexual selection, their reproductive signals would have been prime mechanisms for rewarding more attentive 'investor' males and punishing philanderers.

HUMAN FEMALE REPRODUCTIVE PHYSIOLOGY

Optimal foraging theory predicts that a roving or philandering male should aim to reduce the time spent searching for a fertilizable female, and then reduce the time spent waiting for access to the female at her fertile moment – 'search' time and 'handling' time (cf. Srivastava and Dunbar, submitted). The human female appears 'well-designed' to waste the time of philanderers by withholding accurate information about her true fertility state.

Concealment of ovulation and loss of oestrus with continuous receptivity have eliminated any reliable cue by which to judge whether a female is likely to have been impregnated. The longer a male must remain with one female to ensure fertilization, the smaller his chances of being able to fertilize another within one breeding season (Dunbar 1988: 160). These features are not unique to humans as against other primates (Hrdy 1981: 158). However, in some species with apparently concealed ovulation, males can track female cycles through olfactory cues (e.g. cotton-top tamarins, Ziegler et al. 1993). Studies of variation in human ejaculates (Baker and Bellis 1993: 880) confirm that men are unable to track women's peri-ovulatory periods. Ovulation in women is well concealed. Alexander and Noonan (1979) argued that through concealment of ovulation and continuous receptivity alone, males would have been forced into prolonged consortships; that even in multi-male group contexts, pair-bonds would have been reinforced; and hence that males would have had greater confidence in paternity, leading to greater parental investment. Against this, Hrdy (1981) proposed that these features could function in a context of promiscuity to deprive males of information about paternity, so reducing risks of infanticide. Sillen-Tullberg and Møller (1993) estimate that visual ovulatory signs have been lost several times in non-monogamous mating systems, and never within monogamous systems of anthropoid primates. They contend that this supports Hrdy's hypothesis of the original function of ovulation concealment, but that monogamy – with the implication of increased paternity confidence – is far more likely to evolve in lineages where ovulation signs have been lost. While ovulation may be concealed in the first place to counter infanticide risk, once evolved this feature can be exapted to serve a female strategy of increasing male investment.

A further key means of thwarting philanderers is reproductive cycle synchrony. Knowlton (1979) formulated a general model of synchrony as a strategy by the sex which invests most in offspring to secure greater parental investment from their mates. If females synchronize their fertile moments, no single male will be able to cope with guarding and impregnating any group of females. Local, previously excluded males are attracted into groups by potentially fertile females (cf. Dunbar 1988: 140–2). More male energy, support and protection becomes available to the synchronizing females.

Cycle synchrony, manifested as synchrony of menstrual onset, has been documented among humans (McClintock 1971, and reviews in Graham 1991, Weller and Weller 1993). However, several of these studies have been criticized on methodological grounds (see Wilson 1992). Knowlton, following Maynard-Smith (1977), Ralls (1977) and Emlen and Oring (1977), observes that 'the spread of female synchrony is likely to increase the ESS for male parental investment because the payoffs to searching for new mates are reduced' (1979: 1029). Given the large range sizes predicted for Pleistocene hominids (Leonard and Robertson 1992), synchrony would be effective to the extent it was widespread in populations, rather than restricted to local troops, as observed in various baboon species (Dunbar 1988). The modern human female appears well designed for such widespread cycle synchrony, since she has the capacity for cyclicity linked to an environmental cue. Her mean length of menstrual cycle corresponds to the mean lunar synodic period at 29.5 days (Gunn *et al.* 1937, McClintock 1971, Vollman 1977, Cutler *et al.* 1980); and her mean length of gestation at 266 days is a precise nine times multiple of the mean lunar synodic period (Menaker and Menaker 1959, and see Martin 1992: 263–4). In ancestral populations, any tendency to cycle synchrony aligned by lunar phase would have been further constrained by seasonal and ecological factors, affecting nutritional status and fertility rates (Ellison *et al.* 1989, Ellison 1990). Significant seasonality of births has been documented for hunter-gatherer populations (Wilmsen 1978, Hurtado and Hill 1990).

Synthesizing Alexander and Noonan's argument on ovulation conceal-ment with Knowlton's synchrony model, Turke (1984, 1988) originally proposed that 'ovulatory synchrony' formed an important component of hominid mating systems under selection pressures for encephalization. He argued that ovulation concealment (with continuous receptivity) functioned to draw males into longer consortships, depriving would-be philanderers of accurate information about fertility. A pattern of ovulatory synchrony in local populations had the further effect of punishing male attempts to philander. This should drive the ratio of sexually active males to females in groups towards one-to-one. Sustained male/female bonds on a one-to-one basis should lead to greater paternity confidence, and greater inclination on the part of males to invest care in offspring.

THE PROBLEM OF MENSTRUAL BLEEDING

The difficulty with the synchrony model of encephalization is that reproductive synchrony will never be perfect on the ground. Even if significant numbers of adult females tend to synchronize fertile cycles during a particular season, others will be at various stages of lactation. We would expect staggering of overall reproductive synchrony by birth season. To the extent that a degree of synchrony was an important female strategy for undermining male philandering, then we would predict minimizing of any signal that gave away information about prospective fertility. If synchrony is not going to be perfect, then the least females can do is not advertise the fact, so giving away information to philanderers.

But one reproductive signal has been amplified in the course of human evolution – women's profuse menstrual bleeding. Profet (1993) puts forward the only functional hypothesis of menstruation yet developed. She hypothesizes that menstruation is adaptive as a defence against sperm-transported pathogens, and predicts that it will be accentuated by either continuous sexual receptivity or promiscuity, citing extensive comparative primate data. Other than women, only common chimpanzees – living in promiscuous multi-male systems – are documented to have 'profuse' bleeding, relative to body size.

Menstrual bleeding as a signal

We do not suggest that signalling constituted the primary function of menstruation. But once ovulation was concealed and oestrus was lost in the human lineage, menstruation would have taken on significance as a cue. It is not an accurate indicator of fertility, because it occurs at the non-fertile time of the cycle. But it *is* a good indicator of impending fertility. Because menstruation is the only cue which gave males positive information about female reproductive condition then we would expect that hominid males came under selection pressure to respond to that cue. This is not the case with chimpanzee males who have more reliable information concerning female fertility state available in the females' 'loud' oestrus signals.

Because menstruation is not accurate as an indicator of ovulatory timing, the information is not very useful for philanderers. Menstruation should make a female attractive to males who are prepared to wait around and mate-guard. Concealment of ovulation withdraws from males any information about when to bring mate-guarding to an end. So the male who responds to menstrual cues has to spend time with the female to increase his chances of paternity.

This implies that pronounced menstrual bleeding functioned to attract extra male attention, procuring mating effort in the form of protection, some food-sharing, grooming and coalitionary support. But the signal does not necessarily secure genuine *parental* effort from males. Reproductive cycle synchrony is required to reliably secure parental investment from males. Once a female was pregnant, she risked losing that extra male attention to other menstruating females in the vicinity. The 'loud' menstrual signal threatens to destabilize a synchrony strategy in local populations, by marking out those females who may be impregnated in the near future. The menstrual 'flag' could have encouraged mate desertion, incited male competition and led to some monopoly of fertile consortships by dominant males.

Male mating effort, associated with relatively high rates of mate desertion, may have been adequate for females during earlier phases of hominid evolution, when encephalization was proceeding at a relatively slow rate. The increased energetic costs of the first phase of brain expansion could have been offset by such factors as reduction in gut size (Aiello and Wheeler 1995) and increased female body size (Aiello, in press, Power and Aiello, in press). Reduction in sexual body size dimorphism may be better explained by female requirement to meet reproductive and thermoregulatory costs, than by significant changes in mating strategy at this stage (cf. McHenry, this volume). In modelling the energetics of hominid encephalization, Foley and Lee suggest that early *Homo* mothers did not rely on systematic male provisioning to meet their increasing reproductive costs. Left to themselves, mothers could find the additional energy from 'higher quality diet, from feeding for longer each day, or from maintaining lactation over a longer period' (1991: 70). Selection for slower rates of development and an extended period of immaturity enabled mothers to spread their energy load. Development of the fat stores characteristic of human females may have subsidized the costs of lactation, especially during periods of resource stress (Prentice and Whitehead 1987).

Shipman and Walker (1989: 388) model early *Homo erectus* patterns of foetal and postnatal brain growth, compared to that of chimps and modern humans, on the basis of the cranial capacity and pelvic diameter of the adolescent male KNM-WT 15000 (dated to 1.6 Myr). They infer an incipient human-type pattern of altriciality, which they link to shifts towards higher quality diet. At later stages, during the exponential increase in brain size associated with archaic *Homo sapiens* (cf. Leigh 1992, Aiello, in press), the postnatal trajectory of foetal brain growth became progressively extended (secondary altriciality). Intensification of energetic costs during lactation would have confronted mothers with problems in balancing their energy budgets. These increased costs had to be met by higher quality diet and more reliable supplies, which ultimately meant extracting greater energetic investment from males. Reproductive stress owing to encephalization would have become acute for late archaic females.

Deceptive sexual signalling

Assuming that archaic *Homo sapiens* females required more reliable male parental effort, how could they have resolved the problem of the salience of menstrual bleeding as a signal of impending fertility?

The logical solution is that, within kin coalitions, non-menstruating females 'borrowed' the blood of menstrual females. To the extent that females were able to confuse the information available to males, by showing the same reproductive signal at the same time, coalition members could retain the advantage of menstruation as an indicator of impending fertility for attracting male attention, and retain the advantage of synchrony for maximizing male parental investment.

Sufficient pressure on females to increase or maintain male provisioning effort resulting from increasing costs of encephalization should lead to females, as coalitions, manufacturing synchrony of signals, by displaying sham menstruation on occasions when one of their number was actually menstruating. Females who adopted such a strategy of borrowing the blood of menstruating relatives would be expected to resort to cosmetic means – blood-coloured pigments that could be used in body-painting to augment their 'sham menstruation' displays.

The co-ordinated female display of menstruation would function as a form of advertising for extra male support. Provided females maintained their menstrual solidarity, even if males were aware of which females were actually menstruating, they would not be able to use the information. If males attempted to fight for access to a particular female, they would incur heavy costs, and there would be no benefit since the female is not immediately fertile. Males would be faced with increasing social costs from female resistance to the male strategy of targeting specific imminently fertile females. In this case, males could more reliably increase fitness by maintaining bonds with and existing levels of investment in current partners.

The 'sham menstruation' model gives a basis for describing behavioural adaptations that prefigure symbolic and ritual activity. What was a signal belonging to an individual, capable of extracting energy from males on a one-to-one basis, has become collectivized among a coalition of females and amplified, broadcasting information of critical importance which males cannot afford to ignore. Quite simply, males are only interested in positive cues to fertility. Sham menstruation is an amplified indicator of the presence of an imminently fertile female in the vicinity. This means that the female coalition now has a powerful signal for manipulating males. To the extent that some females who are not imminently fertile pretend to be, the signal is deceptive. Unlike primate tactical deception, which is always on an individual basis (Byrne and Whiten 1988), in this case, the deception is maintained by a collective. As such, it represents a vital step towards sustaining an imaginary construct and sharing that construct with others – that is, establishing symbolism (Knight *et al.* 1995, Knight, this volume).

PROTO-SYMBOLIC BEHAVIOUR AND THE ORIGINS OF A RITUAL TRADITION

So long as female deceptive displays remain situation-dependent, constrained by the local incidence of real menstruation, they would not be fully symbolic but tied to here-and-now contexts. Symbolic cultural evolution takes off when cosmetic displays are staged as a default – a matter of monthly, habitual performance, irrespective of whether any local female is actually menstruating. Once such regularity has been established, females have effectively created a communal construct of 'Fertility' or 'Blood' – decoupled, finally, from its perceptible counterpart. Body-painting within groups repeatedly creates, sustains and recreates this abstract construct. Such energetically costly repeated ritual must be linked to the level, regularity and kind of male provisioning effort it engenders. We therefore predict that data interpretable as evidence for regular female ritual performance will correlate with the onset of a symbolically structured sexual division of labour.

No matter how amplified, menstrual signalling would not motivate males to embark on logistic hunts; on the contrary, it should promote mate-guarding. We have argued that sham menstruation would have been utilized by archaic female coalitions to attract and retain male support. But it could only function to mobilize male mating effort in contexts of area-intensive foraging, where there were sufficient gatherable resources in the vicinity. It is consistent with fairly similar foraging strategies between the sexes, with females accompanying males for hunting of no more than small to medium game. However, for females burdened with increasingly dependent offspring, and especially for late archaics under-going maximal reproductive stress, there would be pressure to reduce activity levels, particularly the energetic costs of travel (Prentice and Whitehead 1987). Our hypothesis is that symbolism arose in this context. To minimize travel costs, coalitions of women began to invest more heavily in 'campsites'. To secure the strategy, women manipulated their attractive, collective signal in a wholly new way: by signalling refusal of sexual access except to males who returned 'home' with provisions. At this point, collective resistance to potential dominant males – 'counter-dominance' in the terminology of Erdal and Whiten (1994) – constitutes symbolic ritual underwriting the sexual division of labour. Menstruation – real or artificial – while biologically the wrong time for fertile sex, is psychologically the right moment for focusing men's minds on imminent hunting, since it offers successful hunters the prospect of fertile sex soon. Coalitions of women who had already been artificially manipulating information divulged to males, and engaging in a level of collective deception, would have had the preadaptations necessary to construct such a 'no' signal.

Knight's 'sex-strike' theory

Knight (1991) posits a model of symbolic cultural origins based in a female strategy of periodically refusing sex to all males except those who returned 'home' with fatty meat. 'Strike' action organized across a landscape motivated males to collective hunting of big game, and ensured their return to a home base with the product. This strategy was premised on a previously evolved tendency to reproductive cycle synchrony (the Turke ovulatory synchrony scenario). The intense levels of sexual solidarity required, and economic interdependency of female coalitions, would promote optimal conditions for menstrual synchrony (see Graham 1991). Lunar-phase alignment of menstrual cycles would have provided females with the necessary environmental clock for co-ordinating their action. Because of the importance of nocturnal light to long-distance hunters, the optimal time for hunting would have been in the period of waxing moon after first quarter. Hence the preceding 'sex strike' would be organized at dark moon, when women were menstruating, with the hunters' return around full moon, coincident with ovulation. This is the appropriate time for cooking fires to be lit.

Knight argues (this volume) that to signal their non-availability loud and clear, resisting would-be dominant males, women would have inter-fered with the specific mate recognition system. Through pantomime dance, they would have got their message across by indicating 'we are a different species from you!; we are the same sex as you!', and, given their menstrual condition, 'this is the wrong time for fertile sex anyway'. By pantomiming not only that they were animals, but that they were bleeding animals, women automatically constructed their blood as the blood of the game. This rendered all bloody flesh – female and animal – taboo to the hunter.

On the basis of this model, we posit a 'time-resistant' syntax, preserved in the structure of ritual and myth (Knight *et al.* 1995). According to this syntax, ritual power is switched 'on' by blood/wetness; dark/crescent moon; extinguishing of cooking fires; hunger (prior to hunting); abstention from marital sex; and 'animal mode' sexual ambiguity. Ritual power is turned 'off' by light; full moon; cooking fires; feasting; and 'human mode' marital sex.

If we integrate the models of sham menstruation and the sex strike, it can be seen that the later sex-strike strategy would rest on an evolved proto-cultural tradition of female coalitions acting to collectivize and standardize their display of reproductive signals. We posit that pressure to transform proto-cultural sham menstruation strategy into a fully cultural 'sex-strike' tradition built up as females endured acute reproductive stress owing to encephalization in the period 160–140 Kyr BP, this being exacerbated by resource stress during the height of the penultimate glacial cycle.

TESTING THE SHAM MENSTRUATION/ SEX-STRIKE MODEL

This hypothesis of symbolic cultural origins generates a number of tightly specified predictions. For the purpose of this article, these are broken down into two areas: (1) what sham menstruation strategy implies about the record of pigment use; and (2) the predictions of sex-strike theory concerning traditions of female inviolability.

Pigments in the archaeological record

For earlier stages of the brain expansion of archaic *Homo sapiens*, we posit context-dependent sham menstruation displays, triggered by the incidence of menstruation in local populations. Female coalitions used these as opportunity arose to attract and retain male support, securing long-term bonds with mates. This strategy implies less planning depth in obtaining materials for cosmetic usage, with correspondingly greater reliance on biodegradable matter, and only occasional traces of utilized ochre. As late archaic to early anatomically modern females endured acute reproductive stress, we posit the emergence of a habitual and fully symbolic strategy of cosmetic ritual underpinning the sexual division of labour. Greater regularity, planning and organization of performances would lead us to expect abundant and regular use of ochre. Evidence of symbolic ritual activity should correlate with the first indications for a sexual division of labour.

In this section, we present a preliminary summary of the archaeological data on ochre, briefly evaluating contending hypotheses of iron oxide use. We contextualize our conclusions on ochre use with brief comments on early Upper Pleistocene evidence for the sexual division of labour.

Re-evaluation of claims for Lower and Middle Pleistocene use of ochre have called into question several oft-cited instances, most notably

Olduvai Bed II (Butzer 1980), Ambrona (Butzer 1980) and Terra Amata (Wreschner 1983, 1985). Aside from these, globally there remain about ten or eleven instances of hominid use of iron oxides definitely or possibly predating the Upper Pleistocene (Knight *et al.* 1995). None of these instances is thought to be significantly older than about 250–300 Kyr BP, and seven are from Late Acheulian, Fauresmith and early Middle Stone Age (MSA) contexts in sub-Saharan Africa. It seems reasonable to conclude that the earliest use of iron oxides was by archaic grade *Homo sapiens* rather than *Homo erectus* (*contra* Marshack 1981, Cordwell 1985, Velo and Kehoe 1990). Although this behaviour is geographically widespread, it is neither regular nor frequent; in all cases we are dealing with a single or just a few pieces.

From the beginning of the Upper Pleistocene, we have divergent pictures of iron oxide use in Africa and Europe. Focusing on MSA use of iron oxides in Southern Africa (south of the Limpopo), we adopt Volman's (1981, 1984) chronological scheme based on informal changes in lithic technology and typology.

The MSA1 is thought to span the greater part of oxygen isotope stage 6, the penultimate glacial ~200–140 Kyr BP Volman suggests that the MSA2a may begin towards the end of Stage 6 – a glacial maximum (Jouzel *et al.* 1993) – and lasts through the onset of the last interglacial. The MSA2b is placed in the later substages of Stage 5 (approximately 110–75 Kyr BP). The only stage of the MSA which can be considered a formal industry is the Howieson's Poort, believed to date to either a cool, late sub-stage of O.I. Stage 5 or the onset of O.I. Stage 4 (Miller *et al.* 1992, Grun *et al.* 1990a, b). The Howieson's Poort is followed by a return to a more orthodox, albeit highly variable, MSA industry in the MSA3 lasting until the transition to the Later Stone Age, variously placed between 38–25 Kyr BP (cf. Wadley 1993).

Figure 11.1 presents data on the percentage frequency of pigments (as a proportion of unselected lithic assemblages) over time. Being associated with a glacial cycle, the early MSA has a low archaeological visibility in the region. However, the higher archaeological visibility of the MSA2a suggests that the low frequency of iron oxides in the early MSA is a behavioural phenomenon not attributable to low archaeological visibility (Watts n.d.). The graph illustrates an explosion in pigment use across the MSA2a/2b transition, and the maintenance of similarly high levels of pigment use for the duration of the MSA.

Throughout the MSA, red ochres massively predominate over orange-red and brownish-red hues, and reds in general are overwhelmingly predominant over other colours. Blacks are very rarely encountered from the MSA2b onwards, whilst data from Klasies River Mouth and Apollo 11 indicate that whites and yellows first occur in the Howieson's Poort. The rarity of black pigments is notable given the proximity of at least some sites to magnetite and manganese ore deposits. The principal criteria

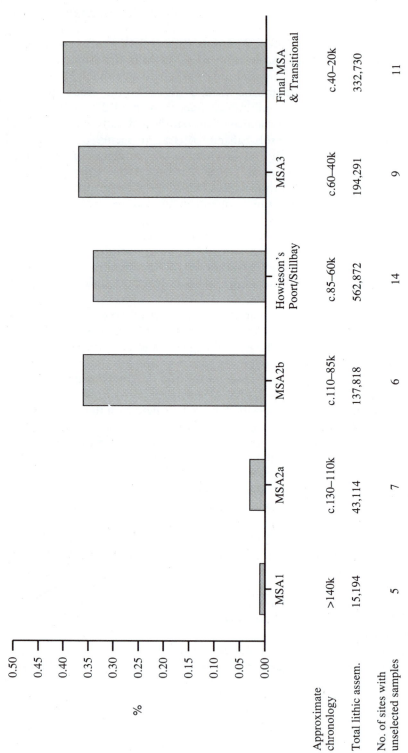

Approximate chronology	MSA1	MSA2a	MSA2b	Howieson's Poort/Stillbay	MSA3	Final MSA & Transitional
	>140k	c.130–110k	c.110–85k	c.85–60k	c.60–40k	c.40–20k
Total lithic assem.	15,194	43,114	137,818	562,872	194,291	332,730
No. of sites with unselected samples	5	7	6	14	9	11

Figure 11.1 The symbolic explosion: ochre frequency as a percentage of total lithic assemblages

used in the selection of raw materials clearly concerned colour and hue, with strong reds occurring earliest and massively predominating. In several MSA2 and Howieson's Poort assemblages there are unique pieces of red ochre which have been notched, drilled or scored with possible 'patterns' which cannot be explained in functional terms of the production of ochre powder (see Knight *et al.* 1995, for illustrations). The 'patterns' consist of parallel, convergent and perpendicular lines, triangles and complex meanders. The notched pieces of ochre in particular, from Stillbay (Evans 1993) and Howieson's Poort (Stapleton and Hewitt 1928) contexts, strongly suggest symbolic traditions. The scale of ochre use in Southern Africa from the MSA2b onwards is unparalleled elsewhere until the Eurasian Upper Palaeolithic. For the rest of Africa this probably reflects the less intensive history of research, as ochre is reported from a number of Last Interglacial or later MSA/Middle Palaeolithic assemblages in Eastern and Central Africa (see Knight *et al.* 1995, for references).

The contrast between this African data and the pre-Upper Palaeolithic European data is marked. Couraud (1991) lists seventeen French Middle Palaeolithic/Mousterian sites where pigments have been reported. Many of these were excavated in the early decades of this century, so details are scanty. However, a few generalizations are possible. The vast majority of occurrences appear to come from late Mousterian (Wurm I and Wurm II) contexts. The quantities involved are slight compared to both the earlier Southern African sites and the Eurasian Upper Palaeolithic, generally consisting of just a few pieces. Equally striking is that the predominant metal oxide is black manganese (Couraud 1991: 38). It is only during the Chatelperronean, when Neanderthals are widely believed to have been in direct competition with the newly arrived 'moderns', that we witness a dramatic increase in the use of red ochre, best illustrated at Arcy-sur-Cure (Couraud 1991).

Competing hypotheses

Before the early 1980s, virtually all archaeologists commenting on the use of iron oxides took a symbolist position, several using post-hoc arguments to suggest menstrual blood as the ultimate referent. Recently, more functional hypotheses have been proposed (e.g. Keeley 1978, 1980, Audouin and Plisson 1982, Moss 1983, Velo 1984, Cordwell 1985, Lavallée *et al.* 1985, Bahn and Vertut 1988, Dumont 1988, Couraud 1991). Many of these more recent commentators have attempted to demonstrate a technical role for ochre in the treatment of hides, primarily on the premise that iron oxides may protect hides from bacterial decay of collagen (e.g. Keeley 1980 citing Mandl 1961). It has also been suggested that iron oxides were used to protect the human body from cold, from the sun, from infestation, and as an astringent medicine (e.g. Keeley 1980, Velo 1984, Cordwell 1985). Bahn has argued that such uses are likely to have preceded and have provided the basis for any subsequent symbolic practice (Bahn and Vertut 1988).

On the possible neutralizing qualities of iron oxides on the action of collagenase, an enzyme responsible for the breakdown of collagen (Keeley 1980, Cordwell 1985: 40), Mandl (1961: 196) noted that *all* metal ions inhibit collagenase. We would expect, therefore:

- that iron oxides would only be selected to the extent that they were more available than other metal oxides, e.g. manganese. Whilst the pre-Chatelperronean classic Neanderthal data appears to meet this expectation, the same cannot be said of the Southern African data.

- that within the class of iron oxides, haematite and red ochres would only be selected to the extent that they were more available than other iron oxides, not necessarily producing a red streak, e.g. magnetite, geothite, limonite and siderite. The African data clearly points to the selection of strong reds; that from Arcy-sur-Cure indicates that calcination of yellow ochre to obtain a red pigment was a practice which, on a small scale, extends back to the pre-Chatelperronean levels (Couraud 1991: 37).

- that the rate of hide deterioration attributable to the enzyme collagenase should be greater than the rate of deterioration attributable solely to wear and tear. No experimental data has been generated, but Silberbauer's (1981: 225–226) assessment of the use-lives of articles of hide clothing amongst the G/wi ranged from 6–18 months. Given such a rapid turnover, it seems improbable that the effects of collagenase would outstrip such use-lives.

In an unpublished but comprehensive evaluation of claims regarding the involvement of ochre in hideworking, Volman (n.d.) argues on both experimental and ethnographic grounds that it is much more likely that where ochre was used in the treatment of hides, it was after all scraping activities were completed – as an optional, *decorative* inclusion in a final, manual application of grease or fat (see Knight *et al.* 1995, for a summary). Volman comments: 'What is particularly disturbing about practically all of the studies considered here are the distortions and misrepresentations of ethnographic and experimental evidence to make it support the archaeological interpretations' (n.d.: 25).

No uniformitarian principle can be considered because despite the claimed neutralizing qualities of iron oxides on collagenase, no technical – as opposed to decorative – role for ochre in the treatment of hides in the ethnographic present can be demonstrated. It is worth noting in this regard that many of the ground pieces of MSA ochre are quite small and that reduction is often to a point or an edge, better suited to applying lines of colour than rubbing over a large surface. Similar criticisms can be raised regarding the claimed use of ochre as a bodily protection against the elements (see Knight *et al.* 1995).

It would seem, therefore, that we have to fall back on the old 'invisible' archaeological stand-by, that Middle Palaeolithic/MSA peoples used ochre primarily as a body paint and possibly in the *aesthetic decoration* of organic materials, a conclusion also reached by Volman. This regular use of pigments, witnessed from at least 130 Kyr BP in Africa, should be regarded as the earliest evidence for a symbolic tradition, as opposed to irregularly expressed capacities (cf. Chase and Dibble 1987, 1992, Soffer 1992).

We have presented a neo-Darwinian processual model which predicts precisely this. To that extent, we are able to go beyond appeals to the universal salience of red (Berlin and Kay 1969, Velo and Kehoe 1990) and the earlier symbolist position which drew on random ethnographic precedents to suggest menstrual blood as the ultimate source of such salience. Our model posits that symbolism can only exist in the context of ritual traditions. Integrating the above data with the model's predictions, 'sham menstruation' behaviour may have been common to all archaic *Homo sapiens*. But it is in Africa, across the Middle/Upper Pleistocene transition, that this context-dependent strategy was raised to the level of habitual performance and a ritual tradition was established. How does this interpretation of ochre data relate to a broader under-standing of the development of the sexual division of labour? We summarize our understanding of some of the differences between early anatomically modern and Neanderthal behaviour (see Knight *et al.* 1995): (1) by the onset of the Last Interglacial, MSA caves/rock-shelters were used in ways more closely approximating camp-sites than Stringer and Gamble's (1993) interpretation of pre-'pioneer' phase cave assemblages; (2) from this period, the regular use of grindstones is suggestive of a higher degree of planning depth among early anatomically modern *Homo sapiens* (eamHs) compared to Neanderthals; (3) there is limited morpho-logical evidence to suggest greater division of labour amongst eamHs compared to Neanderthals (Trinkaus 1993); (4) we reject the assertion that symbolic traditions only developed in the period c. 60 Kyr to 40 Kyr BP Whilst in Europe such a claim appears well founded, in Southern Africa evidence for symbolic traditions, apart from ochre, extends back approximately 100 Kyr. This includes possible recording systems in the form of serially notched bones, symbolically elaborated burial, the trans-port of marine shells over distances of c 100 km, and engraved ostrich eggshell.

Sex-strike theory and ethnographic traditions of 'female inviolability'

If the origins of a symbolically structured sexual division of labour are as late as the last interglacial in Southern Africa, and possibly considerably later in other continents, then it becomes legitimate to ask whether and how the ethnography of contemporary hunter-gatherer societies may illuminate such origins.

We assume that some aspects of culture, such as the structural syntax of myth and ritual, are more conservative than others, such as exchange relations. No extant culture is expected to preserve our postulated 'initial situation' of periodic sex-strike intact. Any concordance with the model in the changeable domain of economic and social behaviour would exceed expectations. The model does specify closely the underlying syntax of ritual signalling, and we expect this to be retained with very high copying fidelity in all cultures up to the ethnographic present. Wherever surviving myth and ritual have anything to say about the moon, menstruation, hunting, sexual abstinence, cooking and so forth, then the symbolic connections should accord with the specified 'time resistant' syntax (Knight et al. 1995).

The model predicts that periodic female inviolability should be discernible as a focus of ritual traditions. Menstrual taboos satisfy this condition, being sufficiently widespread and invariant to indicate extreme antiquity. Predictably, where hunting is practised, the taboos are closely linked with beliefs concerning hunting luck (Knight 1991 and refs). Ritual potency is expected to display everywhere a characteristic signature, revealing its ancestry in menstrual seclusion.

Turning to ethnography, we first review Khoisan data on the use of red pigments, not as ethnographic precedents but in the light of the sham menstruation model. Next, we discuss the interrelations between hunting, sex, menstrual observances and lunar periodicity. Lastly, we test a counter-intuitive prediction derived from the posited 'time-resistant' syntax to the mobilization of ritual power' – that women in menstrual 'power' mode should be engaged in signalling 'we are the wrong sex, and wrong species'.

Pigment use among Khoisan hunter-gatherers

It is clear that ochre and haematite were widely used in Khoisan men-archeal observances (Knight et al. 1995). Among the /Xam the most socially inclusive use of haematite occurred in the context of menarcheal rituals (Lloyd 1870–1879: VI–1, 3969 rev.–3973), when the 'new maiden' presented all the women of the band with lumps of haematite for dressing their cloaks and decorating their faces. A !Kung (Zu'/hoasi) new maiden would have a red ochre design painted on her forehead and cheeks (Marshall 1959). The G/wi or G//ana new maiden would be cut during seclusion and a mixture containing her mother's blood would be rubbed into the cuts (Valiente-Noailles 1993: 96). /Xam and !Kung new maidens treated adolescent boys with red pigment to protect them from accidents when out hunting. Similar uses of red pigment, whether animal, vegetable or mineral, are reported for menarcheal rites among most other Khoisan hunter-gatherer groups (e.g. Thomas 1960: 210; Silberbauer 1965; Viegas Guerreiro 1968: 223, 226).

Most other ochre/haematite uses were ritual, such pigments being prominent in other rites of transition, healing dances, rain magic, hunting magic and rock painting (see Knight *et al.* 1995, for refs). Moreover, ochre-processing seems to have been characteristically a women's activity. A metaphor in Zu/'hoasi oral narratives for impending ritual action was hearing the sound of women pounding red ochre in camp (Biesele 1993: 163, 196). Several ethnographers of the !Kung have remarked on the structural similarity between menarcheal ritual and other rites of transition (see Knight *et al.* 1995, for refs).

We have argued that cosmetic manipulation of menstrual signals – with 'blood' triggering 'periodic seclusion' or 'removal to another world' – provides a basic transformational template from which other patterns of ritual can be understood to derive. Taken in conjunction with our critical assessment of alternative functional hypotheses of prehistoric ochre use, this ethnographic data permits greater confidence in inferring the operation of similar relations of relevance (Wylie 1988, Lewis-Williams 1991) in the early Upper Pleistocene of Southern Africa. Functional uses of iron oxides were then, and remain today, subordinate to ritual and symbolic ones.

Hunting, sex, menstrual observances and lunar periodicity

Over the year, the most productive form of hunting practised by the Hadza, the !Kung of Dobi and !Kubi, and the /Kaicwa San of the Nata River, took place in the dry season. It consisted of night-stand hunts over game trails leading to water-holes or river-pools (Crowell and Hitchcock 1978, Hawkes *et al.* 1991). Because this was a nocturnal activity such hunts were further restricted to moonlit nights (Bunn *et al.* 1988, Crowell and Hitchcock 1978), optimally the second quarter of the waxing moon, possibly including the nights immediately following full moon. Because the hunter was so close to the prey, spears were frequently used; this implies that the strategy was much more ancient than the more common poisoned arrow encounter hunting. This was a more collective form of hunting than most pursuit hunting (Crowell and Hitchcock 1978). There is strong evidence for the practice of dry season, pan-margin hunting extending back to the last interglacial. In line with modern parallels we infer this to have been primarily nocturnal and lunar phase-locked (see Knight *et al.* 1995, for refs).

For the Hadza, the dry season marks the phase of social aggregation when their most sacred rituals are held – the *epeme* dances held on each night of the dark moon for the duration of the aggregation. All camp fires are extinguished and the women call upon each man in turn to dance, referring to him exclusively in consanguineal kinship terms (Woodburn 1964, 1982). In Hadza belief, women synchronize their menstruation with dark moon (Bleek 1930: 700), hence at the time of *epeme* rites. The dance emphasizes gender segregation cross-cut by kinship solidarity. As well as being a healing dance, it is believed to ensure success in forthcoming hunts, when portions of the fattiest meat will be offered in brideservice. A coherent pattern emerges from the following set of Hadza beliefs and practices: first, men should not hunt nor have sex while their wives are bleeding (Woodburn 1964, 1982); second, the most successful hunting in the dry season occurs around full moon; and third, menstruation normatively occurs at dark moon, at the same time as the most sacred ritual. In this case, the specifications of the model are met not only at the level of ritual syntax, but also in actual hunting practice.

Several historical and ethnographic accounts explicitly refer to full-moon hunting by Khoisan, whilst others describe nocturnal hunts where some level of lunar phase-locking has to be presumed. Both the historical and ethnographic accounts are replete with references to a normative belief linking success in the hunt to lunar periodicity. Where details are given, it is always the waxing phase which is associated with hunting success (Knight *et al.* 1995). Like the Hadza, most Khoisan groups had a normative belief associating menstrual with lunar periodicities. Where specified, menstruation is always linked to dark, not full, moon. This linkage structured ritual practice. The /Xam, !Xu, and G/wi and/or G//ana would not release a menarcheal girl from seclusion until the appearance of the new moon (Lloyd 1870–1879: VI–2, 4001–4002, Bleek 1928: 122, Valiente-Noailles 1993: 94–97). The !Kung make explicit their belief that women synchronized menstrual onset (Shostak 1983: 68), while there is indirect evidence for behavioural menstrual synchrony (see Knight *et al.* 1995, for refs).

As with the Hadza, the Khoisan generally believe that a man should not hunt while his wife is menstruating (Biesele 1993: 93), and he should not have sex while she is bleeding or while he is preparing for or engaged in a protracted hunt (Marshall 1959: 354 fn.1, Shostak 1983: 239). As predicted, big-game hunting and marital sex are regarded as incompatible. In an early nineteenth-century account this logic is made explicit, with women going on sex strike to force men to raid for cattle:

> The Bushmen when they will not go out to steal cattle, are by the women deprived of intercourse sexual by them and from this mode of proceeding the men are often driven to steal in opposition to their better inclination. When they have possessed themselves by thieving of a quantity of cattle, the women as long as they exist appear perfectly naked without the kind of covering they at other times employ.
>
> (Smith n.d.: notebook 4, p. 77 rev.)

WRONG SEX, WRONG SPECIES

In summarizing the sex-strike model we drew attention to women's interference with the mate recognition system. They should stress non-availability and resist dominant males by going into animal mode and/or being the wrong sex. As a consequence, the menstruating woman is in a paradoxical position: if by becoming the prey animal she initiates the hunt, she is in some sense not only the quarry but the hunter as well. This paradox permeates the ethnographic material. The Hadza and the !Kung have virtually identical terms for a menarcheal girl. The Hadza say 'She has shot her first zebra' (Woodburn pers. comm.), the !Kung say 'She has shot an eland' (Lewis-Williams 1981: 51). While in seclusion and upon emergence, the girl must keep her eyes down; in this way, the antelopes will do the same and not see the approach of the hunters (Bleek and Lloyd 1911, Lewis-Williams 1981). A !Xo menarcheal girl fires a ritual arrow at a gemsbok shield during seclusion to bring luck to the weapons; but on emergence her face is painted to resemble that of the gemsbok (Heinz 1966). Similarly, among the G/wi, the new maiden is taken by her father to touch her husband's weapons so that 'they will not harm her husband' (Silberbauer 1965: 86). Solomon's (1992) analysis of San rock art focuses on the recurring motif of ambiguously female figures with menstrual flows, ambiguous because of their therianthropic features and/or male attributes such as a penis or hunting equipment.

In the Hadza matriarchy myth of Mambedaka (Woodburn 1964), the original owner of the sacred *epeme* meat is an old woman who dresses as a man, hunts zebra and wears a zebra penis which she uses to have sex with her 'wives'. She demands that men bring the *epeme* meat to her cooking pot which she distributes to the 'wives'. Men have no share in the sacred meat until the violent overthrow of Mambedaka's rule. This is a graphic depiction of the logic of women procuring fatty meat from men by signalling 'wrong sex, wrong species'.

Probably the best-known aspect of Khoisan menarcheal ritual is the 'Eland Bull Dance' (Lewis-Williams 1981, Valiente-Noailles 1993). Men are either totally excluded, or a couple of older men in affinal relation to the menarcheal girl are allowed to remain to play the part of the eland bull. The women pantomime the courtship behaviour of eland cows, dancing around the menarcheal girl, exposing their buttocks both to the girl and to whoever may be playing the bull. Among the Kua the women themselves take the role of the bull (Valientes-Noailles 1993). The !Kung clearly identify the menarcheal girl with the eland bull (Lewis-Williams 1981). Although considered a highly erotic performance, the gender segregation emphasizes displaced sex. In line with the time-resistant syntax specified by our model, displaced, pantomime sex which stresses gender ambiguity may be an integral part in ensuring hunting success. Real marital sex is incompatible with hunting.

CONCLUSION

Our focus in this chapter has been on the ritual function of cosmetics. According to our hypothesis, the symbolic domain arose as a response to increasing levels of reproductive stress experienced by females during the rapid phase of encephalization associated with archaic *Homo sapiens* (from 250 Kyr BP). Ovulation concealment and loss of oestrus had deprived males of precise information about female reproductive status, rendering sex in effect 'time-wasting' for males. As pay-offs to mate-desertion were reduced, females could extract more energy, including provisioning from their partners. Once these signals had been phased out, menstruation remained as the only cue offering males positive information on which females were imminently fertile. Males who responded to menstrual cues were drawn into longer-term consortships and relatively greater investment. Because pronounced menstrual bleeding was valuable for extracting mating effort from males, local non-cycling females would have been motivated to exploit its attractions.

On this basis, we have argued that coalitions of female archaic humans resorted to cosmetic manipulation of menstrual signals, such as body-painting, to secure long-term bonds and parental investment from males. This 'sham menstruation' strategy effectively formed a preadaptation to ritual, exercising a capacity for collective deception. We have argued that the explosion of ochre use witnessed in the MSA2b marks the transcendence of sham menstruation by ritual sex-strike. The MSA obviously does not share in the elaboration of symbolic culture witnessed in the LSA, but all the essential elements of a sexual division of labour appear to be in place by the last interglacial, approximately coincident with the evolution of anatomically modern humans. By the MSA2a, the rituals underpinning the first mode of production had become an embedded part of performance in a context of arbitrary, symbolic constructs. The model as presented improves on the form of analogical argument based on ethnographic precedent used both by 'symbolists' and by 'functionalists'. Having tested the relations of relevance derived from the sex-strike model of cultural origins against Hadza and Khoisan ethnographic data, we conclude, first, that this symbolic usage primarily concerned the mobilization of ritual power; and, second, that the function of such power, linking women's menstrual blood to the blood of the hunt, was to establish rules of distribution governing sexual partners and meat.

ACKNOWLEDGMENTS

Financial support from the University of London Central Research Fund and the British Academy for research in Southern Africa is gratefully acknowledged. For access to ochre collections, thanks are due to Aron Mazel, Natal Museum; Lyn Wadley, Department of Archaeology,

University of Witwatersrand; Peter Beaumont, McGregor Museum, Kimberley; John Kinahan, State Museum, Windhoek; Graham Avery, South African Museum Department of Archaeology; Royden Yates and Ursula Evans, Department of Archaeology, University of Cape Town; and Hilary Deacon, Department of Archaeology, University of Stellenbosch. Thanks are also due to Eric Wendt for permission to examine material from Apollo 11. The South African Museum Library and the African Studies Library gave permission for access to unpublished notebooks. Thomas Volman generously made available unpublished manuscripts. Leslie Aiello and Chris Knight have been helpful with discussion.

REFERENCES

Aiello, L.C. (in press) 'Hominine preadaptations for language and cognition.' In P. Mellars and K. Gibson (eds) *Modelling the Early Human Mind*. Cambridge: McDonald Institute Monograph Series.

Aiello, L.C. and Wheeler, P. (1995) 'The expensive tissue hypothesis: the brain and the digestive system in human and primate evolution.' *Current Anthropology* 36: 199–221.

Alexander, R.D. and Noonan, K.M. (1979) 'Concealment of ovulation, parental care, and human social evolution.' In N. Chagnon and W. Irons (eds) *Evolutionary Biology and Human Social Behavior*, pp. 436–453. North Scituate, MA: Duxbury Press.

Audouin, F. and Plisson, H. (1982) 'Les ocres et leurs témoins au Paléolithique en France: enquête et expériences sur leur validité archéologique.' *Cahiers du Centre de Recherches Préhistoriques* 8: 33–80.

Bahn, P. and Vertut, J. (1988) *Images of the Ice Age*. London: Windward.

Baker, R.R. and Bellis, M.A. (1993) 'Human sperm competition: ejaculate adjustment by males and the function of masturbation.' *Animal Behavior* 46: 861–885.

Berlin, B. and Kay, P. (1969) *Basic Color Terms: Their Universality and Evolution*. Berkeley, CA: University of California Press.

Biesele, M. (1993) *Women Like Meat. The Folklore and Foraging Ideology of the Kalahari Ju/'hoan*. Witwatersrand: University Press.

Bleek, D. (1928) 'Bushmen of Central Angola.' *Bantu Studies* 3: 105–125.

Bleek, D. (1930) Unpublished Hadza notebooks. African Studies Library, University of Cape Town.

Bleek, W.H.I. and Lloyd, L.C. (1911) *Specimens of Bushman Folklore*. London: Allen.

Bunn, H.T., Bartram, L.E. and Kroll, E.M. (1988) 'Variability in bone assemblage formation from Hadza hunting, scavenging, and carcass processing.' *Journal of Anthropological Archaeology* 7: 412–457.

Butzer, K.W. (1980) 'Comment on Wreschner: red ochre and human evolution.' *Current Anthropology* 21: 635.

Byrne, R. and Whiten, A. (eds) (1988) *Machiavellian Intelligence. Social Expertise and the Evolution of Intellect in Monkeys, Apes, and Humans*. Oxford: Clarendon Press.

Chase, P.G. and Dibble, H.L. (1987) 'Middle Palaeolithic symbolism: a review of current evidence and interpretations.' *Journal of Anthropological Archaeology* 6: 263–296.

Chase, P.G. and Dibble, H.L. (1992) 'Scientific archaeology and the origins of symbolism: a reply to Bednarik.' *Cambridge Archaeological Journal* 2: 43–51 .

Clutton-Brock, T.H. and Harvey, P.H. (1977) 'Species differences in feeding and ranging behavior in primates.' In T.H. Clutton-Brock (ed.) *Primate Ecology: Studies of Feeding and Ranging Behavior in Lemurs, Monkeys and Apes*, pp. 557–579. New York: Academic Press.

Cordwell, J.M. (1985) 'Ancient beginnings and modern diversity of the use of cosmetics.' In A. Kligman and J. Graham (eds) *The Psychology of Cosmetic Usage*. New York: Praeger Scientific.

Couraud, C. (1991) 'Les pigments des grottes d'Arcy-sur-Cure (Yonne).' *Gallia Préhistoire* 33: 17–52.

Crowell, A.L. and Hitchcock, R.K. (1978) 'Basarwa ambush hunting in Botswana.' *Botswana Notes and Records* 10: 37–51.

Cutler, W.B., Garcia, C.R. and Krieger, A.M. (1980) 'Sporadic sexual behavior and menstrual cycle length in women.' *Hormones and Behavior* 14: 163–172.

Dawkins, R. and Krebs, J.R. (1984) 'Animal signals: mind-reading and manipulation.' In J.R. Krebs and N.B. Davies (eds) *Behavioural Ecology. An Evolutionary Approach*, pp. 380–402. Oxford: Blackwell Scientific Publications.

Dumont, J. (1988) *A Microwear Analysis of Selected Artifact Types from the Mesolithic Sites of Star Carr and Mount Sandel*. Oxford: British Archaeological Reports, Brit. S. 187.

Dunbar, R.I.M. (1988) *Primate Social Systems*. London and Sydney: Croom Helm.

Ellison, P.T. (1990) 'Human ovarian function and reproductive ecology: new hypotheses.' *American Anthropologist* 92: 933–952.

Ellison, P.T., Peacock, N.R. and Lager, C. (1989) 'Ecology and ovarian function among Lese women of the Ituri Forest, Zaire.' *American Journal of Physical Anthropology* 78: 519–526.

Emlen, S.T. and Oring, L.W. (1977) 'Ecology, sexual selection and the evolution of mating systems.' *Science* 197: 215–223.

Erdal, D. and Whiten, A. (1994) 'On human egalitarianism: an evolutionary product of Machiavellian status escalation?' *Current Anthropology* 35: 175–183.

Evans, U. (1993) 'Hollow rock shelter (Sevilla 48).' Unpublished Honours project for BA degree in Archaeology, University of Cape Town.

Foley, R.A. and Lee, P.C. (1991) 'Ecology and energetics of encephalization in hominid evolution.' *Philosophical Transactions of the Royal Society of London, Series B* 334: 223–232.

Graham, C. (1991) 'Menstrual synchrony: an update and review.' *Human Nature* 2: 293–311.

Grun, R., Shackleton, N.J. and Deacon, H.J. (1990a) 'Electron-spin-resonance dating of tooth enamel from Klasies River Mouth Cave.' *Current Anthropology* 31: 427–432.

Grun, R., Beaumont, P.B. and Stringer, C.B. (1990b) 'ESR dating evidence for early modern humans at Border Cave in South Africa.' *Nature* 344: 537–539.

Gunn, D.L., Jenkin, P.M. and Gunn, A.L. (1937) 'Menstrual periodicity: statistical observations on a large sample of normal cases.' *Journal of Obstetrics and Gynecology of the British Empire* 44: 839.

Hawkes, K., O'Connell, J.F. and Blurton-Jones, N.G. (1991) 'Hunting income patterns among the Hadza: big game, common goods, foraging goals and the evolution of the human diet.' *Philosophical Transactions of the Royal Society of London, Series B* 334: 243–251.

Heinz, H.J. (1966) 'The social organization of the !kõ Bushmen.' Unpublished MA thesis, University of South Africa.

Hardy, S.B. (1981) *The Woman that Never Evolved*. Cambridge, MA: Harvard University Press.

Hurtado, M. and Hill, K. (1990) 'Seasonality in a foraging society: variation in diet, work effort, fertility, and sexual division of labour among the Hiwi of Venezuela.' *Journal of Anthropological Research* 46: 293–346.

Jouzel, J., Barkov, N.I., Barnola, J.I., Bender, M., Chappellaz, J., Genthon, C., Kollyakov, V.M., Lipenkov, V., Lorius, C., Petit, J.R., Raynaud, D., Raisbeck, G., Ritz, C., Sowers, T., Stievenard, M., Yiou, F. and Yiou, P. (1993) 'Extending the Vostok ice-core record of palaeoclimate to the penultimate glacial period.' *Nature* 364: 407–412.

Keeley, L. (1978) 'Preliminary microwear analysis of the Meer assemblages.' In F. Van Noten (ed.) *Les Chasseurs de Meer*, pp. 73–86. Brugge: De Tempel.

Keeley, L. (1980) *Experimental Determination of Stone Tool Uses: A Microwear Analysis*. Chicago: University of Chicago Press.

Knight, C.D. (1991) *Blood Relations. Menstruation and the Origins of Culture*. New Haven and London: Yale University Press.

Knight, C.D., Power, C. and Watts, I. (1995) 'The human symbolic revolution: a Darwinian approach.' *Cambridge Archaeological Journal* 5: 75–114.

Knowlton, N. (1979) 'Reproductive synchrony, parental investment and the evolutionary dynamics of sexual selection.' *Animal Behavior* 27: 1022–1033.

Lavallée, D., Julien, M., Wheeler, J. and Karlin, C. (1985) *Telarmarchay: Chasseurs et Pasteurs Préhistoriques des Andes 1*. Paris: Editions Recherche sur les Civilisations.

Leigh, S. (1992) 'Cranial capacity evolution in *Homo erectus* and early *Homo sapiens*.' *American Journal of Physical Anthropology* 87: 1–13.

Leonard, R.W. and Robertson, M.L. (1992) 'Nutritional requirements and human evolution: a bioenergetics model.' *American Journal of Human Biology* 4: 179–195.

Lewis-Williams, J.D. (1981) *Believing and Seeing. Symbolic Meanings in Southern San Rock Paintings*. London: Academic Press .

Lewis-Williams, J.D. (1991) 'Wrestling with analogy: a methodological dilemma in Upper Palaeolithic art research.' *Proceedings of the Prehistoric Society* 57: 149–162.

Lloyd, L.C. (1870–1879) Unpublished notebooks. Jagger Library, University of Cape Town.

Mandl, I. (1961) 'Collagenases and elastases.' *Advances in Enzymology* 23: 164–264.

Marshack, A. (1981) 'On Paleolithic ochre and the early uses of colour and symbol.' *Current Anthropology* 22: 188–191.

Marshall, L. (1959) 'Marriage among !Kung Bushmen.' *Africa* 29: 335–365.

Martin, R.D. (1992) 'Female cycles in relation to paternity in primate societies.' In R.D. Martin, A.F. Dixson and E.J. Wickings (eds) *Paternity in Primates. Genetic Tests and Theories*, pp. 238–274. Basel: Karger.

Maynard-Smith, J. (1977) 'Parental investment: a prospective analysis.' *Animal Behaviour* 25: 1–9.

McClintock, M.K. (1971) 'Menstrual synchrony and suppression.' *Nature* 229: 244–245.

Menaker, W. and Menaker, A. (1959) 'Lunar periodicity in human reproduction: a likely biological unit of time.' *American Journal of Obstetrics and Gynecology* 77: 905–914.

Miller, G.H., Beaumont, P., Jull, A.J.T. and Johnson, B. (1992) 'Pleistocene geochronology and palaeothermometry from protein diagenesis in ostrich eggshells; implications for the evolution of modern humans.' *Philosophical Transactions of the Royal Society of London, Series B* 337: 149–158.

Moss, E. (1983) *The Functional Analysis of Flint Implements. Pincevent and Point d'Amlon: Two Case Studies from the French Final Paleolithic.* Oxford: British Archaeological Reports, Int. S. 177.

Power, C. and Aiello, L.C. (in press) 'Female proto-symbolic strategies.' In L.D. Hager (ed.) *Women in Human Origins.* New York and London: Routledge.

Prentice, A.M. and Whitehead, R.G. (1987) 'The energetics of human reproduction.' *Symposia of the Zoological Society of London* 57: 275–304.

Profet, M. (1993) 'Menstruation as a defense against pathogens transported by sperm.' *Quarterly Review of Biology* 68: 335–386.

Ralls, K. (1977) 'Sexual dimorphism in mammals: avian models and unanswered questions.' *American Naturalist* 111: 917–938.

Shipman, P. and Walker, A. (1989) 'The costs of becoming a predator.' *Journal of Human Evolution* 18: 373–392.

Shostak, M. (1983) *Nisa. The Life and Words of a !Kung Woman.* Harmondsworth: Penguin.

Silberbauer, G. (1965) *Report to the Government of Bechuanaland on the Bushman Survey.* Gaberones: Bechuanaland Government.

Silberbauer, G. (1981) *Hunter and Habitat in the Central Kalahari Desert.* Cambridge: Cambridge University Press.

Sillen-Tullberg, B. and Møller, A.P. (1993) 'The relationship between concealed ovulation and mating systems in anthropoid primates: a phylogenetic analysis.' *American Naturalist* 141: 1–25.

Smith, A. (n.d.) Unpublished notebook 4. South African Museum Library, Cape Town.

Soffer, O. (1992) 'Social transformations at the Middle and Upper Palaeolithic transition: the implications of the European record.' In G. Brauer and F. Smith (eds) *Continuity and Replacement. Controversies in Homo sapiens Evolution,* pp. 247–259. Rotterdam and Brookfield: Balkema.

Solomon, A. (1992) 'Gender, representation and power in San ethnography and rock art.' *Journal of Anthropological Archaeology* 11: 291–329.

Srivastava, A. and Dunbar, R.I.M. (submitted) 'The mating system of hanuman langurs: a problem in optimal foraging.' *Behavioral Ecology and Sociobiology.*

Stapleton, P. and Hewitt, J. (1928) 'Stone implements from Howieson's Poort.' *South African Journal of Science* 25: 399–409.

Stringer, C. and Gamble, C. (1993) *In Search of the Neanderthals: Solving the Puzzle of Human Origins.* London: Thames and Hudson.

Thomas, E.M. (1960) *The Harmless People.* London: Secker and Warburg.

Trinkaus, E. (1993) 'Femoral neck-shaft angles of the Qafzeh-Skhul early modern humans, and activity levels among immature Near Eastern Middle Palaeolithic hominids.' *Journal of Human Evolution* 25: 393–416.

Turke, P.W. (1984) 'Effects of ovulatory concealment and synchrony on protohominid mating systems and parental roles.' *Ethology and Sociobiology* 5: 33–44.

Turke, P.W. (1988) 'Concealed ovulation, menstrual synchrony and paternal investment.' In E. Filsinger (ed.) *Biosocial Perspectives on the Family*, pp. 119–136. Newbury Park, CA: Sage.

Valiente-Noailles, C. (1993) *The Kua. Life and Soul of the Central Kalahari Bushman.* Rotterdam and Brookfield: Balkema.

Velo, J. (1984) 'Ochre as medicine: a suggestion for the interpretation of the archaeological record.' *Current Anthropology* 25: 674.

Velo, J. and Kehoe, A.B. (1990) 'Red ochre in the Paleolithic.' In M.L. Foster and L.J. Botscharow (eds) *The Life of Symbols*. Boulder, CO: Westview Press.

Viegas Guerreiro, M. (1968) *Bochimanes !khu de Angola; estudo ethnografico.* Lisbon: Instituto de Investigaçao Cientifica de Angola, Hunta de Investigaçoes do Ultramar.

Vollman, R.F. (1977) *The Menstrual Cycle.* New York: Knopf.

Volman, T. (1981) 'The Middle Stone Age in the Southern Cape.' Unpublished PhD thesis, University of Chicago.

Volman, T. (1984) 'Early Prehistory of Southern Africa.' In R.G. Klein (ed.) *Southern African Prehistory and Paleoenvironments*, pp. 169–220. Rotterdam: Balkema.

Volman, T. (n.d.) 'A study in scarlet: red ocher and economy in the Stone Age.' Unpublished manuscript.

Wadley, L. (1993) 'The Pleistocene Later Stone Age south of the Limpopo River.' *Journal of World Prehistory* 7: 243–296.

Watts, I. (n.d.) 'The origins of symbolic culture: The southern African Middle Stone Age and Khoisan ethnography.' PhD thesis, University of London, in prep.

Weller, L. and Weller, A. (1993) 'Human menstrual synchrony: a critical assessment.' *Neuroscience and Biobehavioral Reviews* 17: 427–439.

Wilmsen, E.N. (1978) 'Seasonal effects of dietary intake on Kalahari San.' *Federation Proceedings* 37: 65–72.

Wilson, H.C. (1992) 'A critical review of menstrual synchrony research.' *Psychoneuroendocrinology* 17: 565–591.

Woodburn, J. (1964) 'The social organization of the Hadza of North Tanganyika.' Unpublished PhD thesis, University of Cambridge.

Woodburn, J. (1982) 'Social dimensions of death in four African hunting and gathering societies.' In M. Bloch and J. Parry (eds) *Death and the Regeneration of Life*, pp. 187–210. Cambridge: Cambridge University Press.

Wreschner, E.E. (1983) 'Studies in prehistoric ochre technology.' Unpublished PhD thesis, Hebrew University.

Wreschner, E.E. (1985) 'Evidence and interpretation of red ocher in the early prehistoric sequences.' In P.V. Tobias (ed.) *Hominid Evolution: Past, Present and Future*, pp. 387–394. New York: Alan R. Liss.

Wylie, A. (1988) ' "Simple" analogy and the role of relevance assumptions: implications of archaeological practice.' *International Studies in the Philosophy of Science* 2: 134–150.

Ziegler, T. E., Epple, G., Snowdon, C.T., Porter, T.A., Belcher, A.M. and Küderling, I. (1993) 'Detection of the chemical signals of ovulation in the cotton-top tamarin, *Saguinus oedipus*.' *Animal Behaviour* 45: 313–322.

CHAPTER TWELVE

DARWINISM AND COLLECTIVE REPRESENTATIONS

CHRIS KNIGHT

By 50,000 years ago, the effects of a 'symbolic explosion' – an efflores-cence of human art, song, dance and ritual – were rippling across the globe. The evolution of symbolic culture was now well under way. A testable theory to account for this improbable event is long overdue.

This chapter is in four parts. The first defines symbolism. The second models female strategies amongst late archaic *Homo sapiens* populations. The third applies Darwinian signal evolution theory to the problem of symbolic origins. The fourth suggests predictions and archaeological tests.

DEFINING SYMBOLISM

The brain is a map-making device. It constructs from sensory inputs an internal virtual world, which we respond to as if it were the real one – a private, internal kind of symbolism. There is nothing unusual about this; it is what brains are for. But extraordinarily, through exposure to ritual, art and other 'external memory stores' (Donald 1991), the human brain is able to construct, in addition, a personalized copy of a communal cognitive map, access to which defines membership of a symbolic community.

Our ordinary cognitive map is organism-centred, its co-ordinates measured from the here-and-now of individual experience. The communal map unique to humans is sociocentric, its motivational biases regularly inverting those of ordinary perception – so that onerous social duties (for example) are positively marked, while opportunities for sexual self-indulgence are marked 'danger' or 'taboo'. The representations central to the communal map are intangibles, without perceptual counterparts. 'God', 'Unicorn' and 'Totem' are among the possibilities. Once humans acquire confidence that they share the same gods, they can, naturally, refer to them. Cryptic mutual reference to intangibles is in fact a good preliminary definition of speech. This definition clarifies why other primates have never evolved it. Other primates know of no gods, and seemingly need none. There is therefore nothing for them to vocalize about – except ongoing real events and experiences, for which purpose a gesture/call system (Burling 1993) suffices. Since primates lack a constructed world of commonly acknowledged, morally authoritative intangibles, cryptic mutual reference to them – syntactical or otherwise – is simply unthinkable.

Even under human language training, chimps cannot mutually sustain the motivational biases necessary if speech is to work. Conflicts over coveted items therefore intrude into linguistic exchanges to the point of nullifying them. When, in a classic experiment, 'Booee' and 'Bruno' were taught to beg using American Sign Language, all went well – provided humans were expected to do the giving. Left to themselves, the system collapsed because whenever one animal asked politely for food, the listener would simply run off with the desired item (Fouts 1975: 380). Any seriously hungry chimp had to forget linguistic subtleties and resort to more muscularly persuasive means.

Speech, in other words, is effective only in certain social contexts. Its low-amplitude, 'conspiratorial whispering' design features (Krebs and Dawkins 1978, 1984) indicate an evolutionary origin in gossip (Aiello and Dunbar 1993, Dunbar, this volume), not one-way begging, manipulation or exploitation. Where relations are exploitative, speech in fact tends to lose all relevance, unless its messages are backed up by other means.

Life of a certain kind, then, underpins the effectiveness – the relevance – of speech (cf. Grice 1969, Bennett 1976, Carrithers 1990: 202). This needs stressing because the reverse argument has recently become current among archaeologists, palaeoanthropologists and linguists debating human origins. Given that 'the gods' appear to be symbolic constructs, it has been assumed that such intangibles arose *thanks to* language. The 'human revolution' itself (Mellars and Stringer 1989) has been explained on this basis. Bickerton (1990) postulates a neural macromutation thanks to which the descendants of African Eve spontaneously produced syntacticized language, capable for the first time of displaced reference. From this then stemmed the entirety of symbolic culture (cf. Cavalli-Sforza *et al.* 1988: 6006, Mellars 1991).

Such 'word-magic' scenarios treat speech as unconditionally superior to alternative systems of communication. Darwinian theory, however, does not recognize superiority/inferiority in the abstract – only selection pressures. Speech involves not only benefits but potential costs; among these must be counted the dangers of excessive reliance on uncorroborated information from others and – conversely – the risks of entrusting valuable information to others. Tactical deception theory (Byrne and Whiten 1988) would not predict such trust: within the terms of this paradigm, it is disturbingly anomalous. The human capacity for speech is without doubt a specialized biological adaptation which – no less than stereopsis in monkeys or echolocation in bats – must have evolved through standard processes of Darwinian natural selection (Pinker and Bloom 1990, Lieberman 1991, Pinker 1994). But postulating sudden macro-mutations is not Darwinism.

Primate communication and human speech

Chimpanzees can indicate (through pantomime) possible courses of action, can grasp the nature of the information their own behaviour provides to others, and can modify it accordingly if it suits their purposes (Kendon 1991). Such behaviour is interpreted inferentially, not necessarily through reliance on a code. Vervet monkeys in Kenya, however, possess specific alarm calls for different predators, each call triggering the appropriate flight response (Cheney and Seyfarth 1990). In this case, a code must be assumed. For the system to work, every vervet must share with conspecifics a mental key consisting of a repertoire of potential calls mapped onto a matching set of perceptual schemata for the various predators.

Primates, then, can use overt behaviour to express internal fantasies; they can also use a common code in referring to aspects of the external world. However, no non-human primate can use code terms to refer to internal fantasies. A chimpanzee – for all we know – might be quietly day-dreaming, perhaps remembering some painful event from yesterday. Whatever the details, on waking, she lacks any way of drawing others' attention to such visions. Her companions may detect her mood, but the visions themselves they cannot see. In any case, what benefits would she gain from letting others in on her dreams? Even supposing there was some way – why expend the energy?

We humans, by contrast – as any initiated Aboriginal Australian (Stanner 1956) or San trance dancer (Katz 1982) will confirm – are prepared to suffer immense energetic expenses to externalize and hence share our dreams. It is essential to understand why this became important – why the benefits of tapping into such other-wordly knowledge began to outweigh the extremely high costs. Why did the inner world become so vital, even to the point of partially eclipsing 'reality'? Until such questions are addressed, little progress in understanding the origins of symbolism will be made.

Living in a competitive world, primates face strong pressures to distinguish fantasy from reality. They show no interest in perpetuating illusions. Consequently such illusions never become sufficiently publicized or standardized to qualify for incorporation into a shared code. In this, such illusions differ from primate perceptual schemata, which may qualify. A vervet emits the 'Snake!' alarm only when it sees (or thinks it sees) such a predator. Because vervet mental representations are perceptual, to trigger them is to produce effects analogous to perception, releasing the appropriate set of escape reactions. The internalized 'snake' of a vervet is therefore nothing like a collective representation. It is not socially constructed/replicated – not a communicable concept. If there is any commonality between one monkey's snake-representation and another – and there must be for the call system to work – this stems not from social input but from the fact that snakes, being part of the external world, are equally visible to all.

Quite different would be the problem of assigning cryptic vocal labels to internal fantasies. These are normally so fluid and idiosyncratic as to defy all attempts at communal labelling. Yet humans, in the course of evolution, have evidently managed to label at least certain stable kinds of fantasies, central among which have traditionally been 'religious' constructs or 'collective representations' (Durkheim 1912/1965). Our task is to discover how and why such illusions should ever have evolved.

Deception: individual and collective

At this point, primatologists may counter that too sharp a contrast has been drawn between primate and human forms of consciousness and communication. It is untrue that primates can refer only to real things. They can, after all, deceive – as in the case of the sub-adult male baboon found harassing a youngster and then pursued by the victim's adult protectors. Unexpectedly, the culprit stood on its hindlegs, staring as if watching a distant predator; although this did not exist, it distracted the pursuers' attention long enough for the deceiver to escape (Byrne and Whiten 1985). It might be claimed that the 'false' predator was in effect a symbolic predator (cf. Sperber 1975). It was not, because having checked it out, the victims of the deceit lost all interest in the unreal phenomenon. The fiction expired at that point. The human symbolic domain by contrast is a realm of indefinitely maintained collective deceits, *collective* fantasies (Sperber 1975: 93–95). It is as if the gang of baboons all looked across the valley, saw no leopard – but then joined in with their deceiver in pretending to see one. Clearly, they could only be predicted to do this if they shared some collective interest in perpetuating the fantasy, for example in the course of deceiving a third party. There are no non-human primate examples of this. And it is because other primates' deceptions are never collectively perpetuated that they cannot be labelled by the community. Private lies, private fantasized experiences, are simply not the kinds of things to which agreed, collective labels can be attached.

In this light, it seems misguided to imagine that even highly intelligent archaic humans who stumbled upon the supposedly self-evident 'advantages' of symbolic language would necessarily have appreciated those advantages. Whatever their undoubted symbolic capacities (Marshack 1989,

Soffer 1992), unless they already had powerful reasons for sharing pure fantasies, the point of making the switch to true language would have escaped them. Symbolic speech would have been redundant for the same reason that teaching chimps how to say 'God' is a waste of time. For evolving late archaic *Homo sapiens*, choosing a verbal label for a construct such as 'Spirit' or 'Supernatural Potency' would have been a small challenge compared with the difficulties inherent in establishing a construct of this kind in the first place. More than a linguistic revolution would have been required, after all, to generate the need for constructs of that kind.

To summarize, non-human primates can vocally label reality, individually deceive, and fantasize. They cannot collectively deceive, or label their fantasies. These capacities and incapacities are connected. It is because non-human primate deceptions are not communal that they are not cryptically communicable. Our task, then, is to elucidate the conditións necessary for collective deception to evolve, and – since no better paradigm exists – to do so within a neo-Darwinian, behavioural ecological framework.

ORIGINS OF THE SEXUAL DIVISION OF LABOUR

My hypothesis is that the crucial preconditions for the appearance of symbolic behaviour were found with the appearance of a sexual division of labour, late in the course of hominid evolution and coincident with the appearance of anatomically modern humans.

How do we explain the establishment of an ethnographically recognizable 'hunter-gatherer' sexual division of labour? Previous evolutionary hypotheses have linked changes in human female reproductive physiology with the emergence of such patterns (Lovejoy 1981, Hill 1982, Parker 1987). However, such models locate the crucial events in the Plio-Pleistocene rather than the Upper Pleistocene; more recent models of symbolic culture as a relatively late development (Binford 1989, Gamble 1993) require new thinking in this area.

In fact, a 'hunter-gatherer' type of sexual division of labour should not be assumed even for Neanderthal populations (Soffer 1992, cf. Binford 1989, Binford quoted in Fischman 1992). Whilst differing little from early anatomically modern *Homo sapiens* (eamHs) in their dependence on meat, Neanderthal females appear to have been more self-reliant and more continuously mobile than their eamHs female counterparts. There are suggestions that Eastern European Neanderthal females came under stress following the onset of the last glacial, leading to high rates of juvenile mortality and driving females to retain or accentuate their robust features (Soffer 1992). There is also suggestive evidence that subsets of Levantine early anatomically modern *Homo sapiens* populations were receiving greater provisioning than Neanderthals in the region, and may have been occupying sites more intensively (Trinkaus 1993, Tchernov 1984).

In the absence of the complex logistic arrangements characteristic of modern hunter-gatherers, hunting requires mobility not only of adult males but of all group members. For heavily child-burdened evolving human females, the energetic costs of such mobility (Prentice and Whitehead 1987) must have been considerable. Consorting as frequently as possible with mobile, meat-possessing males has been visualized as an early hominid female strategy (Hill 1982, Parker 1987), but this could only have been optimal where child-carrying burdens were minimal and/or distances short. I have recently suggested that females solved their problems by going periodically on 'sex-strike' to coerce male provisioning of females and offspring at a 'home base' (Knight 1991, Knight *et al.* 1995); this, however, is not the only solution conceivable. Alternative solutions might include a move in the opposite direction, towards female robusticity and increased female foraging autonomy *from* males, as some archaeologists (e.g. Binford quoted in Fischman 1992, Soffer 1992) posit for the Neanderthals in Europe. A further option might be to restrict movements to biotically rich environments, permitting area-intensive foraging (cf. Soffer 1992 for data on Eastern European Neanderthals). But common to all these strategies is an overriding constraint: any increased seasonal dependence on meat will increase the energetic costs incurred by females by compelling them either to hunt for themselves or to travel alongside mobile male hunters.

The radical alternative is to make the meat move. This will involve investing more heavily in camp sites and refusing sex to all males except those returning 'home' with provisions. Where we find archaeological evidence for structured hearths or other signs of investment in home bases (Stringer and Gamble 1993: 154–158), an implication is that females were establishing greater residential stability, with the corollary that they were motivating their mates to take on proportionately more of the energetic costs of foraging.

The idea that home bases were established under female pressure may seem a novel one. But neither structured hearths nor well-built dwellings can be regarded as absolute advances, useful to males and females equally and therefore bound to emerge as brains grew larger. A commitment to return consistently to one and the same base camp would drastically restrict the foraging range of any hunting band which had to move everywhere as a group. The costs of such a commitment could have been outweighed by benefits only given some sexual–political arrangement liberating active males to depart and (where necessary) stay out overnight on long-distance hunting trips, free of sexual distractions and child care encumbrances. Such a 'logistic' configuration (cf. Binford 1989) involves a restructuring of sexual relations and therefore implies a definite female strategy in which sexual access is made dependent on males bringing meat 'home'. Some such pattern is standard among contemporary hunters and gatherers (Collier and Rosaldo 1981, Knight 1991: 139–153). Recent ethnographic work confirms that hunters focus on large game because marital and extramarital relations are best pursued by such means (Hill and Kaplan 1988, Hawkes 1990, Hawkes *et al.* 1991).

Why is this model preferable to more familiar evolutionary scenarios? What of male parental investment, monogamy, paternity certainty? Given strong pair-bonding, would not hunters have provisioned their mates and offspring spontaneously? Why bring in female sexual manipulation?

Male primates differ from many bird species in that they do not provision their mates or offspring. Our task, therefore, is to explain why human males began doing what no primate counterpart had done before. Paternity certainty is rare not only among mammals (Møller and Birkhead 1989) but even among many supposedly 'monogamous' birds (Payne and Payne 1989). Measurements of our evolved human patterns of sexual behaviour – variation in male ejaculates, women's timing of extra-pair copulations, and orgasm under varying conditions – undermine any notion that humans in the evolutionary past expected fidelity of their partners (Baker and Bellis 1989, 1993a, 1993b, Bellis and Baker 1990). Even to the extent that paternity certainty among evolving humans might theoretically have been guaranteed, this would have depended by definition on female sexual behaviour. Modelling such an evolutionary process would entail drawing on neo-Darwinian sexual selection theory, which treats females as discriminating, active strategists in their own right, seeking to maximize their own fitness.

What matters to the female is extracting energy from the current partner – not whether he is really the father of the infant. Human females in fact appear poorly designed to confer genuine paternity certainty on males; patterns of human extra-pair copulation (Bellis and Baker 1990) may reflect an evolutionary background of females insuring against infanticide risk (cf. Hrdy 1981). Certainly, the divulging of precise paternity information can be costly to mothers: it means informing a male when he is *not* the father (Power 1994). A mother then exposes particular infants to severe risk of infanticide should she acquire a new male partner. In particular, a female who confers too much paternity confidence on any one partner, relying uniquely on him, becomes extremely vulnerable in the event of that partner's death. Among the Ache, the leading cause of death for children, including 40 per cent of mortality in the age range 0–3 years, is infanticide/homicide perpetrated by men after the child's father has died (Hill and Kaplan 1988, Hill and Hurtado in press). Given the high adult mortality rates that we can expect for the Pleistocene (cf. Trinkaus 1995), with fathers not infrequently dying before their offspring had matured, females would have been under pressure to develop strategies minimizing infanticide and ensuring that partners helped in ways which benefited both current and previous dependent offspring.

It might be objected that all this is to overestimate the significance of female strategies: why not give male priorities equal weight? Any focus on evolutionary change obliges us to adopt something of a female bias. This is because, according to standard socioecological models, changing ecological variables drive changes in mammalian mating systems via changes in *female* strategies, not male ones (e.g. Jarman 1974). Primates are no exception (Crook and Gartlan 1966, Clutton-Brock and Harvey 1977, Wrangham 1979). Male primates tend to prioritize the search for fertile females over the search for food. Prioritizing the acquisition of resources to feed their young, mothers by contrast distribute themselves, independently of males, in accordance with ecological variables. Within limits set by phylogenetic history, the mating system which emerges depends, consequently, on whether females forage in isolation or in groups and on the nature of interfemale resource competition (van Hooff and van Schaik 1992). Whether such factors as paternity certainty are high or low depends, then, on a mating system whose essential features have been for the most part female-defined.

Unless there exist good reasons for making an exception, we must assume that human groups during the Pleistocene conformed with standard models. Not only Plio-Pleistocene processes but those leading up to the 'symbolic explosion' require analysis in the light of Darwinian theory. In particular, researchers locating the emergence of human symbolic culture in a 'social revolution' (Gamble 1993, Stringer and Gamble 1993, 1994) should suspect that female strategies were driving this (cf. Power and Aiello, in press). If females burdened with the increasing reproductive costs of encephalization (i.e. extended gestation and greatly extended period of postnatal immaturity in offspring) are to drive up male parental investment, they must make philandering more costly. One method is to 'waste the time' of philanderers: ancestral human females achieved this by evolving features of sexual physiology which divulge minimal information about the timing of fertility (concealed oestrus, continuous sexual receptivity). The effect is to correlate the amount of continuous time a male spends with a female with his chances of impregnating her. It is on this basis that Turke (1984, 1988), Knight *et al.* (1995), Power and Watts (this volume) and Power and Aiello (in press) have linked the evolution of human female reproductive physiology to the energetics of human encephalization.

With respect to the socioecological conditions for the appearance of *symbolism*, perhaps the most decisive advantage of a 'female manipulation' model is that it can explain the emergence of collective deception – hence ritual, language and symbolic culture generally. It is this which previous male-biased models have been unable to achieve.

THE SYMBOLIC REVOLUTION

Krebs and Dawkins (1978, 1984) distinguish between two kinds of signal in the animal world, each following a different path of co-evolution.

Where there is a conflict between 'manipulator' and 'victim', evolution takes the form of an arms race between persuasion by the actor and 'sales resistance' by the reactor, leading to conspicuous, repetitive advertising signals which bear all the hallmarks of 'ritualization'. Other signals, however – which can be called co-operative because they occur between communicators sharing an interest in the same signal outcomes – will be selected to be the opposite of ritualized. For reasons of economy of production, they will evolve towards diminished amplitude, diminished conspicuousness and heightened receiver sensitivity. If it pays the reactor to receive and respond to a signal, it will be straining its ears or eyes so that the actor has no need to produce a loud blast of sound or bright colours (Krebs 1991). The outcome is hushed 'conspiratorial whispering' (Krebs and Dawkins 1978, 1984, Krebs 1991).

Human speech displays the design hallmarks of 'conspiratorial whispering' – an adaptation to communicate 'good' information. Speech transmits much information with minimum time and effort (Lieberman 1988, Aiello and Dunbar 1993). Over the generations, listeners in the human case have evidently needed to know: otherwise they would not have evolved such highly specialized neurophysiological adaptations for decoding messages accurately at low amplitudes, requiring minimal redundancy and at astonishingly high speeds (Pinker and Bloom 1990, Lieberman 1991, Pinker 1994). Krebs and Dawkins' Darwinian theory of animal communication therefore indicates that selection for speech occurred in collectives of co-operating individuals.

By contrast, ritual in human cultures demands seemingly disproportionate energetic investments (Sperber 1975). Like their animal counterparts, human rituals are loud, multi-media displays, stereotyped and prone to massive redundancy (Rappaport 1979: 173–246). They are also characteristically illusion-inducing or 'deceptive' (Sperber 1975, Lattas 1989). The difference is that animal manipulative displays are individualistic and competitive, whereas their most potent human counterparts in traditional cultures are quintessentially *collective* performances. They demarcate social relations of power, identifying groups with common interests and setting them in opposition to other groups (Leach 1954, Cohen 1985). But despite this collectivity, they are also highly manipulative performances; the whole aim is to produce an illusion (Leach 1954, Lattas 1989). Human groups throughout recorded history have exploited others by using elaborate ritual to overcome their victims' 'sales resistance'. We might infer – in view of the energy expended in relation to the paucity of reliable information conveyed (Sperber 1975: 8) – that such rituals arose as *coalitions of conspirators* strove to 'exploit the muscle power' of others who tended to resist the message.

We are now in a position to begin putting all this together. Hunter-gatherers, and by implication humans since the origins of symbolism, produce both speech and ritual – both co-operative and exploitative signals. If we attempt to relate these two patterns within an evolutionary framework, they appear at first sight to be mutually incompatible. If the relationships at the root of symbolic origins were exploitative, how could they have been co-operative at the same time? Our earlier discussion of female strategies suggests a solution. What was exploited as the 'human revolution' got under way was the foraging effort of adult males. Those who benefited – the coalitions of conspirators – were females with their kin and offspring.

Evolutionary conditions of displaced reference

There are grounds for linking an intensifying reliance on vocal-auditory communication (in place of gestures and grooming) with evolving *Homo's* need to service increasingly complex networks of potential allies (Aiello and Dunbar 1993, Dunbar, this volume). But 'keeping in touch' through vocal reference to ongoing moods and events is not yet symbolic speech. Coded other-worldly reference, by definition, is not needed to converse about a world which is perceptually manifest. Symbolic speech is a system of coded references to communal fantasies – non-perceptible constructs such as a 'Unicorn' (Bickerton 1990, Kendon 1991). Only humans can gossip about these – and hence about anything imaginable.

When we speak, we use coded terms to successively trigger imaginative acts of identification of pre-existent constructs, each distributed throughout the speech community, the more morally authoritative ones ('God', 'Supernatural Potency', etc.) being central to the whole system. Without such universally distributed modular blocks for the building of symbolic imagery, including a shared understanding of the locus of moral authority, the co-operative signalling which is characteristic of speech simply would not work. But while cryptic signals can trigger morally authoritative constructs, they are powerless to do the initial work of implanting and replicating them throughout a community of speakers. To rely on coded signals to implant a construct such as 'Supernatural Potency' would be hopeless – as futile as using cryptic nods and winks to instil belief in 'God'. Intangibles, by definition, are not self-evident. One cannot just refer to them. They have first to be emotively experienced.

Social anthropologists have extensively documented the elaborate ways in which, within traditional cultures, collective representations such as 'God' are emotionally charged, made fearsome and given both structure and experiential authority. The only known agency capable of doing this is *communal ritual* (Durkheim 1912/1965, cf. Gellner 1992: 36–37). Ritual collectivizes dreams. Representations of events in the inner world are externalized, socially standardized and replicated. To the extent that a performance has succeeded, every participant should share the same set of fantasies. Subsequent to their ritual implantation, these variegated gods, goblins and other beings then comprise an entire world of illusion, within which everyone is immersed. From then on, cryptic mutual reference to these particular illusions can work.

The human revolution

It is now possible to explain the goblins. Recent models of hominid socio-ecology associate the rapid evolutionary expansion of the hominid brain with greater Machiavellian intelligence (e.g. Dunbar 1993). It has been suggested that hunter-gatherer type egalitarianism was eventually established because the capacities of dominant individuals to exploit subordinates became increasingly well matched by group members' 'counterdominance' capacities; under such conditions, a strategy of playing fair – resisting dominance by others whilst not attempting to achieve dominance oneself – became evolutionarily stable (Erdal and Whiten 1994).

Knauft (1994) notes the pronounced behavioural displays of submission central to the signalling repertoire of the social great apes, contrasting such patterns of obsequiousness with the 'don't mess with me' norms of human hunter-gatherers. 'Aversion to submission in human evolution', comments Knauft (1994: 182), 'both between males and between males and females, is particularly important.' The key ape-human distinction, he concludes, 'may be the apes' *willingness* to demonstrate *subordination*'. Such insights accord closely with 'sex-strike' theory (cf. Knight 1991, Power and Watts, this volume). Our hypothesis is that human females assert 'counter-dominant' responses to males by inverting the signs of subordination, and female counterdominance is a prerequisite for the coercion of male provisioning effort. The unique socioecological conditions for this required both selection pressure for encephalization (with its energetic costs for females), and a resource focus which made continuous female mobility and ranging behaviour as part of a mixed-sex foraging band prohibitively costly. Under these conditions, symbolism based in collective deception appeared as an adaptive female-driven strategy.

Female mammals, including primates, recurrently signal subordination with a gesture known as 'presenting', in which the most vulnerable organs are offered to a dominant individual for inspection or for copulation (real or simulated). On this basis, we would predict 'counterdominance' to be signalled by reversing such signals. Courtship ritual in the animal world is central to the functioning of the specific mate recognition system (Paterson 1978, 1982); minimally, this involves signalling to prospective partners, 'right species; right sex; right time'. Systematic reversal yields '*wrong* species/sex/time'. This, then, is the predicted signature of counterdominance. It need hardly be stressed that for human females to signal to males that they were themselves in fact males, and of a non-human species, would be a fantasy not easy to convey. To overcome listener-resistance (consistent with Krebs and Dawkins' theory of exploitative signals), such signalling will be amplified rather than whispered. Transmission will involve energetically expensive, repetitive, highly iconographic pantomime. Between conspirators, on the other hand, the reverse logic will apply. Interests being shared, 'conspiratorial whispering' – i.e. low-amplitude, energy-saving, information-rich, highly encoded signalling – should suffice. Such whispering will now govern the staging of those public, amplified and deceptive signals expressive of counterdominance. The corresponding fantasies, being shared, will now be communicable for the first time.

In this model, female counterdominance behaviour is not exclusively political. It is also economic – a means of compelling *potential* dominant males to depart, join with other males, hunt and bring back meat. 'Ritual' in this context appears as the energy-expensive, amplified collective pantomime of signalling 'no'. But what is a 'no' to dominance is experienced positively – as a whispered 'yes' to synchronized action – within the counterdominance camp. Speech is this 'yes'. In short, while ritual emerged as a system of pantomimed representations – collectively acted-out fantasies – speech was the means through which conspirators communicated to one another about these. Within this perspective, the two most easily distinguished ethnographically documented ways of communicating – one vocal, the other gestural, one 'speech', the other 'ritual' – appear not as successive stages but as interdependent aspects of one and the same symbolic domain. Speech is required for the organization of *ritual*, in turn initiating hunting, while in turn ritual generates an entire world of amplified deceptions which can now be gossiped about for the first time.

TESTING THE MODEL

This hypothesis, although speculative, generates precise predictions potentially falsifiable across a range of disciplines. Ritual traditions focused on female inviolability (Knight 1991), residual elements of 'sex-strike' practices in hunter-gatherer ethnography (Power and Watts, this volume, Knight *et al.* 1995) and evidence for a time-resistant syntax to the mobilization of ritual power (Knight 1987) matching with precision the 'universal structures' of myth uncovered by Lévi-Strauss (1970, 1973, 1978, 1981), offer provisional confirmation.

Evidence that ritual focused on marital relations would falsify the model. Pair-bonding should *not* be a focus of rock art. Our model, which roots symbolic behaviour in female collective action to coerce male provisioning effort, predicts instead that images of power should feature all-female groups engaged in dancing, or all-male groups hunting or preparing for hunting. 'Art' traditionally expresses ritual priorities (Lewis-Williams 1981); rock-artists according to this model should be concerned to fantasize 'animal' roles. If human females are depicted, these should not be 'sociobiological'

– that is, narrow-waisted, big-hipped, big-bosomed, nubile and available (cf. Low *et al.* 1987). Rather, they should be 'ritually potent'. They should include figures interpretable as menstruating, pregnant and/or nursing; as gender-ambivalent; and as pantomiming 'animal' courtship behaviour or attributes.

REFERENCES

Aiello, L.C. and Dunbar, R. (1993) 'Neocortex size, group size, and the evolution of language.' *Current Anthropology* 34: 184–193.

Baker, R.R. and Bellis, M.A. (1989) 'Number of sperm in human ejaculates varies in accordance with sperm competition.' *Animal Behaviour* 37: 867–869.

Baker, R.R. and Bellis, M.A. (1993a) 'Human sperm competition: ejaculate adjustment by males and the function of masturbation.' *Animal Behaviour* 46: 861–885.

Baker, R.R. and Bellis, M.A. (1993b) 'Human sperm competition: ejaculate manipulation by females and a function for the female orgasm.' *Animal Behaviour* 46: 887–909.

Bellis, M.A. and Baker, R.R. (1990) 'Do females promote sperm competition?: data for humans.' *Animal Behaviour* 40: 997–999.

Bennett, J. (1976) *Linguistic Behaviour*. Cambridge: Cambridge University Press.

Bickerton, D. (1990) *Language and Species*. Chicago: University of Chicago Press.

Binford, L.R. (1989) 'Isolating the transition to cultural adaptations: an organizational approach.' In E. Trinkaus (ed.) *The Emergence of Modern Humans. Biocultural Adaptations in the Later Pleistocene*, pp. 18–41. Cambridge: Cambridge University Press.

Burling, R. (1993) 'Primate calls, human language, and nonverbal communication.' *Current Anthropology* 34: 25–53.

Byrne, R. and Whiten, A. (1985) 'Tactical deception of familiar individuals in baboons.' *Animal Behaviour* 33: 669–673 .

Byrne, R. and Whiten, A. (eds) (1988) *Machiavellian Intelligence. Social Expertise and the Evolution of Intellect in Monkeys, Apes, and Humans*. Oxford: Clarendon Press.

Carrithers, M. (1990) 'Why humans have cultures.' *Man* (n.s.) 25: 189–206.

Cavalli-Sforza, L.L., Piazza, A., Menozzi, P. and Mountain, J. (1988) 'Reconstruction of human evolution: bringing together genetic, archaeological, and linguistic data.' *Proceedings of the National Academy of Sciences (USA)* 85: 6002–6006.

Cheney, D.L. and Seyfarth, R.M. (1990) *How Monkeys See the World*. Chicago: University of Chicago Press.

Clutton-Brock, T.H. and Harvey, P.H. (1977) 'Primate ecology and social organization.' *Journal of Zoology* 183: 1–39.

Cohen, A.P. (1985) *The Symbolic Construction of Community*. London: Tavistock.

Collier, J.F. and Rosaldo, M.Z. (1981) 'Politics and gender in simple societies.' In S.B. Ortner and H. Whitehead (eds) *Sexual Meanings. The Cultural Construction of Gender and Sexuality*, pp. 275–329. Cambridge: Cambridge University Press.

Crook, J.H. and Gartlan, J.S. (1966) 'Evolution of primate societies.' *Nature* 210: 1200–1203.

Donald, M. (1991) *Origins of the Modern Mind. Three Stages in the Evolution of Culture and Cognition.* Cambridge, MA: Harvard University Press.

Dunbar, R.I.M. (1993) 'Coevolution of neocortex size, group size and language in humans.' *Behavioural and Brain Sciences* 16: 681–735.

Durkheim, E. (1912/1965) *The Elementary Forms of the Religious Life.* New York: Free Press.

Erdal, D. and Whiten, A. (1994) 'On human egalitarianism: an evolutionary product of Machiavellian status escalation?' *Current Anthropology* 35: 175–183.

Fischman, J. (1992) 'Hard evidence. By re-creating Stone Age behavior, researchers are learning that the Neanderthals were nothing like the people we imagined.' *Discover* February.

Fouts, R.S. (1975) 'Capacities for language in great apes.' In R.H. Tuttle (ed.) *Socioecology and Psychology of Primates*, pp. 371–390. The Hague: Mouton.

Gamble, C. (1993) *Timewalkers. The Prehistory of Global Colonization.* Stroud, Gloucestershire: Alan Sutton.

Gellner, E. (1992) *Reason and Culture.* Oxford: Blackwell.

Grice, H. (1969) 'Utterer's meanings and intentions.' *Philosophical Review* 78: 147–177.

Hawkes, K. (1990) 'Showing off. Tests of an hypothesis about men's foraging goals.' *Ethology and Sociobiology* 12: 29–54.

Hawkes, K., O'Connell, J.F. and Blurton-Jones, N.G. (1991) 'Hunting income patterns among the Hadza: big game, common goods, foraging goals and the evolution of the human diet.' *Philosophical Transactions of the Royal Society of London, Series B* 334: 243–251.

Hill, K. (1982) 'Hunting and human evolution.' *Journal of Human Evolution* 11: 521–544.

Hill, K. and Hurtado, A.M. (in press) *Demographic/Life History of Ache Foragers.* New York: Aldine.

Hill, K. and Kaplan, H. (1988) 'Tradeoffs in male and female reproductive strategies among the Ache, I and II.' In L.L. Betzig, M. Borgerhoff Mulder and P. Turke (eds) *Human Reproductive Behaviour*, pp. 227–305. Cambridge: Cambridge University Press.

Hrdy, S. B. (1981) *The Woman that Never Evolved.* Cambridge, MA: Harvard University Press.

Jarman, P. J. (1974) 'The social organization of antelope in relation to their ecology.' *Behaviour* 48: 215–267.

Katz, R. (1982) *Boiling Energy. Community Healing among the Kalahari !Kung.* Cambridge, MA: Harvard University Press.

Kendon, A. (1991) 'Some considerations for a theory of language origins.' *Man* (n.s.) 26: 199–221.

Knauft, B. (1994) 'Comment on "On human egalitarianism: an evolutionary product of Machiavellian status escalation?" by David Erdal and Andrew Whiten.' *Current Anthropology* 35: 181–182.

Knight, C.D. (1987) 'Menstruation and the origins of culture. A reconsideration of Lévi-Strauss's work on symbolism and myth.' Unpublished PhD thesis, University of London.

Knight, C.D. (1991) *Blood Relations. Menstruation and the Origins of Culture.* New Haven and London: Yale University Press.

Knight, C.D., Power, C. and Watts, I. (1995) 'The human symbolic revolution: a Darwinian approach.' *Cambridge Archaeological Journal* 5: 75–114.

Krebs, J.R. (1991) 'Animal communication: ideas derived from Tinbergen's activities.' In M.S. Dawkins, T.R. Halliday and R. Dawkins (eds) *The Tinbergen Legacy*, pp. 60–74. London: Chapman and Hall.

Krebs, J.R. and Dawkins, R. (1978) 'Animal signals: information or manipulation?' In J.R. Krebs and N.B. Davies (eds) *Behavioural Ecology. An Evolutionary Approach*, pp. 282–309. Oxford: Blackwell Scientific Publications.

Krebs, J.R. and Dawkins, R. (1984) 'Animal signals: mindreading and manipulation.' In J.R. Krebs and N.B. Davies (eds) *Behavioural Ecology. An Evolutionary Approach*, pp. 380–402. Oxford: Blackwell.

Lattas, A. (1989) 'Trickery and sacrifice: tambarans and the appropriation of female reproductive powers in male initiation ceremonies in west New Britain.' *Man* (n.s.) 24: 451–469.

Leach, E. (1954) *Political Systems of Highland Burma*. London: Bell.

Lévi-Strauss, C. (1970) *The Raw and the Cooked. Introduction to a Science of Mythology 1*. London: Cape.

Lévi-Strauss, C. (1973) *From Honey to Ashes. Introduction to a Science of Mythology 2*. London: Cape.

Lévi-Strauss, C. (1978) *The Origin of Table Manners. Introduction to a Science of Mythology 3*. London: Cape.

Lévi-Strauss, C. (1981) *The Naked Man. Introduction to a Science of Mythology 4*. London: Cape.

Lewis-Williams, J.D. (1981) *Believing and Seeing. Symbolic Meanings in Southern San Rock Paintings*. London: Academic Press.

Lieberman, P. (1988) 'On human speech, syntax, and language.' *Human Evolution* 3: 3–18.

Lieberman, P. (1991) *Uniquely Human. The Evolution of Speech, Thought and Selfless Behavior*. Cambridge, MA: Harvard University Press.

Lovejoy, C.O. (1981) 'The origin of man.' *Science* 211: 341–350.

Low, B.S., Alexander, R.D. and Noonan, K.M. (1987) 'Human hips, breasts and buttocks: is fat deceptive?' *Ethology and Sociobiology* 8: 249–257.

Marshack, A. (1989) 'Evolution of the human capacity: the symbolic evidence.' *Yearbook of Physical Anthropology* 32: 1–34.

Mellars, P. (1991) 'Cognitive changes and the emergence of modern humans in Europe.' *Cambridge Archaeological Journal* 1: 63–76.

Mellars, P. and Stringer, C. (1989) 'Introduction.' In P. Mellars and C. Stringer (eds) *The Human Revolution. Behavioural and Biological Perspectives on the Origins of Modern Humans*. Edinburgh: Edinburgh University Press.

Møller, A.P. and Birkhead, T.R. (1989) 'Copulation behaviour in mammals: evidence that sperm competition is widespread.' *Biological Journal of the Linnaean Society* 38: 119–131.

Parker, S. T. (1987) 'A sexual selection model for hominid evolution.' *Human Evolution* 2: 235–253.

Paterson, H.E.H. (1978) 'More evidence against speciation by reinforcement.' *South African Journal of Science* 74: 369–371.

Paterson, H.E.H. (1982) 'Perspective on speciation by reinforcement.' *South African Journal of Science* 78: 537.

Payne, R.B. and Payne, L.L. (1989) 'Heritability estimates and behaviour observations: extra-pair mating in Indigo Buntings.' *Animal Behaviour* 38: 457–467.

Pinker, S. (1994) *The Language Instinct.* London: Penguin.

Pinker, S. and Bloom, P. (1990) 'Natural language and natural selection.' *Behavioural and Brain Sciences* 13: 707–784.

Power, C. (1994) 'The costly business of male philandering and how to stop it.' Paper delivered to the conference, 'Ritual and the Origins of Culture', School of Oriental and African Studies, London, 18–19 March.

Power, C. and Aiello, L.C. (in press) 'Female protosymbolic strategies.' In L.D. Hager (ed.) *Women in Human Origins.* New York and London: Routledge.

Prentice, A.M. and Whitehead, R.G. (1987) 'The energetics of human reproduction.' *Symposia of the Zoological Society of London* 57: 275–304.

Rappaport, R.A. (1979) *Ecology, Meaning, and Religion.* Berkeley: North Atlantic Books.

Soffer, O. (1992) 'Social transformations at the Middle and Upper Palaeolithic transition: the implications of the European record.' In G. Brauer and F. Smith (eds) *Continuity and Replacement. Controversies in Homo sapiens Evolution*, pp. 247–259. Rotterdam and Brookfield: Balkema.

Sperber, D. (1975) *Rethinking Symbolism.* Cambridge: Cambridge University Press.

Stanner, W.E.H. (1956) 'The Dreaming.' In T.A.G. Hungerford (ed.) *Australian Signpost.* Melbourne: Cheshire.

Stringer, C. and Gamble, C. (1993) *In Search of the Neanderthals: Solving the Puzzle of Human Origins.* London: Thames and Hudson.

Stringer, C. and Gamble, C. (1994) 'Review feature: In search of the Neanderthals: solving the puzzle of human origins.' *Cambridge Archaeological Journal* 4: 95–119.

Tchernov, E. (1984) 'Commensal animals and human sedentism in the Middle East.' In J. Clutton-Brock and C. Grigson (eds) *Animals and Archaeology 3.* British Archaeological Reports, Int. S. 202: 91–115.

Trinkaus, E. (1993) 'Femoral neck-shaft angles of the Qafzeh-Skhul early modern humans, and activity levels among immature Near Eastern Middle Palaeolithic hominids.' *Journal of Human Evolution* 25: 393–416.

Trinkaus, E. (1995) 'Neanderthal mortality patterns.' *Journal of Archaeological Science* 22: 121–142.

Turke, P.W. (1984) 'Effects of ovulatory concealment and synchrony on protohominid mating systems and parental roles.' *Ethology and Sociobiology* 5: 33–44.

Turke, P.W. (1988) 'Concealed ovulation, menstrual synchrony and paternal investment.' In E. Filsinger (ed.) *Biosocial Perspectives on the Family*, pp. 119–136. Newbury Park, CA: Sage.

van Hooff, J. and van Schaik, C. (1992) 'Cooperation in competition: the ecology of primate bonds.' In A.H. Harcourt and F.B. de Waal (eds) *Coalitions and Alliances in Humans and Other Animals*, pp. 357–389. Oxford: Oxford University Press.

Wrangham, R.W. (1979) 'Sex differences in chimpanzee dispersion.' In D.A. Hamburg and E.R. McCown (eds) *The Great Apes. Perspectives on Human Evolution*, pp. 481–490. Menlo Park, CA: Benjamin/Cummings.

CHAPTER THIRTEEN

THEIR COMMONWEALTHS ARE NOT AS WE SUPPOSED

Sex, gender and material culture in human evolution

PAUL GRAVES-BROWN

INTRODUCTION

Jan Swammerdam, seventeenth-century naturalist and pioneer of dissection, made a startling discovery – that the ant-hill's Lord, the beehive's King are in fact females. Sadly, he did not receive the recognition that posterity accorded to Galileo (Byatt 1990). The Sun does not revolve around the Earth, nor does the ant-hill or beehive revolve around the male of the species. In the words of A.S. Byatt's fictional poet, Randolph Henry Ash, the 'commonwealths' of these creatures were not as 'man' had supposed. Yet Swammerdam remains an obscure historical figure. Why? Perhaps because questions of sex and gender have had a limited impact on science until the last 10–15 years (Conkey and Gero 1991, Diamond 1991), and then only marginally. Indeed, as the editors of *Engendering Archaeology* (Conkey and Gero 1991) suggest, gender is still regarded as something of an optional extra.

But how can we examine gender in human evolution or prehistory? In historic periods, or where figurative art and/or sexed skeletons exist, inference can be relatively direct. Yet, despite their rhetoric, studies in *Engendering Archaeology* are repeatedly obliged to fall back on conventional attributions: women gather, men hunt; women work in the domestic sphere. Conkey and Gero (1991: 11) claim that:

> While it would be extremely helpful to attribute specific features to a specific gender, and while gender associations are integral to research that takes gender as a subject, we refuse to feel limited by the notion that we *must* provide gender attributions and must do so with a certain fixity.

Can we, in fact, produce reliable gender attributions without dependence on conventional views of male and female roles? Most feminist writers claim not to accept any equation between biological sex and gender. 'One is not born a woman,' said Simone de Beauvoir, 'one *becomes* a woman' (quoted in Keefe 1993), a sentiment echoed by Bender (1989: 93) – 'societies attempt to reproduce themselves as societies, not as biological units' – even though she uses biological arguments (from Hamilton 1984) to support her own position. But should we simply reject biological causation out of hand? Although one may not be born a woman, it is a striking coincidence that almost every person born with a sexually female body ends up becoming one. Logically one cannot have a concept of gender without the existence of biological sex. While Conkey and Gero (1991: 8) rightly argue for 'a rejection of the biological determinism that is implicit in many models of sex role differentiation', we have to accept that biology does play some part in the formation of gender. The point is that recognizing sexual differences should not entail the legitimation of social inequality.

The key word here is determinism. Biological sex is a functional attribute of character; I have a penis, testicles, facial hair and nipples, but no ovaries or uterus. These facts define a certain range of possibilities for me; appropriation of my biological potentials and functions by myself and others is a social matter, but I cannot change them (see Vygotskii 1934/1986). Moreover, sexual characteristics must have an evolutionary ontology: however their salience is modified by sociocultural factors, they are the product of millions of years of natural selection. This fact can be useful to us in explaining the evolution of human gender, provided we keep in mind that social, ecological and economic factors articulate with our physiology to generate quite distinct cultural forms.

This chapter, then, has the following structure. I have already made the uncontentious assertion that humans *are* sexually dimorphic. This assumption is then considered in the light of ecological factors: how do different reproductive biologies relate to subsistence activities in male and female hominids? Next I consider both biological and ecological factors in an economic context, and here I stress that economy derives from the articulation between social organization and ecology. We should not always presume that truly economic concepts such as the 'division of labour' are appropriate to the analysis of early humans. Finally, I consider these comparative analyses in relation to the archaeological record. Should archaeologists form their hypotheses entirely on the basis of comparative biological/ethnographic evidence, or can the archaeological record of hominid and human material culture make a positive contribution to our understanding of the evolution of gender relations? Here I suggest that gender issues form part of a wider problematic concerning the distributed, social nature of human activity, and hence the fundamentally social nature of material culture itself. I conclude that the integration of activity within a social context tends to obscure gender autonomy.

ONE MAN'S MEAT IS ANOTHER WOMAN'S VEGETABLE

How did/do male and female feeding ecologies relate to distinct reproductive priorities? During the last twenty years, the debate about hunting, gathering and the relative primacy of the two in human evolution has generated a heated debate. Some feminist theorists (e.g. Tanner 1981, Zihlman 1981) have sought to topple Man the Hunter and replace him with Woman the Gatherer. Yet as Ingold (1986: 87) says, 'to put "woman the gatherer" at the cutting edge of hominization is simply to reverse the order of dominance.' Conversely, some (e.g. Binford 1985, Knight 1991) still regard hunting as a magic amulet in evolutionary explanation, and one that is a purely male concern. In such works, gathering is either downplayed or simply omitted from discussion.

The distinction between hunting and gathering is one with which we have lived so long as to accept it without any thought. It is usually implied that gathered resources are low-value plant matter that could not support a population without meat. However, as Hamilton (1980: 12) says, 'the stress in the literature on women as gatherers of vegetable food has, I think, been overdone, and the importance of small protein sources such as eggs, birds, lizards, burrowing animals and grubs has been greatly underestimated'. This point is reflected by Ingold's observation that (1986: 87) 'the pursuit of small mobile animals by women is . . . widely reported, although its extent has been obscured by systematic observer's bias towards regarding such pursuit, which would usually be called hunting if performed by men, as mere "gathering" or "collecting" if performed by women'.

Thus the hunting/gathering distinction is overstated. Claims for the exclusive importance of hunting were weakened by the Man the Hunter symposium itself (Lee and DeVore 1968), and have been further discounted by numerous subsequent studies (see e.g. Dahlberg 1981, Hamilton 1980, Misonda 1991; see also Hawkes, this volume). Yet male provision of meat is still paraded as a defining social force in evolution. It can still be asserted that gathered resources (read 'vegetables') can be obtained without effort or ingenuity, and hence have no efficacy in the origin of culture. The argument runs that female hominids have been dependent upon males because they themselves have dependent offspring (Lovejoy 1981, Knight 1991, Washburn 1960). Thus, it is said, females must be provisioned (with meat) in order to survive. Hence the pair-bond. Hence the 'sex-strike' (in the formulation of Knight and colleagues, e.g. this volume). But is this model of human sociality really credible?

LIVERPOOL JOHN MOORES UNIVERSITY
LEARNING SERVICES

Adult females of other primate species have dependent offspring, carry their young (often for several years), and yet are not provisioned. According to Goodall (1971) the young common chimpanzee does not take its first independent step until the age of 5 months, and is dependent on its mother until the age of 6. Moreover, women can carry their young and still feed themselves. If women could organize a sex-strike they could organize themselves to get their own food, and of course they do. It is too easy to see all young children as entirely dependent, yet as Zeller (1987, see also Hamilton 1980 and Hawkes, this volume) points out, children in indigenous societies take an increasingly active part in their mother's foraging activities from the age of 3–6 years onwards. The very young have always been the most vulnerable to predation: yet defence against predators is better accomplished in a group than a pair bond (Clutton-Brock and Harvey 1977).

In general, the provisioning/pair-bonding model represents a quite bizarre analogy with birds (see Lovejoy 1981). As Engels (1972: 98) remarked, 'examples of faithful monogamy in birds prove nothing about man for the simple reason that men are not descended from birds'. In ethnographically recorded 'collector' societies, we should rather propose what Hamilton (1980) calls a dual economic system in which men and women go their separate ways and in which child care is socially organized among women (and sometimes maybe even men?). The basic ecology of hominids probably reflected this dual system (for a related, but somewhat different view see Hawkes, this volume).

What the traditional hunting vs. gathering, animal vs. plant distinctions obscure is a more evolutionarily coherent pattern of resource procurement. Female reproductive success is predicated upon continuous and reliable sources of nutrition (Hamilton 1984). Clearly, the pursuit of diverse vegetable, insect and 'slow' game resources represents just such a reliable, stable strategy. Conversely, of course, the pursuit of large game, or scavenging for that matter, is a risky strategy in terms of the probability of finding game, and the dangers both of the pursuit itself and of competition with other large predators (Clutton-Brock 1983, Hamilton 1984). Males pursue such a risk-laden strategy to gain the high-yield resources that would enable them to compete with other males. Ironically, the concentration on 'Man the Hunter' as provider obscures another set of choices: 'there are strong reasons to suspect that the preference for economically successful mates might often have a bigger genetic pay-off for males than for females. When men fail to invest in children, their reproductive success requires mates who can and do' (Smuts 1989: 33). Or, in terms of a saying among indigenous Australian women, 'A man is indeed a man but sometimes like a child. When it comes to eating, a man hopes you will feed him like his mother did' (in Hamilton 1980: 13).

SHARE AND SHARE ALIKE? COMPLEMENTARITY AS A FORCE IN HUMAN EVOLUTION

Thus far, then, I have discussed male and female foraging priorities. These reflect the different, autonomous interests of male and female that are obscured by traditional ascriptions of hunting vs. gathering. Ecological relations precede economic ones: male and female evolutionary histories have been shaped by different selection pressures, and thus their subsistence activities have, in the past, diverged. However, during the process of human evolution ecological relations have been transformed into *economic* ones. Our ancestors began to share resources and co-operate in their activities. Cultural institutions evolved governing the collection and distribution of food. Sharing implies reciprocity, and hence that each partner has something to give and something to gain. Giving food for sex is not truly 'sharing'. A woman giving sex for food surrenders a great deal in exchange for very little if she subsequently becomes pregnant. What is distinct about human action is its complementarity (Reynolds 1993): individuals or groups fulfil different roles in the completion of a task. In the increasingly diverse habitats that hominids have exploited, and the increasingly diverse ways they have exploited them, the different 'ecological profiles' of male and female form the basis for a social, economic reciprocity of roles, an exchange of products and skills.

From this starting point we may infer the potential existence of two sets of gender-based socioeconomic relations (and of course there would be many others not linked to gender). There are relations of intrasexual co-operation, likely to arise first in the evolutionary sequence since members of the same sex share common interests. Thus one would expect co-operative hunting and gathering by single-sex groups (both male and female), and co-operative child care among females. There are also intersexual relations of co-operation: the fact that male and female have autonomous interests and pursue different activities facilitates an exchange and a reciprocity between the sexes. Thus the importance of women's 'gathering' activities in the Western Desert of Australia 'can be understood when it is recalled that men's hunting activities at certain times of the year . . . are often fruitless'. By contrast, 'Women's gathering groups always produce an amount of food, even in the hardest times' (Hamilton 1980). The same, I suggest, can be seen in other accounts of collector/forager activities (e.g. in Dahlberg 1981, Lee and DeVore 1968).

This complementarity of roles does not mean that men never gather, nor that women never hunt. Indeed, there are many documented examples of women's participation in hunting large game (e.g. the Agta – Estioko-Griffin and Griffin 1981; Ojibwa – Landes 1938; Meiscalero Apaches and Eastern Cree – Flannery 1935; Copper Eskimo – Jennes 1922; and Tiwi – Goodale 1971). But, as Stoczkowski (1991) points out, with the notable exception of the Agta, most cases of female 'big-game' hunting are associated with individuals whose husbands are either sick or dead. Arguments about women's role in hunting large animals usually centre on whether women can or cannot hunt 'fast' game: perhaps we should better ask if they would want to, for perhaps they only do so when the complementary role is not filled by men, or by collective hunting groups (Gero 1991). In a wide variety of societies, women have been excluded from hunting and the tools of the hunt (e.g. Hamilton 1980, Petrequin and Petrequin 1993, Testart 1986, although see Gero 1991). In many cases, according to Testart, the excuse for this exclusion is an '*idéologie du sang*', an argument that female menstrual blood should not mix with the blood of the prey, or that females' presence would spoil the hunt. But need this exclusion have any practical consequences? If women's own economic activities do not depend upon men, then clearly the answer is no. For it is only when men have control over women's means of subsistence that they can exercise complete power over them: as Smuts (1989: 33) suggests, 'in the long view, the recent sharp increase in paid employment of wives and mothers throughout the developed world might well be regarded as a return to, rather than a departure from, the historical economic role of women'.

To conclude this section, then, I suggest that what distinguishes human society is the exercise of complementary roles. In any social group, different individuals have different skills which reinforce each other. Such a *distribution* of skills, knowledge and abilities is founded on the capacity to organize activity through social relations, but says nothing of necessity about dominance or control. Here the key question is one of property.

POSSESSION

It is the concept of possession which, I think, generates so much heat in questions of sex and gender (Byatt 1990). The ideology of monogamy and the language we use to describe mating systems are redolent with notions of ownership. We describe chimpanzee mating systems as 'promiscuous', a term heavy with Victorian disapproval; the Judeo-Christian and Islamic traditions of morality and law link marriage with ownership to the extent that there is more than an etymological link between property and propriety. In Britain, until the Married Women's Property Acts of the 1880s, women were virtually the property of their husbands. But to what extent are our conceptions of property, ownership, and hence control, applicable in a broader context? Many theories of human evolution concentrate upon such notions of control: control of sexuality, control of aggression, control of resources. Yet does the control of social forces require the ownership of things or persons? Among pygmy chimpanzees (*Pan paniscus*) control of social tensions is accomplished through frequent, relatively casual (bi-)sexual interactions (Kano 1992).

Sexual activity is a force that holds society together. Thus we should exercise some care when considering our own ancestors or ourselves.

Concepts of ownership and tenure are subtly different in hunter-gatherer societies from those that prevail in agricultural and pastoral communities (Ingold 1980, 1986). There is no sense of ownership of land or of the game that inhabit a given territory. Indeed, the products of 'hunting' (and one might add 'gathering') *must* be shared (Hamilton 1980, Ingold 1986), although *how* they are shared is a complex matter. This is not to say that there is no ownership in any sense: such communities have tenure over certain pathways, or waterholes or sacred sites, and individuals may exercise ownership of tools. But access to resources is largely open, such that even those from outside a local group cannot be refused access provided they seek permission. This, I think, explains why Hamilton's 'dual system' is possible, and why we should be cautious of talking about a 'division of labour'. For clearly no one has property rights to the extent that they can decree who does what or has access to given resources. Whilst men may control the tools of the hunt, this is not an absolute, and in any case it does not prevent women from controlling their own means of production. Social dominance *can* be exercised in hunter-gatherer societies, but here society does not appropriate the objects of labour, so much as labour itself (and in gender relations, particularly the labour of women, see Hamilton 1980). It is not a matter of owning the means of production, but of controlling persons as the forces of production. The situation in agricultural societies is somewhat different. As Bender (1989) suggests, land becomes the object of collective labour both in space and time; each generation inherits not only land but the labour of past generations (see also Meillassoux 1972). Thus, 'land takes on value and therefore becomes something material, something to be possessed' (Bender 1989: 83).

The progressive convergence of male and female activities in first agricultural and then industrial societies has obvious implications for archaeology. As the means of production of each sex coalesce, so the objects involved in that production are not the exclusive domain of male or female. Unless, that is, we make the simple assumption that the domestic sphere remains the exclusive product and property of women.

MATERIAL CULTURE AS THE MEDIUM OF JOINT ACTION

Can the archaeological record make a positive contribution to our understanding of the evolution of gender relations? To be sceptical, one might conclude that archaeologists can only consume the analyses of the life sciences, fitting the material culture into predetermined patterns. Clearly this is not a desirable situation, since, as I have tried to emphasize, biological factors constrain but do not determine action. How then, should we proceed? What criteria might effect a gender division in material culture? One position might be to suggest that superior strength gave males an exclusive ability to make stone tools. As Gero (1991) argues, this is unlikely; flint knapping is not simply a matter of strength but of skill. However, as Gero acknowledges, there are some contexts in which women's strength might be a disadvantage: quarrying raw materials, for example. Equally, producing some very large flakes might be beyond the strength of the 'average' female knapper (indeed, some Middle Palaeolithic flakes are equally beyond the strength of the average modern *male* knapper– Francis Wenban-Smith, pers. comm.). But physical strength alone is not a sufficient criterion for differentiating gender roles in tool production, any more than it is in the case of hunting.

Drawing on our previous discussions, then, it may be more sensible to seek domains where male and female pursued *autonomous* goals. As Gero asks, 'under what circumstances would females and males have separate charge of distinct production spheres . . . and under what circumstances would gender tasks be specialized and complementary, towards a shared production goal?' (1991: 173). Here, we must be careful to distinguish three domains within the *chaîne operatoire* of stone tool production and use: (1) procurement of raw materials, (2) production of artefacts and (3) use of artefacts. For there may well be autonomy of goals in some domains and not in others.

To begin in the middle, can one distinguish autonomous gender goals in the domain of tool production? Gero (1991) has suggested that flakes and utilized flakes, as opposed to 'fabricated' (*sensu* Böeda 1991) or retouched tools, may be the product of women's activities. Whilst this might apply for later periods, can it be supported for the Lower and Middle Palaeolithic? For the earliest technologies, the answer appears to be negative. The Oldowan, for example, is an exclusively flake-based technology. Similarly, one might suggest that the Acheulian is also a largely flake-based production, with the exception, of course, of the biface. But what was the biface for? There is no plausible reason to conclude that this was an exclusively male (= hunting?) artefact (or for that matter an exclusively female artefact).

Turning to Levalloisian and Mousterian industries, the same applies. Whilst the Levallois technique did produce retouched flakes and points, the entire *chaîne operatoire* can be seen as an 'economy of débitage' (Perlès 1991) in which the debitage by-products were themselves an integral product in their own right. Indeed, as far as the developed '*Levallois recourante*' technique is concerned, it is clear that the goal was to produce a series of flakes/blades from the same core (Böeda 1988, 1991). Before the Upper Palaeolithic then, we have little ground for inferring autonomous gender roles from the production of lithic artefacts. Were these tools used for hunting, making wooden spears, scavenging, processing meat and skins, or making digging sticks? Any or all might equally be the case and any conclusive evidence would, presumably, have been made of perishable materials. The essential problem is that for these early periods there is not enough differentiation or specialization of technical activities for us to detect gender-specific activities in the material cultural record.

We must conclude, then, that while biological and ethnographic evidence leads us to expect autonomous gender roles in the *use* of material culture by hominids preceding the appearance of modern humans, production itself cannot be differentiated except in those few cases where it could be shown to be a matter of brute strength. There is no *a priori* reason to assume a differentiation in the production of handaxes or Levallois flakes, scrapers, or other types of tool. However, the Upper Palaeolithic presents us with a slightly different situation. In the various stages of the Upper Palaeolithic we see a concern with very specific production strategies, including manufacture of projectile points, bone pins, needles, awls, probably specialized clothing, and decorative art. These strategies reflect increasing technical specialization, and it is becoming clear from some Magdalenian material that only some within a kin group or family practised stone tool production to the highest standards (Karlin *et al.* 1993).

Moreover, of course, the clear emphasis on projectile points, harpoons and spear-throwers makes it apparent that a distinct hunting technology had developed (and here I use the word 'hunting' advisedly). Considering what we know from biology and ethnography, we may infer here a clear gender differentiation in the *use* of artefacts, if we accept that women, on the whole, were not engaged in hunting large game. However, we cannot say the same for production. Were the stone tools made by men or women? Who made the bone tools? One might argue that where lithic production involved 'exotic' materials, male exchange networks furnished these materials, and indeed, this situation is seen ethnographically (Hamilton 1980, Petrequin and Petrequin 1993 – but see discussion in Gero 1991). Similarly, one might assume that bone and antler would be the products of male hunting. But we cannot assume that exclusivity of *procurement* determined production and use. For example, the Aurignacian lithic assemblage seems to be entirely concerned with scrapers, burins and some bladelets, with points and pins being made in bone and antler (Chazan, pers. comm., Mellars 1989) . Where 'exotic' lithic raw materials were used (and this was far from always the case) could we expect this to be an entirely male concern? Scrapers and burins could serve both male and female purposes in terms of end use: were the highly skilled knappers men, women or both?

Interestingly, ethnographic examples suggest that there is often a complex web of procurement and use in hunter-gatherer societies. In the eastern Western Desert of Australia (Hamilton 1980) women use grindstones to make a kind of bread from wild grasses; the grindstones are obtained through male exchange networks, but become exclusively female 'property', passing between generations along matrilines. Similarly, whilst men are almost exclusively the possessors of axes, women make their own stone tools and may borrow axes to facilitate their own production of wooden bowls. In Irian Jaya (Petrequin and Petrequin 1993) the procurement of raw materials is highly complex, depending on what sources of raw materials are locally available and what materials must be traded or physically collected from other territories. Here it is the case that whilst quarrying and roughing out of axes and adzes is open to most individuals in a group (where there are locally available raw materials), only a few have the skills required to produce the finished tool.

In general, then, increasing complementarity in subsistence activities is paralleled, and perhaps facilitated, by similar complementarity in the procurement and production of tools. Thus an increased specialization in techniques is accompanied by a loss of autonomy in the domains of procurement and production, where only some members of society can procure certain raw materials, and only some develop the requisite skills to engage in time-consuming technical activities. However, as I have already suggested, what we may be seeing in the Upper Palaeolithic and later hunter-gatherer societies is an increased integration of production and procurement but (despite the development of more specialized techniques) a continuation of the autonomy of gender roles in the domain of *use*.

By contrast, one may suggest, agricultural and industrial societies are characterized by an increasing integration of technological processes at all levels. As Ingold (1993a) suggests, technology (as opposed to technique) is an objectification in which individual autonomy of skill and know-how is taken away: the skilled author of technique becomes merely the operator of a technology. In this sense later prehistoric societies did not allow for an autonomy of gender activity: material culture became disengendered. Buildings, storage pits, ceramics, querns, etc. are not the tools of autonomous production, but the means of collective labour. Here I feel that Gero (1991), like most other authors in the *Engendering Archaeology* volume, is unjustified in falling back on the weak assumption that the domestic domain is entirely female. The division of labour that arises in domestic contexts is not the product of autonomy. Rather it is the integration of production through the use of *owned* material culture; of property.

We can speculate upon the exact effects of more specialized technologies in the Upper Palaeolithic. Would glacial conditions in Europe have curtailed women's autonomous subsistence activities, in that more stable, reliable gathered resources would have been more scarce? Perhaps, and yet the increasing diversity of subsistence activities in some areas (e.g. the use of shellfish – see Conkey 1991) might have limited the effects of this. Could more efficient hunting techniques have enabled the development of male social dominance through ritual activities (see Bender 1989)? Such a process has ethnographic analogues (Hamilton 1980) and might explain the appearance of 'aggregation sites' and information networks (Gamble 1980, 1982), Venus figurines and other art/ritual activities. But engendering the archaeological record is beset with problems. As material culture becomes more differentiated and specialized, to the extent that one might distinguish engendered activities, it necessarily becomes more integrated. Thus the distribution of skills and complementarity of roles comes to obscure or preclude any autonomous, engendered action.

CONCLUSIONS

The aim of this article has been to examine evidence of gender differentiation in human evolution and prehistory, and to ask whether archaeological evidence can make a positive contribution to our understanding. I contend that the potential is limited, but that the scope for enquiry would be even more marginal if, as some feminist writers argue, biological factors were to be excluded from discussion. In the course of this account I have argued that a basic biological pattern can be perceived: male and female hominids have been subject to different selective pressures, associated with a degree of sexual dimorphism. Yet I have also emphasized that this evolutionary heritage has no absolutely determining role on human behaviour; it represents only part of the resources with which we confront the world.

On the basis of these differences, I have suggested that male and female have pursued autonomous ecological strategies, associated with their different interests. These differences can be poorly understood by simple distinctions between hunting meat and gathering vegetables, and should rather be considered as a contrast between a female strategy centred on stable/reliable moderate yield resources, and a male preference for high-yield but unreliable resources. It is not a matter of what is sought (in terms of meat versus plant matter), but of how these resources are pursued and why.

Thus I have argued that gender roles are an example of the distinctively complementary nature of human activity. Only by an articulation between pre-existing social and ecological relations can an economy come into existence, in which distributed skills and labour form the commonwealth of society. I have suggested that in hunter-gatherer societies this does not constitute a 'division of labour', since individuals (male or female) are free to collect subsistence material from the natural world, but are obliged to distribute their products within the social world. That is to say that resources are not owned, but rather under the 'stewardship' of social groups (Ingold 1993b). It is only through social obligations, such as those arising from polygyny, that women's labour can be appropriated by men. Conversely, I have argued that in sedentary societies the ownership of land creates a situation in which both distribution and production are controlled by social obligations. For here land becomes the common object of production for male and female irrespective of whose labour is involved.

When considering the archaeological record, I propose we accept some fairly negative conclusions. Whilst our biological heritage fossilizes certain evolutionary trajectories, and whilst the ethnography gives us some idea of gender roles, archaeology can, in my view, tell us little that we don't already know from these other sources. I have argued that, in order to engender material culture, we must be able to demonstrate an autonomy of male and female activities. However, since the diversity of material culture necessary to record this autonomy depends on a differentiation of techniques, and such a differentiation of technique in turn requires increasingly integrated and complementary roles, there is limited opportunity to detect autonomous, engendered techniques. Here one exception may be in more 'complex' hunting and gathering societies where integration of material culture production takes place, whilst autonomy of subsistence use continues. Perhaps other similar situations can be identified, but the degree to which material culture becomes objectified property in later periods would appear to make this extremely difficult. Many writers simply fall back on traditional distinctions between the domestic/non-domestic roles. But, I suggest, the commonwealths of prehistoric peoples were not as we have supposed.

ACKNOWLEDGEMENTS

I thank Steve Shennan and James Steele for their invitation to participate in this project and their comments on this chapter. Likewise I would thank the following for discussions and/or encouragement at various times; Michael Chazan, Clive Gamble, Jean-Claude Gardin, Linda Hurcombe, Tim Ingold, Siân Jones, Andy Lock, Grahame Richards, Wiktor Stoczkowski and Francis Wenban-Smith. I also thank the Fondation Fyssen, whose grant has given me time to write this. As always the ideas and opinions expressed herein are entirely my own responsibility.

REFERENCES

Bender, B. (1989) 'The roots of inequality.' In D. Miller, M. Rowlands and C. Tilley (eds) *Domination and Resistance*, pp. 83–95. London: Unwin Hyman.

Binford, L.R. (1985) 'Human ancestors: changing views of their behaviour.' *Journal of Archaeological Anthropology* 4: 292–327.

Böeda, E. (1988) 'Le concept laminaire: rupture et filiation avec le concept Levallois.' In M. Otte (ed.) *L'Homme de Néandertal. v.8. La Mutation*, pp. 41–59. Liège: Université de Liège.

Böeda, E. (1991) 'Approche de la variabilité des systèmes de production lithique des industries du Paléolithique Inférieur et Moyen: Chronique d'une variabilité attendue.' *Techniques et Culture* 17–18: 37–79.

Byatt, A.S. (1990) *Possession*. London: Vintage.

Clutton-Brock, T.H. (1983) 'Selection in relation to sex.' In D.S. Bendall (ed.) *Evolution from Molecules to Men*, pp. 457–482. Cambridge: Cambridge University Press

Clutton-Brock, T.H. and Harvey, P.H. (1977) 'Primate ecology and social organization.' *Journal of the Zoological Society of London* 183: 1–39.

Conkey, M. (1991) 'Contexts of action, contexts for power: material culture and gender in the Magdalenian.' In J. Gero and M. Conkey (eds) *Engendering Archaeology. Women and Prehistory*, pp. 57–92. Oxford: Blackwell.

Conkey, M. and Gero, J. (1991) 'Tensions, pluralities and engendering archaeology: an introduction to women and prehistory.' In J. Gero and M. Conkey (eds) *Engendering Archaeology. Women and Prehistory*, pp. 3–31. Oxford: Blackwell.

Dahlberg, F. (ed.) (1981) *Woman the Gatherer*. New Haven: Yale University Press.

Diamond, J. (1991) *The Rise and Fall of the Third Chimpanzee*. London: Vintage.

Engels, F. (1972) *The Origin of the Family, Private Property and the State*. London: Lawrence and Wishart.

Estioko-Griffin, A. and Griffin, P.B. (1981) 'Woman the hunter: the Agta.' In F. Dahlberg (ed.) *Woman the Gatherer*, pp. 121–152. New Haven, CT: Yale University Press.

Flannery, R. (1935) 'The position of woman among the Eastern Cree.' *Primitive Man* 8: 81–86.

Gamble, C.S. (1980) 'Information exchange in the Palaeolithic.' *Nature* 283: 522–523.

Gamble, C.S. (1982) 'Interaction and alliance in Palaeolithic society.' *Man* (n.s.) 17: 92–107.

Gero, J. (1991) 'Genderlithics: women's roles in stone tool production.' In J. Gero and M. Conkey (eds) *Engendering Archaeology. Women and Prehistory*, pp. 163–193. Oxford: Blackwell.

Goodale, J.C. (1971) *Tiwi Wives*. Seattle: University of Washington.

Goodall, J. Van Lawick (1971) *In the Shadow of Man*. London: Fontana.

Hamilton, A. (1980) 'Dual social systems: technology, labour and women's secret rites in the eastern Western Desert of Australia.' *Oceania* 51: 4–19.

Hamilton, M.E. (1984) 'Revising evolutionary narratives: a consideration of alternative assumptions about sexual selection and competition for mates.' *American Anthropologist* 86: 651–662.

Ingold, T. (1980) 'The principles of individual autonomy and the collective appropriation of nature.' In *Proceedings of the 2nd International Conference on Hunting and Gathering Societies 19 to 24 September 1980*. Quebec: Université Laval, Département d'Anthropologie.

Ingold, T. (1986) *The Appropriation of Nature*. Manchester: Manchester University Press.

Ingold, T. (1993a) 'Tool use, sociality and intelligence.' In K.R. Gibson and T. Ingold (eds) *Tools, Language and Cognition in Human Evolution*, pp. 429–446. Cambridge: Cambridge University Press.

Ingold, T. (1993b) 'Tools and hunter-gatherers.' In A. Berthelet and J. Chavaillon (eds) *The Use of Tools by Human and Non-human Primates*. Oxford: Clarendon.

Jennes, D. (1922) 'The life of the Copper Eskimos.' *Report of the Canadian Arctic Expedition 1913–1916 Vol 12*. Ottawa: Acland.

Kano, T. (1992) *The Last Ape: Pygmy Chimpanzee Behaviour and Ecology*. Stanford: Stanford University Press.

Karlin, C., Ploux, S., Bodu, P. and Pigeot, N. (1993) 'Some socio-economic aspects of the knapping process among groups of hunter-gatherers in the Paris Basin area.' In A. Berthelet and J. Chavaillon (eds) *The Use of Tools by Human and Non-human Primates*, pp. 318–337. Oxford: Clarendon.

Keefe, T. (1993) 'The flawed bible.' *Times Higher Education Supplement* 1064: 19.

Knight, C. (1991) *Blood Relations*. New Haven, CT: Yale University Press.

Landes, R. (1938) *The Ojibwa Women*. New York: AMS Press.

Lee, R.B. and DeVore, I. (eds) (1968) *Man the Hunter*. Chicago: Aldine.

Lovejoy, C.O. (1981) 'The origin of man.' *Science* 211: 341–350.

Meillassoux, C. (1972) 'From reproduction to production.' *Economy and Society* 1: 93–105.

Mellars, P. (1989) 'Major issues in the emergence of modern humans.' *Current Anthropology* 30: 349–385.

Misonda, F.B. (1991) 'The significance of modern hunter-gatherers in the study of early human behaviour.' In R.A. Foley (ed.) *The Origins of Human Behaviour*. London: Unwin Hyman.

Perlès, C. (1991) 'Économie des matières premières et économie du débitage: deux conceptions opposées?' In C. Perlès (ed.) *25 Ans D'Études Technologiques en Préhistoire*, pp. 36–45. Juan-les-Pins: Éditions APDCA.

Petrequin, P. and Petrequin, A.M. (1993) 'From polished stone tool to sacred axe: the axes of the Danis of Irian Jaya, Indonesia.' In A. Berthelet and J. Chavaillon (eds) *The Use of Tools by Human and Non-human Primates*, pp. 359–379. Oxford: Clarendon.

Reynolds, P.C. (1993) 'The complementation theory of language and tool use.' In K.R. Gibson and T. Ingold (eds) *Tools, Language and Cognition in Human Evolution*, pp. 429–446. Cambridge: Cambridge University Press.

Smuts, R.W. (1989) 'Behaviour depends on context.' *Behavioural and Brain Sciences* 12: 33–34.

Stoczkowski, W. (1991) 'De l'origine de la division sexuelle du travail: quelques fossiles vivants de l'imaginaire.' *Les Nouvelles de l'Archéologie* 44: 15–18.

Tanner, N.M. (1981) *On Becoming Human*. Cambridge: Cambridge University Press.

Testart, A. (1986) *Essai sur les fondaments de la division sexuelle du travail chez les chasseurs-cueilleurs*. Paris: Editions de l'Ecole des Hautes Etudes en Sciences Sociales.

Vygotskii, L.S. (1934/1986) *Thought and Language*. Boston: MIT Press.

Washburn, S.L. (1960) 'Tools and human evolution.' *Scientific American* 203: 3–15.

Zeller, A.C. (1987) 'A role for children in hominid evolution.' *Man* (n.s.) 22: 528–557.

Zihlman, A.L. (1981) 'Women as shapers of human adaptation.' In F. Dahlberg (ed.) *Woman the Gatherer*, pp. 75–120. New Haven, CT: Yale University Press.

PART IV

COGNITION AND CULTURAL DYNAMICS IN MODERN HUMAN SOCIETIES

Editors' note

In this final section, four contributors locate human cultural capacities and the micro-scale dynamics of cultural evolution in theoretical and comparative perspective. But whereas a conventional social science model might presume that language and encephalization have simply liberated human behaviour from the constraints of genetic determination, these authors point to some evolutionary *constraints* on human social cognition and cultural learning.

Shennan suggests that social inequality has been an enduring and pervasive feature of foraging societies, and links this both to the dynamics of social co-operation in large groups and to the role of cultural authority in reproducing persistent behavioural traditions. He suggests that by the early Upper Palaeolithic, symbolic reproduction of ritual and artistic traditions had evolved in a runaway transmission process which may have become partly decoupled from the adaptive interests of social group members themselves.

Dunbar proposes that symbolic language evolved from mechanisms for servicing social relations in large groups, and suggests that a natural cognitive human group size of up to about 150 individuals can be seen empirically across cultures, reflecting limitations of the human brain's capacity for monitoring relationships. He suggests that the same 'magic number' can be found in analysis of kinship network structures.

Chance argues that creativity and exploratory behaviour, themselves promoters of cognitive development, are constrained by the structure of social ties within social groups. He proposes a set of parallels with 'hedonic' and 'agonic' social systems of non-human primates. Thus while Shennan proposes that robust cultural transmission of symbolic traditions is associated with hierarchy formation, chance contends that creativity (and by implication the quality of individual learning) is suppressed in social systems characterized by authoritarianism and a centripetal dominance rank.

Finally, Cullen develops the argument that cultural transmission can evolve virus-like by its own rules, given a 'host community' of human agents linked into dense interaction networks. His model invites further research on the epidemiology of runaway processes of cultural diffusion, and their relationship to group structure, mobility patterns, social motivations, and the extent to which creativity has been traded off against structures of symbolic authority in human societies at different times and places (as they have left their traces in the archaeological and historical records).

CHAPTER FOURTEEN

SOCIAL INEQUALITY AND THE TRANSMISSION OF CULTURAL TRADITIONS IN FORAGER SOCIETIES

STEPHEN SHENNAN

The object of this chapter is to sketch out the basis of an archaeological approach to examining the interrelationships between cultural traditions, inequality and the maintenance of social groups through time. The approach is intended to be of general relevance, but the discussion will be concentrated on the anthropology of foraging societies, since, for a variety of reasons, these are generally agreed to be of most relevance to providing a perspective for the analysis and discussion of inferred patterns of long-term human evolution.

The idea that there are links between patterns of social inequality and how groups define and organize themselves is familiar enough, but that these should be connected in some way to cultural traditions is perhaps less obvious. The fact that it now seems a worthwhile issue to raise can be ascribed to the development of what Durham (1990, 1992) has called 'evolutionary culture theory', in effect the study of 'cultural descent with modification', based on recent accounts of the mechanisms of cultural transmission and the factors affecting it (Cavalli-Sforza and Feldman 1981, Boyd and Richerson 1985, and see Introduction). However, with the exception of a recent paper by Aldenderfer (1993), the subject of hierarchy and inequality has not been much discussed in this context, even though debates about their nature and extent are regarded by many as central to any understanding of long-term social change. The aim of this chapter is to outline a model which suggests that hierarchy and the cultural transmission process are in some respects closely linked, even in foraging societies, which have tended to be seen as relatively egalitarian.

CULTURAL TRADITIONS

It has long been argued that what differentiates humans from other animals is the existence of cultural traditions, which mean that cultural responses to change have largely superseded genetic ones. The presumption has always been that such cultural traditions were adaptive, in that they enabled people to survive more successfully, and therefore gave a selective advantage in terms of reproductive success over populations which did not have such traditions. A great deal of attention has been devoted to identifying the functional-adaptive role that particular traditions, for example, the production of artefacts, might have had, but the processes by which they are handed on from one (cultural) generation to the next have been considered self-evident and unproblematic. However, the cultural learning on which traditions depend has costs as well as benefits and until recently there has been little attempt to evaluate these and their implications. It turns out that in some circumstances there will be selection for cultural learning even though it does not give any adaptive advantage over trial-and-error learning (see Rogers 1989 and Introduction). Moreover, a variety of factors affect the process of transmitting knowledge from one generation to the next which are largely independent of any adaptive role the knowledge may have. For these reasons the processes of cultural learning and the factors which affect them cannot be left out of any consideration of the role of cultural products in human evolution.

The view taken here is that cultural transmission involves a *sui generis* set of processes, including language transmission, which have the effect of giving cultural attributes a considerable degree of independence from any specific set of bearers of those attributes (Cavalli-Sforza and Feldman 1981, Boyd and Richerson 1985, Shennan 1989, 1991, see also Cullen, this volume, and the introduction to this section). Given that this is the case, the object of this chapter is to examine some relationships between the social arrangements of populations and the transmission of certain kinds of cultural information, beyond the obvious point that social arrangements have an impact on the biological survival and reproductive success of populations, and thus of the cultural attributes associated with them.

EGALITARIANISM AND AUTHORITY IN FORAGER SOCIETIES

From the beginnings of the study of the development of human societies until very recently, foragers have been regarded as the baseline of human social organization (cf. Gamble 1992), from which subsequent social 'complexity' developed. This tendency for such societies to be seen as a rhetorical antithesis to our own reached its apogee in the characterization of the !Kung Bushmen as a totally egalitarian society without any forms of institutionalized leadership, characterized by an ethic of sharing and canonized by Sahlins (1968) as 'the original affluent society'.

More recently, the idea of forager egalitarianism has been taken up by authors interested in developing Darwinian models of the evolution of human social behaviour. Thus, Erdal and Whiten (1994) argue that what they regard as the universality of egalitarianism in forager societies is an ancient evolved pattern contrasting with the hierarchical patterning of other primate societies, and suggest that there must have been a fitness advantage to individuals in resisting domination by other group members but not attempting to achieve domination themselves. Erdal and Whiten propose that egalitarianism may have been associated with the appearance of big-game hunting and the importance of sharing, seen as deriving from the desirability of dividing up large meat packages. A similar point is made by Boehm (1993), who argues for the existence of 'reverse-dominance hierarchies' in which a strong anti-dominance ethic prevails, again suggesting that adult males in particular give up their individual possibilities of domination over others in order to be certain that no one may dominate them, and that egalitarian political arrangements derive not from special ecological or social structural circumstances but from moral sanctions (but contrast Gulbrandsen 1991). Knauft (1991) too has argued for a strong tendency towards egalitarian behaviour over a significant proportion of human evolution, proposing that a significant primate tendency towards social dominance was not extinguished but effectively constrained by strong counter-measures during much of this period, until the appearance of 'complex hunter-gatherer' adaptations relatively recently.

In fact, it has become increasingly apparent since the early 1980s that assertions of forager egalitarianism are much overdone. It is not simply that 'complex hunter-gatherers' (Price and Brown 1985) emerge in later pre-history with a subsistence system based on sedentism and storage, and thus a foundation for material inequalities, or that transport technology makes a very significant difference to the possibilities of material accumulation among foraging groups, as Burch (1988) has shown in the case of the role of the *umiak* and the dog sled among the Inuit groups of north-west Alaska. More important is the impact of so-called revisionist accounts of the Bushmen and similar foraging groups (Wilmsen 1989, Shott 1992). Conceptually central to this discussion is the idea of 'encapsulation' (Woodburn 1988), which in turn depends on a distinction made earlier by Woodburn (1980, 1982) between immediate-return and delayed-return foraging systems:

> An immediate-return system is one in which activities oriented to the present (rather than to the past or the future) are stressed; in which people deploy their labour to obtain food and other resources which will be used on the day they were obtained or casually over the days that follow . . . in which people do not hold valued assets which represent a yield, a return for labour

applied over time, or valued assets which are held and managed in a way which resembles and has similar social implications to delayed yields on labour; in which people are systematically disengaged from assets, from the potential in assets for creating dependency.

A delayed-return system is one in which, in contrast, activities are oriented to the past and the future as well as to the present; in which people hold rights over valued assets of some sort, which either represent a yield, a return for labour applied over time, or, if not, are held and managed in a way which resembles and has similar social implications to delayed yields on labour.

(Woodburn 1988: 32)

In his discussion of 'encapsulation' Woodburn raises the issue of whether the immediate-return system and associated egalitarianism of the !Kung, the Mbuti or the Hadza are not a response to the fact that their societies have had hundreds of years of contact with outside societies and are, in effect, encapsulated within them. On this view, the existence of adjacent agricultural and pastoralist groups and the establishment of relations with them would have led on the one hand to the demise of existing delayed-return foraging systems and on the other to the emergence of oppositional forms of organization. In this way sharing and egalitarian levelling mechanisms analogous to the egalitarian solidarity present in some working-class or millenarian movements would have developed, as a reaction against the possibility that some members of the group might want to increase their power by establishing alliances with outsiders, who in turn might see this as a possibility of exercising control over the foraging group (Woodburn 1988: 62). In the event, Woodburn concludes that encapsulation is insufficient as a general explanation of immediate-return systems, which have probably long been a viable social form, but that in no sense can they be considered as a universal social evolutionary baseline; rather, in fact, that the past saw a greater variety of systems, among which delayed-return systems with their inequalities were certainly more frequent.

Woodburn's analysis raises doubts about 'egalitarianism' as an 'ancient evolved pattern' and may be developed further. Most of the arguments in favour of forager egalitarianism centre on the importance of food-sharing as evidence of equality (e.g. Boehm 1993, Kent 1993), and when they acknowledge the existence of hierarchically organized forager societies account for these in terms of ecologically specific possibilities for the control of material resources. While the relevance of material resources cannot be denied, the assumption that they are the only resources that matter arises from an entrenched view derived from nineteenth-century analyses of social class that material disparities are the only significant ones, so the lack of concern with them on the part of most foragers, combined with the importance of food-sharing, means that they must be egalitarian.

Such arguments neglect two important areas crucial to any evolutionary account. In the first place, there is some evidence of differential reproductive success, at least among males, related to hunting prestige (Hill and Kaplan 1993). Second, and much more important from the point of view of the argument presented here, there are inequalities in access to ritual 'knowledge' in foraging societies. Such 'knowledge' (even if it is not construed as having a large propositional content, Bloch 1974, Boyer 1990), and differential access to it, play a central social role. In many such societies the transmission of ritual 'knowledge' and control over it through initiation and other rites are one of the main social focuses of the people concerned. In fact, the control of cultural transmission of such knowledge is often the only legitimate locus for the generation of inequality among the members of forager societies, not the material goods or food with which anthropologists have been so obsessed (cf. Giddens 1984: 260–262, on authoritative versus allocative power resources and the importance of information storage). Furthermore, in some contexts such control is actually hereditary, again in complete contrast to what are usually asserted as the key characteristics of forager societies.

RITUAL AND INEQUALITY IN FORAGER SOCIETIES: SOME EXAMPLES

Examples of the link between ritual and inequality in forager societies are widespread. Thus, Myers (1988), in a discussion of Pintupi land 'owner-ship' in Australia, argues that 'ownership' is control over stories, objects and ritual associated with mythological ancestors at a particular place, and because such knowledge is highly valued and vital to social reproduction men seek to gain it and be associated with its display and transmission:

> From the Pintupi point of view, the emphasis is just as much on the social production of persons who can 'hold' the country, that is, on initiating young men and teaching them the ritual knowledge necessary to look after the country, as it is on getting the country. The Pintupi image of social continuity is effectively one in which 'country' as an object is passed down – 'given' – from generation to generation. The Pintupi regard this 'giving' as a contribution to the substance and identity of the recipient, a kind of transmission of one gener-ation's (or person's) identity to the next. By learning about the Dreaming and seeing the rituals, one's very being is altered . . . . Certainly, while younger recipients are supposed to reciprocate the gift of knowledge – hunting meat for those who give the knowledge and deferring to them – they cannot really repay what has been given . . . Pintupi stress that men must hold the Law and pass it on. In fact, men are enormously concerned to pass on their knowledge and their identification with places to their 'sons' and 'sister's sons'.

> (1988: 66)

But even among those claiming identity with a particular place only a certain number control the relevant rituals and decide whether particular individuals should be 'taught', a privilege easily granted to close kin but not necessarily to others: 'With its origin in the Dreaming, "country" constitutes a form of valued knowledge that is esoteric, transmitted . . . to younger men, but restricted in access' (1988: 67), although it may also be exchanged between equal men.

Even among the Mardujarra in Western Australia, where ecological conditions are such that significant secular inequalities do not emerge, there are relations of inequality in the sphere of ritual and specifically initiation:

> In the Mardujarra case, the control exerted by older men over their younger counterparts is a generalised one. It is based on the older men's monopoly of esoteric knowledge, which will be transmitted only if young men conform to the dictates of the Law, and are willing to hunt meat in continuing reciprocal payment for the major secrets that are progressively revealed to them. . .
>
> What is being indelibly imprinted on the novices is the imperative that they ensure, through conformity and active participation in the religious life, the continued release of power from the realm of the Dreaming into the physical and social world.
>
> (Tonkinson 1988)

Again, we have the same emphasis on the importance of transmitting the tradition, associated with relations of authority. Even among the Hadza, one of his archetypal 'immediate-return' societies, Woodburn notes, 'the initiated men's group maintains important privileges over certain joints of meat of large game animals. These privileges are linked with exclusive possession of secret sacred knowledge and ritual to which all women and young men are denied access' (Woodburn 1988: 21).

The same point can be made in relation to the foragers of the North American Great Basin. As described by Julian Steward (e.g. 1936, 1938), they are generally regarded as one of the classic egalitarian societies. However, Whitley (1994) presents a different view. Not only was there inequality between men and women, but also among men, in particular between those who were shamans, and thus had access to supernatural power, and those who weren't. Village and band headmen were almost always shamans, and shamanism, like headship, was largely hereditary:

> It was only through the acquisition of shamanistic power that men could truly become political actors and gain prestige and status in Numic society. In turn, this advantaged them in a number of ways: women desired such men as preferred marriage partners, and the population at large respected them, largely out of fear of their potentially malevolent [power]. And in that shamanistic power was partly inherited, but in any case limited to a small segment of the population (estimated at about 2%), it is apparent that a very restricted, incipient elite group, comprised of shaman/headmen, existed within the ostensibly egalitarian Numic society.
>
> (Whitley 1994: 366–367)

A related argument has been developed at length by Riches (1992) in his discussion of the role and significance of shamanism. He points out that 'the cosmologies of nomadic hunting and gathering societies are predominantly shamanistic' (1992: 383) and associates the presence of shamanism with relatively decentralized forms of organization, where descent principles are not strongly emphasized. However, this is not to say that they are thoroughly egalitarian. Among the Canadian Inuit on whom his discussion is mainly focused, although superior hunting ability is not allowed to form a basis for the development of social inequalities, the role of shaman does provide such a basis. The success or failure of hunters is seen as depending on the community's relations with the spirit world and maintaining these in good order depends on the observation of taboos. The shaman is the mediator between these two worlds and has the responsibility for the cultural evaluation process in terms of which some actions are regarded as taboo. The role is seen as a highly skilled one requiring a specialist and the skills are passed on from expert to novice through an apprenticeship. As a result of his mediating position with the spirit world, the shaman has power, privileges and position which are unavailable to anyone else. Riches argues that such cultural forms as taboos and systems of classification are sustained through the strategic work of individuals, in this case shamans; that is to say, they have a key role in determining what are approved and disapproved modes of behaviour, and in transmitting these and the cultural framework on which they are based.

AUTHORITY AND CULTURAL STABILITY

The kind of situation described in the previous section, in which there is a strong association between the transmission of ritual knowledge and relations of authority has been contrasted by Brunton (1989) with the observed cultural instability of certain tropical forest egalitarian foraging societies. These are immediate-return or encapsulated societies in Woodburn's terms (see p. 367) and are indeed strictly egalitarian, in that there is an automatic entitlement to equality of social outcomes. Such societies, tend to be culturally fluid in many respects, Brunton argues, susceptible to acculturation and relatively limited in their collective representations. The Paliyan, for example, have no formalized bodies of knowledge, their rituals are highly variable and may not be performed at all; their knowledge is based on personal experience rather than collective representations and their transmission (Brunton 1989: 676). This arises because of the structural nature of genuine egalitarianism, since it can never provide a basis for ensuring a correct version or interpretation of that which is communicated. Any attempt to distinguish what is valuable from what is not requires an act of evaluation, which in itself implies inequality:

> To the extent that evaluation, and exclusion on the basis of evaluation, takes place, egalitarianism is compromised. To the extent that egalitarianism is

thoroughgoing, such cultures can be little more than heaps of randomly associated elements, whose persistence is always fortuitous.

(Brunton 1989: 678)

On this view, egalitarianism can only be maintained by according little value to cultural products, which indeed accounts for the general indifference to such products in the egalitarian societies Brunton discusses. In delayed-return systems on the other hand, as we have seen, 'inter-generational inequality, as well as inequality between household heads in terms of power, wealth and status are commonly present' (Brunton 1989: 674). These circumstances not only presuppose social group continuity, they are also closely linked with cultural continuity in ritual and other spheres since, as we have seen, the transmission process is often the locus of inequality and strong cultural evaluation takes place; furthermore, group continuity itself provides a better basis for the consistent transmission of particular sets of social practices than a situation in which large numbers of individuals move at frequent intervals from one group to another (cf. Braun 1991). In summary, what is being postulated here, other things being equal, is a relationship between the strength of authority relations and the persistence and linkage of cultural elements, and another relationship between group continuity and cultural continuity (cf. Douglas 1978 and her concepts of 'grid' and 'group', where social arrangements related to the importance of the group as a unit and to within-group, usually hierarchical, distinctions, are similarly seen as having important cultural consequences). Group continuity in this context refers to the continued co-association of a group of people and their descendants over a period of time.

Such a suggestion raises interesting issues for the study of cultural and social continuity and change in the evolution of human societies. If some cultural feature emerged which had the effect of encouraging the process of cultural evaluation, through which some cultural variants rather than others are designated as acceptable or even mandatory, and of encouraging a positive evaluation of itself as acceptable or mandatory in particular, it would spread at the expense of others in the same sphere of relevance which did not have this effect. Furthermore, the potential could exist for a runaway process analogous to sexual selection, in which the development of authority relations encouraging cultural evaluation and accurate transmission went hand in hand with the selection of cultural attributes encouraging authority relations, at least until some selective pressure from elsewhere cut in (see Figure 14.1). The links we have seen above between inequality and transmission processes in foraging societies are in keeping with these suggestions; other things being equal, cultural attributes not linked in this way would generally be less successful in terms of their reproduction through cultural generations.

But a further aspect of groups relevant to their continuity must also be considered. The possibility of group fission in the face of co-operation

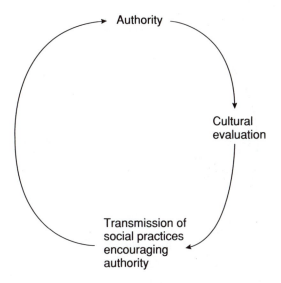

Figure 14.1 Links between authority and cultural/ritual transmission

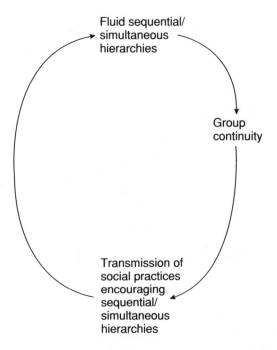

Figure 14.2 Links between group continuity and cultural/ritual transmission

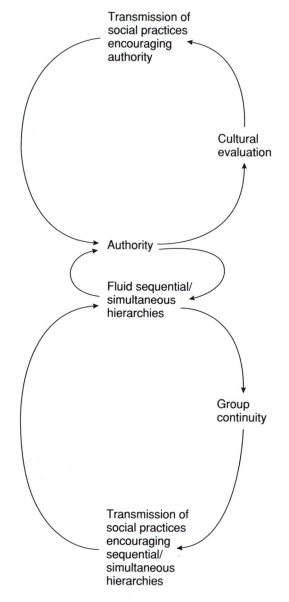

Transmission of
social practices
encouraging
authority

Cultural
evaluation

Authority

Fluid sequential/
simultaneous
hierarchies

Group
continuity

Transmission of
social practices
encouraging
sequential/
simultaneous
hierarchies

Figure 14.3 Authority, group continuity and cultural/ritual transmission linked together

problems is always present. Simulation studies of the maintenance of co-operation in the face of social dilemmas (e.g. Glance and Huberman 1994a) have shown that it will be promoted in situations where individuals have a long future expectation of co-operation and where groups are structured flexibly but hierarchically; not necessarily in the manner of a conventional social hierarchy but in the sense that members of a large group do not interact equally with one another. They interact closely with members of a small group and small groups interact with one another via representative individuals and organizations (Glance and Huberman 1994b, cf. Johnson 1982). Groups based on such forms of organization will tend to be perpetuated through time more successfully than those which are not and thus so will their particular sets of cultural practices. Furthermore, those practices will be more successful which themselves are conducive to this form of group organization and thus to group continuity. So here too a positive feedback loop may be created – in this case between cultural practices and group continuity (Figure 14.2). This loop may in turn be linked to the authority and inequality loop discussed above, in that those who are authoritative guardians of cultural traditions are also likely to be the group representatives in the interactions between groups discussed above, more often than not older males (Figure 14.3).

However, the two linked loops will only be mutually reinforcing up to a point, in that the unbridled expansion of authority and inequality may be detrimental to some group members' interests and thus create tensions which lead, for example, to group fission (cf. Aldenderfer 1993, Steele, chapter 4 this volume). How such incompatibilities play themselves out over time will be a contingent process, dependent among other things on how closely particular attributes are tied to particular groups by processes such as conformant transmission (Boyd and Richerson 1985; see also Introduction to this volume and Editors' Note). In addition to group fission, other possibilities include the destruction of authority and the maintenance of an equilibrium in which negative feedbacks emerge to counter the continuing development of authority beyond a certain point. In all cases there will be implications for the fidelity with which transmission occurs and for the content which is transmitted, both of which will in turn have an impact on the social processes, because of the existence of the links described above.

CONCLUSION

The argument of this chapter may be summarized as follows. I have tried to show, following the work of Woodburn and others, that many if not most forager societies are not as egalitarian as traditionally assumed (cf. also Flanagan 1989, Paynter 1989). The traditional view derives from a belief that inequality must be based on differential access to material resources, of which foragers, for good reasons, possess little, or to food, which is largely shared and thus again provides no basis for inequality. In fact, the locus of inequality is the cultural transmission of ritual knowledge and the link between inequality and transmission has runaway properties. Authority which defines the 'correct' version is important for transmission and at the same time cultural attributes which act to enhance authority tend to be preferentially adopted; authority and conformant transmission in the sphere of ritual go together. However, in the context of foraging societies there are usually fairly strict ecological limits to such processes, arising, for example, from the importance of mobility, which mean that inequalities will not easily extend to other spheres (cf. Aldenderfer 1993).

But further limits arise from the fact that group continuity will also have a positive feedback relationship with successful cultural transmission: group continuity will be conducive to fidelity of transmission but attributes which encourage group continuity will increase their own chance of success. Such groups may well be genetically related sets of individuals and their descendants through time but need be no more than the set of people subscribing to a particular ritual tradition through conformant transmission.

Up to a point, hierarchy, group continuity and successful transmission will all be positively associated with one another. However, as Aldenderfer (1993) among others as pointed out, there comes a point when the growth of ritually based hierarchy and authority becomes incompatible with the maintenance of group continuity, because it leads to group fission, which has the further effect of increasing the probability of cultural loss through small sample drift effects. It was only with the rise of the state that this incompatibility was overcome.

This line of argument accords cultural transmission the importance it might be expected to have if cultural traditions are so central to the evolutionary success of the human species and acknowledges the fact that cultural attributes, or 'memes' as Dawkins (1976) calls them, are not just aspects of people's phenotypes as 'interactors' but have their own lineages as 'replicators', more independent of their bearers than in the genetic case because of the asymmetries of cultural transmission (Boyd and Richerson 1985, Cullen, this volume). However, as with biological evolution, both 'interactors' and 'replicators' are necessary entities in any account of evolutionary change; neither can be reduced to the other (cf. Mitchell 1987).

In some respects the argument presented here is similar to that made by Aldenderfer (1993), who also accords ritual a priority as a basis for hierarchy in foraging societies and sees hierarchy and inequality as being extended to other spheres of life as a result of various kinds of circumscription processes. However, despite his professed adherence to the cultural evolutionary framework adopted here, he sees ritual from a more traditional anthropological perspective in which ritual is a source of both individual and group benefits and of ideological manipulation, and does not assign the active role to the transmission process and the cultural replicators themselves which is at the core of this chapter.

When might such processes have arisen? The answer surely must be the Upper Palaeolithic, when the evidence for ritual and artistic traditions in the archaeological record first becomes compelling. Although there are indications of symbolic/ritual behaviour before this (see e.g. Hayden 1993), they are infrequent and isolated (cf. Rolland 1990). However, as Hayden (1993) argues, we should be careful about assuming a qualitative break between the Upper Palaeolithic and what went before. If the origins of symbolism are associated with the kinds of runaway transmission processes discussed here, we would expect the chronological trend of its uptake to be sigmoid in form, with an earlier stage in which ritual and symbolic behaviour were low in frequency and a later one in which they were widely prevalent, separated by a relatively short phase of exponential growth. In terms of the degree of resolution of archaeological evidence, points near the beginning and the end of this single trend could easily be taken as relating to two qualitatively different states, before or after some event or state change in a different system, such as hominid biology.

But why did it not occur earlier? The answer may be connected with points made by Cullen and Gamble elsewhere in this volume. Successful transmission is partly a function of population density and encounter frequency: when populations are small, there is a high probability of random loss of cultural attributes. It may be that it was only at this time that population densities in many regions were sufficiently high that ritual traditions, which may have started many times before, had a chance to take hold, while the greater spatial extent of contact which Gamble (this volume) documents for the Upper Palaeolithic indicates that the potential for spreading such traditions now existed to an extent previously unparalleled.

ACKNOWLEDGEMENTS

An earlier version of this paper was presented at the LSE conference on Evolution and the Human Sciences in June 1993 and I am grateful for comments and questions on that occasion, in particular from James Woodburn. I also wish to thank Clive Gamble and James Steele for their critical comments on an earlier draft, although I have not been able to follow up all their suggestions.

REFERENCES

Aldenderfer, M. (1993) 'Ritual, hierarchy and change in foraging societies.' *Journal of Anthropological Archaeology* 12: 1–40.

Bloch, M. (1974) 'Symbols, song, dance and features of articulation: is religion an extreme form of traditional authority?' *Archives Européennes de Sociologie* 15: 55–81.

Boehm, C. (1993) 'Egalitarian behaviour and reverse dominance hierarchy.' *Current Anthropology* 34: 227–254.

Boyd, R. and Richerson, P.J. (1985) *Culture and the Evolutionary Process.* Chicago: University of Chicago Press.

Boyer, P. (1990) *Tradition as Truth and Communication*. Cambridge: Cambridge University Press.

Braun, D.P. (1991) 'Are there cross-cultural regularities in tribal social practices?' In S.A. Gregg (ed.) *Between Bands and States*, pp. 423–444. Carbondale: Center for Archaeological Investigations, Southern Illinois University at Carbondale.

Brunton, R. (1989) 'The cultural instability of egalitarian societies.' *Man* (n.s.) 24: 673–681.

Burch, E.S. (1988) 'Modes of exchange in north-west Alaska.' In T. Ingold, D. Riches and J. Woodburn (eds) *Hunters and Gatherers, Volume 2: Property, Power and Ideology*, pp. 95–109. Oxford: Berg.

Cavalli-Sforza, L.L. and Feldman, M.W. (1981) *Cultural Transmission and Evolution: A Quantitative Approach*. Princeton: Princeton University Press.

Dawkins, R. (1976) *The Selfish Gene*. Oxford: Oxford University Press.

Durham, W.H. (1990) 'Advances in evolutionary culture theory.' *Annual Review of Anthropology* 19: 187–210.

Durham, W.H. (1992) 'Applications of evolutionary culture theory.' *Annual Review of Anthropology* 21: 331–355.

Douglas, M. (1978) *Cultural Bias*. London: Royal Anthropological Institute (Occasional Paper No. 35).

Erdal, D. and Whiten, A. (1994) 'On human egalitarianism: an evolutionary product of Machiavellian status escalation.' *Current Anthropology* 35: 175–178.

Flanagan, J. (1989) 'Hierarchy in simple "egalitarian" societies.' *Annual Review of Anthropology* 18: 245–266.

Gamble, C.S. (1992) 'Archaeology, history and the uttermost ends of the earth – Tasmania, Tierra del Fuego and the Cape.' *Antiquity* 66: 712–720.

Giddens, A. (1984) *The Constitution of Society*. Cambridge: Polity.

Glance, N.S. and Huberman, B. (1994a) 'Dynamics of social dilemmas.' *Scientific American* 270: 76–81.

Glance, N.S. and Huberman, B. (1994b) 'Social dilemmas and fluid organisations.' In K. Carley and M. Prietula (eds) *Computational Organisation Theory*, pp. 217–239. New Jersey: Lawrence Erlbaum.

Gulbrandsen, O. (1991) 'On the problem of egalitarianism: the Kalahari San in transition.' In R. Grønhaug, G. Haaland and G. Henriksen (eds) *The Ecology of Choice and Symbol*, pp. 81–110. Bergen: Alma Mater Forlag.

Hayden, B. (1993) 'The cultural capacity of Neandertals – a review and re-evaluation.' *Journal of Human Evolution* 24: 113–146

Hill, K. and Kaplan, H. (1993) 'On why male foragers hunt and share food.' *Current Anthropology* 34: 701–706.

Johnson, G. (1982) 'Organisational structure and scalar stress.' In C. Renfrew, M.J. Rowlands and B.A. Segraves (eds) *Theory and Explanation in Archaeology*, pp. 389–421. New York: Academic.

Kent, S. (1993) 'Sharing in an egalitarian Kalahari community.' *Man* (n.s.) 28: 479–514.

Knauft, B. (1991) 'Violence and sociality in human evolution.' *Current Anthropology* 32: 391–428.

Mitchell, S.D. (1987) 'Competing units of selection? A case of symbiosis.' *Philosophy of Science* 54: 351–367.

Myers, F. (1988) 'Burning the truck and holding the country: property, time and the negotiation of identity among Pintupi Aborigines.' In T. Ingold, D.

Riches and J. Woodburn (eds) *Hunters and Gatherers Volume 2: Property, Power and Ideology*, pp. 52–74. Oxford: Berg.

Paynter, R. (1989) 'The archaeology of equality and inequality.' *Annual Review of Anthropology* 18: 369–399.

Price, T.D. and Brown, J. (eds) (1985) *Prehistoric Hunter-gatherers: The Emergence of Cultural Complexity*. Orlando: Academic.

Riches, D. (1992) 'Shamanism: the key to religion.' *Man* (n.s.) 29: 381–405.

Rogers, A. (1989) 'Does biology constrain culture?' *American Anthropologist* 90: 819–831.

Rolland, N. (1990) 'Middle Palaeolithic socio-economic formations in western Eurasia: an exploratory survey.' In P. Mellars (ed.) *The Emergence of Modern Humans: An Archaeological Perspective*, pp. 347–388. Edinburgh: Edinburgh University Press.

Sahlins, M. (1968) 'Notes on the original affluent society.' In R. Lee and I. DeVore (eds) *Man the Hunter*, pp. 85–89. Chicago: Aldine.

Shennan, S.J. (1989) 'Cultural transmission and cultural change.' In S.E. van der Leeuw and R. Torrence (eds) *What's New? A Closer Look at the Process of Innovation*, pp. 330–346. London: Unwin Hyman.

Shennan, S.J. (1991) 'Tradition, rationality and cultural transmission.' In R. Preucel (ed.) *Processual and Postprocessual Archaeologies: Multiple Ways of Knowing the Past*, pp. 197–208. Carbondale: Center for Archaeological Investigations Southern Illinois University at Carbondale (Occasional Paper No. 10).

Shott, M.J. (1992) 'On recent trends in the anthropology of foragers: Kalahari revisionism and its archaeological implications.' *Man* (n.s.) 27: 843–871.

Steward, J.H. (1936) 'Shoshoni polyandry.' *American Anthropologist* 38: 561–564.

Steward, J.H. (1938) 'Basin Plateau Aboriginal sociopolitical groups.' *Bureau of American Ethnology Bulletin* 120.

Tonkinson, R. (1988) 'Ideology and domination in Aboriginal Australia: a Western Desert test case.' In T. Ingold, D. Riches and J. Woodburn (eds) *Hunters and Gatherers Volume 2: Property, Power and Ideology*, pp. 150–164. Oxford: Berg.

Whitley, D. (1994) 'By the hunter, for the gatherer: art, social relations and subsistence change in the prehistoric Great Basin.' *World Archaeology* 25: 356–373.

Wilmsen, E.N. (1989) *Land Filled with Flies: A Political Economy of the Kalahari*. Chicago: University of Chicago Press.

Woodburn, J. (1980) 'Hunters and gatherers today and reconstruction of the past.' In E. Gellner (ed.) *Soviet and Western Anthropology*, pp. 95–117. London: Duckworth.

Woodburn, J. (1982) 'Egalitarian societies.' *Man* (n.s.) 17: 431–451.

Woodburn, J. (1988) 'African hunter-gatherer social organisation: is it best understood as a product of encapsulation?' In T. Ingold, D. Riches and J. Woodburn (eds) *Hunters and Gatherers Volume 1: History, Evolution and Social Change*, pp. 31–64. Oxford: Berg.

CHAPTER FIFTEEN

ON THE EVOLUTION OF LANGUAGE AND KINSHIP

ROBIN DUNBAR

If anything can be said to demarcate humans from other animals, it must surely be language. Language has enabled us to produce culture, literature, religion and science. Nonetheless, discussions of language invariably tend to assume its existence; worse still, perhaps, they assume that it arose in order to make culture possible. But, biologically speaking, this is a very peculiar (and all but indefensible) claim, for it rests on the assumption that things can evolve in order to serve a purpose that has not yet come into existence, for without language culture cannot exist.

The mere fact that a phenomenon exists raises two key questions. One is why it came to be; the other is when. Social scientists in general have been reluctant to ask both these kinds of questions, preferring to concentrate their efforts on exploring the more tractable questions of how language (and culture) are used on a day-to-day basis. But we cannot ignore the evolutionary problem: none of our closest relatives in the Animal Kingdom possess languages of the complexity that characterizes all human language, and we must therefore assume that at some point in our evolutionary history a non-linguistic ancestor gave rise to a linguistic descendant. When and why that happened remains a problem of legitimate interest in its own right. Moreover, a proper understanding of the evolutionary background to language may give us valuable clues as to how and why language is used by living humans.

In this chapter, I outline a new theory for the evolution of language (answering the 'why it evolved' question) and use the results of this theory to explore the timing of its appearance (the 'when it evolved' question). I then go on to examine some of the implications that these new ideas might have for the structure of human groups.

WHY DID LANGUAGE EVOLVE?

How do we use language?

Even a cursory acquaintance with the content of human conversations suggests that language is used in, at minimum, three very different ways (Table 15.1). At one end of the spectrum lie those conversations whose semantic content is virtually nil: they typically involve speech acts like 'Lovely weather for ducks!', 'Good morning' and 'Have a nice day!'. These speech acts are grammatically well formed and the words themselves have proper meanings, but the phrase as a whole is not *intended* to carry the meaning implied by the words. 'Do you come here often?' (as in the context of a dance or club) is not intended as a question; rather, it is correctly interpreted (in most cases) by the addressee just as the speaker intended, namely as an opening gambit. Much of this form of language is highly ritualized, and probably says no more than '*I* think you're important enough to be worth wasting time on'. It is what I refer to as 'vocal grooming', and is particularly characteristic of well-established relationships.

Table 15.1 The ways in which we typically use language

Type	Semantic content
'Vocal grooming'	Minimal (formulaic usages)
'Gossip'	Social information
Symbolic language	Literature, religion, science

At the other end of the spectrum lie the complex highly technical utterances we hear in lectures and sermons or read in serious books. The content here is all-important: were we to miss the odd word here and there, much of what follows may be unintelligible. Often we cannot understand the content of a sentence on the first pass and we have to read it again more carefully. This highly technical use of language is associated with science and religion, but may also surface in the analytical side of high-brow novels in which a character's social circumstances and state of mind are analysed in some detail. This is what I term the 'Shakespeare-and-Einstein' version of language. It is the form of language that linguists, literary theorists and social anthropologists tend to concentrate their attention on.

Sandwiched between these two levels is, however, a third level. The content is far from being zero, yet the technical content is not so difficult that we struggle to understand it. Indeed, we handle this form of language with effortless ease. It is, of course, that form of social gossip concerning our own behaviour and that of others that so often excites our interest.

Table 15.2 Mean proportions of time individuals spent talking about different topics

Topic	% of time
Personal relationships	38.3
Personal experiences	23.7
Academic matters	14.3
Future activities	11.3
Culture	4.7
Sport/leisure	4.0
Politics, religion, ethics	3.5

Source: 19 conversations (24 male and 27 female speakers) sampled at 30-sec. intervals (from Dunbar and Duncan, submitted).

We have sampled the content of naturally occurring conversations and find that, for people who obviously know each other well, most conversation time is taken up with topics that are largely concerned with their own behaviour or that of other people, the motivations that underlie this behaviour and the relationships that it underpins. A sample of conversations by undergraduates in a refectory, for example, showed that about 65 per cent of conversation time was taken up with these topics (Table 15.2). In contrast, matters of weight and importance such as culture and the arts, politics and religion, or discussions of academic matters accounted for an almost insignificant proportion of time. These results are far from unique to the peculiar situation from which they derive. Other studies have obtained similar results in a variety of contexts (e.g. Emler 1992).

I suggest, then, that the fact that we invest so much of our time in social gossip (and I use the term broadly, as do others working in this area, to refer to anything pertaining to the behaviour of individuals) points to the function for which language originally evolved. The fact that, in contrast, we find discussions of matters of fact about the external world tedious (if not downright difficult) merely serves to reinforce this inference. Some empirical evidence to support this claim is provided by the experimental studies of Cosmides (1989). These have shown that when abstract logical tests that subjects find difficult to solve (such as the so-called 'Wason test') are presented as stories about human behaviour, the solutions are invariably easy to identify. Language evolved, I suggest, to allow humans to exchange social information about themselves and each other so as to facilitate the integration of social groups.

Why did language evolve?

My claim is that language evolved to facilitate bonding in social groups whose size was too large to be bonded using the conventional primate

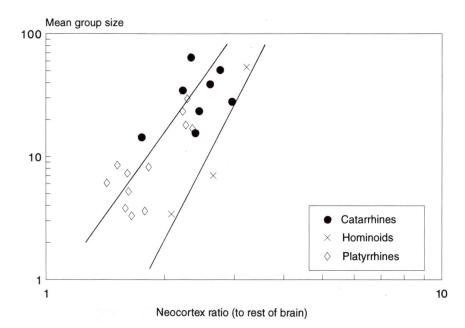

Figure 15.1 Mean group size plotted against relative neocortex size (measured as the ratio of the neocortex volume to the volume of the rest of the brain) in anthropoid primates. Separate regression lines are shown for monkeys and apes (*Source*: Dunbar 1992)

mechanism (namely, social grooming). In order to understand why this should be so, it is necessary to know two key facts. One is that group size appears to be a simple linear function of relative neocortex size in primates (Figure 15.1). If we extrapolate from this relationship to the actual size of the human neocortex, the regression equation yields a predicted mean group size for humans in the order of about 150. This is approximately three times larger than the mean group size observed for any other species of primate.

The second fact is that grooming is the primary communication channel through which social relationships are serviced in non-human primates. We do not yet really understand how grooming is involved in this process, but it is the case that grooming time increases more or less linearly with increasing group size, at least within the Catarrhine primates (the Old World monkeys and apes). If we interpolate the predicted group size for humans based on our neocortex size into the relationship between group size and grooming time, we find that humans would have to spend something in the order of 40 per cent of the day engaged in social grooming in order to maintain the cohesion of their groups to the same level.

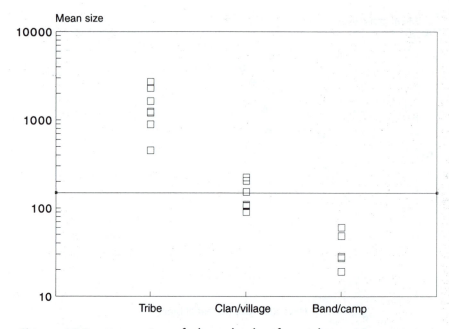

Figure 15.2 Mean size of three levels of social grouping in seven hunter-gatherer and traditional horticulturalist societies, for those tribes listed by Dunbar (1993) for which censuses of all three are available. The horizontal line indicates the predicted group for modern humans based on relative neocortex size.

There is considerable evidence suggesting that groups of about 150 are in fact a regular feature of human societies (see Dunbar 1993). It occurs, for example, in most military organizations (being equivalent to the company in modern armies) and it occurs in many commercial organizations (where it demarcates the upper limit for unstructured groups). In traditional societies, this number reappears in the guise of ritual groupings like the clan or in the villages of settled groups who have adopted a 'slash-and-burn' horticulturalist lifestyle. Figure 15.2 gives data on mean group sizes at different levels of social organization for a set of traditional societies, based on properly censused populations. These show quite clearly a trimodal distribution of group sizes, with small (often unstable) groups of 30–50, groupings of about 150 and large groupings of about 1,000–2,000 individuals (the latter associated with tribal or linguistic divisions). (In fact, the data suggest that the last of these groupings can probably be subdivided in most larger-scale societies into mega-bands of about 500 and tribal groupings of about 1,500.)

The group size of 150 seems to mark the limit within which individuals know each other well enough to manage their social relationships on a strictly personal basis. There is some circumstantial evidence to suggest that it corresponds to the limit at which peer pressure alone can be used to manage and control the behaviour of group members. A quaint example of this is provided by the great Mormon trek out of Illinois in 1846 in the prelude to the founding of Salt Lake City and the settlement of Utah. Faced with the monumental task of trying to co-ordinate the travel of his 5,000 followers, Brigham Young apparently divided his people up into a number of smaller self-contained units of about 150 people each.

It should be made clear that I am not claiming that humans only go about in groups of 150. Indeed, even chimpanzees do not go about in the groups of 55 that correspond to their neocortex size (they spend most of their time in foraging parties of 1–5 individuals). The point being made here concerns a specific kind of group, namely that in which all individuals know each other personally. This group is a cognitive grouping, not an ecological grouping. Hunter-gatherers spend most of their time foraging in small unstable bands of 30–40 individuals, but these bands are made up from a pool of about 150 individuals who have a special relationship with each other: they know each other well enough to be able to join a temporary camp without being invited and without fear of precipitating animosity or resentment, even though they may not have seen each other for many months.

Given that such groups exist, the central problem is how to maintain their cohesion. If humans had to do this using only primate-like grooming, then the time required to service the relationships involved would be prohibitive (about 40 per cent of the total time budget). For any species that has to eke out a living in the real world, this would be an impossible requirement even in the most benign habitats. How, then, could the ancestral humans seeking to live in groups approaching 150 in size hope to co-ordinate the behaviour of so many individuals so as to maintain the cohesion of these groups through time?

The answer, I suggest, is language. Language allows us to solve two of the key constraints to which grooming is subject. One is the fact that grooming is a strictly one-on-one activity (whereas we can speak to several individuals at once); the other is that grooming excludes all other activities (whereas we can walk and talk at the same time). But language also has another important advantage. Non-human primates are limited to direct experience for the acquisition of social knowledge about other individuals. In contrast, language allows us to exchange information not only about ourselves (I can tell you about my likes and dislikes, the kind of person I am, so passing on in a matter of minutes information that would otherwise take months to establish by direct observation), but it also allows us to exchange similar information about third parties.

Some further evidence

In addition to the evidence from the content of conversations, we have some additional evidence to suggest that other aspects of speech and conversation are structured in just the way we might expect if this hypothesis is true. One such prediction relates to the effectiveness of language as a mechanism for interacting with other group members. Grooming, remember, is a purely dyadic activity: there is only ever a single groomer and a single groomee in any given interaction. If this relationship is sufficient to service groups of the size observed with primate societies, we might expect its replacement in humans to allow a speaker ('groomer') to reach proportionately as many interactees as is necessary to increase group size from the largest seen in non-human primates to those found in modern humans.

The largest mean group size in non-human primates is about 55 (typical of both baboons and chimpanzees). The groups of 150 found in humans are thus about 2.8 times larger than those of chimpanzees and baboons. Conversational speech should thus involve a single speaker and about 2.8 listeners. Data collected from a number of different situations reveal that freely forming conversational groups have a skewed size distribution that approaches its asymptotic value of zero at a group size of 4–5 individuals: only 5.7 per cent of the 1,057 conversational groups sampled were larger than four individuals (Figure 15.3). It seems that conversational groups tend to break up into subgroups once the number of members exceeds four individuals.

The reason for this seems to be related to the detectability of speech. Work on the detectability of speech under different levels of background noise and at different inter-individual distances suggests that the maximum possible number of people who can be involved in a conversation is seven under perfect conditions of no background noise, and that this falls off rapidly as noise levels increase. At normal everyday background noise levels and with normal inter-individual distances (about 0.5 m shoulder to shoulder), it is possible to fit only 4–5 individuals into a circle so that conversation is possible (see Cohen 1971). This problem may be compounded by the fact that humans find it difficult to co-ordinate turn-taking in conversations when they are not facing each other (as quickly happens when a circle of talkers becomes too large). There is no intrinsic reason why the machinery for speech production and detection should be so limited: voice boxes could have been designed to produce louder signals without the strain we now experience when shouting, and ears could have been designed to detect quieter signals against higher back-ground noise levels. Instead, it seems that the auditory system as a whole has been designed to permit the exchange of signals at just about the right group size required to allow the jump in groups seen in modern humans.

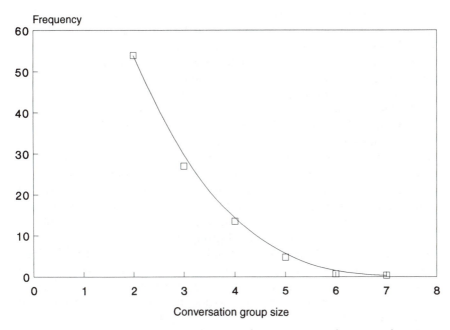

Figure 15.3 Proportional distribution of conversational groups by size, based on a total of 1,057 groups sampled under four different conditions (*Source*: Dunbar *et al.* 1995)

WHEN DID LANGUAGE EVOLVE?

If language evolved for the function outlined above, it did so under circumstances that were quite unique. No other species of primate has ever successfully evolved group sizes as large as those seen in modern humans, and so no other primate species has been under the selection pressure necessary to make the transition to speech and language. We have no idea at this point why the ancestral humans should have needed such large groups. The likely possibilities are either (i) a move into a much more open environment where trees were not available as refuges from predators (so making very large groups the only practical alternative as an anti-predator strategy), (2) defence against other human groups at a time of increasing population densities (a problem that would rapidly generate an arms race for ever-increasing group size) or (3) the need to exchange information or defend access to key resources (such as waterholes) over a very wide area (a problem faced by a highly nomadic species or one living in very poor quality environments) (see Aiello and Dunbar 1993).

This leaves us with one final question, namely *when* did language evolve? Conventional wisdom on this takes one of two views. By and large the palaeoanatomists favour a relatively early date (not later than the appearance of *Homo sapiens* about 250 Kyr BP, with some even favouring the late

H. erectus period), whereas the archaeologists and neuroanatomists tend to favour a later date (corresponding to the Upper Palaeolithic revolution around 50 Kyr BP). We could use the data on neocortex size, group size and grooming time to try to differentiate between these two alternatives in a rather straightforward way providing we could determine relative neocortex sizes for fossil hominids (see also Steele, chapter 8 this volume).

The logic of the analysis is very simple. We know that living primates can cope quite happily with 20 per cent of their daily time budget devoted to social grooming (this is the maximum observed for any given primate population), and we know that modern humans would have to spend around 40 per cent of their time grooming (with a minimum of 30 per cent set by the lower limit in the variation in neocortex size observed within living humans). Somewhere between these two values there must lie the crucial rubicon at which groups of a larger size would simply be impossible to sustain. Once hominid group sizes had reached this barrier, further increases could have evolved only if language evolved to facilitate cohesion. If we can identify the point in the fossil record at which the neocortex reached the size corresponding to a grooming time of about 25–30 per cent, we would be able to identify precisely when the push to language came.

As it turns out, relative neocortex size is very closely related to total brain size in primates (including modern humans). Since the one thing we invariably know about fossil hominids is their brain size, it is a very simple matter to determine relative neocortex size for each fossil, and from this group size and then the grooming time requirement. Our only real trouble lies in not being precisely sure where the critical rubicon is.

The data presented in full in Aiello and Dunbar (1993) show quite clearly that group size would have been well over the threshold by the appearance of *Homo sapiens* approximately 250 Kyr BP. Although some of the later *H. erectus* fossils may also have been within the 'language zone', it is unlikely that a time-budgeting crisis could have triggered the evolution of language much before that.

However, the data show a more interesting trend than simply the crossing of some kind of rubicon. It is clear that while the australo-pithecines as a group were well within the range for living great apes, the appearance of *Homo* marked the beginning of a steady increase in brain size (and hence group size). This growth, however, has more the character of a gradual increase through time than the catastrophic step-function that we would expect of a true rubicon.

The most parsimonious interpretation would seem to be that language evolved not at a sudden crisis point but by a series of more gradual stages in which existing channels of communication (such as grooming) were supplemented by additional and increasingly sophisticated forms of communication. Aiello and Dunbar (1993) suggest that at least three general stages should be distinguished: the early more complex form of contact calling (a form of vocal grooming such as can already be seen in some living species), gossip (or social) language at around 250 Kyr BP and fully symbolic language at the Upper Palaeolithic transition about 50 Kyr BP.

GROUP SIZE AND KINSHIP STRUCTURE

One of the more obvious functions of language in a social group must be to enable individuals to identify third parties during conversations. Without the possibility of naming other individuals, the exchange of social information would be limited to a 'me/you' format. The ability to name individuals, however, raises another important consideration, namely the possibility of specifying abstract relationships ('Jim is my cousin', 'Jane is related to me in the same way that Emily is related to you'). The ability to specify relationships of this kind is crucial for maintaining cohesion in large social groups, as well as for planning and plotting social strategies. Indeed, this seems to be a capacity that is already present among the higher primates (or at least the Old World monkeys and apes). Dasser (1988) and Harcourt (1988) summarize experimental and observational evidence suggesting that Old World monkeys and apes can recognize relationships like relative rank and 'kinship' (probably in the sense of 'is friends with') and use these concepts in everyday social contexts.

It seems that the only element that language adds to this capacity is the ability to transfer conceptual information between individuals. I can explain to you that 'Fred is related to me in the same way that Peter is related to you' even though you have never met Fred. For a non-human primate, such knowledge can only be acquired through direct personal observation. This imposes a very severe limitation on the number of individuals who can be firmly placed in any kind of mental social space. Naming individuals' kinship relationships allows us to go beyond mere individual identities to classes of individuals, and so to class-specific roles.

If an important part of language lies in the ability to name kin (and others) within a group, what kinds of kinship structure might we expect of groups of about 150? Given the general importance of kinship as an organizing principle in primate societies (see Dunbar 1988, 1989), we might expect kinship to have been just as important at the point in human evolutionary history when our present brain (and neocortex) size evolved (about 250 Kyr BP). One observation in support of this is the fact that most traditional human societies are structured around descent lineages of some kind, and we might thus expect to see the residual effects of any such cognitive constraint reflected in the pedigrees in common use in these societies.

If the ancestral group size reflects lineage size, we can ask how large a pedigree would have to be to produce the groups of about 150 predicted for anatomically modern humans. The depth of the pedigree will depend on the typical completed family size. Assuming that only members of the

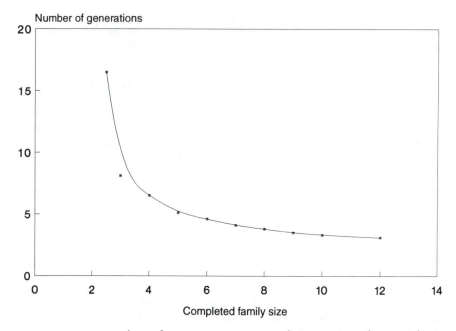

Figure 15.4   Number of generations in a pedigree required to produce 150 living descendants (defined as the members of the three most recent generations) as a function of completed family size (defined as number of offspring survivng to reproductive age). The analysis assumes that descent is recognized through one sex only, and that members of the other sex transfer between groups as spouses

three most recent generations in a pedigree count towards the size of a contemporary group, Figure 15.4 plots the number of generations required to produce group sizes of 150 for different completed family sizes. Note that for present purposes, completed family size includes only those offspring that survive to reproductive age. In addition, I have ignored mode of descent here on the assumption that it is group membership that is important, even though the group is given its *identity* by lineal descent through one sex, just as happens in most non-human primate groups.

It can be seen that this value falls rapidly at first, but then reaches an asymptote at around 3.5 generations once completed family size reaches eight offspring. Although pedigrees have to be deeper when family sizes are smaller, they do not exceed six generations unless family size falls below four surviving offspring. Since a family size of two represents demographic stasis (i.e. zero growth), this is close to the lower limit for population survival.

What evidence is there to suggest that pedigrees are typically of this depth in human societies? Hughes (1988) gives a number of pedigrees

Table 15.3 Pedigree depths and mean completed family size for the grandparental generation for individual pedigrees in traditional societies

Society	Location	Pedigree depth [1]	Source
!Kung San	Botswana	4.5 [2]	Lee 1979
Nuer	E. Africa	5	Evans-Pritchard 1951
Jie	E. Africa	4	Gulliver 1955
Taravad	S. India	5	Kutty 1972
Buryat	Mongolia	5	Humphrey 1983
Garia	New Guinea	5	Lawrence 1984
Rapan	Polynesia	5	Hanson 1970
Navajo	USA	4	Reichard 1928
E. Tennessee	USA	7	Bryant 1981
Makuna	S. America	5	Arhem 1981
Trio	S. America	5	Riviere 1969

Source: Hughes (1988).

Notes
1 Number of generations represented in pedigree.
2 Mean of two pedigrees given by Lee (1979) based on compositions of camp groups; I have added one generation to each pedigree since the dependent offspring were not included in the originals.

drawn from recent and contemporary ethnographic sources. Table 15.3 shows that the modal depth for these pedigrees is five generations (i.e. back to the grandparents of the current grandparental generation). The only example to exceed this depth is the pedigree for a contemporary East Tennessee rural community where Bryant's (1981) pedigree suggests a depth of about seven generations: significantly, perhaps, this is the only case drawn from a literate population.

Unfortunately, ethnographers do not often give examples of real pedigrees (mainly because their interests are limited to kinship naming practices and hence idealized pedigrees), so I have not been able to track down many examples. However, lineage systems that involve pedigree depths of 4–5 generations from a single founder are not uncommon in the ethnological literature. Among the Kikuyu of East Africa, for example, the basic landholding unit, the *mbari*, typically consists of all the descendants of a single great-grandparent (Middleton and Kershaw 1965). Among the Turkana (an East African pastoralist people), the extended family, the *ewowe* or *nitunakothi*, is the largest group of individuals who can trace agnatic links, these usually covering a pedigree of 3–4 generations depth (Gulliver and Gulliver 1953).

If pedigree depths are habitually of about five generations, then this would suggest that family sizes would need to be about 5–5.5 offspring to produce a living descent group of 150 individuals. Estimates of natural family sizes can be obtained from historical records for natural fertility

Table 15.4 Mean completed family size in pre-industrial societies

Sample	Period	Number of children per female	Equivalent pedigree depth [1]	Source
Quakers	1650–1699	7.0	4.1	Landers 1990
(London)	1700–1749	7.2	4.0	Landers 1990
Mennonites	1870s	7–8	c.3.9	Stevenson &
(USA)	1880s	5.8	4.5	Evanson 1990
Papua New Guinea	1982	5.0	5.2	Taufa *et al.* 1990
Krummhorn (Germany)	1720–1750	4.8	5.5	Voland 1990
Ladhak (India)	1930–80	3.8	6.2	Crook & Crook 1988
!Kung San (Botswana)	c. 1915–1930	4.7	5.5	Howell 1976

Note
1 Number of generations in pedigree required to produce a set of 150 living descendants.

populations (i.e. those for which there is no evidence of widespread use of contraception). Estimates of completed family sizes for three early modern populations in Europe and the USA are given in Table 15.4, together with values for one New Guinea population obtained from censuses carried out shortly after contact and for the !Kung San bushmen from Howell's (1976) demographic censuses. These studies consistently give completed family sizes in the order of 5–7 children. In the two cases where survival rates are also given, the mean number of children surviving to reproductive age is 3.7 (Krummhorn) and c. 2.8 (!Kung San), respectively. These values would yield a value of about 150 for the number of living descendants with pedigrees of 4–6 generations depth. The !Kung San probably inhabit what is atypically marginal habitat.

These data suggest there is a correlation between a 'natural' group size in humans (itself related to our cognitive capacities) and the depth of pedigree that could be maintained through direct personal familiarity with the apical ancestor (or ancestral pair). This suggests that one of the proximate limitations to human group sizes may be the number of individuals whose relatedness with respect to each other can be remembered and described. This, in turn, is likely to be a function of the time-depth of human memories in relation to typical generation lengths. Being able to remember back beyond one's grandparents seems to be the exception rather than the rule.

One reason why this may be so is that it is unnecessary to go back further than the fifth generation to identify those individuals who are, from a biological point of view, most important in the currently living generations. Hughes (1988) has pointed out that, from the point of view of biological kin selection theory, the important individuals are not those to whom one is related by certain degrees of relatedness, but those individuals in the current pubertal generation where one's foci of future inclusive fitness are concentrated. This is simply a consequence of the fact that an individual will maximize his or her inclusive fitness by fostering the interests of those individuals who are going to produce most offspring that carry copies of his/her genes, not by fostering the interests of those individuals currently alive who are most closely related to that individual. The issue is not who is most closely related to you biologically (a post-reproductive parent, perhaps), but which of your relatives represents the highest concentration of future gene replication when relatedness and future reproductive potential are taken into account (for example, the puberty-aged offspring of a sibling or a cousin). Hughes' point is that most of the discussions of whether or not kin selection theory is relevant to human societies (e.g. Sahlins 1976) have completely missed the point of kin selection theory.

It turns out that, in most cases, the outer limits on the range of repro-ductively relevant individuals are represented by the offspring of one's cousins (i.e. those individuals who share at least one grandparent with you). Beyond that, it makes little difference who is included in the pedigree, since their impact on one's foci of relatedness in the pubertal generation is negligible. Indeed, Hughes (1988) used simulations to demonstrate that the inclusion of more remote mythical ancestors such as the sun or the moon made no difference at all to individuals' preferences about whom they should associate with socially. It seems that the inclusion of more remote or mythical ancestors is simply a device to provide a stable anchor point by which the pedigree members can identify each other under circumstances where the pubertal generation constantly moves forward as new cohorts are born.

One possible implication of the results in Figure 15.4 is that group size (or even kinship group size) might be a function of mean family size. In other words, the number of individuals who are considered to be 'kin' (as opposed to non-kin) may be constant, irrespective of actual biological relatedness, because an individual can only remember the degrees of kinship between a limited number of dyads. Consequently, in populations where family sizes are typically small (normally ecologically marginal habitats), a relatively large number of generations may be included in the kinship group because a wider range of kinship classes can be included within the set of 150 individuals whose relatedness can be remembered; in contrast, in populations where family sizes are large (generally equitable environments), there will be more individuals in closer kinship categories and the figure of 150 will be reached in pedigrees with smaller depth. There is some evidence from modern British populations that the number of kin contacted on a regular basis is inversely related to the number of non–kin contacted, suggesting that individuals can only cope with a limited number of close relationships (Dunbar and Spoor, submitted).

Note that this does not necessarily imply that individuals base kinship classifications on pedigrees of a certain depth. The point is simply that the kinship relationships that can be remembered within the living generations are the product of a pedigree of a certain depth (which depends on the fecundity of the population). Pedigrees of five generations' depth may be common in practice only because family sizes are typically of the size that produces pedigrees of this depth.

CONCLUSIONS

I have suggested that there is a natural limit on the size of a certain kind of human group. This limit occurs at about 150 individuals and corresponds to a cognitive constraint on the number of individuals with whom you can maintain a coherent well-structured social relationship. This tells us nothing about the function of this kind of grouping: it simply says that should you wish to have a group that requires its members to be socially bonded together (in the sense that they know each other well), then there is an upper limit on the size that group can be. Humans, like other primates, live in multi-tiered social systems with different layers corresponding to different functions (most of which will be ecology- and culture-specific), so this form of group will only be one of a number of different types of group found in any given society.

Given that this kind of grouping does exist, however, a number of implications seem to follow. One concerns the way such groups are bonded. I have suggested that the normal mechanisms that primates use in the flow of social information (namely, grooming and direct personal observation) impose an upper limit on group size at about 70–80 animals. The origins of language can thus be seen as a means of overcoming the constraints imposed by grooming when the ancestral hominids needed to increase group sizes. Consideration of the pattern of changing brain size among fossil hominids suggests that the point of transition to language occurred at around the time of the transition to *Homo sapiens*, about 250 Kyr BP (see Aiello and Dunbar 1993).

Groups of 150 have another interesting property in the context of primate social systems. If such groups arise by natural growth, then it would require a pedigree of about five generations' depth to produce groups of 150 among the living descendants of an ancestral apical pair when completed family sizes are those typical of modern natural fertility populations. In practice, natural human pedigrees are very seldom deeper than five generations. This suggests that the ability to identify kinship relations might have been important. A pedigree of five generations' depth is itself interesting because it is as far back as any living member can be expected to remember (the current grandparents' grandparents). It is possible that some aspects of human memory capacity have been shaped by these demands.

REFERENCES

Aiello, L.C. and Dunbar, R.I.M. (1993) 'Neocortex size, group size and the evolution of language.' *Current Anthropology* 34: 184–193.

Arhem, K. (1981) *Makuna Social Organisation*. Stockholm: Almqvist and Wiksell.

Bryant, F.C. (1981). *We're All Kin: A Cultural Study of a Mountain Neighbourhood*. Knoxville: University of Tennessee Press.

Cohen, J.E. (1971) *Casual Groups of Monkeys and Men*. Cambridge, MA: Harvard University Press.

Cosmides, L. (1989) 'The logic of social exchange: has natural selection shaped how humans reason?' *Cognition* 31: 187–276.

Crook, J.H. and Crook, S.J. (1988) 'Tibetan polyandry: problems of adaptation and fitness.' In L. Betzig, M. Borgerhoff Mulder and P. Turke (eds) *Human Reproductive Behaviour*, pp. 97–114. Cambridge: Cambridge University Press.

Dasser, V. (1988) 'Mapping social concepts in monkeys.' In R. Byrne and A. Whiten (eds) *Machiavellian Intelligence*, pp. 85–93. Oxford: Oxford University Press.

Dunbar, R.I.M. (1988). *Primate Social Systems*. London: Chapman and Hall.

Dunbar, R.I.M. (1989). 'Social systems as optimal strategy sets: costs and benefits of sociality.' In V. Standen and R. Foley (eds) *Comparative Socioecology*, pp. 131–149. Oxford: Blackwell Scientific.

Dunbar, R.I.M. (1992) 'Neocortex size as a constraint on group size in primates.' *Journal of Human Evolution* 20: 469–493.

Dunbar, R.I.M. (1993) 'Coevolution of neocortex size, group size and language in humans.' *Behavioural and Brain Sciences* 16: 681–735.

Dunbar, R.I.M. and Duncan, N. (submitted) 'Human conversational behaviour.' *Ethology and Sociobiology*.

Dunbar, R.I.M., Duncan, N. and Nettle, D. (1995) 'Size and structure of freely forming conversational groups.' *Human Nature* (in press).

Dunbar, R.I.M. and Spoor, M. (submitted) 'Social networks, support cliques and kinship.' *Human Nature*.

Emler, N. (1992) 'The truth about gossip.' *Social Psychology Section Newsletter* No. 27, pp. 23–37.

Evans-Pritchard, E.E. (1951) *Kinship and Marriage among the Nuer*. Oxford: Oxford University Press.

Gulliver, P.H. (1955) *The Family Herds: A Study of Two Pastoral Tribes in East Africa, the Jie and Turkana*. London: Routledge and Kegan Paul.

Gulliver, P. and Gulliver, P.H. (1953) *The Central Nilo-Hamites*. Ethnographic Surveys of Africa. London: International African Institute.

Hanson L.A. (1970) *Rapan Lifeways: Society and History on a Polynesian Island*. Boston: Little Brown.

Harcourt, A.H. (1988) 'Alliances in contests and social intelligence.' In R. Byrne and A. Whiten (eds) *Machiavellian Intelligence*, pp. 132–152. Oxford: Oxford University Press.

Howell, N. (1976) 'The population of the Dobe area !Kung.' In R.B. Lee and I. DeVore (eds) *Kalahari Hunter-gatherers*, pp. 137–151. Cambridge, MA: Harvard University Press.

Hughes, A. (1988) *Evolution and Human Kinship*. Oxford: Oxford University Press.

Humphrey, C. (1983) *Karl Marx Collective: Economy, Society and Religion in a Siberian Collective Farm*. Cambridge: Cambridge University Press.

Kutty, A.R. (1972) *Marriage and Kinship in an Island Society*. Delhi: National Publications House.

Landers, J. (1990) 'Fertility decline and birth spacing among London Quakers.' In J. Landers and V. Reynolds (eds) *Fertility and Resources*, pp. 92–117. Cambridge: Cambridge University Press.

Lawrence, P. (1984) *The Garia: The Ethnography of a Traditional Cosmic System in Papua New Guinea*. Manchester: Manchester University Press.

Lee, R.B. (1979) *The !Kung San: Men, Women and Work in a Foraging Society*. Cambridge: Cambridge University Press.

Middleton, J. and Kershaw, G. (1965) *The Kikuyu and Kamba of Kenya*. Ethnographic Surveys of Africa. London: International African Institute.

Reichard, G.A. (1928) *Social Life of the Navajo Indians*. New York: Columbia University Press.

Riviere, P. (1969) *Marriage Among the Trio*. Oxford: Clarendon Press.

Sahlins, M. (1976) *The Use and Abuse of Biology*. Ann Arbor: University of Michigan Press.

Stevenson, J.C. and Evanson, P.M. (1990) 'The cultural context of fertility transition in immigrant Mennonites.' In J. Landers and V. Reynolds (eds) *Fertility and Resources*, pp. 47–61. Cambridge: Cambridge University Press.

Taufa, T., Mea, V. and Lourie, J. (1990) 'A preliminary report on fertility and socioeconomic changes in two Papua New Guinea communities.' In J. Landers and V. Reynolds (eds) *Fertility and Resources*, pp. 35–46. Cambridge: Cambridge University Press.

Voland, E. (1990) 'Differential reproductive success within the Krummhorn population (Germany, 18th and 19th centuries).' *Behavioral Ecology and Sociobiology* 26: 65–72.

CHAPTER SIXTEEN

A SOCIO-MENTAL BIMODALITY

A pre-hominid inheritance

MICHAEL CHANCE

INTRODUCTION TO THE 'TWO MODES'

It has not been sufficiently realized that we possess an inherent mental bimodality which is, at one and the same time, a property of our minds and also of the corresponding social relations; either one capable of engendering the other.

The agonic social mode

It is often remarked that where there is a 'bad atmosphere' in a department of an organization, there is always present an authoritarian person, usually in authority, who will be over-controlling the group by intimidation varying in intensity from barely perceptible insinuation to periodic outright abuse. 'Subordinated' individuals are often unconscious of their reaction and find themselves unable to resist because they are unaware of the source of their emotional disturbance.

In a less marked manner, in such situations we become primarily concerned with self-security and our attention is much taken up with being part of a group and with what others think of us so as to assure acceptance by the group. We become concerned about rank hierarchy, convention and maintaining good order. In this mode our concerns are predominantly self-protective and our minds engage information-processing systems in our brains that are specifically designed to attend, recognize and respond to potential threats to ourselves, our status and social presentation.

The hedonic social mode

The hedonic mode is marked by the absence of agonic features: since members of a group may not have experienced anything else they do not necessarily know that they are in the hedonic mode. In the hedonic mode people come together in order to enjoy each other's company as such, or to enjoy some common activity or undertake a specific task. There will be a free flow of information between the members, one aspect of which is consultation by leaders with operatives (often with an interchange of roles). This prevents the handing out of excessively detailed instructions (over-control). Individuals are valued or esteemed for their qualities rather than being classified by signs of rank.

Being valued reinforces the individual's sense of social security. This underpins a freedom of association which creates a social network rather than a hierarchy of social rank. As a result the hedonic human being has a flexibility of arousal and attention that allows time for the integration of reality, interpersonal relations, private feelings and thoughts – prerequisites for the operation of intelligence.

These two modes are part of our evolutionary inheritance as primates and can, therefore, be studied by the objective description of social behaviour across species – that is, by the methods of comparative ethology. This was why I undertook a comparison of the social structures of several species of Old World monkeys and apes (our nearest zoological relatives) (see Chance and Jolly 1970). During this study it became evident that social cohesion is brought about by manipulating attention. The logic of this discovery enabled us to see that there is such a thing as a structure to the pattern of attention within a group. Out of the study emerged the model of two contrasting ways of bringing about social cohesion in primate social groups: the *agonic* and *hedonic*. This was extensively explored in an earlier book, *The Social Structure of Attention* (Chance and Larsen 1976). We established that two types of social system exhibiting two types of social cohesion, based on the way in which social attention is manipulated, are to be found in the two closest groups of our Old World phylogenetic relatives – namely, the monkeys and the great apes.

During the study it became evident that low-ranking members of a group of macaques or baboons were always aware of the location of a dominant individual and that a *predominant orientation of attention* could be recognized. Either it was directed within the group (centric attention) or it was directed towards protective features of the environment where, in danger, individuals sought refuge and the group split up (acentric attention). When it was directed within the group, the group cohered and itself afforded protection – high-ranking baboons or macaques according less and receiving more attention than those lower down. In these groups threats passed, on the whole, down the rank order and were socially binding in the hamadryas baboon (Kummer and Kurt 1963, Kummer 1968) and in macaques (Chance 1956, Emory 1975, 1988, Pitcairn 1976, 1988, Waterhouse and Waterhouse 1976). These characteristics of social attention and social structure comprise the *agonic mode*. If we look at the differentiation within the agonic rank order, we see that both dominant individuals and their subordinates are reacting to each other. Whereas the subordinates are dependent upon and restricted by the dominant, the dominant himself (for it is usually but not exclusively a male) controls the subordinates by actively corralling them to maintain a degree of social cohesion. This he does by (1) threatening, (2) neck-biting (a controlled nip, followed by clasping and hugging by hamadryas males) and, in several species of baboon and macaque, by the occasional herding of recalcitrant (i.e. non-responsive) individuals – which clearly indicates a deliberate act directed at circumscribing the movement of other individuals and thereby exerting control.

Contrasting with the way in which the agonic, centric societies of the baboons and macaques cohere is the attractive nature of display which brings together members of separate chimpanzee bands when they meet up after periods of foraging for fruiting trees, constituting their *hedonic* type of society as reported by Reynolds and Reynolds (1965) and Reynolds and Luscombe (1969). Male gorillas use display to alert and attract the members of a troop before setting off on a day's foraging and are another example of the hedonic society.

SUPPORTING EVIDENCE FOR THE 'TWO MODES': A REVIEW

For evidence to be construed as independent support for this model, it must be the result of a separate research programme in a separate discipline: if not an actual though differently worded description of the same phenomenon, then the material should be seen to be coextensive with my description of the two socio-mental modes. So I shall describe those examples which provide the first kind of evidence, and then list the studies which are merely coextensive (see also Chance and Jolly 1970).

Agonic mode in non-human primates

Seen most clearly in baboons and macaques, hierarchically-ranked individuals are arranged in a series of levels one above the other. This rank differentiation is manifest in the structure of attention between them as each individual accords and receives attention as a function of their rank. Higher-ranking individuals accord less and receive more attention than those lower in the social scale. In this way, channels of attention develop, binding those who accord more attention to those of higher rank. This has several consequences. The first is that dominant members of the society are able thereby to exert *control* over those lower in rank, simply, but not solely, through the proximity of the lower-ranking to the centrally dominant figure, and because the channel of communication is always open to the subordinate from the dominant.

In a typically cohesive, hierarchical social system, in which reverted escape brings back the low-ranking individuals towards the source of threat and hence back into the society, escape itself is consummated by proximity to a supportive referent. If this positive referent is of the same rank the individual can relax close to them or, by gaining an affiliation with an individual of higher rank, may use that higher-ranking referent as an ally to maintain or achieve higher rank vis-à-vis another individual through the deployment of protected threat (i.e. threatening another individual using the higher-rank individual as a backdrop). This strategy may be used when females are competing for a male consort or during the maturation of the individual in the society. The maturing male, in the wild, is displaced to the periphery of the group, and may leave it altogether (to which the term exit may be applied) to join bachelor bands, become a lone male or re-enter another group later on. When escape is no longer reverted, a break in this fundamental social vector occurs and exit takes place. This may occur as a result of persistent persecution by a more dominant monkey using protected threat, or simply through the high propensity for escape in the low-ranking individuals, as their sensitivity to threat increases.

In the *agonic mode*, individuals are always together in a group yet spread out, separate from one another, keeping their distance from the more dominant ones to whom they are constantly attentive. They are ready, at an instant, to avoid punishment by reacting to those threats that are dealt out from time to time down the rank order. This they do with various submissive and/or appeasing gestures, and by spatial equilibration which, arising from withdrawal followed by the reversion of escape, serves to prevent escalation of threat into agonistic conflict while tension and arousal remain at a high level. In the agonic mode, partial tension in all the limb muscles is seen directly in the monkey's posture. The continuous high tension combined with centric social attention and without the accompanying agonistic behaviour, is the unique characteristic of this mode, for which the term *agonic* is reserved – as arousal must be balanced by inhibition to preserve this state (Chance 1984).

It has long been known from the work of Sir Charles Sherrington (1906) at the turn of the century that the neocortex inhibited lower parts of the brain, partial disinhibition of which produces specific motor outflows and consequent actions. The evidence for a neurophysiological mechanism capable of sustaining the level of arousal characteristic of the agonic mode has been reviewed by Paul Gilbert (1984). He supports others in referring to this neurophysiological state as one of 'braking', because it 'implies an unabated state of arousal which does not provide any effective behaviour as long as the powerful brakes (controlled by the hippocampus) are applied' (1984: 109–111).

Hedonic mode in non-human primates

The *hedonic mode* in non-human primates is typical of the great apes (chimpanzee, gorilla and orangutan) and is most clearly seen in the social structure of chimpanzees. It is seen in the languid, relaxed, often slow, movements of these creatures except when excited in pursuit of some specific activity requiring muscular exertion (e.g. hunting, throwing, climbing, etc.). This relaxed state may well be a reflection of enhanced powers of neocortical inhibition consequent on their relatively large neocortex which also makes it easier for them to develop hedonic social relations, in which many types of body contact which keep arousal low are frequently present in their social relations.

The chimpanzees' hedonic-type social system is very flexible: Margaret Power (1991) and Frans de Waal (1982, 1989) show how the assuaging qualities of appeasement become transformed into reconciliatory and reassuring gestures between individuals who are mutually dependent. This is seen as the group splits up into twos or threes to go foraging, when the less confident individuals seek and are offered reassurance by contact gestures usually from older, more confident, leaders. Chimpanzee groups mix temporarily without conflict. After the chimpanzees have been foraging in small groups they will come together in response to contact calls, when 'carnivals' of competitive display will focus attention upon the most demonstrative individual. Display actions include jumping up and down, or throwing things into the air. These congregations are one of many different occasions which give opportunities for contact greetings between group members. The most significant occasion for maintaining socialization follows threat from a more dominant individual – although if Power (1991) is right, this is not a frequent occurrence in the wild. Then either party may initiate reconciliation through touch. As de Waal (1989) explains, touching and especially kissing bring about reconciliation among chimpanzees: the contact reduces tension and relaxation occurs. This means that except during moments of excitement the arousal level of the individual is low – this is the hedonic condition (Chance 1980), and is responsible for the flexibility of the hedonic mode. This flexibility is a manifestation not only of absence of the fear of punishment in the relationship between individuals, but also of a freeing of an individual's attention from being the medium or channel of the social bond between them and the rest of the society. Because it is no longer active as a bonding element, attention is freed for detailed investigations and manipulations of objects in the physical environment, thus facilitating the development and expansion of intelligence (Chance 1984).

Coextensive evidence of the two modes in non-human primates

Two studies of semi-feral colonies of rhesus macaques have shown that glancing from a distance is the characteristic mechanism of social attention between agonistically ranked individuals: the lack of this behaviour combined with sitting close together and engaging in relaxed grooming

LIVERPOOL
JOHN MOORES UNIVERSITY
AVRIL ROBARTS LRC
TEL. 0151 231 4022

was evidence of hedonic relations between individuals. Using these measures, Waterhouse and Waterhouse (1976) showed that there were two separate networks of agonic and hedonic attention in a colony at the Bristol Zoo. Pitcairn (1976, 1988) discovered the same dichotomy in a very elaborate study, in which mother/infant relationships were known from a fifteen-year study of the colony at the Basel Zoo.

Agonic mode in humans

The two social modes in human social relations are expressed and communicated between individuals by overt behaviour and non-verbal as well as verbal signals. Both are expressed in modern society through the mass media, especially television, and hence operate not only between individuals in close proximity, but over great distances.

In non-human primates the agonic mode brings about social cohesion in such a way that it interferes with and hence controls to some extent the form of the ongoing behaviour of the individual. Similarly in human agonic groups, when integrated task behaviour is required the form of the direction can be seen to rely more on instruction and less on understanding of the nature of the co-operative task. This has been recently identified by Alvin Toffler (1991) as 'over-control' and can be seen not only to be a more rigid form of control, but also one which interferes with efficiency. Emotional interference with task performance also reduces efficiency. This effect of over-control is common in marriage (Price 1992). It takes many forms, but in essence consists of intimidating or humiliating another person, who because they have allowed this to happen and involuntarily submitted when it first occurred have found themselves unable to extricate themselves from being put down.

Warren Bennis, in his writing on patterns and vicissitudes in T Group development (in Bradford *et al.* 1964: 251), was able to formulate a conclusion that goes some way to describing the features of agonic groups, namely:

> that the core of the theory of group development is that the principal problems or issues the group must solve are to be found in the orientations towards authority and intimacy which members bring to the group. Rebelliousness, submissiveness, or withdrawal, as the characteristic responses to authority figures; destructive competitiveness, emotional exploitativeness, or withdrawal as the characteristic response to peers, prevent consensual validation of experience.

Hedonic mode of humans

Most people will find it rather more difficult to understand the new insight an understanding of this mode gives, because (like good health) it is a part of our normal condition, and thus remains below the threshold of reflective awareness – although with media reports daily providing examples of breakdown in smooth human relationships, people may be increasingly likely to see the point of investigating what keeps human beings happy and competent. As has already been explained, people experiencing any form of intimidation are living in hierarchically ranked social relations with their associates; but there are entirely non-hierarchical societies among hunter-gatherers, which maintain exclusive hedonic social relations.

Woodburn (1982: 434–435) emphasizes that in immediate-return human societies a mobile, flexible nomadism is fundamental: there is an absence of institutionalized leadership and of specialized or formalized institutions that can be distinguished as, say, economic, political, judicial or religious, in function. Kinship concepts and terms are generally a great deal broader than our own, and they designate social relationships rather than actual kin. Leadership is not sought after (Service 1966, Turnbull 1968). According to Woodburn (1982), the social organization of immediate-return foraging societies has the following basic characteristics:

1 Social groups are flexible and constantly changing in composition.
2 Individuals have a choice of whom they associate with in camp gatherings, in the food quest and when travelling.
3 People do not depend on *specific* other people for access to basic requirements.
4 Transactions between people, whether in relationships of kinship or other relationships, stress sharing and mutuality, but do not involve long-term binding commitments and dependencies of the sort that are so familiar in delayed-return systems.

Hence in the hedonic mode (characteristic also of modern Western societies) we are more free to form a network of personal relationships that typically offer mutual support. Then we can also give free rein to our intelligence, our creativity and the creation of systems of order in our thoughts and in our social relations. This is because attention, when released from self-protective needs, can be used to explore and integrate many new domains. The healthy human individual in the hedonic mode has a flexibility of arousal and attention that allows time for integration of reality, interpersonal relations, and private feelings and thoughts, providing prerequisites for the operation of creativity and inventiveness.

Stability of the hedonic mode in humans in hunter-gatherer societies

The essence of the stability of the hunter-gatherer societies referred to above is that they possess several ways of reducing aggression, and this is also the essence of the hedonic mode – namely that there is an absence of overt aggression and of social rank organized by covert aggression. This is achieved by several processes:

1 The young infant is gradually familiarized with its total environment. Colin Turnbull (1968) writes of the Mbuti hunter-gatherers, 'for true non-aggressivity and non-violence to be learned the individual has to gain confidence in his relationship with all the various segments of his experience, and perceive it as a single totality rather than as the mere sum total of separate relationships'.

2 Aggression is not responded to by hunter-gatherers. Richard Sorenson (1978) writes of the Fore of New Guinea, 'when older children were the subject of attack by young children they typically received it with amusement and affection. If the attack became painful they sometimes moved away or more often tried to divert the young child by affectionate playfulness or engaging him in other interests', i.e.:

3 the aggressive child's attention is diverted.

4 The child is indoctrinated into the cultural norm of the tribe. Norms serve as substitutes for the exercise of personal influence.

5 Sanctions act on a person's self-esteem, negatively by shunning, shaming, mocking, group ostracism.

Play is the distinguishing feature of the young of all mammals and much is made of the fact that when it takes the form of rough-and-tumble play between siblings it serves the purpose of practice of the means by which social rank is established between adults. Even in classes of mammals other than primates, individuals in the wild play with physical objects like leaves and pieces of stick, and foxes have been seen to bat tennis balls left on a lawn! Piaget (1952) established parallels between assimilation of information and play and White (1959), re-examining Piaget's findings, discovered that competence was achieved by contented children in play. This is especially evident in studies of the young in three groups – the Mbuti hunter-gatherers of the tropical rain forest of N.E. Zaire (Turnbull 1978), the !Kung hunter-gatherers of the Kalahari desert (Draper 1978), and the Fore hunter-gardeners of New Guinea (Sorenson 1978).

Like the Mbuti child, young infants of the Fore 'remained in almost continual bodily contact with their mother, her housemates or her gardening associates', which led throughout childhood to unrestricted exploratory activity. Once the child can crawl, the young child will explore the floor and the dwelling just as thoroughly as he explored his mother's body. If he comes to minor harm in his explorations of space, she quickly comforts him before turning him loose to try again. Thus the child learns a subtle combination of dependence and independence.

Beyond the relationship with mother there are relationships with other children. !Kung children, like children anywhere, will argue, tease, cry, lose their tempers and strike out at each other (Draper 1978). There are frustrations in this society for even the youngest age groups. The !Kung have a special way of handling anger and physical assaults by one child against another. When two small children quarrel and begin to fight, adults don't punish them or lecture them; they separate them and physically carry each child off in an opposite direction. The adult tries to soothe and distract the child and to get him interested in other things. The strategy is to interrupt misbehaviour before it gets out of hand; for older children, adults use the same interventionist technique.

This way of disciplining children has important consequences for aggressiveness in childhood and later in adulthood. Since parents do not use physical punishment, and since aggressive postures are avoided by adults and devalued by the society at large, children have relatively little opportunity to observe or imitate overtly aggressive behaviour. This situation, of course, is made possible by the fact that children and adults occupy the same close living space and by the fact that on any typical day there will be many adults in camp who are keeping an informal watch on the children.

EVIDENCE OF THE TWO MODES IN INDUSTRIAL SOCIETIES

Small group research

In the era immediately after the Second World War investigators, armed with coding protocols, observed numerous small groups of humans in search of the fundamental dimensions of social behaviour. Carter (1954) concluded that three dimensions were needed to describe the behaviour of members of small groups; he named these dimensions 'group goal facilitation', 'individual prominence and achievement' and 'group sociability'.

These three dimensions are found in several dozen studies of social inter-action, and in analyses of social dimensions of human personality (for a review, see Kemper 1978, Fromme and O'Brien 1982). 'Group goal facili-tation' was derived from items (aggregated across different studies) that included efficiency, co-operation, adaptability, 'work with' skills, behaviour directed at group solution and the like. This dimension reflects the *task* the actors have gathered to do. 'Individual prominence and achievement' was based on such qualities as aggressiveness, authoritarian leadership, being forceful and not timid, physical ability, being quick to take the lead. This set of behavioural characteristics appears to reflect a controlling and dominating stance toward others. This is the *power* dimension. The final factor, 'group sociability', emerged on the basis of such items as sociability, behaviour that is socially agreeable to group members, behaviour directed toward group acceptance, genial, cordial and the like. This is the *status* factor.

When we consider two of the factors (individual prominence/achievement and group sociability) found by Carter, we see that they are of a different order. Foremost is the fact that these two behaviours are oriented not to task completion, but to the other actors. To be forceful and authoritarian, or sociable and cordial, is to orient one's conduct towards others. Hence the *power* and *status* factors are fundamentally descriptive of relational conduct. Power is defined as the ability of one actor to realize his/her interests against the opposition of another actor. This follows closely the important formulation of the sociologist Max Weber (1946). Human actors are, on the other hand, capable of voluntary compliance with the wishes, desires and interests of other actors, even at what may appear to be some sacrifice to themselves. Carter's factor of 'group sociability' stands for the whole range of behaviours in which actors willingly accord each other benefits and compliance.

Kemper (1978) has also analysed the structure of an individual's emotions within a social interactional framework, which is the context in which most emotions are experienced. The description of these outcomes can follow a relatively simple analytic assumption: each actor's power and/or status may increase, decrease or remain the same, as a result of an interaction. In broad outline, the following will ordinarily result. Elevation of one's own power will lead to a greater sense of ease and security, as will decline in the power of the other. Elevation of the other's power will lead to fear/anxiety, as will a decline in one's own power. The effect of no change in power for either self or other is complicated by the state of anticipatory emotions (Kemper 1978). The discovery of the agonic and hedonic modes as the biological roots of Carter's and of Kemper's work underpins and redefines their own binary distinctions between power and status.

Studies of children's social behaviour

Independent evidence from studies of Western industrial societies that an individual's social predispositions fall into one of these two categories is most likely to be found in children's groups, as these will have been formed more through face-to-face interactions in the family and especially with the mother before wider cultural influences have shaped the individual's character. Fortunately there are a cluster of studies made by ethologists in England and France which supply information which is comparable with those supplied by the ethological studies of the social structure of non-human primates and also with Woodburn's (1982) analysis of hunter-gatherer society. The most extensive of these comes from the school led by Hubert Montagner (Montagner *et al.* 1978, 1988) at the Laboratory of Psychophysiology (Faculty of Science, Besançon, France) and an English group prominent amongst which is the work of Vernon Reynolds and A. Guest (1975) from the Department of Biological Anthropology, University of Oxford.

Montagner spent six years studying by ethological methods

how the young child of one to six years organizes his behavioural and physiological responses when confronted with questions that are posed to him by various natural or cultural environments imposed on him. . . . we managed to isolate the most probable act sequences of each child in a communication situation. Thus we were able to show behaviour that *links and appeases* and behaviour that brings about aggression, *breaking of contact*, retreat or escape.

(1988)

Montagner identified a series of non-verbal exchange sequences corresponding to a set of fundamental dimensions of social interaction, and was also able to organize the behavioural profiles of individual children using a similar classification.

Montagner's classification of non-verbal exchange sequences included the following types:

Linking and appeasement behaviour

1 *Offering*. It is often by an offering behaviour or a simulated offering that a child of 2 to 3 years establishes or re-establishes contact with other children. This behaviour causes the receiving child either to stop crying, to accept the presence of the offerer, or there is a sequence of appeasing acts (see 2) followed by one child imitating the other, or a return to exchanging appeasement acts or reciprocal imitation after a conflict, or a channelling of the threat. Offering and offering simulation are already frequently found when children of 14 to 20 months and up to 2 to 3 years play together and it is especially so when they are in a competitive situation.

2 *Linking and appeasement acts*. The stroke, kiss, certain bodily contacts such as taking another child by the hand, or putting his head on another's shoulder, bending the head sideways on to the shoulder, sideward movements of the body, swinging and waddling, jumping and hopping, turning round oneself, smiling and offering, form sequences and regulate the establishing and maintenance of non-aggressive communication between children from 2 to 3 years.

Behaviour which brings about refusal, breaking of contact or aggression

1 *Absence of response to offerings and to soliciting sequences*. The child who has received a refusal or who has not received a response to his offering or soliciting has a tendency to isolate himself, to threaten or become aggressive towards the child he has solicited or another child.

2 *Threatening behaviour*. The desire for an object, competition and conflict bring about behavioural sequences which have a threat value and which bring about: acts of the same kind; the receiver abandoning the desired object; turning the top of the body away; retreating; escaping or fleeing.

The same division between linking behaviour and behaviour which breaks the links is found in the behavioural profiles. Those who make the closest linking sequences become leaders who attract the largest number of other children around them initiating play activities. These *leader* types, who are also dominant, express themselves in non-ambiguous sequences of appeasement acts which become more and more complex from 2 to 3 years; their offerings are frequent and spontaneous aggression is rare. There are also *dominated* children who do not participate in competitive activities, but who have leader behavioural sequences when they approach another child or see another child approaching them and who are followed by a smaller number of children. These two types are the likely progenerative profiles of later *hedonic adults* – placed here in the position of leaders because they are the most relaxed (also reflected in stress hormone profiles) and because using appeasement, showing and linking behaviour they find themselves surrounded by other children.

Then there are four agonistic profiles made up of various mixtures of aggressive and flight behaviours. These are the progenerative profiles of *agonic adults* once they acquire the power to inhibit this instantaneous expression. Finally there are those whose behaviour is to escape social involvement who become isolated or keep apart from the others. This enables them to relax, as confirmed by their stress hormone profiles and some can re-affiliate to participate in social activities if approached by another child.

The factors which influence the establishment of these profiles clearly arises in the home as was discovered by evaluating parental influence. There was a high positive correlation between the ratio of appeasement and aggression behaviours of the dominant children and the appeasement/ threat and aggression ratio in the behaviour toward the children by the mother. There was no correlation with that of the father.

Reynolds and Guest (1975) observed twelve children in a group from which they built up a catalogue of contact body postures which fell into 'associative', 'aggressive' and 'solo' forms listed below. These categories are broadly comparable with those found by Montagner described above, and the 'associative' and 'aggressive' categories are the progenerative items of behaviour for adult 'hedonic' and 'agonic' personalities respectively.

The list of social behaviour units recorded by Reynolds and Guest (1975) was as follows:

1 *Associative.* Arm round neck, embrace, hug, kiss, lean on, link hands, pat head/face/back/bottom, tickle, touch hand/arm, touch elbow/shoulder, touch face/hair/mouth/ears/eyes, share object.
2 *Aggressive.* Bite, bump into, dig in ribs, grab/tug, hit, tick, fight, pinch, punch, push, twist arm, wrestle, slap, fight over object.

3 *Solo*
  • Solitary: stand alone, sit alone.
  • Groom self: bite hand, rub eyes, rub genitals, run hand through hair, scratch, bite nails, chew lips, comb hair, pat hair, pick nostrils/ear, pull ear, suck hand/hair.
  • Display self: dance, chest thump, grimace with tongue out, jump up, skip and hop, stamp, toss head, wave arms, display object.
  • Vocalisation: hum/sing, grunt, squeak, talk to self.

Thus we see that the two socio-mental modes appear in the difference between appeasing and linking behaviour (the hedonic mode) and behaviour which brings about aggression, breaking of contact, retreat or escape (agonistic mode). Children operate agonistically and not agonically as they have not yet developed the necessary inhibitory mental powers to convert agonistic behaviour to agonic. The addition of the central nervous inhibitory activity establishes the agonic linking mode of the adult. It should be noted how important the establishment of social links are to the child as the absence of a response to offering and soliciting sequences immediately brings about a swing into an agonistic response.

Psychiatric studies

Having once grasped the nature of the two modes it is possible to see that some psychiatric authors provide evidence consistent with the model. Maslow (1943) was convinced that the exclusion of psychological features of individuals from attempts to understand society has distorted our view. Too exclusive attention to economic, political, social and other cultural forces has failed to recognize that human psychological types permeate all of these areas. His study revealed that the 'authoritarian' type is basically insecure, regarding 'most or all other human beings as challenging rivals who are seen as either superior and feared, resented, bootlicked or admired; or inferior and therefore to be scorned, humiliated and dominated' (1943). The 'authoritarian' person expresses hatred and hostility against some definable outgroup, usually specified by historical aspects of the culture (e.g. anti-Catholicism, anti-semitism or colour prejudice), making a scapegoat over which to assert his superiority. This corresponds to the 'agonic personality'. Maslow contrasts this type with the 'democratic' person who tends to respect other people as being different rather than better or worse. He is able to perceive and appreciate differences. He is also more task oriented. This corresponds to the 'hedonic personality'. George Vaillant (1977) summarized the evidence of an investigation into the long term health of a batch of men graduates from Harvard University started by the Grant Study in the late 1940s. Briefly, he found the subjects of the study divided into those who responded to crises by finding solutions and meeting challenges (i.e.

hedonic personalities), and those who adopted various psychological defence mechanisms (i.e. agonic personalities). Pearce and Newton (1963) formulated an interpersonal theory of human personality and concluded that this was divided between 'the integral personality' (hedonic mode) and the 'security apparatus' (agonic mode).

THE PHYLOGENETIC INCREASE IN EXPLORATORY VARIABILITY

We have seen that intellectual creativity is promoted by the hedonic type of social system and personality, and now we turn to examining the phylogeny of creativity in primates. Combinatorial competence – a cognitive psychological indicator of creative ability – is expressed in at least two forms, namely technology (the hierarchical assembly of elements into a composite tool) and mental modelling (the cognitive manipulation of abstract representations of sensory phenomena to generate blueprints for novel actions). What are the factors influencing these capabilities?

Manipulative creativity

Christopher Parker (1974, 1980) gave a rope to semi-feral caged members of several primate species and recorded the way they behaved towards it. His conclusions were that in general, the great apes were more diverse than other species in their manipulative behaviour in at least six ways: (1) they used more different body parts to contact the object; (2) they performed more different actions while in contact; (3) they formed a greater number of unique combinations of body part and action; (4) their degree of behavioural predictability was far less, as indexed by the information-theory measure of uncertainty (H), which integrated the number of different combinations of body part and action categories with their relative frequencies of occurrence; (5) the proportion of total behaviours accounted for by the thirty most frequent categories of behaviour was less for the apes; (6) the apes also performed more actions in which the object was grasped and then applied to other body parts or to other objects in the environment, that is, the apes used the object in a tool-like way; whereas the other species were much more likely to perform actions directly on the rope itself. Figure 16.1 contains the results of Parker's analysis in which an increment on the vertical axis means that more combinations were formed by performing more actions with the same body part; and an increment on the horizontal axis indicates that more combinations were created by performing the same action with a greater variety of body parts. Another analysis of his findings indicated that not only did the apes have a greater number of unique combinations of body part and action, but that they were also much more reluctant to repeat a combination once it had been performed. In Figure 16.2 the

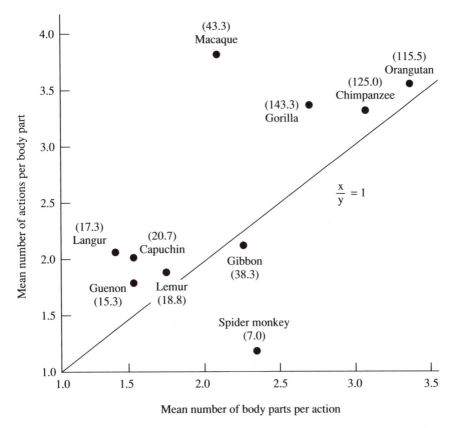

Figure 16.1 Mean number of body parts per action and mean number of actions per body part during manipulation in ten species of non-human primates. Numerals in parentheses indicate the mean number of unique combinations of body parts and actions for each species group

number of combinations of body part and action are plotted as a function of the frequency of the category. The great apes had more combinations of all but the highest frequencies, but for the category 1 they were more than 300 per cent above the next species (macaques). The apes were extremely reluctant to repeat a particular combination once it had been performed. If the animal becomes bored with repetition, but stays interested in the object, this would tend to produce more variation in behaviour. Mittelstaedt (1970) showed that every time an action is undertaken an *output copy* is sent to the sensorium. It is logical to deduce that with an increase in variability evident in the motorium between macaques and the great apes, a corresponding segregation will have taken place in the sensorium.

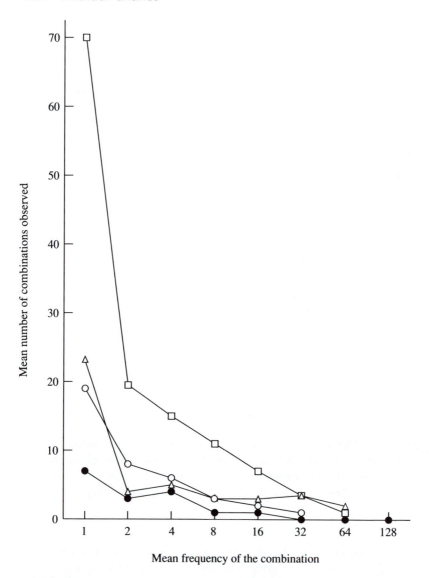

Figure 16.2 Mean number of combinations of body part and action as a function of the frequency of each combination for four groups of non-human primates: □ = great apes; ○ = gibbon; △ = macaque; ● = lemur plus arboreal monkeys

Curiosity and exploring

Rosenzweig, Bennett and Diamond (1972, Bennett *et al.* 1974, Rosenzweig 1984), an ethologist, a biochemist and a neuroanatomist collaborated in a remarkable study of the effects of introducing novel objects into cages of maturing rats each day for a month. They found that this stimulus to exploration brought about marked changes in both the anatomy and biochemistry of the neocortex of these rats, indicating and promoting enhanced exploratory activity. They found a significant migration of glial cells (neuron-nurturing endothelial cells) into the neocortex thereby enhancing and prolonging their capacity to support exploration. The probability is that what is true for rats is true for the higher mammals – especially those which, like the primates, have developed marked powers of exploration – and that the more exploration is encouraged by the lifestyle, the more this ability will be developed (i.e. a feedback process becomes established). Hence those living in an hedonic social setting will exploit more fully the properties of the neocortex.

Attentional interruption

Let us now consider the conditions under which combinatorial competence can be exercised during or as a result of novel experiences encountered during exploration. We should not be surprised that the young child brought up in hedonic ways, typical of the hunter-gatherers, shows a great deal of exploration and finds out what can be done with the objects, e.g. knives, stones, pots, woven materials and even fire, which it comes across. Schneider and Shiffrin (1977) distinguish between automatic processes of response in the long-term memory store triggered by appropriate inputs, and controlled processing which consists of 'temporary' activation of elements of memory not yet fixed, which are easy to set up and modify or utilize in a new situation and which require active control by attention. Clearly this process, guided by attention to new inputs, is the essential requirement of generativity. So we can infer that operating conditions which interrupt the attention span or make overriding demands upon it will attenuate and ultimately stop generativity. This will happen in the agonic mode in which centripetal predominant attention deflects attention towards the dominant centre of the group, while if there is indoctrination with the tenets of a culture attention will also be kept within bounds. Where the organism directs its energies to self-preservation (as in avoiding predators and *dominant interlopers*), conditions necessary for play and manipulative creativity are unavailable.

Interruption of arousal control

When attention is deflected centripetally, the deflection not only interrupts exploratory processes, but also prevents the fluctuation of arousal in the sympathetic nervous system which is essential for the intake of information. This fluctuation was found to be an integral part of information intake in human experiments carried out by Lacey *et al.* (1963). They report that slowing of the heart rate (accompanied by decreased palmar conductance) accompanied and perhaps even facilitated ease of 'environmental intake' in human subjects whereas cardiac acceleration accompanied or facilitated a rejection of the environment (also accompanied by increase in palmar conductance). They

> also reviewed the fragmentary neurophysiological evidence for the notion that cardiac deceleration (if accompanied by lowering of arterial blood pressure) would have the effect of facilitating sensory-motor integration. This effect is mediated by visual afferent mechanisms. Increases in pressure within the *carotid sinus* that result from sympathetic-like cardiovascular changes (i.e. excitement) stimulate the baroreceptors within the carotid sinus. The resulting increase in impulses along Hering's nerve produces inhibition of cortical electrical activity and of sensorimotor activity.
>
> (Lacey *et al.* 1963: 165)

These two pieces of information support the deduction that relaxed social relations combined with fluctuations of arousal accompanying a daily routine, will predispose individuals to take in information while exploring the environment and to develop sensory-motor skills. Both of these would predispose to the establishment of the different cultures found in chimpanzees, each incorporating a different set of skills (e.g. bundles of leaves used as sponges, sticks cleared of side branches and used to extract termites, stones used as hammers to crack nuts on anvils, and the development of hunting skills to kill other species of monkeys) – differences which are found between chimpanzee populations in widely separated habitats of Central and West Africa (McGrew 1993, cf. Kummer and Goodall 1985).

Neocortical evolution and creativity in primates

The longer an individual pays attention to an environmental object the more novel combinations are likely to arise. The enlargement of the neocortex is likely to promote this attention span for the following reasons:

1 enhanced powers of inhibition of lower brain centres will minimize distraction.
2 the migration of glial cells into the neocortex will make it possible for exploratory activity to last longer.

Both of these will potentiate (according to Chris Parker) the likelihood that the great apes will perform different acts in relation to the object and that the object itself will be used in a tool-like way. *Pari passu* with such changes will go enhanced powers of mutualistic or hedonic type social relations which themselves should engender communication about mutual interests in external objects.

It is also possible to see how, in exceptional circumstances, the young of species hitherto regarded as of low intelligence in comparison with apes may be able to perform at a higher level. As already discussed, evidence from a variety of human studies supports the view that we have inherited from our primate ancestors a *socio-mental bimodality* representing two mutually exclusive ways of securing social cohesion in a primate group, and that one, the hedonic, creates the conditions for the expansion of intelligence and the other, the agonic, prevents this. The 'agonic' is a rank–ordered structure of centripetal attention maintained by threat from a dominant individual who thereby exerts a persistent control over the rest of the group. The members of agonic groups remain in a state of emotional and physical tension and receive much of their information from awareness of the dominant's behaviour or, if human, from instructions. The 'hedonic' mode, on the contrary, typically comprises a network of individuals in mutual reciprocity and rewarding social interaction with a free flow of information between nodes of the social network. The evidence, therefore, points to the emergence of creativity only in the hedonic social mode, in which the flexibility of attention and emotional state permits exploration of the environment by the individual.

This is why some species of primate have shown in recent studies unexpected amounts of manipulative inventiveness. Since any restriction on attention and hence freedom to explore will curb creativity, the persistence of a human culture will, of itself, also restrict the opportunities for individual inventiveness. In species of social primate, the social system is an intermediate factor determining the level of individual inventiveness. Westergaard (1988) has reported that lion-tailed macaques (*Macaca silenus*) in captivity, provided with apparatus giving them the opportunity to develop skills appropriate to their mode of feeding in the wild, show an unexpected degree of combinatorial competence, but this may be a consequence of the nature of their social relations which Emory (pers. comm.) has found to be unusually relaxed in a group at the San Diego Zoo. Moreover, Emory has observed inventiveness of a more serendipitous kind in this group, when not constrained by *a priori* experimental design – behaviours such as breaking off a branch from a tree and weaving it into the wire netting before perching on it, and biting a hole in a rubber football to fill with water and then pour the water over another monkey. Bolwig (1964), who then lived in Nigeria, described how a young baboon was brought up as a pet in the family for several years: as she approached maturity (when an adult is normally more aggressive) he tested her problem-solving ability using the methods used by Wolfgang Kohler in Tenerife to study the intelligence of chimpanzees (Chance 1967). He found that she scored very highly, nearly as well as the chimps. The inference is that having been brought up in a human family the baboon was not agonically programmed to be preoccupied with gaining social rank, and that play and rewarding with food and petting may have played their part in engendering an habitually low and fluctuating level of arousal.

If so the neocortex of the baboon possesses properties which in its normal life are suppressed. The contrast between the two modes cannot therefore be reduced to a simple contrast between monkeys and apes, though this comparison is useful as a general illustration of the contrast between the two modes. Even among the Old World monkeys, we can see contrasts in creativity and problem-solving behaviour which reflect differences in behavioural dispositions and in the rearing environment.

CONCLUSION

So exploration is promoted by several factors. The first is an increase in manipulative combinatorial competence tending towards combining one action and object with another. The second is tending towards using the object as a tool. The third factor is that the longer the time devoted to exploration, the more diverse the combinations become. If we make the logical assumption that neuroanatomical and neurochemical changes take place in primates in the same way as in rats (Rosenzweig 1984), then the longer a young ape or a human explores the more it will enhance its capability to explore. Early on, Kirkland (1976) argued persuasively that interest and creativity were closely related to the freedom to indulge in exploration as part of play and we have seen that this combination is a prominent feature of the activities which the young of hunter-gatherers are free to pursue. Their freedom is guaranteed because they are living in and are brought up in an hedonic social group. This (it is argued) is an intermediate factor between a primate and its ability to develop creativity.

Before we leave this theme let us once more tackle the definition of what is going on when creativity is manifest. Beveridge (1950) noted from autobiographical reports of scholarly creativity that intuition into the solution of a problem often comes after a period of intensive work on the problem followed by relaxation when the solution appears with dramatic suddenness. Perkins (1988), in discussing the quest for the mechanism behind creativity, notes of Beethoven 'that he did not just have brilliant ideas; he worked them up and worked them out, as his notebooks testify. In short there were numerous cycles of generation and selection.' One contribution 'purely came from his extensive exploration of motifs around which to construct a whole work – a straightforward example of a plan of problem finding which promotes creativity specifically'. What we are seeing here is an example of a recursive process by which elements retained in memory are repeatedly combined and recombined sometimes with new elements taken in from further awareness. Clearly any overriding calls on attention such as occur in the agonic social mode will interrupt the recursivity of attention and hence prevent creativity.

ACKNOWLEDGEMENTS

My thanks are due to the membership of the Evolutionary Social Systems Institute for inspiration and to Steve Shennan and especially James Steele for excellent guidance in the planning and editing of this chapter.

REFERENCES

Bennett, E.L., Rosenzweig, M.R. and Diamond, M.C. (1974) 'Effects of successive environments on brain measures.' *Physiology and Behaviour* 12: 621–631.

Beveridge, W.D. (1950) *The Art of Scientific Investigation.* New York: Vantage Books.

Bolwig, N. (1964) 'Observations on the mental and manipulative abilities of a captive baboon (*Papio doguera*).' *Behaviour* 22: 24–40.

Bradford, L.P., Gibb, J.R. and Benne, K.D. (1964) *T-group Theory and Laboratory Method; Innovation in Re-education.* New York: John Wiley.

Carter, L.F. (1954) 'Evaluating the performance of individuals as members of small groups.' *Personal Psychology* 7: 477–484.

Chance, M.R.A. (1956) 'Social structure of a colony of *Macaca mulatta*.' *British Journal of Animal Behaviour* 4: 1–13.

Chance, M.R.A. (1967) 'Kohler's chimpanzees: how did they perform?' In A.J. Riopelle (ed.) *Animal Problem Solving*, pp. 91–102. Harmondsworth: Penguin.

Chance, M.R.A. (1980) 'An ethological assessment of emotion.' In R. Plutchik and J. Kellerman (eds) *Emotion Theory, Research and Experience*, pp. 81–111. London: Academic Press.

Chance, M.R.A. (1984) 'Biological systems synthesis of mentality.' *Man Environment Systems* 14: 143–157.

Chance, M.R.A. and Jolly, C. (1970), *Social Groups of Monkeys, Apes and Men.* London: Cape.

Chance, M.R.A. and Larsen, R.R. (eds) (1976) *Social Structure of Attention.* London: John Wiley.

Draper, P. (1978) 'Learning environment for aggression and anti-social behaviour among the !Kung.' in A. Montagu (ed.) *Learning Non-aggression*, pp. 31–53. New York: Oxford University Press.

Emory, G.R. (1975) 'Comparison of spatial and orientational relationships as manifestations of divergent modes of social organization in captive groups of *Mandrillus sphinx* and *Theropithecus gelada*.' *Folia Primatologica* 24: 293–313.

Emory, G.R. (1988) 'Social geometry and cohesion in three primate species.' In M.R.A. Chance (ed.) *Social Fabrics of the Mind*, pp. 47–60. Hillsdale, NJ: Lawrence Erlbaum.

Fromme, D.K. and O'Brien, C.S. (1982) 'A dimensional approach to the circular ordering of emotions.' *Motivation and Emotion* 6: 337–363.

Gilbert, P. (1984) *Depression: From Psychology to Brain State.* Hillsdale, NJ: Lawrence Erlbaum.

Kemper, T.D. (1978) *A Social Interactional Theory of Emotions.* New York: John Wiley.

Kirkland, J. (1976) 'Interest: phoenix in psychology.' *Bulletin of the British Psychological Society* 29: 33–41.

Kummer, H. (1968) 'Social organization of hamadryas baboons – a field study.' *Bibliotheca Primatologica*, No. 6. Basel: S. Karger.

Kummer, H. and Goodall, J. (1985) 'Conditions of innovative behaviour in primates.' *Philosophical Transactions of the Royal Society of London, Series B* 308: 206–213.

Kummer, H. and Kurt, F. (1963) 'Social limits of a free-living population of hamadryas baboons.' *Folia Primatologica* 1: 4–19.

Lacey, J.I., Kagan, J., Lacey, B.C. and Moss, H.A. (1963) 'The visceral level; situational determinants and behavioural correlates of autonomic response patterns.' In P.H. Knapp (ed.) *Expression of the Emotions in Man*, pp. 161–196. New York: International University Press.

Maslow, A.H. (1943) 'The authoritarian character.' *Journal of Social Psychology* 18: 401–411.

McGrew, W.C. (1993) *Chimpanzee Material Culture*. Cambridge: Cambridge University Press.

Mittelstaedt, H. (1970) 'Reafferenzprinzip – Apologie und Critik.' In W.D. Keidel and K.H. Platlig (eds) *Voltage der Erlanger Physiologenstgang*, pp. 162–171. Berlin: Springer.

Montagner, H., Henry, J.C., Lombardot, M., Restoin, A., Bolzoni, D., Duran, M., Humbert, Y. and Moyse, A. (1978) 'Behavioural profile and corticosteroid excretion rhythms in young children. Part 1: non-verbal communication and setting up of behavioural profiles in children from 1–6 years.' In V. Reynolds and N.E. Blurton-Jones (eds) *Human Behaviour and Adaptation*. London: Taylor and Francis.

Montagner, H., Restoin, A., Rodriguez, D., Ullmann, V., Viala, M., Laurent, D. and Godard, D. (1988) 'Social interactions of young children with peers, and their modification in relation to environmental factors.' In M.R.A. Chance (ed.) *Social Fabrics of the Mind*, pp. 237–256. Hillsdale, NJ: Lawrence Erlbaum.

Parker, C.E. (1974) 'The antecedents of man the manipulator.' *Journal of Human Evolution* 3: 493–500.

Parker, C.E. (1980) 'Opportunism and the rise of intelligence.' In E. Sunderland and M.T. Smith (eds) *The Exercise of Intelligence*, pp. 19–36. New York: Garland STMP Press.

Pearce, J. and Newton, S. (1963) *The Conditions of Human Growth*. New York: Citadel Press.

Perkins, D.N. (1988) 'Creativity and the quest for mechanism.' In R.J. Sternberg and E.E. Smith (eds) *The Psychology of Human Thought*, pp. 310–337. Cambridge: Cambridge University Press.

Piaget, J. (1952) *The Origins of Intelligence in Children* (trans. M. Cook). New York: International University Press.

Pitcairn, T.K. (1976) 'Attention and social structure in *Macaca fascicularis*.' In M.R.A. Chance and R. Larsen (eds) *Social Structure of Attention*, pp. 51–81. London: John Wiley.

Pitcairn, T.K. (1988) 'Social attention and social awareness.' In M.R.A. Chance (ed.) *Social Fabrics of the Mind*, pp. 61–74. Hillsdale, NJ: Lawrence Erlbaum.

Power, M. (1991) *The Egalitarians. Human and Chimpanzee*. Cambridge: Cambridge University Press.

Price, J. (1992) 'The agonic and hedonic modes: definition, usage and the promotion of health.' *World Futures* 35: 72–87.

Reynolds, V. and Guest, A. (1975) 'An ethological study of 6–7-year-old school children.' *Biology and Human Affairs* 41: 16–29.

Reynolds, V. and Luscombe, G. (1969) 'Chimpanzee rank order and function of displays.' In C.R. Carpenter (ed.) *Second Conference of the International Primatological Society*, Vol. 1. Basel: S. Karger.

Reynolds, V. and Reynolds, F. (1965) 'Chimpanzees of the Budongo Forest.' In I. DeVore (ed.) *Primate Behaviour*, pp. 368–424. New York: Holt, Rinehart and Winston.

Rosenzweig, M.R. (1984) 'Experience, memory and the brain.' *American Psychologist* 39: 365–376.

Rosenzweig, M.R., Bennett, E.L. and Diamond, M.C. (1972) 'Brain changes in response to experience.' *Scientific American* 226(2): 22–29.

Schneider, W. and Shiffrin, R. (1977) 'Controlled and automatic human information processing: 1. Detection, search and attention.' *Psychological Review* 84: 1–66.

Service, E.R. (1966) *The Hunters*. Englewood Cliffs, NJ: Prentice Hall.

Sherrington, C.S. (1906) *The Integrative Action of the Nervous System*. London: Constable.

Sorenson, E.R. (1978) 'Co-operation and freedom among the Fore of New Guinea.' In A. Montagu (ed.) *Learning Non-Aggression*, pp. 12–30. New York: Oxford University Press.

Toffler, A. (1991) *Power Shift*. London: Bantam Books.

Turnbull, C.M. (1968) 'Contemporary societies: the hunters.' *International Encyclopaedia of Social Sciences* 7: 21–26.

Turnbull, C. (1978) 'The politics of non-aggression.' In A. Montagu (ed.) *Learning Non-aggression*, pp. 161–221. New York: Oxford University Press.

Vaillant, G. (1977) *Adaptation to Life*. Boston: Little, Brown and Co.

de Waal, F. (1982) *Chimpanzee Politics*. London: Allen and Unwin.

de Waal, F. (1989) *Peacemaking Among Primates*. London: Harmondsworth.

Waterhouse, M.J. and Waterhouse, H.B. (1976) 'The development of social organization in rhesus monkeys (*Macaca mulatta*) – an example of bimodal attention structure.' In M.R.A. Chance and R. Larsen (eds) *Social Structure of Attention*, pp. 83–104. New York: John Wiley.

Weber, M. (1946) *Max Weber: Essays in Sociology*. New York: Oxford University Press.

Westergaard, G. (1988) 'Lion-tailed macaques (*Macaca silenus*) manufacture and use tools.' *Journal of Comparative Psychology* 102: 152–159.

White, R.W. (1959) 'Motivation reconsidered: the concept of competence.' *Psychological Review* 66: 297–333.

Woodburn, J. (1982) 'Egalitarian societies.' *Man* (n.s.) 17: 431–451.

CHAPTER SEVENTEEN

SOCIAL INTERACTION AND VIRAL PHENOMENA

BEN CULLEN

INTRODUCTION

Recently, Gardin has written of 'the amazing convergence between the positions defended ... by C. Renfrew, I. Hodder, and others, under various names (cognitive archaeology, symbolic archaeology, contextual archaeology), and the major theses which characterize the hermeneutic current in contemporary semiotics' (Gardin 1992). More archaeologists are choosing to emphasize that the symbolic and economic aspects of human existence are intimately related, and perhaps even inseparable. Examples would include discussions of the intimate relationship between religion and trade (Flannery and Marcus 1993: 262), and between subjective perception and the physical landscape (Bender 1993: 257). Yet, although Renfrew also hints at the possibility of a new synthesis, discussing the role of symbols in a wide range of human activities (Renfrew 1993b: 249, 1994), he has been careful to qualify his remarks:

> Perhaps we shall soon see some convergence between such fields as cognitive psychology, studies in artificial intelligence, computer simulation and cognitive archaeology. The time may be ripe for a great leap forward. But I don't see this happening until those archaeologists interested in the symbolic and cognitive dimensions devote more attention to the formation of a coherent, explicit and in that sense scientific methodology by which that dimension can be systematically explored through the examination and analysis of the archaeological record.
>
> (Renfrew 1993b: 250)

In light of such rumours of a new theoretical synthesis in the making, it is pertinent to consider the recent revival in Darwinian culture theory, and to consider whether any parallels may be drawn between the two philosophical trends. Ultimately, any new synthesis will need to align itself with some kind of general model of culture, humanity and cultural process. A number of candidates for this role can be found within the growing body of neo-Darwinian literature which focuses on the nature of cultural change.

There are a number of different aspects of human culture which neo-Darwinian theory (concerning the influence of selective forces on the reproductive success of independently generated variants) must ultimately address. One is the problem of the origin of the *capacity* for culture, which was so carefully distinguished from other issues by Rindos (1986a, b, 1989) in the 1980s. The cultural capacity must be genetically advantageous to its bearers in some sense, or it could never have evolved as a hominid trait.

A second and closely related problem is that of the origin of *modern human culture*, which may or may not be synonymous with the first. Knight (1991, and see this volume) has shown how it is conceivable that the cultural capacity might only have yielded practically oriented cultural traditions, oriented around knowledge of palpable social relations, food/shelter procurement and relatively simple artefacts such as the handaxe, for many millennia (Knight 1991: 258) – cultures of practical reason. Early hominid, and non-human animal cultures are more limited than those of modern humans from the Upper Palaeolithic onwards. The collective dimension, which for Knight truly warrants the name *human* culture, requires not only the capacity, but the right social conditions, where co-operative interaction becomes extensive enough for the sustained reproduction of the new kinds of cultural phenomena we associate with the Upper Palaeolithic, such as art, to occur (Knight 1991: 17–21).

The third problem of neo-Darwinian culture theory is that of the explanation of cultural change; all those changes which have occurred *since* the origin of culture. Although theories which concern the origin of the human cultural capacity, and of modern human culture, contribute immensely to our understanding of the parameters of human existence, they can never tell the whole story. We also need a neo-Darwinian metaphysic which can explain cultural change on an archaeological timescale, in addition to one which explains genetic evolution on a palaeontological timescale.

While a number of other chapters in this volume are concerned at least partly with the first two problems, this chapter is oriented toward the third: the development of an explanatory framework for cultural change. To use an alternative and more postmodernist turn of phrase, one might say that this chapter is concerned with developing a psychobiology of cultural phenomena, human agency, cultural tradition, social constraint and historical contingency. The particular kind of framework advocated is cultural virus theory (Cullen 1990, 1993a), which can be regarded as a distinctive variety of dual inheritance theory or cultural selectionism (Rindos 1986b: 315), or of evolutionary culture theory (Durham 1991). This is a rapidly growing body of literature in these traditions, both within archaeology (Dunnell 1980, 1989, Fletcher 1992, Leonard and Jones 1987, Neff 1993, O'Brien and Holland 1992, Shennan 1991), and in other disciplines (Ball 1984, Boyd and Richerson 1985, Braun 1990, Corning

1987, Dawkins 1989, Durham 1991, Heylighen 1992, Moritz 1990, Sperber 1985). Such approaches are united by the common goal of applying neo-Darwinian metaphysics to cultural change, where culture is explicitly viewed as both historically contingent, and genealogically independent of the human genome.

Cultural selectionism should be distinguished from the other main body of neo-Darwinian anthropological literature, which is sometimes termed 'sociobiology'. Work in that perspective focuses on the universal, genetically emergent capacities for culture, creative decision-making, and domain-specific reasoning, and on the role that such capacities play in increasing the genetic fitness of their bearers under certain social or environmental conditions (e.g. Brown 1991, Cosmides and Tooby 1987, Freeman 1992, Hinde 1991, Lee 1991, Mithen 1990, Steele in press). Although none of these frameworks exclude the cultural domain altogether, human cultures are not explicitly modelled as neo-Darwinian inheritance systems in their own right. In such approaches neo-Darwinian principles are applied primarily to the understanding of the evolved structures of the human brain. This means that such approaches are most suited to explaining the kinds of phenomena which are determined by the biology of human cognition, such as the phenomena discussed by Jung, Freud, Kant or Lévi-Strauss (Miller 1993: 139), and not to explaining the culturally influenced aspects of human psychology as discussed by Durkheim, Marx, Locke, Boas, Kroeber or Mead (Freeman 1992: 3–6).

WHY WE NEED A DARWINIAN METAPHYSIC FOR CULTURAL PROCESS

Just as each mammalian gene pool is subject to phylogenetic constraints, which limit the range of mutations which can be produced, so must each cultural tradition place limitations on the production of new ideas which transcend that tradition. A common cultural heritage may then yield widespread distributions of cultural phenomena which are based purely in the historical contingencies of that shared cultural ancestry. Such 'universals' could easily have been otherwise; they would be the legacy of an original culture which just happened to be at the right place and the right time. Since then many new ideas may have arisen, new ideas which, by definition, transcended the cultural traditions of which they were part. But each new idea would be a thematic derivative of a pre-existing structure in the tradition from which it emerged. Such heritage constraint can be offered as a non-genetic explanation not only for 'human universals', but for all sorts of less widespread similarities between cultures which share more recent common cultural ancestors.

The variant of cultural selectionism proposed here would therefore predict that a kind of 'constrained viral phenomenon' pattern should occur in archaeological and ethnographic variation, where artefact morphology loosely and intermittently co-varies with human morphology. Such patterns are a direct corollary of the cultural selectionist notion that bones and stones are products of two independent but superimposed Darwinian systems: the spatially or socially constrained patterns of social interaction which permit genetic evolution can also channel cultural transmission. On the other hand, non-cultural selectionist Darwinian frameworks, being based on species-specific, genetically emergent universals, would predict a pattern of either total correlation, or no correlation at all.

There is a growing body of archaeological and anthropological literature which relates this ubiquitous pattern of cultural tradition to a fundamentally selective process (cf. Cullen 1993b: Chapter 8, for an extensive review). Fletcher (1992) and Shennan (1991), for example, have discussed the implications of cultural tradition or heritage for selective explanatory frameworks. Moreover Renfrew (1993a, 1994) has published extensively on the problem of reconciling large-scale geographic patterns in archaeology, language and genetics. Since descent-with-modification patterns are widely recognized to occur in the linguistic and genetic systems, any correlation would imply that a descent-with-modification pattern also occurs in the archaeological record. Renfrew's analysis identifies a number of ways in which genetic and cultural inheritance can either correlate with each other or become decoupled (for example, 1994: 106), which in turn suggests a temperamental and historically contingent association between the three kinds of data. The potential independence of cultural traditions from factors relating to genetic relatedness in populations, coupled with their potential for periodic strong correlation, would suggest a cultural selectionist rather than universalist interpretation of correlations between material cultural change and genetic change in modern human social systems.

Cultural selectionist interpretations of the nature of cultural tradition may also be found in anthropology. Knight (1991) has identified common elements of modern cultures which he sees as a result of the purely cultural descent of modern myths from prototypes in the Upper Palaeolithic. And, finally, anthropologists such as Cavalli-Sforza (1991) and Durham (1991) have explicitly described cultural data as the products of a Darwinian inheritance system which exhibits an intermittent rather than comprehensive correlation with genetic inheritance. If archaeological and ethnographic variation does display a pattern of descent with modification, but one which, at best, only exhibits a *partial or intermittent* correspondence with variation in biological traits, then it would seem to follow that archaeology needs a cultural selectionist approach of some sort.

SOCIAL INTERACTION AND THE SPREAD
OF CULTURAL PHENOMENA

As mentioned briefly above, Knight (1991: 17–21, 258, and this volume) has argued that human culture as we know it may have required more than the mere existence of the human capacity for culture to be brought into being. For Knight, extensive social interaction is itself an additional necessary condition, which in turn implies a social structure capable of facilitating a high rate of social interaction. Although apes have the genetic ability to acquire a variety of cultural phenomena in the context of intense social interaction in modern human communities, Knight questions whether ape societies or Early and Middle Palaeolithic hominid/human societies would often have yielded the extensive social networks of *Homo sapiens sapiens*. Only much later, at the end of the Middle Palaeolithic, did social conditions enable the sustained reproductive success of the new kinds of ideas, behaviour patterns and artefacts (such as art, and the elaboration of ritual) which characterize Upper Palaeolithic and more recent cultural assemblages:

> Memes had to be able to circulate freely over vast areas. Only this could guarantee that they did not die out with the extinction of particular local populations ... The late Neanderthals in each inhabited European district seem to have been in principle capable of almost any symbolic invention. But each of their most unexpectedly 'modern'-seeming artistic or other advances – many of which Marshack (1989) has beautifully documented for us – seems to have occurred only in a localised way, usually disappearing in the place of its origin *before* it could become part of the cultural heritage of the Neanderthals as such. This was the Neanderthals' handicap.
>
> (Knight 1991: 269)

This decoupling of the evolution of the cultural capacity and the appearance of sophisticated cultural phenomena can be visualized via the metaphor of a forest, a metaphor which I call 'the jungle of human sentiment'. A forest is a potentially continuous ecological assemblage, composed of many different populations of organisms in a kaleidoscope of symbiotic, predatory and parasitic relationships.

Within this general ecological assemblage, the tree may be viewed as a convenient representation of the development and differentiation of a human phenotype with a fully developed capacity for culture, from seed to towering giant. The form taken by each phenotype is highly dependent upon environmental factors such as light, climate, nutrition and interaction with other trees, just as the human phenotype is affected by developmental conditions in the manner discussed by Ingold (1986, 1990, 1991, 1993). The extent of social interaction can be visually represented in terms of the closeness of the trees and the degree to which their branches interlock to form a canopy. Cultural phenomena are represented in the form of the various animals and plants which inhabit the canopy. Together, the phenotypes of the trees provide a convoluted and highly structured living landscape, representing the genetically emergent phenomena of the brains of a human community.

Any decoupling of the individual capacity for culture and the explosion of certain kinds of cultural phenomena in the Upper Palaeolithic can be represented in terms of the degree to which fully evolved trees are grouped together in such a way as to provide an interlocking canopy. At one point, trees, as such, evolve, and represent individual hominid phenotypes with a fully developed capacity for culture. However, as long as each tree stands alone, like a tree in a savannah environment, specialized arboreal fauna – being unable to survive by moving from tree to tree – will die when the tree dies. Many intermediate states between savannah and woodland can then represent correspondingly intermediate states in the extent of social interaction and in the cohesion of the networks thereby created. An open woodland with a loose, intermittent canopy of interlocking branches, for example, might be a suitable metaphor for the degree of social interaction involved in Neanderthal social networks, while much of the earlier Palaeolithic could well have involved contingent oscillation between open woodland and the social interaction equivalent of tree-dotted savannah. Phenomena such as handaxes could still survive indefinitely through parent to child enculturation.

Thus, if Knight's hypothesis is to be pursued within the metaphor, we may suggest that the habitat or niche to which cultural phenomena are adapted (communities of hominids with a fully developed cultural capacity) was unevenly distributed and highly unreliable throughout most of the Lower and Middle Palaeolithic. When new ideas appeared in one community there may have been very few opportunities for that idea to have been taught to individuals of other communities some distance away. Under such circumstances, a cultural phenomenon which had a negative effect on the genetic reproductive success of human individuals would be unlikely to survive for long, quickly plunging the small group to which it belonged and itself into extinction. The relationship between human and artefact would have tended to evolve toward stable, symbiotic, ecological relationships, which are perhaps indicated by the long associations between *Homo erectus* and Acheulian assemblages, and between archaic *Homo sapiens* and Mousterian assemblages. The long-term survival of the distinctive cultural phenomena which characterize Upper Palaeolithic and later assemblages would, I propose, have required the existence of extensive coalitions between people distributed over a wide area, and maintained through a continuous fabric of social interaction. Such coalitions would involve, among other things, a fully developed capacity for language; societies where 'verbal grooming' (Aiello and Dunbar 1993) had become the primary means of maintaining large numbers of ongoing relationships, and an indispensable medium for the education of apprentices and novices.

CULTURALLY REPRODUCED ENTITIES
AS VIRAL PHENOMENA

I have used the 'forest' metaphor to make the point that even given a capacity for cultural learning, cultural phenomena still survive only while their human 'hosts' remain extensively networked into widespread social communities. However, my preferred metaphor for the intrinsic dynamic of cultural evolution is that of the *virus*. There are a number of reasons why the general category of viral phenomena provides a better starting point for representing cultural traditions in Darwinian terms, than the more familiar kinds of organisms such as parasites. First, despite the fact that they have elaborate mechanisms for concealing themselves within the human body (Paul 1993), 'fully organismic' parasites never actually become part of their hosts. Viruses, on the other hand, inject naked hereditary material into human cells (Greene 1993: 69): in the case of retroviruses, that genetic material can then insert itself into a human chromosome (Kuby 1992: 463–466). At certain stages of their existence the distinction between viral phenomenon and host becomes very confusing indeed. Despite this blurring effect, microbial viruses are still classified according to their phylogenetic relationships independently of the taxa to which their hosts belong (Postgate 1989). The concept of a viral phenomenon is therefore convenient in that it implies periodic episodes of integration into host minds and genealogical independence from host cells. Knowledge, once learned, can be viewed as physically existing within the brain as a body of altered neuronal structures (Cullen 1993b: Chapter 9, cf. Delius 1991, Edelman 1989, 1992, Levine 1988). But the virus analogy also allows cultural phenomena to be classified phylogenetically, according to cultural tradition, independently of human or hominid phylogeny.

Another advantage of the concept of viral phenomena is that cultural entities and microbial viruses share the potential for separation of hereditary material from phenotype, a quality which true organisms do not possess. In the process of parasitizing a cell, the non–genetic parts of the virus, its phenotype, are left attached to the cell membrane (Greene 1993: 69), while its hereditary material enters the interior of the host cell. Similarly, the phenotype of a cultural phenomenon, the manufacturing behaviour and the artefact itself, are separated from their hereditary material, the manufacturing knowledge residing in human minds. There are many additional qualities which support the joint inclusion of viruses and cultural phenomena in a general category of viral phenomena, as 'sub-organismic' biological individuals. Such qualities include a lack of any intrinsic metabolism or life process (despite the protests of some virologists, Slap 1991), and the lack of the ability to self-reproduce without the help of some proximate reproductive agency. There are also a number of reasons why a cultural entity is better viewed as a viral phenomenon than as a *trait*: cultural phenomena display genealogical independence from genetically emergent traits, and the geographic distribution of a population of cultural phenomena need not be anywhere near as extensive as the geographic distribution of the human population within which it is found.

THE DOMESTIC BEHEMOTH

The chapters in this volume focus on the evolution of hominid social systems, and the appearance in the archaeological record of cultural traditions and of modern human societies. As I indicated earlier, my concern here is to develop an informal verbal model of cultural selection dynamics; and in view of my contention that social systems facilitating rapid cultural evolution only appeared in the Upper Palaeolithic, I shall restrict illustrations of the model to an illustrative reinterpretation of a familiar instance of cultural evolution in modern human populations for whom a good material record exists. Thus in the space that remains I would like to present a brief outline of how one of the most commonly referred to kinds of prehistoric artefact, the megalithic phenomena of the European archaeological record, may be viewed as a class of viral phenomena surviving in a psychological environment made up both of other cultural phenomena and of genetically emergent psychological factors. The aim is to translate the general principles of cultural virus theory into a more familiar set of archaeological categories. Axiomatic to my interpretation is the assumption that megalith-builders inhabited social systems of the requisite level of complexity for cultural phenomena to be propagated through an extensive and frequent pattern of social interactions.

In cultural virus theory each megalithic tomb or stone circle of the European Neolithic would be viewed as an instance of a megalithic phenotype, the physical product of a body of knowledge about the techniques of megalith-making. This knowledge is the hereditary material of the megalithic tradition, the basic megalithic 'thing' whose primary 'goal' is to get reproduced by bringing new apprentices to the megalith-building trade. As I have suggested, knowledge, once learned, can be viewed as physically existing within the brain as a body of altered neuronal structures. Like a retrovirus which has been reverse-transcribed, knowledge of a particular cultural production process like megalith-building is lost amongst a vast assemblage of other neuronal structures inside the mind of its host, except when it is being used to make megalithic artefacts, or being taught to an apprentice megalith-maker. Megalith-manufacturing behaviour patterns are also part of the phenotype of this knowledge. The megalithic viral phenomenon, then, is a three-tiered phenomenon consisting of manufacturing knowledge, manufacturing behaviour and the megaliths themselves.

The above constitutes a brief outline of what megalithic phenomena *are* in cultural virus theory. What was their relationship to the contexts in which they are found, and how did that relationship affect their continued survival as a living tradition within Neolithic society? One important thing to bear in mind in interpreting the 'cultural virus theory' approach to context, is that megalith is to brain as virus is to cell: cultural phenomena are found in ecological relationships with individual humans or social groups, whereas microbial viruses parasitize individual cells rather than whole organisms. Moreover, just as in the case of human microbial viruses (Mitchison 1993: 105), the relationship between megalithic phenomena and the Neolithic communities in which they are found could have varied all the way from beneficial to harmful. Which strategy emerged at any particular time would have been highly contingent and could have varied from century to century, or even from decade to decade, throughout the Neolithic.

In 'cultural virus theory' a large number of knowledge–behaviour–artefact combinations are *domestic* viral phenomena – that is, they are maintained and reproduced actively and deliberately, either by the whole community, or by some specialist group of individuals. Given the great amount of organized labour, however unskilled, involved in the building of megalithic phenomena (Sherratt 1990: 147), it would be ridiculous to consider their manufacture as anything other than active and deliberate. In terms of the possible ways in which such cultural viruses may propagate themselves they are, therefore, ecologically equivalent to domesticated animals and plants in terms of the adaptive strategies available to them. However, this is not to say that megalithic phenomena were always symbiotic or genetically beneficial to the people who manufactured them. It is perfectly conceivable that a group of people might continue in a lifestyle based around one or more domesticated animal or plant species long after the emotional and economic costs have come to outweigh the benefits, particularly if the imbalance of cost and benefit is for some reason difficult to calculate. Such may have been the case, from time to time, with the human activity associated with the building and maintenance of megalithic phenomena. For a domesticate, parasitic ecological relationships emerge through the subjective assessment of the value of that domesticate, whereby people are simply not able to 'see the cost' involved in its support. This allows the cost, in terms of the genetic reproductive success of megalith builders and their kin, to fluctuate through time without making any immediate impact upon the cultural fitness of megaliths.

Even active human agents in charge of their own destiny will not automatically make 'genetically correct' choices to maximize their inclusive fitness: rather, they will make those choices which seem to them to be the best at the time, subjective choices which could be termed 'culturally correct' and 'individually correct'. An assemblage of megalithic phenomena, like a herd of domesticates, cannot be maintained unless individual actors choose to do so. But since all choices are informed by the values, morals and measurements of one or more cultural traditions, it is highly unlikely that any given choice which (by definition) must be correct in terms of the culturally and experientially informed judgements of individuals, will also be the best in *genetic* terms. Every cultural tradition can be expected to produce characteristic 'distortions' of the value of different human activities and artefacts, since systems of evaluation are themselves cultural phenomena. Such distortions need not be catastrophic or genetically suicidal, only small and persistent. Through their inherent dependency on value-laden assessment of the importance of artefacts, people become vulnerable to the possibility of passive exploitation by overvalued cultural phenomena. Other artefacts, which involve less genetic cost to their manufacturers, may simply not hold the same fascination, the same 'magic', the same aesthetic charisma, within the various culturally specific and historically contingent world views of the European Neolithic.

All evidence would seem to suggest that megalithic phenomena were extremely well adapted to Neolithic states of mind: their appeal was the sum of a long list of positive and mutually supportive connotations. They had an initial similarity to the dwellings of some communities of the period, as discussed by Sherratt (in press) and Hodder (1985, 1990, in press), which also constitute a likely cultural ancestor for the megaliths themselves. At a time when so many cultural categories, anxieties and aspirations revolved around images of domestication and its contrast with the wild (Hodder 1990), houses, as artefacts, were preadapted to a new cognitive niche as tombs and monuments. A series of innovations produced new 'megalithic' versions of the houses, which fitted the new symbolic niches of the tomb even better than the houses themselves. The subsequent elaborations of various aspects of megalithic phenomena, such as various forms of art, the association with the additional domesticating imagery of the axe (Hodder in press, Thomas and Tilley in press) and the possible use of narcotics, could only have enhanced their contextual 'charisma' even further. Before very long, megalithic phenomena must have become an indispensable part of the cultural ecology of Neolithic communities.

CONCLUSION

In the last decade, neo-Darwinian theory has often been thought to be incompatible with a variety of interrelated aspects of the postmodernist inspired interpretive archaeology, such as notions of the active, self-determining individual (Hodder 1985: 1, Shanks and Tilley 1987a: 56, 1987b: 175), of the influence of society on such individuals (Shanks and Tilley 1987b: 177), of cultural tradition and historical contingency (Thomas 1991b: 15, Shanks and Tilley 1987b: 176), and of active material

430 Ben Cullen

culture and contextual interpretation (Hodder 1991, 1992: 12–14, in press, Barrett 1987: 10, 1990: 179, Thomas 1991a, 1991b: 17, in press, Thomas and Tilley, in press). Such opinions are an understandable result of the fact that the explanatory frameworks against which they reacted, like much of Darwinian anthropology and indeed sociobiology in general, ignored interpretive factors, being based around pan-human, genetically emergent human capacities and their role in promoting human reproductive success. In this chapter an attempt has been made to outline an alternative Darwinian perspective, cultural virus theory, which has been able to accommodate postmodernist principles by viewing artefacts as cultural organisms adapting in such a way as to take advantage of human agency in a particular cultural context.

ACKNOWLEDGEMENTS

I would like to thank Ian Hodder, Colin Renfrew, Andrew Sherratt and Julian Thomas for kindly sending me unpublished manuscripts.

REFERENCES

Aiello, L.C. and Dunbar, R.I.M. (1993) 'Neocortex size, group size, and the evolution of language.' *Current Anthropology* 34: 184–193.

Ball, J.A. (1984) 'Memes as replicators.' *Ethology and Sociobiology* 5: 145–161.

Barrett, J.C. (1987) 'Fields of discourse.' *Critique of Anthropology* 7: 5–16.

Barrett, J.C. (1990) 'The monumentality of death: the character of Early Bronze Age mortuary mounds in southern Britain.' *World Archaeology* 22: 179–189.

Bender, B. (1993) 'Cognitive archaeology and cultural materialism.' *Cambridge Archaeological Journal* 3: 257–260.

Boyd, R. and Richerson, P.J. (1985) *Culture and the Evolutionary Process*. Chicago: University of Chicago Press.

Braun, D.P. (1990) 'Selection and evolution in nonhierarchical organization.' In S. Upham (ed.) *The Evolution of Political Systems*, pp. 63–86. Cambridge: Cambridge University Press.

Brown, D. (1991) *Human Universals*. New York: McGraw-Hill.

Cavalli-Sforza, L.L. (1991) 'Genes, people and languages.' *Scientific American* 265: 72–78.

Corning, P.A. (1987) 'Evolution and political control: a synopsis of a general theory of politics.' In M. Schmidt and F.M. Wuketits (eds) *Evolutionary Theory in Social Science*, pp. 127–170. Lancaster: Reidel.

Cosmides, L. and Tooby, J. (1987) 'From evolution to behaviour: evolutionary psychology as the missing link.' In J. Dupre (ed.) *The Latest on the Best: Essays on Evolution and Optimality*, pp. 277–306. Cambridge, MA: MIT Press.

Cullen, B.R.S. (1990) 'Darwinian views of history: Betzig's virile psychopath versus the cultural virus.' *Crosscurrents* 4: 61–68.

Cullen, B.R.S. (1993a) 'The Darwinian resurgence and the cultural virus critique.' *Cambridge Archaeological Journal* 3: 179–202.

Cullen, B.R.S. (1993b) 'The cultural virus'. PhD thesis, Prehistoric and Historical Archaeology, University of Sydney.

Dawkins, R. (1989) *The Selfish Gene*, 2nd edn. Oxford: Oxford University Press.

Delius, J.D. (1991) 'The nature of culture.' In M.S. Dawkins, T.R. Halliday and R. Dawkins (eds) *The Tinbergen Legacy*, pp. 75–99. London: Chapman and Hall.

Dunnell, R.C. (1980) 'Evolutionary theory and archaeology.' *Advances in Archaeological Method and Theory* 3: 38–99.

Dunnell, R.C. (1989) 'Aspects of the application of evolutionary theory in archaeology.' In C.C. Lamberg-Karlovsky (ed.) *Archaeological Thought in America*, pp. 35–49. Cambridge: Cambridge University Press.

Durham, W.H. (1991) *Coevolution: Genes, Culture, and Human Diversity*. Stanford, CA: Stanford University Press.

Edelman, G.M. (1989) *Neural Darwinism: The Theory of Neuronal Group Selection*. Oxford: Oxford University Press.

Edelman, G.M. (1992) *Bright Air, Brilliant Fire*. London: Allen Lane, The Penguin Press.

Flannery, K.V. and Marcus, J. (1993) 'Cognitive archaeology.' *Cambridge Archaeological Journal* 3: 260–267.

Fletcher, R.J. (1992) 'Time perspectivism, *Annales*, and the potential of archaeology.' In A.B. Knapp (ed.) *Archaeology, Annales, and Ethnohistory*, pp. 35–49. Cambridge: Cambridge University Press.

Freeman, D. (1992) *Paradigms in Collision: The Far-reaching Controversy over the Samoan Researches of Margaret Mead and its Significance for the Human Sciences*. Research School of Pacific Studies, The Australian National University.

Gardin, J. C. (1992) 'Semiotic trends in archaeology.' In J.C. Gardin and C.S. Peebles (eds) *Representations in Archaeology*. Bloomington and Indianapolis: Indiana University Press.

Greene, W.C. (1993) 'Aids and the immune system.' *Scientific American* 269: 66–73.

Heylighen, F. (1992) ' "Selfish" memes and the evolution of co-operation.' *Journal of Ideas* 2: 77–84.

Hinde, R.A. (1991) 'A biologist looks at anthropology.' *Man* (n.s.) 26: 583–608.

Hodder, I. (1985) 'Post-processual archaeology.' *Advances in Archaeological Method and Theory* 8: 1–25.

Hodder, I. (1990) *The Domestication of Europe: Structure and Contingency in Neolithic Societies*. Oxford: Basil Blackwell.

Hodder, I. (1991) 'Interpretive archaeology and its role.' *American Antiquity* 56: 7–18.

Hodder, I. (1992) 'Symbolism, meaning and context.' In I. Hodder (ed.) *Theory and Practice in Archaeology*, pp. 11–23. London: Routledge.

Hodder, I. (in press) 'Megaliths: production and reproduction.' Ms.

Ingold, T. (1986) *Evolution and Social Life*. Cambridge: Cambridge University Press.

Ingold, T. (1990) 'An anthropologist looks at biology.' *Man* (n.s.) 25: 208–228.

Ingold, T. (1991) 'Comment on "Biology and behaviour in human evolution".' *Cambridge Archaeological Journal* 1: 219–221.

Ingold, T. (1993) 'Comment: on "The Darwinian resurgence and the cultural virus critique".' *Cambridge Archaeological Journal* 3: 194–195.

Knight, C. (1991) *Blood Relations: Menstruation and the Origins of Culture*. New Haven and London: Yale University Press.

Kuby, J. (1992) *Immunology*. New York: W.H. Freeman.

Lee, P.C. (1991) 'Biology and behaviour in human evolution.' *Cambridge Archaeological Journal* 1: 207–226.

Leonard, R.P. and Jones, G.T. (1987) 'Elements of an inclusive evolutionary model for archaeology.' *Journal of Anthropological Archaeology* 6: 199–219.

Levine, D.S. (1988) 'Survival of the synapses.' *The Sciences* 28: 46–52.

Miller, J. (1993) *The Passion of Michel Foucault*. London: Harper/Collins.

Mitchison, A. (1993) 'Will we survive?' *Scientific American* 269: 102–108.

Mithen, S. (1990) *Thoughtful Foragers: A Study of Prehistoric Decision-Making*. Cambridge: Cambridge University Press.

Moritz, E. (1990) 'Memetic science: I – general introduction.' *Journal of Ideas* 1: 1–23.

Neff, H. (1993) 'Theory, sampling, and analytical techniques in the archaeological study of prehistoric ceramics.' *American Antiquity* 58: 23–44.

O'Brien, M.J. and Holland, T.D. (1992) 'The role of adaptation in archaeological explanation.' *American Antiquity* 57: 36–59.

Paul, W.E. (1993) 'Infectious diseases and the immune system.' *Scientific American* 269: 56–65.

Postgate, J. (1989) 'Microbial happy families.' *New Scientist* 21 January: 40–44.

Renfrew, C. (1993a) *The Roots of Ethnicity. Archaeology, Genetics and the Origins of Europe*. Rome: Unione Internationale Degli Instituti di Archeologia Storia e Storia Dell'arte in Roma.

Renfrew, C. (1993b) 'Cognitive archaeology: some thoughts on the archaeology of thought.' *Cambridge Archaeological Journal* 3: 248–250.

Renfrew, C. (1994) 'Explaining world linguistic diversity: towards a new synthesis.' *Scientific American* 270 (January): 104–112.

Rindos, D. (1986a) 'The genetics of cultural anthropology: toward a genetic model of the origin of the capacity for culture.' *Journal of Anthropological Archaeology* 5: 1–38.

Rindos, D. (1986b) 'The evolution of the capacity for culture: sociobiology, structuralism and cultural selectionism.' *Current Anthropology* 27: 315–331.

Rindos, D. (1989) 'Undirected variation and the Darwinian explanation of cultural change.' *Archaeological Method and Theory* 1: 1–48.

Shanks, M. and Tilley, C. (1987a) *Reconstructing Archaeology: Theory and Practice*. Cambridge: Cambridge University Press.

Shanks, M. and Tilley, C. (1987b) *Social Theory and Archaeology*. Cambridge: Polity Press.

Shennan, S. (1991) 'Tradition, rationality and cultural transmission.' In R.W. Preucel (ed.) *Processual and Postprocessual Archaeologies*, pp. 197–208. Center for Archaeological Investigations, Occasional Paper No. 10. Southern Illinois University.

Sherratt, A.G. (1990) 'The genesis of megaliths: monumentality, ethnicity, and social complexity in Neolithic North-West Europe.' *World Archaeology* 22: 147–167.

Sherratt, A.G. (in press) 'Instruments of conversion? The role of megaliths in the mesolithic/neolithic transition in North West Europe.' In K. von Welck (ed.) *Comparative Studies of Megalithics: Progress Reports and Ethnoarchaeological Approaches. Proceedings of the International Symposium*, pp. 1–13. Mannheim: Reiss-Museum, Museum for Archaeologie and Volkerkunde.

Slap, J.K. (1991) 'Virile viruses.' *Australian Natural History* 23: 668.

Sperber, D. (1985) 'Anthropology and psychology: towards an epidemiology of representations.' *Man* (n.s.) 20: 73–89.

Steele, J. (in press) 'Weak modularity and the evolution of human social behaviour.' In H. Maschner (ed.) *Darwinian Archaeologies*. New York: Plenum.

Thomas, J. (1991a) *Rethinking the Neolithic*. Cambridge: Cambridge University Press.

Thomas, J. (1991b) 'The hollow men? A reply to Steven Mithen.' *Proceedings of the Prehistoric Society* 57: 15–20.

Thomas, J. (in press) 'The hermeneutics of megalithic space.' In C. Tilley (ed.) *Interpretive Archaeologies*. London: Berg.

Thomas, J. and Tilley, C. (in press) 'The axe and the torso: symbolic structures in the Neolithic of Brittany.' In C. Tilley (ed.) *Interpretive Archaeologies*. London: Berg.

INDEX

Acheulian 212; contrasts with
Oldowan 219–20; evidence of
imitation in 216; group sizes of
222–3; rules of biface production
165, 167
agonic social mode: characteristics of
397–9, 415; evidence of in humans
402; evidence of in non-human
primates 399–400; presence of in
industrial societies 405–6, 408–9;
psychiatric evidence of 409–10;
see also hedonic social mode
anatomically modern humans:
evidence of agonic social mode in
402, 405–6, 408–9; evidence of
hedonic social mode in 402–6,
408–9; evidence of sexual
dimorphism among 98, 101; mating
systems of and sexual dimorphism
98–9; sexual division of labour
among 335–6
anthropology: role of ethnographic
data in the reconstruction of
hominid social systems 4–5,
143
apes: see chimpanzee, gorilla,
primates
archaeology: archaeological
conceptions of time 267–8;
archaeological evidence of hominid
group size 248–50; inferential
framework of hominid archaeology
185–92; role of modelling in
137–42, 155; study of gender from
the archaeological record, discussion
of 347–8, 353–9; see also
Palaeolithic
australopithecines: debate over their
relationship with Oldowan stone
tools 141–2; relationship to modern
humans 62

Australopithecus afarensis: body size
variation and evidence of sexual
dimorphism among 91–5, 101, 102;
mating system of 100–1
Australopithecus africanus: body size
variation and evidence of sexual
dimorphism among 95, 102; mating
system of 100–1
Australopithecus boisei: body size
variation among 95–6
Australopithecus robustus: body size
variation among 96, 102

behavioural ecology: hominid
behavioural ecology 160–1; theory
of 285–6, 289
bifaces: rules of production of
Acheulian bifaces 165, 167
Binford, L.R.: criticism of home base
model 156–7, 159–60; significance
of bone studies to 161; view of
Clark's *Prehistory of Southern Africa*
142
bipedalism: among non-human
primates 149–50; origins of 9, 10,
149–50, 153; significance of in
human evolution 148–9
body size: see sexual dimorphism
bonding: among chimpanzees 70–1;
among gorillas 70–1; comparison of
chimpanzee and gorilla tie patterns
70–1, 74–8; effects of group size on
the mechanisms of social bonding
384–6; and the evolution of
language 382–3; factors favouring
long-term male and female bonding
62–4; hominoid female kin-bonding
61–3, 80; male kin-bonding 79, 80;
language and the facilitation of
social bonding 382–3, 385–6, 394;
impact of on models of hominid